STREET & SMITH'S
GUIDE TO PRO FOOTBALL
1994

Also by the editors of Street & Smith's
Published by Ballantine Books:

STREET & SMITH'S GUIDE TO BASEBALL 1994
STREET & SMITH'S GUIDE TO PRO BASKETBALL 1994–'95*

*Forthcoming

STREET & SMITH'S GUIDE TO PRO FOOTBALL 1994

by the editors of
Street & Smith's

Consulting Editor: Reuben Lattimore

BALLANTINE BOOKS · NEW YORK

Copyright © 1994 by Condé Nast Publications, Inc.

All rights reserved under International and Pan-American Copyright Conventions. Published in the United States of America by Ballantine Books, a division of Random House, Inc., New York, and simultaneously in Canada by Random House of Canada Limited, Toronto.

Library of Congress Catalog Card Number: 94–94190

ISBN 0–345–38618–3

Manufactured in the United States of America

Cover photo © Focus on Sports

National Football League player names and images used with permission of the National Football League Players Association.

First Edition: September 1994

10 9 8 7 6 5 4 3 2 1

TABLE OF CONTENTS

ACKNOWLEDGMENTS

Trying to fit an entire football season into one book is a challenge, and we could never have done it without a great deal of support.

First, we must thank the Directors of Public Relations and Media Relations for the NFL, the NFL Players Association, and all 28 teams. They and their staffs were consistently helpful and responsive, and provided the information and photographs that make this handbook so complete.

We're indebted to Myles McDonnell, a true sports fan, and to the staff at Creative Graphics, who worked so diligently as we rushed to put this book together in time for the upcoming season.

Also, our editor at Ballantine Books, Jeff Doctoroff, contributed immensely to this guide. His hard work and constant attention to our project have made this book what it is. Finally, we'd like to thank everyone else at Ballantine, especially Caron Harris, George Davidson, Nora Reichard, and Scott Gray.

Editor's Note

Statistical projections for 1994 are based on the individual player's 1993 performance, combined with the degree of change in an individual category (on a per game basis) over a player's career. We take into account the rate of increase in a player's playing time in creating our projection. Stats for 1993 were thrown out in projecting 1994 stats for projected 1994 starters who were injured for most of 1993 (such as Randall Cunningham). But players with a history of injuries, or who have seen a steady decline in playing time for other reasons, are projected to continue that decline in playing time and stats. There are no projections for rookies and second year players, because they lack the statistical differences over two or more years that form the basis of our projections.

Our 1994 projections are just that—projections. They indicate continuations of past trends. Although projected numbers could be used as a forecast of a player's 1994 performance, they are best used as an general indication of whether or not a player is likely to improve on his 1993 numbers. This is particularly true for players entering their third and fourth years in the NFL. The longer a player's career, the less likely our projections are to be skewed by a one-time spike in a player's performance (e.g., Craig Erickson in 1993). When we project that Erickson will pass for over 5700 yards in 1994, or that Bryan Paup will record 15 sacks, we're not necessarily predicting that they will—we're just saying that, if they continue to improve as they have over their short careers, they would reach these milestones.

We have tried to make the rosters in this guide as up-to-date and informative as possible, including returning veterans, recent signings, and all draft picks. In this year of unprecedented player movement, unsigned unrestricted free agents are still listed with their team from last year—they are indicated by a "**" before their names. Unsigned restricted free agents are included in their team's roster with no special mark, since they'll most likely re-sign. We have used the standard abbreviations for teams, positions and statistics, and most of these will be obvious to any fan. For instance, in the rosters, under "How Acquired", a "W" means waivers, a "T" signifies trade, a "D" indicates draft, and "FA" is a free agent. Similarly, the "GP/GS" column in the roster indicates how many games the player played in during '93, and how many he started. Of course, rookies do not have an entry in this column. We have provided the uniform number for as many players as possible.

This guide should give you a comprehensive preview of the 1994 season from training camp to the Super Bowl. Due to a tight schedule, we've probably missed some late free-agent signings, trades, and other developments. Still, we believe this is the most thorough, up-to-date guide of its kind available, so dive in and enjoy the season.

AMERICAN FOOTBALL CONFERENCE

1993 RECAP

EASTERN DIVISION

	W	L	T	PF	PA	HOME	ROAD	NFC	AFC	DIV
x-BUFFALO	12	4	0	329	242	6-2	6-2	4-0	8-4	7-1
MIAMI	9	7	0	349	351	4-4	5-3	3-1	6-6	4-4
N.Y. JETS	8	8	0	270	247	3-5	5-3	2-2	6-6	5-3
NEW ENGLAND	5	11	0	238	286	3-5	2-6	1-1	4-10	2-6
INDIANAPOLIS	4	12	0	189	378	2-6	2-6	0-4	4-8	2-6

CENTRAL DIVISION

	W	L	T	PF	PA	HOME	ROAD	NFC	AFC	DIV
x-HOUSTON	12	4	0	368	238	7-1	5-3	2-2	10-2	6-0
y-PITTSBURGH	9	7	0	308	281	6-2	3-5	2-2	7-5	3-3
CLEVELAND	7	9	0	304	307	4-4	3-5	3-1	4-8	3-3
CINCINNATI	3	13	0	187	319	3-5	0-8	2-2	1-11	0-6

WESTERN DIVISION

	W	L	T	PF	PA	HOME	ROAD	NFC	AFC	DIV
x-KANSAS CITY	11	5	0	328	291	7-1	4-4	2-2	9-3	7-1
y-L.A. RAIDERS	10	6	0	306	326	5-3	5-3	3-1	7-5	5-3
y-DENVER	9	7	0	373	284	5-3	4-4	1-3	8-4	4-4
SAN DIEGO	8	8	0	322	290	4-4	4-4	2-2	6-6	3-5
SEATTLE	6	10	0	280	314	4-4	2-6	0-2	6-8	1-7

x-Division Winner, y-Wild Card

AFC East

Buffalo defied the odds and critics by charging out to a 7-1 start, including a win over Dallas, and won their last 4 games to post the best record in the conference. They then dispatched the Raiders and the Chiefs at home at Rich Stadium, but they still couldn't win the big one.

Miami had one of the league's strongest starts, going 9-2 despite injuries to Dan Marino (in game 5) and his backup Scott Mitchell (in game 8). Then the defense collapsed down the stretch, and they dropped their last 5 games, including the embarrassing loss at home to the Patriots on the season's final weekend that cost Miami a wild card spot.

At the beginning of December, the Jets looked unbeatable—they were 7-4 and had won 5 straight games. Then the offense fell apart, averaging only 6 points per game as New York lost 4 of their last 5 to miss the playoffs. They finished at .500, and it cost coach Bruce Coslet his job.

After a slow start, Bill Parcells got good results from his young Patriots in his first season as their coach. The Patriots lost 11 of their first 12, including 7 straight. Then, New England came together behind rookie QB Drew Bledsoe to win their final 4 games and finish an almost respectable 5-11.

Indianapolis showed that 1992's 9-7 record was merely an aberration, as they plunged to an abysmal 4-12 mark in '93. They struggled on both sides of the ball, and had two losing streaks of 4 games and one of 3 games.

AFC Central

The Oilers got off to an awful start, losing 4 of their first 5 games, but the defense gelled and Houston won a team-record 11 straight games to close the season. They won the division easily, but lost another playoff heartbreaker, this time to Kansas City at home.

Pittsburgh had an inconsistent season last year, beating Buffalo and Miami, but losing to Cleveland and the Rams. Still, the Steelers made the playoffs, only to lose a thrilling first round game in overtime to the more experienced Chiefs.

Browns fans had a tough '93. Beloved QB Bernie Kosar was abruptly released by coach Bill Belichick, setting off a near revolt in Cleveland. Vinny Testaverde stepped in and performed well, but the dispirited Browns lost 7 of their last 9 games to finish below .500 again.

Cincinnati continued to move in the wrong direction. The Bengals were the worst team in the NFL last year, with a 3-13 record. They lost their first 10 games of the season and didn't win a road game all year. At least they got the first draft pick.

AFC West

Division winner Kansas City looked wise for adding veterans Joe Montana and Marcus Allen, as the Chiefs won 5 of their first 6 games. Overall Kansas City went 7-1 against divisional opponents and made it all the way to the AFC title game, where they lost to the Bills.

The Raiders' terrific air attack, featuring new QB Jeff Hostetler and WR Tim Brown, was enough to carry a suspect rushing game and an aging defense in '93. Los Angeles won 4 of its last 5 to take a wild card spot, then beat Denver handily before falling to Buffalo in a nail-biter.

In the first year of the post-Reeves era, the Broncos split two games with the Chiefs but lost to the Raiders twice. All Pro John Elway and a strong defense were enough to put the 9-7 Broncos back in the playoffs, where they lost to (who else?) the Raiders in the first round.

The Chargers slumped to 8-8 in '93 after their stellar 11-5 finish in '92. The Chargers were mediocre in every way (4-4 at home, 4-4 on the road); they couldn't keep up with the top three teams in the division and fell out of contention early.

Seattle improved dramatically over their disastrous 2-14 record of 1992, largely thanks to rookie QB Rick Mirer. They started 4-3, but only won two more games the rest of the way. Still, their 6-10 finish gave Seattle the most improved record in the AFC.

1994 AFC PROJECTIONS

AFC East	AFC Central	AFC West
Buffalo†	Pittsburgh†	L.A. Raiders†
Miami*	Houston	Denver*
New England	Cleveland	Kansas City*
N.Y. Jets	Cincinnati	Seattle
Indianapolis		San Diego

†Division Winner, *Wild Card

Round 1:	Pittsburgh over Kansas City, Miami over Denver
Round 2:	Buffalo over Miami, L.A. Raiders over Pittsburgh
Title Game:	Buffalo over L.A. Raiders
Super Bowl XXIX:	Dallas over Buffalo

Once again, critics are saying that the Bills' dominance of the AFC is over, and the challengers are lining up for a shot at Buffalo. Granted, the Bills lost a few more players and they are getting a bit older, but they've still got the core that's won 4 straight AFC titles, and they're still the odds-on favorite in the East. If anyone can catch them, it's Miami, especially if Dan

Marino comes back strong. New England will take another step forward in '94, but the playoffs seem too much to ask—8-8 would be a good finish for the Pats. The Jets couldn't score at the end of '93, and nothing much seems to have changed. Their defense will win some games, but not enough. In Indy, Jim Harbaugh's not the answer, and the Colts have lost too many starters to improve in '93—they should take up their familiar position in last place.

The Oilers were hit as hard as anyone in the AFC by free agency, and the young Steelers are ready to step into the void at the top of the Central. Houston, with untested Cody Carlson at the helm, should come in second, but their time has come and gone. Cleveland could improve if Vinny Testaverde has a stellar year at QB, but it's more likely that the Browns will put their fans through another sub-.500 season. Top draft pick Dan Wilkinson represents the Bengals' future, but Cincinnati still has too many holes to climb out of the cellar before 1995.

The AFC West will be fun to watch in '94, but that makes it hard to predict. The Raiders, with a fearsome passing attack and an improving defense, should have enough to rise to the top. Denver may give them a run, since John Elway has two scary new targets in Anthony Miller and Mike Pritchard, even though there are a number of question marks on defense. Last year's winner, Kansas City, will also contend, especially if the defense performs, but this may be the year that superstars Joe Montana and Marcus Allen show their age. The Seahawks should continue to improve and might reach .500, but they won't be able to keep up with the division's top threesome. San Diego looks to be in trouble—the defense is still strong, but their two biggest weapons on offense (Anthony Miller and Marion Butts) are gone, so they should be out of the race by mid-November.

Buffalo
BILLS

1994 Scouting Report

Offense

The Bills offense was one of football's most effective in 1993, gaining 5,260 yards (fifth in the NFL)—1,943 rushing yards (eighth in the league) and 3,317 passing yards (eleventh in the NFL). Jim Kelly struggled a bit last year, but figures to bounce back in '94. If he doesn't, Frank Reich is one of the best backups in the NFL, and some in Buffalo would like to see him start. Whoever plays QB has an impressive array of receivers in RB Thurman Thomas, WRs Andre Reed and Bill Brooks, and TE Pete Metzelaars. The Bills are deep at RB with Thomas, who led the AFC in yards gained from scrimmage, and backup Kenneth Davis. They might have problems on the OL, with the loss of free agent T Howard Ballard following '93's loss of Will Wolford.

Defense

Despite the continued strong play of DT Bruce Smith and LBs Cornelius Bennett and Darryl Talley, the Bills defense is not what it once was. Statistically, the AFC champs ranked next to last in the league in '93, allowing 5,554 total yards. They were equally bad against the rush and the pass; Buffalo allowed 1,921 rushing yards (twenty-first in the NFL) and 3,633 passing yards (twenty-fourth in the NFL). The Bills will press No. 1 pick DB Jeff Burris into action after losing James Williams and Nate Odomes.

Special Teams

The Bills are strong on special teams. Steve Christie is one of the league's better kickers, and P Chris Mohr continues to improve. Steve Tasker is an All-Pro cover man and Russell Copeland is a solid punt returner.

1994 Prospects

The Bills have seemed due for a fall for a couple of years, but they've continued to defy the experts and return to the Super Bowl. The team's collective grit and resolve cannot be underestimated, and the Super Bowl losing streak seems to have developed an "us against the world" mindset. Granted, the defense is mediocre, but Thomas, Kelly, and the offense will pile on the points. Unless someone else in the AFC takes a big step forward, the Bills have as good a chance as anyone to get to the Super Bowl again

Team Directory

President: Ralph C. Wilson, Jr.
General manager: John Butler
Director of pro personnel: A. J. Smith
Director of media relations: Scott Berchtold

1993 Review			1994 Schedule		
Sep. 5	NEW ENGLAND	W 38-14	Sep. 4	N.Y. JETS	4:00
Sep. 12	at Dallas	W 13-10	Sep. 11	at New England	1:00
Sep. 19	OPEN DATE		Sep. 18	at Houston	1:00
Sep. 26	MIAMI	L 22-13	Sep. 26	DENVER (Mon.)	9:00
Oct. 3	N.Y. GIANTS	W 17-14	Oct. 2	at Chicago	4:00
Oct. 11	HOUSTON	W 35-7	Oct. 9	MIAMI	1:00
Oct. 17	OPEN DATE		Oct. 16	INDIANAPOLIS	1:00
Oct. 24	at N.Y. Jets	W 19-10	Oct. 23	OPEN DATE	
Nov. 1	WASHINGTON	W 24-10	Oct. 30	KANSAS CITY	1:00
Nov. 7	at New England	W 13-10 (OT)	Nov. 6	at N.Y. Jets	4:00
Nov. 15	at Pittsburgh	L 23-0	Nov. 14	at Pittsburgh (Mon.)	9:00
Nov. 21	INDIANAPOLIS	W 23-9	Nov. 20	GREEN BAY	1:00
Nov. 28	at Kansas City	L 23-7	Nov. 24	at Detroit (Thank.)	12:30
Dec. 5	L.A. RAIDERS	L 25-24	Dec. 4	at Miami	8:00
Dec. 12	at Philadelphia	W 10-7	Dec. 11	MINNESOTA	1:00
Dec. 19	at Miami	W 47-34	Dec. 18	NEW ENGLAND	1:00
Dec. 26	N.Y. JETS	W 16-4	Dec. 24	at Indianapolis	1:00
Jan. 2	at Indianapolis	W 30-10			

1993 finish: 12-4 (6-2 home, 6-2 away), first in AFC East

Team Leaders

PASSING	ATT	COM	COM%	YDS	YPA	TD	TD%	INT	INT%	RTG
Kelly	470	288	61.3	3382	7.20	18	3.8	18	3.8	79.9
Reich	26	16	61.5	153	5.88	2	7.7	0	0.0	103.5
Thomas	1	0	0.0	0	0.00	0	0.0	0	0.0	39.6
TEAM	497	304	61.2	3535	7.11	20	4.0	18	3.6	81.0
OPPONENTS	582	323	55.5	3889	6.68	18	3.1	23	4.0	70.0

RECEIVING	REC	YDS	AVG	TD	RUSHING	ATT	YDS	AVG	TD
Metzelaars	68	609	9.0	4	Thomas	355	1315	3.7	6
Brooks	60	714	11.9	5	Davis, K.	109	391	3.6	6
Reed	52	854	16.4	6	Kelly	36	102	2.8	0
Thomas	48	387	8.1	0	Gardner	20	56	2.8	0
Beebe	31	504	16.3	3	Turner	11	36	3.3	0
TEAM	304	3535	11.6	20	TEAM	550	1943	3.5	12
OPPONENTS	323	3889	12.0	18	OPPONENTS	500	1921	3.8	7

INTERCEPTIONS	INT	YDS	AVG	LG	TD	SACKS	NO
Odomes	9	65	7.2	25	0	Smith	13.5
Talley	3	74	24.7	61t	1	Wright	5.5
Jones	2	92	46.0	85t	1	Bennett	4.5
TEAM	23	308	13.3	83t	3	TEAM	37.0
OPPONENTS	18	174	9.7	35	0	OPPONENTS	31.0

KICK RETURNS	NO	YDS	AV	LG	TD	PUNT RETURNS	NO	FC	YDS	AV	LG	TD
Copeland	24	436	18.2	28	0	Copeland	31	7	274	8.8	47t	1
Beebe	10	160	16.0	22	0	Brooks	1	0	3	3.0	3	0
Davis, K.	8	100	12.5	18	0	Tasker	1	0	0	0.0	0	0
TEAM	45	746	16.6	28	0	TEAM	33	7	277	8.4	47t	1
OPPONENTS	43	850	19.8	49	0	OPPONENTS	29	24	247	8.5	27	0

KICKING	XPM	XPA	FGM	FGA	LG	PTS
Christie	36	37	23	32	59	105
TEAM	36	37	23	32	59	105
OPPONENTS	23	25	23	35	47	92

PUNTING	NO	YDS	LG	AVG	TB	BLK	RET	RYD	IN20	NAV
Mohr	74	2991	58	40.4	4	0	29	247	19	36.0
TEAM	74	2991	58	40.4	4	0	29	247	19	36.0
OPPONENTS	65	2719	58	41.8	8	0	33	277	20	35.1

FUMBLES	FUM	OFF.FUM.REC.	REC	TD	DEF.FUM.REC.	REC	TD
Kelly	7	Kelly	3	0	Patton	3	0
Thomas	6				Maddox	2	0
Davis, K.	3				Talley	2	0
TEAM	26	TEAM	9	0	TEAM	24	1
OPPONENTS	35	OPPONENTS	11	0	OPPONENTS	17	0

1994 Draft Choices

ROUND	NAME	POS	SCHOOL	OVERALL SELECTION
1	Jeff Burris	DB	Notre Dame	27
2	Bucky Brooks	WR	North Carolina	48
2	Lonnie Johnson	TE	Florida State	61
2	Sam Rogers	LB	Colorado	64
3	Marlo Perry	LB	Jackson State	81
3	Corey Loucheiy	T	South Carolina	98
4	Sean Crocker	DB	North Carolina	130
5	A. J. Ofodile	TE	Missouri	158
6	Anthony Abrams	DT	Clark (GA)	188
6	Kevin Knox	WR	Florida State	192
7	Filmel Johnson	DB	Illinois	221

HISTORY

TITLES

1964	AFL Championship
1965	AFL Championship
1966	AFL East Championship
1980	AFC East Championship
1988	AFC East Championship
1989	AFC East Championship
1990	AFC Championship
1991	AFC Championship
1992	AFC Championship
1993	AFC Championship

ALL-TIME TEAM RECORDS

Rushing

Most yards, game:	273	O.J. Simpson	11/25/76
Most yards, season:	2,003	O.J. Simpson	1973
Most yards, career:	10,183	O.J. Simpson	1969-1977

Passing

Most yards, game:	419	Joe Ferguson	10/9/83
Most yards, season:	3,844	Jim Kelly	1991
Most yards, career:	27,590	Joe Ferguson	1973-1984

Receiving

Most catches, game:	13	Greg Bell	9/8/85
		Andre Reed	9/15/89
		Thurman Thomas	9/15/91
Most catches, season:	88	Andre Reed	1989
Most catches, career:	586	Andre Reed	1985-1993

Scoring

Most points, game:	30	Cookie Gilchrist	12/8/67
Most points, season:	138	O.J. Simpson	1975
Most points, career:	670	Scott Norwood	1985-1991

COACHES

NAME	RECORD	YEARS
Buster Ramsey	11-16-1	1960-61
Lou Saban	70-47-4	1962-65, 72-76
Joe Collier	13-17-1	1966-68
Harvey Johnson	2-23-1	1968, 1971
John Rauch	7-20-1	1969-70
Jim Ringo	3-20-0	1976-77
Chuck Knox	38-38-0	1978-82
Kay Stephenson	10-26-0	1983-84
Hank Bullough	4-17-0	1985-86
Marv Levy	87-44-0	1986-93

BUFFALO BILLS
1994 TRAINING CAMP ROSTER

No.	Quarterbacks		Ht.	Wt.	Born	NFL Exp.	College	How acq.	93 GP/GS
12	Kelly, Jim	QB	6-3	220	2-14-60	9	Miami (FL)	D1b '83	16/16
14	Reich, Frank	QB	6-4	205	12-4-61	10	Maryland	D3a '85	13/0
11	Strom, Rick	QB	6-2	197	3-11-65	5	Georgia Tech	FA '94	0/0
	Running backs								
23	Davis, Kenneth	RB	5-10	208	4-16-62	9	Texas Christian	Plan B '89	16/0
33	Fuller, Eddie	RB	5-9	201	6-22-68	5	Louisiana State	D4 '90	7/0
35	Gardner, Carwell	FB	6-2	244	11-27-66	5	Louisville	D2 '90	13/2
34	Thomas, Thurman	RB	5-10	198	5-16-66	7	Oklahoma St.	D2 '88	16/16
21	Turner, Nate	RB	6-1	255	5-28-69	3	Nebraska	D6 '92	13/0
	Wide receivers								
82	Beebe, Don	WR	5-11	180	12-18-64	6	Chadron State	D3 '89	14/14
80	Brooks, Bill	WR	6-0	189	4-6-64	9	Boston University	FA '93	16/13
81	Brooks, Bucky	WR	6-0	190	1-22-71	R	North Carolina	D2a '94	
85	Copeland, Russell	WR	6-0	200	11-4-71	2	Memphis State	D4 '93	16/2
18	Knox, Kevin	WR	6-3	195	1-30-71	R	Florida State	D6b '94	
83	Reed, Andre	WR	6-2	190	1-29-64	10	Kutztown	D4a '85	15/15
89	Tasker, Steve	WR	5-9	183	4-10-62	10	Northwestern	W-HOU '86	15/0
	Tight ends								
**	Awalt, Robert	TE	6-5	238	4-9-64	8	San Diego State	FA '92	12/1
84	Johnson, Lonnie	TE	6-3	230	2-14-71	R	Florida State	D2b '94	
**	McKeller, Keith	TE	6-4	242	7-9-64	8	Jacksonville St.	D9 '87	8/1
88	Metzelaars, Pete	TE	6-7	250	5-24-60	13	Wabash	T-SEA '85	16/16
86	Ofodile, A.J.	TE	6-7	260	10-9-73	R	Missouri	D5 '94	
	Offensive linemen								
66	Crafts, Jerry	T	6-6	351	1-6-68	3	Louisville	FA '92	16/0
65	Davis, John	G	6-4	310	8-22-65	8	Georgia Tech	Plan B '89	16/16
62	Devlin, Mike	C	6-1	293	11-16-69	2	Iowa	D5 '93	12/0
70	Fina, John	OL	6-4	282	3-11-69	3	Arizona	D1 '92	16/16
67	Hull, Kent	C	6-5	284	1-13-61	9	Mississippi St.	FA '86	14/13
68	Lacina, Corbin	OL	6-4	300	11-2-70	1	Augustana (SD)	D6 '93	0/0
63	Lingner, Adam	C	6-4	268	11-2-60	12	Illinois	Plan B '89	16/0
72	Loucheiy, Corey	T	6-7	305	10-10-71	R	South Carolina	D3b '94	
74	Parker, Glenn	G-T	6-5	305	4-22-66	5	Arizona	D3 '90	16/9
**	Ritcher, Jim	G	6-3	273	5-21-58	15	North Carolina St.	D1 '80	12/10
	Defensive linemen								
95	Abrams, Anthony	DT	6-3	298	2-16-71	R	Clark Atlanta	D6a '94	
77	Barnett, Oliver	DE	6-3	292	4-9-66	5	Kentucky	FA '93	16/6
90	Hansen, Phil	DE	6-5	275	5-20-68	4	North Dakota St.	D2 '91	11/9
73	Lodish, Mike	NT	6-3	280	8-11-67	5	UCLA	D10 '90	16/1
92	Parrella, John	DL	6-3	296	11-22-69	2	Nebraska	D2 '93	10/0
99	Patton, James	DL	6-3	287	1-5-70	3	Texas	D2 '92	2/0
78	Pike, Mark	DE	6-4	272	12-27-63	9	Georgia Tech	D7b '86	14/0
78	Smith, Bruce	DE	6-4	273	6-18-63	10	Virginia Tech	D1a '85	16/16
91	Wright, Jeff	NT	6-3	270	6-13-63	7	Central Missouri St.	D8b '88	15/15
	Linebackers								
97	Bennett, Cornelius	LB	6-2	238	8-25-65	8	Alabama	T-IND '87	16/16
96	Brown, Monty	LB	6-0	228	4-13-70	2	Ferris State	FA '93	13/0
50	Goganious, Keith	LB	6-2	239	12-7-68	3	Penn State	D3 '92	16/7
55	Maddox, Mark	LB	6-1	233	3-23-68	4	Northern Michigan	D9 '91	11/8
53	Patton, Marvcus	LB	6-2	243	5-1-67	5	UCLA	D8 '90	16/16
58	Perry, Marlo	LB	6-4	250	8-25-72	R	Jackson State	D2a '94	
93	Rogers, Sam	LB	6-3	245	5-30-70	R	Colorado	D2c '94	
56	Talley, Darryl	LB	6-4	235	7-10-60	12	West Virginia	D2 '83	16/16
	Defensive backs								
22	Burris, Jeff	DB	6-0	204	6-7-72	R	Notre Dame	D1 '94	
27	Crocker, Sean	DB	5-9	191	6-14-71	R	North Carolina	D4 '94	
43	Darby, Matt	S	6-1	200	11-19-68	3	UCLA	D5 '92	16/3
36	Henderson, Jerome	DB	5-10	189	8-8-69	4	Clemson	FA '93	2/0
39	Johnson, Filmel	DB	5-10	187	12-24-70	R	Illinois	D7 '94	
20	Jones, Henry	S	5-11	197	12-29-67	4	Illinois	D1 '91	16/16
**	Kelso, Mark	FS	5-11	185	7-23-63	9	William and Mary	FA '86	14/14
28	Smith, Thomas	CB	5-11	188	12-5-70	2	North Carolina	D1 '93	16/1
25	Washington, Mickey	CB	5-9	191	7-8-68	4	Texas A&M	FA '93	16/6
	Specialists								
2	Christie, Steve	K	6-0	185	11-13-67	5	William and Mary	Plan B '92	16/0
9	Mohr, Chris	P	6-5	215	5-11-66	5	Alabama	FA '91	16/0

Jim Kelly   No. 12/QB

Full name: James Edward Kelly
HT: 6-3 **WT:** 226
Born: 2-14-60, Pittsburgh, PA
High school: East Brady (PA)
College: Miami (FL)
Kelly led the Bills to their fourth straight AFC title with a 61.3% completion rate, second in the conference.

YEAR	TEAM	G	PASSING										RUSHING			
			ATT	CPL	CPL%	YDS	AVG	TDS	TD%	INT	INT%	RTG	ATT	YDS	AVG
1986	Buffalo	16	480	285	59.4	3593	7.5	22	4.6	17	3.5	83.3	41	199	4.9
1987	Buffalo	12	419	250	59.7	2798	6.7	19	4.5	11	2.6	83.8	29	133	4.6
1988	Buffalo	16	452	269	59.5	3380	7.5	15	3.3	17	3.8	78.2	35	154	4.4
1989	Buffalo	13	391	228	58.3	3130	8.0	25	6.4	18	4.6	86.2	29	137	4.7
1990	Buffalo	14	346	219	63.3	2829	8.2	24	6.9	9	2.6	101.2	22	63	2.9
1991	Buffalo	15	474	304	64.1	3844	8.1	33	7.0	17	3.6	97.6	20	45	2.3
1992	Buffalo	16	462	269	58.2	3457	7.5	23	5.0	19	4.1	81.2	31	53	1.7
1993	Buffalo	16	470	288	61.3	3382	7.2	18	3.8	18	3.8	79.9	36	102	2.8
8 YR TOTALS		118	3494	2112	60.4	26413	7.8	179	5.1	126	3.6		243	886	3.6
1993 RANK NFL QB			7	5	15		21	6	25	4	29	27	10	14	31
1994 PROJECTIONS		16	473	292	61.7	3256	6.9	13	2.7	18	3.8		40	119	3.0

Kenneth Davis   No. 23/RB

Full name: Kenneth Earl Davis
HT: 5-10 **WT:** 208
Born: 4-16-62, Temple, TX
High school: Temple (TX)
College: Texas Christian
Davis tied for the team lead with 6 rushing TDs, which matched his career-high.

YEAR	TEAM	G	RUSHING				RECEIVING				KICK RETURNS			
			ATT	YDS	AVG	TD	REC	YDS	AVG	TD	RET	YDS	AVG	TD
1986	Green Bay	16	114	519	4.6	0	21	142	6.8	1	12	231	19.3	0
1987	Green Bay	10	109	413	3.8	3	14	110	7.9	0	---	---	---	---
1988	Green Bay	9	39	121	3.1	1	11	81	7.4	0	---	---	---	---
1989	Buffalo	16	29	149	5.1	1	6	92	15.3	2	3	52	17.3	0
1990	Buffalo	16	64	302	4.7	4	9	78	8.7	1	---	---	---	---
1991	Buffalo	16	129	624	4.8	4	20	118	5.9	1	4	73	18.3	0
1992	Buffalo	16	139	613	4.4	6	15	80	5.3	0	14	251	17.9	0
1993	Buffalo	16	109	391	3.6	6	21	95	4.5	0	8	100	12.5	0
8 YR TOTALS		115	732	3132	4.3	25	117	796	6.8	5	41	707	17.2	0
1993 RANK NFL RB			43	44	79	14	43	65	105	40	20	25	51	
1994 PROJECTIONS		16	108	329	3.0	7	25	97	3.9	0	8	77	9.6	0

Thurman Thomas No. 34/RB

Full name: Thurman Lee Thomas
HT: 5-10 **WT:** 198
Born: 5-16-66, Houston, TX
High school: Willowridge (Missouri City, TX)
College: Oklahoma State
Thomas led the AFC in rushing and total yards from scrimmage, and went to his fifth straight Pro Bowl.

YEAR TEAM	G	RUSHING ATT	YDS	AVG	TD	RECEIVING REC	YDS	AVG	TD	KICK RETURNS RET	YDS	AVG	TD
1988 Buffalo	15	207	881	4.3	2	18	208	11.6	0	---	---	---	---
1989 Buffalo	16	298	1244	4.2	6	60	669	11.2	6	---	---	---	---
1990 Buffalo	16	271	1297	4.8	11	49	532	10.9	2	---	---	---	---
1991 Buffalo	15	288	1407	4.9	7	62	631	10.2	5	---	---	---	---
1992 Buffalo	16	312	1487	4.8	9	58	626	10.8	3	---	---	---	---
1993 Buffalo	16	355	1315	3.7	6	48	387	8.1	0	---	---	---	---
6 YR TOTALS	94	1731	7631	4.4	41	295	3053	10.3	16	0	0	NA	0
1993 RANK NFL RB		1	3	72	14	13	13	50	40	65	65	65	
1994 PROJECTIONS	16	382	1255	3.3	5	42	262	6.2	0	0	0	NA	0

Bill Brooks   No. 80/WR

Full name: William Brooks Jr.
HT: 6-0 **WT:** 189
Born: 4-6-64, Boston, MA
High school: Framingham (MA)
College: Boston University
In his first year with Buffalo, Brooks was second on the team in catches (60) and receiving yards (714).

YEAR TEAM	G	RECEIVING REC	YDS	AVG	TD	RUSHING ATT	YDS	AVG	TD	PUNT RETURN RET	YDS	AVG
1991 Indianapolis	16	72	888	12.3	4	---	---	---	---	---	---	---
1992 Indianapolis	14	44	468	10.6	1	2	14	7.0	0	---	---	---
1993 Buffalo	16	60	714	11.9	5	3	30	10.0	0	1	3	3.0
8 YR TOTALS	122	471	6532	13.9	33	18	106	5.9	0	44	295	6.7
1993 RANK NFL WR		24	36	103	19	12	10	8		27	29	28
1994 PROJECTIONS	16	61	715	11.7	6	4	42	10.5	0	2	5	2.5

Don Beebe　　No. 82/WR

Full name: Don Lee Beebe
HT: 5-11 **WT:** 180
Born: 12-18-64, Aurora, IL
High school: Kaneland (Maple Park, IL)
College: W. Illinois; Chadron State (NE)
The dependable Beebe racked up 504 yards as Buffalo's third wideout.

YEAR	TEAM	G	RECEIVING REC	YDS	AVG	TD	RUSHING ATT	YDS	AVG	TD	PUNT RETURN RET	YDS	AVG
1989	Buffalo	14	17	317	18.6	2	---	---	---	---	---	---	---
1990	Buffalo	12	11	221	20.1	1	1	23	23.0	0	---	---	---
1991	Buffalo	11	32	414	12.9	6	---	---	---	---	---	---	---
1992	Buffalo	12	33	554	16.8	2	1	-6	-6.0	0	---	---	---
1993	Buffalo	14	31	504	16.3	3	---	---	---	---	---	---	---
	5 YR TOTALS	63	124	2010	16.2	14	2	17	8.5	0	0	0	NA
1993	RANK NFL WR		61	55	27	41	42	42	42		30	30	29
1994	PROJECTIONS	16	35	569	16.3	3	0	0	NA	0	0	0	NA

Andre Reed　　No. 83/WR

Full name: Andre Darnell Reed
HT: 6-2 **WT:** 190
Born: 1-29-64, Allentown, PA
High school: Dieruff (Allentown, PA)
College: Kutztown
Reed had a team-high 854 yards on just 52 catches, for an impressive 16.4 yards/catch.

YEAR	TEAM	G	RECEIVING REC	YDS	AVG	TD	RUSHING ATT	YDS	AVG	TD	PUNT RETURN RET	YDS	AVG	TD
1986	Buffalo	15	53	739	13.9	7	3	-8	-2.7	0	---	---	---	---
1987	Buffalo	12	57	752	13.2	5	1	1	1.0	0	---	---	---	---
1988	Buffalo	15	71	968	13.6	6	6	64	10.7	0	---	---	---	---
1989	Buffalo	16	88	1312	14.9	9	2	31	15.5	0	---	---	---	---
1990	Buffalo	16	71	945	13.3	8	3	23	7.7	0	---	---	---	---
1991	Buffalo	16	81	1113	13.7	10	12	136	11.3	0	---	---	---	---
1992	Buffalo	16	65	913	14.0	3	8	65	8.1	0	---	---	---	---
1993	Buffalo	15	52	854	16.4	6	9	21	2.3	0	---	---	---	---
	9 YR TOTALS	137	586	8233	14.0	58	47	0.8	53.6	1	5	12	NA	0
1993	RANK NFL WR		32	20	25	13	2	14	30		30	30	29	
1994	PROJECTIONS	15	44	804	18.3	6	10	0	0.0	0	0	0	NA	0

Pete Metzelaars No. 88/TE

Full name: Peter Henry Metzelaars
HT: 6-7 **WT:** 250
Born: 5-24-60, Three Rivers, MI
High school: Portage Central (MI)
College: Wabash
Metzelaars became the first TE to lead the Bills in receptions since 1962.

			RECEIVING			
YEAR	TEAM	G	REC	YDS	AVG	TD
1986	Buffalo	16	49	485	9.9	3
1987	Buffalo	12	28	290	10.4	0
1988	Buffalo	16	33	438	13.3	1
1989	Buffalo	16	18	179	9.9	2
1990	Buffalo	16	10	60	6.0	1
1991	Buffalo	16	5	54	10.8	2
1992	Buffalo	16	30	298	9.9	6
1993	Buffalo	16	68	609	9.0	4
12 YR TOTALS		174	280	2797	10.0	21
1993 RANK NFL TE			2	8	47	8
1994 PROJECTIONS		16	93	829	8.9	4

Bruce Smith   No. 78/DE

Full name: Bruce Bernard Smith
HT: 6-4 **WT:** 273
Born: 6-18-63, Norfolk, VA
High school: B. T. Washington (Norfolk, VA)
College: Virginia Tech
Smith had a team-high 13.5 sacks; his 12 career postseason sacks are an all-time NFL record.

YEAR	TEAM	G	INT	YDS	AVG	TD	SACKS	FUM REC	TD
1985	Buffalo	16	---	---	---	---	6.5	4	0
1986	Buffalo	16	---	---	---	---	15.0	---	---
1987	Buffalo	12	---	---	---	---	12.0	2	1
1988	Buffalo	12	---	---	---	---	11.0	---	---
1989	Buffalo	16	---	---	---	---	13.0	---	---
1990	Buffalo	16	---	---	---	---	19.0	---	---
1991	Buffalo	5	---	---	---	---	1.5	---	---
1992	Buffalo	15	---	---	---	---	14.0	---	---
1993	Buffalo	16	1	0	0.0	0	13.5	1	0
9 YR TOTALS		124	1	0	0.0	0	105.5	7	1
1993 RANK NFL DL			2	10	10	3	2	25	5
1994 PROJECTIONS		16	2	0	0.0	0	14	2	0

Cornelius Bennett No. 97/LB

Full name: Cornelius O'landa Bennett
HT: 6-2   **WT:** 238
Born: 8-25-65, Birmingham, AL
High school: Ensley (Birmingham, AL)
College: Alabama
5-time Pro Bowler Bennett was fourth on the team in tackles (102) and third in sacks (4.5).

YEAR	TEAM	G	INT	YDS	AVG	TD	SACKS	FUM REC	TD
1987	Buffalo	8	---	---	---	---	8.5	---	---
1988	Buffalo	16	2	30	15.0	---	9.5	3	0
1989	Buffalo	12	2	5	2.5	---	5.5	2	0
1990	Buffalo	16	---	---	---	---	4.0	2	0
1991	Buffalo	16	---	---	---	---	9.0	2	1
1992	Buffalo	15	---	---	---	---	4.0	3	0
1993	Buffalo	16	1	5	5.0	0	4.5	1	0
	7 YR TOTALS	99	5	40	8.0	0	45.0	13	1
1993	RANK NFL LB		17	32	30	5	25	24	8
1994	PROJECTIONS	16	1	7	7.0	0	4	0	0

Henry Jones No. 20/S

HT: 5-11 **WT:** 197
Born: 12-29-67, St. Louis, MO
High school: University (St. Louis)
College: Illinois
Jones was second on the team with 12 passes defensed. His 83 tackles led the secondary.

YEAR	TEAM	G	INT	YDS	AVG	TD	SACKS	FUM REC	TD
1991	Buffalo	15	---	---	---	---	---	1	0
1992	Buffalo	16	8	263	32.9	2	---	2	0
1993	Buffalo	16	2	92	46.0	1	2.0	1	0
	3 YR TOTALS	47	10	355	35.5	3	2.0	4	0
1993	RANK NFL DB		54	13	8	2	4	37	14
1994	PROJECTIONS	16	0	0	NA	1	4	0	0

Steve Christie   No. 2/K

Full name: Geoffrey Stephen Christie
HT: 6-0   **WT:** 185
Born: 11-13-67, Oakville, ONT
High school: Trafalgar (Oakville, ONT)
College: William and Mary
Christie hit the longest FG in Super Bowl history—54 yards against Dallas in '94.

YEAR	TEAM	G	XP	XPA	XP Pct.	FG	FGA	FG Pct.	PTS
1990	Tampa Bay	16	27	27	100.0	23	27	85.2	96
1991	Tampa Bay	16	22	22	100.0	15	20	75.0	67
1992	Buffalo	16	43	44	97.7	24	30	80.0	115
1993	Buffalo	16	36	37	97.3	23	32	71.9	105
	4 YR TOTALS	64	128	130	98.5	85	109	78.0	383
1993	RANK NFL		8	5	17	17	11	24	14
1994	PROJECTIONS	16	37	38	97.4	24	35	68.6	109

Marv Levy   Head Coach

Full name: Marvin Daniel Levy
Born: 8-3-28, Chicago, IL
High school: South Shore (Chicago, IL)
College: Coe (IA)
Levy's Bills have won six straight division titles (tying for first in '92) and four straight AFC titles.

		REGULAR SEASON					POSTSEASON		
YEAR	TEAM	W	L	T	PCT	FINISH	W	L	FINISH
1978	Kansas City	4	12	0	.250	5th/AFC West			
1979	Kansas City	7	9	0	.438	5th/AFC West			
1980	Kansas City	8	8	0	.500	T3rd/AFC West			
1981	Kansas City	9	7	0	.563	3rd/AFC West			
1982	Kansas City	3	6	0	.333	11th/AFC			
1986	Buffalo	2	5	0	.286	4th/AFC East			
1987	Buffalo	7	8	0	.467	4th/AFC East			
1988	Buffalo	12	4	0	.750	1st/AFC East	1	1	lost AFC Title game to Cinn., 21-10
1989	Buffalo	9	7	0	.563	1st/AFC East	0	1	lost 1st Rnd. game to Cleve., 34-30
1990	Buffalo	13	3	0	.813	1st/AFC East	2	1	lost Super Bowl XXV to NY Giants, 20-19
1991	Buffalo	13	3	0	.813	1st/AFC East	2	1	lost Super Bowl XXVI to Wash., 37-24
1992	Buffalo	11	5	0	.688	T1st/AFC East	3	1	lost Super Bowl XVII to Dallas, 52-17
1993	Buffalo	12	4	0	.750	1st/AFC East	2	1	lost Super Bowl XVIII to Dallas, 30-13
	13 YR TOTALS	110	81	0	.576		10	6	

Frank Reich   No. 14/QB

Full name: Frank Michael Reich
HT: 6-4   **WT:** 205
Born: 12-4-61, Freeport, NY
High school: Cedar Crest (Lebanon, PA)
College: Maryland
Reich had a sparkling 103.5 QB rating in 1993.

YEAR	TEAM	G	PASSING									RUSHING		
			ATT	CPL	CPL%	YDS	AVG	TDS	TD%	INT	INT%	RTG	ATT	YDS	AVG
1991	Buffalo	16	41	27	65.9	305	7.4	6	14.6	2	4.9	107.2	13	6	0.5
1992	Buffalo	16	47	24	51.1	221	4.7	0	0.0	2	4.3	46.5	9	-9	-1.0
1993	Buffalo	15	26	16	61.5	153	5.9	2	7.7	0	0.0	103.5	8	-8	-1.0
8	YR TOTALS	77	284	166	58.5	1972	6.9	17	6.0	8	2.8		56	42	0.8
1993	RANK NFL QB		58	58	13	58	48	48	3	61	61		4	46	65	56
1994	PROJECTIONS	15	7	6	85.7	15	2.1	1	14.3	0	0.0		3	0	0.0

Russell Copeland No. 85/WR

Full name: Russell Copeland
HT: 6-0   **WT:** 200
Born: 11-4-71, Tupelo, MS
High school: Tupelo (MS)
College: Memphis State
Copeland posted a team-high 18.6 yards/catch.

YEAR	TEAM	G	RECEIVING				RUSHING				PUNT RETURN		
			REC	YDS	AVG	TD	ATT	YDS	AVG	TD	RET	YDS	AVG
1993	Buffalo	16	13	242	18.6	0	---	---	---	---	31	274	8.8
1	YR TOTALS	16	13	242	18.6	0	0	0	NA	0	31	274	8.8
1993	RANK NFL WR		90	79	11	95	42	42	42		8	8	11

Steve Tasker   No. 89/WR

Full name: Steven Jay Tasker
HT: 5-9   **WT:** 183
Born: 4-10-62, Smith Center, KS
High school: Wichita County (Leoti, KS)
College: Northwestern
Tasker is the NFL's best special teams player.

YEAR	TEAM	G	RECEIVING				RUSHING				PUNT RETURN		
			REC	YDS	AVG	TD	ATT	YDS	AVG	TD	RET	YDS	AVG
1991	Buffalo	16	2	39	19.5	1	---	---	---	---	---	---	---
1992	Buffalo	15	2	24	12.0	0	1	9	9.0	---	---	---	---
1993	Buffalo	15	2	26	13.0	0	---	---	---	---	1	0	0.0
9	YR TOTALS	120	10	152	15.2	3	3	25	8.3	0	1	0	0.0
1993	RANK NFL WR		128	131	82	95	42	42	42		27	30	29
1994	PROJECTIONS	15	2	26	13.0	0	0	0	NA	0	2	0	0.0

Kent Hull

No. 67/C

Full name: James Kent Hull
HT: 6-5 **WT:** 284
Born: 1-13-61, Ponotoc, MS
High school: Greenwood (MS)
College: Mississippi State
The OL will miss departed Howard Ballard.

YEAR	TEAM	G	RUSHING ATT	YDS	AVG	RANK AV RUSH	PASS YDS	RANK PASS YDS	SACKS	YDS. LOST
1991	Buffalo	16	505	2381	4.7	3	4140	3	35	269
1992	Buffalo	16	549	2436	4.4	5	3678	5	29	221
1993	Buffalo	14	550	1943	3.5	23	3535	11	31	218
8 YR TOTALS		122								

Phil Hansen

No. 90/DE

Full name: Philip Allen Hansen
HT: 6-5 **WT:** 275
Born: 5-20-68, Ellendale, ND
High school: Oakes (ND)
College: North Dakota State
Hansen had 3.5 sacks and 14 QB pressures.

YEAR	TEAM	G	NO	YARDS	LONG	AVG	BLK	IN20
1990	New England	16	90	3752	NA	41.7	2	NA
1991	Cleveland	16	80	3397	65	42.5	0	20
1992	Cleveland	16	74	3083	73	41.7	1	28
1993	Cleveland	16	82	3632	72	44.3	2	15
9 YR TOTALS		140	689	29120	73	42.3	8	63
1993 RANK NFL Ps			8	6	5	5		23
1994 PROJECTIONS		16	87	3965	73	45.6	3	7

Jeff Wright

No. 91/NT

Full name: Jeff Dee Wright
HT: 6-3 **WT:** 270
Born: 6-13-63, San Bernadino, CA
High school: Lawrence (KS)
College: Central Missouri St.
Wright's 79 tackles ranked sixth on the team.

YEAR	TEAM	G	INT	YDS	AVG	TD	SACKS	FUM REC	TD
1991	Buffalo	9	---	---	---	---	6.0	---	---
1992	Buffalo	16	---	---	---	---	6.0	1	0
1993	Buffalo	15	---	---	---	---	5.5	1	0
6 YR TOTALS		86	1	0	0.0	0	30.5	5	0
1993 RANK NFL DL			16	NA	NA	NA	43	25	5
1994 PROJECTIONS		16	0	0	0	0	8	1	0

Darryl Talley   No. 56/LB

Full name: Darryl Victor Talley
HT: 6-4   **WT:** 235
Born: 7-10-60, Cleveland, OH
High school: Shaw (East Cleveland, OH)
College: West Virginia
Talley led the team with 136 tackles.

YEAR	TEAM	G	INT	YDS	AVG	TD	SACKS	FUM REC	TD
1991	Buffalo	16	5	45	9.0	0	4.0	2	0
1992	Buffalo	16	---	---	---	---	4.0	---	---
1993	Buffalo	16	3	74	24.7	1	2.0	2	0
11 YR TOTALS		172	11	179	16.3	2	38.5	11	0
1993 RANK NFL LB			2	1	6		37	9	8
1994 PROJECTIONS		16	4	102	25.5	1	1	3	0

Thomas Smith   No. 28/CB

Full name: Thomas Lee Smith Jr.
HT: 5-11   **WT:** 188
Born: 12-5-70, Gates, NC
High school: Gates (NC)
College: North Carolina
'93 draft pick Smith should replace Nate Odomes.

YEAR	TEAM	G	INT	YDS	AVG	TD	SACKS	FUM REC	TD
1993	Buffalo	16	---	---	---	---	---	1	0
1 YR TOTALS		16	0	0	NA	0	0.0	1	0
1993 RANK NFL DB			156	NA	NA	NA	49	37	14

Chris Mohr   No. 9/P

Full name: Christopher Garrett Mohr
HT: 6-5   **WT:** 215
Born: 5-11-66, Atlanta, GA
High school: Briarwood Academy (Thomson, GA)
College: Alabama
Mohr had 19 punts inside the 20 in 1993.

YEAR	TEAM	G	NO	YARDS	LONG	AVG	BLK	IN20
1989	Tampa Bay	16	84	3311	NA	39.4	2	NA
1991	Buffalo	10	54	2085	58	38.6	0	12
1992	Buffalo	16	60	2531	61	42.2	0	13
1993	Buffalo	15	74	2991	58	40.4	0	19
4 YR TOTALS		57	272	10918	61	40.1	2	44
1993 RANK NFL Ps			14	20	25	25		15
1994 PROJECTIONS		16	87	3484	55	40.0	0	24

Cincinnati *BENGALS*

1994 Scouting Report

Offense

Surprisingly, the Bengals signed no major free agents on offense, aside from ex-Bengal Tim McGee, who returns after a year in Washington. Cincinnati is still counting on David Klingler at QB. The Bengals have good WRs in Jeff Query, the team leader in catches, and Carl Pickens, '92's AFC Offensive Rookie of the Year. Also, RB Derrick Fenner and TE Tony McGee both have very good hands. On the ground, Cincinnati will look for a rebound from RB Harold Green, a 1,000-yard back in '92 who gained only 589 yards in '93. T Joe Walter is a steady performer for Cincinnati, but the Bengals will miss T Randy Kirk, who left for Arizona.

Defense

The Bengals ranked second in pass defense with just 2,798 passing yards allowed, but that's because opponents could run against them almost at will. Cincinnati gave up 2,220 rushing yards, next to last in the NFL. The Bengals moved to bolster their run defense by taking big, fast DT Dan Wilkinson with the draft's first pick. He impressed the scouts at the combine, but most think he's a year or two away. NT Tim Krumrie is still one of the best in the league. The LB corps is mediocre, but they're young and should improve— Ricardo McDonald and Steve Tovar may be the team's best. Veteran Louis Oliver, who started at safety for Miami in '93, will bolster the secondary.

Special Teams

Lee Johnson is an above-average punter, who is sometimes called on to attempt long FGs. K Doug Pelfrey is fairly accurate, but main returner Patrick Robinson is only average.

1994 Prospects

There's a shortage of talent and depth on this team. For the first time since 1980, Cincinnati failed to place a player in the Pro Bowl. The Bengals need to upgrade their LB corps before their overall defense can improve dramatically. Offensively, David Klingler hasn't proven he can be a quality NFL QB, and Green or someone else must step up and establish a running game. The Bengals may improve slightly over '93, but fans can expect another long season.

Team Directory

Chairman of the board: Austin E. Knowlton
President: John Sawyer
VP/General manager: Mike Brown
Director of player personnel: Pete Brown
Director of public relations: Allan Heim

1993 Review

Sep. 5	at Cleveland	L 27-14
Sep. 12	INDIANAPOLIS	L 9-6
Sep. 19	at Pittsburgh	L 34-7
Sep. 26	SEATTLE	L 19-10
Oct. 3	OPEN DATE	
Oct. 10	at Kansas City	L 17-15
Oct. 17	CLEVELAND	L 28-17
Oct. 24	at Houston	L 28-12
Oct. 31	OPEN DATE	
Nov. 7	PITTSBURGH	L 24-16
Nov. 14	HOUSTON	L 38-3
Nov. 21	at N.Y. Jets	L 17-12
Nov. 28	L.A. RAIDERS	W 16-10
Dec. 5	at San Francisco	L 21-8
Dec. 12	at New England	L 7-2
Dec. 19	L.A. RAMS	W 15-3
Dec. 26	ATLANTA	W 21-17
Jan. 2	at New Orleans	L 20-13

1994 Schedule

Sep. 4	CLEVELAND	1:00
Sep. 11	at San Diego	4:00
Sep. 18	NEW ENGLAND	1:00
Sep. 25	at Houston	4:00
Oct. 2	MIAMI	8:00
Oct. 9	OPEN DATE	
Oct. 16	at Pittsburgh	1:00
Oct. 23	at Cleveland	1:00
Oct. 30	DALLAS	1:00
Nov. 6	at Seattle	1:00
Nov. 13	HOUSTON	1:00
Nov. 20	INDIANAPOLIS	1:00
Nov. 27	at Denver	4:00
Dec. 4	PITTSBURGH	1:00
Dec. 11	at N.Y. Giants	1:00
Dec. 18	at Arizona	4:00
Dec. 24	PHILADELPHIA	1:00

1993 finish: 3-13 (3-5 home, 0-8 away), fourth in AFC Central

Team Leaders

PASSING	ATT	COM	COM%	YDS	YPA	TD	TD%	INT	INT%	RTG
Klingler	343	190	55.4	1935	5.64	6	1.7	9	2.6	66.6
Schroeder	159	78	49.1	832	5.23	5	3.1	2	1.3	70.0
Wilhelm	6	4	66.7	63	10.50	0	0.0	0	0.0	101.4
TEAM	510	272	53.3	2830	5.55	11	2.2	11	2.2	67.9
OPPONENTS	457	251	54.9	2952	6.46	20	4.4	12	2.6	78.4

RECEIVING	REC	YDS	AVG	TD	RUSHING	ATT	YDS	AVG	TD
Query	56	654	11.7	4	Green	215	589	2.7	0
Fenner	48	427	8.9	0	Fenner	121	482	4.0	1
McGee, To.	44	525	11.9	0	Klingler	41	282	6.9	0
Pickens	43	565	13.1	6	Miles	22	56	2.5	1
Green	22	115	5.2	0	Schroeder	10	41	4.1	0
TEAM	272	2830	10.4	11	TEAM	423	1511	3.6	3
OPPONENTS	251	2952	11.8	20	OPPONENTS	521	2220	4.3	15

INTERCEPTIONS	INT	YDS	AVG	LG	TD	SACKS		NO
Brim	3	74	24.7	30	1	Stubbs		5.0
Williams	2	126	63.0	97t	1	Williams		4.0
White	2	19	9.5	14	0	Copeland		3.0
TEAM	12	272	22.7	97t	2	TEAM		22.0
OPPONENTS	11	49	4.5	30	0	OPPONENTS		53.0

KICK RETURNS	NO	YDS	AV	LG	TD	PUNT RETURNS	NO	FC	YDS	AV	LG	TD
Robinson	30	567	18.9	42	0	Robinson	43	6	305	7.1	36	0
Ball	23	501	21.8	45	0	Pickens	4	2	16	4.0	9	0
Benjamin	4	78	19.5	24	0	Simmons	1	0	0	0.0	0	0
TEAM	61	1211	19.9	45	0	TEAM	48	8	321	6.7	36	0
OPPONENTS	38	831	21.9	66	0	OPPONENTS	47	13	416	8.9	39	0

KICKING	XPM	XPA	FGM	FGA	LG	PTS
Pelfrey	13	16	24	31	53	85
TEAM	13	16	24	31	53	85
OPPONENTS	37	37	20	28	53	97

PUNTING	NO	YDS	LG	AVG	TB	BLK	RET	RYD	IN20	NAV
Johnson	90	3954	60	43.9	12	0	47	416	24	36.6
TEAM	90	3954	60	43.9	12	0	47	416	24	36.6
OPPONENTS	74	3123	72	42.2	6	1	48	321	20	36.2

FUMBLES	FUM	OFF.FUM.REC.	REC	TD	DEF.FUM.REC.	REC	TD
Klingler	7	Fenner	2	0	Vinson	3	0
Schroeder	5	Klingler	2	0	Williams	2	0
TEAM	24	TEAM	13	0	TEAM	14	0
OPPONENTS	22	OPPONENTS	5	0	OPPONENTS	9	2

1994 Draft Choices

ROUND	NAME	POS	SCHOOL	OVERALL SELECTION
1	Dan Wilkinson	DT	Ohio State	1
2	Darnay Scott	WR	San Diego State	30
3	Jeff Cothran	RB	Ohio State	66
3	Steve Shine	LB	Northwestern	86
4	Corey Sawyer	CB	Florida State	104
5	Trent Pollard	T	Eastern Washington	132
6	Kimo Von Oelhoffen	DT	Boise State	162
6	Jerry Reynolds	T	Nevada-Las Vegas	184
7	Ramondo Stallings	DE	San Diego State	195

HISTORY

TITLES

1970	AFC Central Championship
1973	AFC Central Championship
1981	AFC Championship
1988	AFC Championship
1990	AFC Central Championship

ALL-TIME TEAM RECORDS

Rushing

Most yards, game:	201	James Brooks	12/23/90
Most yards, season:	1,239	James Brooks	1989
Most yards, career:	6,393	James Brooks	1984-1991

Passing

Most yards, game:	490	Boomer Esiason	10/7/90
Most yards, season:	3,959	Boomer Esiason	1986
Most yards, career:	32,838	Ken Anderson	1971-1986

Receiving

Most catches, game:	11	Tim McGee	11/9/89
Most catches, season:	71	Dan Ross	1981
Most catches, career:	420	Isaac Curtis	1973-1984

Scoring

Most points, game:	24	Larry Kinnebrew	10/28/84
Most points, season:	120	Jim Breech	1985
Most points, career:	1,059	Jim Breech	1980-1992

COACHES

NAME	RECORD	YEARS
Paul Brown	55-59-1	1968-75
Bill Johnson	18-15-0	1976-78
Homer Rice	8-19-0	1978-79
Forrest Gregg	34-27-0	1980-83
Sam Wyche	64-68-0	1984-91
David Shula	8-24-0	1992-93

CINCINNATI BENGALS
1994 TRAINING CAMP ROSTER

No.	Quarterbacks		Ht.	Wt.	Born	NFL Exp.	College	How acq.	93 GP/GS
12	Hollas, Don	QB	6-3	215	11-22-67	3	Rice	D4 '91	0/0
7	Klingler, David	QB	6-2	205	2-17-69	3	Houston	D1 '92	14/13
10	Schroeder, Jay	QB	6-4	215	6-28-61	11	UCLA	FA '93	8/3
	Running backs								
42	Ball, Eric	RB	6-2	220	7-1-66	6	UCLA	D2 '89	15/1
21	Benjamin, Ryan	RB	5-7	183	4-23-70	2	Pacific	FA '93	2/0
33	Broussard, Steve	RB	5-7	201	2-22-67	5	Washington St.	FA '94	8/0
46	Cothran, Jeff	FB	6-2	231	6-28-71	R	Ohio State	D3a '94	
44	Fenner, Derrick	RB	6-3	228	4-6-67	6	North Carolina	FA '92	14/14

No.	Name	Pos	Ht	Wt	Birthdate	Yr	College	How acq.	G/GS
28	Green, Harold	RB	6-2	222	1-29-68	5	South Carolina	D2 '90	15/15
36	Miles, Ostell	RB	6-0	236	8-6-71	3	Houston	D9 '92	15/3
	Wide receivers								
85	McGee, Tim	WR	5-10	183	8-7-64	9	Tennessee	FA '94	13/12
80	Pickens, Carl	WR	6-2	206	3-23-70	3	Tennessee	D2 '92	14/14
89	Query, Jeff	WR	6-0	165	3-7-67	6	Millikin	W-HOU '92	16/16
88	Rambert, Bennie	WR	6-5	200	12-25-66	3	West Virginia	FA '94	0/0
81	Robinson, Patrick	WR	5-8	176	10-3-69	2	Tennessee St.	W-HOU '93	13/2
86	Scott, Darnay	WR	6-1	180	7-7-72	R	San Diego State	D2 '94	
84	Stegall, Milt	WR	6-0	184	1-25-70	3	Miami (OH)	FA '92	0/0
83	Turner, Elbert	WR	5-11	165	3-19-68	1	Illinois	FA '92	0/0
	Tight ends								
47	Frisch, David	TE	6-7	260	6-22-70	2	Colorado State	FA '93	12/2
82	McGee, Tony	TE	6-3	246	4-21-71	2	Michigan	D2 '93	15/15
87	Sadowski, Troy	TE	6-5	250	12-8-65	5	Georgia	FA '94	13/0
49	Thomason, Jeff	TE	6-4	233	12-30-69	3	Oregon	FA '92	2/1
48	Thompson, Craig	TE	6-2	244	1-13-69	3	N. Carolina A&T	D5 '92	13/2
	Offensive linemen								
60	Bradley, Chuck	T	6-5	296	4-9-70	2	Kentucky	W-HOU '93	1/0
65	Brilz, Darrick	G	6-3	287	2-14-64	8	Oregon State	FA '94	16/16
72	Brumfield, Scott	T	6-8	320	8-19-70	2	Brigham Young	FA '93	16/7
68	Johnson, Donnell	T	6-7	310	12-24-69	2	Johnson C. Smith	FA '93	6/0
66	Jones, Dan	T	6-7	298	7-22-70	2	Maine	FA '93	15/8
64	Kozerski, Bruce	G	6-4	287	4-2-62	11	Holy Cross	D9 '84	15/15
62	Moore, Eric	G	6-5	290	1-21-65	7	Indiana	FA '94	7/5
73	Moyer, Ken	T	6-7	297	11-19-66	5	Toledo	FA '89	16/15
76	Pollard, Trent	OL	6-4	325	11-20-72	R	Eastern Washington	D5 '94	
61	Reynolds, Jerry	OL	6-6	300	4-2-70	R	Nevada-Las Vegas	D6b '94	
77	Sargent, Kevin	T	6-6	284	3-31-69	3	East. Washington	FA '92	N/A
74	Scott, Tom	T	6-6	330	6-25-70	2	East Carolina	D6 '93	14/12
63	Walter, Joe	T	6-7	292	6-18-63	10	Texas Tech	D7 '85	16/16
	Defensive linemen								
92	Copeland, John	DT	6-3	286	9-20-70	2	Alabama	D1 '93	14/14
97	Frier, Mike	DE	6-5	299	3-20-69	3	Appalachian St.	W-SEA '92	16/5
98	Hinkle, George	DT	6-5	288	3-17-65	7	Arizona	FA '93	13/11
71	Howe, Garry	NT	6-1	298	6-20-68	3	Colorado	FA '93	1/0
69	Krumrie, Tim	NT	6-2	274	5-20-60	12	Wisconsin	D10 '83	16/16
93	Parten, Ty	NT	6-4	272	10-13-69	2	Arizona	D3a '93	N/A
79	Stallings, Ramondo	DE	6-7	285	11-21-71	R	San Diego State	D7 '94	
96	Stubbs, Daniel	DE	6-4	264	1-3-65	7	Miami (FL)	W-DAL '91	16/0
67	Von Oelhoffen, Kimo	DT	6-4	300	1-30-71	R	Boise State	D6a '94	
99	Wilkinson, Dan	DT	6-5	300	3-13-73	R	Ohio State	D1 '94	
	Linebackers								
	Braxton, David	LB	6-2	240	5-26-65	6	Wake Forest	FA '94	16/0
50	Francis, James	LB	6-5	252	8-4-68	5	Baylor	D1 '90	14/12
	Johnson, John	LB	6-3	230	5-8-68	4	Clemson	FA '94	15/12
56	McDonald, Ricardo	LB	6-2	235	11-8-69	3	Pittsburgh	D4 '92	N/A
59	McGill, Karmeeleyah	LB	6-3	224	1-11-71	2	Notre Dame	FA '93	4/0
90	Shaw, Eric	LB	6-3	248	9-17-71	3	Louisiana Tech	D12 '92	13/11
52	Shine, Steve	LB	6-6	232	11-28-70	R	Northwestern	D3b '94	
53	Stephens, Santo	LB	6-4	232	6-16-69	2	Temple	W-KC '94	16/0
51	Tovar, Steve	LB	6-3	244	4-25-70	2	Ohio State	D3 '93	16/9
94	Williams, Alfred	LB	6-6	240	11-6-68	4	Colorado	D1 '91	16/16
	Defensive backs								
43	Brim, Mike	CB	6-0	192	1-23-66	7	Virginia Union	FA '93	16/16
32	Carpenter, Ron	S	6-1	188	1-20-70	2	Miami (OH)	W-MIN '93	7/0
41	Duckett, Forey	CB	6-3	195	2-5-70	1	Nevada	D5 '93	0/0
24	Grant, Alan	CB	5-10	187	10-1-66	5	Stanford	W-SF '93	9/1
25	Jones, Rod	CB	6-0	185	3-31-64	9	So. Methodist	T-TB '90	16/16
29	Oliver, Louis	S	6-2	224	3-9-66	6	Florida	FA '94	11/11
23	Sawyer, Corey	CB	5-11	171	10-4-71	R	Florida State	D4 '94	
22	Simmons, Marcello	CB	6-1	180	8-8-71	2	So. Methodist	D4 '93	16/3
34	Vinson, Fernandus	S	5-10	197	11-3-68	4	North Carolina St.	D7 '91	16/7
37	Wheeler, Leonard	CB	5-11	189	1-15-69	3	Troy State	D3 '92	16/3
31	Williams, Darryl	S	6-0	191	1-7-70	3	Miami (FL)	D1 '92	16/16
	Specialists								
11	Johnson, Lee	P-K	6-2	200	11-27-61	10	Brigham Young	W-CLE '88	16/0
9	Pelfrey, Doug	K	5-11	185	9-25-70	2	Kentucky	D8 '93	16/0

David Klingler   No. 7/QB

HT: 6-2   **WT:** 205
Born: 2-17-69, Stratford, TX
High school: Stratford (Houston)
College: Houston

The Bengals cast a vote of confidence in Klingler when, despite his difficult sophomore year, they drafted DT Dan Wilkinson, not a QB, with the first pick.

		PASSING										RUSHING		
YEAR	TEAM	G	ATT	CPL	CPL%	YDS	AVG	TDS	TD%	INT	INT%	RTG	ATT	YDS	AVG
1992	Cincinnati	4	98	47	48.0	530	5.4	3	3.1	2	2.0	66.3	11	53	4.8
1993	Cincinnati	14	343	190	55.4	1935	5.6	6	1.7	9	2.6	66.6	41	282	6.9
	2 YR TOTALS	18	441	237	53.7	2465	5.6	9	2.0	11	2.5		52	335	6.4
1993	RANK NFL QB		18	20	48	22	53	31	54	19	41	45	9	2	2
1994	PROJECTIONS	16	392	246	62.8	2303	5.9	2	0.5	13	3.3		50	433	8.7

Jay Schroeder   No. 10/QB

Full name: Jay Brian Schroeder
HT: 6-4   **WT:** 215
Born: 6-28-61, Milwaukee, WI
High school: Pacific Palisades (CA)
College: UCLA

Schroeder started 3 games for Cincinnati. He's a former Pro Bowler with a Super Bowl ring from the '87 Redskins.

		PASSING										RUSHING		
YEAR	TEAM	G	ATT	CPL	CPL%	YDS	AVG	TDS	TD%	INT	INT%	RTG	ATT	YDS	AVG
1986	Washington	16	541	276	51.0	4109	7.6	22	4.1	22	4.1	72.9	38	47	1.3
1987	Washington	11	267	129	48.3	1878	7.0	12	4.5	10	3.7	71.0	26	120	4.6
1988	LA Raiders	9	256	113	44.1	1839	7.2	13	5.1	13	5.1	64.6	29	109	3.8
1989	LA Raiders	11	194	91	46.9	1550	8.0	8	4.1	13	6.7	60.3	15	38	2.5
1990	LA Raiders	16	334	182	54.5	2849	8.5	19	5.7	9	2.7	90.8	37	81	2.2
1991	LA Raiders	15	357	189	52.9	2562	7.2	15	4.2	16	4.5	71.4	28	76	2.7
1992	LA Raiders	13	253	123	48.6	1476	5.8	11	4.3	11	4.3	63.3	28	160	5.7
1993	Cincinnati	8	159	78	49.1	832	5.2	5	3.1	2	1.3	70.0	10	41	4.1
	9 YR TOTALS	108	2570	1293	50.3	18553	7.2	110	4.3	101	3.9		226	702	3.1
1993	RANK NFL QB		35	38	64	39	55	35	38	53	60	42	34	27	16
1994	PROJECTIONS	5	98	47	48.0	424	4.3	2	2.0	0	0.0		4	17	4.3

Harold Green　No. 28/RB

HT: 6-2　**WT:** 222
Born: 1-29-68, Ladson, SC
High school: Stratford (Goose Creek, SC)
College: South Carolina
Green was a Pro Bowl selection in '92. He gained 1,170 yards that year, but dropped to 589 in '93. Green also slumped from 41 catches in '92 to just 22 in '93.

YEAR	TEAM	G	RUSHING ATT	YDS	AVG	TD	RECEIVING REC	YDS	AVG	TD	KICK RETURNS RET	YDS	AVG	TD
1990	Cincinnati	12	83	353	4.3	1	12	90	7.5	1	---	---	---	---
1991	Cincinnati	14	158	731	4.6	2	16	136	8.5	0	4	66	16.5	0
1992	Cincinnati	16	265	1170	4.4	2	41	214	5.2	0	---	---	---	---
1993	Cincinnati	15	215	589	2.7	0	22	115	5.2	0	---	---	---	---
	4 YR TOTALS	57	721	2843	3.9	5	91	555	6.1	1	4	66	16.5	0
1993	RANK NFL RB		13	30	121	89	42	56	97	40	65	65	65	
1994	PROJECTIONS	16	239	431	1.8	0	19	87	4.6	0	0	0	NA	0

Derrick Fenner　No. 44/RB

Full name: Derrick Steven Fenner
HT: 6-3　**WT:** 228
Born: 4-6-67, Washington, DC
High school: Oxon Hill (MD)
College: North Carolina
In '93, Fenner caught 48 passes (second highest on the team), more than he'd totaled in his 4 previous NFL seasons.

YEAR	TEAM	G	RUSHING ATT	YDS	AVG	TD	RECEIVING REC	YDS	AVG	TD	KICK RETURNS RET	YDS	AVG	TD
1989	Seattle	5	11	41	3.7	1	3	23	7.7	0	---	---	---	---
1990	Seattle	16	215	859	4.0	14	17	143	8.4	1	---	---	---	---
1991	Seattle	11	91	267	2.9	4	11	72	6.5	0	---	---	---	---
1992	Cincinnati	16	112	500	4.5	7	7	41	5.9	1	2	38	19.0	0
1993	Cincinnati	14	121	482	4.0	1	48	427	8.9	0	---	---	---	---
	5 YR TOTALS	62	550	2149	3.9	27	86	706	8.2	2	2	38	19.0	0
1993	RANK NFL RB		36	36	53	58	13	10	34	40	65	65	65	
1994	PROJECTIONS	15	137	548	4.0	0	73	658	9.0	0	0	0	NA	0

Carl Pickens   No. 80/WR

Full name: Carl McNally Pickens
HT: 6-2   **WT:** 206
Born: 3-23-70, Murphy, NC
High school: Murphy (NC)
College: Tennessee

Pickens improved on his rookie season (when he was named AFC Offensive Rookie of the Year) by snagging 43 passes.

YEAR	TEAM	G	RECEIVING REC	YDS	AVG	TD	RUSHING ATT	YDS	AVG	TD	PUNT RETURN RET	YDS	AVG
1992	Cincinnati	16	26	326	12.5	1	---	---	---	---	18	229	12.7
1993	Cincinnati	14	43	565	13.1	6	---	---	---	---	4	16	4.0
2	YR TOTALS	30	69	891	12.9	7	0	0	NA	0	22	245	11.1
1993	RANK NFL WR		41	47	78	13	42	42	42		21	25	26
1994	PROJECTIONS	12	54	724	13.4	10	0	0	NA	0	0	0	NA

Jeff Query   No. 89/WR

Full name: Jeff Lee Query
HT: 6-0   **WT:** 165
Born: 3-7-67, Decatur, IL
High school: Maroa-Forsyth (Maroa, IL)
College: Millikin

A fast, exciting WR, Query was the team's leading receiver in '93 with 56 catches for 654 yards, including a 51-yarder.

YEAR	TEAM	G	RECEIVING REC	YDS	AVG	TD	RUSHING ATT	YDS	AVG	TD	PUNT RETURN RET	YDS	AVG
1989	Green Bay	16	23	350	15.2	2	---	---	---	---	30	247	8.2
1990	Green Bay	16	34	458	13.5	2	3	39	13.0	0	32	308	9.6
1991	Green Bay	16	7	94	13.4	0	---	---	---	---	14	157	11.2
1992	Cincinnati	10	16	265	16.6	3	1	1	1.0	0	---	---	---
1993	Cincinnati	16	56	654	11.7	4	2	13	6.5	0	---	---	---
5	YR TOTALS	74	136	1821	13.4	11	6	53	8.8	0	76	712	9.4
1993	RANK NFL WR		30	40	106	28	22	20	14		30	30	29
1994	PROJECTIONS	16	74	817	11.0	5	2	16	8.0	0	0	0	NA

Tony McGee   No. 82/TE

HT: 6-3 **WT:** 246
Born: 4-21-71, Terre Haute, IN
High school: South (Terre Haute, IN)
College: Michigan

A superb blocker with fine hands, rookie McGee's 44 catches placed third on the Bengals in '93.

YEAR	TEAM	G	RECEIVING REC	YDS	AVG	TD
1993	Cincinnati	15	44	525	11.9	0
1 YR TOTALS		15	44	525	11.9	0
1993 RANK NFL TE			8	11	19	46

Tim Krumrie   No. 69/NT

HT: 6-2 **WT:** 274
Born: 5-20-60, Eau Claire, WI
High school: Mondovi (WI)
College: Wisconsin

A rugged defensive player, Krumrie is the cornerstone of the Bengal defense. He led the team in tackles in '92, and was fourth in '93 with 78.

YEAR	TEAM	G	INT	YDS	AVG	TD	SACKS	FUM REC	TD
1985	Cincinnati	16	---	---	---	---	3.5	2	0
1986	Cincinnati	16	---	---	---	---	1.0	2	0
1987	Cincinnati	12	---	---	---	---	3.5	---	---
1988	Cincinnati	16	---	---	---	---	3.0	3	0
1989	Cincinnati	16	---	---	---	---	3.0	1	0
1990	Cincinnati	16	---	---	---	---	2.0	1	0
1991	Cincinnati	16	---	---	---	---	4.0	1	0
1992	Cincinnati	16	---	---	---	---	4.0	1	0
1993	Cincinnati	16	---	---	---	---	3.0	---	---
11 YR TOTALS		172	0	0	NA	0	33.5	13	0
1993 RANK NFL DL			16	NA	NA	NA	75	71	NA
1994 PROJECTIONS		16	0	0	0	0	3	0	0

Alfred Williams No. 94/LB

HT: 6-6 **WT:** 240
Born: 11-6-68, Houston, TX
High school: Jesse H. Jones Sr. (Houston)
College: Colorado
Williams (10 sacks in '92) had just 4 in '93.
His tackles also dropped to 28, although he
started every game.

YEAR	TEAM	G	INT	YDS	AVG	TD	SACKS	FUM REC	TD
1991	Cincinnati	16	---	---	---	---	3.0	2	0
1992	Cincinnati	15	---	---	---	---	10.0	---	---
1993	Cincinnati	16	---	---	---	---	4.0	---	---
	3 YR TOTALS	47	0	0	NA	0	17.0	2	0
1993	RANK NFL LB		47	NA	NA	NA	26	81	NA
1994	PROJECTIONS	16	0	0	0	0	1	0	0

Louis Oliver No. 29/S

Full name: Louis Oliver III
HT: 6-2 **WT:** 224
Born: 11-3-68, Belle Glade, FL
High school: Glades Central (Belle Glade)
College: North Carolina St.
Oliver missed Miami's last 5 games due to a
sprained right ankle.

YEAR	TEAM	G	INT	YDS	AVG	TD	SACKS	FUM REC	TD
1989	Miami	15	4	32	8.0	0	—	—	—
1990	Miami	16	5	87	17.4	0	1.0	—	—
1991	Miami	16	5	80	16.0	0	—	1	0
1992	Miami	16	5	200	40.0	1	—	1	0
1993	Miami	11	2	60	30.0	1	—	1	0
	5 YR TOTALS	74	21	459	21.9	2	1.0	3	0
1993	RANK NFL DB		54	30	17	2	49	37	14
1994	PROJECTIONS	9	1	36	36.0	1	0	1	0

Doug Pelfrey   No. 9/K

Full name: Thomas Douglas Pelfrey
HT: 5-11 **WT:** 185
Born: 9-25-70, Fort Thomas, KY
High school: Scott (Taylor Mill, KY)
College: Kentucky
Pelfrey has an exceptionally strong leg and consistently sails towering kickoffs out of the end zone.

YEAR	TEAM	G	XP	XPA	XP Pct.	FG	FGA	FG Pct.	PTS
1993	Cincinnati	16	13	16	81.3	24	31	77.4	85
	1 YR TOTALS	16	13	16	81.3	24	31	77.4	85
1993	RANK NFL		28	26	28	15	13	15	21

David Shula   Head Coach

Full name: David Donald Shula
Born: 5-28-59, Lexington, KY
High school: Chaminade (Hollywood, FL)
College: Dartmouth
Shula, the youngest head coach in the NFL, received a contract extension despite having an 8-24 record in 2 years in Cincinnati.

YEAR	TEAM	REGULAR SEASON					POSTSEASON		
		W	L	T	PCT	FINISH	W	L	FINISH
1992	Cincinnati	5	11	0	.313	4th/AFC Central			
1993	Cincinnati	3	13	0	.188	4th/AFC Central			
	2 YR TOTALS	8	24	0	.250		0	0	

Patrick Robinson   No. 81/WR

Full name: Patrick Lavel Robinson
HT: 5-8   **WT:** 176
Born: 10-3-69, Memphis, TN
High school: Northside (Memphis)
College: Tennessee State
He is the Bengals' leading punt and kick returner.

			RECEIVING				RUSHING				PUNT RETURN		
YEAR	TEAM	G	REC	YDS	AVG	TD	ATT	YDS	AVG	TD	RET	YDS	AVG
1993 Cincinnati		15	8	72	9.0	0	1	6	6.0	0	43	305	7.1
1 YR TOTALS		15	8	72	9.0	0	1	6	6.0	0	43	305	7.1
1993 RANK NFL WR			103	111	133	95	31	26	16		1	4	18

Craig Thompson   No. 48/TE

Full name: Craig Thompson
HT: 6-2   **WT:** 224
Born: 1-13-69, Hartsville, SC
High school: Hartsville (SC)
College: North Carolina A&T
Thompson's receiving stats dropped in '93.

			RECEIVING			
YEAR	TEAM	G	REC	YDS	AVG	TD
1992 Cincinnati		16	19	194	10.2	2
1993 Cincinnati		13	17	87	5.1	1
2 YR TOTALS		29	36	281	7.8	3
1993 RANK NFL TE			30	44	64	22
1994 PROJECTIONS		10	14	13	0.9	0

Joe Walter   No. 63/T

Full name: Joseph Follmann Walter Jr.
HT: 6-7   **WT:** 292
Born: 6-18-63, Dallas, TX
High school: North (Garland, TX)
College: Texas Tech
Walter has been an 8-year fixture at RT.

			RUSHING			RANK	PASS	RANK		YDS.
YEAR	TEAM	G	ATT	YDS	AVG	AV RUSH	YDS	PASS YDS	SACKS	LOST
1991 Cincinnati		15	449	1811	4.0	12	3413	13	33	255
1992 Cincinnati		16	454	1976	4.4	7	2284	28	45	341
1993 Cincinnati		16	423	1511	3.6	21	2830	26	53	289
9 YR TOTALS		130								

John Copeland   No. 92/DT

HT: 6-3   **WT:** 286
Born: 9-20-70, Lanett, AL
High school: Valley (Lanett, AL)
College: Alabama
A tremendous run-stuffer with quick feet and great mobility. He posted 48 tackles in his rookie year.

YEAR	TEAM	G	INT	YDS	AVG	TD	SACKS	FUM REC	TD
1993	Cincinnati	14	---	---	---	---	3.0	---	---
1 YR TOTALS		14	0	0	NA	0	3.0	0	0
1993 RANK NFL DL			16	NA	NA	NA	75	71	NA

Steve Tovar   No. 51/LB

HT: 6-3   **WT:** 244
Born: 4-25-70, Elyria, OH
High school: West (Elyria, OH)
College: Ohio State
Tovar finished third in tackles on the Bengals with 85—72 of them solo.

YEAR	TEAM	G	INT	YDS	AVG	TD	SACKS	FUM REC	TD
1993	Cincinnati	16	1	0	0.0	0	---	1	0
1 YR TOTALS		16	1	0	0.0	0	0.0	1	0
1993 RANK NFL LB			17	38	38	5	91	24	8

Ricardo McDonald No. 56/LB

Full name: Ricardo Milton McDonald
HT: 6-2   **WT:** 235
Born: 11-8-69, Kingston, Jamaica
High school: Eastside (Paterson, NJ)
College: Pittsburgh
His 102 tackles ranked second on the Bengals.

YEAR	TEAM	G	INT	YDS	AVG	TD	SACKS	FUM REC	TD
1992	Cincinnati	16	1	0	0.0	0	---	1	0
1993	Cincinnati	14	---	---	---	---	1.0	---	---
2 YR TOTALS		14	0	0	NA	1	0.0	0	0
1993 RANK NFL LB			47	NA	NA	NA	62	81	NA
1994 PROJECTIONS		12	0	0	0	0	2	0	0

Steve Broussard   No. 33/RB

HT: 5-7   **WT:** 201
Born: 2-22-67, Los Angeles, CA
High school: Manual Arts (Los Angeles)
College: Washington State
In 8 games, Broussard had 206 yards on just 39 carries for Atlanta in '93.

		RUSHING				RECEIVING				KICK RETURNS			
YEAR	TEAM	G	ATT	YDS	AVG	TD	REC	YDS	AVG	TD	RET	YDS	AVG	TD
1991	Atlanta	14	99	449	4.5	4	12	120	10.0	1	---	---	---	---
1992	Atlanta	15	84	363	4.3	1	11	98	8.7	1	---	---	---	---
1993	Atlanta	8	39	206	5.3	1	1	4	4.0	0	---	---	---	---
	4 YR TOTALS	50	348	1472	4.2	10	48	380	7.9	2	3	45	15.0	0
1993	RANK NFL RB		81	70	11	58	111	115	109	40	65	65	65
1994	PROJECTIONS	6	22	145	6.6	1	0	0	NA	0	0	0	NA	0

Darryl Williams   No. 31/S

Full name: Darryl Edwin Williams
HT: 6-0   **WT:** 191
Born: 1-7-70, Miami, FL
High school: American (Hialeah, FL)
College: Miami (FL)
Williams led the Bengals with 123 tackles.

YEAR	TEAM	G	INT	YDS	AVG	TD	SACKS	FUM REC	TD
1992	Cincinnati	16	4	65	16.3	0	2.0	1	0
1993	Cincinnati	16	2	126	63.0	1	2.0	2	0
	2 YR TOTALS	32	6	191	31.8	1	4.0	3	0
1993	RANK NFL DB		54	6	4	2	4	10	14
1994	PROJECTIONS	16	0	0	NA	0	2	3	0

Lee Johnson   No. 11/P

HT: 6-2   **WT:** 200
Born: 11-27-61, Dallas, TX
High school: McCullough (The Woodlands, TX)
College: Brigham Young
Veteran Johnson's 43.9 yard average was the best of his 9-year career.

YEAR	TEAM	G	NO	YARDS	LONG	AVG	BLK	IN20
1990	Cincinnati	16	64	2705	70	42.3	0	12
1991	Cincinnati	16	64	2795	62	43.7	0	15
1992	Cincinnati	16	76	3196	64	42.1	0	15
1993	Cincinnati	16	90	3954	60	43.9	0	24
	9 YR TOTALS	129	607	25389	70	41.8	2	146
1993	RANK NFL Ps		2	2	17	7		8
1994	PROJECTIONS	16	104	4623	58	44.5	0	31

Cleveland
BROWNS

1994 Scouting Report

Offense

QB Vinny Testaverde had the best year of his career in an injury-shortened season. The question is whether '93 was a one-season fluke for Testaverde, who led the AFC in yards per pass. WR Michael Jackson was among the AFC leaders in TDs and yards per catch, and WR Mark Carrier had one of his best seasons. Derrick Alexander, the last pick of the draft's first round, may also help at WR. RB Eric Metcalf is a tremendous asset who can run, catch, and return punts. FB Tommy Vardell shows promise, but Cleveland could use a go-to back. T Tony Jones and C Steve Everitt anchor an offensive line that allowed just 10 sacks in the team's last 7 games.

Defense

Cleveland had the league's twelfth-ranked defense in '93, with 4,778 yards allowed. But Cleveland lost their best LB, Mike Johnson, to Detroit in free agency, and there isn't much depth left at that position. The defensive line is strong—DEs Anthony Pleasant and Rob Burnett combined for 20 sacks in '93. Plus. they've got 4-time Pro Bowler DT Michael Dean Perry and third round pick DT Romeo Bandison, who could be a great one. S Stevon Moore was a standout in the Cleveland secondary, and S Eric Turner is solid. Cleveland has tried to fill their need for steady CBs by drafting Antonio Langham and acquiring ex-49er Don Griffin and ex-Charger Donny Frank.

Special Teams

Matt Stover is an accurate kicker, especially from inside the 40. But punter is unsettled, since Brian Hansen left as a free agent. Eric Metcalf is one of the most dangerous and exciting return men in the game.

1994 Prospects

There are a lot of questions facing Bill Belichick's Browns in '94. Can Testaverde have another season like '93? Can the team fill the holes at LB? Who's going to punt? And will they survive 4 games against the tough NFC East? If all of the pieces fall into place, Cleveland could go 9-7 in the weak AFC Central. But if Testaverde falters, new backup Mark Rypien can't fill the void, and the new draft picks don't contribute much, Cleveland could duel with the Bengals for last place in the division.

Team Directory

Owner/President: Arthur B. Modell
Director of player personnel: Michael Lombardi
VP of public relations: Kevin Byrne

1993 Review

Sep. 5	CINCINNATI	W 27-14
Sep. 13	SAN FRANCISCO	W 23-13
Sep. 19	at L.A. Raiders	W 19-16
Sep. 26	at Indianapolis	L 23-10
Oct. 3	OPEN DATE	
Oct. 10	MIAMI	L 24-14
Oct. 17	at Cincinnati	W 28-17
Oct. 24	PITTSBURGH	W 28-23
Oct. 31	OPEN DATE	
Nov. 7	DENVER	L 29-14
Nov. 14	at Seattle	L 22-5
Nov. 21	HOUSTON	L 27-20
Nov. 28	at Atlanta	L 17-14
Dec. 5	NEW ORLEANS	W 17-13
Dec. 12	at Houston	L 19-17
Dec. 19	NEW ENGLAND	L 20-17
Dec. 26	at L.A. Rams	W 42-14
Jan. 2	at Pittsburgh	L 16-9 (OT)

1994 Schedule

Sep. 4	at Cincinnati	1:00
Sep. 11	PITTSBURGH	1:00
Sep. 18	ARIZONA	1:00
Sep. 25	at Indianapolis	1:00
Oct. 2	N.Y. JETS	1:00
Oct. 9	OPEN DATE	
Oct. 13	at Houston (Thurs.)	8:00
Oct. 23	CINCINNATI	1:00
Oct. 30	at Denver	4:00
Nov. 6	NEW ENGLAND	1:00
Nov. 13	at Philadelphia	1:00
Nov. 20	at Kansas City	1:00
Nov. 27	HOUSTON	1:00
Dec. 4	N.Y. GIANTS	4:00
Dec. 10	at Dallas (Sat.)	4:00
Dec. 18	at Pittsburgh	1:00
Dec. 24	SEATTLE	1:00

1993 finish: 7-9 (4-4 home, 3-5 away), third in AFC Central

Team Leaders

PASSING	ATT	COM	COM%	YDS	YPA	TD	TD%	INT	INT%	RTG
Testaverde	230	130	56.5	1797	7.81	14	6.1	9	3.9	85.7
Kosar	138	79	57.2	807	5.85	5	3.6	3	2.2	77.2
Philcox	108	52	48.1	699	6.47	4	3.7	7	6.5	54.5
TEAM	478	262	54.8	3328	6.96	23	4.8	19	4.0	76.2
OPPONENTS	541	306	56.6	3466	6.41	19	3.5	13	2.4	77.6

RECEIVING	REC	YDS	AVG	TD	RUSHING	ATT	YDS	AVG	TD
Metcalf	63	539	8.6	2	Vardell	171	644	3.8	3
Carrier	43	746	17.3	3	Metcalf	129	611	4.7	1
Jackson	41	756	18.4	8	Hoard	56	227	4.1	0
Hoard	35	351	10.0	0	Testaverde	18	74	4.1	0
Kinchen	29	347	12.0	2	Baldwin	18	61	3.4	0
TEAM	262	3328	12.7	23	TEAM	425	1701	4.0	8
OPPONENTS	306	3466	11.3	19	OPPONENTS	451	1654	3.7	9

INTERCEPTIONS	INT	YDS	AVG	LG	TD	SACKS	NO
Turner	5	25	5.0	19	0	Pleasant	11.0
Jones	3	0	0.0	0	0	Burnett	9.0
Mustafaa	1	97	97.0	97t	1	Perry	6.0
TEAM	13	208	10.0	97t	1	TEAM	46.0
OPPONENTS	19	246	12.9	69	0	OPPONENTS	45.0

KICK RETURNS	NO	YDS	AV	LG	TD	PUNT RETURNS	NO	FC	YDS	AV	LG	TD
Baldwin	24	444	18.5	31	0	Metcalf	36	11	464	12.9	91t	2
Metcalf	15	318	21.2	47	0	Carrier	6	1	92	15.3	56t	1
Hoard	13	286	22.0	39	0	Turner	0	0	7	—	7	0
TEAM	58	1119	19.3	47	0	TEAM	42	12	563	13.4	91t	3
OPPONENTS	46	814	17.7	49	0	OPPONENTS	49	14	438	8.9	36	0

KICKING	XPM	XPA	FGM	FGA	LG	PTS
Stover	36	36	16	22	53	84
TEAM	36	36	16	22	53	84
OPPONENTS	30	30	31	38	53	123

PUNTING	NO	YDS	LG	AVG	TB	BLK	RET	RYD	IN20	NAV
Hansen	82	3632	72	44.3	10	2	49	438	15	35.6
TEAM	84	3632	72	43.2	10	2	49	438	15	35.6
OPPONENTS	85	3603	61	42.4	7	0	42	563	24	34.1

FUMBLES	FUM	OFF.FUM.REC.	REC	TD	DEF.FUM.REC.	REC	TD
Hoard	4	Kosar	3	0	Burnett	2	0
Kosar	4	Everitt	2	0	Perry	2	0
Metcalf	4						
TEAM	27	TEAM	8	0	TEAM	9	1
OPPONENTS	29	OPPONENTS	15	0	OPPONENTS	17	2

1994 Draft Choices

ROUND	NAME	POS	SCHOOL	OVERALL SELECTION
1	Antonio Langham	DB	Alabama	9
1	Derrick Alexander	WR	Michigan	29
3	Romeo Bandison	DT	Oregon	75
5	Isaac Booth	DB	California	141
6	Robert Strait	RB	Baylor	171
7	Hamza Hewitt	T	Clemson	203

HISTORY

TITLES

1946	AAFC Championship	1964	NFL Championship
1947	AAFC Championship	1965	NFL East Championship
1948	AAFC Championship	1967	NFL Century Division
1949	AAFC Championship	1968	NFL East Championship
1950	NFL Championship	1969	NFL East Championship
1951	NFL American Conference	1971	AFL Central Championship
1952	NFL American Conference	1980	AFL Central Championship
1953	NFL East Championship	1985	AFL Central Championship
1954	NFL East Championship	1986	AFL Central Championship
1955	NFL Championship	1987	AFL Central Championship
1957	NFL East Championship	1989	AFL Central Championship

ALL-TIME TEAM RECORDS

Rushing

Most yards, game:	237	Jim Brown	11/24/57
			11/19/61
Most yards, season:	1,863	Jim Brown	1963
Most yards, career:	12,312	Jim Brown	1957-1965

Passing

Most yards, game:	489	Bernie Kosar	1/3/87
Most yards, season:	4,132	Brian Sipe	1980
Most yards, career:	23,713	Brian Sipe	1974-1983

Receiving

Most catches, game:	14	Ozzie Newsome	10/14/84
Most catches, season:	89	Ozzie Newsome	1983
			1984
Most catches, career:	662	Ozzie Newsome	1978-1990

Scoring

Most points, game:	36	Dub Jones	11/25/51
Most points, season:	126	Jim Brown	1965
Most points, career:	1,349	Lou Groza	1950-1959,
			1961-1967

COACHES

NAME	RECORD	YEARS	NAME	RECORD	YEARS
Paul Brown	115-49-5	1950-62	Sam Rutigliano	47-52-0	1978-84
Blanton Collier	79-38-2	1963-70	Marty Schottenheimer	46-31-0	1984-88
Nick Skorich	30-26-2	1971-74	Bud Carson	12-14-1	1989-90
Forrest Gregg	18-23-0	1975-77	Jim Shofner	1-6-0	1990
Dick Modzelewski	0-1-0	1977	Bill Belichick	20-28-0	1991-93

CLEVELAND BROWNS
1994 TRAINING CAMP ROSTER

No.	Quarterbacks		Ht.	Wt.	Born	NFL Exp.	College	How acq.	93 GP/GS
**	Philcox, Todd	QB	6-4	225	9-25-66	5	Syracuse	Plan B '91	5/4
11	Kypien, Frank	QB	6-1	221	11-2-69	0	Millikin	FA '94	17/10
12	Testaverde, Vinny	QB	6-5	215	11-13-63	8	Miami (FL)	FA '93	10/6
7	Tupa, Tom	QB-P	6-4	230	2-6-66	6	Ohio State	FA '94	0/0
	Running backs								
23	Byner, Earnest	RB	5-10	215	9-15-62	11	East Carolina	FA '94	16/3
33	Hoard, Leroy	RB	5-11	225	5-15-68	5	Michigan	D2 '90	16/7
**	Mack, Kevin	FB	6-0	225	8-9-62	9	Clemson	D1 Sup '84	4/0
21	Metcalf, Eric	RB	5-10	190	1-23-68	6	Texas	D1 '89	16/9
35	Strait, Robert	FB	6-1	255	11-14-69	R	Baylor	D6 '94	
44	Vardell, Tommy	FB	6-2	230	2-20-69	3	Stanford	D1 '92	16/12
26	Wolfley, Ron	RB	6-0	220	10-14-62	10	West Virginia	Plan B '92	16/5
	Wide receivers								
89	Alexander, Derrick	WR	6-2	195	11-6-71	R	Michigan	D1b '94	
83	Carrier, Mark	WR	6-0	185	10-28-65	8	Nicholls State	FA '93	16/16
81	Jackson, Michael	WR	6-4	195	4-12-69	4	So. Mississippi	D6 '91	15/11
87	McCardell, Keenan	WR	6-1	175	1-6-70	3	Nevada-Las Vegas	Plan B '92	4/3
86	Rowe, Patrick	WR	6-1	195	2-17-69	3	San Diego State	D2 '92	5/0
84	Smith, Rico	WR	6-0	185	1-14-69	3	Colorado	D6a '92	10/1
**	Tillman, Lawyer	WR	6-5	230	5-20-66	6	Auburn	D2 '89	7/0
	Tight ends								
88	Kinchen, Brian	TE	6-2	240	8-6-65	7	Louisiana State	FA '91	16/15
80	McLemore, Tom	TE	6-5	250	3-14-70	3	Southern	W-DET '93	4/0
49	Reeves, Walter	TE	6-4	270	12-15-65	6	Auburn	FA '94	16/15
	Offensive linemen								
73	Arvie, Herman	T	6-4	305	10-12-70	2	Grambling	D5 '93	16/0
72	Dahl, Bob	G	6-5	300	11-5-68	3	Notre Dame	FA '92	16/16
61	Everitt, Steve	C	6-5	292	8-21-70	2	Michigan	D1 '93	16/16
70	Hewitt, Hamza	T	6-6	285	4-26-71	R	Clemson	D7 '94	
64	Hoover, Houston	G	6-2	300	2-6-65	7	Jackson St.	FA '93	16/16
66	Jones, Tony	T	6-5	295	5-24-66	7	Western Carolina	FA '88	16/16
68	King, Ed	T-G	6-4	300	12-3-69	4	Auburn	D2 '91	6/2
62	Williams, Gene	T-G	6-2	305	10-14-68	4	Iowa State	T-MIA '93	16/14
60	Withycombe, Mike	OL	6-6	300	11-18-64	7	Fresno State	FA '94	0/0
	Defensive linemen								
97	Bandison, Romeo	DT	6-5	290	2-12-71	R	Oregon	D3 '94	
90	Burnett, Rob	DE	6-4	280	8-27-67	5	Syracuse	D5 '90	16/16
78	Footman, Dan	DE	6-5	285	1-13-69	2	Florida State	D2 '93	8/0
94	Johnson, Bill	DL	6-4	290	12-9-68	3	Michigan State	D3a '92	10/0
96	Jones, James	DT	6-2	294	2-6-69	4	Northern Iowa	D3 '91	16/12
92	Perry, Michael D.	DT	6-1	285	8-27-65	7	Clemson	D2 '88	16/13
98	Pleasant, Anthony	DE	6-5	280	1-27-68	5	Tennessee St.	D3 '90	16/13
	Linebackers								
	Banks, Carl	LB	6-4	235	8-29-62	11	Michigan State	FA '94	15/15
56	Caldwell, Mike	LB	6-2	235	8-31-71	2	Middle Tenn. St.	D3 '93	15/1
51	Dixon, Gerald	LB	6-3	252	6-20-69	3	South Carolina	D3b '92	11/0
53	Johnson, Pepper	LB	6-3	248	7-29-64	9	Ohio State	FA '93	16/11
55	Stams, Frank	LB	6-2	240	7-17-65	6	Notre Dame	T-RAM '92	15/0
54	Sutter, Eddie	LB	6-3	235	10-3-69	2	Northwestern	W-NE '93	15/0
	Defensive backs								
36	Booth, Isaac	DB	6-3	190	5-23-71	R	California	D5 '94	
26	Fields, Floyd	S	6-0	208	1-7-69	3	Arizona State	FA '94	13/2
37	Frank, Donald	CB	6-0	192	10-24-65	5	Winston-Salem	T-SD '94	16/16
28	Griffin, Don	CB	6-0	176	3-17-64	9	Middle Tenn. St.	FA '94	12/12
31	Hairston, Stacey	CB	5-9	180	8-16-67	3	Ohio Northern	FA '93	16/0
22	Jones, Selwyn	CB	6-0	185	5-13-70	3	Colorado State	D7 '92	11/2
38	Langham, Antonio	CB	6-0	180	7-31-72	R	Alabama	D1a '94	
27	Moore, Stevon	S	5-11	210	2-9-67	6	Mississippi	Plan B '92	16/16
48	Mustafaa, Najee	CB	6-1	190	6-20-64	8	Georgia Tech	FA '93	14/14
42	Riddick, Louis	S	6-2	217	3-15-69	3	Pittsburgh	FA '93	15/0
43	Speer, Del	S	6-0	196	2-1-70	2	Florida	FA '93	16/2
29	Turner, Eric	S	6-1	207	9-20-68	4	UCLA	D1 '91	16/16
	Specialists								
3	Stover, Matt	K	5-11	178	1-27-68	5	Louisiana Tech	Plan B '91	16/0

Vinny Testaverde   No. 12/QB

Full name: Vincent Frank Testaverde
HT: 6-5   **WT:** 215
Born: 11-13-63, Brooklyn, NY
High school: Sewanhaka (Floral Park, NY) and Fort Union Military Academy (VA)
College: Miami (FL)
Testaverde's 85.7 QB rating was third in the AFC behind Joe Montana and John Elway.

YEAR	TEAM	G	PASSING										RUSHING		
			ATT	CPL	CPL%	YDS	AVG	TDS	TD%	INT	INT%	RTG	ATT	YDS	AVG
1987	Tampa Bay	6	165	71	43.0	1081	6.6	5	3.0	6	3.6	60.2	13	50	3.8
1988	Tampa Bay	15	466	222	4.7	3240	7.0	13	2.8	35	7.5	48.8	28	138	4.9
1989	Tampa Bay	14	480	258	53.8	3133	6.5	20	4.2	22	4.6	68.9	25	139	5.6
1990	Tampa Bay	14	365	203	55.6	2818	7.7	17	4.7	18	4.9	75.6	38	280	7.4
1991	Tampa Bay	13	326	166	50.9	1994	6.1	8	2.5	15	4.6	59.0	32	101	3.2
1992	Tampa Bay	14	358	206	57.5	2554	7.1	14	3.9	16	4.5	74.2	38	197	5.5
1993	Cleveland	10	230	130	56.5	1797	7.8	14	6.1	9	3.9	85.7	18	74	4.1
7	YR TOTALS	86	2390	1056	44.2	16817		91	3.8	121	5.1		190	979	5.2
1993	RANK NFL QB		29	28	40	24	9	13	6	19	27	16	27	21	15
1994	PROJECTIONS	9	190	109	57.4	1600	8.4	15	7.9	7	3.7		13	40	3.1

Mark Rypien   No. 11/QB

Full name: Mark Robert Rypien
HT: 6-4   **WT:** 234
Born: 10-2-62, Calgary, Alberta
High school: Shadle Park (Spokane, WA)
College: Washington State
Rypien was released by the Redskins, reportedly after refusing to take a pay cut. He started 10 games in '93.

YEAR	TEAM	G	PASSING									RUSHING		
			ATT	CPL	CPL%	YDS	AVG	TDS	TD%	INT	INT%	RTG	ATT	YDS	AVG
1988	Washington	9	208	114	54.8	1730	8.3	18	8.7	13	6.3	85.2	9	31	3.4
1989	Washington	14	476	280	58.8	3768	7.9	22	4.6	13	2.7	88.1	26	58	2.2
1990	Washington	10	304	166	54.6	2070	6.8	16	5.3	11	3.6	78.4	15	4	0.3
1991	Washington	16	421	249	59.1	3564	8.5	28	6.7	11	2.6	97.9	15	6	0.4
1992	Washington	16	479	269	56.2	3282	6.9	13	2.7	17	3.5	71.7	36	50	1.4
1993	Washington	12	319	166	52.0	1514	4.7	4	1.3	10	3.1	56.3	9	4	0.4
6	YR TOTALS	77	2207	1244	56.4	15928	7.2	101	4.6	75	3.4		110	151	1.4
1993	RANK NFL QB		22	24	55	29	64	38	57	15	38	57	38	45	49
1994	PROJECTIONS	11	275	135	49.1	866	3.1	0	0.0	8	2.9		2	0	0.0

Eric Metcalf   No. 21/RB

Full name: Eric Quinn Metcalf
HT: 5-10 **WT:** 190
Born: 1-23-68, Seattle, WA
High school: Bishop O'Connell (Arlington, VA)
College: Texas

A Pro Bowler, Metcalf led the NFL with 1,932 combined yards. He returned 2 punts for TDs vs. Pittsburgh, tying an NFL record.

YEAR	TEAM	G	RUSHING ATT	YDS	AVG	TD	RECEIVING REC	YDS	AVG	TD	KICK RETURNS RET	YDS	AVG	TD
1989	Cleveland	16	187	633	3.4	6	54	397	7.4	4	31	718	23.2	0
1990	Cleveland	16	80	248	3.1	1	57	452	7.9	1	52	1052	20.2	2
1991	Cleveland	8	30	107	3.6	0	29	294	10.1	0	23	351	15.3	0
1992	Cleveland	16	73	301	4.1	1	47	614	13.1	5	9	157	17.4	0
1993	Cleveland	16	129	611	4.7	1	63	539	8.6	2	15	318	21.2	0
	5 YR TOTALS	72	499	1900	3.8	9	250	2298	9.2	12	130	2596	20.0	2
1993	RANK NFL RB		35	28	25	58	6	6	38	7	11	10	11	
1994	PROJECTIONS	16	152	767	5.0	1	69	530	7.7	1	9	224	24.9	0

Tommy Vardell   No. 44/FB

Full name: Thomas Arthur Vardell
HT: 6-2 **WT:** 238
Born: 2-20-69, El Cajon, CA
High school: Granite Hills (El Cajon, CA)
College: Stanford

Vardell recorded 45 first downs, second on the team, and his 644 yards rushing ranked 14th in the AFC.

YEAR	TEAM	G	RUSHING ATT	YDS	AVG	TD	RECEIVING REC	YDS	AVG	TD	KICK RETURNS RET	YDS	AVG	TD
1992	Cleveland	14	99	369	3.7	0	13	128	9.8	0	2	14	7.0	0
1993	Cleveland	16	171	644	3.8	3	19	151	7.9	1	4	58	14.5	0
	2 YR TOTALS	30	270	1013	3.8	3	32	279	8.7	1	6	72	12.0	0
1993	RANK NFL RB		27	27	66	21	49	51	54	13	28	34	44	
1994	PROJECTIONS	16	229	866	3.8	6	23	156	6.8	2	6	100	16.7	0

Michael Jackson No. 81/WR

Full name: Michael Dwayne Jackson
HT: 6-4 **WT:** 195
Born: 4-12-69, Tangipahoa, LA
High school: Kentwood (LA)
College: Southern Mississippi
Jackson tied for second in the AFC with 8 TD receptions. His 18.4 yards per catch ranked third in the NFL.

YEAR	TEAM	G	REC	YDS	AVG	TD	ATT	YDS	AVG	TD	RET	YDS	AVG
			RECEIVING				RUSHING				PUNT RETURN		
1991	Cleveland	16	17	268	15.8	2	---	---	---	---	---	---	---
1992	Cleveland	16	47	755	16.1	7	1	-21	21.0	0	---	---	---
1993	Cleveland	15	41	756	18.4	8	1	1	1.0	0	---	---	---
	3 YR TOTALS	47	105	1779	16.9	17	2	22	11.0	0	0	0	NA
1993	RANK NFL WR		44	29	12	6	31	34	33		30	30	29
1994	PROJECTIONS	16	49	967	19.7	11	1	0	0.0	0	0	0	NA

Mark Carrier No. 83/WR

Full name: John Mark Carrier
HT: 6-0 **WT:** 185
Born: 10-28-65, Lafayette, LA
High school: Church Point (LA)
College: Nicholls State
Carrier's '93 average of 17.3 yards per catch was a career high, and his 43 catches ranked second on the Browns.

YEAR	TEAM	G	REC	YDS	AVG	TD	ATT	YDS	AVG	TD	RET	YDS	AVG
			RECEIVING				RUSHING				PUNT RETURN		
1987	Tampa Bay	10	26	423	16.3	3	---	---	---	---	---	---	---
1988	Tampa Bay	16	57	970	17.0	5	---	---	---	---	---	---	---
1989	Tampa Bay	16	86	1422	16.5	9	---	---	---	---	---	---	---
1990	Tampa Bay	16	49	813	16.6	4	---	---	---	---	---	---	---
1991	Tampa Bay	16	47	698	14.9	2	---	---	---	---	---	---	---
1992	Tampa Bay	14	56	692	12.4	4	---	---	---	---	---	---	---
1993	Cleveland	16	43	746	17.3	3	4	26	6.5	0	6	92	15.3
	7 YR TOTALS	104	364	5764	15.8	30	4	26	6.5	0	6	92	15.3
1993	RANK NFL WR		41	31	18	41	9	11	14		18	17	2
1994	PROJECTIONS	16	34	693	20.4	2	6	40	6.7	0	9	140	15.6

Brian Kinchen   No. 88/TE

Full name: Brian Douglas Kinchen
HT: 6-2   **WT:** 232
Born: 8-6-65, Baton Rouge, LA
High school: University (Baton Rouge, LA)
College: Louisiana State
In his first season as the starting TE, Kinchen had 19 catches for first downs, including 5 on third down.

			RECEIVING			
YEAR	TEAM	G	REC	YDS	AVG	TD
1988	Miami	16	1	3	3.0	0
1989	Miami	16	1	12	12.0	0
1990	Miami	4	---	---	---	---
1991	Cleveland	14	---	---	---	---
1992	Cleveland	16	---	---	---	---
1993	Cleveland	16	29	347	12.0	2
	6 YR TOTALS	82	31	362	11.7	2
1993	RANK NFL TE		16	16	18	15
1994	PROJECTIONS	16	44	527	12.0	3

Tony Jones   No. 66/T

Full name: Tony Edward Jones
HT: 6-5   **WT:** 290
Born: 5-24-66, Royston, GA
High school: Franklin Cty. (Carnesville, GA)
College: Western Carolina
Jones has started 67 straight games, tops on the Browns. The last 47 have been at left tackle.

			RUSHING			RANK	PASS	RANK		YDS.
YEAR	TEAM	G	ATT	YDS	AVG	AV RUSH	YDS	PASS YDS	SACKS	LOST
1991	Cleveland	16	389	1360	3.5	23	3547	9	42	243
1992	Cleveland	16	451	1607	3.6	26	3102	20	34	217
1993	Cleveland	16	425	1701	4.0	12	3328	19	45	289
	6 YR TOTALS	77								

Anthony Pleasant   No. 98/DE

HT: 6-5   **WT:** 280
Born: 1-27-68, Century, FL
High school: Century (FL)
College: Tennessee State
Pleasant had a career-high 11 sacks, the ninth highest total in team history and more than he'd recorded in the previous 3 years combined.

YEAR	TEAM	G	INT	YDS	AVG	TD	SACKS	FUM REC	TD
1990	Cleveland	16	---	---	---	---	3.5	---	---
1991	Cleveland	16	---	---	---	---	2.5	1	0
1992	Cleveland	16	---	---	---	---	4.0	---	---
1993	Cleveland	16	---	---	---	---	11.0	---	---
	4 YR TOTALS	64	0	0	NA	0	21.0	1	0
1993	RANK NFL DL		16	NA	NA	NA	13	71	NA
1994	PROJECTIONS	16	0	0	0	0	16	0	0

Eric Turner   No. 29/S

Full name: Eric Ray Turner
HT: 6-1   **WT:** 207
Born: 9-20-68, Ventura, CA
High school: Ventura (CA)
College: UCLA
Turner's 5 INTs were a career high, and the most by a Brown since Felix Wright snagged 9 in 1989.

YEAR	TEAM	G	INT	YDS	AVG	TD	SACKS	FUM REC	TD
1991	Cleveland	8	2	42	21.0	1	---	1	0
1992	Cleveland	15	1	6	6.0	0	1.0	2	0
1993	Cleveland	16	5	25	5.0	0	---	---	---
	3 YR TOTALS	39	8	73	9.1	1	1.0	3	0
1993	RANK NFL DB		14	73	104	27	49	94	NA
1994	PROJECTIONS	16	7	20	2.9	0	0	0	0

Matt Stover No. 3/K

Full name: John Matthew Stover
HT: 5-11 **WT:** 178
Born: 1-27-68, Dallas, TX
High school: Lake Highlands (Dallas)
College: Louisiana Tech
Stover's FG percentage (72.6%) ranks second on Cleveland's all-time list, behind Matt Bahr (74.1%).

YEAR	TEAM	G	XP	XPA	XP Pct.	FG	FGA	FG Pct.	PTS
1991	Cleveland	16	33	34	97.1	16	22	72.7	81
1992	Cleveland	16	29	30	96.7	21	29	72.4	92
1993	Cleveland	16	36	36	100.0	16	22	72.7	84
	3 YR TOTALS	48	98	100	98.0	53	73	72.6	257
1993	RANK NFL		8	9	1	22	26	21.	22
1994	PROJECTIONS	16	40	40	100.0	14	22	63.6	82

Bill Belichick Head Coach

Full name: William Stephen Belichick
Born: 4-16-52, Nashville, TN
High school: Annapolis (MD) and Phillips Academy (Andover, MA)
College: Wesleyan
Many fans wanted Belichick's scalp after he dumped popular QB Bernie Kosar last year, but owner Art Modell backed him.

		REGULAR SEASON					POSTSEASON		
YEAR	TEAM	W	L	T	PCT	FINISH	W	L	FINISH
1991	Cleveland	6	10	0	.375	3rd/AFC Central			
1992	Cleveland	7	9	0	.438	3rd/AFC Central			
1993	Cleveland	7	9	0	.438	3rd/AFC Central			
	3 YR TOTALS	20	28	0	.417		0	0	

Leroy Hoard   No. 33/RB

HT: 5-11 **WT:** 230
Born: 5-15-68, New Orleans, LA
High school: St. Augustine (New Orleans)
College: Michigan
Hoard is a double threat—he gained 227 yards on 56 carries, and added 351 yards on 35 catches.

| YEAR | TEAM | G | RUSHING | | | | RECEIVING | | | | KICK RETURNS | | | |
			ATT	YDS	AVG	TD	REC	YDS	AVG	TD	RET	YDS	AVG	TD
1991	Cleveland	16	16	154	9.6	2	48	567	11.8	9	---	---	---	---
1992	Cleveland	16	16	236	14.8	0	26	310	11.9	1	2	34	17.0	(
1993	Cleveland	16	56	227	4.1	0	35	351	10.0	0	13	286	22.0	(
	4 YR TOTALS	46	88	675	7.7	151	112	1238	11.1	83	15	322	21.5	18
1993	RANK NFL RB		66	65	46	89	25	16	19	40	12	11	5	
1994	PROJECTIONS	16	86	241	2.8	0	36	318	8.8	0	22	484	22.0	(

Keenan McCardell No. 87/WR

HT: 6-1 **WT:** 175
Born: 1-6-70, Houston, TX
High school: Waltrip (Houston)
College: Nevada-Las Vegas
He caught 13 passes—11 for first downs—for 234 yards and 4 TDs in Cleveland's last 4 games.

| YEAR | TEAM | G | RECEIVING | | | | RUSHING | | | | PUNT RETURN | | |
			REC	YDS	AVG	TD	ATT	YDS	AVG	TD	RET	YDS	AVG
1992	Cleveland	2	1	8	8.0	0	---	---	---	---	---	---	---
1993	Cleveland	4	13	234	18.0	4	---	---	---	---	---	---	---
	2 YR TOTALS	6	14	242	17.3	4	0	0	NA	0	0	0	NA
1993	RANK NFL WR		90	81	15	28	42	42	42		30	30	29
1994	PROJECTIONS	6	36	678	18.8	12	0	0	NA	0	0	0	NA

Steve Everitt   No. 61/C

HT: 6-5 **WT:** 292
Born: 8-21-70, Miami, FL
College: Michigan
Cleveland's first round pick in '93, Everitt started all 16 games for the Browns and established himself as a powerful blocker in the middle of the line.

| YEAR | TEAM | G | RUSHING | | | RANK | PASS | RANK | | YDS. |
			ATT	YDS	AVG	AV RUSH	YDS	PASS YDS	SACKS	LOST
1993	Cleveland	16	425	1701	4.0	12	3328	19	45	289
	1 YR TOTALS	16								

Rob Burnett   No. 90/DE

Full name: Robert Barry Burnett
HT: 6-4   **WT:** 270
Born: 8-27-67, Livingston, NJ
High school: Newfield (Selden, NY)
College: Syracuse
His 9 sacks were second best on the team in '93.

YEAR	TEAM	G	INT	YDS	AVG	TD	SACKS	FUM REC	TD
1990	Cleveland	16	---	---	---	---	2.0	---	---
1991	Cleveland	13	---	---	---	---	3.0	1	0
1992	Cleveland	16	---	---	---	---	9.0	2	0
1993	Cleveland	16	---	---	---	---	9.0	2	0
	4 YR TOTALS	61	0	0	NA	0	23.0	5	0
1993	RANK NFL DL		16	NA	NA	NA	19	8	5
1994	PROJECTIONS	16	0	0	0	0	11	2	0

Michael Dean Perry   No. 92/DT

Full name: Michael Dean Perry
HT: 6-1   **WT:** 285
Born: 8-27-65, Aiken, SC
High school: South Aiken (SC)
College: Clemson
Perry was named to his fourth Pro Bowl.

YEAR	TEAM	G	INT	YDS	AVG	TD	SACKS	FUM REC	TD
1991	Cleveland	16	---	---	---	---	8.5	---	---
1992	Cleveland	14	---	---	---	---	8.5	---	---
1993	Cleveland	16	---	---	---	---	6.0	2	0
	6 YR TOTALS	94	0	0	NA	0	47.5	7	1
1993	RANK NFL DL		16	NA	NA	NA	37	8	5
1994	PROJECTIONS	16	0	0	0	0	4	3	0

Donny Frank   No. 37/CB

Full name: Donald Lee Frank
HT: 6-0   **WT:** 192
Born: 10-24-65, Edgcombe County, NC
High school: Tarboro (NC)
College: Winston-Salem State (NC)
Frank started all 16 Charger games in '93.

YEAR	TEAM	G	INT	YDS	AVG	TD	SACKS	FUM REC	TD
1990	San Diego	16	2	8	4.0	0	---	---	---
1991	San Diego	16	1	71	71.0	1	---	---	---
1992	San Diego	16	4	37	9.3	0	---	---	---
1993	San Diego	16	3	119	39.7	1	---	---	---
	4 YR TOTALS	64	10	235	23.5	2	0.0	0	0
1993	RANK NFL DB		33	7	12	2	49	94	NA
1994	PROJECTIONS	16	3	167	55.7	1	0	0	0

Stevon Moore   No. 27/S

HT: 5-11   **WT:** 210
Born: 2-9-67, Wiggins, MS
High school: Stone County (Wiggins, MS)
College: Mississippi
Moore's 96 solo tackles led Cleveland in 1993.

YEAR	TEAM	G	INT	YDS	AVG	TD	SACKS	FUM REC	TD
1990	Miami	7	---	---	---	---		1	0
1992	Cleveland	14	---	---	---	---	2.0	3	1
1993	Cleveland	16	---	---	---	---		1	1
3 YR	TOTALS	37	0	0	NA	0	2.0	5	2
1993	RANK NFL DB		156	NA	NA	NA	49	37	2
1994	PROJECTIONS	16	0	0	0	0	0	0	1

Pepper Johnson   No. 53/LB

HT: 6-3   **WT:** 248
Born: 7-29-64, Detroit, MI
High school: MacKenzie (Detroit)
College: Ohio State
Johnson had 87 tackles (fourth on the team) after joining the Browns just before their '93 opener.

YEAR	TEAM	G	INT	YDS	AVG	TD	SACKS	FUM REC	TD
1991	NY Giants	16	2	5	2.5	0	6.5	—	—
1992	NY Giants	16	2	42	21.0	0	1.0	2	0
1993	Cleveland	16	—	—	—	—	1.0	—	—
8 YR	TOTALS	122	10	153	15.3	0	20.0	6	0
1993	RANK NFL LB		47	NA	NA	NA	62	81	NA
1994	PROJECTIONS	16	0	0	NA	0	0	0	0

Earnest Byner   No. 21/RB

Full name: Earnest Alexander Byner
HT: 5-10   **WT:** 218
Born: 9-15-62, Milledgeville, GA
High school: Baldwin (Milledgeville, GA)
College: East Carolina
Byner spent 5 years with the Redskins.

			RUSHING				RECEIVING				KICK RETURNS			
YEAR	TEAM	G	ATT	YDS	AVG	TD	REC	YDS	AVG	TD	RET	YDS	AVG	TD
1991	Washington	16	274	1048	3.8	5	34	308	9.1	0	---	---	---	---
1992	Washington	16	262	998	3.8	6	39	338	8.7	1	---	---	---	---
1993	Washington	16	23	105	4.6	1	27	194	7.2	0	---	---	---	---
10 YR	TOTALS	147	1662	6663	4.0	48	389	3611	9.3	12	23	417	18.1	0
1993	RANK NFL RB		98	94	34	58	34	40	75	40	65	65	65	
1994	PROJECTIONS	16	0	0	NA	0	21	120	5.7	0	0	0	NA	0

Denver
BRONCOS

1994 Scouting Report

Offense

In '93, the Broncos ranked fourth in the NFL with 3,768 passing yards. They could be even better in '94, since QB John Elway will have an improved corps of receivers. The Broncos added free agent WR Anthony Miller, and traded with Atlanta for WR Mike Pritchard. They join Shannon Sharpe, arguably the best TE in football, who caught 81 passes, third highest in the NFL in '93. Overall, the Bronco offense gained 1,693 rushing yards, eighteenth in the league. RB Rod Bernstine was sixth in the AFC in rushing, and RB Robert Delpino was solid in his first season for Denver. Offensive line standouts include G Brian Habib and T Gary Zimmerman.

Defense

The Broncos were strong against the run, allowing just 1,418 rushing yards (good for fourth in the NFL), but their weak pass defense was burned for 3,731 yards, next to last in the league. To bolster their secondary, Denver added CBs Ben Smith and Ray Crockett, who join Pro Bowler Steve Atwater. But Smith is attempting to come back from a serious knee injury, and '93 was one of Crockett's worst seasons. Free agent DT Ted Washington will help on the defensive line, where NT Greg Kragen is coming off of one of his poorest seasons in years. LBs Simon Fletcher and Mike Croel and DE Shane Dronett pressure opposing QBs, and top pick LB Allen Aldridge should contribute.

Special Teams

P Tom Rouen's 45.0 average was the second highest in the NFL. K Jason Elam showed impressive accuracy on FG attempts beyond the 50 in his rookie year. Punt returner Glyn Milburn was ranked fifth in the AFC last year.

1994 Prospects

Denver will contend with Kansas City and the Raiders for the division title. They've certainly got the offense, but Denver's defense, especially the secondary, will determine whether the Broncos will challenge for the Super Bowl or be just another run-of-the-mill playoff also-ran. Denver, normally a strong home team, did not play particularly well at Mile High Stadium in '93, and improved play at home could result in an AFC West title.

Team Directory

President/CEO: Pat Bowlen
General manager: John Beake
Director of football operations & player personnel: Bob Ferguson
Director of media relations: Jim Saccomano

<table>
<tr><td colspan="3">### 1993 Review</td><td colspan="2">### 1994 Schedule</td></tr>
<tr><td>Sep. 5</td><td>at N.Y. Jets</td><td>W 26-20</td><td>Sep. 4</td><td>SAN DIEGO</td><td>8:00</td></tr>
</table>

1993 Review				1994 Schedule	
Sep. 5	at N.Y. Jets	W 26-20	Sep. 4	SAN DIEGO	8:00
Sep. 12	SAN DIEGO	W 34-17	Sep. 11	at N.Y. Jets	4:00
Sep. 20	at Kansas City	L 15-7	Sep. 18	L.A. RAIDERS	4:00
Sep. 26	OPEN DATE		Sep. 26	at Buffalo (Mon.)	9:00
Oct. 3	INDIANAPOLIS	W 35-13	Oct. 2	OPEN DATE	
Oct. 10	at Green Bay	L 30-27	Oct. 9	at Seattle	4:00
Oct. 18	L.A. RAIDERS	L 23-20	Oct. 17	KANSAS CITY (Mon.)	9:00
Oct. 24	OPEN DATE		Oct. 23	at San Diego	4:00
Oct. 31	SEATTLE	W 28-17	Oct. 30	CLEVELAND	4:00
Nov. 7	at Cleveland	W 29-14	Nov. 6	at L.A. Rams	4:00
Nov. 14	MINNESOTA	L 26-23	Nov. 13	SEATTLE	4:00
Nov. 21	PITTSBURGH	W 37-13	Nov. 20	ATLANTA	4:00
Nov. 28	at Seattle	W 17-9	Nov. 27	CINCINNATI	4:00
Dec. 5	at San Diego	L 13-10	Dec. 4	at Kansas City	4:00
Dec. 12	KANSAS CITY	W 27-21	Dec. 11	at L.A. Raiders	4:00
Dec. 18	at Chicago	W 13-3	Dec. 17	at San Francisco (Sat.)	4:00
Dec. 26	TAMPA BAY	L 17-10	Dec. 24	NEW ORLEANS	4:00
Jan. 2	at L.A. Raiders	L 33-30			

1993 finish: 9-7 (5-3 home, 4-4 away), third in AFC West

Team Leaders

PASSING	ATT	COM	COM%	YDS	YPA	TD	TD%	INT	INT%	RTG
Elway	551	348	63.2	4030	7.31	25	4.5	10	1.8	92.8
Maddox	1	1	100.0	1	1.00	1	100.0	0	0.0	118.8
Marshall	1	1	100.0	30	30.00	1	100.0	0	0.0	158.3
TEAM	553	350	63.3	4061	7.34	27	4.9	10	1.8	94.2
OPPONENTS	562	314	55.9	3969	7.06	21	3.7	18	3.2	77.2

RECEIVING	REC	YDS	AVG	TD	RUSHING	ATT	YDS	AVG	TD
Sharpe	81	995	12.3	9	Bernstine	223	816	3.7	4
Russell	44	719	16.3	3	Delpino	131	445	3.4	8
Bernstine	44	372	8.5	0	Milburn	52	231	4.4	0
Milburn	38	300	7.9	3	Elway	44	153	3.5	0
Johnson, V.	36	517	14.4	5	Rivers	15	50	3.3	1
TEAM	350	4061	11.6	27	TEAM	468	1693	3.6	13
OPPONENTS	314	3969	12.6	21	OPPONENTS	397	1418	3.6	6

INTERCEPTIONS	INT	YDS	AVG	LG	TD	SACKS	NO
Smith	3	57	19.0	36	0	Fletcher	13.5
Braxton	3	37	12.3	25	0	Mecklenburg	9.0
Atwater	2	81	40.5	68	0	Dronett	7.0
TEAM	18	230	13.1	08	1	TEAM	48.0
OPPONENTS	10	79	7.9	19	0	OPPONENTS	39.0

KICK RETURNS	NO	YDS	AV	LG	TD	PUNT RETURNS	NO	FC	YDS	AV	LG	TD
Russell	18	374	20.8	49	0	Milburn	40	11	425	10.6	54	0
Milburn	12	188	15.7	26	0	Bradford	1	0	0	0.0	0	0
Delpino	7	146	20.9	49	0							
TEAM	39	717	18.4	49	0	Team	41	11	425	10.4	54	0
OPPONENTS	63	1119	17.8	68	0	OPPONENTS	33	8	337	10.2	37	0

KICKING	XPM	XPA	FGM	FGA	LG	PTS
Elam	41	42	26	35	54	119
TEAM	41	42	26	35	54	119
OPPONENTS	27	27	31	36	53	120

PUNTING	NO	YDS	LG	AVG	TB	BLK	RET	RYD	IN20	NAV
Rouen	67	3017	62	45.0	8	1	33	337	17	37.1
TEAM	68	3017	62	44.4	8	1	33	337	17	37.1
OPPONENTS	81	3541	61	43.7	10	2	41	425	22	36.0

FUMBLES	FUM	OFF.FUM.REC.	REC	TD	DEF.FUM.REC.	REC	TD
Milburn	9	Elway	5	0	Braxton	2	0
Elway	8				Croel	2	0
Bernstine	3				Mecklenburg	2	0
TEAM	29	TEAM	10	1	TEAM	13	0
OPPONENTS	27	OPPONENTS	13	0	OPPONENTS	18	0

1994 Draft Choices

ROUND	NAME	POS	SCHOOL	OVERALL SELECTION
2	Allen Aldridge	LB	Houston	51
4	Randy Fuller	CB	Tennessee State	123
7	Keith Burns	LB	Oklahoma State	210
7	Butler By'not'e	RB	Ohio State	212
7	Tom Nalen	C	Boston College	218

HISTORY

TITLES

1977	AFC Championship
1978	AFC West Championship
1984	AFC West Championship
1986	AFC Championship
1987	AFC Championship
1989	AFC Championship
1991	AFC West Championship

ALL-TIME TEAM RECORDS

Rushing

Most yards, game:	183	Otis Armstrong	12/8/74
Most yards, season:	1,407	Otis Armstrong	1974
Most yards, career:	6,323	Floyd Little	1967-1975

Passing

Most yards, game:	447	Frank Tripucka	9/15/62
Most yards, season:	4,030	John Elway	1993
Most yards, career:	34,246	John Elway	1983-1993

Receiving

Most catches, game:	13	Lionel Taylor	11/29/64
		Bobby Anderson	9/30/73
Most catches, season:	100	Lionel Taylor	1961
Most catches, career:	543	Lionel Taylor	1960-1966

Scoring

Most points, game:	21	Gene Mingo	12/10/60
Most points, season:	137	Gene Mingo	1962
Most points, career:	742	Jim Turner	1971-1979

COACHES

NAME	RECORD	YEARS
Frank Filchock	7-20-1	1960-61
Jack Faulkner	9-22-1	1962-64
Mac Speedie	6-19-1	1964-66
Ray Malavasi	4-8-0	1966
Lou Saban	20-42-3	1967-71
Jerry Smith	2-3-0	1971
John Ralston	34-33-3	1972-76
Red Miller	42-25-0	1977-80
Dan Reeves	117-79-1	1981-92
Wade Phillips	9-7-0	1993

DENVER BRONCOS
1994 TRAINING CAMP ROSTER

No.	Quarterbacks		Ht.	Wt.	Born	NFL Exp.	College	How acq.	93 GP/GS
7	Elway, John	QB	6-3	215	6-28-60	12	Stanford	T-BAL '83	16/16
8	Maddox, Tommy	QB	6-4	193	9-2-71	3	UCLA	D1 '92	10/0
12	Moore, Shawn	QB	6-2	213	4-4-68	4	Virginia	D11 '91	0/0
	Running backs								
33	Bernstine, Rod	RB	6-3	238	2-8-65	8	Texas A&M	FA '93	15/14
28	By'not'e, Butler	RB	5-9	190	9-29-72	R	Ohio State	D7b '94	
39	Delpino, Robert	RB	6-0	205	11-2-65	7	Missouri	FA '93	16/3
37	Lynn, Anthony	RB	6-2	230	12-21-68	2	Texas Tech	FA '93	13/0
22	Milburn, Glyn	RB	5-8	177	2-19-71	2	Stanford	D2 '93	16/2
38	Rivers, Reggie	RB	6-1	215	2-22-68	4	SW Texas State	FA '91	16/2
	Wide receivers								
83	Bonner, Melvin	WR	6-3	207	2-18-70	2	Baylor	D6 '93	4/0
10	Campbell, Jeff	WR	5-8	167	3-26-68	5	Colorado	FA '94	10/0
80	Kimbrough, Tony	WR	6-2	192	9-17-70	2	Jackson St.	D7b '93	15/0
83	Miller, Anthony	WR	5-11	189	4-15-65	7	Tennessee	FA '94	16/16
81	Pritchard, Mike	WR	5-10	180	10-25-69	4	Colorado	T-ATL '94	15/14
85	Russell, Derek	WR	6-0	179	6-22-69	4	Arkansas	D4 '91	13/12
87	Tilman, Cedric	WR	6-2	204	7-22-70	3	Alcorn State	D11 '92	14/3
	Tight ends								
88	Evans, Jerry	TE	6-4	250	9-28-68	2	Toledo	FA '93	14/11
89	Johnson, Reggie	TE	6-2	256	1-27-68	4	Florida State	D2 '91	13/12
84	Sharpe, Shannon	TE	6-2	230	6-28-68	5	Savannah State	D7 '90	16/12
	Offensive linemen								
66	Nalen, Tom	OL	6-2	280	5-13-71	R	Boston College	D7c '94	
68	Freeman, Russell	T	6-7	290	9-2-69	3	Georgia Tech	FA '92	14/14
75	Habib, Brian	G	6-7	299	12-2-64	6	Washington	FA '93	16/16
72	Kartz, Keith	C	6-4	270	5-5-63	8	California	FA '87	12/11
61	Meeks, Bob	C	6-2	279	5-28-69	3	Auburn	D10 '92	7/0
**	Melander, Jon	G	6-7	280	12-27-66	4	Minnesota	W-CIN '93	12/7
**	Scrafford, Kirk	T	6-6	265	3-13-67	5	Montana	W-CIN '93	16/0
79	Widell, Dave	G-C	6-6	292	5-14-65	7	Boston College	T-DAL '91	15/15
65	Zimmerman, Gary	T	6-6	294	12-13-61	9	Oregon	T-MIN '93	16/16
	Defensive linemen								
99	Dronett, Shane	DE	6-6	275	1-12-71	3	Texas	D2 '92	16/16
97	Drozdov, Darren	DT	6-3	280	4-7-69	2	Maryland	FA '93	6/2
71	Kragen, Greg	NT	6-3	265	3-4-62	10	Utah State	FA '85	14/14
91	Oshodin, Willie	DE	6-4	260	9-16-69	3	Villanova	FA '92	15/5
94	Robinson, Jeff	DE	6-4	265	2-20-70	2	Idaho	D4 '93	16/0
98	Washington, Ted	NT	6-4	295	4-13-68	4	Louisville	T-SF '94	12/12
90	Williams, Dan	DE	6-4	290	12-15-69	2	Toledo	D1 '93	13/11
	Linebackers								
57	Aldridge, Allen	LB	6-1	245	5-30-72	R	Houston	D2 '94	
58	Alexander, Elijah	LB	6-2	230	8-8-70	3	Kansas State	W-TB '93	16/0
56	Burns, Keith	LB	6-2	245	5-16-72	R	Oklahoma State	D7a '94	
51	Croel, Mike	LB	6-3	231	6-6-69	4	Nebraska	D1 '91	16/16
54	Donahue, Mitch	LB	6-2	254	2-4-68	4	Wyoming	W-SF '93	13/0
73	Fletcher, Simon	LB	6-6	240	2-18-62	10	Houston	D2b '85	16/16
93	Harvey, Richard	LB	6-1	242	9-11-66	5	Tulane	FA '94	15/0
**	Mecklenburg, Karl	LB	6-3	235	9-1-60	12	Minnesota	D12 '83	16/16
92	Wyman, Dave	LB	6-2	248	3-31-64	8	Stanford	FA '93	16/16
	Defensive backs								
27	Atwater, Steve	S	6-3	217	10-28-66	6	Arkansas	D1 '89	16/16
23	Bradford, Ronnie	CB	5-10	188	10-1-70	2	Colorado	FA '93	10/3
20	Crockett, Ray	CB	5-10	185	1-5-67	6	Baylor	FA '94	15/15
24	Fuller, Randy	CB	5-9	173	6-2-70	R	Tennessee State	D4 '94	
40	Hall, Darryl	S	6-2	210	8-1-66	2	Washington	FA '93	16/2
	Hilliard, Randy	CB	5-11	160	2-6-67	5	Northwestern State	FA '94	12/5
31	Jones, Rondell	S	6-2	210	5-7-71	2	North Carolina	D3 '93	16/0
**	Lang, Le-Lo	CB	5-11	185	1-23-67	5	Washington	D5a '90	16/0
36	Robinson, Frank	CB	5-11	174	1-11-69	3	Boise State	D5 '92	16/2
26	Smith, Ben	CB	5-11	185	5-14-67	5	Georgia	T-PHI '94	13/3
**	Smith, Dennis	S	6-3	200	2-3-59	14	Southern California	D1 '81	14/14
	Specialists								
1	Elam, Jason	K	5-11	192	3-8-70	2	Hawaii	D3a '93	16/0
16	Rouen, Tom	P	6-3	215	6-9-68	2	Colorado	FA '93	16/0

John Elway No. 7/QB

Full name: John Albert Elway
HT: 6-3 **WT:** 215
Born: 6-28-60, Port Angeles, WA
High school: Granada Hills (Los Angeles)
College: Stanford
Pro Bowl starter Elway led the AFC in QB rating (92.8), completions (348) and passing yards (4,030).

| YEAR | TEAM | G | PASSING | | | | | | | | | | | | RUSHING | | | SACKS |
			ATT	CPL	CPL%	YDS	AVG	TDS	TD%	INT	INT%	RTG	ATT	YDS	AVG	NO
1986	Denver	16	504	280	55.6	3485	6.9	19	3.8	13	2.6	79.0	52	257	4.9	N/A
1987	Denver	12	410	224	54.6	3198	7.8	19	4.6	12	2.9	83.4	66	304	4.6	N/A
1988	Denver	15	496	274	55.2	3309	6.7	17	3.4	19	3.8	71.4	54	234	4.3	N/A
1989	Denver	15	416	223	53.6	3051	7.3	18	4.3	18	4.3	73.7	48	244	5.1	N/A
1990	Denver	16	502	294	58.6	3526	7.0	15	3.0	14	2.8	78.5	50	258	5.2	N/A
1991	Denver	16	451	242	53.7	3253	7.2	13	2.9	12	2.7	75.4	55	255	4.6	45
1992	Denver	12	316	174	55.1	2242	7.1	10	3.2	17	5.4	65.7	34	94	2.8	36
1993	Denver	16	551	348	63.2	4030	7.3	25	4.5	10	1.8	92.8	44	153	3.5	39
11 YR TOTALS		160	4620	2723	58.9	34246	7.4	183	4.0	167	3.6		538	2435	4.5	120
1993 RANK NFL QB			1	1	8	1	17	2	16	15	52	10	8	8	24	5
1994 PROJECTIONS		16	607	402	66.2	4478	7.4	31	5.0	6	0.9		41	132	3.2	42

Tommy Maddox No. 8/QB

Full name: Thomas Alfred Maddox
HT: 6-4 **WT:** 195
Born: 9-1-71, Shreveport, LA
High school: L.D. Bell (Hurst, TX)
College: UCLA
Maddox's only pass of 1993 went for a 1-yard touchdown on a fake field goal.

| YEAR | TEAM | G | PASSING | | | | | | | | | | RUSHING | | |
			ATT	CPL	CPL%	YDS	AVG	TDS	TD%	INT	INT%	RTG	ATT	YDS	AVG
1992	Denver	13	121	66	54.5	757	6.3	5	4.1	9	7.4	58.4	9	20	2.2
1993	Denver	16	1	1	100.0	1	1.0	1		0	0.0	118.8	2	-2	-1.0
2 YR TOTALS		29	122	67	54.9	758	6.2	6	4.9	9	7.4		11	18	1.6
1993 RANK NFL QB			73	71	1	72	71	54	1	61	61	1	54	56	56
1994 PROJECTIONS		16	0	0	NA	0	NA	0	NA	0	NA		0	0	NA

Robert Delpino   No. 39/RB

Full name: Robert Lewis Delpino
HT: 6-0   **WT:** 205
Born: 11-2-65, Dodge City, KS
High school: Dodge City (KS)
College: Missouri

Delpino's 8 TDs ranked second on the team and fourth in the AFC. He had no rushing TDs in '92.

		RUSHING				RECEIVING				KICK RETURNS			
YEAR	TEAM	G	ATT	YDS	AVG	TD	REC	YDS	AVG	TD	RET	YDS	AVG	TD
1988	LA Rams	15	34	147	4.3	0	30	312	10.4	2	14	333	23.8	0
1989	LA Rams	16	78	368	4.7	1	34	334	9.8	1	17	334	19.6	0
1990	LA Rams	15	13	52	4.0	0	15	172	11.5	4	20	389	19.5	0
1991	LA Rams	16	214	688	3.2	9	55	617	11.2	1	4	54	13.5	0
1992	LA Rams	10	32	115	3.6	0	18	139	7.7	1	6	83	13.8	0
1993	Denver	16	131	445	3.4	8	26	195	7.5	0	7	146	20.9	0
6 YR TOTALS		88	502	1815	3.6	18	178	1769	9.9	9	68	1339	19.7	0
1993 RANK NFL RB			33	39	92	6	36	38	64	40	24	20	12	
1994 PROJECTIONS		16	154	517	3.4	11	22	128	5.8	0	5	127	25.4	0

Rod Bernstine   No. 33/RB

Full name: Rod Earl Bernstine
HT: 6-3   **WT:** 238
Born: 2-8-65, Fairfield, CA
High school: Bryan (TX)
College: Texas A&M

Bernstine finished sixth in the AFC in rushing with a career-best 816 yards.

		RUSHING				RECEIVING				KICK RETURNS			
YEAR	TEAM	G	ATT	YDS	AVG	TD	REC	YDS	AVG	TD	RET	YDS	AVG	TD
1987	San Diego	10	1	9	9.0	0	10	76	7.6	1	1	13	13.0	0
1988	San Diego	14	2	7	3.5	0	29	340	11.7	0	---	---	---	---
1989	San Diego	5	15	137	9.1	1	21	222	10.6	1	---	---	---	---
1990	San Diego	12	124	589	4.8	4	8	40	5.0	0	---	---	---	---
1991	San Diego	13	159	766	4.8	8	11	124	11.3	0	1	7	7.0	0
1992	San Diego	9	106	499	4.7	4	12	86	7.2	0	---	---	---	---
1993	Denver	15	223	816	3.7	4	44	372	8.5	0	---	---	---	---
7 YR TOTALS		78	630	2823	4.5	21	135	1260	9.3	2	2	20	10.0	0
1993 RANK NFL RB			10	14	74	18	15	14	42	40	65	65	65	
1994 PROJECTIONS		16	273	891	3.3	3	59	497	8.4	0	0	0	NA	0

Mike Pritchard No. 81/WR

Full name: Michael Robert Pritchard
HT: 5-10 **WT:** 190
Born: 10-25-69, Shaw AFB (SC)
High school: Rancho (N. Las Vegas, NV)
College: Colorado
Pritchard had 201 catches in his first 3 years, the fifth-best total in NFL history.

YEAR	TEAM	G	RECEIVING REC	YDS	AVG	TD	RUSHING ATT	YDS	AVG	TD	PUNT RETURN RET	YDS	AVG
1991	Atlanta	16	50	624	12.5	2	---	---	---	---	---	---	---
1992	Atlanta	16	77	827	10.7	5	5	37	7.4	0	---	---	---
1993	Atlanta	15	74	736	9.9	7	2	4	2.0	0	---	---	---
	3 YR TOTALS	47	201	2187	10.9	14	7	41	5.9	0	0	0	NA
1993	RANK NFL WR		11	32	129	7	22	30	31		30	30	29
1994	PROJECTIONS	16	87	804	9.2	10	1	0	0.0	0	0	0	NA

Anthony Miller No. 83/WR

Full name: Lawrence Anthony Miller
HT: 5-11 **WT:** 189
Born: 4-15-65, Los Angeles, CA
High school: John Muir (Pasadena, CA)
College: San Diego State, Tennessee
With San Diego in 1993, Miller placed second in the AFC in catches (84) and receiving yards (1162).

YEAR	TEAM	G	RECEIVING REC	YDS	AVG	TD	RUSHING ATT	YDS	AVG	TD	PUNT RETURN RET	YDS	AVG	TD
1988	San Diego	16	36	526	14.6	3	7	45	6.4	0	---	---	---	---
1989	San Diego	16	75	1252	16.7	10	4	21	5.3	0	---	---	---	---
1990	San Diego	16	63	933	14.8	7	3	13	4.3	0	---	---	---	---
1991	San Diego	13	44	649	14.8	3	---	---	---	---	---	---	---	---
1992	San Diego	16	72	1060	14.7	7	1	-1	-1.0	0	---	---	---	---
1993	San Diego	16	84	1162	13.8	7	---	---	---	---	---	---	---	---
	6 YR TOTALS	93	374	5582	14.9	37	15	0.4	15.0	0	0	0	NA	0
1993	RANK NFL WR		7	6	62	7	42	42	42		30	30	29	
1994	PROJECTIONS	16	93	1246	13.4	7	0	0	NA	0	0	0	NA	0

Shannon Sharpe   No. 84/TE

HT: 6-2   **WT:** 230
Born: 6-28-68, Chicago, Il
High school: Glenville (GA)
College: Savannah State
Sharpe led the Broncos with 81 catches
(third-best in the league) and 9 TDs (second
in the AFC).

			RECEIVING			
YEAR	TEAM	G	REC	YDS	AVG	TD
1990	Denver	16	7	99	14.1	1
1991	Denver	16	22	322	14.6	1
1992	Denver	16	53	640	12.1	2
1993	Denver	16	81	995	12.3	9
4 YR TOTALS		64	163	2056	12.6	13
1993 RANK NFL TE			1	1	15	1
1994 PROJECTIONS		16	108	1325	12.3	14

Shane Dronett   No. 99/DE

HT: 6-6   **WT:** 275
Born: 1-12-71, Orange, TX
High school: Bridge City (Orange, TX)
College: Texas
A ferocious rusher, Dronett has registered
13.5 sacks over his first 2 years in the league
and started all 16 games in 1993.

YEAR	TEAM	G	INT	YDS	AVG	TD	SACKS	FUM REC	TD
1992	Denver	16	---	---	---	---	6.5	2	0
1993	Denver	16	2	13	6.5	0	7.0	---	---
2 YR TOTALS		32	2	13	6.5	0	13.5	2	0
1993 RANK NFL DL			1	4	7	3	29	71	NA
1994 PROJECTIONS		16	4	26	6.5	0	8	0	0

Simon Fletcher   No. 73/LB

Full name: Simon Raynard Fletcher
HT: 6-6   **WT:** 240
Born: 2-18-62, Bay City, TX
High school: Bay City (TX)
College: Houston

Veteran Fletcher set a new NFL mark in 1993, recording at least 1 sack in 10 consecutive games.

YEAR	TEAM	G	INT	YDS	AVG	TD	SACKS	FUM REC	TD
1985	Denver	16	---	---	---	---	1.0	---	---
1986	Denver	16	---	---	---	---	5.5	2	0
1987	Denver	12	---	---	---	---	4.0	1	0
1988	Denver	16	1	4	4.0	---	9.0	1	0
1989	Denver	16	---	---	---	---	12.0	1	0
1990	Denver	16	---	---	---	---	11.0	1	0
1991	Denver	16	---	---	---	---	13.5	1	0
1992	Denver	16	---	---	---	---	16.0	---	---
1993	Denver	16	---	---	---	---	13.5	1	0
	9 YR TOTALS	140	1	4	4.0	0	85.5	8	0
1993 RANK NFL LB			47	NA	NA	NA	1	24	8
1994 PROJECTIONS		16	0	0	0	0	13	1	0

Steve Atwater   No. 27/S

Full name: Stephen Dennis Atwater
HT: 6-3   **WT:** 217
Born: 10-28-66, Chicago, IL
High school: Lutheran North (St. Louis)
College: Arkansas

Pro Bowler Atwater led the squad with 141 tackles, 80 of them solo. He has had at least 2 INTs in each of his pro seasons.

YEAR	TEAM	G	INT	YDS	AVG	TD	SACKS	FUM REC	TD
1989	Denver	16	3	34	11.3	0	—	1	0
1990	Denver	15	2	32	16.0	0	1.0	—	—
1991	Denver	16	5	104	20.8	0	1.0	1	0
1992	Denver	15	2	22	11.0	0	1.0	2	0
1993	Denver	16	2	81	40.5	0	1.0	—	—
	5 YR TOTALS	78	14	273	19.5	0	4.0	4	0
1993 RANK NFL DB			54	18	10	27	13	94	NA
1994 PROJECTIONS		16	2	99	49.5	0	1	0	0

Jason Elam   No. 1/K

Full name: Jason Elam
HT: 5-11 **WT:** 192
Born: 3-08-70, Ft. Walton Beach, FL
High school: Brookwood (Snellville, GA)
College: Hawaii

As a rookie, Elam racked up 119 points and was an impressive 4-for-6 in FGs from beyond 50 yards.

YEAR	TEAM	G	XP	XPA	XP Pct.	FG	FGA	FG Pct.	PTS
1993	Denver	16	41	42	97.6	26	35	74.3	119
	1 YR TOTALS	16	41	42	97.6	26	35	74.3	119
1993	RANK NFL		2	2	15	10	6	19	7

Wade Phillips   Head Coach

Born: 7-21-47, Orange, TX
High school: Port Neches-Groves (TX)
College: Houston

'93 was his first full season as a head coach at any level—high school, college, or pro—although he coached 4 games after his father Bum was fired as Saints' coach in '85.

		REGULAR SEASON				POSTSEASON		
YEAR	TEAM	W	L	T	PCT	FINISH	W	L	FINISH
1985	New Orleans	1	3	0	.250	3rd/NFC West			
1993	Denver	9	7	0	.563	3rd/AFC West	0	1	lost wild card game to LA Raiders, 42-24
	2 YR TOTALS	10	10	0	.500		0	1	

Glyn Milburn   No. 22/RB

Full name: Glyn Milburn
HT: 5-8   **WT:** 177
Born: 2-19-71, Santa Monica, CA
High school: Santa Monica (CA)
College: Stanford
His 10.6 yards/punt return was fifth in the AFC.

YEAR	TEAM	RUSHING					RECEIVING				KICK RETURNS			
		G	ATT	YDS	AVG	TD	REC	YDS	AVG	TD	RET	YDS	AVG	TD
1993	Denver	16	52	231	4.4	0	38	300	7.9	3	12	188	15.7	0
1 YR TOTALS		16	52	231	4.4	0	38	300	7.9	3	12	188	15.7	0
1993 RANK NFL RB			68	62	36	89	19	23	56	2	13	14	39	

Derek Russell   No. 85/WR

Full name: Derek Dwayne Russell
HT: 6-0   **WT:** 179
Born: 6-22-69, Little Rock, AR
High school: Central (Little Rock, AR)
College: Arkansas
Russell averaged an impressive 16.3 yard/catch.

YEAR	TEAM	RECEIVING				RUSHING				PUNT RETURN		
		G	REC	YDS	AVG	TD	ATT	YDS	AVG	TD	RET	YDS	AVG
1991	Denver	13	21	317	15.1	1	---	---	---	---	---	---	---
1992	Denver	12	12	140	11.7	0	---	---	---	---	---	---	---
1993	Denver	13	44	719	16.3	3	---	---	---	---	---	---	---
3 YR TOTALS		38	77	1176	15.3	4	0	0	NA	0	0	0	NA
1993 RANK NFL WR			38	35	26	41	42	42	42		30	30	29
1994 PROJECTIONS		16	80	1358	17.0	6	0	0	NA	0	0	0	NA

Reggie Johnson   No. 89/TE

Full name: Reggie Johnson
HT: 6-2   **WT:** 256
Born: 1-27-68, Pensacola, FL
High school: Escambia (Pensacola, FL)
College: Florida State
Johnson caught a career-high 20 passes in 1993.

YEAR	TEAM	RECEIVING				
		G	REC	YDS	AVG	TD
1991	Denver	16	6	73	12.2	1
1992	Denver	15	10	139	13.9	1
1993	Denver	13	20	243	12.2	1
3 YR TOTALS		44	36	455	12.6	3
1993 RANK NFL TE			29	23	16	22
1994 PROJECTIONS		15	34	404	11.9	1

Brian Habib

No. 75/G

Full name: Brian Richard Habib
HT: 6-7   **WT:** 299
Born: 12-2-64, Ellensburg, WA
High school: Ellensburg (WA)
College: Washington

Habib started all 16 games at RG for Denver.

YEAR	TEAM	G	RUSHING ATT	YDS	AVG	RANK AV RUSH	PASS YDS	RANK PASS YDS	SACKS	YDS. LOST
1991	Minnesota	16	464	2201	4.7	2	3016	24	28	133
1992	Minnesota	16	497	2030	4.1	14	3162	17	40	293
1993	Denver	16	468	1693	3.6	18	4061	4	39	293
	5 YR TOTALS	80								

Greg Kragen

No. 71/NT

Full name: Greg John Kragen
HT: 6-3   **WT:** 265
Born: 3-4-62, Chicago, IL
High school: Amador Valley (Pleasanton, CA)
College: Utah State

Kragen's 3.0 sacks were his fewest since 1990.

YEAR	TEAM	G	INT	YDS	AVG	TD	SACKS	FUM REC	TD
1991	Denver	16	---	---	---	---	3.5	---	---
1992	Denver	16	---	---	---	---	5.5	---	---
1993	Denver	14	---	---	---	---	3.0	1	0
	9 YR TOTALS	136	0	0	NA	0	22.5	12	1
1993	RANK NFL DL		16	NA	NA	NA	75	25	5
1994	PROJECTIONS	13	0	0	0	0	3	1	0

Mike Croel

No. 51/LB

Full name: Mike Croel
HT: 6-3   **WT:** 231
Born: 6-6-69, Detroit, MI
High school: Lincoln-Sudbury (MA)
College: Nebraska

Croel was fourth on the Broncos in tackles (110).

YEAR	TEAM	G	INT	YDS	AVG	TD	SACKS	FUM REC	TD
1991	Denver	13	---	---	---	---	10.0	---	---
1992	Denver	16	---	---	---	---	5.0	1	0
1993	Denver	16	1	22	22.0	1	5.0	2	0
	3 YR TOTALS	45	1	22	22.0	1	20.0	3	0
1993	RANK NFL LB		17	13	9	1	22	9	8
1994	PROJECTIONS	16	2	39	19.5	2	3	3	0

Dave Wyman   No. 57/LB

HT: 6-2   **WT:** 248
Born: 3-31-64, San Diego, CA
High school: Wooster (Reno, NV)
College: Stanford
Wyman's 91 solo tackles led the Broncos.

YEAR	TEAM	G	INT	YDS	AVG	TD	SACKS	FUM REC	TD
1991	Seattle	6	---	---	---	---	---	---	---
1992	Seattle	11	---	---	---	---	---	1	---
1993	Denver	16	1	9	9.0	0	2.0	2	0
	7 YR TOTALS	77	3	33	11	0	5.5	6	0
1993	RANK NFL LB		17	23	20	5	37	9	8
1994	PROJECTIONS	16	1	10	10.0	0	3	3	0

Ray Crockett   No. 20/CB

Full name: Donald Ray Crockett
HT: 5-10   **WT:** 185
Born: 1-5-67, Dallas, TX
High school: Duncanville (TX)
College: Baylor
His 2 INTs for Detroit were his fewest since '89.

YEAR	TEAM	G	INT	YDS	AVG	TD	SACKS	FUM REC	TD
1990	Detroit	16	3	17	5.7	0	1.0	2	1
1991	Detroit	16	6	141	23.5	1	1.0	---	---
1992	Detroit	15	4	50	12.5	0	1.0	1	0
1993	Detroit	16	2	31	15.5	0	1.0	1	0
	5 YR TOTALS	79	16	244	15.3	1	4.0	5	1
1993	RANK NFL DB		54	60	48	27	13	37	14
1994	PROJECTIONS	16	0	0	NA	0	1	1	0

Tom Rouen   No. 16/P

HT: 6-3   **WT:** 215
Born: 6-9-68, Hindsdale, IL
High school: Heritage (Littleton, CO)
College: Colorado
His 45.0 yard average ranked second in the NFL.

YEAR	TEAM	G	NO	YARDS	LONG	AVG	BLK	IN20
1993	Denver	16	67	3017	62	45	1	17
	1 YR TOTALS	16	67	3017	62	45.0	1	17
1993	RANK NFL		21	18	11	7	16	20

Houston
OILERS

1994 Scouting Report

Offense
Overall, Houston's offense ranked third in the NFL in 1993 with 5,658 total yards gained, including 3,866 passing yards (third in the league). But QB Cody Carlson steps in this year for '93 starter Warren Moon, and ex-Viking Sean Salisbury will back him up. Haywood Jeffires, Ernest Givins, Webster Slaughter, and Curtis Duncan are all first-rate WRs, and Gary Wellman proved an able reserve. The Oiler offense hasn't featured a TE, but Houston signed ex-Ram TE Pat Carter, whose blocking helped Jerome Bettis gain 1,000 yards. Backfield depth is thin, behind second-half surprise Gary Brown, and this could be a problem as the season progresses. All-Pro Bruce Matthews and T Brad Hopkins anchor the offensive line.

Defense
Typical of a Buddy Ryan defense, Houston's defense in '93 was the league's best against the run, with just 1,273 rushing yards allowed, and only twenty-third against the pass, giving up 3,601 passing yards. But Houston will have a difficult time maintaining that level in '94. The Oilers have to replace pass-rushing DEs Sean Jones and William Fuller. That's why Houston used their first 2 draft picks to take DEs Henry Ford and Jeremy Nunley and signed ex-Steeler Kenny Davidson. But Pro Bowl DL Ray Childress returns, along with DT Glenn Montgomery. Lamar Lathon and Eddie Robinson are solid LBs. The defensive backfield is first-rate, with Cris Dishman, one of the best CBs in the NFL, and top safeties Bubba McDowell and Marcus Robertson.

Special Teams
Veteran K Al Del Greco had a career-high 125 points in '93, making 85.3% of his FG attempts. Houston signed veteran P Rich Camarillo, who was second in the NFC in net yards per punt for Phoenix in '93, to replace departing free agent Greg Montgomery. TE John Henry Mills returned kicks, averaging 20.9 yards per return, and also posted 10 special teams tackles.

1994 Prospects
There's still a lot of talent here, but the running game is suspect, Carlson has never been a full-time NFL starter, and there's only Sean Salisbury to back him up. The Oilers could very well watch the playoffs on TV this year.

Team Directory

Chairman of the board/President: K. S. (Bud) Adams, Jr.
Executive VP/General manager: Mike Holovak
Director of player relations: Willie Alexander
Director of media services: Chip Namias

1993 Review

Sep. 5	at New Orleans	L 33-21
Sep. 12	KANSAS CITY	W 30-0
Sep. 19	at San Diego	L 18-17
Sep. 26	L.A. RAMS	L 28-13
Oct. 3	OPEN DATE	
Oct. 11	at Buffalo	L 35-7
Oct. 17	at New England	W 28-14
Oct. 24	CINCINNATI	W 28-12
Oct. 31	OPEN DATE	
Nov. 7	SEATTLE	W 24-14
Nov. 14	at Cincinnati	W 38-3
Nov. 21	at Cleveland	W 27-20
Nov. 28	PITTSBURGH	W 23-3
Dec. 5	ATLANTA	W 33-17
Dec. 12	CLEVELAND	W 19-17
Dec. 19	at Pittsburgh	W 26-17
Dec. 25	at San Francisco	W 10-7
Jan. 2	N.Y. JETS	W 24-0

1993 finish: 12-4 (7-1 home, 5-3 away), first in AFC Central

1994 Schedule

Sep. 4	at Indianapolis	1:00
Sep. 11	at Dallas	4:00
Sep. 18	BUFFALO	1:00
Sep. 25	CINCINNATI	4:00
Oct. 3	at Pittsburgh (Mon.)	9:00
Oct. 9	OPEN DATE	
Oct. 13	CLEVELAND (Thurs.)	8:00
Oct. 24	at Philadelphia (Mon.)	9:00
Oct. 30	at L.A. Raiders	4:00
Nov. 6	PITTSBURGH	1:00
Nov. 13	at Cincinnati	1:00
Nov. 21	N.Y. GIANTS (Mon.)	9:00
Nov. 27	at Cleveland	1:00
Dec. 4	ARIZONA	4:00
Dec. 11	SEATTLE	4:00
Dec. 18	at Kansas City	4:00
Dec. 24	N.Y. JETS	4:00

Team Leaders

PASSING	ATT	COM	COM%	YDS	YPA	TD	TD%	INT	INT%	RTG
Moon	520	303	58.3	3485	6.70	21	4.0	21	4.0	75.2
Carlson	90	51	56.7	605	6.72	2	2.2	4	4.4	66.2
Richardson	4	3	75.0	55	13.75	0	0.0	0	0.0	116.7
TEAM	614	357	58.1	4145	6.75	23	3.7	25	4.1	74.2
OPPONENTS	582	302	51.9	3914	6.73	16	2.7	26	4.5	63.9

RECEIVING	REC	YDS	AVG	TD	RUSHING	ATT	YDS	AVG	TD
Slaughter	77	904	11.7	5	Brown	195	1002	5.1	6
Givins	68	887	13.0	4	White	131	465	3.5	2
Jeffires	66	753	11.4	6	Moon	48	145	3.0	1
Duncan	41	456	11.1	3	Tillman	9	94	10.4	0
White	34	229	6.7	0	Carlson	14	41	2.9	2
TEAM	357	4145	11.6	23	TEAM	409	1792	4.4	11
OPPONENTS	302	3914	13.0	16	OPPONENTS	369	1273	3.4	9

INTERCEPTIONS	INT	YDS	AVG	LG	TD	SACKS	NO
Robertson	7	137	19.6	69	0	Jones	13.0
Dishman	6	74	12.3	30	0	Fuller	10.0
Jackson	3	34	10.8	22t	1	Childress	9.0
TEAM	26	412	15.8	69	3	TEAM	52.0
OPPONENTS	25	309	12.4	42	0	OPPONENTS	43.0

KICK RETURNS	NO	YDS	AV	LG	TD	PUNT RETURNS	NO	FC	YDS	AV	LG	TD
Drewrey	15	293	19.5	34	0	Drewrey	41	19	275	6.7	18	0
Mills	11	230	20.9	37	0							
Coleman	3	37	12.3	16	0							
TEAM	31	589	19.0	37	0	TEAM	41	19	275	6.7	18	0
OPPONENTS	60	1062	17.7	36	0	OPPONENTS	28	5	249	8.9	30	0

KICKING	XPM	XPA	FGM	FGA	LG	PTS
Del Greco	39	40	29	34	52	126
TEAM	39	40	29	34	52	126
OPPONENTS	25	26	19	28	53	82

PUNTING	NO	YDS	LG	AVG	TB	BLK	RET	RYD	IN20	NAV
Montgomery	54	2462	77	45.6	5	0	28	249	13	39.1
Sullivan	2	73	37	36.5	1	0	0	0	1	26.5
TEAM	56	2535	77	45.3	6	0	28	249	14	38.7
OPPONENTS	79	3454	71	43.7	13	1	41	275	15	36.9

FUMBLES	FUM	OFF.FUM.REC.	REC	TD	DEF.FUM.REC.	REC	TD
Moon	13	Moon	5	0	Childress	3	1
Jeffires	5	Brown	2	0	Montgomery	3	0
Brown	4	Carlson	2	0	Robertson	3	1
Slaughter	4						
TEAM	37	TEAM	12	0	TEAM	17	3
OPPONENTS	32	OPPONENTS	12	0	OPPONENTS	20	1

1994 Draft Choices

ROUND	NAME	POS	SCHOOL	OVERALL SELECTION
1	Henry Ford	DE	Arkansas	26
2	Jeremy Nunley	DE	Alabama	60
3	Malcolm Seabron	WR	Fresno State	101
4	Michael Davis	CB	Cincinnati	119
4	Sean Jackson	RB	Florida State	129
5	Roderick Lewis	TE	Arizona	157
5	Jim Reid	T	Virginia	161
6	Lee Gissendaner	WR	Northwestern	187
6	Barron Wortham	LB	Texas-El Paso	194
7	Lemanski Hall	LB	Alabama	220

HISTORY

TITLES

1960	AFL Championship
1961	AFL Championship
1962	AFL East Championship
1967	AFL East Championship
1991	AFC Central Championship
1993	AFC Central Championship

ALL-TIME TEAM RECORDS

Rushing

Most yards, game:	216	Billy Cannon	12/10/61
Most yards, season:	1,934	Earl Campbell	1980
Most yards, career:	8,574	Earl Campbell	1978-1984

Passing

Most yards, game:	527	Warren Moon	12/16/90
Most yards, season:	4,690	Warren Moon	1991
Most yards, career:	33,685	Warren Moon	1984-1993

Receiving

Most catches, game:	13	Charlie Hennigan	10/13/61
		Haywood Jeffires	10/13/91
Most catches, season:	101	Charlie Hennigan	1964
Most catches, career:	506	Ernest Givens	1986-1993

Scoring

Most points, game:	30	Billy Cannon	12/10/61
Most points, season:	126	Al Del Greco	1993
Most points, career:	596	George Blanda	1960-1966

COACHES

NAME	RECORD	YEARS
Lou Rymkus	12-7-1	1960-61
Wally Lemm	38-40-4	1961, 1966-70
Pop Ivy	17-12-0	1962-63
Sammy Baugh	4-10-0	1964
Hugh Taylor	4-10-0	1965
Ed Hughes	4-9-1	1971
Bill Peterson	1-18-0	1972-73
Sid Gillman	8-15-0	1973-74
Bum Phillips	59-38-0	1975-80
Ed Biles	8-23-0	1981-83
Chuck Studley	2-8-0	1983
Hugh Campbell	8-22-0	1984-85
Jerry Glanville	35-35-0	1985-89
Jack Pardee	43-25-0	1990-93

HOUSTON OILERS
1994 TRAINING CAMP ROSTER

No	Quarterbacks		Ht	Wt	Born	NFL Exp	College	How acq	93 GP/GS
14	Carlson, Cody	QB	6-3	202	11-5-63	8	Baylor	D3 '87	8/2
7	Richardson, Bucky	QB	6-1	228	2-7-69	3	Texas A&M	D8 '92	2/0
12	Salisbury, Sean	QB	6-5	217	3-9-63	6	Southern California	FA '94	10/5
	Running backs								
33	Brown, Gary	RB	5-11	233	7-1-69	4	Penn State	D8 '91	16/8
41	Jackson, Sean	RB	6-1	222		R	Florida State	D4b '94	
47	Maston, LeShai	RB	6-1	232	10-7-70	2	Baylor	FA '93	10/0
32	Tillman, Spencer	RB	5-11	206	4-21-64	8	Oklahoma	Plan B '92	15/0
**	White, Lorenzo	RB	5-11	222	4-12-66	7	Michigan State	D1 '88	8/8
	Wide receivers								
87	Coleman, Pat	WR	5-7	173	4-8-67	4	Mississippi	FA '91	13/1
80	Duncan, Curtis	WR	5-11	184	1-26-65	8	Northwestern	D10 '87	12/12
86	Gissendaner, Lee	WR	5-9	175		R	Northwestern	D6a '94	
81	Givins, Ernest	WR	5-9	172	9-3-64	9	Louisville	D2 '86	16/16
82	Hannah, Travis	WR	5-7	161	1-31-70	2	Southern California	D4 '93	12/0
84	Jeffires, Haywood	WR	6-2	201	12-12-64	8	North Carolina St.	D1b '87	16/16
83	Seabron, Malcolm	WR	6-0	194		R	Fresno State	D3 '94	
89	Slaughter, Webster	WR	6-1	175	10-19-64	10	San Diego State	FA '92	14/14
88	Wellman, Gary	WR	5-9	168	8-9-67	3	Southern California	D5 '91	11/3
	Tight ends								
46	Carter, Pat	TE	6-4	255	8-1-66	7	Florida State	FA '94	11/10
49	Lewis, Roderick	TE	6-5	254		R	Arizona	D5a '94	
48	Mills, John Henry	TE	6-1	222	10-31-69	2	Wake Forest	D5 '93	16/0
	Offensive linemen								
**	Dawson, Doug	G	6-3	288	12-27-61	8	Texas	FA '90	16/16
77	Donnalley, Kevin	T	6-5	305	6-10-68	4	North Carolina	D3 '91	16/6
72	Hopkins, Brad	T	6-3	306	9-5-70	2	Illinois	D1 '93	16/11
74	Matthews, Bruce	C	6-5	298	8-6-61	12	Southern California	D1 '83	16/16
**	Munchak, Mike	G	6-3	284	3-5-60	13	Penn State	D1 '82	13/12
64	Norgard, Erik	C-G	6-1	282	11-4-65	5	Colorado	FA '90	16/4
67	Reid, Jim	T	6-6	306		R	Virginia	D5b '94	
70	Thomas, Stan	T	6-5	295	10-28-68	4	Texas	FA '93	14/0
73	Williams, David	T	6-5	292	6-21-66	6	Florida	D1 '89	15/15
	Defensive linemen								
79	Childress, Ray	DT	6-6	272	10-20-62	10	Texas A&M	D1a '85	16/16
	Davidson, Kenny	DE	6-5	286	8-17-67	5	Louisiana State	FA '94	16/9
92	Ford, Henry	DE	6-3	284		R	Arkansas	D1 '94	
78	McCants, Keith	DE	6-3	265	4-19-68	5	Alabama	FA '93	13/0
94	Montgomery, Glenn	DT	6-0	282	3-31-67	6	Houston	D5 '89	16/11
93	Nunley, Jeremy	DE	6-5	278		R	Alabama	D2 '94	
68	Roberts, Tim	DT	6-6	318	4-14-69	3	So. Mississippi	D5 '92	5/0
71	Teeter, Mike	DE	6-3	272	10-4-67	3	Michigan	FA '93	14/0
97	Williams, Lee	DE-DT	6-6	271	10-15-62	11	Bethune-Cookman	T-SD '91	14/5
	Linebackers								
51	Barrow, Micheal	LB	6-1	236	4-19-70	2	Miami (FL)	D2 '93	16/0
59	Bowden, Joe	LB	5-11	227	2-25-70	3	Oklahoma	D5a '92	16/6
53	Hall, Lemanski	LB	6-0	229		R	Alabama	D7 '94	
56	Kozak, Scott	LB	6-3	222	11-28-65	6	Oregon	D2 '89	16/0
57	Lathon, Lamar	LB	6-3	252	12-23-67	5	Houston	D1 '90	13/1
**	Marshall, Wilber	LB	6-1	240	4-18-62	11	Florida	T-WAS '93	10/10
50	Robinson, Eddie	LB	6-1	242	4-13-70	3	Alabama State	D2 '92	16/15
54	Smith, Al	LB	6-1	244	11-26-64	8	Utah State	D6a '87	16/16
52	Wortham, Barron	LB	5-11	244		R	Texas-El Paso	D6b '94	
	Defensive backs								
23	Bishop, Blaine	DB	5-9	197	7-24-70	2	Ball State	D8 '93	16/2
22	Brown, Tony	CB	5-9	182	5-15-70	3	Fresno State	D5 '92	16/0
30	Davis, Michael	CB	6-1	192		R	Cincinnati	D4a '94	
28	Dishman, Cris	CB	6-0	188	8-13-65	7	Purdue	D5a '88	16/16
24	Jackson, Steve	CB	5-8	182	4-8-69	4	Purdue	D3a '91	16/12
29	Lewis, Darryll	CB	5-9	183	12-16-68	4	Arizona	D2 '91	4/4
25	McDowell, Bubba	S	6-1	198	11-4-68	6	Miami (FL)	D3 '89	14/14
26	Orlando, Bo	S	5-10	180	4-3-66	5	West Virginia	FA '90	16/3
31	Robertson, Marcus	S	5-11	197	10-2-69	4	Iowa State	D4 '91	13/13
	Specialists								
16	Camarillo, Rich	P	5-11	200	11-29-59	14	Washington	FA '94	16/0
3	Del Greco, Al	K	5-10	200	3-2-62	11	Auburn	FA '91	16/0

Cody Carlson   No. 14/QB

Full name: Matthew Cody Carlson
HT: 6-3 **WT:** 202
Born: 11-5-63, Dallas, TX
High school: Churchill (San Antonio)
College: Baylor

Carlson inherits the starting QB slot with Warren Moon's trade to Minnesota. The Oilers are 10-4 in games he's started.

YEAR	TEAM		PASSING											RUSHING		
		G	ATT	CPL	CPL%	YDS	AVG	TDS	TD%	INT	INT%	RTG	ATT	YDS	AVG
1988	Houston	6	112	52	46.4	775	6.9	4	3.6	6	5.4	59.2	12	36	3.0
1989	Houston	6	31	15	48.4	155	5.0	0	0.0	1	3.2	49.8	3	-3	-1.0
1990	Houston	6	55	37	67.3	383	7.0	4	7.3	2	3.6	96.3	11	52	4.7
1991	Houston	6	12	7	58.3	114	9.5	1	8.3	0	0.0	118.1	4	-3	-0.8
1992	Houston	11	227	149	65.6	1710	7.5	9	4.0	11	4.8	81.2	27	77	2.9
1993	Houston	3	90	51	56.7	605	6.7	2	2.2	4	4.4	66.2	1	0	0.0
	6 YR TOTALS	38	527	311	59.0	3742	7.1	20	3.8	24	4.6		58	159	2.7
1993	RANK NFL QB		45	45	39	45	28	48	50	40	19		48	82	51	51
1994	PROJECTIONS	1	39	22	55.3	259	6.6	1	1.9	2	4.4		0	0	NA

Gary Brown   No. 33/RB

Full name: Gary Leroy Brown
HT: 5-11 **WT:** 233
Born: 7-1-69, Williamsport, PA
High school: Williamsport Area (PA)
College: Penn State

Brown came off the bench to rush for over 1,000 yards in only 10 games. His 5.1 yards/rush led the AFC.

YEAR	TEAM		RUSHING				RECEIVING				KICK RETURNS			
		G	ATT	YDS	AVG	TD	REC	YDS	AVG	TD	RET	YDS	AVG	TD
1991	Houston	11	8	85	10.6	1	2	1	0.5	0	3	30	10.0	0
1992	Houston	16	19	87	4.6	1	1	5	5.0	0	1	15	15.0	0
1993	Houston	16	195	1002	5.1	6	21	240	11.4	2	2	29	14.5	0
	3 YR TOTALS	43	222	1174	5.3	8	24	246	10.3	2	6	74	12.3	0
1993	RANK NFL RB		19	11	14	14	43	32	12	7	44	47	44	
1994	PROJECTIONS	16	329	1679	5.1	10	36	417	11.6	4	2	32	16.0	0

Curtis Duncan No. 80/WR

Full name: Curtis Everett Duncan
HT: 5-11 **WT:** 184
Born: 1-26-65, Detroit, MI
High school: Redford (Detroit)
College: Northwestern

Duncan finished fourth on the team with 41 catches for 465 yards. He's sixth on the all-time Oilers list for both receptions and yards.

YEAR	TEAM	G	RECEIVING					RUSHING				PUNT RETURN		
			REC	YDS	AVG	TD	ATT	YDS	AVG	TD	RET	YDS	AVG
1987	Houston	10	13	237	18.2	5	---	---	---	---	8	23	2.9
1988	Houston	16	22	302	13.7	1	---	---	---	---	4	47	11.8
1989	Houston	16	43	613	14.3	5	1	0	0.0	0	---	---	---
1990	Houston	16	66	785	11.9	1	---	---	---	---	---	---	---
1991	Houston	16	55	588	10.7	4	---	---	---	---	1	-1	-1.0
1992	Houston	16	82	954	11.6	1	---	---	---	---	---	---	---
1993	Houston	12	41	456	11.1	3	---	---	---	---	---	---	---
	7 YR TOTALS	102	322	3935	12.2	20	1	0	0.0	0	13	69	5.3
1993	RANK NFL WR		44	61	114	41	42	42	42		30	30	29
1994	PROJECTIONS	11	33	350	10.6	3	0	0	NA	0	0	0	NA

Ernest Givins No. 81/WR

Full name: Ernest Pastell Givins Jr.
HT: 5-9 **WT:** 172
Born: 9-3-64, St. Petersburg, FL
High school: Lakewood (St. Petersburg)
College: Louisville

Givins became the all-time Oiler leader in passes caught with 506, and his 7,414 yards rank second to Drew Hill's 7,477.

YEAR	TEAM	G	RECEIVING					RUSHING				PUNT RETURN		
			REC	YDS	AVG	TD	ATT	YDS	AVG	TD	RET	YDS	AVG
1986	Houston	15	61	1062	17.4	3	9	148	16.4	1	---	---	---
1987	Houston	12	53	933	17.6	6	1	-13	-13.0	0	---	---	---
1988	Houston	16	60	976	16.3	5	4	26	6.5	0	---	---	---
1989	Houston	15	55	794	14.4	3	---	---	---	---	---	---	---
1990	Houston	16	72	979	13.6	9	3	65	21.7	0	---	---	---
1991	Houston	16	70	996	14.2	5	4	30	7.5	0	11	107	9.7
1992	Houston	16	67	787	11.7	10	7	75	10.7	0	---	---	---
1993	Houston	16	68	887	13.0	4	6	19	3.2	0	---	---	---
	8 YR TOTALS	122	506	7414	14.7	45	34	350	10.3	1	11	107	9.7
1993	RANK NFL WR		13	18	80	28	5	15	26		30	30	29
1994	PROJECTIONS	16	68	893	13.1	2	7	1	0.1	0	0	0	NA

Haywood Jeffires No. 84/WR

Full name: Haywood Franklin Jeffires
HT: 6-2   **WT:** 201
Born: 12-12-64, Greensboro, NC
High school: Page (Greensboro, NC)
College: North Carolina St.
Jeffires saw his 3-year streak of leading the AFC in receptions snapped in '93, as his catches dropped to just 66 last season.

YEAR	TEAM	G	RECEIVING REC	YDS	AVG	TD	RUSHING ATT	YDS	AVG	TD	PUNT RETURN RET	YDS	AVG
1987	Houston	9	7	89	12.7	0	---	---	---	---	---	---	---
1988	Houston	2	2	49	24.5	1	---	---	---	---	---	---	---
1989	Houston	16	47	619	13.2	2	---	---	---	---	---	---	---
1990	Houston	16	74	1048	14.2	8	---	---	---	---	---	---	---
1991	Houston	16	100	1181	11.8	7	---	---	---	---	---	---	---
1992	Houston	16	90	913	10.1	9	---	---	---	---	---	---	---
1993	Houston	16	66	753	11.4	6	---	---	---	---	---	---	---
7 YR TOTALS		91	386	4652	12.1	33	0	0	NA	0	0	0	NA
1993 RANK NFL WR			14	30	108	13	42	42	42		30	30	29
1994 PROJECTIONS		16	56	643	11.5	5	0	0	NA	0	0	0	NA

Pat Carter   No. 46/TE

Full name: Wendell Patrick Carter
HT: 6-4   **WT:** 255
Born: 8-1-66, Sarasota, FL
High school: Riverview (Sarasota, FL)
College: Florida State
Carter started 10 games at TE for the Rams last season. His blocking should benefit Gary Brown.

YEAR	TEAM	G	RECEIVING REC	YDS	AVG	TD
1988	Detroit	15	13	145	11.2	0
1989	LA Rams	16	—	—	—	—
1990	LA Rams	16	8	58	7.3	0
1991	LA Rams	16	8	69	8.6	2
1992	LA Rams	16	20	232	11.6	3
1993	LA Rams	11	14	166	11.9	1
6 YR TOTALS		90	63	670	10.6	6
1993 RANK NFL TE			36	31	20	22
1994 PROJECTIONS		9	14	166	11.9	1

Bruce Matthews No. 74/C

Full name: Bruce Rankin Matthews
HT: 6-5 **WT:** 298
Born: 8-6-61, Arcadia, CA
High school: Arcadia (CA)
College: Southern California
Matthews earned his sixth straight Pro Bowl berth in '93. He's played 168 games as an Oiler, third on the team's all-time list.

YEAR	TEAM	G	RUSHING ATT	YDS	AVG	RANK AV RUSH	PASS YDS	RANK PASS YDS	SACKS	YDS. LOST
1991	Houston	16	331	1366	4.1	10	4804	1	24	183
1992	Houston	16	353	1626	4.6	3	4231	1	32	202
1993	Houston	16	409	1792	4.4	4	4145	3	43	279
11 YR TOTALS		168								

Ray Childress No. 79/DT

Full name: Raymond Clay Childress Jr.
HT: 6-6 **WT:** 272
Born: 10-20-62, Memphis, TN
High school: J.J. Pearce (Richardson, TX)
College: Texas A&M
Childress earned his fifth Pro Bowl berth in '93. He was also named AP second-team All-Pro. His 9 sacks placed third on the team.

YEAR	TEAM	G	INT	YDS	AVG	TD	SACKS	FUM REC	TD
1985	Houston	16	---	---	---	---	3.5	1	0
1986	Houston	16	---	---	---	---	5.0	1	0
1987	Houston	13	---	---	---	---	6.0	1	0
1988	Houston	16	---	---	---	---	8.5	7	0
1989	Houston	14	---	---	---	---	8.5	1	0
1990	Houston	16	---	---	---	---	8.0	1	0
1991	Houston	15	---	---	---	---	7.0	1	0
1992	Houston	16	---	---	---	---	13.0	2	1
1993	Houston	16	---	---	---	---	9.0	3	1
9 YR TOTALS		138	0	0	NA	0	68.5	18	2
1993	RANK NFL DL		16	NA	NA	NA	19	2	1
1994	PROJECTIONS	16	0	0	0	0	8	4	1

Eddie Robinson No. 50/LB

Full name: Eddie Joseph Robinson
HT: 6-1   **WT:** 242
Born: 4-13-70, New Orleans, LA
High school: Brother Martin (New Orleans)
College: Alabama State

Robinson's 57 tackles ranked sixth on the team, and he added 7 special-teams hits. He's started in both of his NFL seasons.

YEAR	TEAM	G	INT	YDS	AVG	TD	SACKS	FUM REC	TD
1992	Houston	16	---	---	---	---	1.0	---	---
1993	Houston	16	---	---	---	---	1.0	---	---
2 YR TOTALS		32	0	0	NA	0	2.0	0	0
1993 RANK NFL LB			47	NA	NA	NA	62	81	NA
1994 PROJECTIONS		16	0	0	0	0	1	0	0

Cris Dishman   No. 28/CB

Full name: Cris Edward Dishman
HT: 6-0   **WT:** 188
Born: 8-13-65, Louisville, KY
High school: DeSales (Louisville, KY)
College: Purdue

Dishman ended up third on the team in tackles with a career high 78. He tied for seventh in the NFL with 6 INTs.

YEAR	TEAM	G	INT	YDS	AVG	TD	SACKS	FUM REC	TD
1988	Houston	15	---	---	---	---	---	1	0
1989	Houston	16	4	31	7.8	0	---	1	0
1990	Houston	16	4	50	12.5	0	---	---	---
1991	Houston	15	6	61	10.2	0	---	3	1
1992	Houston	15	3	34	11.3	0	---	---	---
1993	Houston	16	6	74	12.3	0	---	2	1
6 YR TOTALS		93	23	250	10.9	0	0.0	7	2
1993 RANK NFL DB			7	22	64	27	49	10	2
1994 PROJECTIONS		16	7	89	12.7	0	0	3	1

Al Del Greco　　No. 3/K

Full name: Albert Louis Del Greco Jr.
HT: 5-10 **WT:** 200
Born: 3-2-62, Providence, RI
High school: Coral Gables (FL)
College: Auburn

Del Greco ranked second in the AFC, and fourth in the NFL, with a team record 126 points. He made 85.3% of his FG attempts.

YEAR	TEAM	G	XP	XPA	XP Pct.	FG	FGA	FG Pct.	PTS
1986	Green Bay	16	29	29	100.0	17	27	63.0	80
1987	GB (5)-St.L (3)	8	19	20	95.0	9	15	60.0	46
1988	Phoenix	16	42	44	95.5	12	21	57.1	78
1989	Phoenix	16	28	29	96.6	18	26	69.2	82
1990	Phoenix	16	31	31	100.0	17	27	63.0	82
1991	Houston	7	16	16	100.0	10	13	76.9	46
1992	Houston	16	41	41	100.0	21	27	77.8	104
1993	Houston	16	39	40	97.5	29	34	85.3	126
	10 YR TOTALS	136	317	324	97.8	161	228	70.6	800
1993	RANK NFL		3	3	16	5	9	3	4
1994	PROJECTIONS	16	40	42	95.2	33	37	89.2	139

Jack Pardee　Head Coach

Full name: John Perry Pardee
Born: 4-19-36, Exira, IA
High school: Christoval (TX)
College: Texas A&M

Houston has made the playoffs in each of Pardee's four years at the helm. He was NFL Coach of the Year in '79 with Washington.

		REGULAR SEASON					POSTSEASON			
YEAR	TEAM	W	L	T	PCT	FINISH	W	L	FINISH	
1978	Washington	8	8	0	.500	/NFC East				
1979	Washington	10	6	0	.625	/NFC East				
1980	Washington	6	10	0	.375	/NFC East				
1990	Houston	9	7	0	.563	T1st/AFC Central	0	1	lost 1st Rnd. game to Cinn., 41-14	
1991	Houston	11	5	0	.688	1st/AFC Central	1	1	lost 2nd Rnd. game to Denver, 26-24	
1992	Houston	10	6	0	.625	2nd/AFC Central	0	1	lost 1st Rnd. game to Buffalo, 41-38	
1993	Houston	12	4	0	.750	1st/AFC Central	0	1	lost 2nd Rnd. game to KC, 28-20	
	7 YR TOTALS	66	46	0	.589		1	4		

Sean Salisbury   No. 12/QB

Full name: Richard Sean Salisbury
HT: 6-5   **WT:** 217
Born: 3-9-63, Escondido, CA
High school: Orange Glen (Escondido, CA)
College: Southern California
Ex-Vike starter Salisbury will back up Carlson.

| YEAR | TEAM | G | PASSING | | | | | | | | | | RUSHING | | |
			ATT	CPL	CPL%	YDS	AVG	TDS	TD%	INT	INT%	RTG	ATT	YDS	AVG
1987	Indianapolis	2	12	8	66.7	68	5.7	0	0.0	2	^^^^^^	41.7	---	---	N/A
1992	Minnesota	10	175	97	55.4	1203	6.9	5	2.9	2	1.1	81.7	11	0	0.0
1993	Minnesota	10	195	115	59.0	1413	7.2	9	4.6	6	3.1	84.0	10	-1	-0.1
	3 YR TOTALS	22	382	220	57.6	2684	7.0	14	3.7	10	2.6		21	-1	-0.0
1993	RANK NFL QB		30	30	29	30	19	22	13	31	40	20	34	53	53
1994	PROJECTIONS	13	310	186	60.0	2322	7.5	17	5.5	9	2.9		16	0	0.0

Gary Wellman   No. 88/WR

Full name: Gary James Wellman
HT: 5-9   **WT:** 168
Born: 8-9-67, Syracuse, NY
High school: Westlake (CA)
College: Southern California
Wellman led the Oilers with 13.9 yards/catch.

| YEAR | TEAM | G | RECEIVING | | | | RUSHING | | | | PUNT RETURN | | |
			REC	YDS	AVG	TD	ATT	YDS	AVG	TD	RET	YDS	AVG
1992	Houston	9	---	---	---	---	---	---	---	---	---	---	---
1993	Houston	11	31	430	13.9	1	2	6	3.0	0	---	---	---
	2 YR TOTALS	20	31	430	13.9	1	2	6	3.0	0	0	0	NA
1993	RANK NFL WR		61	63	61	72	22	26	27		30	30	29
1994	PROJECTIONS	13	73	1016	13.9	2	5	14	2.8	0	0	0	NA

John Henry Mills   No. 48/TE

Full name: John Henry Mills
HT: 6-0   **WT:** 222
Born: 10-31-69, Jacksonville, FL
High school: Godby (Tallahassee, FL)
College: Wake Forest
This rookie TE emerged as Houston's top KR.

| YEAR | TEAM | G | RECEIVING | | | | KICK RETURNS | | | |
			REC	YDS	AVG	TD	RET	YDS	AVG	TD
1993	Houston	16	---	---	---	---	11	230	20.9	0
	1 YR TOTALS	16	0	0	NA	0	11	230	20.9	0
1993	RANK NFL TE		64	62	---	46				

Brad Hopkins — No. 72/T

Full name: Bradley D. Hopkins
HT: 6-3   **WT:** 306
Born: 9-5-70, Columbia, SC
High school: Moline (IL)
College: Illinois
He's the first Oiler rookie OL to start since '84.

YEAR	TEAM	G	RUSHING ATT	YDS	AVG	RANK AV RUSH	PASS YDS	RANK PASS YDS	SACKS	YDS. LOST
1993	Houston	16	409	1792	4.4	4	4145	3	43	279
	1 YR TOTALS	16								

Glenn Montgomery — No. 94/DT

Full name: Glenn Steven Montgomery
HT: 6-0   **WT:** 282
Born: 3-31-67, New Orleans, LA
High school: West Jefferson (Harvey, LA)
College: Houston
Montgomery recovered a team-high 3 fumbles.

YEAR	TEAM	G	INT	YDS	AVG	TD	SACKS	FUM REC	TD
1991	Houston	16	—	—	—	—	—	1	0
1992	Houston	16	—	—	—	—	0.5	2	0
1993	Houston	16	—	—	—	—	6.0	3	0
	5 YR TOTALS	78	0	0	NA	0	8.5	6	0
1993	RANK NFL DL		16	NA	NA	NA	37	2	5
1994	PROJECTIONS	16	0	0	0	0	9	4	0

Lamar Lathon — No. 57/LB

Full name: Lamar Lavantha Lathon
HT: 6-3   **WT:** 252
Born: 12-23-67, Wharton, TX
High school: Wharton (TX)
College: Houston
A hard-hitting LB with great speed, Lathon missed
the first 3 games of '93 due to a fractured forearm.

YEAR	TEAM	G	INT	YDS	AVG	TD	SACKS	FUM REC	TD
1990	Houston	11	---	---	---	---	---	1	0
1991	Houston	16	3	77	25.7	1	2.0	---	---
1992	Houston	11	---	---	---	---	1.5	---	---
1993	Houston	13	---	---	---	---	2.0	1	0
	4 YR TOTALS	51	3	77	25.7	1	5.5	2	0
1993	RANK NFL LB		47	NA	NA	NA	37	24	8
1994	PROJECTIONS	15	0	0	NA	0	3	2	0

Bubba McDowell   No. 25/S

Full name: Leonard McDowell
HT: 6-1   **WT:** 198
Born: 11-4-66, Fort Gaines, GA
High school: Merritt Island (FL)
College: Miami (FL)
McDowell was fourth on the team with 75 tackles.

YEAR	TEAM	G	INT	YDS	AVG	TD	SACKS	FUM REC	TD
1991	Houston	16	4	31	7.8	0	1.0	2	0
1992	Houston	16	3	52	17.3	1	1.5	—	—
1993	Houston	14	3	31	10.3	0	1.0	—	—
5 YR TOTALS		77	16	190	11.9	1	5.0	4	0
1993 RANK NFL DB			33	60	77	27	13	94	NA
1994 PROJECTIONS		14	3	28	9.3	0	1	0	0

Marcus Robertson   No. 31/S

Full name: Marcus Aaron Robertson
HT: 5-11   **WT:** 197
Born: 10-2-69, Pasadena, CA
High school: Muir (Pasadena, CA)
College: Iowa State
Robertson was named AP first-team All Pro.

YEAR	TEAM	G	INT	YDS	AVG	TD	SACKS	FUM REC	TD
1991	Houston	16	---	---	---	---	1.0	---	---
1992	Houston	16	1	27	27.0	0	---	---	---
1993	Houston	13	7	137	19.6	0	---	3	1
3 YR TOTALS		45	8	164	20.5	0	1.0	3	1
1993 RANK NFL DB			4	3	33	27	49	1	2
1994 PROJECTIONS		15	14	264	18.9	0	0	6	2

Rich Camarillo   No. 16/P

Full name: Richard Jon Camarillo
HT: 5-11   **WT:** 200
Born: 3-29-68, Chicago, IL
High school: El Rancho (Pico Rivera, CA)
College: Michigan
His 37.8 net yards/punt was second in the NFC.

YEAR	TEAM	G	NO	YARDS	LONG	AVG	BLK	IN20
1990	Phoenix	16	67	2865	NA	42.8	0	NA
1991	Phoenix	16	76	3445	60	45.3	1	19
1992	Phoenix	15	54	2317	73	42.9	0	23
1993	Phoenix	16	73	3189	61	43.7	0	23
13 YR TOTALS		172	854	36615	73	42.9	5	65
1993 RANK NFL Ps			16	14	13	8		10
1994 PROJECTIONS	16		80	3484	53	43.6	0	23

Indianapolis
COLTS

1994 Scouting Report

Offense

Indianapolis was eighth in the NFL in passing, gaining 3,417 yards, while the running game gathered only 1,288 yards, worst in the league. Unfortunately, with Jim Harbaugh replacing the much-maligned Jeff George at QB, prospects are poor for a repeat of last season's passing performance. Also, star WRs Reggie Langhorne and Jesse Hester (who totaled 149 catches in '93) will not be back. One bright spot—TE Kerry Cash has caught 40+ passes for 2 straight years. Indianapolis hopes first round draft pick Marshall Faulk will turn into a Barry Sanders type of back. RB Roosevelt Potts was the team's leading rusher in '93, but failed to post a TD, and RB Rodney Culver has been the team's main scoring threat. T Will Wolford is the OL's best player, but he'll be coming off a torn rotator cuff.

Defense

The Colts defense was, statistically, the worst in the NFL in 1993, surrendering 5,638 total yards, including a league-worst 2,521 rushing yards. The defensive line is weak aside from star DE Jon Hand. Indianapolis is deepest at LB, with Quentin Coryatt (the team's best defensive player) and Jeff Herrod. Plus, the Colts hope first-round pick Trev Alberts and ex-Packer Tony Bennett make big contributions. In the defensive backfield, S Jason Belser was a standout, and Ray Buchanan emerged as a starter late last year.

Special Teams

Reliable Dean Biasucci is Indianapolis' all-time leading scorer, and Rohn Stark is one of the NFL's all-time punting leaders.

1994 Prospects

Colt expectations for the upcoming season cannot be high with Bear reject Jim Harbaugh slotted as the starting QB. Even major improvement would put the Colts in the middle of the pack in rushing offense and defense, and with Harbaugh and the depleted wideout crew, the team's passing prospects are dim. The Colts do have some good young players, and in a few years, a QB may be the last piece of the puzzle. This season, though, the Colts are standing still while the rest of the division is moving ahead. Look for them to repeat at the bottom of the AFC East.

Team Directory

President and treasurer: Robert Irsay   Vice president: Bill Tobin
General manager: James Irsay   Dir., pro player personnel: Clyde Powers
Dir., college player personnel: Geo. Boone   Dir., public relations: Craig Kelley

## 1993 Review			## 1994 Schedule		
Sep. 5	MIAMI	L 24-20	Sep. 4	HOUSTON	1:00
Sep. 12	at Cincinnati	W 9-6	Sep. 11	at Tampa Bay	1:00
Sep. 19	OPEN DATE		Sep. 18	at Pittsburgh	1:00
Sep. 26	CLEVELAND	W 23-10	Sep. 25	CLEVELAND	1:00
Oct. 3	at Denver	L 35-13	Oct. 2	SEATTLE	1:00
Oct. 10	DALLAS	L 27-3	Oct. 9	at N.Y. Jets	1:00
Oct. 17	OPEN DATE		Oct. 16	at Buffalo	1:00
Oct. 24	at Miami	L 41-27	Oct. 23	WASHINGTON	1:00
Oct. 31	NEW ENGLAND	W 9-6	Oct. 30	N.Y. JETS	4:00
Nov. 7	at Washington	L 30-24	Nov. 6	at Miami	1:00
Nov. 14	N.Y. JETS	L 31-17	Nov. 13	OPEN DATE	
Nov. 21	at Buffalo	L 23-9	Nov. 20	at Cincinnati	1:00
Nov. 29	SAN DIEGO	L 31-0	Nov. 27	NEW ENGLAND	8:00
Dec. 5	at N.Y. Jets	W 9-6	Dec. 4	at Seattle	4:00
Dec. 12	at N.Y. Giants	L 20-6	Dec. 11	at New England	1:00
Dec. 19	PHILADELPHIA	L 20-10	Dec. 18	MIAMI	1:00
Dec. 26	at New England	L 38-0	Dec. 24	BUFFALO	1:00
Jan. 2	BUFFALO	L 30-10			

1993 finish: 4-12 (2-6 home, 2-6 away), fifth in AFC East

Team Leaders

PASSING	ATT	COM	COM%	YDS	YPA	TD	TD%	INT	INT%	RTG
George	407	234	57.5	2526	6.21	8	2.0	6	1.5	76.3
Trudeau	162	85	52.5	992	6.12	2	1.2	7	4.3	57.4
Majkowski	24	13	54.2	105	4.38	0	0.0	1	4.2	48.1
TEAM	594	332	55.9	3623	6.10	10	1.7	15	2.5	69.2
OPPONENTS	454	270	59.5	3238	7.13	22	4.8	10	2.2	88.3

RECEIVING	REC	YDS	AVG	TD	RUSHING	ATT	YDS	AVG	TD
Langhorne	85	1038	12.2	3	Potts	179	711	4.0	0
Hester	64	835	13.0	1	Johnson	95	331	3.5	1
Johnson	55	443	8.1	0	Culver	65	150	2.3	3
Cash	43	402	9.3	3	George	13	39	3.0	0
Dawkins	26	430	16.5	1	Verdin	3	33	11.0	0
TEAM	332	3623	10.9	10	TEAM	365	1288	3.5	4
OPPONENTS	270	3238	12.0	22	OPPONENTS	575	2521	4.4	20

INTERCEPTIONS	INT	YDS	AVG	LG	TD	SACKS	NO
Buchanan	4	45	11.3	28	0	Hand	5.0
Baylor	3	11	3.7	7	0	Bickett	4.0
Herrod	1	29	29.0	29	0	Herrod	2.0
Daniel	1	17	17.0	17	0	Peguese	2.0
Belser	1	14	14.0	11	0	McClendon	1.5
TEAM	10	116	11.6	29	0	TEAM	21.0
OPPONENTS	15	247	16.5	56t	1	OPPONENTS	29.0

KICK RETURNS	NO	YDS	AV	LG	TD	PUNT RETURNS	NO	FC	YDS	AV	LG	TD
Verdin	50	1050	21.0	38	0	Verdin	30	17	173	5.8	24	0
Culver	3	51	17.0	20	0							
Butcher	2	2	1.0	2	0							
TEAM	57	1124	19.7	38	0	TEAM	30	17	173	5.8	24	0
OPPONENTS	37	551	14.9	37	0	OPPONENTS	41	12	352	8.6	71t	1

KICKING	XPM	XPA	FGM	FGA	LG	PTS
Biasucci	15	16	26	31	53	93
TEAM	15	16	26	31	53	93
OPPONENTS	43	45	21	30	49	106

PUNTING	NO	YDS	LG	AVG	TB	BLK	RET	RYD	IN20	NAV
Stark	83	3595	65	43.3	13	0	41	352	18	35.9
TEAM	83	3595	65	43.3	13	0	41	352	18	35.9
OPPONENTS	71	2855	59	40.2	6	0	30	173	30	36.1

FUMBLES	FUM	OFF.FUM.REC.	REC	TD	DEF.FUM.REC.	REC	TD
Potts	8	Johnson	2	0	Belser	3	0
Johnson	5	Potts	2	0	McClendon	2	0
George	4						
Langhorne	4						
TEAM	34	TEAM	11	0	TEAM	11	2
OPPONENTS	25	OPPONENTS	13	0	OPPONENTS	20	1

1994 Draft Choices

ROUND	NAME	POS	SCHOOL	OVERALL SELECTION
1	Marshall Faulk	RB	San Diego State	2
1	Trev Alberts	LB	Nebraska	5
2	Eric Mahlum	G	California	32
3	Jason Mathews	T	Texas A&M	67
4	Bradford Banta	TE	Southern California	106
5	John Covington	DB	Notre Dame	133
6	Lamont Warren	RB	Colorado	164
7	Lance Teichelman	DL	Texas A&M	196

HISTORY

TITLES

1958	NFL Championship
1959	NFL Championship
1964	NFL East Championship
1968	NFL Championship
1970	Super Bowl Winner
1975	AFC East Championship
1976	AFC East Championship
1977	AFC East Championship
1987	AFC East Championship

ALL-TIME TEAM RECORDS

Rushing

Most yards, game:	198	Norm Bulaich	9/19/71
Most yards, season:	1,659	Eric Dickerson	1988
Most yards, career:	5,487	Lydell Mitchell	1972-1977

Passing

Most yards, game:	401	Johnny Unitas	9/17/67
Most yards, season:	3,481	Johnny Unitas	1963
Most yards, career:	39,768	Johnny Unitas	1956-1972

Receiving

Most catches, game:	13	Lydell Mitchell	12/15/74
		Joe Washington	9/2/79
Most catches, season:	85	Reggie Langhorne	1993
Most catches, career:	631	Raymond Berry	1955-1967

Scoring

Most points, game:	24	Many Times	
		Eric Dickerson	10/31/88
Most points, season:	120	Lenny Moore	1964
Most points, career:	698	Dean Biasucci	1984-1993

COACHES

NAME	RECORD	YEARS	NAME	RECORD	YEARS
Keith Molesworth	3-9-0	1953	Ted Marchibroda	54-55-0	1975-79,
Weeb Ewbank	61-52-1	1954-62			1992-93
Don Shula	73-26-4	1963-69	Mike McCormack	9-23-0	1980-81
Don McCafferty	26-11-1	1970-72	Frank Kush	11-28-1	1982-84
John Sandusky	4-5-0	1972	Hal Hunter	0-1-0	1984
H. Schnellenberger	4-13-0	1973-74	Rod Dohower	5-24-0	1985-86
Joe Thomas	2-9-0	1974	Ron Meyer	36-36-0	1986-91
			Rick Venturi	1-10-0	1991

INDIANAPOLIS COLTS
1994 TRAINING CAMP ROSTER

No	Quarterbacks		Ht	Wt	Born	NFL Exp	College		GP/GS
7	Majkowski, Don	QB	6-3	208	2-25-64	8	Virginia	FA '93	3/0
12	Harbaugh, Jim	QB	6-3	215	12-23-64	8	Michigan	FA '94	15/15
	Running backs								
35	Culver, Rodney	RB	5-9	224	12-23-69	3	Notre Dame	D4 '92	16/1
28	Faulk, Marshall	RB	5-10	200		R	San Diego State	D1a '94	
25	Humphrey, Ronald	RB	5-10	211	3-3-69	1	Miss. Valley St.	FA '93	0/0
42	Potts, Roosevelt	RB	6-0	245	1-8-71	2	NE Louisiana	D2 '93	16/15
44	Toner, Ed	RB	6-0	240	3-22-68	3	Boston College	FA '92	16/1
21	Warren, Lamont	RB	5-11	194		R	Colorado	D6 '94	
	Wide receivers								
86	Baker, Shannon	WR	5-9	185	7-20-70	1	Florida State	FA '93	0/0
9	Carroll, Wesley	WR	6-0	195	9-6-67	4	Miami (FL)	FA '94	12/0
80	Cox, Aaron	WR	5-10	178	3-13-65	7	Arizona State	FA '93	11/0
87	Dawkins, Sean	WR	6-4	213	2-3-71	2	California	D1 '93	16/7
85	Turner, Floyd	WR	5-11	198	5-29-66	6	Northwestern St.	FA '94	10/2
	Tight ends								
81	Arbuckle, Charles	TE	6-3	248	9-13-68	4	UCLA	FA '92	16/2
49	Banta, Bradford	TE	6-6	255		R	Southern California	D4 '94	
88	Cash, Kerry	TE	6-4	252	8-7-69	4	Texas	D5 '91	16/14
48	Etheredge, Carlos	TE	6-5	259	8-10-70	1	Miami (FL)	D6 '93	0/0
	Offensive linemen								
69	Dixon, Randy	G	6-3	305	3-12-65	8	Pittsburgh	D4 '87	15/15
75	Gray, Cecil	T	6-4	305	2-16-68	5	North Carolina	FA '93	6/2
63	Lowdermilk, Kirk	C	6-4	280	4-10-63	10	Ohio State	FA '93	16/16
65	Mahlum, Eric	G	6-4	285		R	California	D2 '94	
74	Mathews, Jason	T	6-5	284		R	Texas A&M	D3 '94	
73	Moss, Zefross	T	6-6	338	8-17-66	6	Alabama State	T-DAL '89	16/16
68	Ray, John	T	6-8	350	6-5-69	2	West Virginia	FA '93	2/0
79	Staysniak, Joe	T	6-5	302	12-8-66	4	Ohio State	FA '92	14/1
72	Vander Poel, Mark	T	6-7	303	3-5-68	4	Colorado	D4 '91	0/0
67	Wolford, Will	T	6-5	300	5-18-64	9	Vanderbilt	FA '93	12/12
	Defensive linemen								
93	Brown, Robert	DE	6-3	287	5-21-60	12	Virginia Tech	FA '94	0/0
90	Emtman, Steve	DT	6-4	300	4-16-70	3	Washington	D1 '92	5/5
78	Hand, Jon	DE	6-7	310	11-13-63	9	Alabama	D1 '86	15/14
61	McCoy, Tony	NT	6-0	279	6-10-69	3	Florida	D4 '92	6/0
96	Peguese, Willis	DE	6-4	273	12-18-66	5	Miami (FL)	W-HOU '92	13/4
92	Sims, Thomas	DL	6-2	308	8-15-67	5	Pittsburgh	FA '93	5/3
98	Siragusa, Tony	NT	6-3	325	5-14-67	5	Pittsburgh	FA '90	14/14
99	Teichelman, Lance	DL	6-4	276		R	Texas A&M	D7 '94	
	Linebackers								
51	Alberts, Trev	LB	6-4	243		R	Nebraska	D1b '94	
56	Bennett, Tony	LB	6-2	243	7-1-67	5	Mississippi	FA '94	10/7
53	Butcher, Paul	LB	6-0	240	11-8-63	8	Wayne State	FA '93	16/0
55	Coryatt, Quentin	LB	6-3	250	8-1-70	3	Texas A&M	D1 '92	16/16
59	Grant, Stephen	LB	6-0	242	12-23-69	3	West Virginia	D10 '92	16/0
54	Herrod, Jeff	LB	6-0	249	7-29-66	7	Mississippi	D9 '88	14/14
57	McDonald, Devon	LB	6-4	248	11-8-69	2	Notre Dame	D4 '93	16/0
52	Ratigan, Brian	LB	6-4	241	12-27-70	1	Notre Dame	FA '93	0/0
94	Thomas, Marquise	LB	6-4	255	5-25-71	1	Mississippi	D8 '93	0/0
	Defensive backs								
33	Ambrose, Ashley	DB	5-10	185	9-17-70	3	Miss. Valley St.	D2 '92	14/6
29	Belser, Jason	DB	5-9	187	4-28-70	3	Oklahoma	D8 '92	16/16
34	Buchanan, Ray	DB	5-9	193	9-29-71	2	Louisville	D3 '93	16/5
39	Covington, John	DB	6-0	198		R	Notre Dame	D5 '94	
38	Daniel, Eugene	DB	5-11	188	5-4-61	11	Louisiana State	D8 '84	16/16
**	Goode, Chris	DB	6-0	199	9-17-63	8	Alabama	D10 '87	14/10
30	Gray, Derwin	DB	5-10	198	4-9-71	2	Brigham Young	D4 '93	11/0
32	O'Neal, Robert	DB	6-1	199	8-12-71	1	Clemson	FA '93	0/0
	Specialists								
4	Biasucci, Dean	K	6-0	190	7-25-62	10	Western Carolina	FA '86	16/0
3	Stark, Rohn	P	6-3	203	5-4-59	13	Florida State	D2 '82	16/0

Jim Harbaugh   No. 12/QB

Full name: James Joseph Harbaugh
HT: 6-3   **WT:** 215
Born: 12-23-64, Toledo, OH
High school: Pioneer (Ann Arbor, MI) and Palo Alto (CA)
College: Michigan

Ex-Bear Harbaugh's 61.5% completion rate in '93 was his best since 1989.

YEAR	TEAM	PASSING										RUSHING		
		G	ATT	CPL	CPL%	YDS	AVG	TDS	TD%	INT	INT%	RTG	ATT	YDS	AVG
1987	Chicago	6	11	8	72.7	62	5.6	0	0.0	0	0.0	98.2	4	15	3.8
1988	Chicago	10	97	47	48.5	514	5.3	0	0.0	2	2.1	55.9	19	110	5.8
1989	Chicago	12	178	111	62.4	1204	6.8	5	2.8	9	5.1	70.5	45	276	6.1
1990	Chicago	14	312	180	57.7	2178	7.0	10	3.2	6	1.9	81.9	51	321	6.3
1991	Chicago	16	478	275	57.5	3121	6.5	15	3.1	16	3.3	73.7	70	338	4.8
1992	Chicago	16	358	202	56.4	2486	6.9	13	3.6	12	3.4	76.2	47	272	5.8
1993	Chicago	15	325	200	61.5	2002	6.2	7	2.2	11	3.4	72.1	60	277	4.6
	7 YR TOTALS	89	1759	1023	58.2	11567	6.6	50	2.8	56	3.2		296	1609	5.4
1993	RANK NFL QB		20	18	13	19	40	29	52	13	36	38	2	3	8
1994	PROJECTIONS	16	333	213	64.0	1928	5.8	5	1.5	12	3.6		68	288	4.2

Don Majkowski   No. 7/QB

Full name: Donald Vincent Majkowski
HT: 6-3   **WT:** 208
Born: 2-25-64, Buffalo, NY
High school: Depew (NY) and Fork Union Military (VA)
College: Virginia

Former Green Bay starter Majkowski played in just 3 games in 1993 behind Jeff George.

YEAR	TEAM	PASSING										RUSHING		
		G	ATT	CPL	CPL%	YDS	AVG	TDS	TD%	INT	INT%	RTG	ATT	YDS	AVG
1987	Green Bay	7	127	55	43.3	875	6.9	5	3.9	3	2.4	70.2	15	127	8.5
1988	Green Bay	13	336	178	53.0	2119	6.3	9	2.7	11	3.3	67.8	47	225	4.8
1989	Green Bay	16	599	353	58.9	4318	7.2	27	4.5	20	3.3	82.3	75	358	4.8
1990	Green Bay	9	264	150	56.8	1925	7.3	10	3.8	12	4.5	73.5	29	186	6.4
1991	Green Bay	9	226	115	50.9	1362	6.0	3	1.3	8	3.5	59.3	3	11	3.7
1992	Green Bay	14	55	38	69.1	271	4.9	2	3.6	2	3.6	77.2	8	33	4.1
1993	Indianapolis	3	24	13	54.2	105	4.4	0	0.0	1	4.2	48.1	2	4	2.0
	7 YR TOTALS	71	1631	902	55.3	10975	6.7	56	3.4	57	3.5		179	944	5.3
1993	RANK NFL QB		59	59	48	59	67	59	59	56	23	65	54	45	37
1994	PROJECTIONS	0	0	0	NA	0	NA	0	NA	0	NA		0	0	NA

Rodney Culver   No. 35/RB

Full name: Rodney Dwayne Culver
HT: 5-9   **WT:** 224
Born: 12-23-69, Detroit, MI
High school: St. Martin dePorres (Detroit)
College: Notre Dame

Culver has scored 14 of the Colts' last 38 TDs, and led the team with 5 TDs in 1993.

YEAR	TEAM	G	RUSHING ATT	YDS	AVG	TD	RECEIVING REC	YDS	AVG	TD	KICK RETURNS RET	YDS	AVG	TD
1992	Indianapolis	16	121	321	2.7	7	26	210	8.1	2	---	---	---	---
1993	Indianapolis	16	65	150	2.3	3	11	112	10.2	1	3	51	17.0	0
	2 YR TOTALS	32	186	471	2.5	10	37	322	8.7	3	3	51	17.0	0
1993	RANK NFL RB		59	83	127	21	67	58	16	13	36	38	28	
1994	PROJECTIONS	16	9	0	0.0	0	0	0	NA	0	6	102	17.0	0

Roosevelt Potts No. 42/RB

Full name: Roosevelt Bernard Potts
HT: 6-0   **WT:** 245
Born: 1-8-71, Rayville, LA
High school: Rayville (LA)
College: Northeast Louisiana

Rookie RB Potts had a team-high 711 yards on the ground but no TDs in 1993.

YEAR	TEAM	G	RUSHING ATT	YDS	AVG	TD	RECEIVING REC	YDS	AVG	TD	KICK RETURNS RET	YDS	AVG	TD
1993	Indianapolis	16	179	711	4.0	0	26	189	7.3	0	---	---	---	---
	1 YR TOTALS	16	179	711	4.0	0	26	189	7.3	0	0	0	NA	0
1993	RANK NFL RB		23	19	55	89	36	41	70	40	65	65	65	

Floyd Turner   No. 88/WR

HT: 5-11 **WT:** 198
Born: 5-29-66, Shreveport, LA
High school: Mansfield (LA)
College: Northwestern State
Turner peaked with 64 catches for the Saints in '91—he's totaled 17 receptions in the last 2 years.

			RECEIVING				RUSHING				PUNT RETURN		
YEAR	TEAM	G	REC	YDS	AVG	TD	ATT	YDS	AVG	TD	RET	YDS	AVG
1989	New Orleans	13	22	279	12.7	1	2	8	4.0	0	1	7	7.0
1990	New Orleans	16	21	396	18.9	4	---	---	---	---	---	---	---
1991	New Orleans .	16	64	927	14.5	8	---	---	---	---	---	---	---
1992	New Orleans	2	5	43	8.6	0	---	---	---	---	3	10	3.3
1993	New Orleans	10	12	163	13.6	1	---	---	---	---	---	---	---
	5 YR TOTALS	57	124	1808	14.6	14	2	8	4.0	0	4	17	4.3
1993	RANK NFL WR		94	95	67	72	42	42	42		30	30	29
1994	PROJECTIONS	11	5	96	19.2	1	0	0	NA	0	0	0	NA

Sean Dawkins   No. 87/WR

Full name: Sean Russell Dawkins
HT: 6-4 **WT:** 213
Born: 2-3-71, Red Bank, NJ
High school: Homestead (CA)
College: California
Rookie Dawkins' 16.5 yards/catch led the Colts. He will definitely see more action in '94.

			RECEIVING				RUSHING				PUNT RETURN		
YEAR	TEAM	G	REC	YDS	AVG	TD	ATT	YDS	AVG	TD	RET	YDS	AVG
1993	Indianapolis	16	26	430	16.5	1	---	---	---	---	---	---	---
	1 YR TOTALS	16	26	430	16.5	1	0	0	NA	0	0	0	NA
1993	RANK NFL WR		70	63	23	72	42	42	42		30	30	29

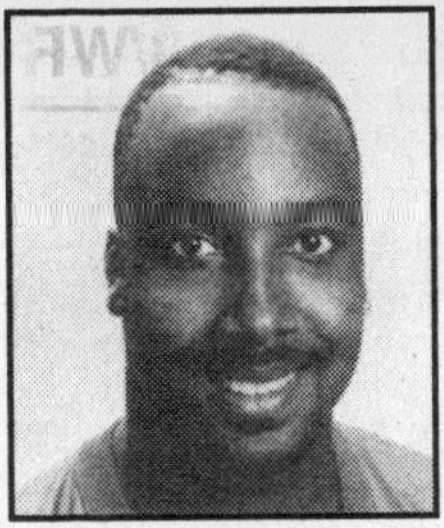

Kerry Cash No. 88/TE

Full name: Kerry Lenard Cash
HT: 6-4 **WT:** 252
Born: 8-7-69, San Antonio, TX
High school: Holmes (San Antonio)
College: Texas
Cash became the first Colts TE to post consecutive 40+ catch seasons since John Mackey in 1967-8.

			RECEIVING			
YEAR	TEAM	G	REC	YDS	AVG	TD
1991	Indianapolis	4	1	18	18.0	0
1992	Indianapolis	16	43	521	12.1	3
1993	Indianapolis	16	43	402	9.3	3
3	YR TOTALS	36	87	941	10.8	6
1993	RANK NFL TE		10	15	44	12
1994	PROJECTIONS	16	53	425	8.0	4

Jon Hand No. 78/DE

Full name: Jon Thomas Hand
HT: 6-7 **WT:** 310
Born: 11-13-63, Sylacauga, AL
High school: Sylacauga (AL)
College: Alabama
Hand led the Colts with 5.5 sacks and 8 QB pressures; his 78 tackles were tops on the DL.

YEAR	TEAM	G	INT	YDS	AVG	TD	SACKS	FUM REC	TD
1986	Indianapolis	15	1	8	8.0	0	5.0	—	—
1987	Indianapolis	12	—	—	—	—	1.0	—	—
1988	Indianapolis	15	—	—	—	—	5.0	1	0
1989	Indianapolis	16	—	—	—	—	10.0	2	0
1990	Indianapolis	12	—	—	—	—	3.0	1	0
1991	Indianapolis	16	—	—	—	—	5.0	1	0
1992	Indianapolis	15	—	—	—	—	1.0	—	—
1993	Indianapolis	15	—	—	—	—	5.0	—	—
8	YR TOTALS	116	1	8	8.0	0	35.0	5	0
1993	RANK NFL DL		16	NA	NA	NA	51	71	NA
1994	PROJECTIONS	15	0	0	0	0	6	0	0

Quentin Coryatt No. 55/LB

Full name: Quentin John Coryatt
HT: 6-3   **WT:** 250
Born: 8-1-70, St. Croix, VI
High school: Lee (Baytown, TX)
College: Texas A&M

Coryatt, the second pick in the '92 draft, led Indy with 150 tackles (96 solo) and 8 QB pressures.

YEAR	TEAM	G	INT	YDS	AVG	TD	SACKS	FUM REC	TD
1992	Indianapolis	7	—	—	—	—	2.0	1	0
1993	Indianapolis	16	—	—	—	—	1.0	—	—
	2 YR TOTALS	23	0	0	NA	0	3.0	1	0
1993	RANK NFL LB		47	NA	NA	NA	62	81	NA
1994	PROJECTIONS	16	0	0	0	0	0	0	0

Ray Buchanan   No. 34/DB

Full name: Raymond Louis Buchanan
HT: 5-9   **WT:** 193
Born: 9-29-71, Chicago, IL
High school: Proviso East (IL)
College: Louisville

Rookie Buchanan won a starting job in Week 12 and led the team in INTs with 4.

YEAR	TEAM	G	INT	YDS	AVG	TD	SACKS	FUM REC	TD
1993	Indianapolis	16	4	45	11.3	0	---	---	---
	1 YR TOTALS	16	4	45	11.3	0	0.0	0	0
1993	RANK NFL DB		21	44	71	27	49	94	NA

Dean Biasucci   No. 4/K

HT: 6-0   **WT:** 190
Born: 7-25-62, Niagara Falls, NY
High school: Miramar (FL)
College: Western Carolina
After leading the Colts in scoring for 8 straight seasons, Biasucci is the team's all-time leading scorer.

YEAR	TEAM	G	XP	XPA	XP Pct.	FG	FGA	FG Pct.	PTS
1984	Indianapolis	15	13	14	92.9	3	5	60.0	22
1986	Indianapolis	16	26	27	96.3	13	25	52.0	65
1987	Indianapolis	12	24	24	100.0	24	27	88.9	96
1988	Indianapolis	16	39	40	97.5	25	32	78.1	114
1989	Indianapolis	16	31	32	96.9	21	27	77.8	94
1990	Indianapolis	16	32	33	97.0	17	24	70.8	83
1991	Indianapolis	16	14	14	100.0	15	26	57.7	59
1992	Indianapolis	16	24	24	100.0	16	29	55.2	72
1993	Indianapolis	16	15	16	93.8	16	31	83.9	93
9 YR TOTALS		139	218	224	97.3	160	226	70.8	698
1993 RANK NFL			26	26	24	10	13		20

Ted Marchibroda   Coach

Full name: Theodore Joseph Marchibroda
Born: 3-15-31, Franklin, PA
High school: Franklin (PA)
College: Detroit and St. Bonaventure
Marchibroda is older than every active NFL head coach except Don Shula (65) and Marv Levy (66). He served as Levy's offensive coordinator before taking the Colts' job in '92.

	REGULAR SEASON					POSTSEASON		
YEAR	TEAM	W	L	T	PCT	FINISH	W	L	FINISH
1975	Baltimore	10	4	0	.714	T1st/AFC East	0	1	lost 1st Rnd. game to Pitt., 28-10
1976	Baltimore	11	3	0	.786	T1st/AFC East	0	1	lost 1st Rnd. game to Pitt., 40-14
1977	Baltimore	10	4	0	.714	T1st/AFC East	0	1	lost 1st Rnd. game to Oakland, 37-31 (OT)
1978	Baltimore	5	11	0	.313	T4th/AFC East			
1979	Baltimore	5	11	0	.313	5th/AFC East			
1992	Indianapolis	9	7	0	.563	3rd/AFC East			
1993	Indianapolis	4	12	0	.250	5th/AFC East			
7 YR TOTALS		54	52	0	.509		0	3	

Aaron Cox No. 80/WR

Full name: Aaron Dion Cox
HT: 5-10 **WT:** 178
Born: 3-13-65, Los Angeles, CA
High school: Dorsey (Los Angeles)
College: Arizona State

Cox (4 catches in '93) could wind up starting in '94.

YEAR	TEAM	G	RECEIVING REC	YDS	AVG	TD	RUSHING ATT	YDS	AVG	TD	PUNT RETURN RET	YDS	AVG
1991	LA Rams	15	15	216	14.4	0	---	---	---	---	---	---	---
1992	LA Rams	10	18	261	14.5	0	---	---	---	---	---	---	---
1993	Indianapolis	11	4	59	14.8	0	---	---	---	---	---	---	---
6 YR TOTALS		82	102	1732	17.0	8	0	0	NA	0	0	0	NA
1993 RANK NFL WR			120	118	48	95	42	42	42		30	30	29
1994 PROJECTIONS		11	0	0	NA	0	0	0	NA	0	0	0	NA

Charles Arbuckle No. 81/TE

Full name: Charles Edward Arbuckle
HT: 6-3 **WT:** 248
Born: 9-13-68, Beaumont, TX
High school: Willowridge (Sugar Land, TX)
College: UCLA

Sure-handed TE Arbuckle is also a fine blocker.

YEAR	TEAM	G	RECEIVING REC	YDS	AVG	TD
1992	Indianapolis	16	13	152	11.7	1
1993	Indianapolis	16	15	90	6.0	0
2 YR TOTALS		32	28	242	8.6	1
1993 RANK NFL TE			34	43	63	46
1994 PROJECTIONS		16	17	28	1.6	0

Will Wolford No. 67/T

Full name: William Charles Wolford
HT: 6-5 **WT:** 300
Born: 5-18-64, Louisville, KY
High school: St. Xavier (Louisville)
College: Vanderbilt

A torn rotator cuff broke his string of 33 starts.

YEAR	TEAM	G	RUSHING ATT	YDS	AVG	RANK AV RUSH	PASS YDS	RANK PASS YDS	SACKS	YDS. LOST
1991	Buffalo	15	505	2381	4.7	3	4140	3	35	269
1992	Buffalo	16	549	2436	4.4	5	3678	5	29	221
1993	Indianapolis	12	365	1288	3.5	24	3623	8	29	206
8 YR TOTALS		114								

Tony Siragusa   No. 98/NT

Full name: Anthony Siragusa
HT: 6-3   **WT:** 325
Born: 5-14-67, Kenilworth, NJ
High school: David Brearly (Kenilworth, NJ)
College: Pittsburgh
Siragusa set a new personal best with 71 tackles.

YEAR	TEAM	G	INT	YDS	AVG	TD	SACKS	FUM REC	TD
1991	Indianapolis	13	---	---	---	---	2.0	1	0
1992	Indianapolis	16	---	---	---	---	3.0	1	---
1993	Indianapolis	14	---	---	---	---	1.5	---	---
4 YR TOTALS		56	0	0	NA	0	7.5	3	0
1993 RANK NFL DL			16	NA	NA	NA	113	71	NA
1994 PROJECTIONS		15	0	0	0	0	1	0	0

Eugene Daniel   No. 38/DB

HT: 5-11   **WT:** 188
Born: 5-4-61, Baton Rouge, LA
High school: Robert E. Lee (Baton Rouge)
College: Louisiana State
Daniel started all 16 games in '93 and led Indy with 15 passes defensed.

YEAR	TEAM	G	INT	YDS	AVG	TD	SACKS	FUM REC	TD
1991	Indianapolis	16	3	22	7.3	0	---	---	---
1992	Indianapolis	14	1	0	0.0	0	2.0	---	---
1993	Indianapolis	16	1	17	17.0	0	---	---	---
10 YR TOTALS		150	27	240	8.89	1	2.0	5	0
1993 RANK NFL DB			95	89	39	27	49	94	NA
1994 PROJECTIONS		16	1	21	21.0	0	0	0	0

Tony Bennett   No. 56/LB

Full name: Tony Lydell Bennett
HT: 6-2   **WT:** 243
Born: 7-1-67, Alligator, MS
High school: Coahoma Cty. (Clarksdale, MS)
College: Mississippi
Ex-Packer Bennett had just 6.5 sacks in 1993.

YEAR	TEAM	G	INT	YDS	AVG	TD	SACKS	FUM REC	TD
1991	Green Bay	16	---	---	---	---	13.0	---	---
1992	Green Bay	16	---	---	---	---	13.5	3	1
1993	Green Bay	10	---	---	---	---	6.5	---	---
4 YR TOTALS		56	0	0	NA	0	36.0	4	1
1990 RANK NFL LB			47	NA	NA	NA	11	81	NA
1994 PROJECTIONS		0	0	0	0	0	0	0	0

Jeff Herrod   No. 54/LB

Full name: Jeff Sylvester Herrod
HT: 6-0   **WT:** 249
Born: 7-29-66, Belle Glade, FL
High school: Belle Glade Central (FL)
College: Mississippi
Herrod's 142 tackles ranked second on the team.

YEAR	TEAM	G	INT	YDS	AVG	TD	SACKS	FUM REC	TD
1991	Indianapolis	14	1	25	25.0	0	2.5	3	0
1992	Indianapolis	16	1	4	4.0	0	2.0	---	---
1993	Indianapolis	14	1	29	29.0	0	2.0	1	1
6 YR TOTALS		88	3	58	19.3	0	13.5	4	1
1993 RANK NFL LB			17	7	2	5	37	24	1
1994 PROJECTIONS		14	1	40	40.0	0	2	1	2

Jason Belser   No. 29/DB

HT: 5-9   **WT:** 187
Born: 4-28-70, Kansas City, MO
High school: Raytown South (MO)
College: Oklahoma
Belser's 127 tackles ranked third on the squad.

YEAR	TEAM	G	INT	YDS	AVG	TD	SACKS	FUM REC	TD
1992	Indianapolis	16	3	27	9.0	0	---	1	0
1993	Indianapolis	16	1	14	14.0	0	---	3	0
2 YR TOTALS		32	4	41	10.3	0	0.0	4	0
1993 RANK NFL DB			95	93	53	27	49	1	14
1994 PROJECTIONS		16	0	0	NA	0	0	5	0

Rohn Stark   No. 3/P

Full name: Rohn Taylor Stark
HT: 6-3   **WT:** 203
Born: 5-4-59, Minneapolis, MN
High school: Pine River (MN)
College: Florida State
Stark is fourth on the NFL's all-time punting list.

YEAR	TEAM	G	NO	YARDS	LONG	AVG	BLK	IN20
1990	Indianapolis	16	71	3084		43.4	1	
1991	Indianapolis	16	82	3492	65	42.6	0	14
1992	Indianapolis	16	83	3716	64	44.8	0	22
1993	Indianapolis	16	83	3595	65	43.3	0	18
12 YR TOTALS		64	319	13887	65	43.5	1	54
1993 RANK NFL			5	7	8	1	9	18
1994 PROJECTIONS		16	85	3629	73	42.7	0	19

Kansas City
CHIEFS

1994 Scouting Report

Offense

Despite the team's 11-5 record, the Chiefs' offense sputtered in 1993. Kansas City's 4,835 yards gained ranked sixteenth in the NFL. Despite their Hall of Fame resumes, QB Joe Montana and RB Marcus Allen are well past their primes. Allen did score an amazing 15 TDs last year, but the Chiefs drafted RBs Greg Hill and Donnell Bennett in the first 2 rounds as insurance. Adding Steve Bono will help; he's a proven backup who can contribute when Montana is sidelined. WRs Willie Davis and J. J. Birden both had strong seasons, and TE Keith Cash's playoff performance shows he could be a valuable contributor in '94. Kimble Anders starts at FB and added 40 catches in '93. The OL features Pro Bowl T John Alt and C Tim Grunhard.

Defense

Defense carried the Chiefs through most of '93; Kansas City allowed only 1,620 rushing yards (ninth in the NFL). Kansas City will be even tougher to run on in '94, with the addition of ex-Cowboy DT Tony Casillas to a defense that already features NT Dan Saleaumua and DE Neil Smith. Smith and LB Derrick Thomas have combined for 62 sacks over the past 2 seasons. Free agency hit the Chiefs' secondary hard, with the defections of top DBs Kevin Ross and Albert Lewis. But Kansas City signed ex-Giant CB Mark Collins.

Special Teams

Citing salary-cap problems, Kansas City waived Nick Lowery and signed journeyman K Lin Elliott. Punting could also be a problem area; the Chiefs added ex-Jet Louie Aguiar, who performed poorly in his last season in New York. Dale Carter handles punt return duties adequately.

1994 Prospects

This may be Joe Montana's last season, and the Chiefs have tried to give him the opportunity to lead them to a Super Bowl. They've even put in grass at Arrowhead Stadium. However, they made no major moves to upgrade their offense, and losing Lowery will hurt. The defense will be strong again, but probably not much better than '93. The Chiefs will definitely be in the playoff hunt, but so will the Raiders and the Broncos. The AFC West keeps getting tougher, and Kansas City might just not have enough to get the job done.

Team Directory

Founder: Lamar Hunt

Chairman of the board: Jack Steadman

President & General manager: Carl Peterson

Director of public relations: Bob Moore

1993 Review			**1994 Schedule**		
Sep. 5	at Tampa Bay	W 27-3	Sep. 4	at New Orleans	1:00
Sep. 12	at Houston	L 30-0	Sep. 11	SAN FRANCISCO	1:00
Sep. 20	DENVER	W 15-7	Sep. 18	at Atlanta	8:00
Sep. 26	OPEN DATE		Sep. 25	L.A. RAMS	1:00
Oct. 3	L.A. RAIDERS	W 24-9	Oct. 2	OPEN DATE	
Oct. 10	CINCINNATI	W 17-15	Oct. 9	at San Diego	4:00
Oct. 17	at San Diego	W 17-14	Oct. 17	at Denver (Mon.)	9:00
Oct. 24	OPEN DATE		Oct. 23	SEATTLE	1:00
Oct. 31	at Miami	L 30-10	Oct. 30	at Buffalo	1:00
Nov. 8	GREEN BAY	W 23-16	Nov. 6	L.A. RAIDERS	8:00
Nov. 14	at L.A. Raiders	W 31-20	Nov. 13	SAN DIEGO	1:00
Nov. 21	CHICAGO	L 19-17	Nov. 20	CLEVELAND	1:00
Nov. 28	BUFFALO	W 23-7	Nov. 27	at Seattle	4:00
Dec. 5	at Seattle	W 31-16	Dec. 4	DENVER	4:00
Dec. 12	at Denver	L 27-21	Dec. 12	at Miami (Mon.)	9:00
Dec. 19	SAN DIEGO	W 28-24	Dec. 18	HOUSTON	4:00
Dec. 26	at Minnesota	L 30-10	Dec. 24	at L.A. Raiders	4:00
Jan. 2	SEATTLE	W 34-24			

1993 finish: 11-5 (7-1 home, 4-4 away), first in AFC West

Team Leaders

PASSING	ATT	COM	COM%	YDS	YPA	TD	TD%	INT	INT%	RTG
Montana	298	181	60.7	2144	7.19	13	4.4	7	2.3	87.4
Krieg	189	105	55.6	1238	6.55	7	3.7	3	1.6	81.4
Blundin	3	1	33.3	2	0.67	0	0.0	0	0.0	42.4
TEAM	490	287	58.6	3384	6.91	20	4.1	10	2.0	84.8
OPPONENTS	525	312	59.4	3379	6.44	18	3.4	21	4.0	73.2

RECEIVING	REC	YDS	AVG	TD	RUSHING	ATT	YDS	AVG	TD
Davis	52	909	17.5	7	Allen	206	764	3.7	12
Birden	51	721	14.1	2	Anders	75	291	3.9	0
Anders	40	326	8.2	1	McNair	51	278	5.5	2
Allen	34	238	7.0	3	Williams	42	149	3.5	0
Hayes	24	331	13.8	1	Montana	25	64	2.6	0
TEAM	287	3384	11.8	20	TEAM	445	1655	3.7	14
OPPONENTS	312	3379	10.8	18	OPPONENTS	453	1620	3.6	11

INTERCEPTIONS	INT	YDS	AVG	LG	TD
Lewis	6	61	10.2	24	0
Mincy	5	44	8.8	20	0
Ross	2	49	24.5	48	0
TEAM	21	225	10.7	48	0
OPPONENTS	10	111	11.1	48	0

SACKS	NO
Smith	15.0
Thomas	8.0
Saleaumua	3.5
TEAM	35.0
OPPONENTS	35.0

KICK RETURNS	NO	YDS	AV	LG	TD
Hughes	14	266	19.0	30	0
Dickerson	11	237	21.5	44	0
Jones	9	156	17.3	29	0
TEAM	45	875	19.4	47	0
OPPONENTS	49	1007	20.6	60	0

PUNT RETURNS	NO	FC	YDS	AV	LG	TD
Carter	27	4	247	9.1	30	0
Birden	5	3	43	8.6	12	0
Hughes	3	0	49	16.3	29	0
TEAM	37	7	348	9.4	30	0
OPPONENTS	43	15	352	8.2	54	0

KICKING	XPM	XPA	FGM	FGA	LG	PTS
Lowery	37	37	23	29	52	106
TEAM	37	37	23	29	52	106
OPPONENTS	27	30	28	32	55	111

PUNTING	NO	YDS	LG	AVG	TB	BLK	RET	RYD	IN20	NAV
Barker	76	3240	59	42.6	8	1	43	352	19	35.4
TEAM	77	3240	59	42.1	8	1	43	352	19	35.4
OPPONENTS	68	3035	67	44.6	6	1	37	348	23	37.8

FUMBLES	FUM	OFF.FUM.REC.	REC	TD	DEF.FUM.REC.	REC	TD
Krieg	6	Carter	2	0	Newton	3	0
Allen	4	Shields	2	0	Smith	3	0
Carter	4						
TEAM	28	TEAM	7	0	TEAM	17	2
OPPONENTS	30	OPPONENTS	11	0	OPPONENTS	18	1

1994 Draft Choices

ROUND	NAME	POS	SCHOOL	OVERALL SELECTION
1	Greg Hill	RB	Texas A&M	25
2	Donnell Bennett	FB	Miami (FL)	58
3	Lake Dawson	WR	Notre Dame	92
3	Chris Penn	WR	Tulsa	96
4	Bracey Walker	S	North Carolina	127
5	James Burton	CB	Fresno State	151
5	Rob Waldrop	DT	Arizona	156
6	Anthony Daigle	RB	Fresno State	185
7	Steve Matthews	QB	Memphis State	199
7	Tracy Greene	TE	Grambling	219

HISTORY

TITLES

1966	AFL Championship
1969	Super Bowl Winner
1971	AFC West Championship
1993	AFC West Championship

ALL-TIME TEAM RECORDS

Rushing

Most yards, game:	200	Barry Ward	10/14/90
Most yards, season:	1,480	Christian Okoye	1989
Most yards, career:	4,897	Christian Okoye	1987-1992

Passing

Most yards, game:	435	Len Dawson	11/1/64
Most yards, season:	4,348	Bill Kenney	1983
Most yards, career:	28,507	Len Dawson	1962-1975

Receiving

Most catches, game:	12	Ed Podolak	10/7/73
Most catches, season:	80	Carlos Carson	1983
Most catches, career:	416	Henry Mitchell	1976-1987

Scoring

Most points, game:	30	Abner Hayes	11/20/61
Most points, season:	139	Nick Lowery	1990
Most points, career:	1,466	Nick Lowery	1980-1993

COACHES

NAME	RECORD	YEARS
Hank Stram	129-79-10	1960-74
Paul Wiggin	11-24-0	1975-77
Tom Bettis	1-6-0	1977
Marv Levy	31-42-0	1978-82
John Mackovic	30-35-0	1983-86
Frank Gansz	8-22-1	1987-88
M. Schottenheimer	51-32-1	1989-93

KANSAS CITY CHIEFS
1994 TRAINING CAMP ROSTER

No.	Quarterbacks	Pos	Ht	Wt	Born	NFL Exp	College	How acq	GP/GS
14	Blundin, Matt	QB	6-6	233	3-7-69	3	Virginia	D2 '92	1/0
13	Bono, Steve	QB	6-4	215	5-11-62	10	UCLA	T-SF '94	8/0
15	Matthews, Steve	QB	6-3	209	10-13-70	R	Memphis State	D7a '94	
19	Montana, Joe	QB	6-2	205	6-11-56	16	Notre Dame	T-SF '93	11/11
	Running backs								
32	Allen, Marcus	RB	6-2	210	3-26-60	13	Southern California	FA '93	16/10
38	Anders, Kimble	FB	5-11	221	9-10-66	4	Houston	FA '91	16/13
35	Bennett, Donnell	FB	6-0	241	9-14-72	R	Miami (FL)	D2 '94	
22	Cobb, Trevor	RB	5-9	209	11-20-70	1	Rice	FA '93	0/0
43	Daigle, Anthony	RB	5-10	203	4-5-70	R	Fresno State	D6 '94	
23	Dickerson, Ron	RB	6-0	206	8-31-71	2	Arkansas	FA '93	6/0
29	Hill, Greg	RB	5-11	205	2-23-72	R	Texas A&M	D1 '94	
21	Stephens, John	RB	6-1	215	2-23-66	7	Northwestern St.	FA '93	7/0
45	Thompson, Ernie	FB	6-0	252	10-25-69	2	Indiana	FA '93	16/2
	Wide receivers								
82	Barnett, Marcus	WR	6-1	199	4-19-68	4	Jackson St.	D3 '91	16/0
88	Birden, J.J	WR	5-10	170	6-16-65	5	Oregon	FA '90	16/16
84	Davis, Willie	WR	6-0	181	10-10-67	3	Central Arkansas	FA '92	16/15
80	Dawson, Lake	WR	6-1	204	1-2-72	R	Notre Dame	D3a '94	
83	Hughes, Danan	WR	6-1	201	12-11-70	2	Iowa	D7 '93	6/0
81	Penn, Chris	WR	6-0	192	4-20-71	R	Tulsa	D3b '94	
	Tight ends								
87	Bartrum, Mike	TE	6-4	247	6-23-70	2	Marshall	FA '93	3/0
89	Cash, Keith	TE	6-4	248	8-7-69	4	Texas	Plan B '92	15/0
93	Greene, Tracy	TE	6-5	275	11-5-72	R	Grambling	D7b '94	
	Offensive linemen								
76	Alt, John	T	6-8	307	5-30-62	11	Iowa	D1b '84	16/16
74	Graham, Derrick	T	6-4	315	3-18-67	5	Appalachian St.	D5a '90	11/2
61	Grunhard, Tim	C	6-2	299	5-17-68	5	Notre Dame	D2 '90	16/16
65	Knapp, Lindsay	G-T	6-6	280	2-25-70	1	Notre Dame	D5 '93	0/0
68	Shields, Will	G	6-2	313	9-15-71	2	Nebraska	D3 '93	16/15
62	Siglar, Ricky	T	6-7	318	5-14-66	3	San Jose State	FA '93	14/14
79	Szott, David	G	6-4	290	12-12-67	5	Penn State	D7 '90	15/13
73	Valerio, Joe	G-C	6-5	293	2-11-69	4	Pennsylvania	D2 '91	13/0
72	Villa, Danny	G	6-5	300	9-21-64	8	Arizona State	FA '93	13/3
	Defensive linemen								
99	Casillas, Tony	DT	6-3	277	10-26-63	9	Oklahoma	FA '94	15/14
77	McDaniels, Pellom	DE	6-3	292	2-21-68	2	Oregon State	FA '93	10/0
92	Mickell, Darren	DT	6-4	268	8-3-70	3	Florida	D2 SUP '92	16/1
96	Newton, Tim	DT	6-0	275	3-23-63	9	Florida	FA '93	16/0
75	Phillips, Joe	DT	6-5	315	7-15-63	9	So. Methodist	FA '92	16/16
97	Saleaumua, Dan	DT	6-0	295	11-25-64	8	Arizona State	Plan B '89	16/16
90	Smith, Neil	DE	6-4	275	4-10-66	7	Nebraska	D1 '88	16/15
98	Waldrop, Rob	DT	6-1	276	12-1-71	R	Arizona	D5b '94	
	Linebackers								
50	Anderson, Erick	LB	6-1	241	10-7-68	3	Michigan	D7 '92	8/1
59	Fields, Jaime	LB	5-11	246	8-28-70	2	Washington	D4 '93	6/1
**	Rogers, Tracy	LB	6-2	241	8-13-67	5	Fresno State	FA '90	14/14
54	Simien, Tracy	LB	6-1	245	5-21-67	4	Texas Christian	FA '91	16/14
58	Thomas, Derrick	LB	6-3	247	1-1-67	6	Alabama	D1 '89	16/15
	Defensive backs								
**	Bayless, Martin	S	6-2	213	10-11-62	11	Bowling Green	Plan B '92	16/10
46	Burton, James	CB	5-9	181	4-22-71	R	Fresno State	D5a '94	
34	Carter, Dale	CB	6-1	188	11-28-69	3	Tennessee	D1 '92	15/11
24	Collins, Mark	CB	5-10	190	1-16-64	9	Cal-Fullerton	FA '94	16/16
42	Mincy, Charles	S	5-11	187	12-16-69	4	Washington	D5 '91	16/4
39	Pickens, Bruce	CB	5-10	190	5-9-68	4	Nebraska	FA '93	3/0
27	Taylor, Jay	CB	5-10	170	11-8-87	6	San Jose State	T-PHO '93	16/1
25	Terry, Doug	S	5-11	204	12-12-69	3	Kansas	FA '92	15/8
40	Walker, Bracey	S	5-11	197	10-28-70	R	North Carolina	D4 '94	
26	Watson, Tim	S	6-1	216	8-13-70	2	Howard	FA '93	5/0
41	Whitmore, David	S	6-0	232	7-6-67	5	Stephen F. Austin	T-SF '93	6/6
	Specialists								
9	Aguiar, Louie	P	6-1	214	6-30-66	4	Utah State	FA '91	16/0
2	Elliott, Lin	K	6-0	182	11-11-68	3	Texas Tech	FA '94	

Joe Montana   No. 19/QB

HT: 6-2   **WT:** 205
Born: 6-11-56, New Eagle, PA
High school: Ringgold (Monongahela, PA)
College: Notre Dame
Perhaps the finest QB in history, Montana has a career QB rating of 92.7 (the best of all time). He led the 49ers to 4 Super Bowl titles, and was named game MVP 3 times.

YEAR	TEAM		PASSING									RUSHING		
		G	ATT	CRL	CPL%	YDS	AVG	TDS	TD%	INT	INTX	RTG	ATT	YDS	AVG
1985	San Francisco	15	494	303	61.9	3653	7.4	27	5.5	13	2.6	91.3	42	153	3.5
1986	San Francisco	8	307	191	62.2	2296	7.3	8	2.6	9	2.9	80.7	17	38	2.2
1987	San Francisco	13	398	266	66.8	3054	7.7	31	7.8	13	3.3	102.1	35	141	4.0
1988	San Francisco	14	397	238	59.9	2981	7.5	18	4.5	10	2.5	87.9	38	132	3.5
1989	San Francisco	13	386	271	70.2	3521	9.1	26	6.7	8	2.1	112.4	49	227	4.6
1990	San Francisco	15	520	321	61.7	3944	7.6	26	5.0	16	3.1	89.0	40	162	4.1
1992	San Francisco	1	21	15	71.4	126	6.0	2	9.5	0	0.0	118.4	3	28	9.3
1993	Kansas City	11	298	181	60.7	2144	7.2	13	4.4	7	2.3	87.4	25	64	2.6
14 YR TOTALS		176	4698	3110	63.5	37258	7.6	257	5.2	130	2.7		439	1659	3.8
1993 RANK NFL QB			24	21	19	18	22	17	16	25	44		15	19	22	34
1994 PROJECTIONS		13	355	205	57.7	2590	7.2	11	3.0	10	2.7		25	-20	-0.8

Marcus Allen   No. 32/RB

HT: 6-2   **WT:** 210
Born: 3-26-60, San Diego, CA
High school: Lincoln (San Diego)
College: Southern California
Allen's 113 TDs are the most by any active AFC player and rank fifth all-time. He still holds the NCAA record for most 200-yard rushing games with 11.

YEAR	TEAM		RUSHING				RECEIVING				KICK RETURNS			
		G	ATT	YDS	AVG	TD	REC	YDS	AVG	TD	RET	YDS	AVG	TD
1986	LA Raiders	13	208	759	3.6	5	46	453	9.8	2	---	---	---	---
1987	LA Raiders	12	200	754	3.8	5	51	410	8.0	0	---	---	---	---
1988	LA Raiders	15	223	831	3.7	7	34	303	8.9	1	---	---	---	---
1989	LA Raiders	8	69	293	4.2	2	20	191	9.6	0	---	---	---	---
1990	LA Raiders	16	179	682	3.8	12	15	189	12.6	1	---	---	---	---
1991	LA Raiders	8	63	287	4.6	2	15	131	8.7	0	---	---	---	---
1992	LA Raiders	16	67	301	4.5	2	28	277	9.9	1	---	---	---	---
1993	Kansas City	16	206	764	3.7	12	34	238	7.0	3	---	---	---	---
12 YR TOTALS		160	2296	9309	4.1	91	480	4496	9.4	21	0	0	NA	0
1993 RANK NFL RB			15	15	71	1	26	33	77	2	65	65	65	
1994 PROJECTIONS		16	257	921	3.6	16	37	220	5.9	4	0	0	NA	0

Kimble Anders   No. 38/RB

Full name: Kimble Lynard Anders
HT. 5-11 **WT.** 221
Born: 9-10-66, Galveston, TX
High school: Ball (Galveston)
College: Houston

Anders had career highs in carries (75), yards gained (291), receptions (40), and receiving yards (326).

YEAR	TEAM	RUSHING					RECEIVING				KICK RETURNS			
		G	ATT	YDS	AVG	TD	REC	YDS	AVG	TD	RET	YDS	AVG	TD
1991	Kansas City	2	---	---	---	---	2	30	15.0	0	---	---	---	---
1992	Kansas City	11	1	1	1.0	0	5	65	13.0	0	1	20	20.0	0
1993	Kansas City	16	75	291	3.9	0	40	326	8.2	1	1	47	47.0	0
	3 YR TOTALS	29	76	292	3.8	0	47	421	9.0	1	2	67	33.5	0
1993	RANK NFL RB		52	52	61	89	16	19	46	13	51	41	1	
1994	PROJECTIONS	16	131	509	3.9	0	62	463	7.5	2	1	68	68.0	0

Willie Davis   No. 84/WR

Full name: Willie Clark Davis
HT: 6-0   **WT:** 181
Born: 10-10-67, Little Rock, AR
High school: Altheimer (AR)
College: Central Arkansas

1993 was Davis' best season, as he led Kansas City with 52 catches for 909 yards. He was Montana's favorite TD target in '93.

YEAR	TEAM	RECEIVING					RUSHING				PUNT RETURN			
		G	REC	YDS	AVG	TD	ATT	YDS	AVG	TD	RET	YDS	AVG	TD
1991	Kansas City	1	---	---	---	---	---	---	---	---	---	---	---	---
1992	Kansas City	16	36	756	21.0	3	1	-11	-11.0	0	---	---	---	---
1993	Kansas City	16	52	909	17.5	7	---	---	---	---	---	---	---	---
	3 YR TOTALS	33	88	1665	18.9	10	1	0.1	-11.0	0	0	0	NA	0
1993	RANK NFL WR		32	16	16	7	42	42	42		30	30	29	
1994	PROJECTIONS	16	73	1213	16.6	11	0	6	NA	0	0	0	NA	0

J.J Birden   No. 88/WR

Full name: LaJourdain J. Birden
HT: 5-10 **WT:** 170
Born: 6-16-65, Portland, OR
High school: Lakeridge (Lake Oswego, OR)
College: Oregon
Birden posted career highs in receptions (51) and yards (721) in '93. He led the team in receiving yards in '92 with 644.

YEAR	TEAM	G	RECEIVING REC	YDS	AVG	TD	RUSHING ATT	YDS	AVG	TD	PUNT RETURN RET	YDS	AVG	TD
1990	Kansas City	11	15	352	23.5	3	---	---	---	---	10	72	7.2	0
1991	Kansas City	15	27	465	17.2	2	---	---	---	---	---	---	---	---
1992	Kansas City	16	42	644	15.3	3	---	---	---	---	0	0		0
1993	Kansas City	16	51	721	14.1	2	---	---	---	---	5	43	8.6	0
	4 YR TOTALS	58	135	2182	16.2	10	0	0.0	0.0	0	15	115	7.7	0
1993	RANK NFL WR		34	34	58	55	42	42	42		20	18	12	
1994	PROJECTIONS	16	61	807	13.2	1	0	0	NA	0	6	58	9.7	0

Keith Cash   No. 89/TE

Full name: Keith Lovell Cash
HT: 6-4 **WT:** 248
Born: 8-7-69, San Antonio, TX
High school: Holmes (San Antonio)
College: Texas
A backup for most of '93, Cash emerged as a key player late in the season. His brother Kerry is a TE with Indianapolis.

YEAR	TEAM	G	RECEIVING REC	YDS	AVG	TD
1991	Pittsburgh	5	7	90	12.9	1
1992	Kansas City	15	12	113	9.4	2
1993	Kansas City	15	24	242	10.1	4
	3 YR TOTALS	35	43	445	10.3	7
1993	RANK NFL TE		20	24	36	8
1994	PROJECTIONS	16	33	319	9.7	6

Neil Smith   No. 90/DE

HT: 6-4   **WT:** 275
Born: 4-10-66, New Orleans, LA
High school: McDonogh 35 (New Orleans)
College: Nebraska
Smith followed '92's 14.5 sacks with a league-high 15.0 in '93. He's been a starter in the Pro Bowl for 3 straight years. His "wing span" is 7 feet, 1½ inches.

YEAR	TEAM	G	INT	YDS	AVG	TD	SACKS	FUM REC	TD
1988	Kansas City	13	---	---	---	---	2.5	---	---
1989	Kansas City	15	---	---	---	---	6.5	2	1
1990	Kansas City	16	---	---	---	---	9.5	1	0
1991	Kansas City	16	---	---	---	---	8.0	2	0
1992	Kansas City	16	1	22	22.0	1	14.5	2	---
1993	Kansas City	16	---	---	---	---	15.0	3	0
6 YR TOTALS		92	1	22	22.0	1	56.0	10	1
1993	RANK NFL DL		16	NA	NA	NA	1	2	5
1994	PROJECTIONS	16	0	0	0	0	17	4	0

Derrick Thomas   No. 58/OLB

Full name: Derrick Vincent Thomas
HT: 6-3   **WT:** 236
Born: 1-1-67, Miami, FL
High school: South (Miami)
College: Alabama
Thomas has had 22.5 sacks over the past 2 seasons. His 7 sacks in 1 game vs. Seattle on November 11, 1990 is an NFL record.

YEAR	TEAM	G	INT	YDS	AVG	TD	SACKS	FUM REC	TD
1989	Kansas City	16	---	---	---	---	10.0	1	0
1990	Kansas City	15	---	---	---	---	20.0	2	0
1991	Kansas City	16	---	---	---	---	13.5	4	1
1992	Kansas City	16	---	---	---	---	14.5	3	0
1993	Kansas City	16	---	---	---	---	8.0	1	1
5 YR TOTALS		79	0	0	NA	0	66.0	11	2
1993	RANK NFL DL		16	NA	NA	NA	25	25	1
1994	PROJECTIONS	16	0	0	0	0	4	0	1

Mark Collins　No. 24/CB

HT: 5-10 **WT:** 190
Born: 1-16-64, San Bernadino, CA
High school: Pacific (San Bernadino, CA)
College: Cal-Fullerton
Collins played with the Giants in '93. He scored his first career TD on a 50 yard interception vs. the Rams last year.

YEAR	TEAM	G	INT	YDS	AVG	TD	SACKS	FUM REC	TD
1986	NY Giants	15	1	0	0.0	0	---	---	---
1987	NY Giants	11	2	28	14.0	0	1.5	---	---
1988	NY Giants	11	1	13	13.0	0	---	---	---
1989	NY Giants	16	2	12	6.0	0	1.0	2	0
1990	NY Giants	13	2	0	0.0	0	---	---	---
1991	NY Giants	16	4	77	19.3	0	---	1	0
1992	NY Giants	14	1	0	0.0	0	---	---	---
1993	NY Giants	16	4	77	19.3	1	1.0	---	---
	8 YR TOTALS	112	17	207	12.2	1	3.5	3	0
1993	RANK NFL DB		21	21	34	2	13	94	NA
1994	PROJECTIONS	16	5	107	21.4	2	1	0	0

Lin Elliott　No. 2/K

Full name: Lindley Franklin Elliott
HT: 6-0 **WT:** 182
Born: 11-11-68, Euless, TX
High school: Waco (TX)
College: Texas Tech
Elliott started '93 with Dallas, but was replaced by Eddie Murray and sat out the rest of the season.

YEAR	TEAM	G	XP	XPA	XP Pct.	FG	FGA	FG Pct.	PTS
1992	Dallas	16	47	48	97.9	24	35	68.6	119
1993	Atlanta	1	2	3	66.7	2	4	50.0	8
	2 YR TOTALS	17	49	51	96.1	26	39	66.7	127
1993	RANK NFL		30	30	30	30	30	30	30
1994	PROJECTIONS	0	0	0	NA	0	0	NA	0

Steve Bono   No. 13/QB

Full name: Steven Christopher Bono
HT: 6-4 **WT:** 215
Born: 5-11-62, Norristown, PA
High school: Norristown (PA)
College: UCLA

Bono was Joe Montana's longtime backup at San Francisco. He's in line to become the Chiefs' starter after Montana retires.

		PASSING									RUSHING		
YEAR	TEAM	G	ATT	CPL	CPL%	YDS	AVG	TDS	TD%	INT	INT%	RTG	ATT	YDS	AVG
1985	Minnesota	1	10	1	10.0	5	0.5	0	0.0	0	0.0	39.6	---	---	N/A
1986	Minnesota	1	1	1	100.0	3	3.0	0	0.0	0	0.0	79.3	---	---	N/A
1987	Pittsburgh	3	74	34	45.9	438	5.9	5	6.8	2	2.7	76.3	8	27	3.4
1988	Pittsburgh	2	35	10	28.6	110	3.1	1	2.9	2	5.7	25.9	---	---	N/A
1989	San Francisco	1	5	4	80.0	62	12.4	1	20.0	0	0.0	157.9	---	---	N/A
1991	San Francisco	9	237	141	59.5	1617	6.8	11	4.6	4	1.7	88.5	17	46	2.7
1992	San Francisco	16	56	36	64.3	463	8.3	2	3.6	2	3.6	87.1	15	23	1.5
1993	San Francisco	8	61	39	63.9	416	6.8	0	0.0	1	1.6	78.9	12	14	1.2
	8 YR TOTALS	41	479	266	55.5	3114	6.5	20	4.2	11	2.3		52	110	2.1
1993	RANK NFL QB		51	48	7	50	27	59	59	58	54	31	33	39	42
1994	PROJECTIONS	7	41	30	73.2	296	7.0	0	0.0	0	0.0		13	12	0.9

M. Schottenheimer   Coach

Full name: Martin Edward Schottenheimer
Born: 9-23-43, Canonsburg, PA
High school: McDonald (PA)
College: Pittsburgh

With a 50-29-1 regular-season record, Schottenheimer's .632 winning percentage is the best in Kansas City Chiefs history. Hank Stram was 124-76-10 for a .614 percentage.

		REGULAR SEASON					POSTSEASON		
YEAR	TEAM	W	L	T	PCT	FINISH	W	L	FINISH
1984	Cleveland	4	4	0	.500	3rd/AFC Central			
1985	Cleveland	8	8	0	.500	1st/AFC Central	0	1	lost 1st Rnd. game to Miami, 24-21
1986	Cleveland	12	4	0	.750	1st/AFC Central	1	1	lost AFC Title game to Denver, 23-20 (OT)
1987	Cleveland	10	5	0	.667	1st/AFC Central	1	1	lost AFC Title game to Denver, 38-33
1988	Cleveland	10	6	0	.625	T2nd/AFC Central	0	1	lost wild card game to Houston 24-23
1989	Kansas City	8	7	1	.531	2nd/AFC West			
1990	Kansas City	11	5	0	.688	2nd/AFC West	0	1	lost 1st Rnd. game to Miami, 17-16
1991	Kansas City	10	6	0	.625	2nd/AFC West	1	1	lost 2nd Rnd. game to Buffalo, 37-14
1992	Kansas City	10	6	0	.625	2nd/AFC West	0	1	lost 1st Rnd. game to San Diego, 17-0
1993	Kansas City	11	5	0	.688	1st/AFC West	2	1	lost AFC Title game to Buffalo, 30-13
	10 YR TOTALS	94	56	1	.626		5	8	

John Alt   No. 76/T

Full name: John Michael Alt
HT: 6-8   **WT:** 307
Born: 5-30-62, Stuttgart, Germany
High school: Columbia Heights (MN)
College: Iowa
Alt's been a Pro Bowl pick for the last 2 years.

YEAR	TEAM	G	RUSHING ATT	YDS	AVG	RANK AV RUSH	PASS YDS	RANK PASS YDS	SACKS	YDS. LOST
1991	Kansas City	16	521	2217	4.3	4	3281	18	21	177
1992	Kansas City	16	446	1532	3.4	27	3115	19	48	323
1993	Kansas City	16	445	1655	3.7	16	3384	15	35	204
	4 YR TOTALS	58								

Tim Barnett   No. 82/WR

Full name: Tim Andre Barnett
HT: 6-1   **WT:** 199
Born: 4-19-68, Gunnison, MS
High school: Rosedale (MS)
College: Jackson State
Barnett had 41 catches his rookie year.

YEAR	TEAM	G	RECEIVING REC	YDS	AVG	TD	RUSHING ATT	YDS	AVG	TD	PUNT RETURN RET	YDS	AVG
1991	Kansas City	16	41	564	13.8	5	---	---	---	---	---	---	---
1992	Kansas City	12	24	442	18.4	4	---	---	---	---	---	---	---
1993	Kansas City	16	17	182	10.7	1	---	---	---	---	---	---	---
	3 YR TOTALS	44	82	1188	14.5	10	0	0	NA	0	0	0	NA
1993	RANK NFL WR		83	89	121	72	42	42	42		30	30	29
1994	PROJECTIONS	16	4	0	0.0	0	0	0	NA	0	0	0	NA

Tim Grunhard   No. 61/C

Full name: Timothy Gerard Grunhard
HT: 6-2   **WT:** 299
Born: 5-17-68, Chicago, IL
High school: St. Laurence (Burbank, IL)
College: Notre Dame
Grunhard started all 16 games for Kansas City.

YEAR	TEAM	G	RUSHING ATT	YDS	AVG	RANK AV RUSH	PASS YDS	RANK PASS YDS	SACKS	YDS. LOST
1991	Kansas City	16	521	2217	4.3	4	3281	18	21	177
1992	Kansas City	12	446	1532	3.4	27	3115	19	48	323
1993	Kansas City	16	445	1655	3.7	16	3384	15	35	204
	4 YR TOTALS	58								

Dan Saleaumua   No. 97/NT

Full name: Raymond Daniel Saleaumua
HT: 6-0   **WT:** 295
Born: 11-25-64, San Diego, CA
High school: Sweetwater (National City, CA)
College: Arizona State
Saleaumua hasn't missed a start since 1990.

YEAR	TEAM	G	INT	YDS	AVG	TD	SACKS	FUM REC	TD
1991	Kansas City	16	---	---	---	---	1.5	2	0
1992	Kansas City	16	---	---	---	---	6.0	---	---
1993	Kansas City	16	1	13	13.0	0	3.5	---	---
7 YR TOTALS		105	2	34	17.0	0	24.0	13	1
1993 RANK NFL DL			2	4	4	3	66	71	NA
1994 PROJECTIONS		16	1	18	18.0	0	3	0	0

Tony Casillas   No. 75/DT

Full name: Tony Steven Casillas
HT: 6-3   **WT:** 277
Born: 10-26-63, Tulsa, OK
High school: East Central (Tulsa, OK)
College: Oklahoma
Casillas had 3 sacks in the '92 NFC title game.

YEAR	TEAM	G	INT	YDS	AVG	TD	SACKS	FUM REC	TD
1986	Atlanta	16	---	---	---	---	1.0	1	0
1987	Atlanta	9	---	---	---	---	2.0	1	0
1988	Atlanta	16	---	---	---	---	2.0	1	0
1989	Atlanta	16	---	---	---	---	2.0	3	0
1990	Atlanta	9	---	---	---	---	1.0	---	---
1991	Dallas	16	---	---	---	---	2.5	1	0
1992	Dallas	15	---	---	---	---	3.0	1	0
1993	Dallas	15	---	---	---	---	2.0	1	0
8 YR TOTALS		112	---	0	NA	0	15.5	9	0
1993 RANK NFL DL			16	NA	NA	NA	99	25	5
1994 PROJECTIONS		15	0	0	0	0	2	1	0

Tracy Simien   No. 54/LB

Full name: Tracy Anthony Simien
HT: 6-1   **WT:** 250
Born: 5-21-67, Bay City, TX
High school: Sweeny (TX)
College: Texas Christian
Simien led the Chiefs with 105 tackles.

YEAR	TEAM	G	INT	YDS	AVG	TD	SACKS	FUM REC	TD
1991	Kansas City	15	---	---	---	---	2.0	1	0
1992	Kansas City	15	3	18	6.0	0	1.0	---	---
1993	Kansas City	16	---	---	---	---	---	---	---
3 YR TOTALS		46	3	18	6	0	3.0	1	0
1993 RANK NFL LB			47	NA	NA	NA	91	81	
1994 PROJECTIONS		16	0	0	0	0	0	0	0

Dale Carter   No. 34/CB

Full name: Dale LaVelle Carter
HT: 6-1   **WT:** 188
Born: 11-28-69, Covington, GA
High school: Newton County (Covington, GA)
College: Tennessee
Carter is Kansas City's primary punt returner.

YEAR	TEAM	G	INT	YDS	AVG	TD	SACKS	FUM REC	TD
1992	Kansas City	16	7	65	9.3	1	---	---	---
1993	Kansas City	15	1	0	0.0	0	---	---	---
	2 YR TOTALS	31	8	65	8.13	1	0.0	0	0
1993	RANK NFL DB		95	124	122	27	49	94	NA
1994	PROJECTIONS	14	0	0	0	0	0	0	0

Charles Mincy   No. 42/S

Full name: Charles Anthony Mincy
HT: 5-11   **WT:** 187
Born: 12-16-69, Los Angeles, CA
High school: Dorsey (Los Angeles)
College: Washington
Mincy became a backup in '93, yet had 5 INTs.

YEAR	TEAM	G	INT	YDS	AVG	TD	SACKS	FUM REC	TD
1992	Kansas City	16	4	128	32.0	2	---	1	---
1993	Kansas City	16	5	44	8.8	0	---	2	0
	2 YR TOTALS	32	9	172	19.1	2	0.0	3	0
1993	RANK NFL DB		14	47	88	27	49	10	14
1994	PROJECTIONS	16	6	0	0.0	0	0	3	0

Louie Aguiar   No. 4/P

HT: 6-2   **WT:** 234
Born: 6-30-66, Livermore, CA
High school: Granada (Livermore, CA)
College: Utah State
Aguiar's 21 punts inside the 20 tied for fourth in the AFC. But his inconsistency drove Jet fans crazy.

YEAR	TEAM	G	NO	YARDS	LONG	AVG	BLK	IN20
1991	NY Jets	16	64	2521	61	39.4	0	14
1992	NY Jets	16	73	2993	65	41	0	22
1993	NY Jets	16	73	2806	71	38.4	0	21
	3 YR TOTALS	48	210	8320	71	39.6	0	57
1993	RANK NFL		16	21	4	10	23	13
1994	PROJECTIONS	16	75	2784	77	37.1	0	22

Los Angeles
RAIDERS

1994 Scouting Report

Offense

Under QB Jeff Hostetler, the Raiders were fifth in the NFL in passing offense with 3,589 yards. Hostetler helped WRs Tim Brown (the AFC leader in reception yardage) and James Jett realize their potential. But the Raiders really missed having a back who could move the ball on the ground; they were twenty-sixth in the NFL in rushing with just 1,425 yards gained. Coach Art Shell hopes ex-Chief Harvey Williams will contribute in '94. Losing TE Ethan Horton and FB Steve Smith, both valuable blockers, will hurt, but new addition G Kevin Gogan will solidify an OL that allowed 50 sacks last year, and ex-49er Jamie Williams could have a big year at TE.

Defense

Although the pass defense unit, led by CB Terry McDaniel, was fifth in the NFL, holding opponents to just 2,858 passing yards, the Raiders ranked just twentieth in run defense, allowing 1,865 yards on the ground. The team's poor showing against the run is a sign of weakness up front on defense, although DEs Anthony Smith and Greg Townsend combined for 20 sacks last year. Now that Howie Long has retired, they could have even more trouble. L.A. remains very thin at LB, but top picks Rob Fredrickson and James Folston should contribute quickly. They have strengthened the secondary, adding Kevin Ross, a top CB from Kansas City.

Special Teams

K Jeff Jaeger led the league with a team-record 132 points scored last year, after totaling just 73 points the year before. P Jeff Gossett averaged a mediocre 41.8 yards/punt. Raghib Ismail led the league with a 24.2 yard kick return average, while Tim Brown is one of the best punt returners in the game.

1994 Prospects

1994 looks to be the Silver-and-Black's year. Hostetler gives them the QB they've needed since Jim Plunkett retired, and he's got the AFC's fastest corps of wideouts. If the defense improves in 1994 (and it should), the Raiders will be able to overcome tough challenges from Kansas City and Denver to take their first division crown since 1990.

Team Directory

President of the General Partner: Al Davis

Executive assistant: Al LoCasale

1993 Review

Sep. 5	MINNESOTA	W 24-7
Sep. 12	at Seattle	W 17-13
Sep. 19	CLEVELAND	L 19-16
Sep. 26	OPEN DATE	
Oct. 3	at Kansas City	L 24-9
Oct. 10	N.Y. JETS	W 24-20
Oct. 18	at Denver	W 23-20
Oct. 24	OPEN DATE	
Oct. 31	SAN DIEGO	L 30-23
Nov. 7	at Chicago	W 16-14
Nov. 14	KANSAS CITY	L 31-20
Nov. 21	at San Diego	W 12-7
Nov. 28	at Cincinnati	L 16-10
Dec. 5	at Buffalo	W 25-24
Dec. 12	SEATTLE	W 27-23
Dec. 19	TAMPA BAY	W 27-20
Dec. 26	at Green Bay	L 28-0
Jan. 2	DENVER	W 33-30 (OT)

1994 Schedule

Sep. 5	at San Francisco (Mon.)	9:00
Sep. 11	SEATTLE	4:00
Sep. 18	at Denver	4:00
Sep. 25	SAN DIEGO	4:00
Oct. 2	OPEN DATE	
Oct. 9	at New England	4:00
Oct. 16	at Miami	1:00
Oct. 23	ATLANTA	4:00
Oct. 30	HOUSTON	4:00
Nov. 6	at Kansas City	8:00
Nov. 13	at L.A. Rams	4:00
Nov. 20	NEW ORLEANS	4:00
Nov. 27	PITTSBURGH	4:00
Dec. 5	at San Diego (Mon.)	9:00
Dec. 11	DENVER	4:00
Dec. 18	at Seattle	8:00
Dec. 24	KANSAS CITY	4:00

1993 finish: 10-6 (5-3 home, 5-3 away), second in AFC West

Team Leaders

PASSING	ATT	COM	COM%	YDS	YPA	TD	TD%	INT	INT%	RTG
Hostetler	419	236	56.3	3242	7.74	14	3.3	10	2.4	82.5
Evans	76	45	59.2	640	8.42	3	3.9	4	5.3	77.7
TEAM	495	281	56.8	3882	7.84	17	3.4	14	2.8	81.7
OPPONENTS	457	258	56.5	3141	6.87	17	3.7	14	3.1	77.4

RECEIVING	REC	YDS	AVG	TD	RUSHING	ATT	YDS	AVG	TD
Brown	80	1180	14.8	7	Robinson	156	591	3.8	1
Horton	43	467	10.9	1	Hostetler	55	202	3.7	5
Jett	33	771	23.4	3	Bell	67	180	2.7	1
Wright	27	462	17.1	4	Smith	47	156	3.3	0
Ismail	26	353	13.6	1	McCallum	37	114	3.1	3
TEAM	281	3882	13.8	17	TEAM	433	1425	3.3	10
OPPONENTS	258	3141	12.2	17	OPPONENTS	494	1865	3.8	17

INTERCEPTIONS	INT	YDS	AVG	LG	TD	SACKS	NO
McDaniel	5	87	17.4	36t	1	Smith	12.5
Anderson	2	52	26.0	27	0	Townsend	7.5
Hoskins	2	34	17.0	20	0	McGlockton	7.0
TEAM	14	199	14.2	36t	1	TEAM	45.0
OPPONENTS	14	289	20.6	102t	2	OPPONENTS	50.0

KICK RETURNS	NO	YDS	AV	LG	TD	PUNT RETURNS	NO	FC	YDS	AV	LG	TD
Ismail	25	605	24.2	66	0	Brown	40	20	465	11.6	74t	1
Wright	10	167	16.7	28	0							
Gault	7	187	26.7	60	0							
TEAM	52	1061	20.4	66	0	TEAM	40	20	465	11.6	74t	1
OPPONENTS	45	783	17.4	49	0	OPPONENTS	35	7	301	8.6	28	0

KICKING	XPM	XPA	FGM	FGA	LG	PTS
Jaeger	27	29	35	44	53	132
TEAM	27	29	35	44	53	132
OPPONENTS	37	37	21	33	57	100

PUNTING	NO	YDS	LG	AVG	TB	BLK	RET	RYD	IN20	NAV
Gossett	71	2971	61	41.8	9	0	35	301	19	35.1
TEAM	71	2971	61	41.8	9	0	35	301	19	35.1
OPPONENTS	80	3369	56	42.1	8	1	40	465	13	34.3

FUMBLES	FUM	OFF.FUM.REC.		REC	TD	DEF.FUM.REC.	REC	TD
Hostetler	6	Smith		3	0	Wallace	2	0
Evans	4	Hostetler		2	0			
Robinson	3							
TEAM	23	TEAM		11	0	TEAM	9	0
OPPONENTS	23	OPPONENTS		13	0	OPPONENTS	11	1

1994 Draft Choices

ROUND	NAME	POS	SCHOOL	OVERALL SELECTION
1	Rob Fredrickson	LB	Michigan State	22
2	James Folston	LB	Northeast Louisiana	52
3	Calvin Jones	RB	Nebraska	80
4	Austin Robbins	DT	North Carolina	120
5	Roosevelt Patterson	T	Alabama	159
7	Rob Holmberg	LB	Penn State	217

HISTORY

TITLES

1967	AFL Championship	1975	AFC West Championship
1968	AFL West Championship	1976	Super Bowl Winner
1969	AFC West Championship	1980	Super Bowl Winner
1970	AFC West Championship	1982	AFC Championship (reg. seas.)
1972	AFC West Championship	1983	Super Bowl Winner
1973	AFC West Championship	1985	AFC West Championship
1974	AFC West Championship	1990	AFC West Championship

ALL-TIME TEAM RECORDS

Rushing

Most yards, game:	221	Bo Jackson	11/30/87
Most yards, season:	1,759	Marcus Allen	1985
Most yards, career:	8,545	Marcus Allen	1982-1992

Passing

Most yards, game:	427	Cotton Davison	10/25/64
Most yards, season:	3,615	Ken Stabler	1979
Most yards, career:	19,078	Ken Stabler	1970-1979

Receiving

Most catches, game:	12	Dave Casper	10/3/76
Most catches, season:	96	Todd Christiansen	1986
Most catches, career:	589	Fed Biletnikoff	1965-1978

Scoring

Most points, game:	24	Art Powell	12/22/63
		Marcus Allen	9/24/84
Most points, season:	132	Jeff Jaeger	1993
Most points, career:	863	George Blanda	1967-1975

COACHES

NAME	RECORD	YEARS	NAME	RECORD	YEARS
Eddie Erdelatz	6-10-0	1960-61	John Madden	112-39-7	1969-78
Marty Feldman	2-15-0	1961-62	Tom Flores	91-56-0	1979-87
Red Cartwright	1-8-0	1962	Mike Shanahan	8-12-0	1988-89
Al Davis	23-16-3	1963-65	Art Shell	46-33-0	1989-92
John Rauch	35-10-1	1966-68			

LOS ANGELES RAIDERS
1994 TRAINING CAMP ROSTER

No.	Quarterbacks		Ht.	Wt.	Born	NFL Exp.	College	How acq.	93 GP/GS
11	Evans, Vince	QB	6-2	210	6-14-55	15	Southern California	FA '92	8/0
12	Hobert, Billy Joe	QB	6-3	225	1-8-71	1	Washington	D3 '93	0/0
15	Hostetler, Jeff	QB	6-3	215	4-22-61	10	West Virginia	FA '93	15/15

Running backs

No.	Name	Pos	Ht	Wt	Birthdate	Exp	College	Draft	G/S
38	Bell, Nick	RB	6-2	250	8-19-68	4	Iowa	D2 '91	10/3
	Jones, Calvin	RB				R	Nebraska	D3 '94	0/0
23	Jordan, Randy	RB	5-10	205	6-6-70	1	North Carolina	FA '93	10/2
41	McCallum, Napoleon	RB	6-2	225	10-6-63	6	Navy	FA '92	13/1
21	Montgomery, Tyrone	RB	6-0	190	8-3-70	2	Mississippi	FA '93	13/0
28	Robinson, Greg	RB	5-10	205	8-7-69	1	NE Louisiana	D8 '93	13/12
39	Smith, Kevin	RB	6-4	255	7-25-69	2	UCLA	D7 '92	10/1
	Williams, Harvey	RB	6-2	222	4-22-67	4	Louisiana State	FA '94	7/16

Wide receivers

No.	Name	Pos	Ht	Wt	Birthdate	Exp	College	Draft	G/S
81	Brown, Tim	WR	6-0	195	7-22-66	6	Notre Dame	D1 '88	16/16
83	Gault, Willie	WR	6-1	175	9-5-60	12	Tennessee	T-CHI '88	15/0
80	Hobbs, Daryl	WR	6-2	180	5-23-68	2	Pacific	FA '93	3/0
86	Ismail, Raghib	WR	5-10	180	11-18-69	1	Notre Dame	FA '93	13/0
82	Jett, James	WR	5-10	165	12-28-70	1	West Virginia	FA '93	16/1
13	Jordan, Charles	WR	5-10	175	10-9-69	1	Long Beach C. C.	FA '93	0/0
89	Wright, Alexander	WR	6-0	190	7-19-67	5	Auburn	T-DAL '92	15/15

Tight ends

No.	Name	Pos	Ht	Wt	Birthdate	Exp	College	Draft	G/S
84	Duff, John	TE	6-7	250	7-31-67	2	New Mexico	FA '93	1/0
87	Glover, Andrew	TE	6-6	245	8-12-67	4	Grambling	D10 '91	15/0
81	Williams, Jamie	TE	6-4	245	2-25-60	11	Nebraska	FA '94	16/0

Offensive linemen

No.	Name	Pos	Ht	Wt	Birthdate	Exp	College	Draft	G/S
66	Gogan, Kevin	G	6-7	317	11-2-64	8	Wisconsin	FA '94	16/16
79	Lanier, Ken	T	6-3	290	7-8-59	14	Florida State	FA '93	2/2
65	Montoya, Max	G	6-5	295	5-12-56	16	UCLA	Plan B '90	16/16
72	Mosebar, Don	C	6-6	305	9-11-65	12	Southern California	D1 '83	16/16
	Patterson, Roosevelt	T	6-3	313		R	Alabama	D5 '94	0/0
64	Peat, Todd	G	6-2	305	5-20-64	6	Northern Illinois	FA '90	16/0
71	Perry, Gerald	T	6-6	300	11-12-64	7	Southern	FA '93	15/15
78	Skrepenak, Greg	T	6-6	310	1-31-70	3	Michigan	D2 '92	0/0
77	Stephens, Rich	G	6-7	310	1-1-65	3	Tulsa	FA '92	16/1
67	Turk, Dan	C	6-4	310	8-25-62	9	Wisconsin	FA '89	16/0
68	Wilkerson, Bruce	T	6-5	305	7-28-64	8	Tennessee	D2 '87	15/15
76	Wisniewski, Steve	G	6-4	295	4-7-67	6	Penn State	D2 '89	14/14

Defensive linemen

No.	Name	Pos	Ht	Wt	Birthdate	Exp	College	Draft	G/S
97	Broughton, Willie	DT	6-5	275	9-9-64	7	Miami (FL)	FA '92	15/0
92	Collons, Ferric	DT	6-6	290	12-4-69	2	California	FA '92	0/0
74	Harrison, Nolan	DT	6-5	290	1-25-69	4	Indiana	D6 '91	16/14
91	McGlockton, Chester	DT	6-4	320	9-16-69	3	Clemson	D1 '92	16/16
	Robbins, Austin	DT	6-6	292		R	North Carolina	D4 '94	0/0
94	Smith, Anthony	DE	6-3	265	6-28-67	4	Arizona	FA '92	16/2
93	Townsend, Greg	DE	6-3	270	11-3-61	12	Texas Christian	D4 '83	16/16

Linebackers

No.	Name	Pos	Ht	Wt	Birthdate	Exp	College	Draft	G/S
54	Biekert, Greg	LB	6-2	235	3-14-69	1	Colorado	D7 '93	16/0
56	Bruce, Aundray	LB	6-5	255	4-30-66	7	Auburn	Plan B '92	16/0
	Folston, James	LB	6-2	235		R	Northeast Louisiana	D2 '94	0/0
	Fredrickson, Rob	LB	6-3	242		R	Michigan State	D1 '94	0/0
	Holmberg, Rob	LB	6-3	214		R	Penn State	D7 '94	0/0
52	Jones, Mike	LB	6-1	235	4-15-69	4	Missouri	FA '91	16/2
99	Moss, Winston	LB	6-3	240	12-24-65	8	Miami (FL)	T-TB '91	16/16
51	Wallace, Aaron	LB	6-3	240	4-17-67	5	Texas A&M	D2 '90	16/14

Defensive backs

No.	Name	Pos	Ht	Wt	Birthdate	Exp	College	Draft	G/S
33	Anderson, Eddie	S	6-1	210	7-22-63	9	Fort Valley State	FA '87	16/16
29	Bates, Patrick	S	6-3	220	11-27-70	1	Texas A&M	D1 '93	13/0
31	Dixon, Rickey	S	5-11	185	12-26-66	7	Oklahoma	T-CIN '93	9/0
46	Dorn, Torin	CB	6-0	190	2-28-68	5	North Carolina	D4 '90	15/0
20	Hoskins, Derrick	S	6-2	200	11-14-70	3	So. Mississippi	D5 '92	16/16
25	Land, Dan	S	6-0	195	7-3-65	6	Albany State	FA '89	15/0
29	Lewis, Albert	CB	6-2	195	10-6-60	12	Grambling	FA '94	14/13
36	McDaniel, Terry	CB	5-10	180	2-8-65	6	Tennessee	D1 '88	16/16
37	Trapp, James	CB	6-0	180	12-28-69	1	Clemson	D3a '93	14/2
48	Washington, Lionel	CB	6-0	185	10-21-60	12	Tulane	T-STL '87	16/16

Specialists

No.	Name	Pos	Ht	Wt	Birthdate	Exp	College	Draft	G/S
7	Gossett, Jeff	P	6-2	195	1-25-57	13	Eastern Illinois	T-HOU '88	16/0
18	Jaeger, Jeff	K	5-11	195	11-26-64	7	Washington	Plan B '89	16/0

Jeff Hostetler   No. 15/QB

Full name: Jeff Hostetler
HT: 6-3   **WT:** 215
Born: 4-22-61, Hollsopple, PA
High school: Conemaugh Valley (Jamestown, PA)
College: West Virginia

In his first year as a Raider, Hostetler threw for a career-best 3,242 yards. He also had a team-high 5 rushing TDs.

YEAR	TEAM	G	ATT	CPL	CPL%	YDS	AVG	TDS	TD%	INT	INT%	RTG	ATT	YDS	AVG
				PASSING										RUSHING	
1985	NY Giants	5	0	0	NA	0	NA	0	NA	0	NA		---	---	NA
1986	NY Giants	13	0	0	NA	0	NA	0	NA	0	NA		1	1	NA
1988	NY Giants	16	29	16	55.2	244	8.4	1	3.4	2	6.9	65.9	5	-3	-0.6
1989	NY Giants	16	39	20	51.3	294	7.5	3	7.7	2	5.1	80.5	11	71	6.5
1990	NY Giants	16	87	47	54.0	614	7.1	3	3.4	1	1.1	83.2	39	190	4.9
1991	NY Giants	16	285	179	62.8	2032	7.1	5	1.8	4	1.4	84.1	42	273	6.5
1992	NY Giants	12	192	103	53.6	1225	6.4	8	4.2	3	1.6	80.8	35	172	4.9
1993	LA Raiders	15	419	236	56.3	3242	7.7	14	3.3	10	2.4	82.5	55	202	3.7
	8 YR TOTALS	109	1051	601	57.2	7651	7.3	34	3.2	22	2.1		188	906	4.8
1993	RANK NFL QB		12	13	42	7	11	13	36	15	43	22	4	6	20
1994	PROJECTIONS	16	570	321	56.3	4527	7.9	19	3.3	15	2.5		68	216	3.2

Vince Evans   No. 11/QB

Full name: Vincent Tobias Evans
HT: 6-2   **WT:** 210
Born: 6-14-55, Greensboro, NC
High school: Benjamin L. Smith (Greensboro, NC)
College: Southern California

Veteran back-up Evans hasn't been a full-time NFL starter since 1981 with Chicago.

YEAR	TEAM	G	ATT	CPL	CPL%	YDS	AVG	TDS	TD%	INT	INT%	RTG	ATT	YDS	AVG
				PASSING										RUSHING	
1982	Chicago	4	28	12	42.9	125	4.5	0	0.0	4	^^^^^^	16.8	2	0	0.0
1983	Chicago	9	145	76	52.4	1108	7.6	5	3.4	7	4.8	69.0	22	142	6.5
1987	LA Raiders	3	83	39	47.0	630	7.6	5	6.0	4	4.8	72.9	11	144	^^^^^^
1989	LA Raiders	1	2	2	100.0	50	25.0	0	0.0	0	0.0	118.8	1	16	^^^^^^
1990	LA Raiders	5	1	1	100.0	38	38.0	0	0.0	0	0.0	118.8	1	-2	-2.0
1991	LA Raiders	4	14	6	42.9	127	9.1	1	7.1	2	^^^^^^	59.8	8	20	2.5
1992	LA Raiders	5	53	29	54.7	372	7.0	4	7.5	3	5.7	78.5	11	79	7.2
1993	LA Raiders	8	76	45	59.2	640	8.4	3	3.9	4	5.3	77.7	14	51	3.6
	13 YR TOTALS	88	1182	586	49.6	8027	6.8	44	3.7	66	5.6		192	1089	5.6
1993	RANK NFL QB		47	47	27	44	4	43	22	40	14	29	29	23	22
1994	PROJECTIONS	10	112	68	60.4	954	8.5	3	3.0	5	4.9		18	42	2.3

Greg Robinson No. 28/RB

HT: 5-10 **WT:** 205
Born: 8-7-69, Grenada, MS
High school: Grenada (MS)
College: Northeast Louisiana
Rookie Robinson was a pleasant surprise for the Raiders. Taken in the eighth round of the '93 draft, he led the team in rushing.

YEAR	TEAM	G	RUSHING ATT	YDS	AVG	TD	RECEIVING REC	YDS	AVG	TD	KICK RETURNS RET	YDS	AVG	TD
1993	LA Raiders	12	155	591	3.8	1	15	142	9.5	0	4	57	14.3	0
	1 YR TOTALS	12	155	591	3.8	1	15	142	9.5	0	4	57	14.3	0
1993	RANK NFL RB		31	29	65	56	59	52	26	40	26	35	47	

Nick Bell No. 38/RB

HT: 6-2 **WT:** 250
Born: 8-19-68, Las Vegas, NV
High school: Clark (Las Vegas)
College: Iowa
Bell struggled along with the rest of the Raider RBs in '93, averaging just 2.7 yards per carry.

YEAR	TEAM	G	RUSHING ATT	YDS	AVG	TD	RECEIVING REC	YDS	AVG	TD	KICK RETURNS RET	YDS	AVG	TD
1991	LA Raiders	9	78	307	3.9	3	6	62	10.3	0	—	—	—	—
1992	LA Raiders	16	81	366	4.5	3	4	40	10.0	0	1	15	15.0	0
1993	LA Raiders	10	67	180	2.7	1	11	111	10.1	0	—	—	—	—
	3 YR TOTALS	35	226	853	3.8	7	21	213	10.1	0	1	15	15.0	0
1993	RANK NFL RB		56	74	122	56	67	59	17	40	65	65	65	
1994	PROJECTIONS	10	70	115	1.6	0	16	165	10.3	0	0	0	NA	0

Tim Brown   No. 81/WR

Full name: Timothy Donnell Brown
HT: 6-0 **WT:** 195
Born: 7-22-66, Dallas, TX
High school: Woodrow Wilson (Dallas)
College: Notre Dame
Brown had the best year of his career in '93, exploding for 1,180 receiving yards (tops in the AFC) on 80 catches (fourth in the AFC).

YEAR	TEAM	G	RECEIVING				RUSHING				PUNT RETURN		
			REC	YDS	AVG	TD	ATT	YDS	AVG	TD	RET	YDS	AVG
1988	LA Raiders	16	43	725	16.9	5	14	50	3.6	1	49	444	9.1
1989	LA Raiders	1	1	8	8.0	0	---	---	---	---	4	43	10.8
1990	LA Raiders	16	18	265	14.7	3	---	---	---	---	34	295	8.7
1991	LA Raiders	16	36	554	15.4	5	5	16	3.2	0	29	330	11.4
1992	LA Raiders	15	49	693	14.1	7	3	-4	-1.3	0	37	383	10.4
1993	LA Raiders	16	80	1180	14.8	7	2	7	3.5	0	40	465	11.6
	6 YR TOTALS	80	227	3425	15.1	27	24	69	2.9	1	193	1960	10.2
1993	RANK NFL WR		8	5	48	7	22	23	24		3	1	4
1994	PROJECTIONS	16	102	1510	14.8	8	2	10	5.0	0	41	496	12.1

James Jett   No. 82/WR

Full name: James Jett
HT: 5-10 **WT:** 165
Born: 12-28-70, Charlestown, WV
High school: Jefferson (Shenandoah Junct., WV)
College: West Virginia
Jett, passed over in the '93 draft, averaged a whopping 23.4 yards/catch last season, best on the team.

YEAR	TEAM	G	RECEIVING				RUSHING				PUNT RETURN		
			REC	YDS	AVG	TD	ATT	YDS	AVG	TD	RET	YDS	AVG
1993	LA Raiders	16	33	771	23.4	3	1	0	0.0	0	---	---	---
	1 YR TOTALS	16	33	771	23.4	3	1	0	0.0	0	0	0	NA
1993	RANK NFL WR		59	28	5	41	31	35	35		30	30	29

Raghib Ismail   No. 86/WR

Full name: Raghib Ramadian Ismail
HT: 6 10 **WT:** 190
Born: 11-18-69, Elizabeth, NJ
High school: Elmer L. Meyers (Wilkes-Barre, PA)
College: Notre Dame
"The Rocket" returned from Canada to average a league-high 24.2 yards per kick return.

		RECEIVING				RUSHING				PUNT RETURN		
YEAR	TEAM	G	REC	YDS	AVG	TD	ATT	YDS	AVG	TD	RET	YDS	AVG
1993	LA Raiders	13	26	353	13.6	1	4	-5	-1.3	0	---	---	---
	1 YR TOTALS	13	26	353	13.6	1	4	-5	-1.3	0	0	0	NA
1993	RANK NFL WR		70	70	68	72	9	40	37		30	30	29

Kevin Gogan   No. 66/G

Full name: Kevin Patrick Gogan
HT: 6-7 **WT:** 319
Born: 11-2-64, San Francisco, CA
High school: Sacred Heart (San Francisco)
College: Michigan
Ex-Cowboy Gogan should help the Raider's develop a more effective running game.

		RUSHING				RANK	PASS	RANK		YDS.
YEAR	TEAM	G	ATT	YDS	AVG	AV RUSH	YDS	PASS YDS	SACKS	LOST
1991	Dallas	16	433	1711	4.0	14	3663	6	38	273
1992	Dallas	16	500	2121	4.2	9	3597	7	23	112
1993	Dallas	16	490	2161	4.4	3	3617	9	29	163
	7 YR TOTALS	103								

Anthony Smith   No. 94/DE

Full name: Anthony Wayne Smith
HT: 6-3   **WT:** 265
Born: 6-28-67, Elizabeth City, NC
High school: Northeastern (Elizabeth City, NC)
College: Alabama and Arizona
After missing all of 1990 with an injury, Smith has racked up an impressive 36 sacks in the last 3 years.

YEAR	TEAM	G	INT	YDS	AVG	TD	SACKS	FUM REC	TD
1991	LA Raiders	16	---	---	---	---	10.5	1	0
1992	LA Raiders	15	---	---	---	---	13.0	---	---
1993	LA Raiders	16	---	---	---	---	12.5	---	---
3 YR TOTALS		47	0	0	NA	0	36.0	1	0
1993 RANK NFL DL			16	NA	NA	NA	5	71	NA
1994 PROJECTIONS		16	0	0	NA	0	12	0	0

Albert Lewis   No. 24/CB

Full name: Albert Ray Lewis
HT: 6-2   **WT:** 195
Born: 10-6-60, Mansfield, LA
High school: DeSote (Mansfield, LA)
College: Clemson
Lewis led the Chiefs with 6 INTs and 16 passes defensed. He has 38 career INTs, tied for third among active players.

YEAR	TEAM	G	INT	YDS	AVG	TD	SACKS	FUM REC	TD
1986	Kansas City	15	4	18	4.5	0	1.0	2	0
1987	Kansas City	12	1	0	0.0	0	---	1	0
1988	Kansas City	14	1	19	19.0	0	---	1	0
1989	Kansas City	16	4	37	9.3	0	1.0	---	---
1990	Kansas City	15	2	15	7.5	0	---	3	0
1991	Kansas City	8	3	21	7.0	0	---	---	---
1992	Kansas City	9	1	0	0.0	0	---	---	---
1993	Kansas City	14	6	61	10.2	0	---	2	0
11 YR TOTALS		150	38	329	8.7	0	4.5	12	1
1993 RANK NFL DB			7	28	78	27	49	10	14
1994 PROJECTIONS		16	9	97	10.8	0	0	0	3

Jeff Jaeger   No. 18/K

Full name: Jeff Todd Jaeger
HT: 5-11 **WT:** 195
Born: 11-26-64, Tacoma, WA
High school: Kent-Meridian (WA)
College: Washington
Jaeger set the all-time Raiders record for points scored with 132 in 1993. He also set the record for FGs made with 27.

YEAR	TEAM	G	XP	XPA	XP Pct.	FG	FGA	FG Pct.	PTS
1987	Cleveland	10	33	33	100.0	14	22	63.6	75
1989	LA Raiders	16	34	34	100.0	23	34	67.6	103
1990	LA Raiders	16	40	42	95.2	15	20	75.0	85
1991	LA Raiders	16	29	30	96.7	29	34	85.3	116
1992	LA Raiders	16	28	28	100.0	15	26	57.7	73
1993	LA Raiders	16	27	29	93.1	35	44	79.5	132
	7 YR TOTALS	90	191	196	97.4	131	180	72.8	584
1993	RANK NFL		20	16	25	1	1	11	1
1994	PROJECTIONS	16	25	28	89.3	43	52	82.7	154

Art Shell   Head Coach

Born: 11-26-46, Charleston, SC
High school: Bonds-Wilson (N. Charleston, SC)
College: Maryland State-Eastern Shore
An underrated coach, Shell has had three playoff teams and just one losing season in five campaigns at the Raider helm.

		REGULAR SEASON					POSTSEASON		
YEAR	TEAM	W	L	T	PCT	FINISH	W	L	FINISH
1989	LA Raiders	7	5	0	.583	3rd/AFC West			
1990	LA Raiders	12	4	0	.750	1st/AFC West	1	1	lost AFC Title game to Buffalo, 51-3
1991	LA Raiders	9	7	0	.563	3rd/AFC West	0	1	lost 1st Rnd. game to Kansas City, 10-6
1992	LA Raiders	7	9	0	.438	4th/AFC West			
1993	LA Raiders	10	6	0	.625	2nd/AFC West	1	1	lost 2nd Rnd. game to Buffalo, 29-23
	5 YR TOTALS	45	31	0	.592		2	3	

Harvey Williams   No. 22/RB

Full name: Harvey Lavance Williams
HT: 6-2   **WT:** 222
Born: 4-22-67, Hempstead, TX
High school: Hempstead (TX)
College: Louisiana State
Williams never lived up to Kansas City's hopes.

YEAR	TEAM	G	RUSHING ATT	YDS	AVG	TD	RECEIVING REC	YDS	AVG	TD	KICK RETURNS RET	YDS	AVG	TD
1991	Kansas City	14	97	447	4.6	1	16	147	9.2	2	24	524	21.8	0
1992	Kansas City	14	78	262	3.4	1	5	24	4.8	0	21	405	19.3	0
1993	Kansas City	7	42	149	3.5	0	7	42	6.0	0	3	53	17.7	0
	3 YR TOTALS	35	217	858	4.0	2	28	213	7.5	2	48	982	20.5	0
1993	RANK NFL RB		60	64	62	69	64	90	92	40	95	37	25	
1994	PROJECTIONS	5	30	100	3.3	0	6	35	5.6	0	0	0	NA	0

Alexander Wright   No. 89/WR

HT: 6-0   **WT:** 190
Born: 7-19-67, Albany, GA
High school: Albany (GA)
College: Auburn
Wright's 4 TD catches were second on the team.

YEAR	TEAM	G	REC	YDS	AVG	TD	ATT	YDS	AVG	TD	RET	YDS	AVG
1990	Dallas	15	11	104	9.5	0	3	26	8.7	0	---	---	---
1991	Dallas	16	10	170	17.0	0	2	-1	-0.5	0	0	0	---
1992	Dallas	3	---	---	---	---	---	---	---	---	---	---	---
1992	LA Raiders	10	12	175	14.6	2	---	---	---	---	---	---	---
1993	LA Raiders	15	27	462	17.1	4	---	---	---	---	---	---	---
	4 YR TOTALS	59	60	911	15.2	6	5	25	5.0	0	0	0	NA
1993	RANK NFL WR		68	59	20	28	42	42	42		30	30	29
1994	PROJECTIONS	16	39	682	17.5	6	0	0	NA	0	0	0	NA

Jamie Williams   No. 88/TE

Full name: Jamie Earl Williams
HT: 6-4   **WT:** 245
Born: 2-25-60, Vero Beach, FL
High school: Central (Davenport, IA)
College: Nebraska
Williams backed up Brent Jones in San Francisco.

YEAR	TEAM	G	RECEIVING REC	YDS	AVG	TD
1991	San Francisco	16	22	235	10.7	1
1992	San Francisco	16	7	76	10.9	1
1993	San Francisco	16	16	132	8.3	1
	11 YR TOTALS	144	178	1955	11.0	11
1993	RANK NFL TE		31	36	49	22
1994	PROJECTIONS	16	18	135	7.5	1

Greg Townsend   No. 93/DE

HT: 6-3   **WT:** 270
Born: 11-3-61, Los Angeles, CA
High school: Dominguez (Compton, CA)
College: Texas Christian
He's never had less than 5 sacks in his career.

YEAR	TEAM	G	INT	YDS	AVG	TD	SACKS	FUM REC	TD
1991	LA Raiders	16	1	31	31.0	0	13.0	1	0
1992	LA Raiders	14	---	---	---	---	5.0	1	0
1993	LA Raiders	16	---	---	---	---	7.5	---	---
	11 YR TOTALS	170	3	117	39.0	1	107.5	7	3
1993	RANK NFL DL		16	NA	NA	NA	27	71	NA
1994	PROJECTIONS	16	0	0	NA	0	7	0	0

Chester McGlockton   No. 91/DT

HT: 6-4   **WT:** 320
Born: 9-16-69, Whiteville, NC
High school: Whiteville (NC)
College: Clemson
McGlockton's 7 sacks were third-best on the team.

YEAR	TEAM	G	INT	YDS	AVG	TD	SACKS	FUM REC	TD
1992	LA Raiders	10	—	—	—	—	3.0	—	—
1993	LA Raiders	16	1	19	19.0	0	7.0	1	0
	2 YR TOTALS	26	1	19	19.0	0	10.0	1	0
1993	RANK NFL DL		2	2	2	3	29	25	5
1994	PROJECTIONS	16	2	38	19.0	0	9	2	0

Aundray Bruce   No. 56/DL

HT: 6-5   **WT:** 255
Born: 4-30-66, Montgomery, AL
High school: G.W. Carver (Montgomery, AL)
College: Auburn
Bruce was the first pick overall in the '88 draft

YEAR	TEAM	G	INT	YDS	AVG	TD	SACKS	FUM REC	TD
1988	Atlanta	16	2	10	5.0	0	6.0	—	—
1989	Atlanta	16	1	0	0.0	0	6.0	—	—
1990	Atlanta	16	—	—	—	—	4.0	—	—
1991	Atlanta	14	—	—	—	—	—	—	—
1992	LA Raiders	16	—	—	—	—	3.5	—	—
1993	LA Raiders	16	—	—	—	—	2.0	1	0
	6 YR TOTALS	94	3	10	3.3	0	21.5	1	0
1993	RANK NFL DL		16	NA	NA	NA	99	25	5
1994	PROJECTIONS	16	0	0	NA	0	1	0	0

Eddie Anderson   No. 33/S

Full name: Eddie Lee Anderson Jr.
HT: 6-1 **WT:** 210
Born: 7-22-63, Warner Robbins, GA
High school: Warner Robbins (GA)
College: Fort Valley State (GA)
He has returned 3 INTs for TDs in his career.

YEAR	TEAM	G	INT	YDS	AVG	TD	SACKS	FUM REC	TD
1991	LA Raiders	16	2	14	7.0	0	---	1	0
1992	LA Raiders	16	3	131	43.7	1	1.0	---	---
1993	LA Raiders	16	2	52	26.0	0	1.0	1	0
	8 YR TOTALS	113	18	531	29.5	3	2.0	4	0
1993	RANK NFL DB		54	40	22	27	13	37	14
1994	PROJECTIONS	16	1	25	25.0	0	1	1	0

Terry McDaniel   No. 36/CB

Full name: Terence Lee McDaniel
HT: 5-10 **WT:** 180
Born: 2-8-65, Saginaw, MI
High school: Saginaw (MI)
College: Tennessee
McDaniel led the team with a career-best 5 INTs.

YEAR	TEAM	G	INT	YDS	AVG	TD	SACKS	FUM REC	TD
1990	LA Raiders	16	3	20	6.7	0	2.0	2	1
1991	LA Raiders	16	—					1	0
1992	LA Raiders	16	4	180	45.0	0	—	1	0
1993	LA Raiders	16	5	87	17.4	1	—	—	—
	6 YR TOTALS	82	15	308	20.5	1	3.0	4	1
1993	RANK NFL DB		14	16	37	2	49	94	NA
1994	PROJECTIONS	16	6	78	13.0	2	0	0	0

Jeff Gossett   No. 7/P

Full name: Jeffrey Alan Gossett
HT: 6-2 **WT:** 195
Born: 1-25-57, Charleston, IL
High school: Charleston (IL)
College: Eastern Illinois
'93's 41.8 yard average was his third-best as a pro.

YEAR	TEAM	G	NO	YARDS	LONG	AVG	BLK	IN20
1990	LA Raiders	16	60	2315	NA	38.6	0	NA
1991	LA Raiders	16	67	2961	61	44.2	0	26
1992	LA Raiders	16	77	3255	56	42.3	0	17
1993	LA Raiders	16	71	2971	61	41.8	0	19
	12 YR TOTALS	168	773	31839	61	41.2	1	62
1993	RANK NFL Ps		21	21	13	20		15
1994	PROJECTIONS	16	69	2832	64	41.0	0	18

Miami
DOLPHINS

1994 Scouting Report

Offense

Amazingly, despite losing Dan Marino and Scott Mitchell to injury, Miami still finished first in the NFL in passing offense with 4,353 yards in the air. Irving Fryar, the team's most dangerous receiver, broke 1,000 yards last year, and TE Keith Jackson made the Pro Bowl for the fifth time. The RBs were best used as receivers last year—Terry Kirby tied for the lead among NFL RBs (and led all rookies) with 75 catches, and Keith Byars had a Pro Bowl year, catching 61 passes. The team ranked just twenty-fifth in rushing with 1,459 yards. Starting in only 8 games, RB Mark Higgs led the team with just 693 rushing yards. Pro Bowlers LT Richmond Webb and G Keith Sims remain on the OL, but C Jeff Uhlenhake left for New Orleans.

Defense

Miami's 1993 defensive stats are deceiving. The team ranked fourteenth in the NFL in rushing defense, allowing 1,665 yards, but during the stretch drive last season, Miami found it difficult to stop the run. Top draft picks DT Tim Bowens and LB Aubrey Beavers should help change this in '94. DE Jeff Cross continues to excel, but the rest of the DL is average. LBs Bryan Cox, Marco Coleman, and Dwight Hollier make a strong unit. The defensive backfield features CB J.B. Brown and newcomers CB Michael Stewart and S Gene Atkins, who has to replace the departed Louis Oliver.

Special Teams

Pete Stoyanovich is one of the most accurate kickers in the NFL, making 83.8% of FGs under 50 yards. The Dolphins punting game was one of the league's worst, but ex-Lion Jim Arnold replaces weak-legged Dale Hatcher. O. J. McDuffie is in the league's top 10 for both punt and kick returns.

1994 Prospects

Miami will move the ball as well as anyone. But unless Higgs proves he can carry the load for a full season and the defense improves dramatically, Miami will have difficulty protecting any leads they can get. Miami could finish anywhere from second to fourth in a competitive and improving division, but if Marino can return from his Achilles tendon tear, the Dolphins should return to the playoffs.

Team Directory

President: Timothy J. Robbie
Assistant general manager: Bryan Wiedmeyer
Director of player personnel: Tom Heckert
Director of media relations: Harvey Greene

1993 Review

Sep. 5	at Indianapolis	W 24-20
Sep. 12	N.Y. JETS	L 24-14
Sep. 19	OPEN DATE	
Sep. 26	at Buffalo	W 22-13
Oct. 4	WASHINGTON	W 17-10
Oct. 10	at Cleveland	W 24-14
Oct. 17	OPEN DATE	
Oct. 24	INDIANAPOLIS	W 41-27
Oct. 31	KANSAS CITY	W 30-10
Nov. 7	at N.Y. Jets	L 27-10
Nov. 14	at Philadelphia	W 19-14
Nov. 21	NEW ENGLAND	W 17-13
Nov. 25	at Dallas	W 16-14
Dec. 5	N.Y. GIANTS	L 19-14
Dec. 13	PITTSBURGH	L 21-20
Dec. 19	BUFFALO	L 47-34
Dec. 27	at San Diego	L 45-20
Jan. 2	at New England	L 33-27 (OT)

1994 Schedule

Sep. 4	NEW ENGLAND	4:00
Sep. 11	vs. Green Bay (Mil.)	1:00
Sep. 18	N.Y. JETS	1:00
Sep. 25	at Minnesota	1:00
Oct. 2	at Cincinnati	8:00
Oct. 9	at Buffalo	1:00
Oct. 16	L.A. RAIDERS	4:00
Oct. 23	OPEN DATE	
Oct. 30	at New England	1:00
Nov. 6	INDIANAPOLIS	1:00
Nov. 13	CHICAGO	1:00
Nov. 20	at Pittsburgh	1:00
Nov. 27	at N.Y. Jets	1:00
Dec. 4	BUFFALO	8:00
Dec. 12	KANSAS CITY (Mon.)	9:00
Dec. 18	at Indianapolis	1:00
Dec. 25	DETROIT	8:00

1993 finish: 9-7 (4-4 home, 5-3 away), second in AFC East

Team Leaders

PASSING	ATT	COM	COM%	YDS	YPA	TD	TD%	INT	INT%	RTG
Mitchell	233	133	57.1	1773	7.61	12	5.2	8	3.4	84.2
DeBerg	188	113	60.1	1521	8.09	6	3.2	7	3.7	81.0
Marino	150	91	60.7	1218	8.12	8	5.3	3	2.0	95.9
TEAM	581	342	58.9	4564	7.86	27	4.6	18	3.1	86.4
OPPONENTS	572	350	61.2	3682	6.44	26	4.5	13	2.3	85.6

RECEIVING	REC	YDS	AVG	TD	RUSHING	ATT	YDS	AVG	TD
Kirby	75	874	11.7	3	Higgs	186	693	3.7	3
Fryar	64	1010	15.8	5	Kirby	119	390	3.3	3
Byars	61	613	10.0	3	Byars	64	269	4.2	3
Ingram	44	707	16.1	6	Mitchell	21	89	4.2	0
Jackson	39	613	15.7	6	Parmalee	4	16	4.0	0
TEAM	342	4564	13.3	27	TEAM	419	1459	3.5	10
OPPONENTS	350	3682	10.5	26	OPPONENTS	460	1665	3.6	12

INTERCEPTIONS	INT	YDS	AVG	LG	TD	SACKS		NO
Brown	5	43	8.6	29	0	Cross		10.5
Oliver	2	60	30.0	56t	1	Coleman		5.5
Vincent	2	29	14.5	23	0	Cox		5.0
TEAM	13	175	13.5	56t	1	TEAM		29.0
OPPONENTS	18	329	18.3	97t	2	OPPONENTS		30.0

KICK RETURNS	NO	YDS	AV	LG	TD	PUNT RETURNS	NO	FC	YDS	AV	LG	TD
McDuffie	32	755	23.6	48	0	McDuffie	28	22	317	11.3	72t	2
Williams	8	180	22.5	39	0	Vincent	0	0	9	—	9	0
Kirby	4	85	21.3	26	0							
TEAM	49	1068	21.8	48	0	TEAM	28	22	326	11.6	72t	2
OPPONENTS	62	1239	20.0	40	0	OPPONENTS	32	12	359	11.2	64t	1

KICKING	XPM	XPA	FGM	FGA	LG	PTS
Stoyanovich	37	37	24	32	52	109
TEAM	37	40	24	32	52	109
OPPONENTS	40	42	17	27	59	91

PUNTING	NO	YDS	LG	AVG	TB	BLK	RET	RYD	IN20	NAV
Hatcher	58	2304	56	39.7	4	0	32	359	13	32.2
TEAM	58	2304	56	39.7	4	0	32	359	13	32.2
OPPONENTS	76	3135	60	41.3	8	1	28	326	19	34.9

FUMBLES	FUM	OFF.FUM.REC.	REC	TD	DEF.FUM.REC.	REC	TD
Kirby	5	Kirby	4	0	Cox	4	0
Marino	4	Marino	2	0	Cross	2	0
McDuffie	4				Williams	2	0
TEAM	32	TEAM	15	0	TEAM	14	0
OPPONENTS	30	OPPONENTS	15	0	OPPONENTS	16	2

1994 Draft Choices

ROUND	NAME	POS	SCHOOL	OVERALL SELECTION
1	Tim Bowens	DT	Mississippi	20
2	Aubrey Beavers	LB	Oklahoma	54
2	Tim Ruddy	C	Notre Dame	65
4	Ronnie Woolfork	LB	Colorado	112
5	William Gaines	DT	Florida	147
6	Brant Boyer	LB	Arizona	177
7	Sean Hill	CB	Montana State	214

HISTORY

TITLES

1971	AFC Championship
1972	Super Bowl Winner
1973	Super Bowl Winner
1974	AFC East Championship
1979	AFC East Championship
1980	AFC East Championship
1982	AFC Championship
1983	AFC East Championship
1984	AFC Championship
1985	AFC East Championship
1992	AFC East Championship

ALL-TIME TEAM RECORDS

Rushing

Most yards, game:	197	Mercury Morris	9/30/73
Most yards, season:	1,258	Delvin Williams	1978
Most yards, career:	6,737	Larry Czonka	1968-1974, 1979

Passing

Most yards, game:	521	Dan Marino	10/23/88
Most yards, season:	5,084	Dan Marino	1984
Most yards, career:	40,720	Dan Marino	1983-1993

Receiving

Most catches, game:	12	Jim Jensen	11/6/88
Most catches, season:	86	Mark Clayton	1988
Most catches, career:	550	Mark Clayton	1983-1992

Scoring

Most points, game:	24	Paul Warfield	12/15/73
Most points, season:	124	Pete Stoyanovich	1992
Most points, career:	830	Garo Yepremian	1970-1978

COACHES

NAME	RECORD	YEARS
George Wilson	15-39-2	1966-69
Don Shula	254-132-2	1970-93

MIAMI DOLPHINS
1994 TRAINING CAMP ROSTER

No.	Quarterbacks		Ht	Wt	Born	NFL Exp.	College	How acq.	'93 GP/GS
19	Kosar, Bernie	QB	6-5	215	11-25-63	10	Miami (FL)	FA '94	4/1
13	Marino, Dan	QB	6-4	224	9-15-61	12	Pittsburgh	D1 '83	5/5
11	Stouffer, Kelly	QB	6-3	222	7-6-94	6	Colorado State	FA '94	0/0
	Running backs								
41	Byars, Keith	FB	6-1	256	10-14-63	9	Ohio State	FA '93	16/16
34	Craver, Aaron	RB	6-0	220	12-18-68	4	Fresno State	D3 '91	0/0
21	Higgs, Mark	RB	5-7	195	4-11-66	7	Kentucky	Plan B '90	16/8
43	Kirby, Terry	RB	6-1	221	1-20-70	2	Virginia	D3 '93	16/8
30	Parmalee, Bernie	RB	5-11	205	9-16-67	3	Ball State	FA '92	16/0
22	Saxon, James	FB	5-11	237	3-23-66	7	San Jose State	Plan B '92	16/0
	Wide receivers								
80	Fryar, Irving	WR	6-0	200	9-28-62	11	Nebraska	T-NE '93	16/16
82	Ingram, Mark	WR	5-11	194	8-23-65	8	Michigan State	FA '93	16/16
81	McDuffie, O.J.	WR-KR	5-10	191	12-2-69	2	Penn State	D1 '93	16/0
83	Miller, Scott	WR	5-11	179	10-20-68	4	UCLA	D9 '93	3/0
87	Williams, Mike	WR	5-11	190	10-9-66	4	Northeastern	FA '91	13/0
	Tight ends								
**	Baty, Greg	TE	6-6	240	8-28-64	8	Stanford	FA '90	16/1
88	Jackson, Keith	TE	6-2	258	4-19-65	7	Oklahoma	FA '92	15/15
85	Williams, Ronnie	TE	6-3	266	1-19-66	2	Oklahoma St.	FA '93	11/0
	Offensive linemen								
66	Blake, Eddie	G	6-4	315	12-18-68	2	Auburn	D2 '91	0/0
65	Dellenbach, Jeff	G-C	6-5	290	2-14-63	10	Wisconsin	D4b '85	16/16
74	Dennis, Mark	T	6-6	292	4-15-65	8	Illinois	D8b '87	16/0
62	Gray, Chris	G-T	6-4	294	6-19-70	2	Auburn	D5 '93	5/0
73	Heller, Ron	T	6-6	293	8-25-62	11	Penn State	FA '93	16/16
67	Novak, Jeff	T-G	6-5	295	7-27-67	1	Southwest Texas St.	FA '93	0/0
61	Ruddy, Tim	C	6-3	286	4-27-72	R	Notre Dame	D2b '94	
69	Sims, Keith	G	6-3	303	6-17-67	5	Iowa State	D2 '90	16/16
78	Webb, Richmond	T	6-6	298	1-11-67	5	Texas A&M	D1 '90	16/16
60	Weidner, Bert	G-C	6-2	290	1-20-66	5	Kent State	D11 '89	16/11
	Defensive linemen								
91	Cross, Jeff	DE	6-4	281	3-25-66	7	Missouri	D9 '88	16/16
95	Bowens, Tim	DT	6-4	317	2-7-73	R	Mississippi	D1 '94	
93	Gaines, William	DT	6-5	300	6-20-71	R	Florida	D5 '94	
99	Klingbeil, Chuck	NT	6-1	295	11-2-65	4	Northern Michigan	FA '91	16/16
94	Veasey, Craig	DT	6-2	300	12-25-66	5	Houston	FA '93	14/0
79	Webster, Larry	DE	6-5	296	1-18-69	3	Maryland	D3 '92	13/9
	Linebackers								
53	Beavers, Aubrey	LB	6-3	233	8-30-71	R	Oklahoma	D2a '94	
52	Boyer, Brant	LB	6-0	233	6-27-71	R	Arizona	D6 '94	
90	Coleman, Marco	LB	6-3	267	12-18-69	3	Georgia Tech	D1b '92	15/15
54	Cox, Bryan	LB	6-4	242	2-17-68	4	Western Illinois	D5a '91	16/16
50	Hollier, Dwight	LB	6-2	257	4-21-69	3	North Carolina	D4 '92	16/10
**	Offerdahl, John	LB	6-3	238	8-17-64	9	Western Michigan	D2 '86	9/8
**	Singleton, Chris	LB	6-2	247	2-2-67	5	Arizona	FA '93	17/4
58	Woolfork, Ronnie	LB	6-3	256	12-21-70	R	Colorado	D4 '94	
	Defensive backs								
**	Alexander, Bruce	CB	5-8	178	9-17-65	6	Stephen F. Austin	Plan B '92	14/0
28	Atkins, Gene	S	5-11	200	11-22-64	8	Florida A&M	FA '94	16/16
**	Braxton, Tyrone	S	5-11	185	12-17-64	8	North Dakota St.	FA '94	16/16
37	Brown, J.B.	CB	6-0	189	1-5-67	6	Maryland	D12 '89	16/16
42	Green, Chris	S	5-11	198	2-26-68	4	Illinois	D7 '91	14/0
31	Hill, Sean	CB	5-10	176	8-14-71	R	Montana State	D7 '94	
**	Jackson, Vestee	CB	6-0	186	8-14-63	9	Washington	T-CHI '91	16/6
47	Malone, Darrell	CB	5-10	182	11-23-67	3	Jacksonville St.	FA '92	16/1
20	Oliver, Muhammad	CB	5-11	185	3-12-69	3	Oregon	FA '93	3/0
28	Smith, Frankie	CB	5-9	191	10-8-68	2	Baylor	FA '93	5/1
35	Stewart, Michael	S	5-11	199	7-12-65	8	Fresno State	FA '94	16/14
24	Vincent, Troy	CB	6-0	197	6-8-70	3	Wisconsin	D1a '92	11/11
**	Williams, Jarvis	S	5-11	200	5-16-65	7	Florida	D2 '88	16/14
	Specialists								
6	Arnold, Jim	P	6-3	235	1-31-61	12	Vanderbilt	FA '94	16/0
10	Stoyanovich, Pete	K	5-11	195	4-28-67	6	Indiana	D8 '89	16/0

Dan Marino   No. 13/QB

Full name: Daniel Constantine Marino Jr.
HT: 6-4   **WT:** 224
Born: 9-15-61, Pittsburgh, PA
High school: Central Catholic (Pittsburgh)
College: Pittsburgh
In '94 Marino should pass Dan Fouts to move into second place on the NFL all-time list for pass attempts and completions.

YEAR	TEAM	G	PASSING ATT	CPL	CPL%	YDS	AVG	TDS	TD%	INT	INT%	RTG	RUSHING ATT	YDS	AVG
1985	Miami	16	567	336	59.3	4137	7.3	30	5.3	21	3.7	84.1	26	-24	-0.9
1986	Miami	16	623	378	60.7	4746	7.6	44	7.1	23	3.7	92.5	12	-3	-0.3
1987	Miami	12	444	263	59.2	3245	7.3	26	5.9	13	2.9	89.2	12	-5	-0.4
1988	Miami	16	606	354	58.4	4434	7.3	28	4.6	23	3.8	80.8	20	-17	-0.9
1989	Miami	16	550	308	56.0	3997	7.3	24	4.4	22	4.0	76.9	14	-7	-0.5
1990	Miami	16	531	306	57.6	3563	6.7	21	4.0	11	2.1	82.6	16	29	1.8
1991	Miami	16	549	318	57.9	3970	7.2	25	4.6	13	2.4	85.8	25	108	4.3
1992	Miami	16	554	330	59.6	4116	7.4	24	4.3	16	2.9	85.1	20	66	3.3
1993	Miami	5	150	91	60.7	1218	8.1	8	5.3	3	2.0	95.9	9	-4	-0.4
11	YR TOTALS	158	5434	3219	59.2	40720	7.5	298	5.5	168	3.1		210	181	0.9
1993	RANK NFL QB		36	34	20.0	34	6.0	24	9.0	43	^^^^^^	8	38	60	^^^^^^
1994	PROJECTIONS	16	555	336	60.6	4212	7.6	24	4.3	16	3.0		20	71	3.6

Bernie Kosar   No. 19/QB

Full name: Bernie Joseph Kosar Jr.
HT: 6-5   **WT:** 215
Born: 11-25-63, Boardman, OH
High school: Boardman (OH)
College: Miami (FL)
University of Miami star Kosar started 6 of 8 games for Cleveland last year, then ended up as Troy Aikman's backup in Dallas.

YEAR	TEAM	G	PASSING ATT	CPL	CPL%	YDS	AVG	TDS	TD%	INT	INT%	RTG	RUSHING ATT	YDS	AVG
1987	Cleveland	12	389	241	62.0	3033	7.8	22	5.7	9	2.3	95.4	15	22	1.5
1988	Cleveland	9	259	156	60.2	1890	7.3	10	3.9	7	2.7	84.3	12	-1	-0.1
1989	Cleveland	16	513	303	59.1	3533	6.9	18	3.5	14	2.7	80.3	30	70	2.3
1990	Cleveland	13	423	230	54.4	2562	6.1	10	2.4	15	3.5	65.7	10	13	1.3
1991	Cleveland	16	494	307	62.1	3487	7.1	18	3.6	9	1.8	87.8	26	74	2.8
1992	Cleveland	7	155	103	66.5	1160	7.5	8	5.2	7	4.5	87.0	5	12	2.4
1993	Cleveland	7	138	79	57.2	807	5.8	5	3.6	3	2.2	77.2	14	19	1.4
1993	Dallas	4	63	36	57.1	410	6.5	3	4.8	0	0.0	92.7	9	7	0.8
9	YR TOTALS	112	3213	1889	58.8	22314	6.9	119	3.7	81	2.5		171	223	1.3
1993	RANK NFL QB		50	50	35	51	34	43	12	61	61		11	38	42	45
1994	PROJECTIONS	11	150	79	52.4	763	5.1	6	4.0	0	0.0		29	25	0.9

Keith Byars No. 41/FB

HT: 6-1 **WT:** 256
Born: 10 11 00, Dayton, OH
High school: Nettie Lee Roth (Dayton)
College: Ohio State

First-time Pro Bowler Byars has caught at least 1 pass in 103 consecutive regular season games, the fourth longest active streak in the NFL.

YEAR	TEAM	RUSHING					RECEIVING				KICK RETURNS			
		G	ATT	YDS	AVG	TD	REC	YDS	AVG	TD	RET	YDS	AVG	TD
1986	Philadelphia	16	177	577	3.3	1	11	44	4.0	0	2	47	23.5	0
1987	Philadelphia	10	116	426	3.7	3	21	177	8.4	1	---	---	---	---
1988	Philadelphia	16	152	517	3.4	6	72	705	9.8	4	2	20	10.0	0
1989	Philadelphia	16	133	452	3.4	5	68	721	10.6	0	1	27	27.0	0
1990	Philadelphia	16	37	141	3.8	0	81	819	10.1	3	---	---	---	---
1991	Philadelphia	16	94	383	4.1	1	62	564	9.1	3	---	---	---	---
1992	Philadelphia	15	41	176	4.3	1	56	502	9.0	2	---	---	---	---
1993	Miami	16	64	269	4.2	3	61	613	10.0	3	---	---	---	---
	8 YR TOTALS	121	814	2941	3.6	20	432	4145	9.6	16	5	94	18.8	0
1993	RANK NFL RB		60	58	40	21	123	122	122	40	65	65	65	
1994	PROJECTIONS	16	63	274	4.3	4	59	615	10.4	3	0	0	NA	0

Terry Kirby No. 43/RB

Full name: Terry Gayle Kirby
HT: 6-1 **WT:** 221
Born: 1-20-70, Hampton, VA
High school: Tabb (VA)
College: Virginia

Kirby tied Herschel Walker for first among catches by an NFL RB in 1993. His 75 catches were the third-most ever by a rookie.

YEAR	TEAM	RUSHING					RECEIVING				KICK RETURNS			
		G	ATT	YDS	AVG	TD	REC	YDS	AVG	TD	RET	YDS	AVG	TD
1993	Miami	16	119	390	3.3	3	75	874	11.7	3	4	85	21.3	1
	1 YR TOTALS	16	119	390	3.3	3	75	874	11.7	3	4	85	21.3	1
1993	RANK NFL RB		39	45	101	21	1	1	10	2	28	27	9	

Irving Fryar   No. 80/WR

Full name: Irving Dale Fryar
HT: 6-0 **WT:** 200
Born: 9-28-62, Mount Holly, NJ
High school: Rancocas Valley (NJ)
College: Nebraska

Fryar is the only Dolphin receiver, other than Mark Clayton or Mark Duper, to have 1,000+ receiving yards in a single season.

YEAR	TEAM	G	RECEIVING				RUSHING				PUNT RETURN		
			REC	YDS	AVG	TD	ATT	YDS	AVG	TD	RET	YDS	AVG
1986	New England	14	43	737	17.1	6	4	80	20.0	0	35	366	10.5
1987	New England	12	31	467	15.1	5	9	52	5.8	0	18	174	9.7
1988	New England	15	33	490	14.8	5	6	12	2.0	0	38	398	10.5
1989	New England	11	29	537	18.5	3	2	15	7.5	0	12	107	8.9
1990	New England	16	54	856	15.9	4	---	---	---	---	28	133	4.8
1991	New England	16	68	1014	14.9	3	2	11	5.5	0	2	10	5.0
1992	New England	15	55	791	14.4	4	1	6	6.0	0	0	0	---
1993	Miami	16	64	1010	15.8	5	3	-4	-1.3	0	---	---	---
10 YR TOTALS		145	427	6736	15.8	43	36	188	5.2	1	206	2055	10.0
1993 RANK NFL WR		17	9	30	19	12	38	38			30	30	29
1994 PROJECTIONS		16	67	1078	16.1	6	4	0	0.0	0	0	0	NA

Mark Ingram   No. 82/WR

Full name: Mark V. Ingram
HT: 5-11 **WT:** 194
Born: 8-23-65, Rockford, IL
High school: Northwestern (Flint, MI)
College: Michigan State

Ingram's reception and reception yardage totals were the second-highest in his career, behind only his totals as a Giant in '91.

YEAR	TEAM	G	RECEIVING				RUSHING				PUNT RETURN		
			REC	YDS	AVG	TD	ATT	YDS	AVG	TD	RET	YDS	AVG
1987	NY Giants	9	2	32	16.0	0	---	---	---	---	---	---	---
1988	NY Giants	7	13	158	12.2	1	---	---	---	---	---	---	---
1989	NY Giants	16	17	290	17.1	1	1	1	1.0	0	---	---	---
1990	NY Giants	16	26	499	19.2	5	1	4	4.0	0	---	---	---
1991	NY Giants	16	51	824	16.2	3	---	---	---	---	8	49	6.1
1992	NY Giants	12	27	408	15.1	1	---	---	---	---	---	---	---
1993	Miami	16	44	707	16.1	6	---	---	---	---	---	---	---
7 YR TOTALS		92	180	2918	16.2	17	2	5	2.5	0	8	49	6.1
1993 RANK NFL WR		38	38	28	13	42	42	42			30	30	29
1994 PROJECTIONS		16	48	777	16.2	8	0	0	NA	0	0	0	NA

Keith Jackson   No. 88/TE

Full name: Keith Jerome Jackson
HT. 6-2   **WT.** 258
Born: 4-19-65, Little Rock, AR
High school: Parkview (Little Rock, AR)
College: Oklahoma

A 5-time Pro Bowler, 4 of Jackson's first 6 catches went for TDs. His reception total has dropped every year since his rookie season.

			RECEIVING			
YEAR	TEAM	G	REC	YDS	AVG	TD
1988	Philadelphia	16	81	869	10.7	6
1989	Philadelphia	14	63	648	10.3	3
1990	Philadelphia	14	50	670	13.4	6
1991	Philadelphia	16	48	569	11.9	5
1992	Miami	13	48	594	12.4	5
1993	Miami	15	39	613	15.7	6
6 YR TOTALS		88	329	3963	12.0	31
1993 RANK NFL TE			14	6	4	3
1994 PROJECTIONS		16	33	630	19.1	7

Jeff Cross   No. 91/DE

Full name: Jeffrey Allen Cross
HT: 6-4   **WT:** 281
Born: 3-25-66, Riverside, CA
High school: Rancho Palos Verde (CA)
College: Missouri

Cross' 93 tackles were fourth on the Dolphins. His 44 career sacks place him fourth on the all-time Dolphin list.

YEAR	TEAM	G	INT	YDS	AVG	TD	SACKS	FUM REC	TD
1988	Miami	16	---	---	---	---	0.0	---	---
1989	Miami	16	---	---	---	---	10.0	---	---
1990	Miami	16	---	---	---	---	11.5	2	0
1991	Miami	16	---	---	---	---	7.0	---	---
1992	Miami	16	---	---	---	---	5.0	---	---
1993	Miami	16	---	---	---	---	10.5	2	0
6 YR TOTALS		96	0	0	NA	0	44.0	4	0
1993 RANK NFL DL			16	NA	NA	NA	14	8	5
1994 PROJECTIONS		16	0	0	0	0	12	3	0

Bryan Cox   No. 51/LB

Full name: Bryan Keith Cox
HT: 6-4   **WT:** 242
Born: 2-17-68, East St. Louis, IL
High school: East St. Louis (IL)
College: Western Michigan
The outspoken Cox led the Dolphins in tackles (122) and forced fumbles (4). He's had 100 tackles in 2 of his 3 NFL seasons.

YEAR	TEAM	G	INT	YDS	AVG	TD	SACKS	FUM REC	TD
1991	Miami	13	---	---	---	---	2.0	---	---
1992	Miami	16	1	0	0.0	0	14.0	1	---
1993	Miami	16	1	26	26.0	0	5.0	4	0
	3 YR TOTALS	45	2	26	13.0	0	21.0	5	0
1993	RANK NFL LB		17	10	4	5	22	1	8
1994	PROJECTIONS	16	1	46	46.0	0	1	7	0

J. B. Brown   No. 37/CB

Full name: James Harold Brown
HT: 6-0   **WT:** 189
Born: 1-5-67, Washington, DC
High school: DeMatha (Hyattsville, MD)
College: Maryland
Brown started all 16 games at CB, posting 72 tackles, sixth best on the team. His 5 INTs were a career high.

YEAR	TEAM	G	INT	YDS	AVG	TD	SACKS	FUM REC	TD
1989	Miami	16	---	---	---	---	---	---	---
1990	Miami	16	---	---	---	---	1.0	---	---
1991	Miami	15	1	0	0.0	0	---	---	---
1992	Miami	16	4	119	29.8	1	---	1	---
1993	Miami	16	5	43	8.6	0	---	---	---
	5 YR TOTALS	79	10	162	16.2	1	1.0	1	0
1993	RANK NFL DB		14	48	89	27	49	94	NA
1994	PROJECTIONS	16	6	36	6.0	0	0	0	0

Pete Stoyanovich   No. 10/K

Full name: Peter Stoyanovich
HT: 5-11 **WT:** 195
Born: 4-28-67, Dearborn, MI
High school: Crestwood (Dearborn Hts., MI)
College: Indiana
Stoyanovich has hit 83.8% of FGs under 50 yards and is the only Miami kicker to score 100+ points in 4 straight seasons.

YEAR	TEAM	G	XP	XPA	XP Pct.	FG	FGA	FG Pct.	PTS
1989	Miami	16	38	39	97.4	19	26	73.1	95
1990	Miami	16	37	37	100.0	21	25	84.0	100
1991	Miami	14	28	29	96.6	31	37	83.8	121
1992	Miami	16	34	36	94.4	30	37	81.1	124
1993	Miami	16	37	37	100.0	24	32	75.0	109
	5 YR TOTALS	78	174	178	97.8	125	157	79.6	549
1993	RANK NFL		5	5	1	15	11	16	11
1994	PROJECTIONS	16	38	38	100.0	22	30	73.3	104

Don Shula   Head Coach

Full name: Donald Francis Shula
Born: 1-4-30, Painesville, OH
High school: Harvey (Painesville, OH)
College: John Carroll (OH)
Shula is now the winningest coach in NFL history. He'll be the first father to face his son when Miami plays Cincinnati in October.

YEAR	TEAM	REGULAR SEASON				POSTSEASON		
		W	L	T	PCT	FINISH	W	L	FINISH
1981	Miami	11	4	1	.719	1st/AFC East	0	1	lost 1st Rnd. game to San Diego, 41-38 (OT)
1982	Miami	7	2	0	.778	T2nd/AFC	3	1	lost Super Bowl XVII to Washington, 27-17
1983	Miami	12	4	0	.750	1st/AFC East	0	1	lost 1st Rnd. game to Seattle, 27-20
1984	Miami	14	2	0	.875	1st/AFC East	2	1	lost Super Bowl XIX to SF, 38-16
1985	Miami	12	4	0	.750	1st/AFC East	1	1	lost AFC Title game to New England, 31-14
1986	Miami	8	8	0	.500	3rd/AFC East			
1987	Miami	8	7	0	.533	T2nd/AFC East			
1988	Miami	6	10	0	.375	5th/AFC East			
1989	Miami	8	8	0	.500	T2nd/AFC East			
1990	Miami	12	4	0	.750	2nd/AFC East	1	1	lost 2nd Rnd. game to Buffalo, 44-34
1991	Miami	8	8	0	.500	T2nd/AFC East			
1992	Miami	11	5	0	.688	T1st/AFC East	1	1	lost 2nd Rnd. game to Buffalo, 29-10
1993	Miami	9	7	0	.563	2nd/AFC East			
	31 YR TOTALS	309	143	6	.681		18	15	

Mark Higgs   No. 21/RB

Full name: Mark Deyon Higgs
HT: 5-7   **WT:** 195
Born: 4-11-66, Chicago, IL
High school: Owensboro (KY)
College: Kentucky
Higgs gained only 134 yards in '93's second half.

YEAR	TEAM	G	RUSHING ATT	YDS	AVG	TD	RECEIVING REC	YDS	AVG	TD	KICK RETURNS RET	YDS	AVG	TD
1991	Miami	14	231	905	3.9	4	11	80	7.3	0	---	---	---	---
1992	Miami	16	256	915	3.6	7	16	142	8.9	0	---	---	---	---
1993	Miami	16	186	693	3.7	3	10	72	7.2	0	---	---	---	---
	6 YR TOTALS	78	732	2764	3.8	14	40	303	7.6	0	28	534	19.1	0
1993	RANK NFL RB		20	22	68	21	71	75	72	40	65	65	65	
1994	PROJECTIONS	16	181	676	3.7	2	9	62	6.9	0	0	0	NA	0

O. J. McDuffie   No. 81/WR

Full name: Otis James McDuffie
HT: 5-10   **WT:** 191
Born: 12-2-69, Marion, OH
High school: Hawken (Gates Mills, OH)
College: Penn State
He was second in the AFC in kick return average.

YEAR	TEAM	G	RECEIVING REC	YDS	AVG	TD	RUSHING ATT	YDS	AVG	TD	PUNT RETURN RET	YDS	AVG
1993	Miami	16	19	197	10.4	0	1	-4	-4.0	0	28	317	11.3
	1 YR TOTALS	16	19	197	10.4	0	1	-4	-4.0	0	28	317	11.3
1993	RANK NFL WR		80	86	123	95	31	38	40		10	3	5

Richmond Webb   No. 78/T

Full name: Richmond Jewel Webb
HT: 6-6   **WT:** 298
Born: 1-11-67, Dallas, TX
High school: Franklin D. Roosevelt (Dallas)
College: Texas A&M
Webb made the Pro Bowl team for the fourth year.

YEAR	TEAM	G	RUSHING ATT	YDS	AVG	RANK AV RUSH	PASS YDS	RANK PASS YDS	SACKS	YDS. LOST
1991	Miami	14	379	1352	3.6	21	4077	4	28	188
1992	Miami	16	407	1525	3.7	20	4148	2	28	173
1993	Miami	16	419	1459	3.5	26	4564	1	30	211
	4 YR TOTALS	62								

Keith Sims   No. 69/G

Full name: Keith A. Sims
HT: 6-3   **WT:** 303
Born: 6-17-67, Baltimore, MD
High school: Watchung Hills (Warren, NJ)
College: Iowa State
Sims made the Pro Bowl for the first time in '93.

		RUSHING			RANK	PASS	RANK		YDS.
YEAR	TEAM	G	ATT	YDS	AVG	AV RUSH	YDS	PASS YDS	SACKS	LOST
1991	Miami	12	379	1352	3.6	21	4077	4	28	188
1992	Miami	16	407	1525	3.7	20	4148	2	28	173
1993	Miami	16	419	1459	3.5	26	4564	1	30	211
	4 YR TOTALS	58								

Dwight Hollier   No. 50/LB

Full name: Dwight Leon Hollier
HT: 6-2   **WT:** 257
Born: 4-21-69, Hampton, VA
High school: Kecoughtan (Hampton, VA)
College: North Carolina
Hollier's 94 tackles ranked third on the Dolphins.

YEAR	TEAM	G	INT	YDS	AVG	TD	SACKS	FUM REC	TD
1992	Miami	16	---	---	---	---	1.0	2	---
1993	Miami	16	---	---	---	---	1	0	
	2 YR TOTALS	32	0	0	NA	0	1.0	3	0
1993	RANK NFL LB		47	NA	NA	NA	91	24	8
1994	PROJECTIONS	16	0	0	0	0	0	0	0

Marco Coleman   No. 90/LB

Full name: Marco Darnell Coleman
HT: 6-3   **WT:** 267
Born: 12-18-69, Dayton, OH
High school: Patterson Co-operative (Dayton)
College: Georgia Tech
Coleman notched 5.5 sacks (second on the team).

YEAR	TEAM	G	INT	YDS	AVG	TD	SACKS	FUM REC	TD
1992	Miami	16	---	---	---	---	6.0	---	---
1993	Miami	15	---	---	---	---	5.5	---	---
	2 YR TOTALS	31	0	0	NA	0	11.5	0	0
1993	RANK NFL DL		16	NA	NA	NA	43	71	NA
1994	PROJECTIONS	14	0	0	0	0	5	0	0

Gene Atkins   No. 28/S

Full name: Gene Reynard Atkins
HT: 5-11 **WT:** 200
Born: 11-26-64, Tallahassee, FL
High school: J. S. Rickards (Tallahassee, FL)
College: Florida A&M
Atkins led the Saints in '93 with 3 INTs.

YEAR	TEAM	G	INT	YDS	AVG	TD	SACKS	FUM REC	TD
1991	New Orleans	16	5	198	39.6	0	3.0	2	0
1992	New Orleans	16	3	0	0.0	0	---	1	0
1993	New Orleans	16	3	59	19.7	0	1.0	2	0
7 YR TOTALS		107	21	324	15.4	0	7.0	6	0
1993 RANK NFL DB			33	31	32	27	13	10	14
1994 PROJECTIONS		16	3	64	21.3	0	1	2	0

Michael Stewart   No. 35/CB

Full name: Michael Anthony Stewart
HT: 5-11 **WT:** 195
Born: 7-12-65, Atascadero, CA
High school: Bakersfield (CA)
College: Fresno State
Stewart's 74 tackles ranked fourth on the Rams.

YEAR	TEAM	G	INT	YDS	AVG	TD	SACKS	FUM REC	TD
1991	LA Rams	16	2	8	4.0	0	1.0	---	---
1992	LA Rams	11	---	---	---	---	2.0	1	---
1993	LA Rams	16	1	30	30.0	0	1.0	---	---
3 YR TOTALS		16	3	38	12.7	0	4.0	1	0
1993 RANK NFL DB			95	64	17	27	13	94	NA
1994 PROJECTIONS		16	1	51	51.0	0	0	0	0

Jim Arnold   No. 6/P

Full name: James Edward Arnold
HT: 6-3 **WT:** 235
Born: 1-31-61, Dalton, GA
High school: Dalton (GA)
College: Vanderbilt
In '93, Arnold's 44.5 yards/punt led the NFC.

YEAR	TEAM	G	NO	YARDS	LONG	AVG	BLK	IN20
1990	Detroit	16	63	2560	NA	40.6	0	NA
1991	Detroit	16	75	3092	63	41.2	0	27
1992	Detroit	16	65	2846	71	43.8	1	12
1993	Detroit	16	72	3207	68	44.5	0	15
11 YR TOTALS		64	275	11705	71	42.6	1	54
1993 RANK NFL			19	12	5	5	7	23
1994 PROJECTIONS		16	74	3345	78	45.2	0	16

New England
PATRIOTS

1994 Scouting Report

Offense

The Patriot offense improved to twelfth in the NFL in 1993 with 5,065 total yards gained, behind QB Drew Bledsoe, the first pick in the 1993 draft, and new coach Bill Parcells. The passing game should continue to improve in '94. Bledsoe has skilled targets in WRs Vincent Brisby, Michael Timpson, and Ray Crittenden and TE Ben Coates (New England's leading receiver). RB Leonard Russell became the first Pats RB to break 1,000 yards since 1989. He's talking holdout, but ex-Charger Marion Butts gives New England insurance at RB. On the OL, T Bruce Armstrong is a two-time Pro Bowler.

Defense

The '93 Patriots surrendered 1,951 rushing yards (twenty-second in the league). But New England started out allowing 185 yards per game, and cut that to less than 85 yards by season's end. The DL is average, and features DE Mike Pitts and NT Mike Goad. The Pats will miss retired LB Andre Tippett, but LB Vincent Brown led the team in tackles, and top pick Willie McGinest could make an immediate impact. The secondary, led by CB Maurice Hurst, allowed just 2,845 passing yards (fourth in the NFL), and the addition of S Myron Guyton and DB Ricky Reynolds should make the defensive backfield even stronger.

Special Teams

New England's kicking game should be more consistent with a full year from veteran Matt Bahr. New England took the top-rated punter in the draft, Pat O'Neill, but Mike Saxon had a good year in '93, putting 25 punts inside the 20 (second best in the league). Ray Crittenden handles kick returns, averaging a strong 20.8 yards per return.

1994 Prospects

The Patriots closed '93 strong, winning their last 4 games as Parcells' coaching began to take hold. Remember, this is a young team and they should continue to improve. If the draft picks and the free agents contribute, New England could hit .500 for the year. If the defense figures out how to stop the run consistently and Bledsoe continues to mature, they have an outside shot at the playoffs. That's much more likely for '95, though.

Team Directory

President/CEO: Robert K. Kraft

VP/Owner's representative: Jonathan A. Kraft

VP of football operations.: Patrick Forte

Director of public relations: Don Lowery

1993 Review			**1994 Schedule**		
Sep. 5	at Buffalo	L 38-14	Sep. 4	at Miami	4:00
Sep. 12	DETROIT	L 19-16 (OT)	Sep. 11	BUFFALO	1:00
Sep. 19	SEATTLE	L 17-14	Sep. 18	at Cincinnati	1:00
Sep. 26	at N.Y. Jets	L 45-7	Sep. 25	at Detroit	4:00
Oct. 3	OPEN DATE		Oct. 2	GREEN BAY	1:00
Oct. 10	at Phoenix	W 23-21	Oct. 9	L.A. RAIDERS	4:00
Oct. 17	HOUSTON	L 28-14	Oct. 16	at N.Y. Jets	1:00
Oct. 24	at Seattle	L 10-9	Oct. 23	OPEN DATE	
Oct. 31	at Indianapolis	L 9-6	Oct. 30	MIAMI	1:00
Nov. 7	BUFFALO	L 13-10 (OT)	Nov. 6	at Cleveland	1:00
Nov. 14	OPEN DATE		Nov. 13	MINNESOTA	1:00
Nov. 21	at Miami	L 17-13	Nov. 20	SAN DIEGO	1:00
Nov. 28	N.Y. JETS	L 6-0	Nov. 27	at Indianapolis	8:00
Dec. 5	at Pittsburgh	L 17-14	Dec. 4	NEW YORK JETS	1:00
Dec. 12	CINCINNATI	W 7-2	Dec. 11	INDIANAPOLIS	1:00
Dec. 19	at Cleveland	W 20-17	Dec. 18	at Buffalo	1:00
Dec. 26	INDIANAPOLIS	W 38-0	Dec. 24	at Chicago	1:00
Jan. 2	MIAMI	W 33-27 (OT)			

1993 finish: 5-11 (3-5 home, 2-6 away), fourth in the AFC East

Team Leaders

PASSING	ATT	COM	COM%	YDS	YPA	TD	TD%	INT	INT%	RTG
Bledsoe	429	214	49.9	2494	5.81	15	3.5	15	3.5	65.0
Secules	134	75	56.0	918	6.85	2	1.5	9	6.7	54.3
Zolak	2	0	0.0	0	0.00	0	0.0	0	0.0	39.6
TEAM	566	289	51.1	3412	6.03	17	3.0	24	4.2	62.1
OPPONENTS	474	280	59.1	3087	6.51	20	4.2	13	2.7	81.1

RECEIVING	REC	YDS	AVG	TD	RUSHING	ATT	YDS	AVG	TD
Coates	53	659	12.4	8	Russell	300	1088	3.6	7
Brisby	45	626	13.9	2	Turner	50	231	4.6	0
Timpson	42	654	15.6	2	Croom	60	198	3.3	1
Turner	39	333	8.5	2	Gash	48	149	3.1	1
Russell	26	245	9.4	0	Bledsoe	32	82	2.6	0
TEAM	289	3412	11.8	17	TEAM	502	1780	3.5	9
OPPONENTS	280	3087	11.0	20	OPPONENTS	505	1951	3.9	9

INTERCEPTIONS	INT	YDS	AVG	LG	TD	SACKS	NO
Hurst	4	53	13.3	24	0	Slade	9.0
Wren	3	-7	-2.3	2	0	Tippett	8.5
Barnett	1	40	40.0	40	0	Jones	3.5
TEAM	13	122	9.4	40	0	TEAM	34.0
OPPONENTS	24	201	8.4	34	1	OPPONENTS	23.0

KICK RETURNS	NO	YDS	AV	LG	TD	PUNT RETURNS	NO	FC	YDS	AV	LG	TD
Crittenden	23	478	20.8	44	0	Brown	25	9	224	9.0	19	0
Brown	15	243	16.2	29	0	Harris	23	4	201	8.7	21	0
Harris	6	90	15.0	19	0	Crittenden	2	1	37	18.5	30	0
TEAM	47	819	17.4	44	0	TEAM	51	14	462	9.1	30	0
OPPONENTS	44	921	20.9	42	0	OPPONENTS	34	6	313	9.2	47t	1

KICKING	XPM	XPA	FGM	FGA	LG	PTS
Bahr (NE/PHI)	28	29	13	18	48	67
Sisson	15	15	14	26	40	57
TEAM	25	25	19	31	40	82
OPPONENTS	32	32	20	24	42	92

PUNTING	NO	YDS	LG	AVG	TB	BLK	RET	RYD	IN20	NAV
Saxon	73	3096	59	42.4	7	3	34	313	25	34.8
TEAM	76	3096	59	40.7	7	3	34	313	25	34.8
OPPONENTS	90	3709	58	41.2	6	0	51	462	19	34.7

FUMBLES	FUM	OFF.FUM.REC.	REC	TD	DEF.FUM.REC.	REC	TD
Bledsoe	8	Bledsoe	5	0	Tippett	4	0
Russell	4	Russell	2	0			
Secules	4	Secules	2	0			
		Turner	2	0			
TEAM	30	TEAM	19	0	TEAM	9	0
OPPONENTS	20	OPPONENTS	8	0	OPPONENTS	10	1

1994 Draft Choices

ROUND	NAME	POS	SCHOOL	OVERALL SELECTION
1	Willie McGinest	LB	Southern California	4
2	Kevin Lee	WR	Alabama	35
3	Ervin Collier	DT	Florida A&M	78
3	Joe Burch	C	Texas Southern	90
4	John Burke	TE	Virginia Tech	121
5	Pat O'Neill	P	Syracuse	135
6	Steve Hawkins	WR	Western Michigan	166
6	Max Lane	T	Navy	168
7	Jay Walker	QB	Howard	198
7	Marty Moore	LB	Kentucky	222

HISTORY

TITLES

1963	AFL East Championship
1978	AFC East Championship
1985	AFC Championship
1986	AFC East Championship

ALL-TIME TEAM RECORDS

Rushing

Most yards, game:	212	Tony Collins	9/18/83
Most yards, season:	1,458	Jim Nance	1966
Most yards, career:	5,453	Sam Cunningham	1973-1979 1981-1982

Passing

Most yards, game:	414	Tony Eason	9/21/86
Most yards, season:	3,465	Babe Parilli	1964
Most yards, career:	26,886	Steve Grogan	1975-1990

Receiving

Most catches, game:	11	Art Graham	11/20/66
		Tony Collins	11/29/87
Most catches, season:	84	Stanley Morgan	1986
Most catches, career:	534	Stanley Morgan	1977-1989

Scoring

Most points, game:	28	Gino Cappelletti	12/18/65
Most points, season:	155	Gino Cappelletti	1964
Most points, career:	1,130	Gino Cappelletti	1960-1970

COACHES

NAME	RECORD	YEARS
Lou Saban	7-12-0	1960-61
Mike Holovak	53-47-9	1961-68
Clive Rush	5-16-0	1969-70
John Mazur	9-21-0	1970-72
Phil Bengston	1-4-0	1972
Chuck Fairbanks	46-41-0	1973-78
Hank Bullough- Ron Ehrhardt*	0-1-0	1978
Ron Ehrhardt	21-27-0	1979-81
Ron Meyer	18-16-0	1983-84
Raymond Berry	51-41-0	1984-89
Rod Rust	1-15-0	1990
Dick MacPherson	8-24-0	1991-92
Bill Parcells	5-11-0	1993

* co–coaches

NEW ENGLAND PATRIOTS
1994 TRAINING CAMP ROSTER

No.	Quarterbacks		Ht.	Wt.	Born	NFL Exp.	College	How acq.	93 GP/GS
11	Bledsoe, Drew	QB	6-5	233	2-14-72	2	Washington St.	D1 '93	13/12
7	Walker, Jay	QB	6-3	230	1-24-72	R	Howard	D7a '94	
16	Zolak, Scott	QB	6-5	222	12-13-67	4	Maryland	D4 '91	3/0
	Running backs								
44	Butts, Marion	RB	6-1	248	8-1-66	6	Florida State	T-SD '94	16/16
26	Croom, Corey	RB	5-11	212	5-22-71	2	Ball State	FA '93	14/1
33	Gash, Sam	FB	5-11	224	3-7-69	3	Penn State	D8a '92	15/4
35	Leggette, Burnie	FB	6-1	243	12-5-70	2	Michigan	FA '93	7/0
32	Russell, Leonard	RB	6-2	235	11-17-69	4	Arizona State	D1a '91	16/15
31	Thomas, Blair	RB	5-10	202	10-7-67	5	Penn State	FA '94	11/6
34	Turner, Kevin	FB	6-1	224	6-12-69	3	Alabama	D3a '92	16/8
	Wide receivers								
82	Brisby, Vincent	WR	6-1	186	1-25-71	2	NE Louisiana	D2b '93	16/13
80	Brown, Troy	WR-KR	5-9	195	7-2-71	2	Marshall	D8 '93	12/0
81	Crittenden, Ray	WR	6-1	188	3-1-70	2	Virginia Tech	FA '93	16/2
19	Hawkins, Steve	WR	6-5	207	3-16-71	R	Western Michigan	D6a '94	
86	Lee, Kevin	WR	6-1	194	1-1-71	R	Alabama	D2 '94	
83	Timpson, Michael	WR	5-10	175	6-6-67	6	Penn State	D4 '89	16/7
	Tight ends								
85	Burke, John	TE	6-3	258	9-7-71	R	Virginia Tech	D4 '94	
87	Coates, Ben	TE	6-5	245	8-16-69	4	Livingstone	D5a '91	16/10
88	Griffith, Richard	TE	6-5	256	7-31-69	2	Arizona	D5a '93	3/0
	Offensive linemen								
78	Armstrong, Bruce	T	6-4	284	9-7-65	8	Louisville	D1 '87	16/16
65	Arthur, Mike	C	6-3	280	5-7-68	4	Texas A&M	W-CIN '93	13/11
60	Burch, Joe	C	6-2	278	8-8-71	R	Texas Southern	D3b '94	
69	Chung, Eugene	G	6-4	295	6-14-69	3	Virginia Tech	D1 '92	16/16
67	Gisler, Mike	G	6-4	300	8-26-69	2	Houston	FA '93	12/0
77	Harlow, Pat	T	6-6	290	3-16-69	4	Southern California	D1 '91	16/16
61	Kratch, Bob	G	6-3	288	1-6-66	6	Iowa	FA '94	16/16
68	Lane, Max	T	6-6	295	2-22-71	R	Navy	D6b '94	
70	Moore, Brandon	T	6-6	290	6-21-70	2	Duke	FA '93	16/0
	Defensive linemen								
92	Agnew, Ray	DE	6-3	272	12-9-67	5	North Carolina St.	D1a '89	16/1
91	Collier, Ervin	NT	6-3	287	5-12-71	R	Florida A&M	D3a '94	
72	Goad, Tim	NT	6-3	280	2-28-66	7	North Carolina	D4 '88	16/15
97	Jones, Aaron	DE	6-5	267	12-18-66	7	East. Kentucky	FA '93	11/1
	Jones, Mike	DE	6-4	295	8-25-69	4	North Carolina St.	FA '94	16/2
93	Pitts, Mike	DE	6-5	277	9-25-60	12	Alabama	FA '93	16/15
76	Washington, John	DE	6-4	290	2-20-63	9	Oklahoma St.	FA '93	16/13
	Linebackers								
52	Bavaro, David	LB	6-1	228	3-27-67	4	Syracuse	FA '94	12/0
59	Brown, Vincent	LB	6-2	245	1-9-65	7	Miss. Valley St.	D2 '88	16/16
54	Collins, Todd	LB	6-2	242	5-27-70	3	Carson-Newman	D3 '92	16/12
50	DeOssie, Steve	LB	6-2	248	11-22-62	11	Boston College	FA '94	15/0
55	McGinest, Willie	LB	6-4	255	12-11-71	R	Southern California	D1 '94	
45	Moore, Marty	LB	6-1	242	3-19-71	R	Kentucky	D7b '94	
95	Sabb, Dwayne	LB	6-4	248	10-9-69	3	New Hampshire	D5 '92	14/7
51	Slade, Chris	LB	6-4	232	1-30-71	2	Virginia	D2 '93	16/5
51	White, David	LB	6-2	235	2-27-70	2	Nebraska	W-BUF '93	6/0
	Defensive backs								
42	Barnett, Harlon	FS	5-11	200	1-2-67	5	Michigan State	W-CLE '93	14/12
30	Brown, Corwin	SS	6-1	192	4-25-70	2	Michigan	D4a '93	15/12
29	Guyton, Myron	SS	6-1	205	8-26-67	7	East. Kentucky	FA '94	16/16
37	Hurst, Maurice	CB	5-10	185	9-17-67	6	Southern University	D4a '89	16/16
24	Lambert, Dion	CB	6-1	185	2-12-69	3	UCLA	D4a '92	14/4
43	Lewis, Vernon	CB	5-10	192	10-27-70	2	Pittsburgh	FA '93	10/0
23	Ray, Terry	SS	6-1	205	10-12-69	3	Oklahoma	W-ATL '93	15/1
21	Reynolds, Ricky	CB	5-11	190	1-19-65	8	Washington St.	FA '94	14/13
22	Smith, Rod	CB	5-11	187	3-12-70	3	Notre Dame	D2 '92	16/9
27	Wren, Darryl	CB	6-1	188	1-25-67	2	Pittsburg St.(KS)	W-BUF '93	12/5
	Specialists								
3	Bahr, Matt	K	5-10	175	7-6-56	16	Penn State	W-PHI '93	3/0
5	O'Neill, Pat	P	6-1	195	2-9-71	R	Syracuse	D5 '94	
5	Saxon, Mike	P	6-3	202	7-10-62	10	San Diego State	FA '94	16/0
9	Sisson, Scott	K	6-0	197	7-21-71	2	Georgia Tech	D5 '93	13/0

Drew Bledsoe　No. 11/QB

HT: 6-5　**WT:** 233
Born: 2-14-72, Ellensburg, WA
High school: Walla Walla (WA)
College: Washington State

The first pick in the 1993 draft, Bledsoe set Patriot rookie records for completions (214), attempts (429), and yards (2,494). His 2,494 yards is fourth on the all-time NFL rookie list.

| YEAR | TEAM | | PASSING | | | | | | | | | | RUSHING | | |
		G	ATT	CPL	CPL%	YDS	AVG	TDS	TD%	INT	INT%	RTG	ATT	YDS	AVG
1993	New England	13	429	214	49.9	2494	5.8	15	3.5	15	3.5	65.0	32	82	2.6
1	YR TOTALS	13	429	214	49.9	2494	5.8	15	3.5	15	3.5		32	82	2.6
1993	RANK NFL QB		11	17	62	16	51	10	34	9	32	50	12	20	33

Leonard Russell　No. 32/RB

Full name: Leonard James Russell
HT: 6-2　**WT:** 235
Born: 11-17-69, Long Beach, CA
High school: Long Beach Polytechnic (CA)
College: Arizona State

Russell's 1,088 rushing yards ranked second in the AFC. He also had career highs in receptions (26) and total yards (1,333).

| YEAR | TEAM | | RUSHING | | | | | RECEIVING | | | | KICK RETURNS | | |
		G	ATT	YDS	AVG	TD	REC	YDS	AVG	TD	RET	YDS	AVG	TD
1991	New England	16	266	959	3.6	4	18	81	4.5	0	---	---	---	---
1992	New England	11	123	390	3.2	2	11	24	2.2	0	---	---	---	---
1993	New England	16	300	1088	3.6	7	26	245	9.4	0	---	---	---	---
3	YR TOTALS	43	689	2437	3.5	13	55	350	6.4	0	0	0	NA	0
1993	RANK NFL RB		2	6	76	9	36	29	27	40	65	65	65	
1994	PROJECTIONS	16	369	1381	3.7	10	33	391	11.8	0	0	0	NA	0

Marion Butts   No. 44/RB

Full name: Marion Stevenson Butts Jr.
HT: 6-1   **WT:** 248
Born: 8-1-66, Worth County, GA
High school: Worth County (Sylvester, GA)
College: NE Oklahoma A&M and Fla. State
Pro Bowl alternate Butts was obtained from
San Diego in a Draft Day trade. He led San
Diego in rushing each of the last 5 years.

		RUSHING				RECEIVING				KICK RETURNS			
YEAR	TEAM	G	ATT	YDS	AVG	TD	REC	YDS	AVG	TD	RET	YDS	AVG	TD
1989 San Diego		15	170	683	4.0	9	7	21	3.0	0	---	---	---	---
1990 San Diego		14	265	1225	4.6	8	16	117	7.3	0	---	---	---	---
1991 San Diego		16	193	834	4.3	6	10	91	9.1	1	1	0	0.0	0
1992 San Diego		15	218	809	3.7	4	9	73	8.1	0	---	---	---	---
1993 San Diego		16	185	746	4.0	4	15	105	7.0	0	---	---	---	---
5 YR TOTALS		76	1031	4297	4.2	31	57	407	7.1	1	1	0	0.0	0
1993 RANK NFL RB			21	17	47	18	59	61	77	40	65	65	65	
1994 PROJECTIONS		16	163	652	4.0	3	17	116	6.8	0	0	0	NA	0

Ray Crittenden No. 81/WR

HT: 6-1   **WT:** 188
Born: 3-1-70, Washington, DC
College: Virginia Tech
A rookie in '93, Crittenden is the Patriots'
third WR and his 18.3 yards/catch led the
team. He was also a 3-year starter on the
soccer team at Virginia Tech.

		RECEIVING				RUSHING				PUNT RETURN		
YEAR	TEAM	G	REC	YDS	AVG	TD	ATT	YDS	AVG	TD	RET	YDS	AVG
1993 New England		16	16	293	18.3	1	1	-3	-3.0	0	2	37	18.5
1 YR TOTALS		16	16	293	18.3	1	1	-3	-3.0	0	2	37	18.5
1993 RANK NFL WR			86	77	13	72	31	37	39		25	19	1

Vincent Brisby No. 82/WR

Full name: Vincent Cole Brisby
HT: 6-1   **WT:** 186
Born: 1-25-71, Lake Charles, LA
High school: Washington-Marion (L. Charles, LA)
College: Northeast Louisiana
Brisby played in all 16 Patriot games, starting 12. His 45 receptions were second on the team, and second among all NFL rookies.

YEAR	TEAM	G	RECEIVING REC	YDS	AVG	TD	RUSHING ATT	YDS	AVG	TD	PUNT RETURN RET	YDS	AVG
1993	New England	16	45	626	13.9	2	---	---	---	---	---	---	---
1	YR TOTALS	16	45	626	13.9	2	0	0	NA	0	0	0	NA
1993	RANK NFL WR		36	44	60	55	42	42	42		30	30	29

Ben Coates   No. 87/TE

Full name: Ben Terrence Coates
HT: 6-5   **WT:** 245
Born: 8-16-69, Greenwood, SC
High school: Greenwood (SC)
College: Livingstone (NC)
Coates led the team with 53 catches. His 8 TD catches were the most by a Patriots TE since Russ Francis had 8 in 1980.

YEAR	TEAM	G	RECEIVING REC	YDS	AVG	TD
1991	New England	16	10	95	9.5	1
1992	New England	16	20	171	8.6	3
1993	New England	16	53	659	12.4	8
3	YR TOTALS	48	83	925	11.1	12
1993	RANK NFL TE		7	4	14	2
1994	PROJECTIONS	16	80	1044	13.1	12

Bruce Armstrong No. 78/T

Full name: Bruce Charles Armstrong
HT: 6-4 **WT:** 284
Born: 9-7-65, Miami, FL
High school: Central (Miami)
College: Louisville
Armstrong went to the Pro Bowl in 1990 and 1991. He suffered torn knee ligaments in 1992, but started all 16 Patriot games in '93.

YEAR	TEAM	G	RUSHING ATT	YDS	AVG	RANK AV RUSH	PASS YDS	RANK PASS YDS	SACKS	YDS. LOST
1991	New England	16	433	1467	3.4	24	3442	10	63	436
1992	New England	8	419	1550	3.7	23	2492	26	65	458
1993	New England	16	502	1780	3.5	22	3412	14	23	127
7 YR TOTALS		100								

Mike Pitts No. 93/DE

Full name: Michael Pitts
HT: 6-5 **WT:** 277
Born: 9-25-60, Pell City, AL
High school: Polytechnic (Baltimore)
College: Alabama
Pitts started New England's final 15 games. His 75 tackles ranked sixth on the team.

YEAR	TEAM	G	INT	YDS	AVG	TD	SACKS	FUM REC	TD
1985	Atlanta	16	1	1	1.0	0	7.0	1	0
1986	Atlanta	16	---	---	---	---	5.5	2	1
1987	Philadelphia	12	---	---	---	---	2.0	4	0
1988	Philadelphia	16	---	---	---	---	1.5	---	---
1989	Philadelphia	16	---	---	---	---	7.0	2	0
1990	Philadelphia	4	---	---	---	---	3.0	---	---
1991	Philadelphia	16	---	---	---	---	2.0	1	0
1992	Philadelphia	11	---	---	---	---	4.0	---	---
1993	New England	16	---	---	---	---	3.0	---	---
11 YR TOTALS		153	1	1	1.0	0	47.5	13	1
1993	RANK NFL DL		16	NA	NA	NA	75	71	NA
1994	PROJECTIONS	16	0	0	0	0	1	0	0

Vincent Brown   No. 59/LB

Full name: Vincent Bernard Brown
HT: 6-2   **WT:** 245
Born: 1-9-65, Atlanta, GA
High school: W. F. George (Decatur, GA)
College: Miss. Valley St.
Brown's career-high 158 tackles led the Patriots in '93. He was named the team's Player of the Year.

YEAR	TEAM	G	INT	YDS	AVG	TD	SACKS	FUM REC	TD
1988	New England	16	---	---	---	---	---	---	---
1989	New England	14	1	-1	-1.0	0	4.0	2	0
1990	New England	16	---	---	---	---	2.5	---	---
1991	New England	16	---	---	---	---	3.0	1	0
1992	New England	13	1	49	49.0	1	0.5	2	---
1993	New England	16	1	24	24.0	0	1.0	---	---
	6 YR TOTALS	91	3	72	24.0	1	11.0	5	0
1993	RANK NFL LB		17	12	7	5	62	81	NA
1994	PROJECTIONS	16	1	21	21.0	0	0	0	0

Maurice Hurst   No. 37/CB

Full name: Maurice Roy Hurst
HT: 5-10   **WT:** 185
Born: 9-17-67, New Orleans, LA
High school: Fortier (New Orleans)
College: Southern University
Hurst led the Patriots with 4 INTs. He posted 50 solo tackles, a career high.

YEAR	TEAM	G	INT	YDS	AVG	TD	SACKS	FUM REC	TD
1989	New England	16	5	31	6.2	1	---	---	---
1990	New England	16	4	61	15.3	0	---	---	---
1991	New England	15	3	21	7.0	0	---	---	---
1992	New England	16	3	29	9.7	0	---	---	---
1993	New England	16	4	53	13.3	0	1.0	---	---
	5 YR TOTALS	79	19	195	10.3	1	1.0	0	0
1993	RANK NFL DB		21	39	57	27	13	94	NA
1994	PROJECTIONS	16	4	64	16.0	0	2	0	0

Matt Bahr   No. 3/K

Full name: Matthew David Bahr
HI: 5-10 **WI:** 175
Born: 7-6-56, Philadelphia, PA
High school: Neshaminy Langhorne (PA)
College: Penn State
Bahr joined the team near the end of 1993 after being waived by the Eagles and kicked flawlessly (5-5 FGs, 10-10 PATs).

YEAR	TEAM	G	XP	XPA	XP Pct.	FG	FGA	FG Pct.	PTS
1986	Cleveland	12	30	30	100.0	20	26	76.9	90
1987	Cleveland	3	9	10	90.0	4	5	80.0	21
1988	Cleveland	16	32	33	97.0	24	29	82.8	104
1989	Cleveland	16	40	40	100.0	16	24	66.7	88
1990	NY Giants	13	29.	30	96.7	17	23	73.9	80
1991	NY Giants	13	24	25	96.0	22	29	75.9	90
1992	NY Giants	12	29	29	100.0	16	21	76.2	77
1993	Philadelphia	11	18	19	94.7	8	13	61.5	42
1993	New England	3	10	10	100.0	5	5	100.0	25
15 YR TOTALS		203	459	471	97.5	250	348	71.8	1209
1993 RANK NFL			17	16	19	28	28	23	27

Bill Parcells   Head Coach

Full name: Duane Charles Parcells
Born: 8-22-41, Englewood, NJ
High school: River Dell (Oradell, NJ)
College: Wichita State
Parcells' 82 career regular season victories are eighth among active coaches, but no active coach has more Super Bowl wins.

YEAR	TEAM	REGULAR SEASON					POSTSEASON		
		W	L	T	PCT	FINISH	W	L	FINISH
1983	NY Giants	3	12	1	.219	5th/NFC East			
1984	NY Giants	9	7	0	.563	T2nd/NFC East			
1985	NY Giants	10	6	0	.625	T1st/NFC East	1	1	lost 1st Rnd. game to SF, 21-10
1986	NY Giants	14	2	0	.875	1st/NFC East	1	1	lost 1st Rnd. game to Chicago, 21-0
1987	NY Giants	6	9	0	.400	5th/NFC East	3	0	won Super Bowl XXI over Denver, 39-20
1988	NY Giants	10	6	0	.625	T1st/NFC East			
1989	NY Giants	12	4	0	.750	1st/NFC East	0	1	lost 1st Rnd. game to LA Rams, 19-13 (OT)
1990	NY Giants	13	3	0	.813	1st/NFC East	3	0	won Super Bowl XXV over Buffalo, 20-19
1993	New England	5	11	0	.313	4th/AFC East			
9 YR TOTALS		82	60	1	.577		8	3	

Scott Zolak   No. 16/QB

Full name: Scott David Zolak
HT: 6-5   **WT:** 222
Born: 12-13-67, Pittsburgh, PA
High school: Ringgold (Monongahela, PA)
College: Maryland
Zolak started 4 games in 1992.

YEAR	TEAM	G	PASSING										RUSHING		
			ATT	CPL	CPL%	YDS	AVG	TDS	TD%	INT	INT%	RTG	ATT	YDS	AVG
1992	New England	6	100	52	52.0	561	5.6	2	2.0	4	4.0	58.8	18	71	3.9
1993	New England	3	2	0	0.0	0	0.0	0	0.0	0	0.0	39.6	1	0	0.0
	2 YR TOTALS	9	102	52	51.0	561	5.5	2	2.0	4	3.9		19	71	3.7
1993	RANK NFL QB		72	73	73	73	73	59	59	61	61	70	62	51	51
1994	PROJECTIONS	0	0	0	NA	0	NA	0	NA	0	NA		0	0	NA

Kevin Turner   No. 34/RB

Full name: Paul Kevin Turner
HT: 6-0   **WT:** 224
Born: 6-12-69, Prattville, AL
High school: Prattville (AL)
College: Alabama
Turner had a career high in yards rushing (231).

YEAR	TEAM	G	RECEIVING			RUSHING				PUNT RETURN		
			REC	YDS	AVG	TD	ATT	YDS	AVG	TD	RET	YDS	AVG
1989	New Orleans	13	22	279	12.7	1	2	8	4.0	0	1	7	7.0
1990	New Orleans	16	21	396	18.9	4	---	---	---		---	---	---
1991	New Orleans	16	64	927	14.5	8	---	---	---		---	---	---
1992	New Orleans	2	5	43	8.6	0	---	---	---		3	10	3.3
1993	New Orleans	10	12	163	13.6	1	---	---	---		4	17	4.3
	5 YR TOTALS	57	124	1808	14.6	14	2	8	4.0	0	4	17	4.3
1993	RANK NFL WR		94	95	67	72	42	42	42		30	30	29
1994	PROJECTIONS	11	5	96	19.2	1	0	0	NA	0	0	0	NA

Bob Kratch   No. 61/G

HT: 6-3   **WT:** 288
Born: 1-6-66, Brooklyn, NY
High school: Mahwah (NJ)
College: Iowa
Kratch, a part-time starter and backup with the Giants, became the starting RG in '93.

YEAR	TEAM	G	RUSHING			RANK	PASS	RANK		SACKS	YDS.
			ATT	YDS	AVG	AV RUSH	YDS	PASS YDS			LOST
1991	NY Giants	15	487	2064	4.2	6	3025	23		36	181
1992	NY Giants	16	458	2077	4.5	4	2628	25		45	283
1993	NY Giants	16	560	2210	3.9	14	3180	22		40	245
	5 YR TOTALS	65									

Tim Goad
No. 72/NT

Full name: Timothy Ray Goad
HT: 6-3   **WT:** 280
Born: 2-28-66, Claudville, VA
High school: Patrick County (Stuart, VA)
College: North Carolina
Goad's 77 tackles tied for third on the team.

YEAR	TEAM	G	INT	YDS	AVG	TD	SACKS	FUM REC	TD
1991	New England	16	—	—	—	—	—	—	—
1992	New England	16	—	—	—	—	2.5	1	0
1993	New England	16	—	—	—	—	0.5	1	0
6 YR TOTALS		96	0	0	NA	0	8.5	3	0
1993 RANK NFL DL			16	NA	NA	NA	157	25	5
1994 PROJECTIONS		16	0	0	0	0	0	1	0

Chris Slade
No. 53/LB

Full name: Christopher Carroll Slade
HT: 6-4   **WT:** 232
Born: 1-30-71, Newport News, VA
High school: Tabb (VA)
College: Virginia
Slade was a *Football News* All-Rookie pick.

YEAR	TEAM	G	INT	YDS	AVG	TD	SACKS	FUM REC	TD
1993	New England	16	---	---	---	---	9.0	1	0
1 YR TOTALS		16	0	0	NA	0	9.0	1	0
1993 RANK NFL LB			47	NA	NA	NA	7	24	8

Myron Guyton
No. 29/S

Full name: Myron Mynard Guyton
HT: 6-1   **WT:** 205
Born: 8-26-67, Metcalf, GA
High school: Central (Thomasville, GA)
College: Pittsburgh
He had 5 or more tackles in 8 games last year.

YEAR	TEAM	G	INT	YDS	AVG	TD	SACKS	FUM REC	TD
1990	NY Giants	16	1	0	0.0	0	---	2	0
1991	NY Giants	16	---	---	---	---	---	1	0
1992	NY Giants	4	---	---	---	---	---	---	---
1993	NY Giants	16	2	34	17.0	0	---	---	---
5 YR TOTALS		68	5	61	12.2	0	0.0	0	0
1993 RANK NFL DB			34	34	53	27	43	94	NA
1994 PROJECTIONS		16	3	55	18.3	0	0	0	0

Ricky Reynolds   No. 21/CB

Full name: Derrick Scott Reynolds
HT: 5-11   **WT:** 190
Born: 1-19-65, Sacramento, CA
High school: Luther Burbank (Sacramento, CA)
College: Washington State
He's third on the Bucs' all-time list with 17 INTs.

YEAR	TEAM	G	INT	YDS	AVG	TD	SACKS	FUM REC	TD
1991	Tampa Bay	16	2	7	3.5	0	1.0	---	---
1992	Tampa Bay	16	2	0	0.0	0	1.0	2	---
1993	Tampa Bay	14	1	3	3.0	0	1.0	---	---
7 YR TOTALS		105	17	174	10.2	1	3.0	8	0
1993 RANK NFL DB			95	115	110	27	13	94	NA
1994 PROJECTIONS		14	0	0	1	0	1	0	0

Darryl Wren   No. 27/CB

HT: 6-1   **WT:** 188
Born: 1-25-67, Tulsa, OK
High school: Tulsa (OK)
College: Pittsburg St. (KS)
Wren intercepted 2 passes against Detroit. He
also led the Patriots in passes defensed with 9.

YEAR	TEAM	G	INT	YDS	AVG	TD	SACKS	FUM REC	TD
1993	New England	12	3	-7	-2.3	0	---	---	---
1 YR TOTALS		12	3	-7	-2.3	0	0.0	0	0
1993 RANK NFL DB			33	157	155	27	49	94	NA

Mike Saxon   No. 4/P

HT: 6-3   **WT:** 202
Born: 7-10-62, Arcadia, CA
High school: Arcadia (CA)
College: Pasadena City (CA) and San Diego St.
In his first year as a Patriot, Saxon's 42.4 yard
average was the fourth-highest in team history.

YEAR	TEAM	G	NO	YARDS	LONG	AVG	BLK	IN20
1990	Dallas	16	79	3413	62	43.2	0	20
1991	Dallas	16	57	2426	64	42.6	0	16
1992	Dallas	16	61	2620	58	43	0	19
1993	New England	16	73	3096	59	42.4	3	25
9 YR TOTALS		64	270	11555	64	42.8	3	80
1993 RANK NFL			16	16	22	13	15	5
1994 PROJECTIONS		16	79	3331	58	42.2	5	29

New York
JETS

1994 Scouting Report

Offense

Although he placed fourth among AFC QBs with a rating of 84.5, Boomer Esiason's arm is still a question mark—he started strong, but dropped off sharply as New York scored just 84 points in its final 8 games. The Jets aren't deep at WR, with Rob Moore the team leader in receiving yards with 843. New York looks to veteran Art Monk to replace retired Chris Burkett and departed free agent Terence Mathis. TE Johnny Mitchell could be a star of the future. RB Johnny Johnson was the team's MVP, leading the Jets in both rushing and receiving, and FB Brad Baxter is a solid all-around back who can block. T Jeff Criswell anchors a big offensive line which allowed just 21 sacks last year.

Defense

One of the most underrated in the NFL, the Jet defense gave up 4,712 total yards (eighth in the league) in '93, and only 1,473 rushing yards (fifth in the NFL). In fact, the Jets went 3 straight games without allowing a TD. The Jets gave up 3,239 passing yards (seventeenth in the NFL). DE Jeff Lageman came back from reconstructive knee surgery to post 8.5 sacks. Free agent DE Donald Evans should improve the team's weak pass rush. LBs Mo Lewis and Kyle Clifton led the team in tackles. Draft pick CB Aaron Glenn could be a great one; he's been compared to Darrell Green. He'll join veterans SS Brian Washington, S Ronnie Lott, and CB James Hasty in the Jet secondary.

Special Teams

P Louie Aguiar will be replaced in '94 by ex-Brown Brian Hansen. Cary Blanchard is an average kicker; he was 13th in the AFC with 82 kicking points. Top pick Aaron Glenn led the NCAA in punt returns, and should take over those duties for the Jets. RB Adrian Murrell is the kick returner.

1994 Prospects

Last minute collapses cost the Jets as many as 3 wins in '93. If they've matured this year, they could be exciting to watch. Although not a great football team, they might have enough talent to make a run at the playoffs if Esiason has a big year. The Colts always bedevil them, but they always play division powers Buffalo and Miami tough.

Team Directory

Chairman of the board: Leon Hess
President: Steve Gutman
VP & General manager: Dick Steinberg
Director of player personnel: Dick Haley
Director of public relations: Frank Ramos

<table>
<tr><td colspan="3">### 1993 Review</td><td colspan="2">### 1994 Schedule</td></tr>
<tr><td>Sep. 5</td><td>DENVER</td><td>L 26-20</td><td>Sep. 4   at Buffalo</td><td>4:00</td></tr>
<tr><td>Sep. 12</td><td>at Miami</td><td>W 24-14</td><td>Sep. 11   DENVER</td><td>4:00</td></tr>
<tr><td>Sep. 19</td><td>OPEN DATE</td><td></td><td>Sep. 18   at Miami</td><td>1:00</td></tr>
<tr><td>Sep. 26</td><td>NEW ENGLAND</td><td>W 45-7</td><td>Sep. 25   CHICAGO</td><td>8:00</td></tr>
<tr><td>Oct. 3</td><td>PHILADELPHIA</td><td>L 35-30</td><td>Oct. 2   at Cleveland</td><td>1:00</td></tr>
<tr><td>Oct. 10</td><td>at L.A. Raiders</td><td>L 24-20</td><td>Oct. 9   INDIANAPOLIS</td><td>1:00</td></tr>
<tr><td>Oct. 17</td><td>OPEN DATE</td><td></td><td>Oct. 16   NEW ENGLAND</td><td>1:00</td></tr>
<tr><td>Oct. 24</td><td>BUFFALO</td><td>L 19-10</td><td>Oct. 23   OPEN DATE</td><td></td></tr>
<tr><td>Oct. 31</td><td>at N.Y. Giants</td><td>W 10-6</td><td>Oct. 30   at Indianapolis</td><td>4:00</td></tr>
<tr><td>Nov. 7</td><td>MIAMI</td><td>W 27-10</td><td>Nov. 6   BUFFALO</td><td>4:00</td></tr>
<tr><td>Nov. 14</td><td>at Indianapolis</td><td>W 31-17</td><td>Nov. 13   at Green Bay</td><td>4:00</td></tr>
<tr><td>Nov. 21</td><td>CINCINNATI</td><td>W 17-12</td><td>Nov. 20   at Minnesota</td><td>4:00</td></tr>
<tr><td>Nov. 28</td><td>at New England</td><td>W 6-0</td><td>Nov. 27   MIAMI</td><td>1:00</td></tr>
<tr><td>Dec. 5</td><td>INDIANAPOLIS</td><td>L 9-6</td><td>Dec. 4   at New England</td><td>1:00</td></tr>
<tr><td>Dec. 11</td><td>Washington</td><td>W 3-0</td><td>Dec. 10   DETROIT (Sat.)</td><td>12:30</td></tr>
<tr><td>Dec. 18</td><td>DALLAS</td><td>L 28-7</td><td>Dec. 18   SAN DIEGO</td><td>1:00</td></tr>
<tr><td>Dec. 26</td><td>at Buffalo</td><td>L 16-14</td><td>Dec. 24   at Houston</td><td>4:00</td></tr>
<tr><td>Jan. 2</td><td>at Houston</td><td>L 24-0</td><td></td><td></td></tr>
</table>

1993 finish: 8-8 (3-5 home, 5-3 away), third in AFC East

Team Leaders

PASSING	ATT	COM	COM%	YDS	YPA	TD	TD%	INT	INT%	RTG
Esiason	473	288	60.9	3421	7.23	16	3.4	11	2.3	84.5
Nagle	14	6	42.9	71	5.07	0	0.0	0	0.0	58.9
Aguiar	2	0	0.0	0	0.00	0	0.0	1	50.0	0.0
TEAM	489	294	60.1	3492	7.14	16	3.3	12	2.5	82.6
OPPONENTS	497	296	59.6	3434	6.91	15	3.0	19	3.8	74.6

RECEIVING	REC	YDS	AVG	TD	RUSHING	ATT	YDS	AVG	TD
Johnson	67	641	9.6	1	Johnson	198	821	4.1	3
Moore	64	843	13.2	1	Baxter	174	559	3.2	7
Burkett	40	531	13.3	4	Thomas	59	221	3.7	1
Mitchell	39	630	16.2	6	Murrell	34	157	4.6	1
Mathis	24	352	14.7	0	Esiason	45	118	2.6	1
TEAM	294	3492	11.9	16	TEAM	521	1880	3.6	14
OPPONENTS	296	3434	11.6	15	OPPONENTS	420	1473	3.5	8

INTERCEPTIONS	INT	YDS	AVG	LG	TD	SACKS		NO
Washington, B.	6	128	21.3	62t	1	Lageman		8.5
Lott	3	35	11.7	29	0	Washington, M.		5.5
Hasty	2	22	11.0	22	0	Lewis		4.0
TEAM	19	233	12.3	62t	1	TEAM		32.0
OPPONENTS	12	310	25.8	94t	3	OPPONENTS		21.0

KICK RETURNS	NO	YDS	AV	LG	TD	PUNT RETURNS	NO	FC	YDS	AV	LG	TD
Murrell	23	342	14.9	23	0	Hicks	17	4	157	9.2	20	0
Prior	9	126	14.0	27	0	Mathis	14	8	99	7.1	16	0
Mathis	7	102	14.6	28	0							
TEAM	46	675	14.7	28	0	TEAM	31	12	256	8.3	20	0
OPPONENTS	47	911	19.4	45	0	OPPONENTS	26	12	156	6.0	36	0

KICKING	XPM	XPA	FGM	FGA	LG	PTS
Blanchard	31	31	17	26	45	82
TEAM	31	31	17	26	45	82
OPPONENTS	26	26	21	26	48	89

PUNTING	NO	YDS	LG	AVG	TB	BLK	RET	RYD	IN20	NAV
Aguiar	73	2806	71	38.4	7	0	26	156	21	34.4
TEAM	73	2806	71	38.4	7	0	26	156	21	34.4
OPPONENTS	66	2859	68	43.3	6	0	31	256	17	37.6

FUMBLES	FUM	OFF.FUM.REC.	REC	TD	DEF.FUM.REC.	REC	TD
Esiason	13	Esiason	5	0	Pickel	3	0
Johnson	5	Baxter	2	0	Clifton	2	0
Mathis	5	Johnson	2	0	Frase	2	0
		Murrell	2	0	Hasty	2	0
					Lott	2	0
TEAM	38	TEAM	20	0	TEAM	18	0
OPPONENTS	30	OPPONENTS	12	0	OPPONENTS	16	0

1994 Draft Choices

ROUND	NAME	POS	SCHOOL	OVERALL SELECTION
1	Aaron Glenn	CB	Texas A&M	12
2	Ryan Yarborough	WR	Wyoming	41
3	Lou Benfatti	DT	Penn State	94
4	Orlando Parker	WR	Troy State	117
5	Horace Morris	LB	Tennessee	152
6	Fred Lester	FB	Alabama A&M	173
7	Glenn Foley	QB	Boston College	208

HISTORY

TITLES

1968   Super Bowl Winner
1969   AFL East Championship

ALL-TIME TEAM RECORDS

Rushing

Most yards, game:	192	Freeman McNeil	9/15/85
Most yards, season:	1,331	Freeman McNeil	1985
Most yards, career:	8,074	Freeman McNeil	1981-1992

Passing

Most yards, game:	496	Joe Namath	9/24/72
Most yards, season:	4,007	Joe Namath	1967
Most yards, career:	27,057	Joe Namath	1965-1976

Receiving

Most catches, game:	17	Clark Gaines	9/21/80
Most catches, season:	93	Al Toon	1988
Most catches, career:	627	Don Maynard	1960-1972

Scoring

Most points, game:	24	Wesley Walker	9/21/86
Most points, season:	145	Jim Turner	1968
Most points, career:	1,470	Pat Leahy	1974-1991

COACHES

NAME	RECORD	YEARS
Sammy Baugh	14-14-0	1960-61
Bulldog Turner	5-9-0	1962
Weeb Ewbank	73-78-6	1963-73
Charley Winner	9-14-0	1974-75
Ken Shipp	1-4-0	1975
Lou Holtz	3-10-0	1976
Mike Holovak	0-1-0	1976
Walt Michaels	41-49-1	1977-82
Joe Walton	54-59-1	1983-89
Bruce Coslet	26-39-0	1990-93

NEW YORK JETS
1994 TRAINING CAMP ROSTER

No.	Quarterbacks		Ht.	Wt.	Born	NFL Exp.	College	How acq.	93 GP/GS
9	Blake, Jeff	QB	6-0	202	12-4-70	3	East Carolina	DO 3L	0/0
7	Esiason, Boomer	QB	6-5	220	4-17-61	11	Maryland	T-CIN '93	16/16
14	Foley, Glenn	QB	6-2	205	10-10-70	R	Boston College	D7 '94	
16	Trudeau, Jack	QB	6-3	227	9-9-62	9	Illinois	FA '94	5/5
	Running backs								
20	Anderson, Richie	RB	6-2	225	9-13-71	1	Penn State	D6 '93	0/0
30	Baxter, Brad	RB	6-1	235	5-5-67	5	Alabama State	FA '89	16/16
28	Chaffey, Pat	RB	6-1	220	4-19-67	4	Oregon State	Plan B '92	3/0
	Johnson, Anthony	RB	6-0	222	10-25-67	5	Notre Dame	FA '94	13/8
39	Johnson, Johnny	RB	6-3	220	6-11-68	5	San Jose State	T-PHO '93	15/10
35	Lester, Fred	FB	6-0	232	8-1-71	R	Alabama A&M	D6 '94	
29	Murrell, Adrian	RB	5-11	212	10-16-70	2	West Virginia	D5a '93	16/0
	Wide receivers								
82	Carpenter, Rob	WR	6-2	190	8-1-68	4	Syracuse	Plan B '92	16/0
**	Dawkins, Dale	WR	6-1	190	10-30-66	5	Miami (FL)	D9 '90	4/0
	Monk, Art	WR	6-3	210	12-5-57	15	Syracuse	FA '94	16/5
85	Moore, Rob	WR	6-3	205	9-27-68	5	Syracuse	D1 Sup '90	13/13
89	Parker, Orlando	WR-KR	5-11	190	3-7-72	R	Troy State	D4 '94	
87	Yarborough, Ryan	WR	6-2	190	4-26-71	R	Wyoming	D2 '94	
	Tight ends								
84	Baxter, Fred	TE	6-3	260	6-14-71	2	Auburn	D5 '93	7/0
86	Mitchell, Johnny	TE	6-3	241	1-20-71	3	Nebraska	D1 '92	14/14
80	Thornton, James	TE	6-2	242	2-8-65	7	Cal-State Fullerton	FA '93	13/2
	Offensive linemen								
76	Brown, James	T	6-6	321	1-3-70	2	Virginia State	W-DAL '92	13/1
**	Cadigan, Dave	G	6-4	285	4-6-65	7	Southern California	D1 '88	16/16
69	Criswell, Jeff	T	6-7	291	3-7-64	8	Graceland	FA '88	16/16
52	Dixon, Cal	C	6-4	292	10-11-69	3	Florida	D5 '92	16/0
62	Duffy, Roger	G-C	6-3	294	7-16-67	5	Penn State	D8 '90	16/1
75	Malamala, Siupeli	T	6-5	313	1-15-69	3	Washington	D3 '92	15/15
53	Sweeney, Jim	C-G	6-4	286	8-8-62	11	Pittsburgh	D2a '84	16/16
68	Ware, David	G-T	6-6	285	2-21-70	1	Virginia	D4 '93	0/0
67	White, Dwayne	G	6-2	315	2-10-67	5	Alcorn State	D7a '90	15/15
77	Willig, Matt	T	6-8	305	1-21-69	2	Southern California	FA '92	4/0
	Defensive linemen								
78	Benfatti, Lou	DT	6-4	278	3-9-71	R	Penn State	D3 '94	
60	Evans, Donald	DT-DE	6-2	282	3-14-64	7	Winston-Salem	FA '94	16/16
91	Frase, Paul	DT-DE	6-5	270	5-5-65	6	Syracuse	D6 '88	16/4
96	Gunn, Mark	DT-DE	6-5	279	7-24-68	4	Pittsburgh	D4 '91	12/0
56	Lageman, Jeff	DE	6-5	266	7-18-67	6	Virginia	D1 '89	16/16
**	Pickel, Bill	DT	6-5	265	11-5-59	12	Rutgers	Plan B '91	16/3
92	Rudolph, Coleman	DE-DT	6-4	271	10-22-70	2	Georgia Tech	D2 '93	5/0
97	Washington, Marvin	DE	6-6	272	10-22-65	6	Idaho	D6a '89	16/16
	Linebackers								
98	Barber, Kurt	LB	6-4	249	1-5-69	3	Southern California	D2 '92	13/0
50	Cadrez, Glenn	LB	6-3	245	1-20-70	3	Houston	D6a '92	16/0
59	Clifton, Kyle	LB	6-4	236	8-23-62	11	Texas Christian	D3 '84	16/16
55	Houston, Bobby	LB	6-2	245	10-26-67	4	North Carolina St.	Plan B '91	16/15
54	Jones, Marvin	LB	6-2	240	6-28-72	2	Florida State	D1 '93	9/0
57	Lewis, Mo	LB	6-3	250	10-21-69	4	Georgia	D3 '91	16/16
58	Morris, Horace	LB	6-2	230	5-29-71	R	Tennessee	D5 '94	
	Defensive backs								
33	Glenn, Aaron	CB-KR	5-9	185	9-16-72	R	Texas A&M	D1 '94	
21	Green, Victor	CB	5-9	195	12-8-69	2	Akron	FA '93	11/0
40	Hasty, James	CB	6-0	201	5-23-65	7	Washington St.	D3b '88	16/16
42	Lott, Ronnie	S	6-1	203	5-8-59	14	Southern California	FA '93	16/16
37	Prior, Anthony	CB-S	5-11	185	3-27-70	2	Washington St.	FA '93	16/0
27	Terrell, Pat	FS	6-2	210	3-18-68	5	Notre Dame	FA '94	13/3
23	Turner, Marcus	CB-S	6-0	190	1-13-66	6	UCLA	Plan B '92	16/16
48	Washington, Brian	S	6-1	210	9-10-65	6	Nebraska	W-CLE '89	16/16
	Williams, Perry	CB	6-2	203	5-12-61	12	North Carolina St.	FA '94	12/6
**	Young, Lonnie	S-CB	6-1	196	7-18-63	10	Michigan State	T-PHO '91	8/1
	Specialists								
10	Blanchard, Cary	K	6-1	225	11-5-68	3	Oklahoma St.	W NO '92	16/0
11	Hansen, Brian	P	6-4	215	10-26-60	12	Sioux Falls	FA '94	16/0

Boomer Esiason   No. 7/QB

Full name: Norman Julius Esiason
HT: 6-5   **WT:** 220
Born: 4-17-61, West Islip, NY
High school: East Islip (Islip Terrace, NY)
College: Maryland

Esiason has now gained more passing yards than any other left-handed QB in NFL history, passing Ken Stabler in '93.

YEAR	TEAM	G	PASSING											RUSHING		
			ATT	CPL	CPL%	YDS	AVG	TDS	TD%	INT	INT%	RTG	ATT	YDS	AVG
1986	Cincinnati	16	469	273	58.2	3959	8.4	24	5.1	17	3.6	87.7	44	146	3.3
1987	Cincinnati	12	440	240	54.5	3321	7.5	16	3.6	19	4.3	73.1	52	241	4.6
1988	Cincinnati	16	388	223	57.5	3572	9.2	28	7.2	14	3.6	97.4	43	248	5.8
1989	Cincinnati	16	455	258	56.7	3525	7.7	28	6.2	11	2.4	92.1	47	278	5.9
1990	Cincinnati	16	402	224	55.7	3031	7.5	24	6.0	22	5.5	77.0	49	157	3.2
1991	Cincinnati	14	413	233	56.4	2883	7.0	13	3.1	16	3.9	72.5	24	68	2.8
1992	Cincinnati	12	278	144	51.8	1407	5.1	11	4.0	15	5.4	57.0	21	66	3.1
1993	NY Jets	16	473	288	60.9	3421	7.2	16	3.4	11	2.3	84.5	45	118	2.6
10	YR TOTALS	143	3851	2185	56.7	29092	7.6	190	4.9	140	3.6	.	377	1482	3.9
1993	RANK NFL QB		6	5	18	4	20	9	35	13	45	18	6	11	32
1994	PROJECTIONS	16	506	322	63.6	3849	7.6	15	3.0	7	1.4		51	118	2.3

Brad Baxter   No. 30/RB

Full name: Herman Bradley Baxter
HT: 6-1   **WT:** 235
Born: 5-5-67, Dothan, AL
High school: Slocomb (AL)
College: Alabama State

A good blocker, Baxter started all 16 games at FB. His 7 TDs tied for tenth in the AFC; his 20 catches were a personal best.

YEAR	TEAM	G	RUSHING				RECEIVING				KICK RETURNS			
			ATT	YDS	AVG	TD	REC	YDS	AVG	TD	RET	YDS	AVG	TD
1989	NY Jets	1	---	---	---	---	---	---	---	---	---	---	---	---
1990	NY Jets	16	124	539	4.3	6	8	73	9.1	0	---	---	---	---
1991	NY Jets	16	184	666	3.6	11	12	124	10.3	0	---	---	---	---
1992	NY Jets	15	152	698	4.6	6	4	32	8.0	0	---	---	---	---
1993	NY Jets	16	174	559	3.2	7	20	158	7.9	0	---	---	---	---
5	YR TOTALS	64	634	2462	3.9	30	44	387	8.8	0	0	0	NA	0
1993	RANK NFL RB		25	33	106	9	47	48	55	40	65	65	65	
1994	PROJECTIONS	16	191	536	2.8	7	27	210	7.8	0	0	0	NA	0

Johnny Johnson No. 39/RB

HT: 6-3 **WT:** 220
Born: 6-11-68, Santa Clara, CA
High school: Santa Cruz (CA)
College: San Jose State
The team MVP, Johnson ranked second in the AFC (behind only Thurman Thomas) with 1,462 total yards from scrimmage.

YEAR	TEAM	G	RUSHING ATT	YDS	AVG	TD	RECEIVING REC	YDS	AVG	TD	KICK RETURNS RET	YDS	AVG	TD
1990	Phoenix	14	234	926	4.0	5	25	241	9.6	0	---	---	---	---
1991	Phoenix	15	196	666	3.4	4	29	225	7.8	2	---	---	---	---
1992	Phoenix	12	178	734	4.1	6	14	103	7.4	0	---	---	---	---
1993	NY Jets	15	198	821	4.1	3	67	641	9.6	1	---	---	---	---
	4 YR TOTALS	56	806	3147	3.9	18	135	1210	9.0	3	0	0	NA	0
1993	RANK NFL RB		16	13	41	21	4	3	25	13	65	65	65	
1994	PROJECTIONS	16	197	849	4.3	1	101	985	9.8	1	0	0	NA	0

Art Monk WR

HT: 6-3 **WT:** 210
Born: 12-5-57, White Plains, NY
High school: White Plains (NY)
College: Syracuse
Long-time Redskin Monk couldn't come to terms with Washington. He'll bring experience to a young Jet WR corps.

YEAR	TEAM	G	RECEIVING REC	YDS	AVG	TD	RUSHING ATT	YDS	AVG	TD	PUNT RETURN RET	YDS	AVG
1986	Washington	16	73	1068	14.6	4	4	27	6.8	0	---	---	---
1987	Washington	9	38	483	12.7	6	6	63	10.5	0	---	---	---
1988	Washington	16	72	946	13.1	5	7	46	6.6	0	---	---	---
1989	Washington	16	86	1186	13.8	8	3	8	2.7	0	---	---	---
1990	Washington	16	68	770	11.3	5	7	59	8.4	0	---	---	---
1991	Washington	16	71	1049	14.8	8	9	19	2.1	0	---	---	---
1992	Washington	16	46	644	14.0	3	6	45	7.5	0	---	---	---
1993	Washington	16	41	398	9.7	2	---	---	---	---	---	---	---
1993	Washington	16	41	398	9.7	2	---	---	---	---	---	---	---
	14 YR TOTALS	205	888	12026	13.5	65	62	333	5.4	0	0	0	NA
1993	RANK NFL WR		44	65	131	55	42	42	42		30	30	29
1994	PROJECTIONS	16	36	290	8.1	1	0	0	NA	0	0	0	NA

Rob Moore   No. 85/WR

HT: 6-3   **WT:** 205
Born: 9-27-68, New York, NY
High school: Hempstead (NY)
College: Syracuse
Moore missed 3 games due to injury, but still led the Jets with 843 receiving yards. He had 5 games with 7 catches or more. He's been plagued with knee, ankle, and foot problems.

YEAR	TEAM	G	RECEIVING				RUSHING				PUNT RETURN		
			REC	YDS	AVG	TD	ATT	YDS	AVG	TD	RET	YDS	AVG
1990	NY Jets	15	44	692	15.7	6	2	-4	-2.0	0	---	---	---
1991	NY Jets	16	70	987	14.1	5	---	---	---	---	---	---	---
1992	NY Jets	16	50	726	14.5	4	1	21	21.0	0	---	---	---
1993	NY Jets	13	64	843	13.2	1	1	-6	-6.0	0	---	---	---
	4 YR TOTALS	60	228	3248	14.2	16	4	11	2.8	0	0	0	NA
1993	RANK NFL WR		17	21	77	72	31	41	41		30	30	29
1994	PROJECTIONS	13	76	961	12.6	0	1	0	0.0	0	0	0	NA

Johnny Mitchell No. 86/TE

HT: 6-3   **WT:** 241
Born: 1-20-71, Chicago, IL
High school: Neal F. Simeon (Chicago)
College: Nebraska
Mitchell started 14 games at TE, finishing fourth on the Jets in receptions and third in receiving yards. He tallied 6 TDs in '93, vs. just 1 the year before in his rookie season.

YEAR	TEAM	G	RECEIVING			
			REC	YDS	AVG	TD
1992	NY Jets	11	16	210	13.1	1
1993	NY Jets	13	39	630	16.2	6
	2 YR TOTALS	24	55	840	15.3	7
1993	RANK NFL TE		14	5	2	3
1994	PROJECTIONS	15	68	1167	17.2	12

Jeff Criswell   No. 69/T

HT: 6-7 **WT:** 291
Born: 3-7-64, Grinnell, IA
High school: Lynnville-Sully (IA)
College: Graceland (IA)
Criswell is a 5-year starter at LT on a line that allowed just 21 sacks, best in the NFL in '93.

YEAR	TEAM	G	RUSHING ATT	YDS	AVG	RANK AV RUSH	PASS YDS	RANK PASS YDS	SACKS	YDS. LOST
1991	NY Jets	16	523	2160	4.1	8	3429	11	33	273
1992	NY Jets	14	424	1752	4.1	13	2962	23	39	283
1993	NY Jets	16	521	1880	3.6	20	3492	12	21	160
	7 YR TOTALS	96								

Jeff Lageman   No. 56/DE

Full name: Jeffrey David Lageman
HT: 6-5 **WT:** 266
Born: 7-18-67, Fairfax, VA
High school: Park View (Sterling, VA)
College: Virginia
Lageman's selection was heavily criticized by certain "draft experts" in '89, but he led the team in sacks with 8.5.

YEAR	TEAM	G	INT	YDS	AVG	TD	SACKS	FUM REC	TD
1989	NY Jets	16	---	---	---	---	4.5	---	---
1990	NY Jets	16	---	---	---	---	4.0	---	---
1991	NY Jets	16	---	---	---	---	10.0	---	---
1992	NY Jets	2	---	---	---	---	1.0	---	---
1993	NY Jets	16	1	15	15.0	0	8.5	---	---
	5 YR TOTALS	66	1	15	15.0	0	28.0	0	0
1993	RANK NFL DL		2	3	3	3	22	71	NA
1994	PROJECTIONS	16	2	23	11.5	0	9	0	0

Mo Lewis   No. 57/LB

Full name: Morris Lewis
HT: 6-3   **WT:** 250
Born: 10-21-69, Atlanta, GA
High school: J. C. Murphy (Atlanta)
College: Georgia
Lewis was AFC Defensive Player of the Month in November with 44 tackles, 5 QB pressures, 1 sack and 1 pass deflection.

YEAR	TEAM	G	INT	YDS	AVG	TD	SACKS	FUM REC	TD
1991	NY Jets	16	---	---	---	---	1.0	1	0
1992	NY Jets	16	1	1.0	1.0	0	2.0	4	---
1993	NY Jets	16	2	4.0	2.0	0	4.0	---	---
	3 YR TOTALS	48	3	5.0	1.7	0	7.0	5	0
1993	RANK NFL LB		4	34	36	5	26	81	NA
1994	PROJECTIONS	16	3	7	3	0	6	0	0

Ronnie Lott   No. 42/S

Full name: Ronald Mandel Lott
HT: 6-1   **WT:** 203
Born: 5-8-59, Albuquerque, NM
High school: Eisenhower (Rialto, CA)
College: Southern California
Defying critics who say he's lost a step, Lott was third on the Jets with 123 tackles, and forced 4 fumbles.

YEAR	TEAM	G	INT	YDS	AVG	TD	SACKS	FUM REC	TD
1985	San Francisco	16	6	68	11.3	0	1.5	2	0
1986	San Francisco	14	10	134	13.4	1	2.0	—	—
1987	San Francisco	12	5	62	12.4	0	—	2	0
1988	San Francisco	13	5	59	11.8	0	—	4	0
1989	San Francisco	11	5	34	6.8	0	—	—	—
1990	San Francisco	11	3	26	8.7	0	—	1	0
1991	LA Raiders	16	8	52	6.5	0	1.0	1	0
1992	LA Raiders	16	1	0	0.0	0	—	1	0
1993	NY Jets	16	3	35	11.7	0	1.0	2	0
	13 YR TOTALS	177	63	730	11.6	5	7.5	16	0
1993	RANK NFL DB		33	53	70	27	13	10	14
1994	PROJECTIONS	16	2	40	20.0	0	1	3	0

Cary Blanchard   No. 10/K

HT: 6-1   **WT:** 225
Born: 11-5-68, Fort Worth, TX
High school: L.D. Bell (Hurst, TX)
College: Oklahoma State
Blanchard had only 82 points and 17 FGs in his first full season. His leg strength is suspect—his longest FG in '93 was from just 45 yards.

YEAR	TEAM	G	XP	XPA	XP Pct.	FG	FGA	FG Pct.	PTS
1992	NY Jets	11	17	17	100.0	16	22	72.7	65
1993	NY Jets	16	31	31	100.0	17	26	65.4	82
	2 YR TOTALS	27	48	48	100.0	33	48	68.8	147
1993	RANK NFL		14	15	1	21	22	26	23
1994	PROJECTIONS	16	37	37	100.0	11	20	55.0	70

Pete Carroll   Head Coach

Full name: Peter Carroll
Born: 9-15-51, San Francisco, CA
College: Pacific
Carroll takes over for Bruce Coslet. The fifth youngest head coach in the NFL, he'd been interviewed for other head coaching jobs.

		REGULAR SEASON					POSTSEASON			
YEAR	TEAM	W	L	T	PCT	FINISH	W	L		FINISH
1994	NY Jets	first year in NFL								

Jack Trudeau   No. 16/QB

Full name: Jack Francis Trudeau
HT: 6-3   **WT:** 227
Born: 9-9-62, Forest Lake, MN
High school: Granada (Livermore, CA)
College: Illinois
Trudeau threw 7 INTs in 5 starts at Indianapolis.

YEAR	TEAM		PASSING										RUSHING		
		G	ATT	CPL	CPL%	YDS	AVG	TDS	TD%	INT	INT%	RTG	ATT	YDS	AVG
1991	Indianapolis	2	7	2	28.6	19	2.7	0	0.0	1	^^^^^	0.0	---	---	N/A
1992	Indianapolis	11	181	105	58.0	1271	7.0	4	2.2	8	4.4	68.6	13	6	0.5
1993	Indianapolis	5	162	85	52.5	992	6.1	2	1.2	7	4.3	57.4	5	3	0.6
8 YR TOTALS		61	1536	812	52.9	9647	6.3	41	2.7	62	4.0		91	156	1.7
1993 RANK NFL QB			34	36	54	38	41	48	58	25	22	58	47	47	47
1994 PROJECTIONS		3	123	64	52.0	737	6.0	1	0.8	5	4.1		3	0	0.0

Adrian Murrell   No. 29/RB

HT: 5-11   **WT:** 212
Born: 10-16-70, Wahiawa, HI
High school: Leilehua (HI)
College: West Virginia
Murrell was the fourth leading rusher on the team and led all Jets KRs with 342 yards.

YEAR	TEAM		RUSHING				RECEIVING				KICK RETURNS			
		G	ATT	YDS	AVG	TD	REC	YDS	AVG	TD	RET	YDS	AVG	TD
1993	NY Jets	16	34	157	4.6	1	5	12	2.4	0	23	342	14.9	0
1 YR TOTALS		16	34	157	4.6	1	5	12	2.4	0	23	342	14.9	0
1993 RANK NFL RB			87	79	30	58	92	111	120	40	8	9	43	

James Thornton   No. 80/TE

Full name: James Michael Thornton
HT: 6-2   **WT:** 242
Born: 2-8-65, Santa Rosa, CA
High school: Analy (Sebastopol, CA)
College: Cal-State Fullerton
Thornton started games 10 and 11 and had 2 TDs.

YEAR	TEAM		RECEIVING			
		G	REC	YDS	AVG	TD
1990	Chicago	16	19	254	13.4	1
1991	Chicago	16	17	278	16.4	1
1993	NY Jets	13	12	108	9.0	2
5 YR TOTALS		77	87	1167	13.4	7
1993 RANK NFL TE			39	40	45	15
1994 PROJECTIONS		15	12	28	2.3	3

Marvin Washington   No. 97/DE

Full name: Marvin Andrew Washington
HT: 6-6   **WT:** ???
Born: 10-22-65, Denver, CO
High school: Justin F. Kimball (Dallas)
College: UTEP, Hinds CC (MS) and Idaho
Washington had a team-high 24 QB pressures.

YEAR	TEAM	G	INT	YDS	AVG	TD	SACKS	FUM REC	TD
1991	NY Jets	15	---	---	---	---	6.0	---	---
1992	NY Jets	16	---	---	---	---	8.5	---	---
1993	NY Jets	16	---	---	---	---	5.5	---	---
5 YR TOTALS		79	0	0	NA	0	26.0	1	0
1993 RANK NFL DL			16	NA	NA	NA	43	71	NA
1994 PROJECTIONS		16	0	0	0	0	5	0	0

Donald Evans   No. 60/DT-DE

Full name: Donald Lee Evans
HT: 6-2   **WT:** 282
Born: 3-14-64, Raleigh, NC
High school: Athens Drive (Raleigh, NC)
College: Winston-Salem State (NC)
Evans had a career-best 6.5 sacks in '93.

YEAR	TEAM	G	INT	YDS	AVG	TD	SACKS	FUM REC	TD
1991	Pittsburgh	16	---	---	. ---	---	2.0	1	0
1992	Pittsburgh	16	---	---	---	---	3.0	2	---
1993	Pittsburgh	16	---	---	---	---	6.5	---	---
6 YR TOTALS		70	0	0	NA	0	14.5	6	0
1993 RANK NFL DL			16	NA	NA	NA	34	71	NA
1994 PROJECTIONS		16	0	0	0	0	9	0	0

Kyle Clifton   No. 59/LB

HT: 6-4   **WT:** 236
Born: 8-23-62, Onley, TX
High school: Bridgeport (TX)
College: Texas Christian
Clifton's 143 tackles were second on the team.
He's had 100 or more tackles 9 times.

YEAR	TEAM	G	INT	YDS	AVG	TD	SACKS	FUM REC	TD
1990	NY Jets	16	3	49	16.3	0	0.5	1	0
1991	NY Jets	16	1	3	3.0	0	1.0	---	---
1992	NY Jets	16	1	1	1.0	0	1.0	4	0
1993	NY Jets	16	1	3	3.0	0	1.0	2	0
10 YR TOTALS		156	12	74	6.2	0	5.5	13	0
1993 RANK NFL LB			17	36	35	5	62	9	8
1994 PROJECTIONS		16	1	0	0.0	0	1	2	0

James Hasty No. 40/CB

Full name: James Edward Hasty
HT: 6-0   **WT:** 201
Born: 5-23-65, Seattle, WA
High school: Franklin (Seattle)
College: Central Washington and Washington St.
Defensive captain Hasty has 35 total takeaways.

YEAR	TEAM	G	INT	YDS	AVG	TD	SACKS	FUM REC	TD
1990	NY Jets	16	2	0	—	0	—	3	0
1991	NY Jets	16	3	39	13.0	0	—	4	0
1992	NY Jets	16	2	18	9.0	0	—	2	0
1993	NY Jets	16	2	22	11.0	0	—	2	0
6 YR TOTALS		95	19	161	8.5	1	1.0	16	0
1993 RANK NFL DB			54	80	74	27	49	10	14
1994 PROJECTIONS		16	2	23	11.5	0	0	2	0

Brian Washington No. 48/S

Full name: Brian Wayne Washington
HT: 6-1   **WT:** 210
Born: 9-10-65, Richmond, VA
High school: Highland Springs (VA)
College: Nebraska
Washington has 299 tackles over the past 3 years.

YEAR	TEAM	G	INT	YDS	AVG	TD	SACKS	FUM REC	TD
1990	NY Jets	14	3	22	7.3	0	1.0	1	0
1991	NY Jets	16	1	0	0.0	0	2.0	1	0
1992	NY Jets	16	6	59	9.8	1	1.0	2	0
1993	NY Jets	16	6	128	21.3	1	—	1	0
5 YR TOTALS		78	19	313	16.5	3	4.5	5	0
1993 RANK NFL DB			7	5	29	2	49	37	14
1994 PROJECTIONS		16	7	184	26.3	1	0	1	0

Brian Hansen No. 11/P

HT: 6-4   **WT:** 215
Born: 10-26-60, Hawarden, IA
High school: W. Sioux CC (Hawarden, IA)
College: Sioux Falls (SD)
Hansen had 63 punts inside the 20 during his 3
years with Cleveland.

YEAR	TEAM	G	NO	YARDS	LONG	AVG	BLK	IN20
1990	New England	16	90	3752	NA	41.7	2	NA
1991	Cleveland	16	80	3397	65	42.5	0	20
1992	Cleveland	16	74	3083	73	41.7	1	28
1993	Cleveland	16	82	3632	72	44.3	2	15
9 YR TOTALS		140	689	29120	73	42.3	8	63
1993 RANK NFL Ps			8	6	5	5		23
1994 PROJECTIONS		16	87	3965	73	45.6	3	7

Pittsburgh
STEELERS

1994 Scouting Report

Offense

The Steelers ranked seventh in the NFL in 1993 with 5,235 total yards, thanks to 2,003 yards on the ground (sixth in the NFL). Neil O'Donnell had a steady year, posting a 79.5 QB rating (eighth in the AFC). His favorite targets are star TE Eric Green and WR Dwight Stone. WR Ernie Mills comes in on third down, and Charles Johnson, the first WR taken in this year's draft, should help. The running game features a great duo in RBs Barry Foster (who must come back from an injury) and Leroy Thompson. John L. Williams will replace Merril Hoge as the Steelers' big back. On the OL, C Dermontti Dawson is a past Pro Bowler.

Defense

Pittsburgh's defense was terrific in '93; the new Steel Curtain ranked third in the NFL, allowing just 4,531 total yards. They gave up 1,368 yards on the ground (third in the league) and 3,163 yards in the air (sixth in the NFL). Free agent DE Ray Seals will replace the departed Donald Evans on the DL, where he joins DE Gerald Williams. LB Kevin Greene is one of football's best pass rushers; he's posted 5 straight seasons with 10 sacks or more. Pittsburgh has other quality LBs in Greg Lloyd and Levon Kirkland. The undisputed star of the defense is CB Rod Woodson, Steelers' MVP and AP NFL Defensive Player of the Year. He gets help in the defensive backfield from S Darren Perry (10 INTs in his first 2 seasons) and SS Carnell Lake.

Special Teams

K Gary Anderson's 93.3 FG percentage was the best in the AFC, and P Mark Royals tied for second in the NFL with 28 punts inside the 20. The sure-handed Woodson returns punts and some kickoffs.

1994 Prospects

Pittsburgh is a young team with a solid defense, a good running game, and a lot of promise. If the Steelers have a weakness, it's a lack of depth at WR, but TE Green is a powerful weapon. Considering the weakened state of the AFC Central as a whole, Pittsburgh should win the division going away. They're probably not quite there yet, but smart acquisitions and no serious losses could put the Steelers in the Super Bowl within the next few years.

Team Directory
President: Daniel M. Rooney

Director of football operations.: Tom Donahoe

Director of public relations: Dan Edwards

<table>
<tr><td colspan="4">1993 Review</td><td colspan="3">1994 Schedule</td></tr>
<tr><td>Sep. 5</td><td>SAN FRANCISCO</td><td>L</td><td>24-13</td><td>Sep. 4</td><td>DALLAS</td><td>4:00</td></tr>
<tr><td>Sep. 12</td><td>at L.A. Rams</td><td>L</td><td>27-0</td><td>Sep. 11</td><td>at Cleveland</td><td>1:00</td></tr>
<tr><td>Sep. 19</td><td>CINCINNATI</td><td>W</td><td>34-7</td><td>Sep. 18</td><td>INDIANAPOLIS</td><td>1:00</td></tr>
<tr><td>Sep. 27</td><td>at Atlanta</td><td>W</td><td>45-17</td><td>Sep. 25</td><td>at Seattle</td><td>4:00</td></tr>
<tr><td>Oct. 3</td><td>OPEN DATE</td><td></td><td></td><td>Oct. 3</td><td>HOUSTON (Mon.)</td><td>9:00</td></tr>
<tr><td>Oct. 10</td><td>SAN DIEGO</td><td>W</td><td>16-3</td><td>Oct. 9</td><td>OPEN DATE</td><td></td></tr>
<tr><td>Oct. 17</td><td>NEW ORLEANS</td><td>W</td><td>37-14</td><td>Oct. 16</td><td>CINCINNATI</td><td>1:00</td></tr>
<tr><td>Oct. 24</td><td>at Cleveland</td><td>L</td><td>28-23</td><td>Oct. 23</td><td>at N.Y. Giants</td><td>1:00</td></tr>
<tr><td>Oct. 31</td><td>OPEN DATE</td><td></td><td></td><td>Oct. 30</td><td>at Arizona</td><td>8:00</td></tr>
<tr><td>Nov. 7</td><td>at Cincinnati</td><td>W</td><td>24-16</td><td>Nov. 6</td><td>at Houston</td><td>1:00</td></tr>
<tr><td>Nov. 15</td><td>BUFFALO</td><td>W</td><td>23-0</td><td>Nov. 14</td><td>BUFFALO (Mon.)</td><td>9:00</td></tr>
<tr><td>Nov. 21</td><td>at Denver</td><td>L</td><td>37-13</td><td>Nov. 20</td><td>MIAMI</td><td>1:00</td></tr>
<tr><td>Nov. 28</td><td>at Houston</td><td>L</td><td>23-3</td><td>Nov. 27</td><td>at L.A. Raiders</td><td>4:00</td></tr>
<tr><td>Dec. 5</td><td>NEW ENGLAND</td><td>W</td><td>17-14</td><td>Dec. 4</td><td>at Cincinnati</td><td>1:00</td></tr>
<tr><td>Dec. 13</td><td>at Miami</td><td>W</td><td>21-20</td><td>Dec. 11</td><td>PHILADELPHIA</td><td>1:00</td></tr>
<tr><td>Dec. 19</td><td>HOUSTON</td><td>L</td><td>26-17</td><td>Dec. 18</td><td>CLEVELAND</td><td>1:00</td></tr>
<tr><td>Dec. 26</td><td>at Seattle</td><td>L</td><td>16-6</td><td>Dec. 24</td><td>at San Diego</td><td>4:00</td></tr>
<tr><td>Jan. 2</td><td>CLEVELAND</td><td>W</td><td>16-9</td><td></td><td></td><td></td></tr>
</table>

1993 finish: 9-7 (6-2 home, 3-5 away), second in AFC Central

Team Leaders

PASSING	ATT	COM	COM%	YDS	YPA	TD	TD%	INT	INT%	RTG
O'Donnell	486	270	55.6	3208	6.60	14	2.9	7	1.4	79.5
Tomczak	54	29	53.7	398	7.37	2	3.7	5	9.3	51.3
TEAM	540	299	55.4	3606	6.68	16	3.0	12	2.2	76.7
OPPONENTS	521	277	53.2	3440	6.60	16	3.1	24	4.6	64.9

RECEIVING	REC	YDS	AVG	TD	RUSHING	ATT	YDS	AVG	TD
Green	63	942	15.0	5	Thompson	205	763	3.7	3
Stone	41	587	14.3	2	Foster	177	711	4.0	8
Graham	38	579	15.2	0	Hoge	51	249	4.9	1
Thompson	38	259	6.8	0	Stone	12	121	10.1	1
Hoge	33	247	7.5	4	O'Donnell	26	111	4.3	0
TEAM	299	3606	12.1	16	TEAM	491	2003	4.1	13
OPPONENTS	277	3440	12.4	16	OPPONENTS	399	1368	3.4	6

INTERCEPTIONS	INT	YDS	AVG	LG	TD	SACKS		NO
Woodson	8	138	17.3	63t	1	Greene		12.5
Perry	4	61	15.3	30	0	Evans		6.5
Lake	4	31	7.8	26	0	Lloyd		6.0
TEAM	24	386	16.1	78	1	TEAM		42.0
OPPONENTS	12	216	18.0	97t	2	OPPONENTS		48.0

KICK RETURNS	NO	YDS	AV	LG	TD	PUNT RETURNS	NO	FC	YDS	AV	LG	TD
Woodson	15	294	19.6	44	0	Woodson	42	10	338	8.0	39	0
Hastings	12	177	14.8	22	0	Figures	5	2	15	3.0	6	0
Stone	11	168	15.3	30	0							
TEAM	52	878	16.9	44	0	TEAM	47	12	353	7.5	39	0
OPPONENTS	54	1165	21.6	97t	1	OPPONENTS	50	16	678	13.6	91t	3

KICKING	XPM	XPA	FGM	FGA	LG	PTS
Anderson, G.	32	32	28	30	46	116
TEAM	32	32	28	30	46	116
OPPONENTS	29	30	24	29	54	101

PUNTING	NO	YDS	LG	AVG	TB	BLK	RET	RYD	IN20	NAV
Royals	89	3781	61	42.5	3	0	50	678	28	34.2
TEAM	89	3781	61	42.5	3	0	50	678	28	34.2
OPPONENTS	82	3600	58	43.9	6	0	47	353	23	38.1

FUMBLES	FUM	OFF.FUM.REC.	REC	TD	DEF.FUM.REC.	REC	TD
Thompson	7	Nine Tied With	1	0	Greene	3	0
O'Donnell	5				Figures	2	0
Foster	3				Kirkland	2	1
Green	3				Lake	2	0
TEAM	28	TEAM	9	0	TEAM	14	2
OPPONENTS	37	OPPONENTS	22	1	OPPONENTS	15	1

1994 Draft Choices

ROUND	NAME	POS	SCHOOL	OVERALL SELECTION
1	Charles Johnson	WR	Colorado	17
2	Brentson Buckner	DT	Clemson	50
3	Jason Gildon	DE	Oklahoma State	88
3	Byron Morris	RB	Texas Tech	91
4	Taase Faumui	DL	Hawaii	122
5	Myron Bell	S	Michigan State	140
5	Gary Brown	T	Georgia Tech	148
6	Jim Miller	QB	Michigan State	178
6	Eric Ravotti	LB	Penn State	180
7	Brice Abrams	FB	Michigan State	209

HISTORY

TITLES

1972	AFC Central Championship
1974	Super Bowl Winner
1975	Super Bowl Winner
1976	AFC Central Championship
1977	AFC Central Championship
1978	Super Bowl Winner
1979	Super Bowl Winner
1983	AFC Central Championship
1984	AFC Central Championship
1992	AFC Central Championship

ALL-TIME TEAM RECORDS

Rushing

Most yards, game:	218	John Fuqua	12/20/70
Most yards, season:	1,690	Barry Foster	1992
Most yards, career:	11,950	Franco Harris	1972-1983

Passing

Most yards, game:	409	Bobby Layne	12/3/58
Most yards, season:	3,724	Terry Bradshaw	1979
Most yards, career:	27,989	Terry Bradshaw	1970-1983

Receiving

Most catches, game:	12	J. R. Wilburn	10/22/67
Most catches, season:	80	John Stallworth	1984
Most catches, career:	537	John Stallworth	1974-1987

Scoring

Most points, game:	24	Ray Mathews	10/17/54
		Roy Jefferson	11/3/68
Most points, season:	139	Gary Anderson	1985
Most points, career:	1,239	Gary Anderson	1982-1992

COACHES

NAME	RECORD	YEARS	NAME	RECORD	YEARS
Forrest Dowds	3-6-2	1933	Aldo Donelli	0-5-0	1941
Luby DiMelio	2-10-0	1934	Jim Leonard	2-8-0	1945
Joe Bach	21-27-0	1935-36,	Jock Sutherland	13-10-1	1946-47
		1952-53	Johnny Michelosen	20-26-2	1948-51
John McNalty	6-19-0	1937-39	Raymond Parker	51-47-6	1957-64
Walt Kesling	30-55-5	1939-40,	Mike Nixon	2-12-0	1965
		1941-44,	Bill Austin	11-28-3	1966-68
		1954-56	Chuck Noll	209-156-1	1969-91
Bert Bell	0-2-0	1941	Bill Cowher	20-14-0	1992-93

PITTSBURGH STEELERS
1994 TRAINING CAMP ROSTER

No.	Quarterbacks		Ht.	Wt.	Born	NFL Exp.	College	How acq.	93 GP/GS
16	Miller, Jim	QB	6-2	220		R	Michigan State	D4a '11	
14	O'Donnell, Neil	QB	6-3	230	7-3-66	5	Maryland	D3a '90	16/15
18	Tomczak, Mike	QB	6-1	207	10-23-62	10	Ohio State	FA '93	7/1
	Running backs								
49	Abrams, Brice	FB	6-1	258		R	Michigan State	D7 '94	
42	Cuthbert, Randy	RB	6-3	226	1-16-70	2	Duke	FA '93	10/0
29	Foster, Barry	RB	5-10	214	12-8-68	5	Arkansas	D5 '90	9/9
30	Jones, Victor	FB	5-8	220	12-5-67	5	Louisiana State	FA '93	16/0
33	Morris, Byron	RB	6-0	235		R	Texas Tech	D3b '94	
34	Thompson, Leroy	RB	5-11	221	2-3-69	4	Penn State	D6 '91	15/6
22	Williams, John L.	FB	5-11	231	11-23-64	9	Florida	FA '94	16/9
	Wide receivers								
80	Davenport, Charles	WR	6-3	210	11-22-68	3	North Carolina St.	D4 '92	16/0
88	Hastings, Andre	WR	6-0	185	11-7-70	2	Georgia	D3 '93	6/0
81	Johnson, Charles	WR	6-0	189		R	Colorado	D1 '94	
89	Mills, Ernie	WR	5-11	187	10-28-68	4	Florida	D3 '91	14/5
20	Stone, Dwight	WR-RB	6-0	189	1-28-64	8	Middle Tenn. St.	FA '87	16/15
82	Thigpen, Yancey	WR	6-1	208	8-15-69	3	Winston-Salem	FA '92	12/0
	Tight ends								
86	Green, Eric	TE	6-5	280	6-22-67	5	Liberty	D1 '90	16/16
84	Jorden, Tim	TE	6-3	235	10-30-66	5	Indiana	FA '92	16/1
87	Keith, Craig	TE	6-3	253	4-27-71	2	Lenoir-Rhyne	D7 '93	1/0
	Offensive linemen								
68	Brown, Brentson	T	6-4	288		R	Georgia Tech	D5b '94	
63	Dawson, Dermontti	C	6-2	288	6-17-65	7	Kentucky	D2 '88	16/16
60	Gammon, Kendall	C	6-4	286	10-28-68	3	Pittsburg St.(KS)	D11 '92	16/0
77	Haselrig, Carlton	G	6-1	290	1-22-66	5	Pitt-Johnstown	D12 '89	9/4
65	Jackson, John	T	6-6	300	1-4-65	7	East. Kentucky	D10 '88	16/16
62	Kalis, Todd	G	6-5	296	5-10-65	7	Arizona State	FA '94	16/7
67	Love, Duval	G	6-3	288	6-24-63	10	UCLA	Plan B '92	16/16
66	Palelei, Siulagi	G	6-3	322	10-15-70	2	Nevada-Las Vegas	D5 '93	3/0
72	Searcy, Leon	T	6-3	304	12-21-69	3	Miami (FL)	D1 '92	16/16
69	Solomon, Ariel	C-G	6-5	290	7-16-68	4	Colorado	D10 '91	16/0
73	Strzelczyk, Justin	G-T	6-6	295	8-18-68	5	Maine	D11 '90	16/12
	Defensive linemen								
74	Buckner, Brentson	DT	6-2	305		R	Clemson	D2 '94	
78	Faumui, Taase	DL	6-3	278		R	Hawaii	D4 '94	
76	Henry, Kevin	DE	6-4	269	10-23-68	2	Mississippi St.	D3 '93	12/1
97	Seals, Ray	DE	6-3	309	6-17-65	7	None	FA '94	16/11
93	Steed, Joel	NT	6-2	295	2-17-69	3	Colorado	D3 '92	14/12
96	Sutton, Ricky	DE	6-2	282	4-27-71	2	Auburn	FA '93	7/0
98	Williams, Gerald	DE	6-3	288	9-8-63	9	Auburn	D2 '86	10/8
90	Zgonina, Jeff	DT	6-1	282	5-24-70	2	Purdue	D7 '93	5/0
	Linebackers								
50	Barnes, Reggie	LB	6-1	235	10-23-69	2	Oklahoma	FA '93	16/0
94	Brown, Chad	LB	6-2	240	7-12-70	2	Colorado	D2 '93	16/9
51	Gildon, Jason	LB	6-3	237		R	Oklahoma State	D3a '94	
57	Ravotti, Eric	LB	6-3	254		R	Penn State	D6b '94	
91	Greene, Kevin	LB	6-3	249	7-31-62	10	Auburn	FA '93	16/16
99	Kirkland, Levon	LB	6-1	250	2-17-69	3	Clemson	D2 '92	16/13
95	Lloyd, Greg	LB	6-2	225	5-26-65	8	Fort Valley State	D6 '87	15/15
56	Mack, Rico	LB	6-4	236	2-22-71	2	Appalachian St.	FA '93	8/0
**	Olsavsky, Jerry	LB	6-1	221	3-29-67	6	Pittsburgh	D10 '89	5/0
	Defensive backs								
40	Bell, Myron	S	5-11	203		R	Michigan State	D5a '94	
21	Figures, Deon	CB-PR	6-0	203	1-10-70	2	Colorado	D1 '93	15/4
28	Haller, Alan	CB	5-11	185	8-9-70	2	Michigan State	FA '93	4/0
25	Jones, Gary	S	6-2	213	11-30-67	5	Texas A&M	D9 '90	13/2
37	Lake, Carnell	SS	6-1	209	7-15-67	6	UCLA	D2 '89	14/14
39	Perry, Darren	FS	5-11	194	12-29-68	3	Penn State	D8 '92	16/16
24	Shelton, Richard	S	5-10	202	1-2-66	5	Liberty	FA '91	9/2
27	Williams, Willie	CB	5-9	185	12-26-70	2	Western Carolina	D6 '93	16/0
26	Woodson, Rod	CB-KR	6-0	202	3-10-65	8	Purdue	D1 '87	16/16
	Specialists								
1	Anderson, Gary	K	5-11	179	7-16-59	13	Syracuse	W-BUF '82	16/0
3	Royals, Mark	P	6-5	215	6-22-64	5	Appalachian St.	Plan B '92	16/0

Neil O'Donnell   No. 14/QB

Full name: Neil Kennedy O'Donnell
HT: 6-3   **WT:** 230
Born: 7-3-66, Morristown, NJ
High school: Madison-Boro (Madison, NJ)
College: Maryland

O'Donnell's 486 attempts and 270 completions broke Terry Bradshaw's Steeler records.

YEAR	TEAM	G	PASSING ATT	CPL	CPL%	YDS	AVG	TDS	TD%	INT	INT%	RTG	RUSHING ATT	YDS	AVG
1991	Pittsburgh	12	286	156	54.5	1963	6.9	11	3.8	7	2.4	78.8	18	82	4.6
1992	Pittsburgh	12	313	185	59.1	2283	7.3	13	4.2	9	2.9	83.6	27	5	0.2
1993	Pittsburgh	16	486	270	55.6	3208	6.6	14	2.9	7	1.4	79.5	26	111	4.3
	3 YR TOTALS	40	1085	611	56.3	7454	6.9	38	3.5	23	2.1		71	198	2.8
1993	RANK NFL QB		4	9	44	8	32	13	43	25	59		28	17	12
1994	PROJECTIONS	16	547	297	54.3	3438	6.3	12	2.2	4	0.7		22	164	7.5

Mike Tomczak   No. 18/QB

Full name: Michael John Tomczak
HT: 6-1   **WT:** 207
Born: 10-23-62, Calumet City, IL
High school: Thornton Fractional (IL)
College: Ohio State

Tomczak, Neil O'Donnell's backup, is 27-20 as a starter (0-1 as a Steeler).

YEAR	TEAM	G	PASSING ATT	CPL	CPL%	YDS	AVG	TDS	TD%	INT	INT%	RTG	RUSHING ATT	YDS	AVG
1986	Chicago	13	151	74	49.0	1105	7.3	2	1.3	10	6.6	50.2	23	117	5.1
1987	Chicago	12	178	97	54.5	1220	6.9	5	2.8	10	5.6	62.0	18	54	3.0
1988	Chicago	14	170	86	50.6	1310	7.7	7	4.1	6	3.5	75.4	13	40	3.1
1989	Chicago	16	306	156	51.0	2058	6.7	16	5.2	16	5.2	68.2	24	71	3.0
1990	Chicago	16	104	39	37.5	521	5.0	3	2.9	5	4.8	43.8	12	41	3.4
1991	Green Bay	12	238	128	53.8	1490	6.3	11	4.6	9	3.8	72.6	17	93	5.5
1992	Cleveland	12	211	120	56.9	1693	8.0	7	3.3	7	3.3	80.1	24	39	1.6
1993	Pittsburgh	7	54	29	53.7	398	7.4	2	3.7	5	9.3	51.3	5	-4	-0.8
	8 YR TOTALS	108	1418	731	51.6	9828	6.9	53	3.7	68	4.8		138	454	3.3
1993	RANK NFL QB		53	54	50	52	16	48	28	35	3		63	47	60	55
1994	PROJECTIONS	4	12	7	58.3	100	8.3	0	0.0	3	^^^^^^		1	0	0.0

Leroy Thompson No. 34/RB

Full name: Ulys Leroy Thompson
HT: 5-11 **WT:** 221
Born: 2-3-69, Knoxville, TN
High school: Austin-East (Knoxville, TN)
College: Penn State

Thompson 205 rushes for 763 yards were both team highs and career bests. His 38 catches were a career high.

YEAR	TEAM	RUSHING					RECEIVING				KICK RETURNS			
		G	ATT	YDS	AVG	TD	REC	YDS	AVG	TD	RET	YDS	AVG	TD
1991	Pittsburgh	13	20	60	3.0	0	14	118	8.4	0	1	8	8.0	0
1992	Pittsburgh	15	35	157	4.5	1	22	278	12.6	0	2	51	25.5	0
1993	Pittsburgh	15	205	763	3.7	3	38	259	6.8	0	4	77	19.3	0
	3 YR TOTALS	43	260	980	3.8	4	74	655	8.9	0	7	136	19.4	0
1993	RANK NFL RB		16	16	69	21	19	27	79	40	28	30	20	
1994	PROJECTIONS	16	358	1322	3.7	5	55	299	5.4	0	6	114	19.0	0

Barry Foster No. 29/RB

HT: 5-10 **WT:** 214
Born: 12-8-68, Hurst, TX
High school: Duncanville (TX)
College: Arkansas

Foster is tied for third on the all-time Steeler TD list with 21, along with Merril Hoge and Frenchy Fuqua. He must come back from an ankle injury.

YEAR	TEAM	RUSHING					RECEIVING				KICK RETURNS			
		G	ATT	YDS	AVG	TD	REC	YDS	AVG	TD	RET	YDS	AVG	TD
1990	Pittsburgh	16	36	203	5.6	1	1	2	2.0	0	3	29	9.7	(
1991	Pittsburgh	10	96	488	5.1	1	9	117	13.0	1	---	---	---	---
1992	Pittsburgh	16	390	1690	4.3	11	36	344	9.6	0	---	---	---	---
1993	Pittsburgh	9	177	711	4.0	8	27	217	8.0	1	---	---	---	---
	4 YR TOTALS	51	699	3092	4.4	21	73	680	9.3	2	3	29	9.7	(
1993	RANK NFL RB		24	19	50	6	34	35	52	13	65	65	65	
1994	PROJECTIONS	8	174	660	3.8	9	31	238	7.7	1	0	0	NA	(

John L. Williams   No. 32/FB

HT: 5-11 **WT:** 231
Born: 11-23-64, Palatka, FL
High school: Palatka (FL)
College: Florida
Ex-Seahawk Williams has had at least 58 catches in each of the past 6 seasons.

		RUSHING				RECEIVING				KICK RETURNS			
YEAR	TEAM	G	ATT	YDS	AVG	TD	REC	YDS	AVG	TD	RET	YDS	AVG	TD
1991 Seattle		16	188	741	3.9	4	61	499	8.2	1	---	---	---	---
1992 Seattle		16	114	339	3.0	1	74	556	7.5	2	---	---	---	---
1993 Seattle		16	82	371	4.5	3	58	450	7.8	1	---	---	---	---
8 YR TOTALS		123	1148	4579	4.0	17	471	4151	8.8	16	0	0	NA	0
1993 RANK NFL RB			47	46	35	21	8	8	58	13	65	65	65	
1994 PROJECTIONS		16	40	295	7.4	4	49	385	7.9	1	0	0	NA	0

Dwight Stone No. 20/WR-RB

HT: 6-0 **WT:** 189
Born: 1-28-64, Florala, AL
High school: Florala (AL) and Marion Military Institute (AL)
College: Middle Tennessee State
Stone's 41 receptions, a career high, ranked second on the team. An exceptional athlete, he runs the 40 yard dash in 4.25 seconds.

		RECEIVING				RUSHING				PUNT RETURN		
YEAR	TEAM	G	REC	YDS	AVG	TD	ATT	YDS	AVG	TD	RET	YDS	AVG
1987 Pittsburgh		14	1	22	22.0	0	17	135	7.9	0	---	---	---
1988 Pittsburgh		16	11	196	17.8	1	40	127	3.2	0	---	---	---
1989 Pittsburgh		16	7	92	13.1	0	10	53	5.3	0	---	---	---
1990 Pittsburgh		16	19	332	17.5	1	2	-6	-3.0	0	---	---	---
1991 Pittsburgh		16	32	649	20.3	5	1	2	2.0	0	---	---	---
1992 Pittsburgh		15	34	501	14.7	3	12	118	9.8	0	---	---	---
1993 Pittsburgh		16	41	587	14.3	2	12	121	10.1	1	---	---	---
7 YR TOTALS		109	145	2379	16.4	12	94	550	5.9	1	0	0	NA
1993 RANK NFL WR			44	45	57	55	1	1	7		30	30	29
1994 PROJECTIONS		16	47	645	13.7	2	14	149	10.6	2	0	0	NA

Eric Green   No. 86/TE

Full name: Bernard Eric Green
HT: 6-5   **WT:** 280
Born: 6-22-67, Savannah, GA
High school: A.E. Beach (Savannah)
College: Liberty (VA)

Green's career-high 15.0 yards per catch was fourth best among all players with at least 63 receptions.

			RECEIVING			
YEAR	TEAM	G	REC	YDS	AVG	TD
1990	Pittsburgh	13	34	387	11.4	7
1991	Pittsburgh	11	41	582	14.2	6
1992	Pittsburgh	7	14	152	10.9	2
1993	Pittsburgh	16	63	942	15.0	5
	4 YR TOTALS	47	152	2063	13.6	20
1993	RANK NFL TE		4	2	8	6
1994	PROJECTIONS	16	76	1208	15.9	4

Ray Seals   No. 97/DE

Full name: Raymond Seals
HT: 6-3   **WT:** 309
Born: 6-17-65, Syracuse, NY
High school: Henninger (Syracuse, NY)
College: None

Seals began the year as a pass-rushing substitute but started Tampa Bay's final 11 games.

YEAR	TEAM	G	INT	YDS	AVG	TD	SACKS	FUM REC	TD
1989	Tampa Bay	2	---	---	---	---	1.0	---	---
1990	TB (8)-Det (0)-Ind	8	---	---	---	---	---	---	---
1991	Tampa Bay	10	---	---	---	---	1.0	2	0
1992	Tampa Bay	11	---	---	---	---	5.0	---	---
1993	Tampa Bay	16	1	0	0.0	1	8.5	---	---
	5 YR TOTALS	47	1	0	0.0	1	15.5	2	0
1993	RANK NFL DL		2	10	10	1	22	71	NA
1994	PROJECTIONS	16	2	0	0.0	2	10	0	0

Kevin Greene   No. 91/LB

Full name: Kevin Darwin Greene
HT: 6-3   **WT:** 249
Born: 7-31-62, New York, NY
High school: South (Granite City, IL)
College: Auburn
Greene's 12.5 sacks was the third-highest total in team history and the most since Mike Merriweather's team-record 15 in 1984.

YEAR	TEAM	G	INT	YDS	AVG	TD	SACKS	FUM REC	TD
1985	LA Rams	15	—	—	—	—	—	—	—
1986	LA Rams	16	—	—	—	—	7.0	1	0
1987	LA Rams	9	1	25	25.0	1	6.5	—	—
1988	LA Rams	16	1	10	10.0	0	16.5	—	—
1989	LA Rams	16	—	—	—	—	16.5	2	0
1990	LA Rams	15	—	—	—	—	13.0	4	0
1991	LA Rams	16	—	—	—	—	3.0	—	—
1992	LA Rams	16	—	—	—	—	10.0	4	0
1993	Pittsburgh	16	—	—	—	—	12.5	3	0
	9 YR TOTALS	135	2	35	17.5	1	85.0	14	0
1993	RANK NFL LB		47	NA	NA	NA	3	4	8
1994	PROJECTIONS	16	0	0	0	0	14	3	0

Rod Woodson No. 26/CB-PR

Full name: Roderick Kevin Woodson
HT: 6-0   **WT:** 202
Born: 3-10-65, Fort Wayne, IN
High school: R. N. Snider (Fort Wayne, IN)
College: Purdue
Woodson's 8 INTs were the most by a Steeler since Mel Blount set the team record with 11 in 1975. He was the Steelers' MVP.

YEAR	TEAM	G	INT	YDS	AVG	TD	SACKS	FUM REC	TD
1987	Pittsburgh	8	1	45	45.0	1	---	2	0
1988	Pittsburgh	16	4	98	24.5	0	0.5	3	0
1989	Pittsburgh	15	3	39	13.0	0	---	4	0
1990	Pittsburgh	16	5	67	13.4	0	---	3	0
1991	Pittsburgh	15	3	72	24.0	0	1.0	2	0
1992	Pittsburgh	16	4	90	22.5	0	6.0	1	---
1993	Pittsburgh	16	8	138	17.3	1	2.0	---	---
	7 YR TOTALS	102	28	549	19.6	2	9.5	15	0
1993	RANK NFL DB		3	2	38	2	4	94	NA
1994	PROJECTIONS	16	10	170	17.0	2	1	0	0

Gary Anderson   No. 1/K

Full name: Gary Allan Anderson
HT: 5-11 **WT:** 179
Born: 7-16-59, Parys, South Africa
High school: Brettonwood (South Africa)
College: Syracuse
His 9 straight FGs in postseason play ties for the second-longest streak in playoff history (Dallas' Rafael Septien hit 15 straight).

YEAR	TEAM	G	XP	XPA	XP Pct.	FG	FGA	FG Pct.	PTS.
1985	Pittsburgh	16	40	40	100.0	33	42	78.6	139
1986	Pittsburgh	16	32	32	100.0	21	32	65.6	95
1987	Pittsburgh	12	21	21	100.0	22	27	81.5	87
1988	Pittsburgh	16	34	35	97.1	28	36	77.8	118
1989	Pittsburgh	16	28	28	100.0	21	30	70.0	91
1990	Pittsburgh	16	32	32	100.0	20	25	80.0	92
1991	Pittsburgh	16	31	31	100.0	23	33	69.7	100
1992	Pittsburgh	16	29	31	93.5	28	36	77.8	113
1993	Pittsburgh	16	32	32	100.0	28	30	93.3	116
12 YR TOTALS		181	384	388	99.0	285	366	77.9	1239
1993 RANK NFL			13	14	1	6	16	2	9
1994 PROJECTIONS		16	33	33	100.0	30	29	100.0	123

Bill Cowher   Head Coach

Full name: William Laird Cowher
Born: 5-8-57, Pittsburgh, PA
High school: Carlynton (Crafton, PA)
College: North Carolina State
Named AP NFL Coach of the Year in '92, Cowher was a LB and special teams player with the Browns ('80–82) and Eagles ('83–84).

	REGULAR SEASON					POSTSEASON		
YEAR	TEAM	W	L	T	PCT	FINISH	W	L	FINISH
1992	Pittsburgh	11	5	0	.688	1st/AFC Central	0	1	Lost 1st Rnd. to Buffalo, 24-3
1993	Pittsburgh	9	7	0	.563	2nd/AFC Central	0	1	lost wild card game to KC, 27-24 (OT)
2 YR TOTALS		20	12	0	.625		0	2	

Yancey Thigpen   No. 82/WR

Full name: Yancey Dirk Thigpen
HT: 6-1   **WT:** 208
Born: 8-15-69, Tarboro, NC
High school: SW Edgecombe (Tarboro, NC)
College: Winston-Salem (NC)
Thigpen's 9 catches in '93 were a career high.

YEAR	TEAM	G	RECEIVING REC	YDS	AVG	TD	RUSHING ATT	YDS	AVG	TD	PUNT RETURN RET	YDS	AVG
1992	Pittsburgh	4	1	2	2.0	0	---	---	---	---	---	---	---
1993	Pittsburgh	12	9	154	17.1	3	---	---	---	---	---	---	---
2 YR TOTALS		16	10	156	15.6	3	0	0	NA	0	0	0	NA
1993 RANK NFL WR			100	96	20	41	42	42	42		30	30	29
1994 PROJECTIONS		16	20	403	20.2	8	0	0	NA	0	0	0	NA

Ernie Mills   No. 89/WR

Full name: Ernest Lee Mills III
HT: 5-11   **WT:** 187
Born: 10-28-68, Dunnellon, FL
High school: Dunnellon Senior (FL)
College: Florida
Primarily a third-down receiver, Mills had 29 catches.

YEAR	TEAM	G	RECEIVING REC	YDS	AVG	TD	RUSHING ATT	YDS	AVG	TD	PUNT RETURN RET	YDS	AVG
1991	Pittsburgh	16	3	79	26.3	1	---	---	---	---	1	0	0.0
1992	Pittsburgh	16	30	383	12.8	3	1	20	20.0	0	---	---	---
1993	Pittsburgh	14	29	386	13.3	1	3	12	4.0	0	---	---	---
3 YR TOTALS		46	62	848	13.7	5	4	32	8.0	0	1	0	0.0
1993 RANK NFL WR			65	67	73	72	12	21	21		30	30	29
1994 PROJECTIONS		16	42	561	13.4	0	6	14	2.3	0	0	0	NA

Dermontti Dawson   No. 63/C

Full name: Dermontti Farra Dawson
HT: 6-2   **WT:** 288
Born: 6-17-65, Lexington, KY
High school: Bryan Station (Lexington, KY)
College: Kentucky
Dawson's 84 consecutive starts lead the Steelers.

YEAR	TEAM	G	RUSHING ATT	YDS	AVG	RANK AV RUSH	PASS YDS	RANK PASS YDS	SACKS	YDS. LOST
1991	Pittsburgh	16	394	1627	4.1	9	3313	15	45	359
1992	Pittsburgh	16	518	2156	4.2	11	3046	22	40	296
1993	Pittsburgh	16	491	2003	4.1	9	3606	10	48	374
6 YR TOTALS		88								

Greg Lloyd — No. 95/LB

Full name: Gregory Lenard Lloyd
HT: 6-2 **WT:** 225
Born: 5-26-65, Miami, FL
High school: Peach County (GA)
College: Fort Valley State (GA)
Lloyd led Pittsburgh in tackles with a career-high 111.

YEAR	TEAM	G	INT	YDS	AVG	TD	SACKS	FUM REC	TD
1991	Pittsburgh	16	1	0	0.0	0	8.0	2	0
1992	Pittsburgh	16	1	35	35.0	0	6.5	4	0
1993	Pittsburgh	15	—	—	—	—	6.0	1	0
	6 YR TOTALS	87	7	93	13.3	0	32.5	11	0
1993	RANK NFL LB		47	NA	NA	NA	16	24	8
1994	PROJECTIONS	16	0	0	0	0	6	0	0

Levon Kirkland — No. 99/LB

Full name: Lorenzo Levon Kirkland
HT: 6-1 **WT:** 250
Born: 2-17-69, Lamar, SC
High school: Lamar (SC)
College: Clemson
Kirkland was second on the team with 103 tackles.

YEAR	TEAM	G	INT	YDS	AVG	TD	SACKS	FUM REC	TD
1992	Pittsburgh	16	---	---	---	---	---	---	---
1993	Pittsburgh	16	---	---	---	---	1.0	2	1
	2 YR TOTALS	32	0	0	NA	0	1.0	2	1
1993	RANK NFL LB		47	NA	NA	NA	62	9	1

Darren Perry — No. 39/S

HT: 5-10 **WT:** 194
Born: 12-29-68, Chesapeake, VA
High school: Deep Creek (Chesapeake, VA)
College: Penn State
His 10 INTs over his first 2 years are the most by a
Steeler since Clendon Thomas' 15 in '62 and '63.

YEAR	TEAM	G	INT	YDS	AVG	TD	SACKS	FUM REC	TD
1992	Pittsburgh	16	6	69	11.5	0	—	1	0
1993	Pittsburgh	16	4	61	15.3	0	—	—	—
	2 YR TOTALS	32	10	130	13.0	0	0.0	1	0
1993	RANK NFL DB		21	28	50	27	49	94	NA
1994	PROJECTIONS	16	2	53	26.5	0	0	0	0

Gerald Williams   No. 98/DE

HT: 6-3   **WT:** 288
Born: 9-8-63, Waycross, GA
High school: Valley (AL)
College: Auburn

In his first year at DE, Williams shared the team lead with 3 blocked passes.

YEAR	TEAM	G	INT	YDS	AVG	TD	SACKS	FUM REC	TD
1990	Pittsburgh	16	—	—	—	—	6.0	—	—
1991	Pittsburgh	16	—	—	—	—	2.0	—	—
1992	Pittsburgh	10	—	—	—	—	3.0	—	—
1993	Pittsburgh	10	—	—	.—	—	1.0	—	—
8 YR TOTALS		109	0	0	NA	0	23.0	3	0
1993 RANK NFL DL			16	NA	NA	NA	122	71	NA
1994 PROJECTIONS		10	0	0	NA	0	0	0	0

Carnell Lake   No. 37/SS

Full name: Carnell Augustino Lake
HT: 6-1   **WT:** 209
Born: 7-15-67, Salt Lake City, UT
High school: Culver City (CA)
College: UCLA

Lake's 4 INTs and 6 sacks were both career highs.

YEAR	TEAM	G	INT	YDS	AVG	TD	SACKS	FUM REC	TD
1991	Pittsburgh	16	—	—	—	—	1.0	1	0
1992	Pittsburgh	16	—	—	—	—	2.0	1	0
1993	Pittsburgh	14	4	31	7.8	0	5.0	2	0
5 YR TOTALS		77	6	31	5.2	0	10.0	10	0
1993 RANK NFL DB			21	60	91	27	1	10	14
1994 PROJECTIONS		14	6	47	7.8	0	7	2	0

Mark Royals   No. 3/P

Full name: Mark Alan Royals
HT: 6-5   **WT:** 215
Born: 6-22-64, Hampton, VA
High school: Mathews (VA)
College: Appalachian State

His 3 touchbacks were the fewest by an AFC punter.

YEAR	TEAM	G	NO	YARDS	LONG	AVG	BLK	IN20
1990	Tampa Bay	16	72	2902	62	40.3	0	8
1991	Tampa Bay	16	84	3389	56	40.3	0	22
1992	Pittsburgh	16	73	3119	58	42.7	1	22
1993	Pittsburgh	16	89	3781	61	42.5	0	28
5 YR TOTALS		64	318	13191	62	41.5	1	80
1993 RANK NFL			5	4	14	26	1	2
1994 PROJECTIONS		16	97	4165	63	42.9	0	33

San Diego
CHARGERS

1994 Scouting Report

Offense

The QB controversy has been settled with John Friesz's departure—Stan Humphries is the No. 1 guy—but the Chargers figure to have trouble moving the ball in '94. Already thin at wide receiver, San Diego lost its only deep threat, Anthony Miller, to Denver as a free agent. Ex-Bronco WR Vance Johnson isn't on Miller's level. Opposing defenses will be able to play the run, where San Diego should be weaker since they traded '94's top rusher, Marion Butts. RB Ronnie Harmon (73 receptions) is a good third-down back, but lacks Butts' power, and it's too soon to tell about Natrone Means. C Courtney Hall is one of the few quality linemen remaining, after the departures of Mike Zandofsky and Mike Withycombe.

Defense

The Chargers ranked dead last in pass defense, allowing 3,752 yards in the air. But thanks to a strong DL and LB Junior Seau, a punishing tackler, the team was second in the league vs. the run (1,314 rushing yards allowed). Turnover threatens the defense's effectiveness in '94. DE Leslie O'Neal, the Chargers' all-time sack leader, will be teamed with DE Reuben Davis, who played for Phoenix last season. DE Chris Mims takes over for the departed Burt Grossman. Ex-Lion LB Dennis Gibson and former Dolphin LB David Griggs will replace departed free agents Gary Plummer and Gary Brady. The secondary is a problem area, with S Darren Carrington the lone bright spot.

Special Teams

K John Carney had 124 points in 1993, fifth-best in the NFL. The Chargers have signed inexperienced P Kent Sullivan to replace free agent John Kidd. Darren Gordon averaged an impressive 12.7 yards/punt return.

1994 Prospects

San Diego lost 10 starters during the off-season—from a team that was 8-8. Coach Bobby Ross's Chargers will have trouble this season moving the ball both on the ground and in the air, and they'll continue to have difficulty stopping the pass. That's not good news when you've got to face Denver, the Raiders, and Kansas City twice each during the season. San Diego will be lucky to equal last season's mark in '94.

Team Directory

Chairman of the board: Alex G. Spanos
Vice chairman: Dean A. Spanos
General manager: Bobby Beathard
Director of player personnel: Billy Devaney
Director of public relations: Bill Johnston

1993 Review				1994 Schedule	
Sep. 5	SEATTLE	W 18-12	Sep. 4	at Denver	8:00
Sep. 12	at Denver	L 34-17	Sep. 11	CINCINNATI	4:00
Sep. 19	HOUSTON	W 18-17	Sep. 18	at Seattle	4:00
Sep. 26	OPEN DATE		Sep. 25	at L.A. Raiders	4:00
Oct. 3	at Seattle	L 31-14	Oct. 2	OPEN DATE	
Oct. 10	at Pittsburgh	L 16-3	Oct. 9	KANSAS CITY	1:00
Oct. 17	KANSAS CITY	L 17-14	Oct. 16	at New Orleans	4:00
Oct. 24	OPEN DATE		Oct. 23	DENVER	4:00
Oct. 31	at L.A. Raiders	W 30-23	Oct. 30	SEATTLE	4:00
Nov. 7	at Minnesota	W 30-17	Nov. 6	at Atlanta	1:00
Nov. 14	CHICAGO	L 16-13	Nov. 13	at Kansas City	1:00
Nov. 21	L.A. RAIDERS	L 12-7	Nov. 20	at New England	1:00
Nov. 29	at Indianapolis	W 31-0	Nov. 27	L.A. RAMS	4:00
Dec. 5	DENVER	W 13-10	Dec. 5	L.A. RAIDERS (Mon.)	9:00
Dec. 12	GREEN BAY	L 20-13	Dec. 11	SAN FRANCISCO	4:00
Dec. 19	at Kansas City	L 28-24	Dec. 18	at N.Y. Jets	1:00
Dec. 27	MIAMI	W 45-20	Dec. 24	PITTSBURGH	4:00
Jan. 2	at Tampa Bay	W 32-17			

1993 finish: 8-8 (4-4 home, 4-4 away), fourth in AFC West

Team Leaders

PASSING	ATT	COM	COM%	YDS	YPA	TD	TD%	INT	INT%	RTG
Humphries	324	173	53.4	1981	6.11	12	3.7	10	3.1	71.5
Friesz	238	128	53.8	1402	5.89	6	2.5	4	1.7	72.8
Means	1	0	0.0	0	0.00	0	0.0	0	0.0	39.6
TEAM	563	301	53.5	3383	6.01	18	3.2	14	2.5	72.0
OPPONENTS	556	329	59.2	3958	7.12	17	3.1	22	4.0	74.8

RECEIVING	REC	YDS	AVG	TD	RUSHING	ATT	YDS	AVG	TD
Miller	84	1162	13.8	7	Butts	185	746	4.0	4
Harmon	73	671	9.2	2	Means	160	645	4.0	8
Lewis	38	463	12.2	4	Harmon	46	216	4.7	0
Jefferson	30	391	13.0	2	Bieniemy	33	135	4.1	1
Walker	21	212	10.1	1	Jefferson	5	53	10.6	0
TEAM	301	3383	11.2	18	TEAM	455	1824	4.0	14
OPPONENTS	329	3958	12.0	17	OPPONENTS	414	1314	3.2	10

INTERCEPTIONS	INT	YDS	AVG	LG	TD	SACKS	NO
Carrington	7	104	14.9	28	0	O'Neal	12.0
Frank	3	119	39.7	102t	1	Mims	7.0
Seau	2	58	29.0	42	0	Grossman	4.5
TEAM	22	319	14.5	102t	1	TEAM	32.0
OPPONENTS	14	271	19.4	68	2	OPPONENTS	32.0

KICK RETURNS	NO	YDS	AV	LG	TD	PUNT RETURNS	NO	FC	YDS	AV	LG	TD
Lewis	33	684	20.7	60	0	Gordon	31	15	395	12.7	54	0
Bieniemy	7	110	15.7	18	0	Lewis	3	2	17	5.7	7	0
Hendrickson	2	25	12.5	13	0							
TEAM	47	901	19.2	60	0	TEAM	34	17	412	12.1	54	0
OPPONENTS	64	1063	16.6	48	0	OPPONENTS	36	21	292	8.1	30	0

KICKING	XPM	XPA	FGM	FGA	LG	PTS
Carney	31	33	31	40	51	124
TEAM	31	33	31	40	51	124
OPPONENTS	30	30	26	33	54	108

PUNTING	NO	YDS	LG	AVG	TB	BLK	RET	RYD	IN20	NAV
Kidd	57	2431	67	42.6	7	0	28	243	16	35.9
Sullivan	13	541	50	41.6	0	0	6	33	3	39.1
Carney	4	155	46	38.8	0	0	2	16	1	34.8
TEAM	74	3127	67	42.3	7	0	36	292	20	36.4
OPPONENTS	72	3031	77	42.1	3	0	34	412	23	35.5

FUMBLES	FUM	OFF.FUM.REC.	REC	TD	DEF.FUM.REC.	REC	TD
Gordon	4	Lewis	2	0	Mims	2	0
Friesz	2						
Humphries	2						
TEAM	13	TEAM	7	0	TEAM	12	0
OPPONENTS	19	OPPONENTS	7	0	OPPONENTS	5	1

1994 Draft Choices

ROUND	NAME	POS	SCHOOL	OVERALL SELECTION
2	Isaac Davis	G	Arkansas	43
2	Vaughn Parker	G	UCLA	63
3	Andre Coleman	WR	Kansas State	70
3	Willie Clark	CB	Notre Dame	82
5	Aaron Laing	TE	New Mexico State	137
5	Rodney Harrison	S	Western Illinois	145
5	Darren Krein	DE	Miami (FL)	150
5	Tony Vinson	RB	Towson State	160
7	Zane Beehn	LB	Kentucky	207

HISTORY

TITLES

1960	AFL West Championship
1961	AFL West Championship
1963	AFL Championship
1964	AFL West Championship
1965	AFL West Championship
1979	AFC West Championship
1980	AFC West Championship
1981	AFC West Championship
1992	AFC West Championship

ALL-TIME TEAM RECORDS

Rushing

Most yards, game:	217	Gary Anderson	12/18/88
Most yards, season:	1,225	Marion Butts	1990
Most yards, career:	4,963	Paul Lowe	1960-1967

Passing

Most yards, game:	444	Dan Fouts	10/19/80
			12/11/82
Most yards, season:	4,802	Dan Fouts	1981
Most yards, career:	43,040	Dan Fouts	1973-1987

Receiving

Most catches, game:	15	Kellen Winslow	10/7/84
Most catches, season:	89	Kellen Winslow	1980
Most catches, career:	586	Charlie Joiner	1976-1986

Scoring

Most points, game:	30	Kellen Winslow	11/22/81
Most points, season:	124	John Carney	1993
Most points, career:	766	Rolf Benirschke	1977-1986

COACHES

NAME	RECORD	YEARS
Sid Gillman	87-57-6	1960-69, 1971
Charlie Waller	9-7-3	1969-70
Harland Svare	7-17-2	1971-73
Ron Waller	1-5-0	1973
Tommy Prothro	21-39-0	1974-78
Don Coryell	72-60-0	1978-86
Al Saunders	17-22-0	1986-88
Dan Henning	16-32-0	1989-91
Bobby Ross	20-14-0	1992-93

SAN DIEGO CHARGERS
1994 TRAINING CAMP ROSTER

No.	Quarterbacks		Ht	Wt	Born	NFL Exp.	College	How acq.	93 GP/GS
5	Gilbert, Gale	QB	6-3	210	12-20-61	9	California	FA '89	1/0
7	Green, Trent	QB	6-3	211	7-9-70	1	Indiana	D8 '93	0/0
12	Humphries, Stan	QB	6-2	223	4-14-65	6	NE Louisiana	T-WAS '92	12/10
	Running backs								
32	Bienemy, Eric	RB	5-7	198	8-15-69	4	Colorado	D2a '91	16/0
23	Dunson, Walter	RB	5-9	173	10-24-70	1	Middle Tenn. St.	D5 '93	0/0
33	Harmon, Ronnie	RB	5-11	207	5-7-64	9	Iowa	Plan B '90	16/1
34	Hendrickson, Steve	RB-LB	6-0	258	8-30-66	6	California	FA '90	16/10
20	Means, Natrone	RB	5-10	245	4-26-72	2	North Carolina	D2 '93	16/0
45	Vinson, Tony	RB	6-1	229	3-13-71	R	Towson State	D5d '94	
	Wide receivers								
85	Barnes, Johnnie	WR	6-1	180	7-21-68	3	Hampton (VA)	D9 '92	14/0
83	Coleman, Andre	WR-KR	5-8	185	1-18-71	R	Kansas State	D3a '94	
89	Johnson, Vance	WR	5-11	180	3-13-63	10	Arizona	FA '94	10/8
80	Jefferson, Shawn	WR	5-11	172	2-22-69	4	Central Florida	T-HOU '91	16/4
81	Martin, Tony	WR	6-0	180	9-5-65	5	Mesa	T-MIA '94	12/0
82	Seay, Mark	WR	6-0	175	4-11-67	2	Long Beach State	W-SF '93	1/0
	Tight ends								
15	Boles, Eric	TE	6-3	210	4-29-70	1	Cent. Washington	FA '93	0/0
84	Dyal, Mike	TE	6-2	240	5-20-66	7	Texas A&I	FA '93	10/0
46	Laing, Aaron	TE	6-3	264	7-19-71	R	New Mexico State	D5a '94	
88	May, Deems	TE	6-4	263	3-6-69	3	North Carolina	D7 '92	15/1
86	Pupunu, Alfred	TE	6-2	252	10-17-69	3	Weber State	W-KC '92	16/7
87	Young, Duane	TE	6-1	270	3-29-68	4	Michigan State	D5 '91	16/15
	Offensive linemen								
67	Brock, Stan	T	6-6	295	6-8-58	15	Colorado	FA '93	16/16
68	Cocozzo, Joe	G	6-4	300	8-7-70	2	Michigan	D3 '93	16/5
73	Davis, Isaac	G	6-3	325	4-6-72	R	Arkansas	D2a '94	
53	Hall, Courtney	C-G	6-2	281	8-26-68	6	Rice	D2 '89	16/16
74	Jonassen, Eric	T	6-5	310	8-16-68	3	Bloomsburg (PA)	D5b '92	16/2
71	Milinichik, Joe	G	6-5	300	3-30-63	9	North Carolina St.	FA '93	10/10
77	Moten, Eric	G-T	6-2	306	4-11-68	4	Michigan State	D2b '91	4/4
70	Parker, Vaughn	G-T	6-3	296	6-5-71	R	UCLA	D2b '94	
72	Swayne, Harry	T	6-5	295	2-2-65	8	Rutgers	Plan B '91	11/11
64	Whitley, Curtis	C-G	6-1	288	5-10-69	3	Clemson	D5 '92	15/0
	Defensive linemen								
93	Davis, Rueben	DT	6-5	340	5-7-65	7	North Carolina	FA '94	16/15
99	Johnson, Raylee	DE	6-3	245	6-1-70	2	Arkansas	D4a '93	9/0
97	Krein, Darren	DE	6-4	258	7-7-71	R	Miami (FL)	D5c '94	
98	Lee, Shawn	DT	6-2	280	10-24-66	7	North Alabama	FA '92	16/15
94	May, Chris	DE-DT	6-5	290	9-29-70	3	Tennessee	D1 '92	16/7
91	O'Neal, Leslie	DE	6-4	265	5-7-64	8	Oklahoma St.	D1a '86	16/16
59	Stanley, Israel	DE	6-2	250	4-21-70	1	Arizona State	FA '93	0/0
90	White, Reggie	DT	6-4	300	3-22-70	3	N. Carolina A&T	D6 '92	8/0
	Linebackers								
**	Anno, Sam	LB	6-3	240	1-26-65	8	Southern California	Plan B '92	16/0
96	Beehn, Zane	LB	6-4	252	9-28-71	R	Kentucky	D7 '94	
58	Bush, Lewis	LB	6-2	245	12-2-69	1	Washington St.	D4a '93	16/0
51	Crews, Terry	LB	6-2	245	7-30-68	3	Western Michigan	FA '93	10/0
98	Gibson, Dennis	LB	6-2	243	2-8-64	8	Iowa State	FA '94	15/15
92	Griggs, David	LB	6-3	248	2-5-67	6	Virginia	FA '89	9/0
54	Miller, Doug	LB	6-3	232	10-29-69	1	S. Dakota St.	D7 '93	8/0
55	Seau, Junior	LB	6-3	250	1-19-69	5	Southern California	D1 '90	16/16
	Defensive backs								
29	Carrington, Darren	S	6-2	200	10-10-66	6	Northern Arizona	FA '91	16/14
44	Castle, Eric	S	6-3	212	3-15-70	2	Oregon	D6 '93	5/0
31	Clark, Willie	CB	5-10	186	1-6-72	R	Notre Dame	D3b '94	
40	Fuller, James	S	6-0	208	8-5-69	3	Portland State	D8 '92	10/0
21	Gordon, Darrien	CB	5-11	182	11-14-70	2	Stanford	D1 '93	16/7
28	Harper, Dwayne	CB	5-11	174	3-29-66	7	S. Carolina St.	FA '94	14/14
37	Harrison, Rodney	S	6-0	201	12-15-72	R	Western Illinois	D5b '94	
24	Richard, Stanley	S	6-2	197	10-21-67	4	Texas	D1 '91	16/16
25	Vanhorse, Sean	CB	5-10	180	7-22-68	5	Howard	Plan B '92	15/10
	Specialists								
3	Carney, John	K	5-11	170	4-20-64	5	Notre Dame	FA '90	16/0
1	Sullivan, Kent	P	6-0	202	5-15-67	R	California Lutheran	FA '94	2/0

Stan Humphries   No. 12/QB

Full name: William Stanley Humphries
HT: 6-2   **WT:** 223
Born: 4-14-65, Shreveport, LA
High school: Southwood (Shreveport, LA)
College: LSU and Northeast Louisiana
The Chargers were 6-4 with Humphries starting, 2-4 when he was out with a shoulder injury.

YEAR	TEAM		PASSING										RUSHING		
		G	ATT	CPL	CPL%	YDS	AVG	TDS	TD%	INT	INT%	RTG	ATT	YDS	AVG
1989	Washington	2	10	5	50.0	91	9.1	1	10.0	1	^^^^^^	75.4	5	10	2.0
1990	Washington	7	156	91	58.3	1015	6.5	3	1.9	10	6.4	57.5	23	106	4.6
1992	San Diego	16	454	263	57.9	3356	7.4	16	3.5	18	4.0	76.4	28	79	2.8
1993	San Diego	12	324	173	53.4	1981	6.1	12	3.7	10	3.1	71.5	8	37	4.6
	4 YR TOTALS	37	944	532	56.4	6443	6.8	32	3.4	39	4.1		64	232	3.6
1993	RANK NFL QB		21	23	51	20	42	18	28	15	39	39	41	32	7
1994	PROJECTIONS	13	387	199	51.4	2169	5.8	15	3.9	9	2.3		0	3	NA

Natrone Means   No. 20/RB

Full name: Natrone Jermaine Means
HT: 5-10   **WT:** 245
Born: 4-26-72, Harrisburg, NC
High school: Cent. Cabarrus (Concord, NC)
College: North Carolina
With Marion Butts gone, Means, fifth among rookie RBs with 645 yards, should see more action.

YEAR	TEAM		RUSHING				RECEIVING				KICK RETURNS			
		G	ATT	YDS	AVG	TD	REC	YDS	AVG	TD	RET	YDS	AVG	TD
1993	San Diego	16	160	645	4.0	8	10	59	5.9	0	2	22	11.0	0
	1 YR TOTALS	16	160	645	4.0	8	10	59	5.9	0	2	22	11.0	0
1993	RANK NFL RB		29	26	48	6	71	79	94	40	44	51	57	

Ronnie Harmon No. 33/RB

Full name: Ronnie Keith Harmon
HT: 5-11 **WT:** 207
Born: 5-7-64, Queens, NY
High school: Bayside (Queens, NY)
College: Iowa

Top third-down back Harmon had 73 receptions, good for third among all NFL RBs.

		RUSHING				RECEIVING				KICK RETURNS			
YEAR TEAM	G	ATT	YDS	AVG	TD	REC	YDS	AVG	TD	RET	YDS	AVG	TD
1991 San Diego	16	89	544	6.1	1	59	555	9.4	1	2	25	12.5	0
1992 San Diego	16	55	235	4.3	3	79	914	11.6	1	7	98	13.7	0
1993 San Diego	16	46	216	4.7	0	73	671	9.2	2	1	18	18.0	0
8 YR TOTALS	121	500	2326	4.7	7	401	4103	10.2	16	58	1148	19.8	0
1993 RANK NFL RB		79	67	26	69	3	2	30	7	51	53	23	
1994 PROJECTIONS	16	31	125	4.0	0	74	579	7.8	3	0	0	NA	0

Nate Lewis No. 81/WR

Full name: Nathaniel Lewis
HT: 5-11 **WT:** 198
Born: 10-19-66, Moultrie, GA
High school: Colquitt County (GA)
College: NE Oklahoma A&M, Georgia, and Oregon Tech

Lewis had the AFC's longest kick return of the season: 60 yards.

		RECEIVING				RUSHING				PUNT RETURN		
YEAR TEAM	G	REC	YDS	AVG	TD	ATT	YDS	AVG	TD	RET	YDS	AVG
1990 San Diego	12	14	192	13.7	1	4	25	6.3	1	13	117	9.0
1991 San Diego	16	42	554	13.2	3	3	10	3.3	0	5	59	11.8
1992 San Diego	15	34	580	17.1	4	2	7	3.5	0	13	127	9.8
1993 San Diego	15	38	463	12.2	4	3	2	0.7	0	3	17	5.7
4 YR TOTALS	58	128	1789	14.0	12	12	44	3.7	1	34	320	9.4
1993 RANK NFL WR		51	58	100	28	12	33	34		23	24	23
1994 PROJECTIONS	16	44	469	10.7	5	3	0	0.0	0	0	0	NA

Vance Johnson No. 82/WR

Full name: Vance Edward Johnson
HT: 5-11 **WT:** 180
Born: 3-13-63, Trenton, NJ
High school: Cholla (Tucson, AZ)
College: Arizona
Johnson had 517 receiving yards in only 10 games for Denver in 1993.

YEAR	TEAM	G	RECEIVING				RUSHING				PUNT RETURN		
			REC	YDS	AVG	TD	ATT	YDS	AVG	TD	RET	YDS	AVG
1986	Denver	12	31	363	11.7	2	5	15	3.0	0	3	36	12.0
1987	Denver	11	42	684	16.3	7	1	-8	-8.0	0	1	9	9.0
1988	Denver	16	68	896	13.2	5	1	1	1.0	0	---	---	---
1989	Denver	16	76	1095	14.4	7	---	---	---	---	12	118	9.8
1990	Denver	16	54	747	13.8	3	---	---	---	---	11	92	8.4
1991	Denver	10	21	208	9.9	3	---	---	---	---	24	174	7.3
1992	Denver	11	24	294	12.3	2	---	---	---	---	---	---	---
1993	Denver	10	36	517	14.4	5	---	---	---	---	---	---	---
	9 YR TOTALS	118	403	5525	13.7	37	17	44	2.6	0	81	689	8.5
1993	RANK NFL WR		54	53	55	19	42	42	42		30	30	29
1994	PROJECTIONS	9	37	551	14.9	6	0	0	NA	0	0	0	NA

Derrick Walker   No. 89/TE

Full name: Derrick Norval Walker
HT: 6-5 **WT:** 250
Born: 6-23-67, Glenwood, IL
High school: Bloom Township (Chicago Heights, IL)
College: Michigan
Even though he missed 4 games, Walker ranked fifth on the team in receiving yardage.

YEAR	TEAM	G	RECEIVING			
			REC	YDS	AVG	TD
1991	San Diego	16	20	134	6.7	0
1992	San Diego	16	34	393	11.6	2
1993	San Diego	12	21	212	10.1	1
	4 YR TOTALS	60	98	979	10.0	4
1993	RANK NFL TE		27	26	35	22
1994	PROJECTIONS	13	22	215	9.8	1

Courtney Hall   No. 53/C

Full name: Courtney Caesar Hall
HT: 6-2   **WT:** 281
Born: 8-26-68, Los Angeles, CA
High school: Banning (Wilmington, CA)
College: Rice
Center Hall has started every game in his 5-year NFL career.

YEAR	TEAM	G	RUSHING ATT	YDS	AVG	RANK AV RUSH	PASS YDS	RANK PASS YDS	SACKS	YDS. LOST
1991	San Diego	16	464	2248	4.8	1	2983	25	35	236
1992	San Diego	16	489	1875	3.8	18	3614	6	33	268
1993	San Diego	16	455	1824	4.0	11	3383	16	32	240
	5 YR TOTALS	80								

Leslie O'Neal   No. 91/DE

Full name: Leslie Claudis O'Neal
HT: 6-4   **WT:** 265
Born: 5-7-64, Little Rock, AR
High school: Hall (Little Rock)
College: Oklahoma State
Pro Bowler O'Neal is the Chargers' all-time sack leader with 80.5 in 101 games. He's had at least 9 in each of the last 5 seasons.

YEAR	TEAM	G	INT	YDS	AVG	TD	SACKS	FUM REC	TD
1986	San Diego	13	2	22	11.0	1	12.5	2	0
1988	San Diego	9	---	---	---	---	4.0		
1989	San Diego	16	---	---	---	---	12.5	2	
1990	San Diego	16	---	---	---	---	13.5		
1991	San Diego	16	---	---	---	---	9.0	---	---
1992	San Diego	15	---	---	---	---	17.0	1	---
1993	San Diego	16	---	---	---	---	12.0	1	0
	7 YR TOTALS	101	2	22	11.0	1	80.5	6	0
1993	RANK NFL DL		16	NA	NA	NA	9	25	5
1994	PROJECTIONS	16	0	0	0	0	11	1	0

Junior Seau   No. 55/LB

Full name: Tiaina Seau Jr.
HT: 6-3   **WT:** 250
Born: 1-19-69, San Diego, CA
High school: Oceanside (San Diego)
College: Southern California

Seau was the Chargers' leading tackler in 10 games and had a team-high 19 tackles for losses.

YEAR	TEAM	G	INT	YDS	AVG	TD	SACKS	FUM REC	TD
1990	San Diego	16	---	---	---	---	1.0	---	---
1991	San Diego	16	---	---	---	---	7.0	---	---
1992	San Diego	15	2	51	25.5	0	4.5	1	0
1993	San Diego	16	---	---	---	---	---	1	0
4 YR TOTALS		63	2	51	25.5	0	12.5	2	0
1993 RANK NFL LB			47	NA	NA	NA	91	24	8
1994 PROJECTIONS		16	0	0	0	0	0	1	0

Darren Carrington   No. 29/S

Full name: Darren Russell Carrington
HT: 6-2   **WT:** 200
Born: 10-10-66, New York, NY
High school: James Monroe (Bronx, NY)
College: Pittsburgh and Northern Arizona

Carrington led San Diego with 7 INTs (fourth-best in the AFC) and 14 passes defensed.

YEAR	TEAM	G	INT	YDS	AVG	TD	SACKS	FUM REC	TD
1989	Denver	16	1	2	2.0	0	---	---	---
1990	Detroit	12	---	---	---	---	---	1	0
1991	San Diego	16	3	30	10.0	0	---	---	---
1992	San Diego	16	6	152	25.3	1	---	---	---
1993	San Diego	16	7	104	14.9	0	1.0	1	0
5 YR TOTALS		76	17	288	16.9	1	1.0	2	0
1993 RANK NFL DB			4	9	51	27	13	37	14
1994 PROJECTIONS		16	9	116	12.9	0	2	1	0

John Carney   No. 3/K

Full name: John Michael Carney
HT: 5-11 **WT:** 170
Born: 4-20-64, Hartford, CT
High school: Cardinal Newman (W. Palm Beach)
College: Notre Dame
Carney's 124 points in 1993 (fifth-best in the NFL) set a new San Diego team record.

YEAR	TEAM	G	XP	XPA	XP Pct.	FG	FGA	FG Pct.	PTS
1988	Tampa Bay	4	6	6	100.0	2	5	40.0	12
1989	Tampa Bay	1	0	0	—	0	0	—	0
1990	Rams (1)-SD (12)	13	27	28	96.4	19	21	90.5	84
1991	San Diego	16	31	31	100.0	19	29	65.5	88
1992	San Diego	16	35	35	100.0	26	32	81.3	113
1993	San Diego	16	31	33	93.9	31	40	77.5	124
	6 YR TOTALS	66	130	133	97.7	97	127	76.4	421
1993	RANK NFL		14	12	23	3	3	14	5
1994	PROJECTIONS	16	32	35	91.4	36	47	76.6	140

Bobby Ross   Head Coach

Full name: Robert Joseph Ross
Born: 12-23-36, Richmond, VA
High school: Benedectine (Richmond, VA)
College: Virginia Military Institute
No Ross-coached team has had a losing record since 1988 (his second year at Georgia Tech).

YEAR	TEAM	REGULAR SEASON W	L	T	PCT	FINISH	POSTSEASON W	L	FINISH
1992	San Diego	11	5	0	.688	1st/AFC West	1	1	lost 2nd Rnd. game to Miami, 31-0
1993	San Diego	8	8	0	.500	4th/AFC West			
	2 YR TOTALS	19	13	0	.594		1	1	

Gale Gilbert   No. 5/QB

Full name: Gale Reed Gilbert
HT: 6-3   **WT:** 210
Born: 12-20-61, Red Bluff, CA
High school: Red Bluff (CA)
College: California
Ex-Bill Gilbert has appeared in just 26 games.

YEAR	TEAM	G	ATT	CPL	CPL%	YDS	AVG	TDS	TD%	INT	INT%	RTG	ATT	YDS	AVG
				PASSING										RUSHING	
1985	Seattle	9	40	19	47.5	218	5.5	1	2.5	2	5.0	51.9	7	4	0.6
1986	Seattle	16	76	42	55.3	485	6.4	3	3.9	3	3.9	71.4	3	8	2.7
1990	Buffalo	1	15	8	53.3	106	7.1	2	13.3	2	^^^^^^	76.0	---	---	N/A
3 YR TOTALS		26	131	69	52.7	809	6.2	6	4.6	7	5.3		10	12	1.2
1994 PROJECTIONS		0	0	0	NA	0	NA	0	NA	0	NA		0	0	NA

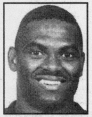

Shawn Jefferson   No. 80/WR

Full name: Vanchi LaShawn Jefferson
HT: 5-11   **WT:** 172
Born: 2-22-69, Jacksonville, FL
High school: Raines (Jacksonville, FL)
College: Central Florida
His 30 catches and 391 yards were career highs.

YEAR	TEAM	G	REC	YDS	AVG	TD	ATT	YDS	AVG	TD	RET	YDS	AVG
			RECEIVING				RUSHING				PUNT RETURN		
1991	San Diego	16	12	125	10.4	1	1	27	27.0	0	---	---	---
1992	San Diego	16	29	377	13.0	2	---	---	---	---	---	---	---
1993	San Diego	16	30	391	13.0	2	5	53	10.6	0	---	---	---
3 YR TOTALS		48	71	893	12.6	5	6	80	13.3	0	0	0	NA
1993 RANK NFL WR			63	66	81	55	6	3	5		30	30	29
1994 PROJECTIONS		16	35	465	13.3	2	9	86	9.6	0	0	0	NA

Tony Martin   No. 81/WR

Full name: Tony Derrick Martin
HT: 6-0   **WT:** 177
Born: 9-5-65, Miami, FL
High school: Miami Northwestern (FL)
College: Bishop (TX) and Mesa State (CO)
His 17.4 yards/catch in 1993 was a career-high.

YEAR	TEAM	G	REC	YDS	AVG	TD	ATT	YDS	AVG	TD	RET	YDS	AVG
			RECEIVING				RUSHING				PUNT RETURN		
1991	Miami	16	27	434	16.1	2	---	---	---	---	1	10	10.0
1992	Miami	16	33	553	16.8	2	1	-2	-2.0	0	1	0	0.0
1993	Miami	12	20	347	17.4	3	1	6	6.0	0	---	---	---
4 YR TOTALS		60	109	1722	15.8	9	3	12	4.0	0	28	150	5.4
1993 RANK NFL WR			77	73	17	41	31	26	16		30	30	29
1994 PROJECTIONS		11	17	306	18.0	4	1	9	9.0	0	0	0	NA

Alfred Pupunu   No. 86/TE

Full name: Alfred Sione Pupunu
HT: 6-2   **WT:** 252
Born: 10-17-69, Tonga
High school: South (Salt Lake City)
College: Dixie JC (UT) and Weber State
Pupunu filled in at TE and had 13 receptions.

YEAR	TEAM	G	REC	YDS	AVG	TD
1992 San Diego		15		---	---	---
1993 San Diego		16	13	142	10.9	0
2 YR TOTALS		31	13	142	10.9	0
1993 RANK NFL TE			38	35	28	46
1994 PROJECTIONS		16	26	284	10.9	0

RECEIVING

Chris Mims   No. 94/DE-DT

Full name: Christopher Eddie Mims
HT: 6-5   **WT:** 290
Born: 9-29-70, Los Angeles, CA
High school: Dorsay (Los Angeles)
College: Pierce JC (CA), Southwest CC (CA) and Tenn.
Mims will be a full-time starter in '94.

YEAR	TEAM	G	INT	YDS	AVG	TD	SACKS	FUM REC	TD
1992 San Diego		16	---	---	---	---	10.0	1	---
1993 San Diego		16	---	---	---	---	7.0	2	0
2 YR TOTALS		16	0	0	NA	0	17.0	3	0
1993 RANK NFL DL			16	NA	NA	NA	29	8	5
1994 PROJECTIONS		16	0	0	0	0	4	3	0

Dennis Gibson   No. 56/LB

Full name: Dennis Michael Gibson
HT: 6-2   **WT:** 243
Born: 2-8-64, Des Moines, IA
High school: Ankeny (IA)
College: Iowa State
Gibson had 62 tackles for the 1993 Lions.

YEAR	TEAM	G	INT	YDS	AVG	TD	SACKS	FUM REC	TD
1987 Detroit		12	1	5	5.0	0	1.0	---	---
1988 Detroit		16	---	---	---	---	0.5	1	0
1989 Detroit		6	1	10	10.0	---	---	3	0
1990 Detroit		11	---	---	---	---	---	1	0
1991 Detroit		16	---	---	---	---	---	---	---
1992 Detroit		16	---	---	---	---	---	---	---
1993 Detroit		15	1	0	0.0	0	1.0	1	0

Dwayne Harper   No. 28/CB

Full name: Dwayne Anthony Harper
HT: 5-11 **WT:** 174
Born: 3-29-66, Orangeburg, SC
High school: Orangeburg-Wilkinson (SC)
College: South Carolina St.
Harper's 67 tackles in '93 ranked sixth on Seattle.

YEAR	TEAM	G	INT	YDS	AVG	TD	SACKS	FUM REC	TD
1988	Seattle	16	---	---	---	---	1.0	1	0
1989	Seattle	16	2	15	7.5	0	---	1	0
1990	Seattle	16	3	69	23.0	0	---	---	---
1991	Seattle	16	4	84	21.0	0	---	---	---
1992	Seattle	16	3	74	24.7	0	---	1	0
1993	Seattle		1	0	0.0	0	---	1	0
6 YR TOTALS		80	13	242	18.6	0	1.0	4	0

Stanley Richard   No. 24/S

Full name: Stanley Palmer Richard
HT: 6-2 **WT:** 197
Born: 10-21-67, Miniola, TX
High school: Hawkins (TX)
College: Texas
Richard calls the plays for the Charger secondary.

YEAR	TEAM	G	INT	YDS	AVG	TD	SACKS	FUM REC	TD
1991	San Diego	15	2	5	2.5	0	---	---	---
1992	San Diego	14	3	26	8.7	0	---	1	---
1993	San Diego	16	1	-2	-2.0	0	2.0	1	0
YR TOTALS		45	6	29	4.8	0	2.0	2	0
1993	RANK NFL DB		95	156	154	27	4	37	14
1994	PROJECTIONS	16	0	0	0	0	4	1	0

Kent Sullivan   No. 1/P

Full name: Kent Allen Sullivan
HT: 6-0 **WT:** 202
Born: 5-15-67, Plymouth, IN
High school: Northridge (Middlebury, IN)
College: California Lutheran
Sullivan has limited NFL experience.

YEAR	TEAM	G	NO	YARDS	LONG	AVG	BLK	IN20
1991	Houston	1	3	106	37	35.3	0	1
1992	Kansas City	1	6	247	59	41.2	0	2
1993	Houston	1	2	73	37	36.5	0	1
1993	San Diego	2	13	541	50	41.6	0	3
3 YR TOTALS		5	24	967	59	40.3	0	7
1993	RANK NFL		32	32	32	32	31	33
1994	PROJECTIONS	3	27	1125	32	41.7	0	5

Seattle
SEAHAWKS

1994 Scouting Report

Offense

Despite QB Rick Mirer's promising debut, rushing was the team's strong suit—2,015 yards gained (fourth in the league). The passing attack generated only 2,654 yards (twenty-fifth in the NFL). Pro Bowl alternate Brian Blades and Kelvin Martin are the team's only proven wideouts. Veteran Ferrell Edmunds returns as the starting TE, but he had just 24 catches last year. Chris Warren sparked the AFC's best rushing attack, gaining 1,000 yards for the second straight year. Seattle is counting on RB Jon Vaughn, a backup in '93, to take over for the departed John L. Williams (58 catches). Seattle hopes ex-Bill Pro Bowl T Howard Ballard will compensate for departed OL Andy Heck. C Ray Donaldson is the anchor of an OL that allowed 48 sacks.

Defense

Seattle had problems defending the pass in '93. Although thirteenth against the run (1,660 rushing yards), the team was twenty-sixth in the NFL against the pass (3,653 yards). Top pick DT Sam Adams and ex-Patriot DE Brent Williams will take some of the pressure off of DT Cortez Kennedy, a 3-time Pro Bowler, and DE Michael Sinclair should develop into a strong pass-rusher. Rod Stephens and Terry Wooden are quality LBs. The secondary features Pro Bowl S Eugene Robinson, who led the NFL with 9 INTs, and CB Patrick Hunter. Newly-signed CB Nate Odomes will miss the season with a knee injury.

Special Teams

Strong-legged John Kasay set the team mark with a 55-yard FG against Kansas City last season, and P Rick Tuten's 44.5 yard gross average was a team record. Michael Bates handles kick returns, and had an impressive 22 tackles on special teams.

1994 Prospects

Seattle plays in a tough division which should put 3 teams in the AFC play-offs, but the Seahawks could improve if they upgrade their WR corps and tighten up their pass defense. However, they don't seem to have made enough moves in these areas. Plus, with just 5 draft picks, they won't have much young, quality talent in camp. Look for Mirer to continue to mature, but Seattle will battle San Diego for cellar-dweller status in the AFC West.

Team Directory

Owner: Ken Behring
President: David Behring
General manager: Tom Flores
Director of player personnel: Mike Allman
VP, administration & public relations: Gary Wright

1993 Review

Sep. 5	at San Diego	L	18-12
Sep. 12	L.A. RAIDERS	L	17-13
Sep. 19	at New England	W	17-14
Sep. 26	at Cincinnati	W	19-10
Oct. 3	SAN DIEGO	W	31-14
Oct. 10	OPEN DATE		
Oct. 17	at Detroit	L	30-10
Oct. 24	NEW ENGLAND	W	10-9
Oct. 31	at Denver	L	28-17
Nov. 7	at Houston	L	24-14
Nov. 14	CLEVELAND	W	22-5
Nov. 21	OPEN DATE		
Nov. 28	DENVER	L	17-9
Dec. 5	KANSAS CITY	L	31-16
Dec. 12	at L.A. Raiders	L	27-23
Dec. 19	PHOENIX	L	30-27 (OT)
Dec. 26	PITTSBURGH	W	16-6
Jan. 2	at Kansas City	L	34-24

1994 Schedule

Sep. 4	at Washington	1:00
Sep. 11	at L.A. Raiders	4:00
Sep. 18	SAN DIEGO	4:00
Sep. 25	PITTSBURGH	4:00
Oct. 2	at Indianapolis	1:00
Oct. 9	DENVER	4:00
Oct. 16	OPEN DATE	
Oct. 23	at Kansas City	1:00
Oct. 30	at San Diego	4:00
Nov. 6	CINCINNATI	4:00
Nov. 13	at Denver	4:00
Nov. 20	TAMPA BAY	4:00
Nov. 27	KANSAS CITY	4:00
Dec. 4	INDIANAPOLIS	4:00
Dec. 11	at Houston	4:00
Dec. 18	L.A. RAIDERS	8:00
Dec. 24	at Cleveland	1:00

1993 finish: 6-10 (4-4 home, 2-6 away), fifth in AFC West

Team Leaders

PASSING	ATT	COM	COM%	YDS	YPA	TD	TD%	INT	INT%	RTG
Mirer	486	274	56.4	2833	5.83	12	2.5	17	3.5	67.0
Gelbaugh	5	3	60.0	39	7.80	0	0.0	1	20.0	45.0
McGwire	5	3	60.0	24	4.80	1	20.0	0	0.0	111.7
TEAM	498	280	56.2	2896	5.82	13	2.6	18	3.6	66.8
OPPONENTS	595	333	56.0	3897	6.55	16	2.7	22	3.7	69.6

RECEIVING	REC	YDS	AVG	TD	RUSHING	ATT	YDS	AVG	TD
Blades	80	945	11.8	3	Warren	273	1072	3.9	7
Williams	58	450	7.8	1	Williams	82	371	4.5	3
Martin	57	798	14.0	5	Mirer	68	343	5.0	3
Edmunds	24	239	10.0	2	Vaughn	36	153	4.3	0
Green	23	178	7.7	1	Blades	5	52	10.4	0
TEAM	280	2896	10.3	13	TEAM	473	2015	4.3	13
OPPONENTS	333	3897	11.7	16	OPPONENTS	452	1660	3.7	12

INTERCEPTIONS	INT	YDS	AVG	LG	TD	SACKS	NO
Robinson	9	80	8.9	28	0	Sinclair	8.0
Hunter	4	54	13.5	34	0	Kennedy	6.5
Clay	5	55	11.0	10	0	McClary	4.0
TEAM	22	196	8.9	34	1	TEAM	38.0
OPPONENTS	18	159	8.8	40	0	OPPONENTS	48.0

KICK RETURNS	NO	YDS	AV	LG	TD	PUNT RETURNS	NO	FC	YDS	AV	LG	TD
Bates	30	603	20.1	46	0	Martin	32	15	270	8.4	33	0
Vaughn	16	280	17.5	31	0	McCloughan	1	0	10	10.0	10	0
Martin	3	38	12.7	15	0							
TEAM	50	931	18.6	46	0	TEAM	33	15	280	8.5	33	0
OPPONENTS	52	967	18.6	95t	1	OPPONENTS	47	21	475	10.1	74t	1

KICKING	XPM	XPA	FGM	FGA	LG	PTS
Kasay	29	29	23	28	55	98
TEAM	29	29	23	28	55	98
OPPONENTS	31	32	29	39	55	118

PUNTING	NO	YDS	LG	AVG	TB	BLK	RET	RYD	IN20	NAV
Tuten	90	4007	64	44.5	7	1	47	475	21	37.3
TEAM	91	4007	64	44.0	7	1	47	475	21	37.3
OPPONENTS	73	3097	60	42.4	11	0	33	280	19	35.6

FUMBLES	FUM	OFF.FUM.REC.	REC	TD	DEF.FUM.REC.	REC	TD
Mirer	13	Mirer	5	0	Hunter	3	0
Warren	3	Heck	2	0	Bates	2	0
Williams	2				Robinson	2	0
TEAM	25	TEAM	10	0	TEAM	15	2
OPPONENTS	23	OPPONENTS	6	0	OPPONENTS	13	1

1994 Draft Choices

ROUND	NAME	POS	SCHOOL	OVERALL SELECTION
1	Sam Adams	DT	Texas A&M	8
2	Kevin Mawae	C	Louisiana State	36
3	Lamar Smith	RB	Houston	73
4	Larry Whigham	S	Northeast Louisiana	110
7	Carlester Crumpler	TE	East Carolina	202

HISTORY

TITLES

1988   AFC West Championship

ALL-TIME TEAM RECORDS

Rushing

Most yards, game:	207	Curt Warner	11/27/83
Most yards, season:	1,481	Curt Warner	1986
Most yards, career:	6,705	Curt Warner	1983-1989

Passing

Most yards, game:	418	Dave Krieg	11/20/83
Most yards, season:	3,671	Dave Krieg	1984
Most yards, career:	26,132	Dave Krieg	1980-1991

Receiving

Most catches, game:	15	Steve Largent	10/18/87
Most catches, season:	80	Brian Blades	1993
Most catches, career:	819	Steve Largent	1976-1989

Scoring

Most points, game:	24	Daryl Turner	9/15/85
		Curt Warner	12/11/88
Most points, season:	110	Norm Johnson	1984
Most points, career:	810	Norm Johnson	1982-1990

COACHES

NAME	RECORD	YEARS
Jack Patera	35-59-0	1976-82
Mike McCormack	4-3-0	1982
Chuck Knox	83-67-0	1983-91
Tom Flores	8-24-0	1992-93

SEATTLE SEAHAWKS
1994 TRAINING CAMP ROSTER

No.	Quarterbacks		Ht.	Wt.	Born	NFL Exp.	College	How acq.	93 GP/GS
18	Gelbaugh, Stan	QB	6-3	207	12-4-62	8	Maryland	Plan B '92	1/0
7	Graham, Jeff	QB	6-5	220	2-5-66	4	Long Beach State	FA '92	0/0
10	McGwire, Dan	QB	6-8	243	12-18-67	4	San Diego State	D1 '91	2/0
3	Mirer, Rick	QB	6-2	216	3-19-70	2	Notre Dame	D1 '93	16/16
	Running backs								
43	Johnson, Tracy	FB	6-0	230	11-29-66	6	Clemson	Plan B '92	16/1
36	Smith, Lamar	RB	5-11	230		R	Houston	D3 '94	
22	Vaughn, Jon	RB	5-9	203	3-12-70	4	Michigan	T-NE '93	16/2
42	Warren, Chris	RB	6-2	225	1-24-67	5	Ferrum	D4 '90	14/14
	Wide receivers								
40	Barrett, Reggie	WR	6-3	215	8-14-69	4	Texas-El Paso	T-DET '94	0/0
81	Bates, Michael	WR	5-10	189	12-19-69	2	Arizona	D6 '92	16/1
89	Blades, Brian	WR	5-11	189	7-24-65	7	Miami (FL)	D2 '88	16/15
84	Martin, Kelvin	WR	5-9	162	5-14-65	8	Boston College	FA '93	16/14
85	Thomas, Doug	WR	5-10	178	9-18-69	4	Clemson	D2 '91	16/0
**	Thomas, Robb	WR	5-11	175	3-29-66	6	Oregon State	FA '92	16/0
88	Warren, Terrence	WR	6-1	200	8-2-69	2	Hampton	D5 '93	2/0
	Tight ends								
48	Crumpler, Carlester	TE	6-6	255		R	East Carolina	D7 '94	
82	Edmunds, Ferrell	TE	6-6	254	4-16-65	7	Maryland	FA '93	16/16
87	Green, Paul	TE	6-3	230	10-8-66	3	Southern California	FA '92	15/8
83	Junkin, Trey	TE	6-2	237	1-23-61	12	Louisiana Tech	FA '90	16/1
	Offensive linemen								
75	Ballard, Howard	T	6-6	336	11-3-63	7	Alabama A&M	FA '94	16/16
69	Blackshear, Jeff	G	6-6	315	3-29-69	2	NE Louisiana	D8 '93	15/2
79	Childs, Jason	T	6-4	285	1-6-69	2	North Dakota	W-SF '93	0/0
53	Donaldson, Ray	C	6-3	300	5-18-58	15	Georgia	FA '93	16/16
76	Hitchcock, Bill	G	6-6	291	8-26-65	4	Purdue	D8 '90	14/14
78	Keim, Mike	T	6-7	301	11-12-65	3	Brigham Young	FA '92	3/0
52	Mawae, Kevin	C	6-4	288		R	Louisiana State	D2 '94	
73	Roberts, Ray	T	6-6	304	6-3-69	3	Virginia	D1 '92	16/16
71	Shaw, Rickie	T	6-4	294	12-26-69	2	North Carolina	W-NO '93	0/0
	Defensive linemen								
68	Adams, Sam	DT	6-3	288		R	Texas A&M	D1 '94	
**	Bryant, Jeff	DT	6-5	281	5-22-60	13	Clemson	D1 '82	16/15
67	Edwards, Antonio	DE	6-3	270	3-10-70	2	Valdosta State	D8 '93	9/0
96	Kennedy, Cortez	DT	6-3	293	8-23-68	5	Miami (FL)	D1 '90	16/16
92	McCrary, Michael	DE	6-4	250	7-7-70	2	Wake Forest	D7 '93	15/0
**	Nash, Joe	DT	6-3	278	10-11-60	13	Boston College	FA '82	16/16
91	Rodgers, Tyrone	DE	6-3	266	4-27-69	3	Washington	FA '92	16/0
70	Sinclair, Michael	DE	6-4	271	1-31-68	3	East. New Mexico	D6 '91	9/1
**	Tuataga loa, Natu	DE	6-4	274	5-25-66	6	California	FA '92	16/15
	Williams, Brent	DE	6-4	275	10-23-64	9	Toledo	FA '94	13/2
	Linebackers								
51	Brandon, David	LB	6-4	230	2-9-65	8	Memphis State	FA '93	13/3
50	Davis, Anthony	LB	6-0	231	3-7-69	2	Utah	FA '92	10/0
**	Junior, E.J.	LB	6-3	242	12-8-59	14	Alabama	FA '92	4/0
98	Murphy, Kevin	LB	6-2	235	9-8-63	9	Oklahoma	FA '93	14/10
97	Porter, Rufus	LB	6-1	227	5-18-65	7	Southern	FA '88	7/5
58	Spitulski, Bob	LB	6-3	235	9-10-69	3	Central Florida	D3 '92	6/0
94	Stephens, Rod	LB	6-1	237	6-14-66	6	Georgia Tech	FA '90	13/13
95	Wells, Dean	LB	6-3	238	7-20-70	2	Kentucky	D4 '93	14/1
90	Wooden, Terry	LB	6-3	236	1-14-67	5	Syracuse	D2a '90	16/16
	Defensive backs								
39	Allred, Brian	CB	5-10	175	3-16-69	2	Sacramento State	FA '93	4/0
25	Blackmon, Robert	S	6-0	197	5-12-67	5	Baylor	D2b '90	16/16
26	Gray, Carlton	CB	6-0	191	6-26-71	2	UCLA	D2 '93	10/2
27	Hunter, Patrick	CB	5-11	186	10-24-64	9	Nevada	D3 '86	15/15
44	McCloughan, Dave	S	6-1	185	11-20-66	4	Colorado	T-GB '93	15/1
	Odomes, Nate	CB	5-10	188	8-25-65	8	Wisconsin	FA '94	16/15
21	Robinson, Rafael	S	5-11	200	6-19-69	3	Wisconsin	FA '92	16/1
41	Robinson, Eugene	S	6-0	191	5-28-63	10	Colgate	FA '85	16/16
23	Whigham, Larry	S	6-2	202		R	Northeast Louisiana	D4 '94	
	Specialists								
	Kasay, John	K	5-10	189	10-27-69	4	Georgia	D4 '91	16/0
14	Tuten, Rick	P	6-2	218	1-5-65	5	Florida State	FA '91	16/0

Rick Mirer   No. 3/QB

HT: 6-2 **WT:** 216
Born: 3-19-70, Goshen, IN
High school: Goshen (IN)
College: Notre Dame
Mirer had better stats that New England's Drew Bledsoe, who was picked before him in the '93 draft.

		PASSING										RUSHING		
YEAR	TEAM	G	ATT	CPL	CPL%	YDS	AVG	TDS	TD%	INT	INT%	RTG	ATT	YDS AVG
1993	Seattle		486	274	56.4	2833	5.8	12	2.5	17	3.5	67.0	---	N/A
1	YR TOTALS	0	486	274	56.4	2833	5.8	12	2.5	17	3.5		0	0 N/A
1993	RANK NFL QB		4	7	41	14	50	18	47	5	31	44	67	67 67

Jon Vaughn   No. 22/RB

Full name: Jonathan Stewart Vaughn
HT: 5-9 **WT:** 203
Born: 3-12-70, Florissant, MO
High school: McCluer North (Florissant, MO)
College: Michigan
Vaughn had just 36 carries in '93; he will take over for the departed John L. Williams.

		RUSHING				RECEIVING					KICK RETURNS			
YEAR	TEAM	G	ATT	YDS	AVG	TD	REC	YDS	AVG	TD	RET	YDS	AVG	TD
1991	New England	16	31	146	4.7	2	9	69	9.9	0	34	717	21.1	1
1992	New England	16	113	451	4.0	1	13	64	6.5	0	20	554	26.2	1
1993	Seattle	16	36	153	4.3	0	—	—	—	—	16	280	17.5	0
3	YR TOTALS	48	180	750	4.2	3	22	173	7.9	0	70	1551	22.3	2
1993	RANK NFL RB		65	61	36	69	123	122	122	40	10	12	27	
1994	PROJECTIONS	16	0	0	NA	0	0	0	NA	0	10	29	2.9	0

Chris Warren   No. 42/RB

Full name: Christopher Collins Warren Jr.
HT: 6 0   **WT:** 006
Born: 1-24-67, Silver Spring, MD
High school: Robinson Secondary (Fairfax, VA)
College: Ferrum (VA)
Warren exploded with 1,017 yards in '92, then broke 1,000 yards again in '93. Seattle would like him to catch more passes.

YEAR	TEAM	G	RUSHING ATT	YDS	AVG	TD	RECEIVING REC	YDS	AVG	TD	KICK RETURNS RET	YDS	AVG	TD
1990	Seattle	16	6	11	1.8	1	---	---	---	---	23	478	20.8	0
1991	Seattle	16	11	13	1.2	0	2	9	4.5	0	35	792	22.6	0
1992	Seattle	16	223	1017	4.6	3	16	134	8.4	0	28	524	18.7	0
1993	Seattle	14	273	1072	3.9	7	15	99	6.6	0	---	---	---	---
	4 YR TOTALS	62	513	2113	4.1	11	33	242	7.3	0	86	1794	20.9	0
1993	RANK NFL RB		7	8	56	9	59	63	84	40	65	65	65	
1994	PROJECTIONS	15	399	1529	3.8	11	21	128	6.1	0	0	0	NA	0

Kelvin Martin   No. 84/WR

Full name: Kelvin Brian Martin
HT: 5-9   **WT:** 162
Born: 5-14-65, San Diego, CA
High school: Ribault (Jacksonville, FL)
College: Boston College
While leading the team with 5 TDs, Martin has a personal best 798 receiving yards.

YEAR	TEAM	G	RECEIVING REC	YDS	AVG	TD	RUSHING ATT	YDS	AVG	TD	PUNT RETURN RET	YDS	AVG
1987	Dallas	7	5	103	20.6	0	---	---	---	---	22	216	9.8
1988	Dallas	16	49	622	12.7	3	4	-4	-1.0	0	44	360	8.2
1989	Dallas	11	46	644	14.0	2	---	---	---	---	4	32	8.0
1990	Dallas	16	64	732	11.4	0	4	-2	-0.5	0	5	46	9.2
1991	Dallas	16	16	243	15.2	0	---	---	---	---	21	244	11.6
1992	Dallas	16	32	359	11.2	3	2	13	6.5	0	42	532	12.7
1993	Seattle	16	57	798	14.0	5	1	0	0.0	0	32	270	8.4
	7 YR TOTALS	98	269	3501	13.0	13	11	7	0.6	0	170	1700	10.0
1993	RANK NFL WR		29	24	59	19	31	35	35	'	7	9	14
1994	PROJECTIONS	16	67	974	14.5	7	1	0	0.0	0	35	240	6.9

Brian Blades   No. 89/WR

Full name: Brian Keith Blades
HT: 5-11 **WT:** 189
Born: 7-24-65, Fort Lauderdale, FL
High school: Piper (Sunrise, FL)
College: Miami (FL)
Pro Bowl alternate Blades broke Steve Largent's team record with 80 catches in 1993.

YEAR	TEAM	G	REC	YDS	AVG	TD	ATT	YDS	AVG	TD	RET	YDS	AVG
			RECEIVING				**RUSHING**				**PUNT RETURN**		
1988 Seattle		16	40	682	17.1	8	5	24	4.8	0	---	---	---
1989 Seattle		16	77	1063	13.8	5	1	3	3.0	0	---	---	---
1990 Seattle		16	49	525	10.7	3	3	19	6.3	0	---	---	---
1991 Seattle		16	70	1003	14.3	2	2	17	8.5	0	---	---	---
1992 Seattle		6	19	256	13.5	1	1	5	5.0	0	---	---	---
1993 Seattle		16	80	945	11.8	3	5	52	10.4	0	---	---	---
6 YR TOTALS		86	335	4474	13.4	22	17	120	7.1	0	0	0	NA
1993 RANK NFL WR			8	11	104	41	6	4	6		30	30	29
1994 PROJECTIONS		16	91	1031	11.3	3	6	72	12.0	0	0	0	NA

Ferrell Edmunds   No. 82/TE

Full name: Ferrell Edmunds Jr.
HT: 6-6   **WT:** 254
Born: 4-16-65, South Boston, VA
High school: G. Washington (Danville, VA)
College: Maryland
Edmunds ranked fourth on the Seahawks in catches (24) and receiving yards (239).

YEAR	TEAM	G	REC	YDS	AVG	TD
			RECEIVING			
1988 Miami		16	33	575	17.4	3
1989 Miami		16	32	382	11.9	3
1990 Miami		16	31	446	14.4	1
1991 Miami		8	11	118	10.7	2
1992 Miami		10	10	91	9.1	1
1993 Seattle		16	24	239	10.0	2
6 YR TOTALS		82	141	1851	13.1	12
1993 RANK NFL TE			20	25	38	15
1994 PROJECTIONS		16	25	237	9.5	2

Howard Ballard   No. 75/T

Full name: Howard Louis Ballard
HT: 6-6   **WT:** 336
Born: 11-3-63, Ashland, AL
High school: Clay County (Ashland, AL)
College: Alabama A&M
Ex-Bill Pro Bowler Ballard should make
Seattle's rushing game even better.

YEAR	TEAM	G	RUSHING ATT	YDS	AVG	RANK AV RUSH	PASS YDS	RANK PASS YDS	SACKS	YDS. LOST
1991	Buffalo	16	505	2381	4.7	3	4140	3	35	269
1992	Buffalo	16	549	2436	4.4	5	3678	5	29	221
1993	Buffalo	.	550	1943	3.5	23	3535	11	31	218
6 YR TOTALS		78								

Cortez Kennedy No. 96/DT

HT: 6-3   **WT:** 293
Born: 8-23-68, Osceola, AR
High school: Rivercrest (Wilson, AR)
College: Miami (FL)
3-time Pro Bowler Kennedy had 77 tackles
and led the team with 14 tackles for a loss.

YEAR	TEAM	G	INT	YDS	AVG	TD	SACKS	FUM REC	TD
1990	Seattle	16	—	—	—	—	1.0	1	0
1991	Seattle	16	—	—	—	—	6.5	1	0
1992	Seattle	16	—	—	—	—	14.0	1	0
1993	Seattle	16	—	—	—	—	6.5	1	0
4 YR TOTALS		64	0	0	NA	0	28.0	4	0
1993 RANK NFL DL			16	NA	NA	NA	34	25	5
1994 PROJECTIONS		16	0	0	NA	0	5	1	0

Terry Wooden   No. 90/LB

Full name: Terrence Tylon Wooden
HT: 6-3 **WT:** 236
Born: 1-14-67, Hartford, CT
High school: Farmington (CT)
College: Syracuse
Wooden racked up 106 tackles (second on the team), 12 of them for a loss.

YEAR	TEAM	G	INT	YDS	AVG	TD	SACKS	FUM REC	TD
1990	Seattle	8	---	---	---	---	---	---	-3
1991	Seattle	16	---	---	---	---	2.0	4	0
1992	Seattle	8	1	3	3.0	0	---	---	-3
1993	Seattle	16	---	---	---	---	2.5	1	0
	4 YR TOTALS	48	1	3	3.0	0	4.5	5	0
1993	RANK NFL LB		47	NA	NA	NA	34	24	8
1994	PROJECTIONS	16	0	0	NA	0	4	1	0

Eugene Robinson   No. 41/S

HT: 6-0 **WT:** 191
Born: 5-28-63, Hartford, CT
High school: Weaver (Hartford)
College: Colgate
Veteran Pro Bowler Robinson, tops in the NFL with 9 INTs, led Seattle with 111 tackles.

YEAR	TEAM	G	INT	YDS	AVG	TD	SACKS	FUM REC	TD
1985	Seattle	16	2	47	23.5	0	—	—	—
1986	Seattle	16	3	39	13.0	0	—	3	0
1987	Seattle	12	3	75	25.0	0	—	1	0
1988	Seattle	16	1	0	0.0	0	1.0	—	—
1989	Seattle	16	5	24	4.8	0	—	1	0
1990	Seattle	16	3	89	29.7	0	—	4	1
1991	Seattle	16	5	56	11.2	0	1.0	1	0
1992	Seattle	16	7	126	18.0	0	—	1	0
1993	Seattle	16	9	80	8.9	0	2.0	2	0
	8 YR TOTALS	140	38	536	14.1	0	4.0	13	1
1993	RANK NFL DB		1	19	87	27	4	10	14
1994	PROJECTIONS	16	11	74	6.7	0	3	2	0

John Kasay No. 4/K

Full name: John David Kasay
HT: 5-10 **WT:** 189
Born: 10-27-69, Athens, GA
High school: Clarke Central (Athens, GA)
College: Georgia
After a poor '92 (56 points), Kasay bounced back to score 98 last season.

YEAR	TEAM	G	XP	XPA	XP Pct.	FG	FGA	FG Pct.	PTS
1991	Seattle	16	27	28	96.4	25	31	80.6	102
1992	Seattle	16	14	14	100.0	14	22	63.6	56
1993	Seattle	16	29	29	100.0	23	28	82.1	98
	3 YR TOTALS	48	70	71	98.6	62	81	76.5	256
1993	RANK NFL		16	16	1	17	18	7	19
1994	PROJECTIONS	16	37	37	100.0	27	30	90.0	118

Tom Flores Head Coach

Full name: Thomas Raymond Flores
Born: 3-21-37, Fresno, CA
High school: Sanger (CA)
College: Fresno CC (CA) and Pacific
Flores is one of only three active coaches who have won two Super Bowls (the others are Bill Parcells and Don Shula).

		REGULAR SEASON					POSTSEASON			
YEAR	TEAM	W	L	T	PCT	FINISH	W	L	FINISH
1979	Oakland	9	7	0	.563	T3rd/AFC West			
1980	Oakland	11	5	0	.688	T1st/AFC West	4	0	won Super Bowl XV over Phila., 27-10
1981	Oakland	7	9	0	.438	4th/AFC West			
1982	LA Raiders	8	1	0	.889	1st/AFC	1	1	lost 2nd Rnd. to NY Jets, 17-14
1983	LA Raiders	12	4	0	.750	1st/AFC West	3	0	won Super Bowl XVIII over Wash., 38-9
1984	LA Raiders	11	5	0	.688	3rd/AFC West	0	1	lost wild-card game to Seattle, 13-7
1985	LA Raiders	12	4	0	.750	1st/AFC West	0	1	lost 1st Rnd. to New England, 27-20
1986	LA Raiders	8	8	0	.500	4th/AFC West			
1987	LA Raiders	5	10	0	.333	4th/AFC West			
1992	Seattle	2	14	0	.125	5th/AFC West			
1993	Seattle	6	10	0	.375	5th/AFC West			
	11 YR TOTALS	91	77	0	.542		8	3	

Dan McGwire   No. 10/QB

Full name: Daniel Scott McGwire
HT: 6-8   **WT:** 243
Born: 12-18-67, Pomona, CA
High school: Claremont (CA)
College: San Diego State
McGwire has attempted just 42 passes in 3 years.

		PASSING										RUSHING		
YEAR	TEAM	G	ATT	CPL	CPL%	YDS	AVG	TDS	TD%	INT	INT%	RTG	ATT	YDS	AVG
1991	Seattle	1	7	3	42.9	27	3.9	0	0.0	1	^^^^^^	14.3	3	14	4.7
1992	Seattle	2	30	17	56.7	116	3.9	0	0.0	3	^^^^^^	25.8	3	13	4.3
1993	Seattle	2	5	3	60.0	24	4.8	1	20.0	0	0.0	111.7	1	-1	-1.0
	3 YR TOTALS	5	42	23	54.8	167	4.0	1	2.4	4	9.5		7	26	3.7
1993	RANK NFL QB		67	66	23	69	62	54	2	61	61	3	62	53	56
1994	PROJECTIONS	3	0	0	NA	0	NA	3	NA	0	NA		0	0	NA

Michael Bates   No. 81/WR-KR

HT: 5-10   **WT:** 189
Born: 12-19-69, Tucson, AZ
High school: Amphitheater (Tucson)
College: Arizona
Bates averaged 20.1 yards per KR, totaling over 600 return yards.

			RECEIVING				RUSHING				PUNT RETURN		
YEAR	TEAM	G	REC	YDS	AVG	TD	ATT	YDS	AVG	TD	RET	YDS	AVG
1993	Seattle	16	1	6	6.0	0	---	---	---	---	---	---	---
	1 YR TOTALS	16	1	6	6.0	0	0	0	NA	0	0	0	NA
1993	RANK NFL WR		138	147	95		42	42	42		30	30	29

Paul Green   No. 87/TE

Full name: Paul Earl Green
HT: 6-3   **WT:** 230
Born: 10-8-66, Coalinga, CA
High school: West (Clovis, CA)
College: Southern California
Back-up Green had 23 catches (fifth on the team).

			RECEIVING			
YEAR	TEAM	G	REC	YDS	AVG	TD
1992	Seattle	4	9	67	7.4	1
1993	Seattle	15	23	178	7.7	1
	2 YR TOTALS	19	32	245	7.7	2
1993	RANK NFL TE		24	29	54	22
1994	PROJECTIONS	16	13	112	8.6	0

Ray Donaldson No. 53/C

Full name: Raymond Canute Donaldson
HT: 6-3 **WT:** 300
Born: 5-18-58, Rome, GA
High school: East (Rome, GA)
College: Georgia
Donaldson didn't miss an offensive down in '93.

YEAR	TEAM	G	RUSHING ATT	YDS	AVG	RANK AV RUSH	PASS YDS	RANK PASS YDS	SACKS	YDS. LOST
1991	Indianapolis	3	354	1169	3.3	27	3066	21	57	487
1992	Indianapolis	16	379	1102	2.9	28	3584	8	44	318
1993	Seattle	16	473	2015	4.3	8	2896	25	48	242
14 YR TOTALS		200								

Michael Sinclair No. 70/DE

Full name: Michael Glenn Sinclair
HT: 6-4 **WT:** 271
Born: 1-31-68, Galveston, TX
High school: Charlton-Pollard (Beaumont, TX)
College: Eastern New Mexico
Sinclair had a team-high 8 sacks in only 9 games.

YEAR	TEAM	G	INT	YDS	AVG	TD	SACKS	FUM REC	TD
1992	Seattle	12	---	---	---	---	1.0	---	---
1993	Seattle	9	---	---	---	---	8.0	---	---
2 YR TOTALS		21	0	0	NA	0	9.0	0	0
1993 RANK NFL DL			16	NA	NA	NA	25	71	NA
1994 PROJECTIONS		6	0	0	NA	0	10	0	0

Rod Stephens No. 94/LB

Full name: Rodrequis La'Vant Stephens
HT: 6-1 **WT:** 237
Born: 6-14-66, Atlanta, GA
High school: North Fulton (Atlanta)
College: Georgia Tech
Stephens (105 tackles) recorded 2 safeties in 1993.

YEAR	TEAM	G	INT	YDS	AVG	TD	SACKS	FUM REC	TD
1991	Seattle	16	---	---	---	---	---	1	0
1992	Seattle	16	---	---	---	---	---	---	---
1993	Seattle	13	---	---	---	---	2.5	1	1
5 YR TOTALS		59	0	0	NA	0	2.5	2	1
1993 RANK NFL LB			47	NA	NA	NA	34	24	1
1994 PROJECTIONS		13	0	0	NA	0	4	1	2

Patrick Hunter   No. 27/CB

Full name: Patrick Edward Hunter
HT: 5-11 **WT:** 186
Born: 10-24-64, San Francisco, CA
High school: South San Francisco (CA)
College: Nevada

Hunter had 11 passes defensed to go with 4 INTs.

YEAR	TEAM	G	INT	YDS	AVG	TD	SACKS	FUM REC	TD
1991	Seattle	15	1	32	32.0	1	—	—	—
1992	Seattle	16	2	0	0.0	0	—	1	0
1993	Seattle	15	4	54	13.5	0	—	3	0
8 YR TOTALS		115	9	89	9.9	1	1.0	5	0
1993 RANK NFL DB			21	35	56	27	49	1	14
1994 PROJECTIONS		16	6	92	15.3	0	0	5	0

Nate Odomes   No. 37/CB

Full name: Nathaniel Bernard Odomes
HT: 5-10 **WT:** 188
Born: 8-25-65, Columbus, GA
High school: Carver (Columbus, GA)
College: Wisconsin

He led Buffalo with 20 passes defensed in '93.

YEAR	TEAM	G	INT	YDS	AVG	TD	SACKS	FUM REC	TD
1990	Buffalo	16	1	0	0.0	0	—	3	1
1991	Buffalo	16	5	120	24.0	1	1.0	1	0
1992	Buffalo	16	5	19	3.8	0	1.0	1	0
1993	Buffalo	16	9	65	7.2	0	—	1	1
7 YR TOTALS		108	26	224	8.6	1	3.0	8	2
1993 RANK NFL DB			1	26	93	27	49	37	2
1994 PROJECTIONS		16	12	78	6.5	0	0	1	1

Rick Tuten   No. 14/P

Full name: Richard Lamar Tuten
HT: 6-2 **WT:** 218
Born: 1-5-65, Perry, FL
High school: Forest (Ocala, FL)
College: Florida State

His 44.5 yard gross average was a team record.

YEAR	TEAM	G	NO	YARDS	LONG	AVG	BLK	IN20
1990	Buffalo	14	53	2107	NA	39.8	0	NA
1991	Seattle	10	49	2106	60	43.0	0	8
1992	Seattle	16	108	4760	65	44.1	0	29
1993	Seattle	16	90	4007	64	44.5	1	21
5 YR TOTALS		58	307	13236	65	43.1	1	58
1993 RANK NFL Ps			2	1	10	4		12
1994 PROJECTIONS		16	84	3790	56	45.1	2	19

NATIONAL FOOTBALL CONFERENCE

1993 RECAP

EASTERN DIVISION

	W	L	T	PF	PA	HOME	ROAD	NFC	AFC	DIV
x-DALLAS	12	4	0	376	229	6-2	6-2	10-2	2-2	7-1
y-N.Y. GIANTS	11	5	0	288	205	6-2	5-3	9-3	2-2	5-3
PHILADELPHIA	8	8	0	293	315	3-5	5-3	6-6	2-2	3-5
PHOENIX	7	9	0	326	269	4-4	3-5	6-8	1-1	4-4
WASHINGTON	4	12	0	230	345	3-5	1-7	3-9	1-3	1-7

CENTRAL DIVISION

	W	L	T	PF	PA	HOME	ROAD	NFC	AFC	DIV
x-DETROIT	10	6	0	298	292	5-3	5-3	8-6	2-0	4-4
y-MINNESOTA	9	7	0	277	290	4-4	5-3	7-5	2-2	6-2
y-GREEN BAY	9	7	0	340	282	6-2	3-5	6-6	3-1	4-4
CHICAGO	7	9	0	234	230	3-5	4-4	5-7	2-2	3-5
TAMPA BAY	5	11	0	237	376	3-5	2-6	4-8	1-3	3-5

WESTERN DIVISION

	W	L	T	PF	PA	HOME	ROAD	NFC	AFC	DIV
x-SAN FRAN.	10	6	0	473	295	6-2	4-4	8-4	2-2	4-2
NEW ORLEANS	8	8	0	317	343	4-4	4-4	6-6	2-2	3-3
ATLANTA	6	10	0	316	385	4-4	2-6	5-7	1-3	4-2
L.A. RAMS	5	11	0	221	367	3-5	2-6	3-9	2-2	1-5

x-Division Winner, y-Wild Card

NFC East

Dallas got off to a slow start in 1993, as Emmitt Smith held out and the Cowboys lost their first 2 games. Then Smith signed and Dallas went 12-2 the rest of the way (including 5 straight wins to end the season) and cruised through the playoffs to their second consecutive Super Bowl victory.

Under new coach Dan Reeves, the Giants rebounded from 2 awful seasons. A ferocious defense, anchored by a strong corps of linebackers, helped New York weather injuries to RB Rodney Hampton and WR Mike Sherrard. They flagged at the end, though, losing the division to Dallas on the last day of the season and getting crushed by the 49ers in the playoffs.

After a 4-0 start the Eagles fell to earth when Randall Cunningham and wideout Fred Barnett went out for the year with injuries.

Philadelphia proceeded to lose 6 straight and only got back to .500 on the last day of the season.

Head coach Joe Bugel, his job on the line, led a much improved Cardinal team in '93. While their record was just 7-9, 8 of Phoenix's losses were by 7 points or less and they closed strong, winning their last 3 games. Still, it wasn't enough, and Bugel was fired after the season.

Washington surprised everyone by being abysmal last year. After an impressive opening day victory over Dallas (minus Emmitt Smith), the 'Skins lost 6 straight, as age and injuries took them out of contention early.

NFC Central

Despite a three-headed QB controversy and a midseason injury to star RB Barry Sanders, the Lions rebounded from an awful '92 to take their second division crown in 3 years behind Eric Kramer. They slumped in the playoffs, though, losing to Green Bay at home in the first round.

The Vikings struggled on the offensive side of the ball last year, but their defense, the best in the NFL, kept them in the race. They won 4 of their last 5 games to earn a wild card spot, but lost to the Giants on the road in the first round.

Green Bay had the league's second ranked defense last year, and looked like the early favorite in the Central. But after a 7-4 start, the Packers lost 3 of their last 5 and watched the division title slip away from them. They salvaged their season with a road playoff win at Detroit before falling to Dallas.

Chicago was the league's streakiest team during Dave Wannstedt's first season as head coach—they lost their first 2, won 3 straight, lost 3 more, won 4 straight, then dropped their last 4. The main problem was at QB, as the Bears had the league's worst passing attack for the second straight year.

Only in Tampa Bay could a 5-11 record be cause for excitement. Remember, the Bucs have had double digit losses for the past 11 years. Coach Sam Wyche's squad did not get blown out often in 1993, and the offense, under Craig Erickson, was putting points on the board by season's end.

NFC West

The 49ers, now firmly Steve Young's team, solidified their position as the second-best team in the NFC last year, coasting to win the West behind the usual stellar year from Jerry Rice. They cruised into the NFC title game, where they were crushed by the Cowboys for the second straight year.

New Orleans had the NFL's best start last year, rocketing to 5-0, with impressive wins over Houston and the 49ers. But they collapsed in October and went 3-8 the rest of the way, losing 4 of their last 5 to blow what looked like a sure playoff berth.

The Falcons were remarkably inconsistent in '93—they beat Dallas and the 49ers, but lost to Washington, Tampa Bay, and even Cincinnati on their way to a disappointing 6-10 record. Management blamed coach Jerry Glanville, and he was fired after the season.

Despite the amazing debut of rookie RB Jerome Bettis, the Rams struggled in '93. Plagued by a poor passing game under Jim Everett, an aging offensive line, and a porous defense, the Rams went 5-11 and never contended.

1994 NFC PROJECTIONS

NFC East	NFC Central	NFC West
Dallas†	Green Bay†	San Francisco†
Arizona*	Minnesota*	New Orleans
N.Y. Giants*	Chicago	Atlanta
Philadelphia	Detroit	L.A. Rams
Washington	Tampa Bay	

†Division Winner, *Wild Card

Round 1:	Green Bay over New York, Arizona over Minnesota
Round 2:	Dallas over Arizona, San Francisco over Green Bay
Title Game:	Dallas over San Francisco
Super Bowl XXIX:	Dallas over Buffalo

Free agency has brought some parity to the NFC, but there should not be any dramatic shakeup in the standings at season's end. Dallas fans are moaning over departed players and the coaching change, but the rest of the East should make vacation plans for late January. Arizona, with a new name and a new coach (Buddy

Ryan), has improved, but the Cowboys still should prevail. The Giants released Phil Simms and lost Lawrence Taylor and Mark Collins; they should squeak into the playoffs, but count on an early exit. Philadelphia has Randall Cunningham back, but they'll miss defensive stalwarts Seth Joyner and Clyde Simmons. The only thing keeping the Eagles out of the basement will be the hapless Redskins. New coach Norv Turner oversaw an extensive revamping of the squad, but a return to respectability is a few seasons away.

The Central Division race should be one of the league's tightest in '94, with four true contenders. But, as always, whoever prevails will be beaten up and will lose to the other division winners in the playoffs. In Green Bay, Sean Jones joins Reggie White on the DL, making a killer pass rush combination. Brett Favre is a year older and hopefully wiser—if he doesn't hold out, he should lead the Pack to their first division crown since 1972. Minnesota will give them a fight, though, as new QB Warren Moon will jump-start the Vikes' moribund offense. Chicago has added offensive firepower as well, although they're probably still a year or two away. Watch for the Bears to gel as the season goes along. The Lions have put all their money ($11 million) on Scott Mitchell at QB. If he performs, they'll be in the race; if not, they'll fall right out of contention. Tampa Bay has improved, but in this division, all they can do is pray for realignment.

No division in football shows less evidence of parity than the NFC West. San Francisco is clearly the class of this division, and should run away early, especially if their defense, bolstered by All Pro LB Ken Norton, performs as it can. They do have a shot at unseating Dallas, especially if they get the home field advantage for the title game. No one else here figures to make the playoffs—New Orleans might be in the wild card hunt for a while, but their defense is getting old and Jim Everett isn't that much of an improvement over Wade Wilson. Atlanta should find consistency under new coach June Jones, but their fans might not like it—with their top '93 receivers (Mike Pritchard and Michael Haynes) gone and Deion Sanders preparing to leave, the Falcons could be consistently bad. The Rams are counting on Chris Miller to carry them to respectability, but they might be wishing they'd taken a top QB prospect in the draft before season's end.

Arizona
CARDINALS

1994 Scouting Report

Offense
Thanks to the acquisition of QB Steve Beuerlein (who set career highs in most categories) and WR Gary Clark, the Cardinals had the ninth-best passing offense in the NFL with 3,404 passing yards gained. In addition to Clark, Beuerlein has RB Larry Centers (whose 66 catches led the team in '93), WR Ricky Proehl, and WR Randal Hill. Last year, Arizona gained 1,809 rushing yards, eleventh in the NFL, as rookie RB Ron Moore became the Cardinals' first 1,000-yard rusher since Stump Mitchell in '85. RB Garrison Hearst was the subject of Draft Day trade rumors. The Arizona OL, in addition to helping Moore gain 1,000 yards, allowed just 33 sacks last year.

Defense
New coach/GM Buddy Ryan has signed former Eagles LB Seth Joyner, DT Clyde Simmons, and P Jeff Feagles as free agents. They, along with ex-Bill CB James Williams, complement a solid defensive core featuring NT Michael Bankston, DT Eric Swann, and ILB Eric Hill. With Ryan's 46 defense and 8-man fronts, the team's overall defensive standing should improve, if they can stop the pass. The flaw in Ryan's defensive schemes has always been that teams that can protect their passer get big plays, because receivers face man-to-man coverage deep.

Special Teams
K Greg Davis has only an average leg, but he was perfect last year from inside the 40. P Jeff Feagles led the NFL with 31 punts inside the 20.

1994 Prospects
Controversial coach Buddy Ryan may be one of the most underrated judges of talent in football. The Eagles added defensive stars like Reggie White, Clyde Simmons, Seth Joyner, and Ben Smith during Ryan's tenure there. And it's indisputable that Ryan gets players to work for him—his defenses won Super Bowls for the Bears and Jets. The Cardinals would be pleased just to make the playoffs, something Ryan did three straight seasons in Philadelphia. Arizona fans should see an improved defense, a winning record, and a playoff team this season.

Team Directory

President: William V. Bidwill

Head coach/General manager: Buddy Ryan

Pro personnel director: Erik Widmark

Director of public relations: Paul Jensen

1993 Review

Sep. 5	at Philadelphia	L 23-17
Sep. 12	at Washington	W 17-10
Sep. 19	DALLAS	L 17-10
Sep. 26	at Detroit	L 26-20
Oct. 3	OPEN DATE	
Oct. 10	NEW ENGLAND	L 23-21
Oct. 17	WASHINGTON	W 36-6
Oct. 24	at San Francisco	L 28-14
Oct. 31	NEW ORLEANS	L 20-17
Nov. 7	PHILADELPHIA	W 16-3
Nov. 14	at Dallas	L 20-15
Nov. 21	OPEN DATE	
Nov. 28	at N.Y. Giants	L 19-17
Dec. 5	L.A. RAMS	W 38-10
Dec. 12	DETROIT	L 21-14
Dec. 19	at Seattle	W 30-27 (OT)
Dec. 26	N.Y. GIANTS	W 17-6
Jan. 2	at Atlanta	W 27-10

1994 Schedule

Sep. 4	at L.A. Rams	4:00
Sep. 11	N.Y. GIANTS	8:00
Sep. 18	at Cleveland	1:00
Sep. 25	OPEN DATE	
Oct. 2	MINNESOTA	4:00
Oct. 9	at Dallas	4:00
Oct. 16	at Washington	1:00
Oct. 23	DALLAS	4:00
Oct. 30	PITTSBURGH	8:00
Nov. 6	at Philadelphia	4:00
Nov. 13	at N.Y. Giants	1:00
Nov. 20	PHILADELPHIA	4:00
Nov. 27	CHICAGO	4:00
Dec. 4	at Houston	4:00
Dec. 11	WASHINGTON	4:00
Dec. 18	CINCINNATI	4:00
Dec. 24	at Atlanta	1:00

1993 finish: 7-9 (4-4 home, 3-5 away), fourth in NFC East

Team Leaders

PASSING	ATT	COM	COM%	YDS	YPA	TD	TD%	INT	INT%	RTG
Beuerlein	418	258	61.7	3164	7.57	18	4.3	17	4.1	82.5
Chandler	103	52	50.5	471	4.57	3	2.9	2	1.9	64.8
Hearst	1	0	0.0	0	0.00	0	0.0	1	100.0	0.0
TEAM	522	310	59.4	3635	6.96	21	4.0	20	3.8	78.0
OPPONENTS	495	281	56.8	3511	7.09	14	2.8	9	1.8	80.8

RECEIVING	REC	YDS	AVG	TD	RUSHING	ATT	YDS	AVG	TD
Centers	66	603	9.1	3	Moore	263	1018	3.9	9
Proehl	65	877	13.5	7	Hearst	76	264	3.5	1
Clark	63	818	13.0	4	Bailey	49	253	5.2	1
Hill	35	519	14.8	4	Centers	25	152	6.1	0
Bailey	32	243	7.6	0	Proehl	8	47	5.9	0
TEAM	310	3635	11.7	21	TEAM	452	1809	4.0	12
OPPONENTS	281	3511	12.5	14	OPPONENTS	433	1861	4.3	13

INTERCEPTIONS	INT	YDS	AVG	LG	TD	SACKS		NO
Lynch	3	13	4.3	13	0	Harvey		9.5
Williams	2	87	43.5	46t	1	Nunn		6.5
Dooty	1	24	12.0	19	0	Swann		5.5
TEAM	9	124	13.8	46t	1	TEAM		34.0
OPPONENTS	20	143	7.2	37	0	OPPONENTS		33.0

KICK RETURNS	NO	YDS	AV	LG	TD	PUNT RETURNS	NO	FC	YDS	AV	LG	TD
Bailey	31	699	22.5	48	0	Bailey	35	5	282	8.1	58t	1
Blount	8	163	20.4	27	0	Blount	9	3	90	10.0	25	0
Edwards	3	51	17.0	20	0	Edwards	3	3	12	4.0	11	0
TEAM	45	951	21.1	48	0	TEAM	47	11	384	8.2	58t	1
OPPONENTS	51	994	19.5	61	0	OPPONENTS	30	19	267	8.9	33	0

KICKING	XPM	XPA	FGM	FGA	LG	PTS
Davis	37	37	21	28	55	100
TEAM	37	37	21	28	55	100
OPPONENTS	27	27	26	35	54	105

PUNTING	NO	YDS	LG	AVG	TB	BLK	RET	RYD	IN20	NAV
Camarillo	73	3189	61	43.7	8	0	30	267	23	37.8
TEAM	73	3189	61	43.7	8	0	30	267	23	37.8
OPPONENTS	78	3333	62	42.7	4	1	47	384	23	36.8

FUMBLES	FUM	OFF.FUM.REC.	REC	TD	DEF.FUM.REC.	REC	TD
Beuerlein	8	Beuerlein	2	0	Bankston	5	0
Bailey	4	Centers	2	0	Lynch	3	1
Moore	3	Smith	2	0			
TEAM	23	TEAM	11	0	TEAM	17	2
OPPONENTS	27	OPPONENTS	8	0	OPPONENTS	11	0

1994 Draft Choices

ROUND	NAME	POS	SCHOOL	OVERALL SELECTION
1	Jamir Miller	LB	UCLA	10
2	Chuck Levy	RB	Arizona	38
3	Rich Braham	G	West Virginia	76
3	Erik England	DE	Texas A&M	89
4	Perry Carter	CB	Southern Mississippi	107
4	John Reece	CB	Nebraska	113
4	Terry Irving	LB	McNeese State	115
5	Anthony Redmon	G	Auburn	139
6	Terry Samuels	TE	Kentucky	172
7	Frank Harvey	FB	Georgia	204

HISTORY

TITLES

1925	NFL Championship	1974	NFC East Championship
1947	NFL Championship	1975	NFC East Championship
1948	NFL West Championship		

ALL-TIME TEAM RECORDS

Rushing

Most yards, game:	203	John David Crow	12/18/60
Most yards, season:	1,605	Ottis Anderson	1979
Most yards, career:	7,999	Ottis Anderson	1979-1986

Passing

Most yards, game:	468	Neil Lomax	12/16/84
Most yards, season:	4,614	Neil Lomax	1984
Most yards, career:	34,639	Jim Hart	1966-1983

Receiving

Most catches, game:	16	Sonny Randle	11/4/62
Most catches, season:	91	J. T. Smith	1987
Most catches, career:	522	Roy Green	1979-1990

Scoring

Most points, game:	40	Ernie Nevers	11/28/29
Most points, season:	117	Jim Bakken	1967
		Neil O'Donoghue	1984
Most points, career:	1,380	Jim Bakken	1962-1978

COACHES

NAME	RECORD	YEARS	NAME	RECORD	YEARS
Paddy Driscoll	13-9-3	1920-22	Curly Lambeau	7-15-0	1950-51
Arnold Horween	13-8-1	1923-24	Phil Handler-*	1-1-0	1951
Norman Barry	16-8-2	1925-26	Cecil Isbell		
Fred Gillies	3-7-1	1927	Joe Kuharich	4-8-0	1952
Guy Chamberlin	1-5-0	1928	Joe Stydahar	3-20-1	1953-54
Dewey Scanlon	6-6-1	1929	Pop Ivy	17-29-2	1958-61
Ernie Nevers	11-18-2	1930-31	Ray Richards	14-21-1	1955-57
		1939	Wally Lemm	27-26-3	1962-65
LeRoy Andrews	0-2-0	1931	Charley Winner	35-30-5	1966-70
Jack Chevigny	2-6-2	1932	Bob Hollway	8-18-2	1971-72
Paul Schissler	6-15-1	1933-34	Don Coryell	42-29-1	1973-77
Milan Creighton	16-26-4	1935-38	Bud Wilkinson	9-20-0	1978-79
Jimmy Conzelman	35-32-3	1940-42,	Larry Wilson	2-1-0	1979
		1946-48	Jim Hanifan	39-50-1	1980-85
Phil Handler	1-29-0	1943-45	Gene Stallings	23-34-1	1986-89
Phil Handler-*	2-4-0	1949	Hank Kuhlmann	0-5-0	1989
Buddy Parker			Joe Bugel	20-44-0	1990-93
Buddy Parker	4-1-1	1949			
*co-coaches					

ARIZONA CARDINALS
1994 TRAINING CAMP ROSTER

No	Quarterbacks		Ht	Wt	Born	NFL Exp	College	How acq	93 GP/GS
7	Beuerlein, Steve	QB	6-3	210	3-7-65	7	Notre Dame	FA '93	16/14
2	Furrer, Will	QB	6-3	210	2-5-68	3	Virginia Tech	W-CHI '93	0/0
9	McMahon, Jim	QB	6-1	195	8-21-59	13	Brigham Young	FA '94	12/12
	Running backs								
**	Bailey, Johnny	RB-KR	5-8	187	3-17-67	5	Texas A&I	Plan B '92	13/0
25	Blount, Eric	RB-KR	5-9	200	9-22-70	3	North Carolina	D8 '92	6/0
37	Centers, Larry	RB	5-11	215	6-1-68	5	Stephen F. Austin	D5 '90	16/9
32	Harvey, Frank	FB	6-0	245	1-19-71	R	Georgia	D7 '94	
23	Hearst, Garrison	RB	5-11	215	1-4-71	2	Georgia	D1 '93	6/5
4	Levy, Chuck	RB-QB	6-0	197	1-7-72	R	Arizona	D2 '94	
30	Moore, Ron	RB	5-10	220	1-26-70	2	Pittsburg State (KS)	D4 '93	16/11
85	Ware, Derek	RB-TE	6-3	250	9-17-67	3	Central State (OK)	D7 '92	16/1
	Wide receivers								
84	Clark, Gary	WR	5-9	175	5-1-62	10	James Madison	FA '93	14/10
83	Edwards, Anthony	WR	5-10	190	5-26-66	6	N. Mex. Highlands	FA '91	16/0
81	Hill, Randal	WR	5-10	180	9-21-69	4	Miami (FL)	T-MIA '91	16/8
87	Proehl, Ricky	WR	6-0	190	3-7-68	5	Wake Forest	FA '92	16/16
	Tight ends								
**	Beach, Pat	TE	6-4	250	8-26-60	13	Washington St.	Plan B '93	15/0
**	Rolle, Butch	TE	6-4	245	8-19-64	9	Michigan State	Plan B '92	16/5
89	Samuels, Terry	TE	6-2	254	9-27-70	R	Kentucky	D6 '94	
	Offensive linemen								
76	Braham, Rich	G	6-4	290	11-6-70	R	West Virginia	D3a '94	
62	Coleman, Ben	T	6-6	335	5-18-71	2	Wake Forest	D2 '93	12/0
70	Cunningham, Ed	C	6-3	285	8-17-69	3	Washington	D3 '92	15/15
64	Cunningham, Rick	T	6-7	*320	1-4-67	4	Texas A&M	FA '92	16/16
65	Dye, Ernest	T	6-6	325	7-15-71	2	South Carolina	D1a '93	7/1
**	May, Mark	T	6-6	290	11-2-59	14	Pittsburgh	Plan B '92	11/11
60	Redmon, Anthony	G-T	6-4	308	4-6-71	R	Auburn	D5 '94	
67	Sharpe, Luis	T	6-5	280	6-16-60	13	UCLA	D1 '82	16/16
68	Wolf, Joe	OL	6-6	296	12-28-66	6	Boston College	D1b '89	8/5
	Defensive linemen								
63	Bankston, Michael	DL	6-3	280	3-12-70	3	Sam Houston St.	D4a '92	16/12
78	Brown, Chad	DE	6-7	265	7-9-71	2	Mississippi	D8 '93	5/0
92	England, Erik	DE	6-2	283	3-25-71	R	Texas A&M	D3b '94	
79	Rucker, Keith	DL	6-4	360	11-20-68	3	Ohio Wesleyan	FA '92	16/15
96	Simmons, Clyde	DE	6-6	280	8-4-64	9	Western Carolina	FA '94	16/16
98	Swann, Eric	DT	6-5	295	8-16-70	4	None	D1 '91	9/9
	Linebackers								
58	Hill, Eric	ILB	6-2	255	11-14-66	6	Louisiana State	D1 '89	13/12
56	Irving, Terry	LB	6-0	224	7-3-71	R	McNeese State	D4c '94	
53	Jax, Garth	ILB	6-2	250	9-16-63	9	Florida State	Plan B '89	16/0
59	Joyner, Seth	OLB	6-2	235	11-18-64	9	Texas-El Paso	FA '94	16/16
57	Kirk, Randy	LB	6-2	231	12-27-64	7	San Diego State	FA '94	16/0
95	Miller, Jamir	OLB	6-4	242	11-19-73	R	UCLA	D1 '94	
**	Nunn, Freddie Joe	LB	6-4	250	4-9-62	10	Mississippi	D1 '85	f6/10
52	Wallerstedt, Brett	LB	6-1	240	11-24-70	2	Arizona State	D6 '93	7/0
	Defensive backs								
40	Carter, Perry	CB	5-11	194	8-15-71	R	Southern Mississippi	D4a '94	
26	Cecil, Chuck	FS	6-0	185	11-8-64	7	Arizona	FA '93	15/7
**	Duerson, Dave	S	6-1	215	11-28-60	13	Notre Dame	FA '91	16/4
31	Harris, Odie	CB	6-0	190	4-16-66	7	Sam Houston St.	W-CLE '92	16/0
28	Lofton, Steve	CB	5-9	185	11-26-68	4	Texas A&M	FA '91	13/0
29	Lynch, Lorenzo	CB	5-11	200	4-6-63	8	Cal-Sacramento	Plan B '90	16/15
27	Oldham, Chris	CB	5-10	195	10-26-68	4	Oregon	FA '92	16/6
41	Reece, John	Cb	6-0	203	1-24-71	R	Nebraska	D4b '94	
35	Williams, Aeneas	CB	5-10	190	1-29-68	4	Southern	D3 '90	16/16
21	Williams, James	CB	5-10	185	3-30-67	5	Fresno State	T-BUF '94	15/11
**	Zordich, Michael	S	6-1	201	10-12-63	8	Penn State	Plan B '90	16/9
	Specialists								
5	Davis, Greg	K	6-0	205	10-29-65	7	Citadel	Plan B '91	16/0
10	Feagles, Jeff	P	6-1	205	3-7-66	7	Miami (FL)	FA '94	16/0

Steve Beuerlein   No. 7/QB

Full name: Stephen Taylor Beuerlein
HT: 6-3   **WT:** 210
Born: 3-7-65, Hollywood, CA
High school: Servite (Anaheim, CA)
College: Notre Dame

In his first year as a starter, Beuerlein set career highs in most categories, including 18 TD passes.

YEAR	TEAM	G	PASSING ATT	CPL	CPL%	YDS	AVG	TDS	TD%	INT	INT%	RTG	RUSHING ATT	YDS	AVG
1988	LA Raiders	10	238	105	44.1	1643	6.9	8	3.4	7	2.9	66.6	30	35	1.2
1989	LA Raiders	10	217	108	49.8	1677	7.7	13	6.0	9	4.1	78.4	16	39	2.4
1991	Dallas	8	137	68	49.6	909	6.6	5	3.6	2	1.5	77.2	7	-14	-2.0
1992	Dallas	16	18	12	66.7	152	8.4	0	0.0	1	5.6	69.7	4	-7	-1.8
1993	Phoenix	16	418	258	61.7	3164	7.6	18	4.3	17	4.1	82.5	22	45	2.0
	5 YR TOTALS	60	1028	551	53.6	7545	7.3	44	4.3	36	3.5		79	98	1.2
1993	RANK NFL QB		13	11	12	9	15	6	19	5	24	22	21	26	35
1994	PROJECTIONS	16	544	347	63.8	4159	7.6	24	4.4	23	4.2		26	65	2.5

Ron Moore   No. 30/RB

HT: 5-10 **WT:** 220
Born: 1-26-70, Spencer, OK
High school: Star Spencer (OK)
College: Pittsburg State (KS)

Rookie Moore outplayed top pick Garrison Hearst, winning the starting job in week 7. His 9 rushing TDs led all NFL rookies.

YEAR	TEAM	G	RECEIVING REC	YDS	AVG	TD	RUSHING ATT	YDS	AVG	TD	PUNT RETURN RET	YDS	AVG
1990	NY Jets	15	44	692	15.7	6	2	-4	-2.0	0	---	---	---
1991	NY Jets	16	70	987	14.1	5	---	---	---	---	---	---	---
1992	NY Jets	16	50	726	14.5	4	1	21	21.0	0	---	---	---
1993	NY Jets	13	64	843	13.2	1	1	-6	-6.0	0	---	---	---
	4 YR TOTALS	60	228	3248	14.2	16	4	11	2.8	0	0	0	NA
1993	RANK NFL WR		17	21	77	72	31	41	41		30	30	29
1994	PROJECTIONS	13	76	961	12.6	0	1	0	0.0	0	0	0	NA

Larry Centers   No. 37/RB

HT: 5-11 **WT:** 215
Born: 6-1-68, Tatum, TX
High school: Tatum (TX)
College: Stephen F. Austin (TX)
Centers' 66 catches led the Cards and ranked fifth among NFC RBs.

		RUSHING				RECEIVING				KICK RETURNS			
YEAR TEAM	G	ATT	YDS	AVG	TD	REC	YDS	AVG	TD	RET	YDS	AVG	TD
1990 Phoenix	6	---	---	---	---	---	---	---	---	16	272	17.0	0
1991 Phoenix	9	14	44	3.1	0	19	176	9.3	0	16	330	20.6	0
1992 Phoenix	16	37	139	3.8	0	50	417	8.3	2	---	---	---	---
1993 Phoenix	16	25	152	6.1	0	66	603	9.1	3	---	---	---	---
4 YR TOTALS	47	76	335	4.4	0	135	1196	8.9	5	32	602	18.8	0
1993 RANK NFL RB		94	82	8.	89	5	5	32	2	65	65	65	
1994 PROJECTIONS	16	24	186	7.8	0	84	780	9.3	4	0	0	NA	0

Garrison Hearst   No. 23/RB

HT: 5-11 **WT:** 215
Born: 1-4-71, Lincolnton, GA
High school: Lincoln County (GA)
College: Georgia
A first-round pick for the Cardinals in '93, Hearst was a disappointment. He had just 264 yards in 6 games before being injured.

		RUSHING				RECEIVING				KICK RETURNS			
YEAR TEAM	G	ATT	YDS	AVG	TD	REC	YDS	AVG	TD	RET	YDS	AVG	TD
1993 Phoenix	6	76	264	3.5	1	6	18	3.0	0	---	---	---	---
1 YR TOTALS	6	76	264	3.5	1	6	18	3.0	0	0	0	NA	0
1993 RANK NFL RB		51	58	88	58	87	104	115	40	65	65	65	

Gary Clark   No. 84/WR

HT: 5-9 **WT:** 175
Born: 5-1-62, Radford, VA
High school: Pulaski County (Dublin, VA)
College: James Madison
Clark is the only NFL player with 50+ catches
in each of the last 9 years.

YEAR	TEAM	G	RECEIVING REC	YDS	AVG	TD	RUSHING ATT	YDS	AVG	TD	PUNT RETURN RET	YDS	AVG
1986	Washington	15	74	1265	17.1	7	2	10	5.0	0	1	14	14.0
1987	Washington	12	56	1066	19.0	7	1	0	0.0	0	---	---	---
1988	Washington	16	59	892	15.1	7	2	6	3.0	0	8	48	6.0
1989	Washington	15	79	1229	15.6	9	2	19	9.5	0	---	---	---
1990	Washington	16	75	1112	14.8	8	1	1	1.0	0	---	---	---
1991	Washington	16	70	1340	19.1	10	1	0	0.0	0	---	---	---
1992	Washington	16	64	912	14.3	5	2	18	9.0	0	---	---	---
1993	Phoenix	14	63	818	13.0	4	---	---	---	---	---	---	---
	9 YR TOTALS	136	612	9560	15.6	62	11	54	4.9	0	9	62.0	6.9
1993	RANK NFL WR		20	23	84	28	42	42	42		30	30	29
1994	PROJECTIONS	13	60	692	11.5	3	0	0	NA	0	0	0	NA

Ricky Proehl   No. 87/WR

Full name: Richard Scott Proehl
HT: 6-0 **WT:** 190
Born: 3-7-68, Belle Mead, NJ
High school: Hillsborough (NJ)
College: Wake Forest
Proehl tied a team record with TD catches in
5 straight games.

YEAR	TEAM	G	RECEIVING REC	YDS	AVG	TD	RUSHING ATT	YDS	AVG	TD	PUNT RETURN RET	YDS	AVG
1990	Phoenix	16	56	802	14.3	4	1	4	4.0	0	1	2	2.0
1991	Phoenix	16	55	766	13.9	2	3	21	7.0	0	4	26	6.5
1992	Phoenix	16	60	744	12.4	3	3	23	7.7	0	---	---	---
1993	Phoenix	16	65	877	13.5	7	8	47	5.9	0	---	---	---
	4 YR TOTALS	64	236	3189	13.5	16	15	95	6.3	0	5	28	5.6
1993	RANK NFL WR		16	19	72	7	3	5	18		30	30	29
1994	PROJECTIONS	16	69	948	13.7	10	11	64	5.8	0	0	0	NA

Randal Hill   No. 81/WR

Full name: Randal Thrill Hill
HT: 5-10 **WT:** 180
Born: 9-21-69, Miami, FL
High school: Miami Killian (FL)
College: Miami (FL)
Hill was fourth on the Cards with 35 catches, and averaged 14.8 yards/catch.

YEAR	TEAM	G	RECEIVING REC	YDS	AVG	TD	RUSHING ATT	YDS	AVG	TD	PUNT RETURN RET	YDS	AVG
1991	Mia (1)-Pho (15)	16	43	495	11.5	1	---	---	---	---	---	---	---
1992	Phoenix	16	58	861	14.8	3	1	4	4.0	0	---	---	---
1993	Phoenix	16	35	519	14.8	4	---	---	---	---	---	---	---
	3 YR TOTALS	48	136	1875	13.8	8	1	4	4.0	0	0	0	NA
1993	RANK NFL WR		56	52	47	28	42	42	42		30	30	29
1994	PROJECTIONS	16	22	354	16.1	5	0	0	NA	0	0	0	NA

Clyde Simmons No. 96/DE

HT: 6-6 **WT:** 280
Born: 8-4-64, Lanes, SC
High school: New Hanover (Wilmington, NC)
College: Western Carolina
Slowed by injuries, Simmons had just 5 sacks, half his career average. He still managed to extend his string of consecutive starts to 108.

YEAR	TEAM	G	INT	YDS	AVG	TD	SACKS	FUM REC	TD
1986	Philadelphia	16	---	---	---	---	2.0	---	---
1987	Philadelphia	12	---	---	---	---	6.0	1	0
1988	Philadelphia	16	---	---	---	---	8.0	3	0
1989	Philadelphia	16	1	60	60.0	1	15.5	---	---
1990	Philadelphia	16	---	---	---	---	7.5	2	1
1991	Philadelphia	16	---	---	---	---	13.0	3	1
1992	Philadelphia	16	---	---	---	---	19.0	1	---
1993	Philadelphia	16	1	0	0.0	0	5.0	---	---
	8 YR TOTALS	124	2	60	30.0	1	76.0	10	2
1993	RANK NFL DL		2	10	10	3	51	71	NA
1994	PROJECTIONS	16	1	0	0.0	0	0	0	0

Seth Joyner   No. 59/LB

HT: 6-2   **WT:** 235
Born: 11-18-64, Spring Valley, NY
High school: Spring Valley (NY)
College: Texas-El Paso
Ex-Eagle Joyner led Philly with 113 tackles in 1993. He also had 20 hurries and started all 16 games at LLB.

YEAR	TEAM	G	INT	YDS	AVG	TD	SACKS	FUM REC	TD
1986	Philadelphia	14	1	4	4.0	0	2.0	—	—
1987	Philadelphia	12	2	42	21.0	0	4.0	2	1
1988	Philadelphia	16	4	96	24.0	0	3.5	1	0
1989	Philadelphia	14	1	0	0.0	0	4.5	—	—
1990	Philadelphia	16	1	9	9.0	0	7.5	—	—
1991	Philadelphia	16	3	41	13.7	0	6.5	4	2
1992	Philadelphia	16	4	88	22.0	2	6.5	1	0
1993	Philadelphia	16	1	6	6.0	0	2.0	—	—
	8 YR TOTALS	120	17	286	16.8	2	36.5	8	3
1993	RANK NFL LB		17	29	25	5	37	81	NA
1994	PROJECTIONS	16	0	0	NA	0	0	0	0

Eric Hill   No. 58/ILB

HT: 6-2   **WT:** 255
Born: 11-14-66, Galveston, TX
High school: Ball (Galveston, TX)
College: Louisiana State
Hill missed 3 early games, but placed second on the team with 92 tackles.

YEAR	TEAM	G	INT	YDS	AVG	TD	SACKS	FUM REC	TD
1989	Phoenix	15	—	—	—	—	1.0	1	0
1990	Phoenix	16	—	—	—	—	1.5	—	—
1991	Phoenix	16	—	—	—	—	—	1	1
1992	Phoenix	16	—	—	—	—	—	1	0
1993	Phoenix	13	—	—	—	—	1.0	1	0
	5 YR TOTALS	76	0	0	NA	0	4.5	4	1
1993	RANK NFL LB		47	NA	NA	NA	62	24	8
1994	PROJECTIONS	12	0	0	0	0	1	1	0

Greg Davis   No. 5/K

Full name: Gregory Brian Davis
HT: 6-0   **WT:** 205
Born: 10-29-65, Rome, GA
High school: Lakeside (Atlanta)
College: The Citadel
Davis was a perfect 13-for-13 on FGs of less than 40 yards.

YEAR	TEAM	G	XP	XPA	XP Pct.	FG	FGA	FG Pct.	PTS
1987	Atlanta	3	6	6	100.0	3	4	75.0	15
1988	Atlanta	16	25	27	92.6	19	30	63.3	82
1989	NE (9)-Atl(6)	15	25	28	89.3	23	34	67.6	94
1990	Atlanta	16	40	40	100.0	22	33	66.7	106
1991	Phoenix	16	19	19	100.0	21	30	70.0	82
1992	Phoenix	16	28	28	100.0	13	26	50.0	67
1993	Phoenix	16	37	37	100.0	21	28	75.0	100
	7 YR TOTALS	98	180	185	97.3	122	185	65.9	546
1993	RANK NFL		5	5	1	20	18	16	18
1994	PROJECTIONS	16	42	42	100.0	23	27	85.2	111

Buddy Ryan   Head Coach

Born: 2-17-34, Frederick, OK
College: Oklahoma State
Better known for clashes with former Eagles' owner Norman Braman and Oilers' offensive coordinator Kevin Gilbride, Ryan's fiery reputation has overshadowed his achievements, including coaching Super Bowl championship defenses in New York and Chicago.

		REGULAR SEASON					POSTSEASON			
YEAR	TEAM	W	L	T	PCT	FINISH	W	L	FINISH
1986	Philadelphia	5	10	1	.344	4th/NFC East			
1987	Philadelphia	7	8	0	.467	4th/NFC East			
1988	Philadelphia	10	6	0	.625	1st/NFC East	0	1	lost 1st Rnd. game to Chicago, 20-12
1989	Philadelphia	11	5	0	.688	2nd/NFC East	0	1	lost wild card game to LA Rams, 21-7
1990	Philadelphia	10	6	0	.625	2nd/NFC East	0	1	lost wild card game to Wash., 20-6
	5 YR TOTALS	43	35	1	.551		0	3	

Anthony Edwards No. 83/WR

HT: 5-10 **WT:** 190
Born: 5-26-66, Casa Grande, AZ
High school: Union (Casa Grande, AZ)
College: New Mexico Highlands
Edwards averaged 25.1 yards/catch in a limited amount of time at wideout.

YEAR	TEAM	G	RECEIVING				RUSHING				PUNT RETURN		
			REC	YDS	AVG	TD	ATT	YDS	AVG	TD	RET	YDS	AVG
1991	Phoenix	13	---	---	---	---	---	---	---	---	1	7	7.0
1992	Phoenix	16	14	147	10.5	1	---	---	---	---	---	---	---
1993	Phoenix	16	13	326	25.1	1	---	---	---	---	3	12	4.0
	5 YR TOTALS	59	29	547	18.9	2	0	0	NA	0	19	143	7.5
1993	RANK NFL WR		90	76	3	72	42	42	42		23	27	26
1994	PROJECTIONS	16	16	451	28.2	1	0	0	NA	0	1	0	0.0

Rick Cunningham   No. 64/T

Full name: Patrick Dante Ross Cunningham
HT: 6-6 **WT:** 320
Born: 1-4-67, Los Angeles, CA
High school: Beverly Hills (CA)
College: Sacramento CC (CA) and Texas A&M
Cunningham's OL allowed just 33 sacks.

YEAR	TEAM	G	RUSHING			RANK	PASS	RANK		YDS.
			ATT	YDS	AVG	AV RUSH	YDS	PASS YDS	SACKS	LOST
1992	Phoenix	8	395	1491	3.8	19	3344	12	36	258
1993	Phoenix	16	452	1809	4.0	13	3635	7	33	231
	2 YR TOTALS	26								

Eric Swann   No. 98/DL

Full name: Eric Jerrod Swann
HT: 6-5 **WT:** 295
Born: 8-16-70, Pinehurst, NC
High school: Western Harnett (Lillington, NC)
College: None
A knee injury ended his season after 9 games.

YEAR	TEAM	G	INT	YDS	AVG	TD	SACKS	FUM REC	TD
1991	Phoenix	12	---	---	---	---	4.0	---	---
1992	Phoenix	16	---	---	---	---	2.0	---	---
1993	Phoenix	9	---	---	---	---	3.5	1	0
	3 YR TOTALS	37	0	0	NA	0	9.5	1	0
1993	RANK NFL DL		16	NA	NA	NA	66	25	5
1994	PROJECTIONS	8	0	0	0	0	4	2	0

Michael Bankston   No. 63/NT

HT: 6-1   **WT:** 280
Born: 3-12-70, East Bernard, TX
High school: East Bernard (TX)
College: Sam Houston State
Bankston's 5 fumble recoveries tied a Cards record.

YEAR	TEAM	G	INT	YDS	AVG	TD	SACKS	FUM REC	TD
1992	Phoenix	16	—	—	—	—	2.0	—	—
1993	Phoenix	16	—	—	—	—	3.0	5	0
2 YR TOTALS		32	0	0	NA	0	5.0	5	0
1993 RANK NFL DL			16	NA	NA	NA	75	1	5
1994 PROJECTIONS		16	0	0	NA	0	4	10	0

Chuck Cecil   No. 26/FS

Full name: Charles Douglas Cecil
HT: 6-0   **WT:** 185
Born: 11-8-64, Red Bluff, CA
High school: Helix (La Mesa, CA)
College: Arizona
Cecil had 61 tackles despite second half injuries.

YEAR	TEAM	G	INT	YDS	AVG	TD	SACKS	FUM REC	TD
1991	Green Bay	16	3	76	25.3	0	—	—	—
1992	Green Bay	16	4	52	13.0	0	—	—	—
1993	Phoenix	15	—	—	—	—	—	—	—
6 YR TOTALS		81	13	200	15.4	0	0.0	1	0
1993 RANK NFL DB			156	NA	NA	NA	49	94	NA
1994 PROJECTIONS		16	0	0	0	0	0	0	0

James Williams   No. 21/CB

Full name: James Earl Williams
HT: 5-10   **WT:** 185
Born: 3-30-67, Osceola, AR
High school: Coalinga (CA)
College: Fresno State
Williams brings playoff experience to the Cards.

			RUSHING				RECEIVING				KICK RETURNS			
YEAR	TEAM	G	ATT	YDS	AVG	TD	REC	YDS	AVG	TD	RET	YDS	AVG	TD
1991	Seattle	16	188	741	3.9	4	61	499	8.2	1	...	...	...	...
1992	Seattle	16	114	339	3.0	1	74	556	7.5	2	...	...	...	...
1993	Seattle	16	82	371	4.5	3	58	450	7.8	1	...	...	...	...
8 YR TOTALS		123	1148	4579	4.0	17	471	4151	8.8	16	0	0	NA	0
1993 RANK NFL RB			47	48	35	21	8	8	58	13	65	65	65	
1994 PROJECTIONS		16	40	295	7.4	4	49	385	7.9	1	0	0	NA	0

Jim McMahon   No. 9/QB

Full name: James Robert McMahon
HT: 6-1 **WT:** 195
Born: 8-21-59, Jersey City, NJ
High school: Roy (UT)
College: Brigham Young
McMahon is reunited with his Eagles coach.

		PASSING										RUSHING		
YEAR	TEAM	G	ATT	CPL	CPL%	YDS	AVG	TDS	TD%	INT	INT%	RTG	ATT	YDS	AVG
1991	Philadelphia	12	311	187	60.1	2239	7.2	12	3.9	11	3.5	80.3	22	55	2.5
1992	Philadelphia	4	43	22	51.2	279	6.5	1	2.3	2	4.7	60.1	6	23	3.8
1993	Minnesota	12	331	200	60.4	1968	5.9	9	2.7	8	2.4	76.2	33	96	2.9
12 YR TOTALS		111	2625	1465	55.8	17884	6.8	99	3.8	87	3.3		328	1600	4.9
1993 RANK NFL QB		19	18		21	21		46	22		44	23	42	33	11	16	30
1994 PROJECTIONS		15	513	315	61.4	2948	5.7	14	2.6	11	2.1		51	141	2.8

Jeff Feagles   No. 10/P

Full name: Jeffrey Allan Feagles
HT: 6-1 **WT:** 205
Born: 3-7-66, Scottsdale, AZ
High school: Gerard Catholic (Phoenix)
College: Scottsdale CC (AZ) and Miami (FL)
Feagles led the NFL with 31 punts inside the 20.

YEAR	TEAM	G	NO	YARDS	LONG	AVG	BLK	IN20
1990	New England	16	72	3026	60	42.0	2	20
1991	Philadelphia	16	87	3640	77	41.8	1	29
1992	Philadelphia	16	82	3459	68	42.2	0	26
1993	Philadelphia	16	83	3323	60	40.0	0	31
6 YR TOTALS		96	478	19322	77	40.4	4	143
1993 RANK NFL Ps		6	10	17	26		1
1994 PROJECTIONS	16	83	3176	52	38.3	0	34

Atlanta
FALCONS

1994 Scouting Report

Offense

Overall, Atlanta gained 5,110 total yards in 1993, eleventh in the NFL. Under new coach June Jones, the Falcons are sticking with the run-and-shoot offense that gained 3,520 passing yards last season, sixth in the NFL. That means Atlanta, once again, will gain a lot of yards in the air and relatively little on the ground. The Falcons have added Jeff George with hopes that he will be more effective than Bobby Hebert, whose arm strength has long been suspect. But the team must replace two key WRs in Mike Pritchard and Michael Haynes. Jones will look to ex-Jet Terance Mathis and rookie Bert Emanuel to have big years. Underrated RB Erric Pegram is a solid runner. The Falcons had 1,590 rushing yards last season, twenty-third in the NFL— Pegram gained 1,185.

Defense

Overall, the Falcons gave up 5,421 total yards, twenty-fifth in the league. The sore spot was pass defense, where (despite Deion Sanders and his NFC-leading 7 INTs) Atlanta allowed 3,637 passing yards, twenty-fifth in the NFL. So they obtained DE Chris Doleman from Minnesota to beef up the pass rush and signed free agent DBs Kevin Ross (from Kansas City) and D. J. Johnson (from Pittsburgh) to bolster the defensive backfield. The Falcons are still weak at LB, and will probably be only average against the run in 1994; in 1993, they gave up 1,784 rushing yards, fifteenth in the NFL.

Special Teams

Norm Johnson is a reliable kicker; he put together a streak of 26 straight field goals between 1992 and 1993 (second longest in NFL history). P Harold Alexander's net punting average was fifth best in the NFL at 37.6. Of course, Deion Sanders (if he returns) is always a TD threat on kick and punt returns.

1994 Prospects

Atlanta will not seriously challenge San Francisco in the NFC West—They just don't have the players. With the improvement in the NFC Central, they probably won't even qualify for a wild card, but they could finish as high as second in their division.

Team Directory

Chairman of the board: Rankin M. Smith, Sr.

President: Taylor Smith

Director of pro personnel: Chuck Connor

Director of public relations: Charlie Taylor

1993 Review			1994 Schedule		
Sep. 5	at Detroit	L 30-13	Sep. 4	at Detroit	1:00
Sep. 12	NEW ORLEANS	L 34-31	Sep. 11	L.A. RAMS	1:00
Sep. 19	at San Francisco	L 37-30	Sep. 18	KANSAS CITY	8:00
Sep. 27	PITTSBURGH	L 45-17	Sep. 25	at Washington	1:00
Oct. 3	at Chicago	L 6-0	Oct. 2	at L.A. Rams	4:00
Oct. 10	OPEN DATE		Oct. 9	TAMPA BAY	1:00
Oct. 14	L.A. RAMS	W 30-24	Oct. 16	SAN FRANCISCO	1:00
Oct. 24	at New Orleans	W 26-15	Oct. 23	at L.A. Raiders	4:00
Oct. 31	TAMPA BAY	L 31-24	Oct. 30	OPEN DATE	
Nov. 7	OPEN DATE		Nov. 6	SAN DIEGO	1:00
Nov. 14	at L.A. Rams	W 13-0	Nov. 13	at New Orleans	1:00
Nov. 21	DALLAS	W 27-14	Nov. 20	at Denver	4:00
Nov. 28	CLEVELAND	W 17-14	Nov. 27	PHILADELPHIA	1:00
Dec. 5	at Houston	L 33-17	Dec. 4	at San Francisco	4:00
Dec. 11	SAN FRANCISCO	W 27-24	Dec. 11	NEW ORLEANS	8:00
Dec. 19	at Washington	L 30-17	Dec. 18	vs. Green Bay (Mil.)	1:00
Dec. 26	at Cincinnati	L 21-17	Dec. 24	ARIZONA	1:00
Jan. 2	PHOENIX	L 27-10			

1993 finish: 6-10 (4-4 home, 2-6 away), third in NFC West

Team Leaders

PASSING	ATT	COM	COM%	YDS	YPA	TD	TD%	INT	INT%	RTG
Hebert	430	263	61.2	2978	6.93	24	5.6	17	4.0	84.0
Tolliver	76	39	51.3	464	6.11	3	3.9	5	6.6	56.0
Miller	66	32	48.5	345	5.23	1	1.5	3	4.5	50.4
TEAM	573	334	58.3	3787	6.61	28	4.9	25	4.4	76.3
OPPONENTS	505	308	61.0	3786	7.50	27	5.3	13	2.6	91.2

RECEIVING	REC	YDS	AVG	TD	RUSHING	ATT	YDS	AVG	TD
Rison	86	1242	14.4	15	Pegram	292	1185	4.1	3
Pritchard	74	736	9.9	7	Broussard	39	206	5.3	1
Haynes	72	778	10.8	4	Dickerson	26	91	3.5	0
Hill	34	384	11.3	0	Hebert	24	49	2.0	0
Pegram	33	302	9.2	0	Tolliver	7	48	6.9	0
TEAM	334	3787	11.3	28	TEAM	395	1590	4.0	4
OPPONENTS	308	3786	12.3	27	OPPONENTS	419	1784	4.3	14

INTERCEPTIONS	INT	YDS	AVG	LG	TD	SACKS	NO
Sanders	7	91	13.0	41	0	Holt	6.5
Walker	3	7	2.3	7	0	Geathers	3.5
Clark	2	59	29.5	38	0	Smith	3.5
Eaton	1	0	0.0	0	0	Agee	2.5
Case	0	3	—	3	0	Gardner	2.0
TEAM	13	160	12.3	44	0	TEAM	27.0
OPPONENTS	25	345	13.8	78	2	OPPONENTS	40.0

KICK RETURNS	NO	YDS	AV	LG	TD	PUNT RETURNS	NO	FC	YDS	AV	LG	TD
Smith, T.	38	948	24.9	97t	1	Smith, T.	32	17	255	8.0	51	0
Sanders	7	169	24.1	31	0	Sanders	2	1	21	10.5	16	0
Pegram	4	63	15.8	28	0	Clark	1	0	0	0.0	0	0
TEAM	55	1300	23.6	97t	1	TEAM	35	18	276	7.9	51	0
OPPONENTS	55	1064	19.3	65	0	OPPONENTS	41	17	350	8.5	30	0

KICKING	XPM	XPA	FGM	FGA	LG	PTS
Johnson	34	34	26	27	54	112
TEAM	34	34	26	27	54	112
OPPONENTS	45	46	20	31	52	105

PUNTING	NO	YDS	LG	AVG	TB	BLK	RET	RYD	IN20	NAV
Alexander	72	3114	75	43.3	3	0	41	350	21	37.6
TEAM	72	3114	75	43.3	3	0	41	350	21	37.6
OPPONENTS	74	3029	66	40.9	5	1	35	276	23	35.9

FUMBLES	FUM	OFF. FUM. REC.	REC	TD	DEF. FUM. REC.	REC	TD
Hebert	11	Pegram	4	0	Smith, C.	2	0
Pegram	6	Hebert	3	0	Washington	2	0
Smith, T.	4	Whitfield	2	0			
TEAM	31	TEAM	13	0	TEAM	11	1
OPPONENTS	25	OPPONENTS	9	0	OPPONENTS	17	3

1994 Draft Choices

ROUND	NAME	POS	SCHOOL	OVERALL SELECTION
2	Bert Emanuel	WR	Rice	45
3	Anthony Phillips	CB	Texas A&M-Kingsville	72
3	Alai Kalaniuvalu	G	Oregon State	99
4	Perry Klein	QB	C.W. Post	111
4	Mitch Davis	LB	Georgia	118
5	Harrison Houston	WR	Florida	138
7	Jamal Anderson	RB	Utah	201

HISTORY

TITLES

1980   NFC West Championship

ALL-TIME TEAM RECORDS

Rushing

Most yards, game:	202	Gerald Riggs	9/2/84
Most yards, season:	1,719	Gerald Riggs	1985
Most yards, career:	6,631	Gerald Riggs	1982-1988

Passing

Most yards, game:	416	Steve Bartkowski	11/15/81
Most yards, season:	3,830	Steve Bartkowski	1981
Most yards, career:	23,468	Steve Bartkowski	1975-1985

Receiving

Most catches, game:	15	William Andrews	11/15/81
Most catches, season:	93	Andre Rison	1992
Most catches, career:	359	Alfred Jenkins	1975-1983

Scoring

Most points, game:	18	Many Times	
		Andre Rison	9/20/93
Most points, season:	114	Mick Luckhurst	1981
Most points, career:	558	Mick Luckhurst	1981-1987

COACHES

NAME	RECORD	YEARS
Norb Hecker	4-26-1	1966-68
Norm Van Brocklin	37-49-3	1968-74
Marion Campbell	17-51-0	1974-76, 87-89
Pat Peppler	3-6-0	1976
Leeman Bennett	47-44-0	1977-82
Dan Henning	22-41-1	1983-86
Jim Hanifan	0-4-0	1989
Jerry Glanville	28-38-0	1990-93

ATLANTA FALCONS
1994 TRAINING CAMP ROSTER

No.	Name	Pos	Ht	Wt	Born	NFL Exp	College	How Acq	GP/GS
1	George, Jeff	QB	6-4	218	12-8-67	5	Illinois	T-IND '94	13/11
3	Hebert, Bobby	QB	6-4	215	8-19-60	9	NW Louisiana	FA '93	14/12
7	Klein, Perry	QB	6-2	218	3-25-71	R	C.W. Post	D4a '94	
Running backs									
38	Anderson, Jamal	RB	5-10	246	3-6-72	R	Utah	D7 '94	
	Heyward, Craig	FB	5-11	260	9-26-66	7	Pittsburgh	FA '94	16/15
33	Pegram, Erric	RB	5-9	188	1-7-69	4	North Texas St.	D6 '91	16/14
28	Smith, Tony	RB	6-1	224	6-29-70	3	Southern Mississippi	D1 '92	15/0
Wide receivers									
87	Emanuel, Bert	WR	5-10	176	10-27-70	R	Rice	D2 '94	
83	Harris, Leonard	WR	5-8	166	11-27-60	9	Texas Tech	FA '94	4/2
89	Houston, Harrison	WR	5-9	174	1-26-72	R	Florida	D5 '94	
81	Mathis, Terance	WR	5-10	177	6-7-67	5	New Mexico	FA '94	16/3
34	Mims, David	WR	5-8	191	7-7-70	2	Baylor	FA '93	15/2
80	Rison, Andre	WR	6-1	188	3-18-67	6	Michigan State	T-IND '90	16/16
Tight ends									
88	Le Bel, Harper	TE	6-4	248	7-14-63	6	Colorado State	Plan B '91	16/0
86	Lyons, Mitch	TE	6-4	255	5-13-70	2	Michigan State	D6 '93	16/8
Offensive linemen									
62	Alex, Keith	G	6-4	307	6-9-69	2	Texas A&M	FA '93	13/0
	Eatman, Irv	T	6-7	300	1-1-61	9	UCLA	FA '94	16/16
65	Fortin, Roman	G-C	6-5	285	2-26-67	5	San Diego State	Plan B '92	16/0
75	Kalaniuvalu, Alai	G	6-3	302	10-23-71	R	Oregon State	D3b '94	
78	Kenn, Mike	T	6-7	280	2-9-56	17	Michigan	D1 '78	16/16
66	Kennedy, Lincoln	G-T	6-6	335	2-12-71	2	Washington	D1 '93	16/16
**	Ruether, Mike	C-G	6-4	286	9-20-62	9	Texas	Plan B '90	16/0
70	Whitfield, Bob	T	6-5	308	10-18-71	3	Stanford	D1 '92	16/16
72	Zandofsky, Mike	C-G	6-2	305	11-30-65	6	Washington	FA '94	16/16
Defensive linemen									
68	Agee, Mel	DL	6-5	298	11-22-68	3	Illinois	FA '92	11/7
92	Archambeau, Lester	DE	6-5	275	6-27-67	5	Stanford	T-GB '93	15/11
59	Doleman, Chris	DE	6-5	275	10-16-61	10	Pittsburgh	T-MIN '94	16/16
76	Gann, Mike	DE	6-5	270	10-19-63	10	Notre Dame	D2 '85	8/8
67	Gardner, Moe	NT	6-2	261	8-10-68	4	Illinois	D4 '91	16/16
97	Geathers, Jumpy	DT	6-7	290	6-26-60	11	Wichita State	FA '93	14/0
71	Goldberg, Bill	DT	6-2	268	12-27-66	2	Georgia	FA '93	5/0
95	Holt, Pierce	DL	6-4	275	1-1-62	7	Angelo State	FA '93	16/15
73	Logan, Ernie	DE	6-3	285	5-18-68	4	East Carolina	FA '93	8/1
90	Smith, Chuck	DE-LB	6-2	254	12-21-69	3	Tennessee	D2 '92	15/1
Linebackers									
**	Conner, Darion	LB	6-2	245	9-28-67	5	Jackson St.	D2 '90	14/10
99	Davis, Mitch	LB	6-3	238	7-7-71	R	Georgia	D4b '94	
51	Dinkins, Howard	LB	6-1	230	4-26-69	3	Florida State	D3 '92	3/0
50	George, Ron	LB	6-2	225	3-20-70	2	Stanford	D5 '93	12/4
53	Gordon, Dwayne	LB	6-1	231	11-2-69	2	New Hampshire	FA '93	5/0
	Matthews, Clay	LB	6-2	245	3-15-56	17	Southern California	FA '94	16/15
**	Solomon, Jesse	LB	6-0	235	11-4-63	9	Florida State	FA '92	16/16
52	Tippins, Ken	LB	6-1	235	7-22-66	6	Middle Tenn. St.	FA '90	14/1
54	Tuggle, Jessie	LB	5-11	230	2-14-65	8	Valdosta State	FA '87	16/16
Defensive backs									
**	Case, Scott	S	6-1	188	5-17-62	11	Oklahoma	D2 '84	16/16
27	Clark, Vinnie	CB	6-0	194	1-22-69	4	Ohio State	T-GB '93	15/9
**	Donaldson, Jeff	S	6-0	190	4-19-62	11	Colorado	Plan B '91	13/2
**	Eaton, Tracey	S	6-1	195	7-19-65	6	Portland State	Plan B '91	16/1
47	Harper, Roger	S	6-2	223	10-26-70	2	Ohio State	D2 '93	16/1
44	Johnson, D.J.	CB	6-0	180	7-14-66	6	Kentucky	FA '94	16/15
22	Montgomery, Alton	S	6-0	202	6-16-68	5	Houston	T-DEN '93	8/0
26	Phillips, Anthony	CB	6-2	217	10-5-70	R	Texas A&M	D3a '94	
36	Ross, Kevin	CB	5-9	182	1-16-62	11	Temple	FA '94	15/15
**	Sanders, Deion	CB	6-0	185	8-9-67	6	Florida State	D1 '89	11/10
**	Shelley, Elbert	S	5-11	185	12-24-64	8	Arkansas State	D11 '87	16/0
45	Walker, Darnell	CB	5-8	164	1-17-70	2	Oklahoma	D7 '93	15/8
46	Washington, Charles	S	6-1	217	10-8-66	6	Cameron (OK)	FA '93	6/0
Specialists									
5	Alexander, Harold	P	6-2	224	10-20-70	2	Appalachian St.	D3 '93	16/0
9	Johnson, Norm	K	6-2	203	5-31-60	13	UCLA	FA '91	15/0

Jeff George   No. 1/QB

Full name: Jeffrey Scott George
HT: 6-4   **WT:** 218
Born: 12-8-67, Indianapolis, IN
High school: Warren Central (Indianapolis)
College: Purdue, Illinois
George was acquired from Indianapolis during the off-season to replace Chris Miller. He threw just 6 INTs in 1993.

YEAR	TEAM	G	PASSING ATT	CPL	CPL%	YDS	AVG	TDS	TD%	INT	INT%	RTG	RUSHING ATT	YDS	AVG
1990	Indianapolis	13	334	181	54.2	2152	6.4	16	4.8	13	3.9	73.8	11	2	0.2
1991	Indianapolis	16	485	292	60.2	2910	6.0	10	2.1	12	2.5	73.8	16	36	2.3
1992	Indianapolis	10	306	167	54.6	1963	6.4	7	2.3	15	4.9	61.5	14	26	1.9
1993	Indianapolis	13	407	234	57.5	2526	6.2	8	2.0	6	1.5	76.3	13	39	3.0
	4 YR TOTALS	52	1532	874	57.0	9551	6.2	41	2.7	46	3.0		54	103	1.9
1993	RANK NFL QB		14	14	33	15	38	24	53	31	58	32	32	29	27
1994	PROJECTIONS	15	485	283	58.4	2984	6.2	8	1.6	0	0.0		13	54	4.2

Bobby Hebert   No. 3/QB

Full name: Bobby Joseph Hebert Jr.
HT: 6-4   **WT:** 215
Born: 8-19-60, Baton Rouge, LA
High school: South Lafourche (LA)
College: Northwestern Louisiana
Slated to back up Jeff George in '94, Hebert set personal bests in 1993 with 24 TD passes and an 84 QB rating.

YEAR	TEAM	G	PASSING ATT	CPL	CPL%	YDS	AVG	TDS	TD%	INT	INT%	RTG	RUSHING ATT	YDS	AVG
1985	New Orleans	6	181	97	53.6	1208	6.7	5	2.8	4	2.2	74.6	12	26	2.2
1986	New Orleans	5	79	41	51.9	498	6.3	2	2.5	8	^^^^^	40.5	5	14	2.8
1987	New Orleans	12	294	164	55.8	2119	7.2	15	5.1	9	3.1	82.9	13	95	7.3
1988	New Orleans	16	478	280	58.6	3156	6.6	20	4.2	15	3.1	79.3	37	79	2.1
1989	New Orleans	14	353	222	62.9	2686	7.6	15	4.2	15	4.2	82.7	25	87	3.5
1991	New Orleans	9	248	149	60.1	1676	6.8	9	3.6	8	3.2	79.0	18	56	3.1
1992	New Orleans	16	422	249	59.0	3287	7.8	19	4.5	16	3.8	82.9	32	95	3.0
1993	Atlanta	14	430	263	61.2	2978	6.9	24	5.6	17	4.0	84.0	24	49	2.0
	8 YR TOTALS	92	2485	1465	59.0	17608	7.1	109	4.4	92	3.7		166	501	3.0
1993	RANK NFL QB		10	10	16	13	25	3	8	5	26	20	20	24	36
1994	PROJECTIONS	15	491	303	61.7	3308	6.7	30	6.1	20	4.1		23	34	1.5

Erric Pegram   No. 33/RB

HT: 5-9   **WT:** 188
Born: 1-7-69, Dallas, TX
High school: Hillcrest (Dallas)
College: North Texas State
Pegram finished fourth in the NFL with 1,185 rushing yards. He fumbled just 6 times, an average of once every 55 plays.

		RUSHING				RECEIVING				KICK RETURNS			
YEAR	TEAM	G	ATT	YDS	AVG	TD	REC	YDS	AVG	TD	RET	YDS	AVG	TD
1991	Atlanta	16	101	349	3.5	1	1	-1	-1.0	0	16	260	16.3	0
1992	Atlanta	16	21	89	4.2	0	2	25	12.5	0	9	161	17.9	0
1993	Atlanta	16	292	1185	4.1	3	33	302	9.2	0	4	63	15.8	0
	3 YR TOTALS	48	414	1623	3.9	4	36	326	9.1	0	29	484	16.7	0
1993	RANK NFL RB		4	4	45	21	28	22	31	40	28	-33	37	
1994	PROJECTIONS	16	475	1942	4.1	5	57	516	9.1	0	0	0	NA	0

Tony Smith   No. 28/RB

HT: 6-1   **WT:** 224
Born: 6-29-70, Chicago, IL
High school: Warren Central (MS)
College: Southern Mississippi
Smith placed second in the NFL in kick return yards, third in kick return average and third in combined kick return/punt return yards.

		RUSHING				RECEIVING				KICK RETURNS			
YEAR	TEAM	G	ATT	YDS	AVG	TD	REC	YDS	AVG	TD	RET	YDS	AVG	TD
1992	Atlanta	14	87	329	3.8	2	2	14	7.0	0	7	172	24.6	0
1993	Atlanta	15	---	---	---	---	---	---	---	---	38	948	24.9	1
	2 YR TOTALS	29	87	329	3.8	2	2	14	7.0	0	45	1120	24.9	1
1993	RANK NFL RB		138	137	137	89	123	122	122	40	1	1	3	

Andre Rison   No. 80/WR

Full name: Andre Previn Rison
HT: 6-1   **WT:** 188
Born: 3-18-67, Flint (MI)
High school: Northwestern (Flint, MI)
College: Michigan State
Rison's 394 catches over his first 5 seasons are more than any NFL player has ever recorded in that span.

YEAR	TEAM	G	RECEIVING				RUSHING				PUNT RETURN		
			REC	YDS	AVG	TD	ATT	YDS	AVG	TD	RET	YDS	AVG
1989	Indianapolis	16	52	820	15.8	4	3	18	6.0	0	2	20	10.0
1990	Atlanta	16	82	1208	14.7	10	---	---	---	---	2	10	5.0
1991	Atlanta	16	81	976	12.0	12	1	-9	-9.0	0	---	---	---
1992	Atlanta	15	93	1121	12.1	11	---	---	---	---	---	---	---
1993	Atlanta	16	86	1242	14.4	15	---	---	---	---	---	---	---
	5 YR TOTALS	79	394	5367	13.6	52	4	9	2.3	0	4	30	7.5
1993	RANK NFL WR		4	4	53	1	42	42	42		30	30	29
1994	PROJECTIONS	16	86	1316	15.3	17	0	0	NA	0	0	0	NA

Terance Mathis   No. 81/WR

HT: 5-10 **WT:** 177
Born: 9-21-69, Detroit, MI
High school: Redan (Stone Mountain, GA)
College: New Mexico
Mathis came back from arthroscopic knee surgery to post career highs in receiving yards (352) and average yards per catch (14.7).

YEAR	TEAM	G	RECEIVING				RUSHING				PUNT RETURN		
			REC	YDS	AVG	TD	ATT	YDS	AVG	TD	RET	YDS	AVG
1990	NY Jets	16	19	245	12.9	0	2	9	4.5	0	11	165	15.0
1991	NY Jets	16	28	329	11.8	1	1	19	19.0	0	23	157	6.8
1992	NY Jets	16	22	316	14.4	3	3	25	8.3	1	2	24	12.0
1993	NY Jets	16	24	352	14.7	0	---	---	---	---	14	99	7.1
	4 YR TOTALS	64	93	1242	13.4	4	6	53	8.8	1	50	445	8.9
1993	RANK NFL WR		73	71	50	95	42	42	42		16	16	19
1994	PROJECTIONS	16	25	380	15.2	0	0	0	NA	0	17	107	6.3

Pierce Holt   No. 95/DL

HT: 6-4 **WT:** 275
Born: 1-1-62, Marlin, TX
High school: Lamar (Rosenberg, TX)
College: Angelo State
Holt, a '93 free-agent acquisition, led the Falcons with 6.5 sacks. His 79 tackles were third on the team.

YEAR	TEAM	G	INT	YDS	AVG	TD	SACKS	FUM REC	TD
1988	San Francisco	9	---	---	---	---	5.0	1	0
1989	San Francisco	16	---	---	---	---	10.5	1	0
1990	San Francisco	16	---	---	---	---	5.5	2	0
1991	San Francisco	13	---	---	---	---	3.0	---	---
1992	San Francisco	16	---	---	---	---	5.5	---	---
1993	Atlanta	16	---	---	---	---	6.5	---	---
	6 YR TOTALS	86	0	0	NA	0	36.0	4	0
1993	RANK NFL DL		16	NA	NA	NA	34	71	NA
1994	PROJECTIONS	16	0	0	0	0	7	0	0

Chris Doleman   No. 59/DE

Full name: Christopher John Doleman
HT: 6-5 **WT:** 275
Born: 10-16-61, Indianapolis, IN
High school: Valley Forge Military Academy (Wayne, PA) and William Penn (York, PA)
College: Pittsburgh
Doleman made the Pro Bowl for the sixth time. He also made second-team AP All-Pro.

YEAR	TEAM	G	INT	YDS	AVG	TD	SACKS	FUM REC	TD
1985	Minnesota	16	1	5	5.0	0	0.5	—	0
1986	Minnesota	16	1	59	59.0	1	3.0	—	0
1987	Minnesota	12	—	—	—	—	11.0	—	—
1988	Minnesota	16	—	—	—	—	8.0	—	—
1989	Minnesota	16	—	—	—	—	21.0	5	0
1990	Minnesota	16	1	30	30.0	0	11.0	—	0
1991	Minnesota	16	—	—	—	—	7.0	2	0
1992	Minnesota	16	1	27	27.0	1	14.5	3	0
1993	Minnesota	16	1	-3	-3.0	0	12.5	1	0
	9 YR TOTALS	140	5	118	23.6	2	88.5	14	0
1993	RANK NFL DL		2	15	15	3	5	25	5
1994	PROJECTIONS	16	1	0	0.0	0	12	0	0

Jessie Tuggle   No. 58/LB

Full name: Jessie Lloyd Tuggle
HT: 5-11 **WT:** 230
Born: 2-14-65, Spalding County, GA
High school: Griffin (GA)
College: Valdosta State
Tuggle has led the Falcons in tackles for 5 straight years. He's returned 4 fumbles for TDs, sharing an NFL record.

YEAR	TEAM	G	INT	YDS	AVG	TD	SACKS	FUM REC	TD
1987	Atlanta	12	---	---	---	---	1.0	---	---
1988	Atlanta	16	---	---	---	---	---	1	1
1989	Atlanta	16	---	---	---	---	1.0	1	0
1990	Atlanta	16	---	---	---	---	5.0	2	1
1991	Atlanta	16	1	21	21.0	0	1.0	2	1
1992	Atlanta	15	1	1	1.0	0	1.0	1	1
1993	Atlanta	16	---	---	---	---	2.0	1	0
7 YR TOTALS		107	2	22	11.0	0	11.0	8	4
1993 RANK NFL LB			47	NA	NA	NA	37	24	8
1994 PROJECTIONS		16	0	0	0	0	2	1	0

Deion Sanders   No. 21/CB

Full name: Deion Luwynn Sanders
HT: 6-0   **WT:** 185
Born: 8-9-67, Fort Myers, FL
High school: North Fort Myers (FL)
College: Florida State
Sanders' 7 INTs led the NFC. A dangerous kick returner, he might choose baseball full-time. Either way, he'll miss the first 4 games.

YEAR	TEAM	G	INT	YDS	AVG	TD	SACKS	FUM REC	TD
1989	Atlanta	15	5	52	10.4	0	---	1	0
1990	Atlanta	16	3	153	51.0	2	---	2	0
1991	Atlanta	15	6	119	19.8	1	1.0	1	0
1992	Atlanta	13	3	105	35.0	0	---	2	0
1993	Atlanta	11	7	91	13.0	0	---	---	---
5 YR TOTALS		70	24	520	21.7	3	1.0	6	0
1993 RANK NFL DB			4	14	58	27	49	94	NA
1994 PROJECTIONS		10	8	86	10.8	0	0	0	0

Norm Johnson   No. 9/K

HT: 6-2   **WT:** 203
Born: 5-31-60, Inglewood, CA
High school: Pacifica (Garden Grove, CA)
College: UCLA
Pro Bowler Johnson had a string of 26 straight FGs, second-longest in NFL history, broken last season. 25 of his 69 kickoffs went into the end zone.

YEAR	TEAM	G	XP	XPA	XP Pct.	FG	FGA	FG Pct.	PTS
1985	Seattle	16	40	41	97.6	14	25	56.0	82
1986	Seattle	16	42	42	100.0	22	35	62.9	108
1987	Seattle	13	40	40	100.0	15	20	75.0	85
1988	Seattle	16	39	39	100.0	22	28	78.6	105
1989	Seattle	16	27	27	100.0	15	25	60.0	72
1990	Seattle	16	33	34	97.1	23	32	71.9	102
1991	Atlanta	14	38	39	97.4	19	23	82.6	95
1992	Atlanta	16	39	39	100.0	18	22	81.8	93
1993	Atlanta	15	34	34	100.0	26	27	96.3	112
12 YR TOTALS		179	444	450	98.7	222	300	74.0	1110
1993 RANK NFL			11	11	1	10	21	1	10
1994 PROJECTIONS		15	33	33	100.0	30	29	100.0	123

June Jones   Head coach

Born: 2-19-53, Portland, OR
High school: Portland (OR)
College: Portland State
A former NFL QB, Jones was in charge of the offense under Jerry Glanville. Atlanta will stick with its version of the run-and-shoot in '94.

YEAR	TEAM	G	INT	YDS	AVG	TD	SACKS	FUM REC	TD
1990	Dallas	16	---	---	---	---	7.5	---	---
1991	Dallas	16	---	---	---	---	2.0	2	0
1992	Dallas	16	---	---	---	---	4.0	---	---
1993	Dallas	15	---	---	---	---	5.5	---	---
4 YR TOTALS		63	0	0	NA	0	19.0	2	0
1993 RANK NFL DL			16	NA	NA	NA	43	71	NA
1994 PROJECTIONS		16	0	0	0	0	7	0	0

David Mims   No. 34/WR

HT: 5-8   **WT:** 191
Born: 7-7-70, Daingerfield, TX
High school: Daingerfield (TX)
College: Baylor
Mims had a personal-best 6 catches and his first TD against the Rams.

		RECEIVING				RUSHING				PUNT RETURN		
YEAR	TEAM	G	REC	YDS	AVG	TD	ATT	YDS	AVG	TD	RET	YDS	AVG
1993	Atlanta	15	12	107	8.9	1	1	3	3.0	0	---	---	---
	1 YR TOTALS	15	12	107	8.9	1	1	3	3.0	0	0	0	NA
1993	RANK NFL WR		94	105	135	72	31	32	27		30	30	29

Mitch Lyons   No. 86/TE

HT: 6-4   **WT:** 255
Born: 5-13-70, Grand Rapids, MI
High school: Forest Hills N. (Grand Rapids, MI)
College: Michigan State
Lyons started 8 games and helped open holes for RB Erric Pegram's 4 100-yard games.

		RECEIVING			
YEAR	TEAM	G	REC	YDS	AVG	TD
1993	Atlanta	16	8	63	7.9	0
	1 YR TOTALS	16	8	63	7.9	0
1993	RANK NFL TE		48	51	53	46

Lincoln Kennedy   No. 66/G

Full name: Tamerlane Lincoln Kennedy
HT: 6-6   **WT:** 335
Born: 2-12-71, York, PA
High school: Morse (San Diego)
College: Washington
Kennedy deserves credit for Erric Pegram's year.

		RUSHING			RANK	PASS	RANK			YDS.
YEAR	TEAM	G	ATT	YDS	AVG	AV RUSH	YDS	PASS YDS	SACKS	LOST
1993	Atlanta	16	395	1590	4.0	10	3787	6	40	267
	1 YR TOTALS	16								

Jumpy Geathers   No. 97/DT

Full name: James Geathers
HT: 6-7   **WT:** 290
Born: 6-26-60, Georgetown, SC
High school: Choppee (Georgetown, SC)
College: Wichita State
Geathers led the Falcons with 36 QB pressures.

YEAR	TEAM	G	INT	YDS	AVG	TD	SACKS	FUM REC	TD
1991	Washington	16	---	---	---	---	4.0	---	---
1992	Washington	16	---	---	---	---	5.0	---	---
1993	Atlanta	14	---	---	---	---	3.5	---	---
10 YR TOTALS		135	0	0	NA	0	41.5	9	0
1993 RANK NFL DL			16	NA	NA	NA	66	71	NA
1994 PROJECTIONS		14	0	0	0	0	3	0	0

Moe Gardner   No. 67/DT

Full name: Morris Gardner Jr.
HT: 6-2   **WT:** 261
Born: 8-10-68, Indianapolis, IN
High school: Cathedral (Indianapolis)
College: Illinois
His 128 total tackles were second on the Falcons.

YEAR	TEAM	G	INT	YDS	AVG	TD	SACKS	FUM REC	TD
1991	Atlanta	16	---	---	---	---	3.0	---	---
1992	Atlanta	16	---	---	---	---	4.5	---	---
1993	Atlanta	16	---	---	---	---	2.0	---	---
3 YR TOTALS		48	0	0	NA	0	9.5	0	0
1993 RANK NFL DL			16	NA	NA	NA	99	71	NA

Harold Alexander   No. 5/P

HT: 6-2   **WT:** 224
Born: 10-20-70, Pickens, SC
High school: Pickens (SC)
College: Appalachian State (Boone, NC)
Alexander's net punting average of 37.6 was fifth best in the NFL. He had 11 punts of 50+ yards.

YEAR	TEAM	G	NO	YARDS	LONG	AVG	BLK	IN20
1993	Atlanta	16	72	3114	75	43.3	0	21
1 YR TOTALS		16	72	3114	75	43.3	0	21
1993 RANK NFL Ps			19	16	4	11		12

D. J. Johnson   No. 44/CB

Full name: David Allen Johnson
HT: 6-0   **WT:** 189
Born: 7-14-66, Louisville, KY
High school: Male (Louisville, KY)
College: Kentucky
Johnson started 15 games for Pittsburgh in 1993.

YEAR	TEAM	G	INT	YDS	AVG	TD	SACKS	FUM REC	TD
1990	Pittsburgh	16	2	60	30.0	1	—	1	0
1991	Pittsburgh	16	1	0	0.0	0	1.0	—	—
1992	Pittsburgh	15	5	67	13.4	0	—	2	0
1993	Pittsburgh	16	3	51	17.0	0	—	—	—
	5 YR TOTALS	79	12	178	14.8	1	1.0	3	0
1993	RANK NFL DB		33	41	39	27	49	94	NA

Kevin Ross   No. 36/CB

Full name: Kevin Lesley Ross
HT: 5-9   **WT:** 185
Born: 1-16-62, Camden, NJ
High school: Paulsboro (NJ)
College: Temple
Ross is known for tight coverage and hard hits.

YEAR	TEAM	G	INT	YDS	AVG	TD	SACKS	FUM REC	TD
1991	Kansas City	14	1	0	0.0	0	---	1	0
1992	Kansas City	16	1	99	99.0	1	0.5	---	---
1993	Kansas City	15	---	---	---	---	0.5	1	0
	10 YR TOTALS	151	28	502	17.9	2	4.0	10	1
1993	RANK NFL DB		156	NA	NA	NA	45	37	14
1994	PROJECTIONS	15	0	0	0	0	1	1	0

Mike Zandofsky   No. 72/G

Full name: Michael Leslie Zandofsky
HT: 6-2   **WT:** 305
Born: 11-30-65, Corvallis, OR
High school: Corvallis (OR)
College: Washington
Zandofsky started all 16 games for San Diego.

YEAR	TEAM	G	RUSHING		AVG	RANK	PASS	RANK	SACKS	YDS.
			ATT	YDS		AV RUSH	YDS	PASS YDS		LOST
1991	San Diego	10	464	2248	4.8	1	2983	25	35	236
1992	San Diego	15	489	1875	3.8	18	3614	6	33	268
1993	San Diego	16	455	1824	4.0	11	3383	16	32	240
	5 YR TOTALS	69								

Chicago
BEARS

1994 Scouting Report

Offense

After gaining just 2,040 passing yards in 1993 (the worst in the NFL), the Bears finally gave up on Jim Harbaugh and signed free agent QB Erik Kramer from Detroit. The problem is that the Bears have no star wideouts— Terry Obee and Tom Waddle are solid, but not spectacular. The team did use the free-agent market to bolster its running game, adding big backs Merril Hoge from Pittsburgh and Lewis Tillman from the Giants, and T Andy Heck from Seattle. These acquisitions should improve Chicago's offensive standings in 1994 (3,717 total yards in 1993, worst in the NFL; 1,677 rushing yards, nineteenth in the NFL). The Bears will need more help on the OL— they're hoping rookie T Marcus Spears will contribute immediately.

Defense

The Bears allowed just 4,653 total yards in 1993, fourth best in the NFL. They gave up 1,835 yards on the ground (seventeenth in the NFL) but their pass defense was the third best in the league, surrendering just 2,818 yards. The Bears couldn't come to terms with Richard Dent, and have said goodbye to his 12 1993 sacks. They still have Trace Armstrong, who had 11.5 sacks last year, LB Dante Jones (189 tackles), DT Chris Zorich, and CB Donnell Woolford. LB John Thierry might be one of the steals of the '94 draft.

Special Teams

Speedy Curtis Conway is the Bears' primary kick returner. Chris Gardocki is a good punter—only 22 of his 80 punts were returned in '93. Maurice Douglass led the Bears in special teams tackles. Kevin Butler is the Bears' longtime place-kicker—he's fairly accurate, although not blessed with a very strong leg.

1994 Prospects

The Bears were a pleasant surprise in 1993, but the rest of their division has improved markedly during the off-season. The Bears have a tough defense, and they've bulked up their running game, so they should be in a lot of close games in '94. But they lack the wide receivers to come back from big deficits or to make it to the playoffs.

Team Directory

Chairman of the board: Ed McCaskey
President/CEO: Michael McCaskey
VP of operations: Ted Phillips
Director of public relations: Bryan Harlan

1993 Review				1994 Schedule		
Sep. 5	N.Y. GIANTS	L 26-20		Sep: 4	TAMPA BAY	1:00
Sep. 12	at Minnesota	L 10-7		Sep. 12	at Philadelphia (Mon.)	9:00
Sep. 19	OPEN DATE			Sep. 18	MINNESOTA	1:00
Sep. 26	TAMPA BAY	W 47-17		Sep. 25	at N.Y. Jets	8:00
Oct. 3	ATLANTA	W 6-0		Oct. 2	BUFFALO	4:00
Oct. 10	at Philadelphia	W 17-6		Oct. 9	NEW ORLEANS	1:00
Oct. 17	OPEN DATE			Oct. 16	OPEN DATE	
Oct. 25	MINNESOTA	L 19-12		Oct. 23	at Detroit	1:00
Oct. 31	at Green Bay	L 17-3		Oct. 31	GREEN BAY (Mon.)	9:00
Nov. 7	L.A. RAIDERS	L 16-14		Nov. 6	at Tampa Bay	1:00
Nov. 14	at San Diego	W 16-13		Nov. 13	at Miami	1:00
Nov. 21	at Kansas City	W 19-17		Nov. 20	DETROIT	1:00
Nov. 25	at Detroit	W 10-6		Nov. 27	at Arizona	4:00
Dec. 5	GREEN BAY	W 30-17		Dec. 1	at Minnesota (Thurs.)	8:00
Dec. 12	at Tampa Bay	L 13-10		Dec. 11	at Green Bay	1:00
Dec. 18	DENVER	L 13-3		Dec. 18	L.A. RAMS	1:00
Dec. 26	DETROIT	L 20-14		Dec. 24	NEW ENGLAND	1:00
Jan. 2	at L.A. Rams	L 20-6				

1993 finish: 7-9 (3-5 home, 4-4 away), fourth in NFC Central

Team Leaders

PASSING	ATT	COM	COM%	YDS	YPA	TD	TD%	INT	INT%	RTG
Harbaugh	325	200	61.5	2002	6.16	7	2.2	11	3.4	72.1
Willis	60	30	50.0	268	4.47	0	0.0	5	8.3	27.6
Gardocki	2	0	0.0	0	0.00	0	0.0	0	0.0	39.6
TEAM	388	230	59.3	2270	5.85	7	1.8	16	4.1	64.7
OPPONENTS	504	306	60.7	3105	6.16	12	2.4	18	3.6	71.4

RECEIVING	REC	YDS	AVG	TD	RUSHING	ATT	YDS	AVG	TD
Waddle	44	552	12.5	1	Anderson	202	646	3.2	4
Anderson	31	160	5.2	0	Worley	110	437	4.0	2
Obee	26	351	13.5	3	Harbaugh	60	277	4.6	4
Conway	19	231	12.2	2	Heyward	68	206	3.0	0
Christian	16	160	10.0	0	Conway	5	44	8.8	0
TEAM	230	2270	9.9	7	TEAM	477	1677	3.5	10
OPPONENTS	306	3105	10.1	12	OPPONENTS	476	1835	3.9	9

INTERCEPTIONS	INT	YDS	AVG	LG	TD	SACKS	NO
Carrier	4	94	23.5	34t	1	Dent	12.5
Jones	4	52	13.0	22	0	Armstrong	11.5
Lincoln	3	109	36.3	80t	1	Zorich	7.0
TEAM	18	300	16.7	86t	2	TEAM	46.0
OPPONENTS	16	105	6.6	25	1	OPPONENTS	48.0

KICK RETURNS	NO	YDS	AV	LG	TD	PUNT RETURNS	NO	FC	YDS	AV	LG	TD
Conway	21	450	21.4	55	0	Obee	35	20	289	8.3	28	0
Green	9	141	15.7	30	0							
Obee	9	159	17.7	34	0							
TEAM	45	811	18.0	55	0	TEAM	35	20	289	8.3	28	0
OPPONENTS	53	918	17.3	35	0	OPPONENTS	22	38	115	5.2	34	0

KICKING	XPM	XPA	FGM	FGA	LG	PTS
Butler	21	22	27	36	55	102
TEAM	21	22	27	36	55	102
OPPONENTS	20	22	26	34	42	98

PUNTING	NO	YDS	LG	AVG	TB	BLK	RET	RYD	IN20	NAV
Gardocki	80	3080	58	38.5	2	0	22	115	28	36.6
TEAM	80	3080	58	38.5	2	0	22	115	28	36.6
OPPONENTS	78	3231	75	41.4	6	1	35	289	22	36.2

FUMBLES	FUM	OFF.FUM.REC.	REC	TD	DEF.FUM.REC.	REC	TD
Harbaugh	15	Harbaugh	4	0	Armstrong	3	0
Worley	3	Wojciechowski	2	0	Baker	2	1
Anderson	2			0	Jones	2	1
TEAM	29	TEAM	14	0	TEAM	12	2
OPPONENTS	24	OPPONENTS	12	0	OPPONENTS	14	0

1994 Draft Choices

ROUND	NAME	POS	SCHOOL	OVERALL SELECTION
1	John Thierry	LB	Alcorn State	11
2	Marcus Spears	T	NW Louisiana	39
3	Jim Flanigan	DT	Notre Dame	74
4	Raymont Harris	RB	Ohio State	114
6	Lloyd Hill	WR	Texas Tech	170
7	Dennis Collier	S	Colorado	205

HISTORY

TITLES

1921	NFL Championship	1946	NFL Championship
1932	NFL Championship	1956	NFL West Championship
1933	NFL Championship	1963	NFL Championship
1934	NFL West Championship	1984	NFC Central Championship
1937	NFL West Championship	1985	Super Bowl Winner
1940	NFL Championship	1986	NFC Central Championship
1941	NFL Championship	1987	NFC Central Championship
1942	NFL West Championship	1988	NFC Central Championship
1943	NFL Championship	1990	NFC Central Championship

ALL-TIME TEAM RECORDS

Rushing

Most yards, game:	275	Walter Payton	11/20/77
Most yards, season:	1,852	Walter Payton	1977
Most yards, career:	16,726	Walter Payton	1975-1987

Passing

Most yards, game:	486	Johnny Lujack	12/11/49
Most yards, season:	3,172	Bill Wade	1962
Most yards, career:	14,686	Sid Luckman	1939-1950

Receiving

Most catches, game:	14	Jim Keane	10/23/49
Most catches, season:	93	Johnny Morris	1964
Most catches, career:	492	Walter Payton	1975-1987

Scoring

Most points, game:	36	Gale Sayers	12/12/65
Most points, season:	144	Kevin Butler	1985
Most points, career:	915	Kevin Butler	1985-1993

COACHES

NAME	RECORD	YEARS
George Halas	324-151-31	1920-29, 33-42, 46-55, 58-67
Ralph Jones	24-10-7	1930-32
Hunk Anderson-*	24-12-2	1942-45
Luke Johnsos		
Paddy Driscoll	14-10-1	1956-57
Jim Dooley	20-36-0	1968-71
Abe Gibron	11-30-1	1972-74
Jack Pardee	20-23-0	1975-77
Neill Armstrong	30-35-0	1978-81
Mike Ditka	112-68-0	1982-92
Dave Wannstedt	7-9-0	1993

* co-coaches

CHICAGO BEARS
1994 TRAINING CAMP ROSTER

No.	Quarterbacks	Pos	Ht	Wt	Born	NFL Exp	College	How acq	93 GP/GS
12	Kramer, Erik	QB	6-1	200	11-6-64	5	North Carolina St.	FA '94	5/4
9	Matthews, Shane	QB	6-3	196	6-1-70	1	Florida	FA '93	0/0
4	Walsh, Steve	QB	6-3	200	12-1-66	6	Miami (FL)	FA '94	2/1
Running backs									
44	Christian, Bob	RB	5-10	225	11-14-68	2	Northwestern	FA '92	14/1
22	Green, Robert	RB	5-8	212	9-10-70	3	William and Mary	W-WAS '93	16/0
29	Harris, Raymont	RB	6-0	225	12-23-70	R	Ohio State	D4 '94	
33	Hoge, Merril	FB	6-2	226	1-26-65	8	Idaho State	FA '94	16/13
27	Tillman, Lewis	RB	6-0	204	4-16-66	6	Jackson St.	FA '94	16/7
38	Worley, Tim	RB	6-2	225	9-24-66	5	Georgia	T-PIT '93	16/3
Wide receivers									
80	Conway, Curtis	WR-KR	6-0	193	3-13-71	2	Southern California	D1 '93	16/6
**	Davis, Wendell	WR	6-0	188	1-3-66	7	Louisiana State	D1 '88	5/4
81	Graham, Jeff	WR	6-2	196	2-14-69	4	Ohio State	T-PIT '94	15/12
14	Hill, Lloyd	WR	6-1	189	1-16-72	R	Texas Tech	D6 '94	
83	Obee, Terry	WR	5-10	188	6-15-68	2	Oregon	FA '93	16/5
87	Waddle, Tom	WR	6-0	190	2-20-67	5	Boston College	FA '89	15/15
Tight ends									
86	Cook, Marv	TE	6-4	234	2-24-66	6	Iowa	FA '94	16/12
84	Gedney, Chris	TE	6-5	265	8-9-70	2	Syracuse	D3 '93	7/3
85	Jennings, Keith	TE	6-4	270	5-19-66	5	Clemson	FA '91	13/11
89	Wetnight, Ryan	TE	6-2	235	11-5-70	2	Stanford	FA '93	10/1
Offensive linemen									
70	Auzenne, Troy	T	6-7	300	6-26-69	3	California	D2 '92	11/11
62	Bortz, Mark	G	6-6	290	2-12-61	12	Iowa	D8 '83	16/16
63	Burger, Todd	G	6-3	296	6-5-70	1	Penn State	FA '93	0/0
67	Fontenot, Jerry	G-C	6-3	285	11-21-66	6	Texas A&M	D3 '89	16/16
64	Heck, Andy	T	6-6	296	1-1-67	6	Notre Dame	FA '94	16/16
58	Leeuwenburg, Jay	OL	6-3	290	6-18-69	3	Colorado	W-KC '92	16/16
60	McGuire, Gene	C	6-2	300	7-17-70	3	Notre Dame	W-NO '93	9/0
69	Myslinski, Tom	G	6-2	289	12-7-68	3	Tennessee	FA '93	1/0
75	Perry, Todd	G	6-5	300	11-28-70	2	Kentucky	D4 '93	13/3
79	Spears, Marcus	T	6-4	302	9-28-71	R	NW Louisiana	D2 '94	
71	Williams, James	T	6-7	335	3-29-68	4	Cheyney State	FA '91	3/0
Defensive linemen									
93	Armstrong, Trace	DE	6-4	270	10-5-65	6	Florida	D1 '89	16/16
65	Epps, Tory	DT	6-1	280	5-28-67	5	Memphis State	FA '93	3/0
68	Flanigan, Jim	DT	6-2	281	8-27-71	R	Notre Dame	D3 '94	
96	Fontenot, Albert	DE	6-4	272	9-17-70	2	Baylor	D4 '93	16/0
99	Ryan, Tim	DT	6-2	275	9-8-67	5	Southern California	D3 '90	11/0
94	Simpson, Carl	DT	6-2	285	4-18-70	2	Florida State	D2 '93	11/0
90	Spellman, Alonzo	DE	6-4	285	9-27-71	3	Ohio State	D1 '92	16/0
94	Thierry, John	DT	6-4	260	9-4-71	R	Alcorn State (MS)	D1 '94	
97	Zorich, Chris	DT	6-1	277	3-13-69	4	Notre Dame	D2 '91	16/16
Linebackers									
91	Baker, Myron	LB	6-1	228	1-6-71	2	Louisiana Tech	D4 '93	16/0
59	Cain, Joe	LB	6-1	233	6-11-65	6	Oregon Tech	FA '93	15/15
54	Cox, Ron	LB	6-2	235	2-27-68	5	Fresno State	D2 '90	16/2
53	Jones, Dante	LB	6-2	236	3-23-65	7	Oklahoma	D2 '88	16/16
92	Minter, Barry	LB	6-2	236	1-28-70	2	Tulsa	T-DAL '93	2/0
55	Smith, Vinson	LB	6-2	247	7-3-65	8	East Carolina	T-DAL '93	16/13
57	Snow, Percy	LB	6-2	240	11-5-67	5	Michigan State	W-KC '93	10/0
Defensive backs									
47	Blaylock, Anthony	CB	5-10	185	2-21-65	7	Winston-Salem St.	FA '93	9/9
20	Carrier, Mark	S	6-1	192	4-28-63	5	Southern California	D1 '90	16/16
32	Collier, Dennis	S	5-9	187	5-17-71	R	Colorado	D7 '94	
37	Douglass, Maurice	CB	5-11	200	2-12-64	8	Kentucky	D8 '86	16/1
23	Gayle, Shaun	S	5-11	202	3-8-62	11	Ohio State	D10 '84	16/16
25	Johnson, Keshon	CB	5-10	183	7-17-70	2	Arizona	D7 '93	15/0
39	Lincoln, Jeremy	CB	5-10	180	4-7-69	3	Tennessee	D3 '92	16/7
26	Mangum, John	CB	5-10	192	3-16-67	5	Alabama	D6 '90	12/1
24	Miniefield, Kevin	CB	5-9	178	5-12-70	2	Arizona State	FA '93	8/0
21	Woolford, Donnell	CB	5-9	188	1-6-66	6	Clemson	D1 '89	16/16
Specialists									
6	Butler, Kevin	K	6-1	205	7-24-62	10	Georgia	D4 '85	16/0
17	Gardocki, Chris	P-K	6-1	196	2-7-70	4	Clemson	D3 '91	16/0

Erik Kramer   No. 12/QB

Full name: William Erik Kramer
HT: 6-1   **WT:** 200
Born: 11-6-64, Encino, CA
High school: Conoga Park (CA)
College: LA Pierce JC, North Carolina State
Kramer started only the last 4 games of 1993 for Detroit, but threw for 8 TDs and led the Lions to the playoffs.

			PASSING										RUSHING		
YEAR	TEAM	G	ATT	CPL	CPL%	YDS	AVG	TDS	TD%	INT	INT%	RTG	ATT	YDS	AVG
1987	Atlanta	3	92	45	48.9	559	6.1	4	4.3	5	5.4	60.0	2	10	5.0
1991	Detroit	13	265	136	51.3	1635	6.2	11	4.2	8	3.0	71.8	35	26	0.7
1992	Detroit	7	106	58	54.7	771	7.3	4	3.8	8	7.5	59.1	12	34	2.8
1993	Detroit	5	138	87	63.0	1002	7.3	8	5.8	3	2.2	95.1	10	5	0.5
	4 YR TOTALS	28	601	326	54.2	3967	6.6	27	4.5	24	4.0		59	75	1.3
1993	RANK NFL QB		37	35	9	35	18	24	7	43	48		9	34	44	48
1994	PROJECTIONS	4	130	87	66.9	978	7.5	8	6.2	1	0.8		9	0	0.0

Merril Hoge   No. 33/FB

Full name: Merril DuAine Hoge
HT: 6-2   **WT:** 226
Born: 1-26-65, Pocatello, ID
High school: Highland (Pocatello, ID)
College: Idaho State
For Pittsburgh in 1993, Hoge had 5 TDs, his best since 1990, and a career-high 4 TD catches.

			RUSHING				RECEIVING				KICK RETURNS			
YEAR	TEAM	G	ATT	YDS	AVG	TD	REC	YDS	AVG	TD	RET	YDS	AVG	TD
1987	Pittsburgh	13	3	8	2.7	0	7	97	13.9	1	1	13	13.0	0
1988	Pittsburgh	16	170	705	4.1	3	50	487	9.7	3	---	---	---	---
1989	Pittsburgh	16	186	621	3.3	8	34	271	8.0	0	---	---	---	---
1990	Pittsburgh	16	203	772	3.8	7	40	342	8.6	3	---	---	---	---
1991	Pittsburgh	16	165	610	3.7	2	49	379	7.7	1	---	---	---	---
1992	Pittsburgh	16	41	150	3.7	0	28	231	8.3	1	2	28	14.0	0
1993	Pittsburgh	16	51	249	4.9	1	33	247	7.5	4	3	33	11.0	0
	7 YR TOTALS	109	819	3115	3.8	21	241	2054	8.5	13	6	74	12.3	0
1993	RANK NFL RB		89	60	17	58	28	28	65	1	38	46	57	
1994	PROJECTIONS	16	18	162	9.0	0	32	225	7.0	5	4	43	10.8	0

Lewis Tillman No. 27/RB

HT: 6-0 **WT:** 204
Born: 1 16 66, Oklahoma City, OK
High school: Hazelhurst (MS)
College: Jackson State
As a backup for the Giants, Tillman rushed for 585 yards on 121 carries, both career-highs.

YEAR	TEAM	G	RUSHING				RECEIVING				KICK RETURNS			
			ATT	YDS	AVG	TD	REC	YDS	AVG	TD	RET	YDS	AVG	TD
1989	NY Giants	16	79	290	3.7	0	1	9	9.0	0	---	---	---	---
1990	NY Giants	16	84	231	2.8	1	8	18	2.3	0	---	---	---	---
1991	NY Giants	16	65	287	4.4	1	5	30	6.0	0	2	29	14.5	0
1992	NY Giants	16	6	13	2.2	0	1	15	15.0	0	---	---	---	---
1993	NY Giants	16	121	585	4.8	3	1	21	21.0	0	---	---	---	---
	5 YR TOTALS	80	355	1406	4.0	5	16	93	5.8	0	2	29	14.5	0
1993	RANK NFL RB		38	31	20	21	111	103	1	40	66	65	65	
1994	PROJECTIONS	16	162	813	5.0	4	0	0	NA	0	0	0	NA	0

Terry Obee No. 83/WR

HT: 5-10 **WT:** 188
Born: 6-15-68, Vallejo, CA
High school: J. F. Kennedy (Richmond, CA)
College: Oregon
Obee led the 1993 Bears with 3 TD catches, and handled every punt return for the team.

YEAR	TEAM	G	RECEIVING				RUSHING				PUNT RETURN		
			REC	YDS	AVG	TD	ATT	YDS	AVG	TD	RET	YDS	AV
1991	Chicago	1	---	---	---	---	---	---	---	---	---	---	---
1993	Chicago	16	26	351	13.5	3	---	---	---	---	35	289	8
	2 YR TOTALS	17	26	351	13.5	3	0	0	NA	0	35	289	8
1993	RANK NFL WR		70	72	70	41	42	42	42		5	5	1
1994	PROJECTIONS	16	52	702	13.5	6	0	0	NA	0	70	578	8

Tom Waddle   No. 87/WR

Full name: Gregory Thomas Waddle
HT: 6-0   **WT:** 190
Born: 2-20-67, Cincinnati, OH
High school: Moeller (Cincinnati)
College: Boston College
Waddle's 44 catches and 552 receiving yards led the Bears, but he had only 1 TD catch.

| | | | RECEIVING | | | | ROSHING | | | | PONT RETURN | | |
YEAR	TEAM	G	REC	YDS	AVG	TD	ATT	YDS	AVG	TD	RET	YDS	AVG
1989	Chicago	3	1	8	8.0	0	---	---	---	---	1	2	2.0
1990	Chicago	5	2	32	16.0	0	---	---	---	---	---	---	---
1991	Chicago	16	55	599	10.9	3	---	---	---	---	5	31	6.2
1992	Chicago	12	46	674	14.7	4	---	---	---	---	8	28	3.5
1993	Chicago	15	44	552	12.5	1	---	---	---	---	---	---	---
	5 YR TOTALS	51	148	1865	12.6	8	0	0	NA	0	14	61	4.4
1993	RANK NFL WR		38	48	91	72	42	42	42		30	30	29
1994	PROJECTIONS	16	48	585	12.2	0	0	0	NA	0	0	0	NA

Andy Heck   No. 64/T

Full name: Andrew Robert Heck
HT: 6-6   **WT:** 296
Born: 1-1-67, Fargo, ND
High school: W.T. Woodson (Fairfax, VA)
College: Notre Dame
Heck played every down at right tackle for Seattle in 1993, helping the Seahawks lead the AFC in rushing.

| | | | RUSHING | | | RANK | PASS | RANK | | | YDS. |
YEAR	TEAM	G	ATT	YDS	AVG	AV RUSH	YDS	PASS YDS	SACKS	LOST
1991	Seattle	16	394	1426	3.6	20	3371	14	42	263
1992	Seattle	13	402	1596	4.0	15	2323	27	67	545
1993	Seattle	16	473	2015	4.3	8	2896	25	48	242
	5 YR TOTALS	77								

Trace Armstrong   No. 93/DE

Full name: Raymond Lester Armstrong
HT: 6-4   **WT:** 270
Born: 10-5-65, Bethesda, MD
High school: John Carroll (Birmingham, AL)
College: Florida
With 11.5 sacks Armstrong trailed only Richard Dent on the Bears, and tied for sixth-best in the NFC.

YEAR	TEAM	G	INT	YDS	AVG	TD	SACKS	FUM REC	TD
1989	Chicago	15	---	---	---	---	5.0	1	0
1990	Chicago	16	---	---	---	---	10.0	2	0
1991	Chicago	12	---	---	---	---	1.5	---	---
1992	Chicago	14	---	---	---	---	6.5	1	0
1993	Chicago	16	---	---	---	---	11.5	3	0
	5 YR TOTALS	73	0	0	NA	0	34.5	7	0
1993	RANK NFL DL		16	NA	NA	NA	10	2	5
1994	PROJECTIONS	16	0	0	NA	0	14	4	0

Dante Jones   No. 53/LB

Full name: Dante Delaneo Jones
HT: 6-2   **WT:** 236
Born: 3-23-65, Dallas, TX
High school: Skyline (Dallas)
College: Oklahoma
Defensive leader Jones signed a big contract after leading the Bears with an impressive 189 tackles in 1993.

YEAR	TEAM	G	INT	YDS	AVG	TD	SACKS	FUM REC	TD
1988	Chicago	13	---	---	---	---	---	---	---
1989	Chicago	10	---	---	---	---	---	---	---
1990	Chicago	2	---	---	---	---	2.0	---	---
1991	Chicago	16	---	---	---	---	---	---	---
1992	Chicago	13	---	---	---	---	---	---	---
1993	Chicago	16	4	52	13.0	0	1.0	2	1
	6 YR TOTALS	70	4	52	13.0	0	3.0	2	1
1993	RANK NFL LB		1	3	16	5	62	9	1
1994	PROJECTIONS	16	6	79	13.2	0	0	3	2

Donnell Woolford   No. 21/CB

HT: 5-9   **WT:** 188
Born: 1-6-66, Baltimore, MD
High school: Douglass Byrd (Fayetteville, NC)
College: Clemson
First-time Pro Bowler Woolford led the Bears with 22 passes defensed and ranked fifth with 101 tackles.

YEAR	TEAM	G	INT	YDS	AVG	TD	SACKS	FUM REC	TD
1989	Chicago	11	3	0	0.0	0	---	---	---
1990	Chicago	13	3	18	6.0	0	2.0	---	---
1991	Chicago	15	2	21	10.5	0	1.0	1	0
1992	Chicago	16	7	67	9.6	0	---	---	---
1993	Chicago	16	2	18	9.0	0	---	---	---
	5 YR TOTALS	71	17	124	7.3	0	3.0	1	0
1993	RANK NFL DB		54	88	85	27	49	94	NA
1994	PROJECTIONS	16	0	0	NA	0	0	0	0

Marv Cook   No. 86/TE

Full name: Marvin Eugene Cook
HT: 6-4   **WT:** 234
Born: 2-24-66, Iowa City, IA
High school: West Branch (IA)
College: Iowa
Cook clashed with Bill Parcells at New England, and lost his starting spot to Ben Coates.

YEAR	TEAM	G	RECEIVING REC	YDS	AVG	TD
1989	New England	16	3	13	4.3	0
1990	New England	16	51	455	8.9	5
1991	New England	16	82	808	9.9	3
1992	New England	16	52	413	7.9	2
1993	New England	16	22	154	7.0	1
	5 YR TOTALS	80	210	1843	8.8	11
1993	RANK NFL TE		26	32	58	22
1994	PROJECTIONS	16	6	0	0.0	0

Kevin Butler

No. 6/K

Full name: Kevin Gregory Butler
HT: 6-1 **WT:** 205
Born: 7-24-62, Savannah, GA
High school: Redan (GA)
College: Georgia

The Bears' all-time leading scorer with 915 points, Butler holds 18 other club records, and has scored in 64 straight games.

YEAR	TEAM	G	XP	XPA	XP Pct.	FG	FGA	FG Pct.	PTS
1985	Chicago	16	51	51	100.0	31	37	83.8	144
1986	Chicago	16	36	37	97.3	28	41	68.3	120
1987	Chicago	12	28	30	93.3	19	28	67.9	85
1988	Chicago	16	37	38	97.4	15	19	78.9	82
1989	Chicago	16	43	45	95.6	15	19	78.9	88
1990	Chicago	16	36	37	97.3	26	37	70.3	114
1991	Chicago	16	32	34	94.1	19	29	65.5	89
1992	Chicago	16	34	34	100.0	19	26	73.1	91
1993	Chicago	16	21	22	95.5	27	36	75.0	102
	9 YR TOTALS	140	318	328	97.0	199	272	73.2	915
1993	RANK NFL		25	25	22	9	5	16	17
1994	PROJECTIONS	16	14	15	93.3	31	40	77.5	107

Dave Wannstedt Head Coach

Full name: David Raymond Wannstedt
Born: 5-21-52, Pittsburgh
High school: Baldwin (Pittsburgh)
College: Pittsburgh

Wannstedt was defensive coordinator for an NCAA champ (Miami in '87-88) and Super Bowl winner (Dallas in '92). He turned down the Giants' opening in '92 for the Bears' job.

YEAR	TEAM	REGULAR SEASON					POSTSEASON		
		W	L	T	PCT	FINISH	W	L	FINISH
1993	Chicago	7	9	0	.438	4th/NFC Central			
	1 YR TOTALS	7	9	0	.438		0	0	

Steve Walsh No. 4/QB

Full name: Stephen John Walsh
HT: 6-3 **WT:** 200
Born: 12-1-66, St. Paul, MN
High school: Cretin (St. Paul)
College: Miami (FL)

He saw action in just 2 games for the Saints in '93.

| YEAR | TEAM | G | PASSING | | | | | | | | | | RUSHING | | |
			ATT	CPL	CPL%	YDS	AVG	TDS	TD%	INT	INT%	RTG	ATT	YDS	AVG
1990	Dal (1)-NO (12)	13	219	110	50.2	1371	12.5	5	4.5	9	8.2	60.5	8	18	2.7
1991	New Orleans	8	255	141	55.3	1638	11.6	11	7.8	6	4.3	79.5	8	0	0.0
1993	New Orleans	1	38	20	52.6	271	13.6	2	10.0	3	^^^^^	60.3	4	-4	-1.0
	4 YR TOTALS	30	731	381	52.1	4651	6.4	23	3.1	27	3.7		24	28	1.2
1993	RANK NFL QB		57	56	53	54	23	48	10	43	6	52	49	60	56
1994	PROJECTIONS	0	0	0	NA	0	NA	0	NA	0	NA		0	0	NA

Tim Worley No. 38/RB

Full name: Timothy Ashley Worley
HT: 6-2 **WT:** 225
Born: 9-24-66, Lumberton, NC
High school: Lumberton (NC)
College: Georgia

Worley started the Bears' final 3 games.

| YEAR | TEAM | G | RUSHING | | | | RECEIVING | | | | KICK RETURNS | | | |
			ATT	YDS	AVG	TD	REC	YDS	AVG	TD	RET	YDS	AVG	TD
1991	Pittsburgh	2	22	117	5.3	0	---	---	---	---	---	---	---	---
1993	Pittsburgh	6	10	33	3.3	0	3	13	4.3	0	4	85	21.3	0
1993	Chicago	10	110	437	4.0	2	8	49	6.1	0	2	36	18.0	0
	5 YR TOTALS	44	446	1775	4.0	7	34	245	7.2	0	6	121	20.2	0
1993	RANK NFL RB		42	40	54	46	81	85	91	40	44	44	23	
1994	PROJECTIONS	15	235	887	3.8	5	17	112	6.6	0	0	0	NA	0

Curtis Conway No. 80/WR-KR

Full name: Curtis LaMont Conway
HT: 6-0 **WT:** 193
Born: 3-13-71, Hawthorne, CA
High school: Hawthorne (CA)
College: Southern California

Conway was the Bears' main kick returner.

| YEAR | TEAM | G | RECEIVING | | | | RUSHING | | | | PUNT RETURN | | |
			REC	YDS	AVG	TD	ATT	YDS	AVG	TD	RET	YDS	AVG
1993	Chicago	16	19	231	12.2	2	5	44	8.8	0	---	---	---
	1 YR TOTALS	16	19	231	12.2	2	5	44	8.8	0	0	0	NA
1993	RANK NFL WR		80	82	101	55	6	6	9		30	30	29

Jeff Graham   No. 81/WR

Full name: Jeffery Todd Graham
HT: 6-2   **WT:** 196
Born: 2-14-69, Dayton, OH
High school: Alter (Kettering, OH)
College: Ohio State

Graham was Pittsburgh's leading receiver in '92.

YEAR	TEAM	G	RECEIVING				RUSHING				PUNT RETURN		
			REC	YDS	AVG	TD	ATT	YDS	AVG	TD	RET	YDS	AVG
1991	Pittsburgh	13	2	21	10.5	0	---	---	---	---	8	46	5.8
1992	Pittsburgh	14	49	711	14.5	1	---	---	---	---	---	---	---
1993	Pittsburgh	15	38	579	15.2	0	---	---	---	---	---	---	---
	3 YR TOTALS	42	89	1311	14.7	1	0	0	NA	0	8	46	5.8
1993	RANK NFL WR		51	46	37	95	42	42	42		30	30	29
1994	PROJECTIONS	16	42	668	15.9	0	0	0	NA	0	0	0	NA

Jay Leeuwenburg   No. 58/OL

Full name: Jay Robert Leeuwenburg
HT: 6-3   **WT:** 290
Born: 6-18-69, St. Louis, MO
High school: Kirkwood (MO)
College: Colorado

He started at both LT and RT during '93.

YEAR	TEAM	G	RUSHING			RANK	PASS	RANK	SACKS	YDS.
			ATT	YDS	AVG	AV RUSH	YDS	PASS YDS		LOST
1992	Chicago	12	427	1871	4.4	6	3334	14	45	264
1993	Chicago	16	477	1677	3.5	25	2270	28	48	230
	2 YR TOTALS	28								

Chris Zorich   No. 97/DT

Full name: Christopher Robert Zorich
HT: 6-1   **WT:** 277
Born: 3-13-69, Chicago, IL
High school: Chicago Vocational (IL)
College: Notre Dame

He ranked third on the team in tackles and sacks.

YEAR	TEAM	G	INT	YDS	AVG	TD	SACKS	FUM REC	TD
1991	Chicago	12	---	---	---	---	---	---	---
1992	Chicago	16	---	---	---	---	2.0	1	1
1993	Chicago	16	---	---	---	---	7.0	2	0
	3 YR TOTALS	44	0	0	NA	0	9.0	3	1
1993	RANK NFL DL		16	NA	NA	NA	29	8	5
1994	PROJECTIONS	16	0	0	0	0	11	3	0

Joe Cain No. 59/LB

Full name: Joseph Harrison Cain Jr.
HT: 6-1 **WT:** 233
Born: 6-11-65, Los Angeles, CA
High school: Compton (CA)
College: Stanford, Oregon Tech

Cain recorded an impressive 108 tackles.

YEAR	TEAM	G	INT	YDS	AVG	TD	SACKS	FUM REC	TD
1991	Seattle	16	1	5	5.0	0	—	—	—
1992	Seattle	16	2	3	1.5	0	—	1	0
1993	Chicago	15	—	—	—	—	—	—	—
	5 YR TOTALS	72	3	8	2.7	0	0.0	1	0
1993	RANK NFL LB		47	NA	NA	NA	91	81	NA
1994	PROJECTIONS	15	0	0	NA	0	0	0	0

Mark Carrier No. 20/S

Full name: Mark Anthony Carrier
HT: 6-1 **WT:** 192
Born: 4-28-68, Lake Charles, LA
High school: Long Beach Polytechnic (CA)
College: Southern California

Carrier had 4 INTs, his best total since 1990.

YEAR	TEAM	G	INT	YDS	AVG	TD	SACKS	FUM REC	TD
1991	Chicago	16	2	54	27.0	0	---	1	0
1992	Chicago	16	---	---	---	---	---	2	0
1993	Chicago	16	4	94	23.5	1	---	---	---
	4 YR TOTALS	64	16	187	11.7	1	0.0	5	0
1993	RANK NFL DB		21	12	24	2	49	94	NA
1994	PROJECTIONS	16	5	138	27.6	2	0	0	0

Chris Gardocki No. 17/P-K

Full name: Christopher Allen Gardocki
HT: 6-1 **WT:** 196
Born: 2-7-70, Stone Mountain, GA
High school: Redan (GA)
College: Clemson

Only 22 of his 80 punts were returned in 1993.

YEAR	TEAM	G	NO	YARDS	LONG	AVG	BLK	IN20
1991	Chicago	4	—	—	—	—	—	—
1992	Chicago	16	79	3393	61	42.9	0	19
1993	Chicago	16	80	3080	58	38.5	0	28
	3 YR TOTALS	36	159	6473	61	40.7	0	47
1993	RANK NFL Ps		9	18	25	30		2
1994	PROJECTIONS	16	101	3694	71	36.6	0	40

Dallas
COWBOYS

1994 Scouting Report

Offense

The Cowboys had the league's fourth best offense in 1993, gaining 5,615 total yards, including 2,161 rushing yards (second in the NFL). Pro Bowl backs Emmitt Smith and Daryl Johnston return, but the offensive line lost free agents Kevin Gogan and John Gesek. Dallas will still rack up the points, but the weakened OL will hurt; they don't figure to control the ball as effectively as they have in the past. Of course, Troy Aikman may be the best QB in the game, and Michael Irvin and Alvin Harper are two of the NFL's top receivers. TE Jay Novacek had an off-year (for him) in '93, but still made the Pro Bowl.

Defense

Overall, Dallas ranked tenth in the NFL in 1993. But free agency cost Dallas several key players, including DT Tony Casillas, LB Ken Norton, and DT Jimmie Jones, so teams could find it easier to run on Dallas in 1994. On the plus side for the 'Boys, Tony Tolbert and Russell Maryland remain to stuff the run and Charles Haley could recover from his back problems to return to form as one of the game's top pass rushers. Opponents will try to pick on CB Larry Brown and avoid CB Kevin Smith (6 INTs in '93).

Special Teams

The Cowboys lost reliable K Eddie Murray, who signed with Philadelphia as a free agent. John Jett is a quality punter who led the NFL in the proportion of punts inside the 20 (39.3%). Kevin Williams handles punt and kick return duties for Dallas, with top ten rankings in both categories.

1994 Prospects

Dallas lost popular and successful coach Jimmy Johnson and offensive coordinator Norv Turner during the off-season. New coach Barry Switzer has no pro experience, is saddled with the remainder of Johnson's staff, and will have an uphill struggle gaining the respect of his players. Plus, no team lost as many significant free agents as did Dallas. But the team still has Aikman, Smith, and Irvin, football's best offensive trio, and most of the defense returns. Until someone else can prove they're on the Cowboys' level, it's hard to see another team representing the NFC at the end of January.

Team Directory

President/General manager: Jerry Jones
Vice-president: Mike McCoy
Vice-president: Stephen Jones
Director of public relations: Rich Dalrymple

1993 Review			1994 Schedule		
Sep. 6	at Washington	L 35-16	SEP. 4	at Pittsburgh	4:00
Sep. 12	BUFFALO	L 13-10	Sep. 11	HOUSTON	4:00
Sep. 19	at Phoenix	W 17-10	Sep. 19	DETROIT (Mon.)	9:00
Sep. 26	OPEN DATE		Sep. 25	OPEN DATE	
Oct. 3	GREEN BAY	W 36-14	Oct. 2	at Washington	1:00
Oct. 10	at Indianapolis	W 27-3	Oct. 9	ARIZONA	4:00
Oct. 17	SAN FRANCISCO	W 26-17	Oct. 16	PHILADELPHIA	4:00
Oct. 24	OPEN DATE		Oct. 23	at Arizona	4:00
Oct. 31	at Philadelphia	W 23-10	Oct. 30	at Cincinnati	1:00
Nov. 7	N.Y. GIANTS	W 31-9	Nov. 7	N.Y. GIANTS (Mon.)	9:00
Nov. 14	PHOENIX	W 20-15	Nov. 13	at San Francisco	4:00
Nov. 21	at Atlanta	L 27-14	Nov. 20	WASHINGTON	1:00
Nov. 25	MIAMI	L 16-14	Nov. 24	GREEN BAY (Thank.)	4:00
Dec. 6	PHILADELPHIA	W 23-17	Dec. 4	at Philadelphia	1:00
Dec. 12	at Minnesota	W 37-20	Dec. 10	CLEVELAND (Sat.)	4:00
Dec. 18	at N.Y. Jets	W 28-7	Dec. 19	at New Orleans (Mon.)	9:00
Dec. 26	WASHINGTON	W 38-3	Dec. 24	at N.Y. Giants	1:00
Jan. 2	at N.Y. Giants	W 16-13 (OT)			

1993 finish: 7-9 (6-2 home, 6-2 away), first in NFC East

Team Leaders

PASSING	ATT	COM	COM%	YDS	YPA	TD	TD%	INT	INT%	RTG
Aikman	392	271	69.1	3100	7.91	15	3.8	6	1.5	99.0
Kosar	63	36	57.1	410	6.51	3	4.8	0	0.0	92.7
Garrett	19	9	47.4	61	3.21	0	0.0	0	0.0	54.9
TEAM	475	317	66.7	3617	7.61	18	3.8	6	1.3	96.8
OPPONENTS	555	334	60.2	3347	6.03	14	2.5	14	2.5	75.3

RECEIVING	REC	YDS	AVG	TD	RUSHING	ATT	YDS	AVG	TD
Irvin	88	1330	15.1	7	Smith	283	1486	5.3	9
Smith	57	414	7.3	1	Lassic	75	269	3.6	3
Johnston	50	372	7.4	1	Coleman	34	132	3.9	2
Novacek	44	445	10.1	1	Aikman	32	125	3.9	0
Harper	36	777	21.6	5	Johnston	24	74	3.1	3
TEAM	317	3617	11.4	18	TEAM	490	2161	4.4	20
OPPONENTS	334	3347	10.0	14	OPPONENTS	423	1651	3.9	7

INTERCEPTIONS	INT	YDS	AVG	LG	TD	SACKS		NO
Smith	6	56	9.3	32t	1	Tolbert		7.5
Bates	2	25	12.5	22	0	Jeffcoat		6.0
Everett	2	25	12.5	17	0	Jones		5.5
TEAM	14	171	12.2	32t	1	TEAM		34.0
OPPONENTS	6	47	7.8	26	0	OPPONENTS		29.0

KICK RETURNS	NO	YDS	AV	LG	TD	PUNT RETURNS	NO	FC	YDS	AV	LG	TD
Williams, K.	31	689	22.2	49	0	Williams, K.	36	14	381	10.6	64t	2
Gant	1	18	18.0	18	0	Washington	1	0	0	0.0	0	0
Hennings	1	7	7.0	7	0	TEAM	37	14	381	10.3	64t	2
TEAM	36	758	21.1	49	0	OPPONENTS	32	12	169	5.3	20	0
OPPONENTS	66	1225	18.6	95t	1							

KICKING	XPM	XPA	FGM	FGA	LG	PTS
Murray	38	38	28	33	52	122
TEAM	40	41	30	37	52	130
OPPONENTS	23	23	22	27	48	89

PUNTING	NO	YDS	LG	AVG	TB	BLK	RET	RYD	IN20	NAV
Jett	56	2342	59	41.8	3	0	32	169	22	37.7
TEAM	56	2342	59	41.8	3	0	32	169	22	37.7
OPPONENTS	78	3219	60	41.3	6	0	37	381	21	34.8

FUMBLES	FUM	OFF.FUM.REC.	REC	TD	DEF.FUM.REC.	REC	TD
Williams, K.	8	Williams, K.	4	0	Woodson	3	0
Aikman	7	Aikman	3	0	Maryland	2	0
Smith	4	Smith	3	0			
TEAM	33	TEAM	14	0	TEAM	14	0
OPPONENTS	22	OPPONENTS	7	0	OPPONENTS	16	1

1994 Draft Choices

ROUND	NAME	POS	SCHOOL	OVERALL SELECTION
1	Shante Carver	DE/LB	Arizona State	23
2	Larry Allen	G	Sonoma State	46
3	George Hegamin	T	North Carolina State	102
4	Willie Jackson	WR	Florida	109
4	DeWayne Dotson	LB	Mississippi	131
6	Darren Studstill	DB	West Virginia	191
7	Todderick McIntosh	DT	Florida State	216

HISTORY

TITLES

1966	NFL East Championship
1967	NFL East Championship
1968	NFL Capitol Division Championship
1969	NFL Capitol Division Championship
1970	NFC Championship
1971	Super Bowl Winner
1973	NFC East Championship
1975	NFC Championship
1976	NFC East Championship
1977	Super Bowl Winner
1978	NFC Championship
1979	NFC East Championship
1981	NFC East Championship
1985	NFC East Championship
1992	Super Bowl Winner
1993	Super Bowl Winner

ALL-TIME TEAM RECORDS

Rushing

Most yards, game:	206	Tony Dorsett	12/4/77
Most yards, season:	1,713	Emmitt Smith	1992
Most yards, career:	12,036	Tony Dorsett	1977-1987

Passing

Most yards, game:	460	Don Meredith	11/10/63
Most yards, season:	3,980	Danny White	1983
Most yards, career:	22,700	Roger Staubach	1969-1979

Receiving

Most catches, game:	13	Lance Rentzel	11/19/67
Most catches, season:	93	Michael Irvin	1991
Most catches, career:	489	Drew Pearson	1973-1983

Scoring

Most points, game:	24	Many Times	
		Emmitt Smith	11/18/90
Most points, season:	123	Rafael Septien	1983
Most points, career:	874	Rafael Septien	1975-1986

COACHES

NAME	RECORD	YEARS
Tom Landry	270-178-6	1960-88
Jimmy Johnson	48-37-0	1989-93

DALLAS COWBOYS
1994 TRAINING CAMP ROSTER

No.	Quarterbacks		Ht.	Wt.	Born	NFL Exp.	College	How acq.	93 GP/GS
8	Aikman, Troy	QB	6-4	228	11-21-66	5	UCLA	D1 '89	14/14
17	Garrett, Jason	QB	6-2	195	3-28-66	2	Princeton	FA '93	5/1
9	Peete, Rodney	QB	6-0	193	3-16-66	6	Southern California	FA '94	10/10
	Running backs								
**	Agee, Tommie	FB	6-0	235	2-22-64	8	Auburn	Plan B '90	12/0
44	Coleman, Lincoln	RB	6-1	249	8-12-69	2	Baylor	FA '93	7/0
48	Johnston, Daryl	FB	6-2	236	2-10-66	6	Syracuse	D2a '89	16/16
25	Lassic, Derrick	RB	5-10	192	1-26-70	2	Alabama	D4 '93	10/3
22	Smith, Emmitt	RB	5-9	209	5-15-69	5	Florida	D1 '90	14/13
	Wide receivers								
81	Daniel, Tim	WR	5-11	192	9-14-69	3	Florida A&M	D11 '92	0/0
80	Harper, Alvin	WR	6-3	208	7-6-67	4	Tennessee	D1a '91	16/15
88	Irvin, Michael	WR	6-2	205	3-5-66	7	Miami (FL)	D1 '88	16/16
1	Jackson, Willie	WR	6-1	205	8-16-71	R	Florida	D4a '94	
82	Smith, Jimmy	WR	6-1	205	2-9-69	3	Jackson St.	D2 '92	0/0
85	Williams, Kevin	WR	5-9	190	1-25-71	2	Miami (FL)	D2 '93	16/1
86	Williams, Tyrone	WR	6-5	220	3-26-70	2	Western Ontario	FA '93	5/0
	Tight ends								
89	Galbraith, Scott	TE	6-2	255	1-6-67	5	Southern California	FA '93	7/0
84	Novacek, Jay	TE	6-4	231	10-24-62	10	Wyoming	Plan B '90	16/16
	Price, Jim	TE	6-4	247	10-2-66	4	Stanford	T-SF '94	8/0
	Offensive linemen								
73	Allen, Larry	G	6-3	325	11-27-71	R	Sonoma State	D2 '94	
**	Cornish, Frank	C-G	6-4	285	9-24-67	5	UCLA	Plan B '92	14/3
69	Hegamin, George	T	6-7	359	2-14-73	R	North Carolina State	D3 '94	
**	Hellestrae, Dale	C-G	6-5	275	7-11-62	10	So. Methodist	T-RAI '90	16/0
66	Kennard, Derek	G	6-3	300	9-9-62	9	Nevada-Reno	FA '94	16/16
61	Newton, Nate	T	6-3	322	12-20-61	9	Florida A&M	FA '86	16/16
62	Parrish, James	T	6-6	310	5-19-68	1	Temple	FA '93	0/0
**	Stepnoski, Mark	C	6-2	264	1-20-67	6	Pittsburgh	D3a '89	16/16
65	Stone, Ron	T	6-5	306	7-20-71	2	Boston College	D4a '93	0/0
71	Tuinei, Mark	T	6-5	305	3-31-60	12	Hawaii	FA '83	16/16
79	Williams, Erik	T	6-6	324	9-7-68	4	Central St. (OH)	D3b '91	16/16
	Defensive linemen								
96	Carver, Shante	DE	6-5	240	2-12-71	R	Arizona State	D1 '94	
94	Haley, Charles	DE	6-5	250	1-6-64	9	James Madison	T-SF '92	14/11
95	Hennings, Chad	DT	6-6	286	10-20-65	3	Air Force	FA '92	13/0
77	Jeffcoat, Jim	DE	6-5	280	4-1-61	12	Arizona State	D1 '83	16/3
78	Lett, Leon	DL	6-6	287	10-12-68	4	Emporia State	D7 '91	11/6
67	Maryland, Russell	DT	6-1	277	3-22-69	4	Miami (FL)	D1 '91	16/12
90	McIntosh, Toddrick	DT	6-3	277	1-22-72	R	Florida State	D7 '94	
92	Tolbert, Tony	DE	6-6	265	12-29-67	6	Texas-El Paso	D4 '89	16/16
	Linebackers								
50	Dotson, Dewayne	LB	6-1	250	6-10-71	R	Mississippi	D4b '94	
58	Edwards, Dixon	LB	6-1	224	3-25-68	4	Michigan State	D2 '91	16/15
55	Jones, Robert	LB	6-2	236	9-27-69	3	East Carolina	D1a '92	13/3
98	Myles, Godfrey	LB	6-1	241	9-22-68	4	Florida	D3 '91	9/0
59	Smith, Darrin	LB	6-1	227	4-15-70	2	Miami (FL)	D2a '93	16/13
**	Vanderbeek, Matt	LB-DE	6-3	243	8-16-67	5	Michigan State	W-IND '93	16/0
	Defensive backs								
**	Bates, Bill	S	6-1	205	6-6-61	12	Tennessee	FA '83	16/0
24	Brown, Larry	CB	5-11	182	11-30-69	4	Texas Christian	D12 '91	16/16
46	Fishback, Joe	S	6-0	212	11-29-67	5	Carson-Newman	FA '93	6/0
29	Gant, Kenneth	S	5-11	188	4-18-67	5	Albany State	D9 '90	12/1
37	Holmes, Clayton	CB	5-10	178	8-23-69	3	Carson-Newman	D3a '92	
31	Marion, Brock	S	5-11	189	6-11-70	2	Nevada-Reno	D7 '93	15/0
26	Smith, Kevin	CB	5-11	180	4-7-70	3	Texas A&M	D1 '92	16/16
30	Studstill, Darren	DB	6-1	186	8-9-70	R	West Virginia	D6 '94	
41	Thomas, Dave	CB	6-2	205	8-25-68	2	Tennessee	D8 '93	12/0
37	Washington, James	S	6-1	209	1-10-65	7	UCLA	Plan B '90	14/1
28	Woodson, Darren	S	6-1	216	4-25-69	3	Arizona State	D2a '92	16/15
	Specialists								
19	Jett, John	P	6-0	184	11-11-68	2	East Carolina	FA '93	16/0

Troy Aikman   No. 8/QB

Full name: Troy Kenneth Aikman
HT: 6-4   **WT:** 222
Born: 11-21-66, West Covina, CA
High school: Henryetta (OK)
College: Oklahoma, UCLA
Pro Bowler Aikman's 69.1% completion rate led the NFL, and was the fourth best mark in league history.

| YEAR | TEAM | G | PASSING | | | | | | | | | | | RUSHING | | |
			ATT	CPL	CPL%	YDS	AVG	TDS	TD%	INT	INT%	RTG	ATT	YDS	AVG
1989	Dallas	11	293	155	52.9	1749	6.0	9	3.1	18	6.1	55.7	38	302	7.9
1990	Dallas	15	399	226	56.6	2579	6.5	11	2.8	18	4.5	66.6	40	172	4.3
1991	Dallas	12	363	237	65.3	2754	7.6	11	3.0	10	2.8	88.7	16	5	0.3
1992	Dallas	16	473	302	63.8	3445	7.3	23	4.9	14	3.0	89.5	37	105	2.8
1993	Dallas	14	392	271	69.1	3100	7.9	15	3.8	6	1.5	99.0	32	125	3.9
	5 YR TOTALS	68	1920	1191	62.0	13627	7.1	69	3.6	66	3.4		163	709	4.3
1993	RANK NFL QB		16	8	3	10	8	10	26	31	57	7	12	10	17
1994	PROJECTIONS	15	413	302	73.1	3450	8.4	18	3.9	2	0.5		34	138	4.1

Emmitt Smith   No. 22/RB

Full name: Emmitt J. Smith III
HT: 5-9   **WT:** 203
Born: 5-15-69, Pensacola, FL
High school: Escambia (Pensacola, FL)
College: Florida
Only 3 other players have led the NFL in rushing 3 straight years—Earl Campbell, Jim Brown, and Steve Van Buren.

| YEAR | TEAM | G | RUSHING | | | | RECEIVING | | | | KICK RETURNS | | | |
			ATT	YDS	AVG	TD	REC	YDS	AVG	TD	RET	YDS	AVG	TD
1990	Dallas	16	241	937	3.9	11	24	228	9.5	0	---	---	---	---
1991	Dallas	16	365	1563	4.3	12	49	258	5.3	1	---	---	---	---
1992	Dallas	16	373	1713	4.6	18	59	335	5.7	1	---	---	---	---
1993	Dallas	14	283	1486	5.3	9	57	414	7.3	1	---	---	---	---
	4 YR TOTALS	62	1262	5699	4.5	50	189	1235	6.5	3	0	0	NA	(
1993	RANK NFL RB		6	1	12	3	9	11	71	13	65	65	65	
1994	PROJECTIONS	15	290	1688	5.8	7	70	546	7.8	1	0	0	NA	(

Daryl Johnston   No. 48/FB

Full name: Daryl Peter Johnston
HT: 6-2 **WT:** 236
Born: 2-10-66, Youngstown, NY
High school: L-P Central (Youngstown, NY)
College: Syracuse
Johnston was fifth in the NFC in receptions among running backs.

YEAR	TEAM	G	RUSHING ATT	YDS	AVG	TD	RECEIVING REC	YDS	AVG	TD	KICK RETURNS RET	YDS	AVG	TD
1989	Dallas	16	67	212	3.2	0	16	133	8.3	3				
1990	Dallas	16	10	35	3.5	1	14	148	10.6	1				
1991	Dallas	16	17	54	3.2	0	28	244	8.7	1	---	---	---	---
1992	Dallas	16	17	61	3.6	0	32	249	7.8	2	---	---	---	---
1993	Dallas	16	24	74	3.1	3	50	372	7.4	1	---	---	---	---
5 YR TOTALS		80	135	436	3.2	4	140	1146	8.2	8	0	0	NA	0
1993 RANK NFL RB			95	99	112	21	12	14	67	13	65	65	65	
1994 PROJECTIONS		16	25	74	3.0	4	62	452	7.3	1	0	0	NA	0

Alvin Harper   No. 80/WR

Full name: Alvin Craig Harper
HT: 6-3 **WT:** 203
Born: 7-6-67, Lake Wells, FL
High school: Frostproof (FL)
College: Tennessee
Harper's 21.6 yards per catch average was the highest by a Cowboy since Bob Hayes' 24.0 in 1971.

YEAR	TEAM	G	RECEIVING REC	YDS	AVG	TD	RUSHING ATT	YDS	AVG	TD	PUNT RETURN RET	YDS	AVG
1990	Detroit	16	---	---	---	---	---	---	---	---	34	361	10.6
1991	Detroit	16	3	42	14.0	0	2	11	5.5	0	25	385	15.4
1992	Detroit	15	---	---	---	---	---	---	---	---	18	175	9.7
1993	Detroit	11	---	---	---	---	---	---	---	---	23	197	8.6
8 YR TOTALS		110	13	164	12.6	0	19	99	5.2	1	160	1851	11.6
1993 RANK NFL WR			151	151	151	95	42	42	42		12	11	13
1994 PROJECTIONS		9	0	0	NA	0	0	0	NA	0	22	171	7.8

Michael Irvin   No. 88/WR

Full name: Michael Jerome Irvin
HT: 6-2   **WT:** 199
Born: 3-5-66, Fort Lauderdale, FL
High school: St. Aquinas (Ft. Lauderdale)
College: Miami (FL)
Irvin is the first Cowboy WR to have 3 straight
seasons with 50+ catches.

			RECEIVING				RUSHING				PUNT RETURN		
YEAR	TEAM	G	REC	YDS	AVG	TD	ATT	YDS	AVG	TD	RET	YDS	AVG
1988	Dallas	14	32	654	20.4	5	1	2	2.0	0	---	---	---
1989	Dallas	6	26	378	14.5	2	1	6	6.0	0	---	---	---
1990	Dallas	12	20	413	20.7	5	---	---	---	---	---	---	---
1991	Dallas	16	93	1523	16.4	8	---	---	---	---	---	---	---
1992	Dallas	16	78	1396	17.9	7	---	---	---	---	---	---	---
1993	Dallas	16	88	1330	15.1	7	2	6	3.0	0	---	---	---
6 YR TOTALS		80	337	5694	16.9	34	4	14	3.5	0	0	0	NA
1993 RANK NFL WR			3	2	39	7	22	26	27		30	30	29
1994 PROJECTIONS		16	96	1374	14.3	7	3	8	2.7	0	0	0	NA

Jay Novacek   No. 84/TE

Full name: Jay McKinley Novacek
HT: 6-4   **WT:** 231
Born: 10-24-62, Martin, SD
High school: Gothenburg (NE)
College: Wyoming
Since 1990, no NFL TE has caught more
passes than Novacek's 230. He's been a Pro
Bowler for 3 straight seasons.

			RECEIVING			
YEAR	TEAM	G	REC	YDS	AVG	TD
1986	St. Louis	8	1	2	2.0	0
1987	St. Louis	7	20	254	12.7	3
1988	Phoenix	16	38	569	15.0	4
1989	Phoenix	16	23	225	9.8	1
1990	Dallas	16	59	657	11.1	4
1991	Dallas	16	59	664	11.3	4
1992	Dallas	16	68	630	9.3	6
1993	Dallas	16	44	445	10.1	1
9 YR TOTALS		127	313	3450	11.0	23
1993 RANK NFL TE			8	14	34	22
1994 PROJECTIONS		16	36	367	10.2	0

Nate Newton   No. 61/T

Full name: Nathaniel Newton Jr.
HT: 6-3 **WT:** 322
Born: 12-20-61, Orlando, FL
High school: Jones (Orlando, FL)
College: Florida A&M
Newton's been a Pro Bowl pick for 2 straight years. He's started 105 games, tops among Cowboy offensive players.

YEAR	TEAM	G	RUSHING				RANK	PASS	RANK		YDS.
			ATT	YDS	AVG	AV	RUSH	YDS	PASS YDS	SACKS	LOST
1991	Dallas	14	433	1711	4.0	14		3663	6	38	273
1992	Dallas	15	500	2121	4.2	9		3597	7	23	112
1993	Dallas	16	490	2161	4.4	3		3617	9	29	163
	8 YR TOTALS	114									

Tony Tolbert   No. 92/DE

Full name: Tony Lewis Tolbert
HT: 6-6 **WT:** 265
Born: 12-29-67, Tuskeegee, AL
High school: Dw. Morrow (Englewood, NJ)
College: Texas El-Paso
Tolbert's 84 tackles led Cowboy defensive linemen. He comes out on third downs when Dallas goes to a nickel defense.

YEAR	TEAM	G	INT	YDS	AVG	TD	SACKS	FUM REC	TD
1989	Dallas	16	---	---	---	---	2.0	---	---
1990	Dallas	16	---	---	---	---	6.0	---	---
1991	Dallas	16	---	---	---	---	7.0	1	0
1992	Dallas	16	---	---	---	---	8.5	---	---
1993	Dallas	16	---	---	---	---	7.5	---	---
	5 YR TOTALS	80	0	0	NA	0	31.0	1	0
1993	RANK NFL DL		16	NA	NA	NA	27	71	NA
1994	PROJECTIONS	16	0	0	0	0	8	0	0

Charles Haley   No. 94/DE

Full name: Charles Lewis Haley
HT: 6-5 **WT:** 230
Born: 1-6-64, Gladys, VA
High school: William Campbell (Naruna, VA)
College: James Madison
Although Haley had only 4 sacks, he led the team with 28 QB pressures. He's played in 4 Super Bowls and 14 playoff games.

YEAR	TEAM	G	INT	YDS	AVG	TD	SACKS	FUM REC	TD
1986	San Francisco	16	1	8	8.0	---	12.0	2	0
1987	San Francisco	12	---	---	---	---	6.5	---	---
1988	San Francisco	16	---	---	---	---	11.5	2	0
1989	San Francisco	16	---	---	---	---	10.5	1	1
1990	San Francisco	16	---	---	---	---	16.0	1	0
1991	San Francisco	14	---	---	---	---	7.0	1	0
1992	Dallas	15	---	---	---	---	6.0	---	---
1993	Dallas	14	---	---	---	---	4.0	1	0
	8 YR TOTALS	119	1	8	8.0	0	73.5	8	1
1993	RANK NFL DL		16	NA	NA	NA	60	25	5
1994	PROJECTIONS	13	0	0	0	0	2	1	0

Kevin Smith   No. 26/CB

Full name: Kevin Rey Smith
HT: 5-11 **WT:** 173
Born: 4-7-70, Orange, TX
High school: West Orange-Stark (TX)
College: Texas A&M
Smith's 6 INTs (tied for second in the NFC) were the most by a Cowboy since Michael Downs had 6 in 1986. His nickname is "Pup."

YEAR	TEAM	G	INT	YDS	AVG	TD	SACKS	FUM REC	TD
1992	Dallas	16	2	10	5.0	0	---	---	---
1993	Dallas	16	6	56	9.3	1	---	1	0
	2 YR TOTALS	32	8	66	8.3	1	0.0	1	0
1993	RANK NFL DB		7	34	84	2	49	37	14
1994	PROJECTIONS	16	10	102	10.2	2	0	2	0

Rodney Peete QB

HT: 6-0 **WT:** 193
Born: 3-16-66, Mesa, AZ
High school: Sahuaro (Tucson, AZ)
College: Southern California
Peete led the Lions to 4 straight wins in the middle of '93, but ended up a third-stringer. Dallas signed him as a free agent.

YEAR	TEAM	G	PASSING ATT	CPL	CPL%	YDS	AVG	TDS	TD%	INT	INT%	RTG	RUSHING ATT	YDS	AVG
1989	Detroit	8	195	103	52.8	1479	7.6	5	2.6	9	4.6	67.0	33	148	4.5
1990	Detroit	11	271	142	52.4	1974	7.3	13	4.8	8	3.0	79.8	47	363	7.7
1991	Detroit	11	194	116	59.8	1339	6.9	5	2.6	9	4.6	69.9	25	125	5.0
1992	Detroit	8	213	123	57.7	1702	8.0	9	4.2	9	4.2	80.0	21	83	4.0
1993	Detroit	10	252	157	62.3	1670	6.6	6	2.4	14	5.6	66.4	45	165	3.7
	5 YR TOTALS	48	1125	641	57.0	8164	7.3	38	3.4	49	4.4		171	884	5.2
1993	RANK NFL QB		26	25	10	26	31	31	49	11	12	46	6	7	21
1994	PROJECTIONS	11	285	185	65.0	1750	6.1	5	1.7	18	6.2		58	189	3.2

Barry Switzer Head Coach

Born: 10-5-37, Crossett, AR
High school: Crossett (AR)
College: Arkansas
A long-time winner at Oklahoma University, Dallas is Switzer's first pro assignment. Switzer was Troy Aikman's first college head coach (Aikman later transferred to UCLA).

YEAR	TEAM	REGULAR SEASON W	L	T	PCT	FINISH	POSTSEASON W	L	FINISH
1994	Dallas	first year in NFL							

Derrick Lassic   No. 25/RB

HT: 5-10   **WT:** 192
Born: 1-26-70, North Rockland, NY
High school: North Rockland (Haverstraw, NY)
College: Alabama
Starting at HB during Emmitt Smith's holdout, he
gained 75 yards on 16 carries in his first game.

YEAR	TEAM	G	RUSHING ATT	YDS	AVG	TD	RECEIVING REC	YDS	AVG	TD	KICK RETURNS RET	YDS	AVG	TD
1993	Dallas	10	75	269	3.6	3	9	37	4.1	0	---	---	---	--
	1 YR TOTALS	10	75	269	3.6	3	9	37	4.1	0	0	0	NA	
1993	RANK NFL RB		52	56	80	21	77	94	108	40	65	65	65	

Kevin Williams   No. 85/WR

HT: 5-9   **WT:** 190
Born: 1-25-71, Dallas, TX
High school: Roosevelt (Dallas)
College: Miami (FL)
Williams is a solid punt and kick returner, and is
the Cowboys' third wideout.

YEAR	TEAM	G	RECEIVING REC	YDS	AVG	TD	RUSHING ATT	YDS	AVG	TD	PUNT RETURN RET	YDS	AVG
1993	Dallas	16	20	151	7.6	2	7	26	3.7	2	36	381	10.6
	1 YR TOTALS	16	20	151	7.6	2	7	26	3.7	2	36	381	10.6
1993	RANK NFL WR		77	97	142	55	4	11	23		4	2	7

Mark Tuinei   No. 71/T

Full name: Mark Pulemau Tuinei
HT: 6-5   **WT:** 299
Born: 3-31-60, Nanakuli, HI
High school: Punahou (Honolulu)
College: Hawaii
No active OL has been in more Dallas games.

YEAR	TEAM	G	RUSHING ATT	YDS	AVG	RANK AV RUSH	PASS YDS	RANK PASS YDS	SACKS	YDS. LOST
1991	Dallas	12	433	1711	4.0	14	3663	6	38	273
1992	Dallas	15	500	2121	4.2	9	3597	7	23	112
1993	Dallas	16	490	2161	4.4	3	3617	9	29	163
	11 YR TOTALS	143								

Jim Jeffcoat   No. 77/DE

Full name: James Wilson Jeffcoat Jr.
HT: 6-5   **WT:** 274
Born: 4-1-61, Long Branch, NJ
High school: Regional (Matawan, NJ)
College: Arizona State

Jeffcoat generally plays in Dallas's nickel defense.

YEAR	TEAM	G	INT	YDS	AVG	TD	SACKS	FUM REC	TD
1991	Dallas	16	---	---	---	---	4.0	---	---
1992	Dallas	16	---	---	---	---	10.5	---	---
1993	Dallas	16	---	---	---	---	6.0	---	---
11 YR TOTALS		172	---	91	45.5	2	86.5	11	2
1993 RANK NFL DL			16	NA	NA	NA	37	71	NA
1994 PROJECTIONS		16	0	0	0	0	5	0	0

Russell Maryland   No. 67/DT

HT: 6-1   **WT:** 277
Born: 3-22-69, Chicago, IL
High school: Whitney-Young (Chicago)
College: Miami (FL)

Maryland was selected to his first Pro Bowl after the '93 season.

YEAR	TEAM	G	INT	YDS	AVG	TD	SACKS	FUM REC	TD
1991	Dallas	16	---	---	---	---	4.5	---	---
1992	Dallas	14	---	---	---	---	2.5	2	1
1993	Dallas	16	---	---	---	---	2.5	2	0
3 YR TOTALS		46	0	0	NA	0	9.5	4	1
1993 RANK NFL DL			16	NA	NA	NA	94	8	5
1994 PROJECTIONS		16	0	0	0	0	2	2	0

James Washington   No. 37/S

Full name: James McArthur Washington
HT: 6-1   **WT:** 197
Born: 1-10-65, Los Angeles, CA
High school: Jordan (Los Angeles)
College: UCLA

Washington plays FS in Dallas's nickel defense.

YEAR	TEAM	G	INT	YDS	AVG	TD	SACKS	FUM REC	TD
1991	Dallas	16	2	9	4.5	0	---	---	---
1992	Dallas	16	3	31	10.3	0	---	1	0
1993	LA Rams	14	1	38	38.0	0	---	1	0
6 YR TOTALS		86	10	109	10.9	0	0.0	6	0
1993 RANK NFL DB			95	51	13	27	49	37	14
1994 PROJECTIONS		14	0	0	NA	0	0	1	0

John Jett   No. 19/P

HT: 6-0   **WT:** 184
Born: 11-11-68, Richmond, VA
High school: Northumberland (Reedville, VA)
College: East Carolina
Jett's net punt average of 37.7 ranked third in the NFC and fourth in the NFL.

YEAR	TEAM	G	NO	YARDS	LONG	AVG	BLK	IN20
1993	Dallas	16	56	2342	59	41.8	0	22
	1 YR TOTALS	16	56	2342	59	41.8	0	22
1993	RANK NFL		24	24	21	24	18	11

Robert Jones   No. 55/LB

HT: 6-2   **WT:** 236
Born: 9-27-69, Blackstone, VA
High school: Fork Union (VA) Military Academy
College: East Carolina
Dallas expects Jones to replace Ken Norton.

YEAR	TEAM	G	INT	YDS	AVG	TD	SACKS	FUM REC	TD
1992	Dallas	15	---	---	---	---	1.0	1	0
1993	Dallas	13	---	---	---	---	---	---	---
	2 YR TOTALS	28	0	0	NA	0	1.0	1	0
1993	RANK NFL LB		47	NA	NA	NA	91	81	NA
1994	PROJECTIONS	11	0	0	NA	0	0	0	0

Darren Woodson   No. 28/S

Full name: Darren Ray Woodson
HT: 6-1   **WT:** 216
Born: 4-25-69, Phoenix, AZ
High school: Maryvale (Phoenix)
College: Arizona State
His 3 defensive fumble recoveries led the team.

YEAR	TEAM	G	INT	YDS	AVG	TD	SACKS	FUM REC	TD
1992	Dallas	16	---	---	---	---	1.0	---	---
1993	Dallas	16	---	---	---	---	---	3	0
	2 YR TOTALS	32	0	0	NA	0	1.0	3	0
1993	RANK NFL DB		156	NA	NA	NA	49	1	14
1994	PROJECTIONS	16	0	0	NA	0	0	6	0

Detroit
LIONS

1994 Scouting Report

Offense

The Lions couldn't pass the ball in 1993. While Detroit's 1,944 rushing yards behind Barry Sanders were good for seventh in the NFL, their 2,714 passing yards ranked just twenty-fourth in the league. The Lions hope free agent Scott Mitchell is the answer at QB, but he's hardly a proven starter and he's coming off an injury. Rodney Peete and Andre Ware have left town, so behind Mitchell is Dave Krieg, who's getting on in years. Running backs don't get any better than Barry Sanders, and Derrick Moore is a strong back-up. WRs Herman Moore and ex-Viking Anthony Carter are solid, proven veterans, and free-agent addition TE Ron Hall will be a safety valve receiver, as well as a blocker for Sanders.

Defense

Detroit's defense is one of the best in the league, allowing 4,669 total yards in 1993 (sixth in the NFL), including 1,649 rushing yards, tenth in the league, and 3,020 passing yards, ninth in the NFL. The defense has returning stars in LB Pat Swilling, S Bennie Blades, and LB Chris Spielman, and free agent LB Mike Johnson will help. Tracy Scroggins and Robert Porcher will further pressure opposing QBs, and DB William White and DE Kelvin Pritchett should have big seasons.

Special Teams

Jason Hanson is a reliable kicker who led the NFC in scoring, and new punter Greg Montgomery is one of the league's best. Veteran Mel Gray is still a top notch punt and kick returner.

1994 Prospects

If defense wins championships, Detroit should be in the thick of things come playoff time. They have several strengths that characterize winning football teams—a fine running game, a good offensive line, solid all-around defense, and a good kicker. But the passing game under Mitchell remains suspect, they're playing in one of football's toughest divisions, and they face non-division road games at Dallas, Miami, and the Giants. The Lions have to be regarded as a long shot to win the division again, and they could miss the playoffs altogether.

Team Directory

Owner/President: William Clay Ford
Director of player personnel: Ron Hughes
Coordinator of media relations: Mike Murray
Director of pro scouting: Kevin Colbert

1993 Review			
Sep. 5	ATLANTA	W	30-13
Sep. 12	at New England	W	19-16 (OT)
Sep. 19	at New Orleans	L	14-3
Sep. 26	PHOENIX	W	26-20
Oct. 3	at Tampa Bay	L	27-10
Oct. 10	OPEN DATE		
Oct. 17	SEATTLE	W	30-10
Oct. 24	at L.A. Rams	W	16-13
Oct. 31	at Minnesota	W	30-27
Nov. 7	TAMPA BAY	W	23-0
Nov. 14	OPEN DATE		
Nov. 21	vs. Green Bay	L	26-17
Nov. 25	CHICAGO	L	10-6
Dec. 5	MINNESOTA	L	13-0
Dec. 12	at Phoenix	W	21-14
Dec. 19	SAN FRANCISCO	L	55-17
Dec. 26	at Chicago	W	20-14
Jan. 2	GREEN BAY	W	30-20

1994 Schedule		
Sep. 4	ATLANTA	1:00
Sep. 11	at Minnesota	1:00
Sep. 19	at Dallas (Mon.)	9:00
Sep. 25	NEW ENGLAND	4:00
Oct. 2	at Tampa Bay	1:00
Oct. 9	SAN FRANCISCO	1:00
Oct. 16	OPEN DATE	
Oct. 23	CHICAGO	1:00
Oct. 30	at N.Y. Giants	1:00
Nov. 6	vs. Green Bay (Mil.)	1:00
Nov. 13	TAMPA BAY	8:00
Nov. 20	at Chicago	1:00
Nov. 24	BUFFALO (Thank.)	12:30
Dec. 4	GREEN BAY	1:00
Dec. 10	at N.Y. Jets (Sat.)	12:30
Dec. 17	MINNESOTA (Sat.)	12:30
Dec. 25	at Miami	8:00

1993 finish: 10-6 (5-3 home, 5-3 away), first in NFC Central

Team Leaders

PASSING	ATT	COM	COM%	YDS	YPA	TD	TD%	INT	INT%	RTG
Peete	252	157	62.3	1670	6.63	6	2.4	14	5.6	66.4
Kramer	138	87	63.0	1002	7.26	8	5.8	3	2.2	95.1
Ware	45	20	44.4	271	6.02	1	2.2	2	4.4	53.1
TEAM	435	264	60.7	2943	6.77	15	3.4	19	4.4	74.1
OPPONENTS	514	309	60.1	3273	6.37	19	3.7	19	3.7	75.6

RECEIVING	REC	YDS	AVG	TD	RUSHING	ATT	YDS	AVG	TD
Moore	61	935	15.3	6	Sanders	243	1115	4.6	3
Perriman	49	496	10.1	2	Moore	88	405	4.6	3
Sanders	36	205	5.7	0	Lynch	53	207	3.9	2
Green	28	462	16.5	2	Peete	45	165	3.7	1
Holman	25	244	9.8	2	Ware	7	23	3.3	0
TEAM	264	2943	11.1	15	TEAM	456	1944	4.3	9
OPPONENTS	309	3273	10.6	19	OPPONENTS	433	1649	3.8	12

INTERCEPTIONS		INT	YDS	AVG	LG	TD	SACKS		NO
Swilling		3	16	5.3	14	0	Porcher		8.5
Jamison		2	48	24.0	35t	1	Scroggins		8.0
Crockett		2	31	15.5	31	0	Swilling		6.5
TEAM		19	156	8.2	35t	1	TEAM		43.0
OPPONENTS		19	177	9.3	63t	1	OPPONENTS		46.0

KICK RETURNS	NO	YDS	AV	LG	TD	PUNT RETURNS	NO	FC	YDS	AV	LG	TD
Gray	28	688	24.6	95t	1	Gray	23	14	197	8.6	35	0
Turner	15	330	22.0	46	0	Turner	17	4	152	8.9	53	0
Anderson	3	51	17.0	24	0							
TEAM	52	1204	23.2	95t	1	TEAM	40	18	349	8.7	53	0
OPPONENTS	30	609	20.3	64	0	OPPONENTS	45	5	377	8.4	21	0

KICKING	XPM	XPA	FGM	FGA	LG	PTS
Hanson	28	28	34	43	53	130
TEAM	28	28	34	43	53	130
OPPONENTS	31	32	23	30	54	100

PUNTING	NO	YDS	LG	AVG	TB	BLK	RET	RYD	IN20	NAV
Arnold	72	3207	68	44.5	9	0	45	377	15	36.8
TEAM	72	3207	68	44.5	9	0	45	377	15	36.8
OPPONENTS	81	3489	57	43.1	7	0	40	349	25	37.0

FUMBLES	FUM	OFF.FUM.REC.		REC	TD	DEF.FUM.REC.		REC	TD
Peete	11	Peete		4	0	Clay		2	2
Moore	4	Moore		3	0	Owens		2	0
Gray	3	Sanders		3	0	Pete		2	0
Sanders	3					Spielman		2	0
						Spindler		2	0
TEAM	29	TEAM		12	0	TEAM		16	2
OPPONENTS	34	OPPONENTS		16	0	OPPONENTS		13	0

1994 Draft Choices

ROUND	NAME	POS	SCHOOL	OVERALL SELECTION
1	Johnnie Morton	WR	Southern California	21
2	Van Malone	DB	Texas	57
3	Shane Bonham	DT	Tennessee	93
4	Vaughn Bryant	DB	Stanford	124
5	Tony Semple	G	Memphis State	154
6	Jocelyn Borgella	DB	Cincinnati	183
7	Thomas Beer	LB	Wayne State	215

HISTORY

TITLES

1935	NFL Championship
1952	NFL Championship
1954	NFL West Championship
1957	NFL Championship
1983	NFC Central Championship
1991	NFC Central Championship
1993	NFC Central Championship

ALL-TIME TEAM RECORDS

Rushing

Most yards, game:	220	Barry Sanders	11/24/91
Most yards, season:	1,548	Barry Sanders	1991
Most yards, career:	6,789	Barry Sanders	1989-1993

Passing

Most yards, game:	374	Bobby Layne	11/5/50
Most yards, season:	3,223	Gary Danielson	1980
Most yards, career:	15,710	Bobby Layne	1950-1958

Receiving

Most catches, game:	12	Cloyce Box	12/3/50
		James Jones	9/28/86
Most catches, season:	77	James Jones	1984
Most catches, career:	336	Charlie Sanders	1968-1977

Scoring

Most points, game:	24	Cloyce Box	12/3/50
Most points, season:	130	Jason Hanson	1993
Most points, career:	1,113	Eddie Murray	1980-1991

COACHES

NAME	RECORD	YEARS	NAME	RECORD	YEARS
Tubby Griffen	5-6-3	1930	George Wilson	55-45-6	1957-64
Potsy Clark	54-25-7	1931-36, 1940	Harry Gilmer	10-16-2	1965-66
			Joe Schmidt	43-35-7	1967-72
Dutch Clark	14-8-0	1937-38	Don McCafferty	6-7-1	1973
Gus Henderson	6-5-0	1939	Rick Forzano	15-17-0	1974-76
Bill Edwards	4-9-1	1941-42	Tommy Hudspeth	11-13-0	1976-77
John Karcis	0-8-0	1942	Monte Clark	43-63-1	1978-84
Gus Dorais	20-31-2	1943-47	Darryl Rogers	18-40-0	1985-88
Bo McMillin	12-24-0	1948-50	Wayne Fontes	43-44-0	1989-93
Buddy Parker	50-24-2	1951-56			

DETROIT LIONS
1994 TRAINING CAMP ROSTER

No.	Quarterbacks		Ht.	Wt.	Born	NFL Exp.	College	How acq.	93 GP/GS
17	Krieg, Dave	QB	6-1	202	10-20-58	15	Milton	FA '94	12/5
16	Long, Chuck	QB	6-4	217	2-18-63	7	Iowa	FA '94	0/0
19	Mitchell, Scott	QB	6-6	230	1-2-68	5	Utah	FA '94	13/7
	Running backs								
**	Anderson, Gary	RB	6-1	190	4-18-61	9	Arkansas	FA '93	4/0
26	Lynch, Eric	RB	5-10	224	5-16-70	2	Grand Valley St.	FA '92	4/2
31	Moore, Derrick	RB	6-1	227	10-13-67	3	Northeast State (OK)	W '93	13/3
20	Sanders, Barry	RB	5-8	203	7-16-68	6	Oklahoma St.	D1 '89	11/11
	Wide receivers								
	Carter, Anthony	WR	5-11	181	9-17-60	10	Michigan	FA '94	15/14
23	Gray, Mel	WR/KR	5-9	171	3-16-61	9	Purdue	FA '89	11/0
**	Matthews, Aubrey	WR	5-7	165	9-15-62	9	Delta State	FA '90	15/1
84	Moore, Herman	WR	6-3	210	10-20-69	4	Virginia	D1 '91	16/15
87	Morton, Johnnie	WR	5-9	190	10-7-71	R	Southern California	D1 '94	
80	Perriman, Brett	WR	5-9	180	10-10-65	7	Miami (FL)	T-NO '91	15/15
	Tight ends								
89	Hall, Ron	TE	6-4	245	3-15-64	8	Hawaii	FA '94	16/16
49	Hallock, Ty	TE	6-3	249	4-30-71	2	Michigan State	D7 '93	16/4
**	Holman, Rodney	TE	6-3	238	4-20-60	13	Tulane	FA '93	16/16
81	Thompson, Marty	TE	6-3	243	12-9-69	2	Fresno State	FA '93	6/2
	Offensive linemen								
66	Bouwens, Shawn	G	6-4	290	5-25-68	4	Nebraska Wesleyan	FA '91	16/1
75	Brown, Lomas	T	6-4	287	3-30-63	10	Florida	D1 '85	11/11
68	Burton, Leonard	C	6-3	275	6-18-64	8	New Orleans	FA '94	0/0
74	Compton, Mike	C-G	6-6	297	9-18-70	2	West Virginia	D3 '93	8/0
53	Glover, Kevin	C	6-2	282	6-17-63	10	Maryland	D2 '85	16/16
	Jetton, Paul	C-G	6-4	295	10-6-64	7	Texas	FA '94	0/0
73	Lutz, Dave	G-T	6-6	305	12-20-59	12	Georgia Tech	FA '93	16/16
67	Richards, Dave	G	6-5	310	4-11-66	7	UCLA	FA '93	15/15
**	Rodenhauser, Mark	C	6-5	280	6-1-61	7	Illinois State	FA '93	16/0
62	Semple, Tony	G	6-4	286	12-20-70	R	Memphis State	D5 '94	
71	Tharpe, Larry	T	6-4	299	11-19-70	3	Tennessee St.	D6 '92	5/3
	Widell, Doug	G	6-4	280	9-23-66	6	Boston College	FA '94	16/9
	Defensive linemen								
97	Bonham, Shane	DL	6-4	260	10-18-70	R	Tennessee	D3 '94	
90	Owens, Dan	DE	6-3	283	3-16-67	5	Southern California	D2 '90	15/11
91	Porcher, Robert	DE	6-3	283	7-30-69	3	S. Carolina St.	D1 '92	16/5
94	Pritchett, Kelvin	DE	6-2	281	10-24-69	4	Mississippi	T-DAL '91	16/5
93	Spindler, Mark	DE	6-5	290	11-28-69	5	Pittsburgh	D3 '90	16/16
	Linebackers								
98	Beer, Tom	LB	6-1	237	3-27-69	R	Wayne State	D7 '94	
**	Caston, Toby	LB	6-1	243	7-17-65	8	Louisiana State	FA '93	9/0
99	Hayworth, Tracy	LB	6-3	260	12-18-67	5	Tennessee	D7 '90	11/2
**	Jamison, George	LB	6-1	235	9-30-62	9	Cincinnati	D2 SUP '84	16/16
51	Johnson, Mike	LB	6-1	230	11-26-62	9	Virginia Tech	FA '94	16/16
57	Jones, Victor	ILB	6-2	250	10-19-66	7	Virginia Tech	FA '89	16/1
55	London, Antonio	LB	6-2	234	4-14-71	2	Alabama	D3 '93	14/0
59	Scroggins, Tracy	LB	6-2	255	9-11-69	3	Tulsa	D2 '92	16/0
54	Spielman, Chris	ILB	6-0	247	10-11-65	7	Ohio State	D2 '88	16/16
56	Swilling, Pat	LB	6-3	242	10-25-64	9	Georgia Tech	T-NO '93	14/14
	Defensive backs								
36	Blades, Bennie	S	6-1	221	9-3-66	7	Miami (FL)	D1 '88	4/4
27	Borgella, Jocelyn	CB	5-10	180	8-26-71	R	Cincinnati	D6 '94	
24	Bryant, Vaughn	CB	5-9	187	3-20-72	R	Stanford	D4 '94	
32	Clay, Willie	CB	5-9	184	9-5-70	3	Georgia Tech	D8 '92	16/1
21	Colon, Harry	S	6-0	203	2-14-69	4	Missouri	FA '92	15/11
22	Jeffries, Greg	CB	5-9	184	10-16-71	2	Virginia	D6 '93	7/0
39	Malone, Van	S	5-11	186	7-1-70	R	Texas	D2 '94	
40	Massey, Robert	CB	5-10	190	2-17-67	6	N. Carolina Cent.	FA '94	10/10
**	McKyer, Tim	CB	6-0	174	9-5-63	9	Texas-Arlington	FA '93	15/3
47	McNeil, Ryan	CB	6-0	175	10-4-70	2	Miami (FL)	D2 '93	16/2
38	Scott, Kevin	CB	5-9	175	5-19-69	4	Stanford	D4 '91	12/10
35	White, William	S	5-10	191	2-19-66	7	Ohio State	D4 '88	16/16
	Specialists								
4	Hanson, Jason	K	5-11	183	6-17-70	3	Washington St.	D2 '92	16/0
9	Montgomery, Greg	P	6-4	215	10-29-64	7	Michigan State	FA '94	15/0

Scott Mitchell   No. 19/QB

HT: 6-6   **WT:** 230
Born: 1-2-68, Salt Lake City, UT
High school: Springville (UT)
College: Utah

Mitchell got a big contract from the Lions after ranking fifth among AFC passers while replacing Dan Marino.

YEAR	TEAM	G	ATT	CPL	CPL%	YDS	AVG	TDS	TD%	INT	INT%	RTG	ATT	YDS	AVG
			PASSING										RUSHING		
1991	Miami	2	0	0	NA	0	NA	0	NA	0	NA	---	---	---	NA
1992	Miami	16	8	2	25.0	32	4.0	0	0.0	1	^^^^^^	4.2	8	10	1.3
1993	Miami	13	233	133	57.1	1773	7.8	12	5.2	8	3.4	84.2	21	89	4.2
3 YR TOTALS		31	241	135	56.0	1805	7.5	12	5.0	9	3.7		29	99	3.4
1993	RANK NFL QB		28	27	37	13	18	11	23	35	19	22	18	12
1994	PROJECTIONS	15	467	268	57.4	3585	7.8	24	5.1	16	3.4		39	175	4.5

Barry Sanders   No. 20/RB

HT: 5-8   **WT:** 203
Born: 7-16-68, Wichita, KS
High school: North (Wichita, KS)
College: Oklahoma State

A 5-time Pro Bowl starter, Sanders missed the last 5 games in '93 due to a knee injury. Before the injury, he was leading the NFL in rushing and total yards from scrimmage.

YEAR	TEAM	G	ATT	YDS	AVG	TD	REC	YDS	AVG	TD	RET	YDS	AVG	TD
			RUSHING				RECEIVING				KICK RETURNS			
1989	Detroit	15	280	1470	5.3	14	24	282	11.8	0	5	118	23.6	0
1990	Detroit	16	255	1304	5.1	13	36	480	13.3	3	---	---	---	---
1991	Detroit	15	342	1548	4.5	16	41	307	7.5	1	---	---	---	---
1992	Detroit	16	312	1352	4.3	9	29	225	7.8	1	---	---	---	---
1993	Detroit	11	243	1115	4.6	3	36	205	5.7	0	---	---	---	---
5 YR TOTALS		73	1432	6789	4.7	55	166	1499	9.0	5	5	118	23.6	0
1993	RANK NFL RB		9	5	32	21	23	37	95	40	65	65	65	
1994	PROJECTIONS	10	234	1072	4.6	0	39	186	4.8	0	0	0	NA	0

Derrick Moore   No. 31/RB

HT: 6-1   **WT:** 227
Born: 10-13-67, Albany, GA
High school: Albany (GA)
College: Northeast State (OK)

Moore was used as a short-yardage runner and scored 3 TDs. After Barry Sanders' injury, fill-in Moore had 261 rushing yards and 19 catches in 3 late-season starts.

| | | RUSHING | | | | RECEIVING | | | | KICK RETURNS | | | |
YEAR	TEAM	G	ATT	YDS	AVG	TD	REC	YDS	AVG	TD	RET	YDS	AVG	TD
1993	Detroit	13	88	405	4.6	3	---	---	---	---	---	---	---	---
1 YR TOTALS		13	88	405	4.6	3	0	0	NA	0	0	0	NA	(
1993 RANK NFL RB			45	42	31	21	123	122	122	40	65	65	65	

Herman Moore   No. 84/WR

Full name: Herman Joseph Moore
HT: 6-3   **WT:** 210
Born: 10-20-69, Danville, VA
High school: G. Washington (Danville, VA)
College: Virginia

Moore led the Lions with 61 catches for 935 yards and 6 TDs. He's caught at least 1 pass in his last 30 games.

| | | RECEIVING | | | | ROSHING | | | | PONT RETURN | | |
YEAR	TEAM	G	REC	YDS	AVG	TD	ATT	YDS	AVG	TD	RET	YDS	AVG
1991	Detroit	13	11	135	12.3	0	---	---	---	---	---	---	---
1992	Detroit	12	51	966	18.9	4	---	---	---	---	---	---	---
1993	Detroit	16	61	935	15.3	6	---	---	---	---	---	---	---
3 YR TOTALS		41	123	2036	16.6	10	0	0	NA	0	0	0	NA
1993 RANK NFL WR			22	14	36	13	42	42	42		30	30	29
1994 PROJECTIONS		16	69	951	13.8	8	0	0	NA	0	0	0	NA

Mike Johnson   No. 51/LB

HT: 6-1   **WT:** 230
Born: 11-26-62, Southport, NC
High school: DeMatha (Hyattsville, MD)
College: Virginia Tech

Johnson led the Browns in tackles 6 times in 8 seasons, including 1993, when he posted a career high 181 tackles.

YEAR	TEAM	G	INT	YDS	AVG	TD	SACKS	FUM REC	TD
1986	Cleveland	16	---	---	---	---	---	2	0
1987	Cleveland	11	1	3	3.0	0	2.0	1	0
1988	Cleveland	16	2	36	18.0	0	---	---	---
1989	Cleveland	16	3	43	14.3	0	1.0	---	---
1990	Cleveland	16	1	64	64.0	1	2.0	---	---
1991	Cleveland	5	1	0	0.0	0	---	---	---
1992	Cleveland	16	1	0	0.0	0	2.0	5	1
1993	Cleveland	16	1	0	0.0	0	4.0	---	---
	8 YR TOTALS	112	10	146	14.6	1	11.0	8	1
1993	RANK NFL LB		17	38	38	5	26	81	NA
1994	PROJECTIONS	16	1	0	0.0	0	5	0	0

Anthony Carter   WR

HT: 5-11 **WT:** 181
Born: 9-17-60, Riviera Beach, FL
High school: Sun Coast (Riviera Beach, FL)
College: Michigan

Former Michigan standout Carter returns to the state as a pro for the first time since his days with the USFL's Michigan Panthers. He's coming off his best year since '90.

			RECEIVING				RUSHING				PUNT RETURN			
YEAR	TEAM	G	REC	YDS	AVG	TD	ATT	YDS	AVG	TD	RET	YDS	AVG	TD
1986	Minnesota	12	38	686	18.1	7	1	12	12.0	0	---	---	---	---
1987	Minnesota	12	38	922	24.3	7	---	---	---	0	3	40	13.3	0
1988	Minnesota	16	72	1225	17.0	6	4	41	10.3	0	1	3	3.0	0
1989	Minnesota	16	65	1066	16.4	4	3	18	6.0	0	1	2	2.0	0
1990	Minnesota	15	70	1008	14.4	8	3	16	5.3	0	---	---	---	---
1991	Minnesota	15	51	553	10.8	5	13	117	9.0	1	---	---	---	---
1992	Minnesota	16	41	580	14.1	2	16	66	4.1	1	---	---	---	---
1993	Minnesota	15	60	775	12.9	5	---	---	---	---	---	---	---	---
	9 YR TOTALS	133	478	7636	16.0	62	40	0.8	46.7	2	14	0.0	31.3	0
1993	RANK NFL WR		24	27	85	19	42	42	42		30	30	29	
1994	PROJECTIONS	15	66	827	12.5	6	0	0	NA	0	0	0	NA	0

Ron Hall   No. 89/TE

Full name: Ronald Edwin Hall
HT: 6-4 **WT:** 245
Born: 3-15-64, Fort Huachuca, AZ
High school: San Pasqual (Escondido, CA)
College: Fresno State

Hall was the starting TE in Tampa Bay. Hall and Keith Jackson are the only NFL TEs with at least 30 catches every year from '88 to '92.

YEAR	TEAM	G	REC	YDS	AVG	TD
			RECEIVING			
1987	Tampa Bay	11	16	169	10.6	1
1988	Tampa Bay	15	39	555	14.2	0
1989	Tampa Bay	16	30	331	11.0	2
1990	Tampa Bay	16	31	464	15.0	2
1991	Tampa Bay	15	31	284	9.2	0
1992	Tampa Bay	12	39	351	9.0	4
1993	Tampa Bay	16	23	268	11.7	1
	7 YR TOTALS	101	209	2422	11.6	10
1993	RANK NFL TE		24	20	25	22
1994	PROJECTIONS	16	13	193	14.8	0

Chris Spielman No. 54/ILB

Full name: Charles Christopher Spielman
HT: 6-0 **WT:** 247
Born: 10-11-65, Canton, OH
High school: Washington (Massillon, OH)
College: Ohio State

Pro Bowl alternate Spielman lost 10 pounds and improved his speed and quickness. His 148 tackles led the team.

YEAR	TEAM	G	INT	YDS	AVG	TD	SACKS	FUM REC	TD
1988	Detroit	16	---	---	---	---	---	1	0
1989	Detroit	16	---	---	---	---	5.0	2	0
1990	Detroit	12	1	12	12.0	0	2.0	2	0
1991	Detroit	16	---	---	---	---	1.0	3	0
1992	Detroit	16	---	---	---	---	1.0	1	0
1993	Detroit	16	2	-2	-1.0	0	0.5	2	0
	6 YR TOTALS	92	3	10	3.3	0	9.5	11	0
1993	RANK NFL LB		4	46	46	5	90	9	8
1994	PROJECTIONS	16	3	0	0.0	0	0	2	0

Robert Porcher No. 91/DE

Full name: Robert Porcher III
HT: 6-3 **WT:** 283
Born: 7-30-69, Wando, SC
High school: Cainhoy (Huger, SC)
College: South Carolina St.
Despite starting only 5 games, Porcher led
the Lions with 8.5 sacks.

YEAR	TEAM	G	INT	YDS	AVG	TD	SACKS	FUM REC	TD
1992	Detroit	16	---	---	---	---	1.0	---	---
1993	Detroit	16	---	---	---	---	8.5	---	---
	2 YR TOTALS	32	0	0	NA	0	9.5	0	0
1993	RANK NFL DL		16	NA	NA	NA	22	71	NA
1994	PROJECTIONS	16	0	0	0	0	16	0	0

William White   No. 35/S

Full name: William Eugene White
HT: 5-10 **WT:** 191
Born: 2-19-66, Lima, OH
High school: Lima (OH)
College: Ohio State
One of the best tacklers on the team, White
was second on the Lions with 84 tackles.

YEAR	TEAM	G	INT	YDS	AVG	TD	SACKS	FUM REC	TD
1988	Detroit	10	---	---	---	---	---	1	0
1989	Detroit	15	1	0	0.0	0	1.0	1	1
1990	Detroit	16	5	120	24.0	1	---	---	---
1991	Detroit	16	2	35	17.5	0	---	---	---
1992	Detroit	16	4	54	13.5	0	---	---	---
1993	Detroit	16	1	5	5.0	0	1.5	---	---
	6 YR TOTALS	95	13	214	16.5	1	2.5	2	1
1993	RANK NFL DB		95	112	104	27	10	94	NA
1994	PROJECTIONS	16	0	0	NA	0	2	0	0

Jason Hanson   No. 4/K

Full name: Jason Douglas Hanson
HT: 5-11 **WT:** 183
Born: 6-17-70, Spokane, WA
High school: Mead (Spokane, WA)
College: Washington State

Hanson established new Detroit records with 31 FGs in a season and 130 points (tops in the NFC).

YEAR	TEAM	G	XP	XPA	XP Pct.	FG	FGA	FG Pct.	PTS
1992	Detroit	16	30	30	100.0	21	26	80.8	93
1993	Detroit	16	28	28	100.0	34	43	79.1	130
	2 YR TOTALS	32	58	58	100.0	55	69	79.7	223
1993	RANK NFL		17	20	1	2	2	13	2
1994	PROJECTIONS	16	26	26	100.0	47	60	78.3	167

Wayne Fontes Head Coach

Full name: Wayne Howard Joseph Fontes
Born: 2-2-40, New Bedford, MA
High school: Wareham (MA) and McKinley (OH)
College: Michigan State

Fontes earned Coach of the Year honors in '91, when the Lions went 12–4, the most wins in franchise history. He's won more games than any Detroit coach since 1964.

YEAR	TEAM	W	L	T	PCT	FINISH	W	L	FINISH
		REGULAR SEASON					POSTSEASON		
1988	Detroit	2	3	0	.400	T4th/NFC Central			
1989	Detroit	7	9	0	.438	3rd/NFC Central			
1990	Detroit	6	10	0	.375	T2nd/NFC Central			
1991	Detroit	12	4	0	.750	1st/NFC Central	1	1	lost NFC Title game to Wash., 41-10
1992	Detroit	5	11	0	.313	T3rd/NFC Central			
1993	Detroit	10	6	0	.625	1st/NFC Central	0	1	lost wild card game to Green Bay 28-24
	6 YR TOTALS	42	43	0	.494		1	2	

Dave Krieg　　No. 17/QB

HT: 6-1　**WT:** 202
Born: 10-20-58, Iola, WS
High school: D.C. Everest (Schofield, WS)
College: Milton College

Krieg backed up Joe Montana last season. He has 217 TD passes, tenth on the all-time list.

| YEAR | TEAM | G | PASSING | | | | | | | | | | RUSHING | | |
			ATT	CPL	CPL%	YDS	AVG	TDS	TD%	INT	INT%	RTG	ATT	YDS	AVG
1990	Seattle	16	448	265	59.2	3194	7.1	15	3.3	20	4.5	73.6	32	115	3.6
1991	Seattle	10	285	187	65.6	2080	7.3	11	3.9	12	4.2	82.5	13	59	4.5
1992	Kansas City	16	413	230	55.7	3115	7.5	15	3.6	12	2.9	79.9	37	74	2.0
1993	Kansas City	12	189	105	55.6	1238	6.6	7	3.7	3	1.6	81.4	21	24	1.1
	14 YR TOTALS	157	4178	2431	58.2	30485	7.3	217	5.2	163	3.9		352	1188	3.4
1993	RANK NFL QB		31	33	44	33	33	29	28	43	56	24	22	35	43
1994	PROJECTIONS	12	107	52	48.6	634	5.0	4	3.8	0	0.0		19	0	0.0

Brett Perriman　　No. 80/WR

HT: 5-9　**WT:** 180
Born: 10-10-65, Miami, FL
High school: Northwestern (Miami)
College: Miami (FL)

Perriman slumped after leading the Lions in catches in '91 and '92.

| YEAR | TEAM | G | RECEIVING | | | | RUSHING | | | | PUNT RETURN | | |
			REC	YDS	AVG	TD	ATT	YDS	AVG	TD	RET	YDS	AVG
1990	Detroit	16	36	382	10.6	2	---	---	---	---	---	---	---
1991	Detroit	15	52	668	12.8	1	---	---	---	---	---	---	---
1992	Detroit	16	69	810	11.7	4	---	---	---	---	---	---	---
1993	Detroit	15	49	496	10.1	2	---	---	---	---	---	---	---
	6 YR TOTALS	92	242	2927	12.1	11	4	7	1.8	0	1	10	10.0
1993	RANK NFL WR		35	57	126	55	42	42	42		30	30	29
1994	PROJECTIONS	16	51	456	8.9	2	0	0	NA	0	0	0	NA

Kelvin Pritchett　　No. 94/DE

Full name: Kelvin Bratodd Pritchett
HT: 6-2　**WT:** 281
Born: 10-24-69, Atlanta, GA
High school: Therrell (Atlanta)
College: Mississippi

30 of his 42 tackles came in the last 5 games.

YEAR	TEAM	G	INT	YDS	AVG	TD	SACKS	FUM REC	TD
1991	Detroit	16	---	---	---	---	1.5	---	---
1992	Detroit	16	---	---	---	---	6.5	---	---
1993	Detroit	16	---	---	---	---	4.0	---	---
	3 YR TOTALS	48	0	0	NA	0	12.0	0	0
1993	RANK NFL DL		16	NA	NA	NA	60	71	NA
1994	PROJECTIONS	16	0	0	0	0	3	0	0

Tracy Scroggins   No. 59/LB

HT: 6-2   **WT:** 255
Born: 9-11-69, Checotah, OK
High school: Checotah (OK)
College: Tulsa
Scroggins posted 8 sacks in '93, second on the team. He's mostly used in passing situations.

YEAR	TEAM	G	INT	YDS	AVG	TD	SACKS	FUM REC	TD
1992	Detroit	16	---	---	---	---	7.5	---	---
1993	Detroit	16	1	0	0.0	0	8.0	1	0
	2 YR TOTALS	32	1	0	0.0	0	15.5	1	0
1993 RANK NFL LB			17	38	38	5	10	24	8
1994 PROJECTIONS		16	2	0	0.0	0	9	2	0

Pat Swilling   No. 56/LB

Full name: Patrick Travis Swilling
HT: 6-3   **WT:** 242
Born: 10-25-64, Toccoa, GA
High school: Stephens County (Toccoa, GA)
College: Georgia Tech
Swilling was selected to his fifth straight Pro Bowl.

YEAR	TEAM	G	INT	YDS	AVG	TD	SACKS	FUM REC	TD
1991	New Orleans	16	1	39	39.0	1	17.0	1	0
1992	New Orleans	16	---	---	---	---	10.5	1	---
1993	Detroit	14	3	16	5.3	0	6.5	1	0
	8 YR TOTALS	121	6	79	13.2	1	83.0	8	0
1993 RANK NFL LB			2	19	29	5	11*	24	8
1994 PROJECTIONS		13	4	18	4.5	0	4	1	0

Dave Lutz   No. 73/G-T

Full name: David Graham Lutz
HT: 6-6   **WT:** 305
Born: 12-20-59, Monroe, NC
High school: Bowman (Wadesboro, NC)
College: Georgia Tech
He started all 16 games in his first year as a Lion.

| YEAR | TEAM | G | RUSHING | | | RANK | PASS | RANK | | YDS. |
			ATT	YDS	AVG	AV RUSH	YDS	PASS YDS	SACKS	LOST
1991	Kansas City	16	521	2217	4.3	4	3281	18	21	177
1992	Kansas City	16	446	1532	3.4	27	3115	19	48	323
1993	Detroit	16	456	1944	4.3	7	2943	24	46	229
	11 YR TOTALS	155								

Bennie Blades No. 36/S

Full name: Horatio Benedict Blades
HT: 6-1 **WT:** 221
Born: 9-3-66, Fort Lauderdale, FL
High school: Piper (Sunrise, FL)
College: Miami (FL)
Blades had 21 tackles before breaking his ankle.

YEAR	TEAM	G	INT	YDS	AVG	TD	SACKS	FUM REC	TD
1988	Detroit	15	2	12	6.0	0	1.0	4	0
1989	Detroit	16	---	---	---	---	---	1	0
1990	Detroit	12	2	25	12.5	0	1.0	1	0
1991	Detroit	16	1	14	14.0	0	---	3	0
1992	Detroit	16	3	56	18.7	0	---	---	---
1993	Detroit	4	---	---	---	---	---	---	---
	6 YR TOTALS	79	8	107	13.4	0	2.0	9	0

Mel Gray No. 23/WR-KR

HT: 5-9 **WT:** 162
Born: 3-16-61, Williamsburg, VA
High school: Lafayette (Williamsburg, VA)
College: Purdue
Gray is second on the NFL all-time list for kickoff
returns (266) and third in combined returns (426).

YEAR	TEAM	G	RECEIVING				RUSHING				PUNT RETURN		
			REC	YDS	AVG	TD	ATT	YDS	AVG	TD	RET	YDS	AVG
1990	Detroit	16	---	---	---	---	---	---	---	---	34	361	10.6
1991	Detroit	16	3	42	14.0	0	2	11	5.5	0	25	385	15.4
1992	Detroit	15	---	---	---	---	---	---	---	---	18	175	9.7
1993	Detroit	11	---	---	---	---	---	---	---	---	23	197	8.6
	8 YR TOTALS	110	13	164	12.6	0	19	99	5.2	0	160	1851	11.6
1993	RANK NFL WR		151	151	151	95	42	42	42		12	11	13
1994	PROJECTIONS	9	0	0	NA	0	0	0	NA	0	22	171	7.8

Greg Montgomery No. 9/P

Full name: Gregory Hugh Montgomery
HT: 6-4 **WT:** 215
Born: 10-29-64, Morristown, NJ
High school: Red Bank Reg. (Little Silver, NJ)
College: Michigan State
His 39.1 yd. net average was second in the NFL.

YEAR	TEAM	G	NO	YARDS	LONG	AVG	BLK	IN20
1988	Houston	16	65	2523	NA	38.8	0	NA
1989	Houston	16	56	2422	NA	43.3	2	NA
1990	Houston	16	34	1530	NA	45.0	0	NA
1991	Houston	15	48	2105	60	43.9	2	13
1992	Houston	16	53	2487	66	46.9	2	14
1993	Houston	15	54	2462	77	45.6	0	13
	6 YR TOTALS	94	310	13529	77	43.6	6	40

Green Bay
PACKERS

1994 Scouting Report

Offense

QB Brett Favre had a disappointing '93. He was plagued by inconsistency and made poor decisions on the field. As a result, the Pack placed just eighteenth in passing offense with 3,131 yards. Favre will need to return to his '92 form for Green Bay to go far. His primary target, Sterling Sharpe, is simply one of the greatest WRs ever—he has set NFL single-season receiving records two straight years. FB Edgar Bennett is a good receiver (59 catches, second on the team). Green Bay's running game ranked twenty-second in the NFL with 1,619 yards gained, but Tampa Bay free agent RB Reggie Cobb and rookie LeShon Johnson should help. Green Bay tried three players at LG last season; they hoped top draft pick Aaron Taylor would fill that hole, but he was injured in minicamp.

Defense

One of the league's best defenses, the Packers allowed 1,582 rushing yards and 2,900 passing yards, both eighth in the league. New DE Sean Jones was one of the prizes of this year's free agent class—he should work well with power rushers DE Reggie White and LB Bryce Paup. Other defensive standouts include LB George Koonce, CBs Roland Mitchell and Terrell Buckley, and S LeRoy Butler.

Special Teams

K Chris Jacke is a first-team All-Pro selection. P Bryan Wagner enjoyed his best year in '93, as he placed sixth among NFC punters. Robert Brooks led the NFL in kick returns (26.6 yards/return), and also handles punts.

1994 Prospects

As good as any team on defense and special teams, Green Bay will go as far as their offense can take them. If Cobb thrives in Green Bay, and Favre bounces back, Green Bay could make a serious run at the Super Bowl, provided they survive three late season games at Buffalo, Dallas, and Detroit. If the offense has another disappointing season, Green Bay could find itself in a dogfight in the tough NFC Central. We think they'll build on last year's success and win their first division crown since 1972.

Team Directory

President/CEO: Robert E. Harlan
Executive VP/General manager: Ron Wolf
Director of pro personnel: Jesse Kaye
Director of public relations & marketing: Lee Remmel

<table>
<tr><td colspan="4">

1993 Review
</td><td colspan="3">

1994 Schedule
</td></tr>
<tr><td>Sep. 5</td><td>L.A. RAMS</td><td>W</td><td>36-6</td><td>Sep. 4</td><td>MINNESOTA</td><td>1:00</td></tr>
<tr><td>Sep. 12</td><td>PHILADELPHIA</td><td>L</td><td>20-17</td><td>Sep. 11</td><td>MIAMI (at Mil.)</td><td>1:00</td></tr>
<tr><td>Sep. 19</td><td>OPEN DATE</td><td></td><td></td><td>Sep. 18</td><td>at Philadelphia</td><td>1:00</td></tr>
<tr><td>Sep. 26</td><td>at Minnesota</td><td>L</td><td>15-13</td><td>Sep. 25</td><td>TAMPA BAY</td><td>1:00</td></tr>
<tr><td>Oct. 3</td><td>at Dallas</td><td>L</td><td>36-14</td><td>Oct. 2</td><td>at New England</td><td>1:00</td></tr>
<tr><td>Oct. 10</td><td>DENVER</td><td>W</td><td>30-27</td><td>Oct. 9</td><td>L.A. RAMS</td><td>1:00</td></tr>
<tr><td>Oct. 17</td><td>OPEN DATE</td><td></td><td></td><td>Oct. 16</td><td>OPEN DATE</td><td></td></tr>
<tr><td>Oct. 24</td><td>at Tampa Bay</td><td>W</td><td>37-14</td><td>Oct. 20</td><td>at Minnesota (Thurs.)</td><td>8:00</td></tr>
<tr><td>Oct. 31</td><td>CHICAGO</td><td>W</td><td>17-3</td><td>Oct. 31</td><td>at Chicago (Mon.)</td><td>9:00</td></tr>
<tr><td>Nov. 8</td><td>at Kansas City</td><td>L</td><td>23-16</td><td>Nov. 6</td><td>DETROIT (at Mil.)</td><td>1:00</td></tr>
<tr><td>Nov. 14</td><td>at New Orleans</td><td>W</td><td>19-17</td><td>Nov. 13</td><td>N.Y. JETS</td><td>4:00</td></tr>
<tr><td>Nov. 21</td><td>DETROIT (at Mil.)</td><td>W</td><td>26-17</td><td>Nov. 20</td><td>at Buffalo</td><td>1:00</td></tr>
<tr><td>Nov. 28</td><td>TAMPA BAY</td><td>W</td><td>13-10</td><td>Nov. 24</td><td>at Dallas (Thank.)</td><td>4:00</td></tr>
<tr><td>Dec. 5</td><td>at Chicago</td><td>L</td><td>30-17</td><td>Dec. 4</td><td>at Detroit</td><td>1:00</td></tr>
<tr><td>Dec. 12</td><td>at San Diego</td><td>W</td><td>20-13</td><td>Dec. 11</td><td>CHICAGO</td><td>1:00</td></tr>
<tr><td>Dec. 19</td><td>MINN. (at Mil.)</td><td>L</td><td>21-17</td><td>Dec. 18</td><td>ATLANTA (at Mil.)</td><td>1:00</td></tr>
<tr><td>Dec. 26</td><td>L.A. RAIDERS</td><td>W</td><td>28-0</td><td>Dec. 24</td><td>at Tampa Bay</td><td>1:00</td></tr>
<tr><td>Jan. 2</td><td>at Detroit</td><td>L</td><td>30-20</td><td></td><td></td><td></td></tr>
</table>

1993 finish: 9-7 (6-2 home, 3-5 away), second in NFC Central

Team Leaders

PASSING	ATT	COM	COM%	YDS	YPA	TD	TD%	INT	INT%	RTG
Favre	522	318	60.9	3303	6.33	19	3.6	24	4.6	72.2
Detmer	5	3	60.0	26	5.20	0	0.0	0	0.0	73.8
Sharpe	1	1	100.0	1	1.00	0	0.0	0	0.0	79.2
TEAM	528	322	61.0	3330	6.31	19	3.6	24	4.5	72.2
OPPONENTS	529	290	54.8	3201	6.05	16	3.0	18	3.4	68.9

RECEIVING	REC	YDS	AVG	TD	RUSHING	ATT	YDS	AVG	TD
Sharpe	112	1274	11.4	11	Thompson	169	654	3.9	3
Bennett	59	457	7.7	1	Bennett	159	550	3.5	9
Harris	42	604	14.4	4	Favre	58	216	3.7	1
Clayton	32	331	10.3	3	Stephens	48	173	3.6	1
West	25	253	10.1	0	Brooks	3	17	5.7	0
TEAM	322	3330	10.3	19	TEAM	448	1619	3.6	14
OPPONENTS	290	3201	11.0	16	OPPONENTS	424	1582	3.7	6

INTERCEPTIONS	INT	YDS	AVG	LG	TD	SACKS		NO
Butler	6	131	21.8	39	0	White		13.0
Holland	2	41	20.5	30	0	Paup		11.0
Buckley	2	31	15.5	31	0	Bennett		6.5
TEAM	18	255	14.2	39	0	TEAM		46.0
OPPONENTS	24	437	18.2	86t	3	OPPONENTS		30.0

KICK RETURNS	NO	YDS	AV	LG	TD	PUNT RETURNS	NO	FC	YDS	AV	LG	TD
Brooks	23	611	26.6	95t	1	Prior	17	3	194	11.4	24	0
Harris	16	482	30.1	65	0	Brooks	16	4	135	8.4	35	0
Thompson	9	171	19.0	42	0	Buckley	11	5	76	6.9	39	0
TEAM	60	1483	24.7	95t	1	TEAM	45	12	404	9.0	39	0
OPPONENTS	70	1407	20.1	68	0	OPPONENTS	38	12	350	9.2	35	0

KICKING	XPM	XPA	FGM	FGA	LG	PTS
Jacke	35	35	31	37	54	128
TEAM	35	35	31	37	54	128
OPPONENTS	27	27	31	40	53	120

PUNTING	NO	YDS	LG	AVG	TB	BLK	RET	RYD	IN20	NAV
Wagner	74	3174	60	42.9	7	0	38	350	19	36.3
TEAM	74	3174	60	42.9	7	0	38	350	19	36.3
OPPONENTS	79	3176	58	40.2	3	0	45	404	20	34.3

FUMBLES	FUM	OFF.FUM.REC.	REC	TD	DEF.FUM.REC.	REC	TD
Favre	14	Favre	2	0	Evans	2	0
Prior	3	Prior	2	0	Holland	2	0
Holland	2	Ruettgers	2	0	Teague	2	0
Thompson	2						
TEAM	26	TEAM	15	0	TEAM	15	1
OPPONENTS	33	OPPONENTS	16	0	OPPONENTS	10	2

1994 Draft Choices

ROUND	NAME	POS	SCHOOL	OVERALL SELECTION
1	Aaron Taylor	T	Notre Dame	16
3	LeShon Johnson	RB	Northern Illinois	84
4	Gabe Wilkins	DE	Gardner-Webb	126
5	Terry Mickens	WR	Florida A&M	146
5	Dorsey Levens	RB	Georgia Tech	149
6	Jay Kearney	WR	West Virginia	169
6	Ruffin Hamilton	LB	Tulane	175
6	Bill Schroeder	WR	Wisconsin-La Crosse	181
6	Paul Duckworth	LB	Connecticut	190

HISTORY

TITLES

1929	NFL Championship	1960	NFL West Championship
1930	NFL Championship	1961	NFL Championship
1931	NFL Championship	1962	NFL Championship
1936	NFL Championship	1965	NFL Championship
1938	NFL West Championship	1966	Super Bowl Winner
1939	NFL Championship	1967	Super Bowl Winner
1944	NFL Championship	1972	NFC Central Championship

ALL-TIME TEAM RECORDS

Rushing

Most yards, game:	186	Jim Taylor	12/3/61
Most yards, season:	1,407	Jim Taylor	1962
Most yards, career:	8,207	Jim Taylor	1958-1966

Passing

Most yards, game:	418	Lynn Dickey	10/12/80
Most yards, season:	4,458	Lynn Dickey	1983
Most yards, career:	23,718	Bart Starr	1956-1971

Receiving

Most catches, game:	14	Don Hutson	11/22/42
Most catches, season:	112	Sterling Sharpe	1993
Most catches, career:	530	James Lofton	1978-1986

Scoring

Most points, game:	33	Paul Hornung	10/8/61
Most points, season:	176	Paul Hornung	1960
Most points, career:	823	Don Hutson	1935-1945

COACHES

NAME	RECORD	YEARS	NAME	RECORD	YEARS
Curly Lambeau	212-106-21	1921-49	Phil Bengston	20-21-1	1968-70
Gene Ronzani	14-31-1	1950-53	Dan Devine	25-28-4	1971-74
H. Devore-S. McLean	0-2-0	1953	Bart Starr	53-77-3	1975-83
Lisle Blackbourn	17-31-0	1954-57	Forrest Gregg	25-37-1	1984-87
Scooter McLean	1-10-1	1958	Lindy Infante	24-40-0	1988-91
Vince Lombardi	98-30-4	1959-67	Mike Holmgren	18-14-0	1992-93

GREEN BAY PACKERS
1994 TRAINING CAMP ROSTER

No.	Quarterbacks		Ht.	Wt.	Born	NFL Exp.	College	How acq.	93 GP/GS
8	Brunell, Mark	QB	6-1	208	9-17-70	1	Washington	D5 '93	0/0
11	Detmer, Ty	QB	6-0	190	10-30-67	3	Brigham Young	D9 '92	3/0
4	Favre, Brett	QB	6-2	218	10-10-69	4	So. Mississippi	T-ATL '92	16/16
	Running backs								
34	Bennett, Edgar	FB	6-0	216	2-15-69	3	Florida State	D4 '92	16/14

No.	Name	Pos	Ht	Wt	Birthdate	Exp	College	Acquired	G/S
32	Cobb, Reggie	RB	6-0	215	7-7-68	5	Tennessee	FA '94	12/10
42	Johnson, LeShon	RB	5-11	204	1-15-71	R	Northern Illinois	D3 '94	
46	Levens, Dorsey	RB	6-1	231	5-21-70	R	Georgia Tech	D5b '94	
44	McNabb, Dexter	FB	6-2	245	7-9-69	3	Florida	D5 '92	16/0
**	Thompson, Darrell	RB	6-0	217	3-5-67	5	Minnesota	D1a '90	16/11
20	Williams, Kevin	RB	6-1	215	2-17-70	2	UCLA	FA '93	3/0
29	Wilson, Marcus	RB	6-1	210	4-18-68	3	Virginia	FA '92	10/0
Wide receivers									
87	Brooks, Robert	WR	6-0	174	6-23-70	3	South Carolina	D3 '92	14/0
**	Clayton, Mark	WR	5-9	185	4-8-61	12	Louisville	FA '93	16/15
30	Harris, Corey	WR	5-11	195	10-25-69	3	Vanderbilt	W-HOU '92	11/0
18	Kearney, Jay	WR	6-1	194	9-29-71	R	West Virginia	D6a '94	
85	Lewis, Ron	WR	5-11	189	3-25-68	5	Florida State	W-SF '92	9/0
88	Mickens, Terry	WR	6-1	203	2-21-71	R	Florida A&M	D5a '94	
**	Milling, James	WR	5-9	160	2-14-65	6	Maryland	T-ATL '93	0/0
81	Morgan, Anthony	WR	6-1	195	11-15-67	4	Tennessee	W-CHI '93	2/0
19	Schroeder, Bill	WR	6-2	195	1-9-71	R	Wisconsin-LaCrosse	D6c '94	
84	Sharpe, Sterling	WR	6-1	210	4-6-65	7	South Carolina	D1 '88	16/16
Tight ends									
89	Chmura, Mark	TE	6-5	242	2-22-69	3	Boston College	D6 '92	14/0
80	Harris, Jackie	TE	6-4	243	1-4-68	5	NE Louisiana	D4 '90	12/12
**	West, Ed	TE	6-1	245	8-2-61	11	Auburn	FA '84	16/7
Offensive linemen									
63	Campen, James	C	6-3	280	6-11-64	8	Tulane	Plan B '89	4/4
72	Dotson, Earl	T	6-4	315	12-17-70	2	Texas A&I	D3 '93	13/0
76	Galbreath, Harry	G	6-1	275	1-1-65	7	Tennessee	FA '93	16/16
67	Hutchins, Paul	T	6-5	335	2-11-70	2	Western Michigan	D6a '93	1/0
**	Ilkin, Tunch	T	6-3	272	9-23-57	15	Indiana State	FA '93	1/0
**	Moran, Rich	G	6-3	280	3-19-62	10	San Diego State	D3 '85	3/3
**	Robbins, Tootie	T	6-5	315	6-2-58	13	East Carolina	T-PHO '92	12/11
75	Ruettgers, Ken	T	6-6	290	8-20-62	10	Southern California	D1 '85	16/16
68	Sims, Joe	T	6-3	310	3-1-69	4	Nebraska	FA '92	13/5
79	Taylor, Aaron	T	6-4	307	1-14-72	R	Notre Dame	D1 '94	
52	Winters, Frank	C/G	6-3	285	1-23-64	8	Western Illinois	Plan B '92	16/16
60	Zeno, Lance	C	6-4	279	4-15-67	3	UCLA	W-TB '93	5/0
Defensive linemen									
**	Brock, Matt	DE	6-6	280	1-14-66	6	Oregon	D3 '89	16/13
71	Brown, Gilbert	NT	6-2	330	2-22-71	2	Kansas	W-MIN '93	2/0
99	Davey, Don	DE	6-4	270	4-8-68	4	Wisconsin	FA '92	9/0
**	Grant, David	DE	6-4	275	9-17-65	6	West Virginia	FA '93	7/0
96	Jones, Sean	DE	6-7	275	12-19-62	11	Northeastern	FA '94	16/16
64	Jurkovic, John	NT	6-2	285	8-18-67	3	Eastern Illinois	FA '91	16/12
97	LaBounty, Matt	DE	6-4	254	1-3-69	2	Oregon	W-SF '93	0/0
77	Maas, Bill	NT	6-5	282	3-2-62	11	Pittsburgh	FA '93	14/3
	McMichael, Steve	DT	6-2	268	10-17-57	15	Texas	FA '94	16/16
94	Scott Merserau	DT	6-3	275	4-8-65	8	S. Connecticut	FA '94	13/13
**	Patterson, Shawn	DE	6-5	270	6-13-64	7	Arizona State	D2 '88	5/3
92	White, Reggie	DE	6-5	290	12-19-61	10	Tennessee	FA '93	16/16
98	Wilkins, Gabe	DE	6-5	292	9-1-71	R	Gardner-Webb	D4 '94	
Linebackers									
54	Coleman, Keo	LB	6-1	255	5-1-70	3	Mississippi St.	FA '93	12/2
46	Duckworth, Paul	LB	6-1	245	3-12-71	R	Connecticut	D6d '94	
49	Hamilton, Ruffin	LB	6-1	230	3-2-71	R	Tulane	D6b '94	
53	Koonce, George	LB	6-1	238	10-15-68	3	East Carolina	FA '92	15/15
57	Merriweather, Mike	LB	6-2	228	11-26-60	12	Pacific	FA '93	0/0
**	Morrissey, Jim	LB	6-3	225	12-24-62	10	Michigan State	FA '93	6/0
**	Mott, Joe	LB	6-4	255	10-6-65	5	Iowa	FA '93	2/0
95	Paup, Bryce	LB	6-5	247	2-29-68	5	Northern Iowa	D6 '90	15/14
59	Simmons, Wayne	LB	6-3	240	12-15-69	2	Clemson	D1 '93	14/8
56	Willis, James	LB	6-2	235	9-2-72	2	Auburn	D5a '93	13/0
Defensive backs									
27	Buckley, Terrell	CB	5-9	174	6-7-71	3	Florida State	D1 '92	16/16
36	Butler, LeRoy	S	6-0	193	7-19-68	5	Florida State	D2 '90	16/16
33	Evans, Doug	CB	6-1	188	5-13-70	2	Louisiana Tech	D6 '93	16/0
**	Hauck, Tim	S	5-11	185	12-20-66	5	Montana	Plan B '91	13/0
47	Mitchell, Roland	CB	5-11	195	3-15-64	7	Texas Tech	Plan B '91	16/16
45	Prior, Mike	S	6-0	215	11-14-63	9	Illinois State	FA '93	16/4
31	Teague, George	S	6-1	187	2-18-71	2	Alabama	D1a '93	16/12
23	Walker, Sammy	CB	5-11	203	1-20-69	4	Texas Tech	W-PIT '93	8/1
Specialists									
13	Jacke, Chris	K	6-0	200	3-12-66	6	Texas El Paso	D6 '89	16/0
9	Wagner, Bryan	P	6-2	200	3-28-62	7	Cal St.-Northridge	FA '92	16/0

Brett Favre   No. 4/QB

Full name: Brett Lorenzo Favre
HT: 6-2   **WT:** 218
Born: 10-10-69, Gulfport, MS
High school: Hancock N. Central (Kiln, MS)
College: Southern Mississippi

Favre is currently the most accurate passer in Green Bay history—62.4% to Bart Starr's 57.4%.

YEAR	TEAM	G	ATT	CPL	CPL%	YDS	AVG	TDS	TD%	INT	INT%	RTG	ATT	YDS	AVG
				PASSING										RUSHING	
1991	Atlanta	2	5	0	0.0	0	0.0	0	0.0	2	^^^^^^	0.0	0	0	N/A
1992	Green Bay	15	471	302	64.1	3227	6.9	18	3.8	13	2.8	85.3	47	198	4.2
1993	Green Bay	16	522	318	60.9	3303	6.3	19	3.6	24	4.6	72.2	58	216	3.7
	3 YR TOTALS	33	998	620	62.1	6530	6.5	37	3.7	39	3.9		105	414	3.9
1993	RANK NFL QB		2	2	17	8	37	5	32	1	15	37	3	5	18
1994	PROJECTIONS	16	652	395	60.6	4059	6.2	24	3.7	31	4.8		76	272	3.6

Edgar Bennett   No. 34/RB

Full name: Edgar Bennett III
HT: 6-0   **WT:** 216
Born: 2-15-69, Jacksonville, FL
High school: Lee (Jacksonville)
College: Florida State

Bennett tied for sixth in the league with 10 TDs. His 59 catches were the most by a Packer RB since '89.

YEAR	TEAM	G	ATT	YDS	AVG	TD	REC	YDS	AVG	TD	RET	YDS	AVG	TD
			RUSHING				RECEIVING				KICK RETURNS			
1992	Green Bay	16	61	214	3.5	0	13	93	7.2	0	5	104	20.8	0
1993	Green Bay	16	159	550	3.5	9	59	457	7.7	1	---	---	---	---
	2 YR TOTALS	32	220	764	3.5	9	72	550	7.6	1	5	104	20.8	0
1993	RANK NFL RB		30	34	89	3	7	7	59	13	65	65	65	
1994	PROJECTIONS	16	257	886	3.4	18	105	821	7.8	2	0	0	NA	0

Sterling Sharpe   No. 84/WR

HT: 6-1   **WT:** 210
Born: 4-6-65, Chicago, IL
High school: Glenville (GA)
College: South Carolina
Sharpe is the only player in NFL history to
have two 100-catch seasons. And he's just
29 behind James Lofton's all-time Packer
mark of 530 career receptions.

YEAR	TEAM	G	RECEIVING REC	YDS	AVG	TD	RUSHING ATT	YDS	AVG	TD	PUNT RETURN RET	YDS	AVG
1988	Green Bay	16	55	791	14.4	1	4	-2	-0.5	0	9	48	5.3
1989	Green Bay	16	90	1423	15.8	12	2	25	12.5	0	---	---	---
1990	Green Bay	16	67	1105	16.5	6	2	14	7.0	0	---	---	---
1991	Green Bay	16	69	961	13.9	4	4	4	1.0	0	---	---	---
1992	Green Bay	16	108	1461	13.5	13	4	8	2.0	0	---	---	---
1993	Green Bay	16	112	1274	11.4	11	4	8	2.0	0	---	---	---
	6 YR TOTALS	96	501	7015	14.0	47	20	57	2.9	0	9	48	5.3
1993	RANK NFL WR		1	3	109	3	9	22	31		30	30	29
1994	PROJECTIONS	16	124	1271	10.3	12	4	7	1.8	0	0	0	NA

Reggie Cobb   No. 32/RB

Full name: Reginald John Cobb
HT: 6-0   **WT:** 215
Born: 7-7-68, Knoxville, TN
High school: Central (Knoxville, TN)
College: Tennessee
Cobb dropped from 1,171 yards rushing in
1992 to 658 in '93, but he's only the third Buc
RB to have 3 straight 500-yard seasons.

YEAR	TEAM	G	RUSHING ATT	YDS	AVG	TD	RECEIVING REC	YDS	AVG	TD	KICK RETURNS RET	YDS	AVG	TD
1990	Tampa Bay	16	151	480	3.2	2	39	299	7.7	0	11	223	20.3	0
1991	Tampa Bay	16	196	752	3.8	7	15	111	7.4	0	2	15	7.5	0
1992	Tampa Bay	16	310	1171	3.8	9	21	156	7.4	0	---	---	---	---
1993	Tampa Bay	12	221	658	3.0	3	9	61	6.8	1	---	---	---	---
	4 YR TOTALS	60	878	3061	3.5	21	84	627	7.5	1	13	238	18.3	0
1993	RANK NFL RB		12	23	118	21	77	78	80	13	65	65	65	
1994	PROJECTIONS	11	221	581	2.6	1	4	19	4.8	1	0	0	NA	0

Robert Brooks   No. 87/WR

Full name: Robert Darren Brooks
HT: 6-0   **WT:** 174
Born: 6-23-70, Greenwood, SC
High school: Greenwood (SC)
College: South Carolina
Brooks led the NFL in kick returns with a 26.6 yard average. He assumed punt return duties from Terrell Buckley and averaged 8.8 yards.

YEAR	TEAM	G	RECEIVING				RUSHING				PUNT RETURN		
			REC	YDS	AVG	TD	ATT	YDS	AVG	TD	RET	YDS	AVG
1992	Green Bay	16	12	126	10.5	1	2	14	7.0	0	11	102	9.3
1993	Green Bay	14	20	180	9.0	0	3	17	5.7	0	16	135	8.4
	2 YR TOTALS	30	32	306	9.6	1	5	31	6.2	0	27	237	8.8
1993	RANK NFL WR		77	90	133	95	12	16	19		14	15	14
1994	PROJECTIONS	12	25	214	8.6	0	4	19	4.8	0	19	155	8.2

Jackie Harris   No. 80/TE

Full name: Jackie Bernard Harris
HT: 6-4   **WT:** 243
Born: 1-4-68, Pine Bluff, AR
High school: Dollarway (Pine Bluff, AR)
College: Northeast Louisiana
Harris led the Packers in yards per catch with 14.4. A restricted free agent, he signed a Tampa Bay offer sheet in the off-season.

YEAR	TEAM	G	RECEIVING			
			REC	YDS	AVG	TD
1990	Green Bay	16	12	157	13.1	0
1991	Green Bay	16	24	264	11.0	3
1992	Green Bay	16	55	595	10.8	2
1993	Green Bay	12	42	604	14.4	4
	4 YR TOTALS	60	133	1620	12.2	9
1993	RANK NFL TE		13	9	9	8
1994	PROJECTIONS	11	46	713	15.5	5

Reggie White   No. 92/DE

Full name: Reginald Howard White
HT: 6-5   **WT:** 290
Born: 12-19-61, Chattanooga, TN
High school: Howard (Chattanooga, TN)
College: Tennessee

In his first year as a Packer, White had 79 tackles (tops on the Green Bay DL) and led the team with 13 sacks and 3 forced fumbles.

YEAR	TEAM	G	INT	YDS	AVG	TD	SACKS	FUM REC	TD
1985	Philadelphia	13	---	---	---	---	13.0	2	0
1986	Philadelphia	16	---	---	---	---	18.0	---	---
1987	Philadelphia	12	---	---	---	---	21.0	1	1
1988	Philadelphia	16	---	---	---	---	18.0	2	0
1989	Philadelphia	16	---	---	---	---	11.0	1	0
1990	Philadelphia	16	1	33	33.0	0	14.0	1	0
1991	Philadelphia	16	1	0	0.0	0	15.0	3	0
1992	Philadelphia	16	---	---	---	---	14.0	1	0
1993	Green Bay	16	---	---	---	---	13.0	1	0
	9 YR TOTALS	137	2	33	16.5	0	137.0	12	1
1993	RANK NFL DL		16	NA	NA	NA	3	25	5

Sean Jones   No. 96/DE

Full name: Dwight Andre Sean-O'Neil Jones
HT: 6-7   **WT:** 275
Born: 12-19-62, Kingston, Jamaica
High school: Montclair-Kimberly (Montclair, NJ)
College: Northeastern

Jones, a free agent pickup from Houston, posted 13 sacks in '93, fourth in the NFL. He started all 16 games for the Oilers.

YEAR	TEAM	G	INT	YDS	AVG	TD	SACKS	FUM REC	TD
1985	Houston	15	---	---	---	---	8.5	1	0
1986	Houston	16	---	---	---	---	15.5	---	---
1987	Houston	12	---	---	---	---	6.0	2	0
1988	Houston	16	---	---	---	---	7.5	---	---
1989	Houston	16	---	---	---	---	6.0	2	0
1990	Houston	16	---	---	---	---	12.5	1	0
1991	Houston	16	---	---	---	---	10.0	---	---
1992	Houston	15	1	0	0.0	0	8.5	---	---
1993	Houston	16	---	---	---	---	13.0	2	0
	10 YR TOTALS	154	1	0	0.0	0	88.5	8	0
1993	RANK NFL DL		16	NA	NA	NA	3	8	5
1994	PROJECTIONS	16	0	0	NA	0	15	3	0

Bryce Paup   No. 95/LB

Full name: Bryce Eric Paup
HT: 6-5   **WT:** 247
Born: 2-29-68, Jefferson, IA
High school: Scranton (IA)
College: Northern Iowa

Paup's 74 total tackles (fifth on the team) were a career high, as were his 11 sacks.

YEAR	TEAM	G	INT	YDS	AVG	TD	SACKS	FUM REC	TD
1990	Green Bay	5	—	—	—	—	—	—	—
1991	Green Bay	12	—	—	—	—	7.5	—	—
1992	Green Bay	16	—	—	—	—	6.5	2	0
1993	Green Bay	15	1	8	8.0	0	11.0	—	—
4	YR TOTALS	48	1	8	8.0	0	25.0	2	0
1993	RANK NFL LB		17	24	22	5	5	81	NA
1994	PROJECTIONS	16	2	14	7.0	0	15	0	0

LeRoy Butler   No. 36/S

Full name: LeRoy Butler III
HT: 6-0   **WT:** 193
Born: 7-19-68, Jacksonville, FL
High school: Robert E. Lee (Jacksonville)
College: Florida State

A first-team AP All-Pro, Butler's 6 INTs (a career high) tied for second in the NFC, and were the most by a Packer since 1989.

YEAR	TEAM	G	INT	YDS	AVG	TD	SACKS	FUM REC	TD
1990	Green Bay	16	3	42	14.0	0	---	---	---
1991	Green Bay	16	3	6	2.0	0	---	1	0
1992	Green Bay	15	1	0	0.0	0	---	1	0
1993	Green Bay	16	6	131	21.8	0	1.0	1	1
4	YR TOTALS	63	13	179	13.8	0	1.0	3	1
1993	RANK NFL DB		7	4	28	27	13	37	2
1994	PROJECTIONS	16	8	205	25.6	0	2	1	2

Chris Jacke   No. 13/K

Full name: Christopher Lee Jacke
HT: 6-0 **WT:** 200
Born: 3-12-66, Richmond, VA
High school: J. J. Pearce (Richardson, TX)
College: Texas-El Paso

A first-team AP All-Pro selection, Jacke's career-high 128 points in '93 ranked third in the NFL.

YEAR	TEAM	G	XP	XPA	XP Pct.	FG	FGA	FG Pct.	PTS
1989	Green Bay	16	42	42	100.0	22	28	78.6	108
1990	Green Bay	16	28	29	96.6	23	30	76.7	97
1991	Green Bay	16	31	31	100.0	18	24	75.0	85
1992	Green Bay	16	30	30	100.0	22	29	75.9	96
1993	Green Bay	16	35	35	100.0	31	37	83.8	128
5	YR TOTALS	80	166	167	99.4	116	148	78.4	514
1993	RANK NFL		10	10	1	3	4	6	3
1994	PROJECTIONS	16	37	37	100.0	36	42	85.7	145

Mike Holmgren Head Coach

Full name: Michael George Holmgren
Born: 6-15-48, San Francisco, CA
High school: Lincoln (San Francisco)
College: Southern California

Holmgren has led the Pack to back-to-back winning seasons for the first time since the Lombardi era.

		REGULAR SEASON					POSTSEASON			
YEAR	TEAM	W	L	T	PCT	FINISH	W	L		FINISH
1992	Green Bay	9	7	0	.563	2nd/NFC Central				
1993	Green Bay	9	7	0	.563	T2nd/NFC Central	1	1		lost 2nd Rnd. game to Dallas, 27-17
2	YR TOTALS	18	14	0	.563		1	1		

Ty Detmer   No. 11/QB

Full name: Ty Hubert Detmer
HT: 6-0   **WT:** 190
Born: 10-30-67, San Marcos, TX
High school: Southwest (San Antonio)
College: Brigham Young
Detmer is Brett Favre's primary backup.

YEAR	TEAM		G	ATT	CPL	CPL%	YDS	AVG	TDS	TD%	INT	INT%	RTG	ATT	YDS	AVG
		PASSING												RUSHING		
1993	Green Bay		3	5	3	60.0	26	5.2	0	0.0	0	0.0	73.8	1	-2	-2.0
1	YR TOTALS		3	5	3	60.0	26	5.2	0	0.0	0	0.0		1	-2	-2.0
1993	RANK NFL QB			67	66	23	68	57	59	59	61	61	35	62	56	66

Mark Chmura   No. 89/TE

Full name: Mark William Chmura
HT: 6-5   **WT:** 242
Born: 2-22-69, Deerfield, MA
High school: Frontier Regional (S. Deerfield, MA)
College: Boston College
Chmura must bounce back from a knee injury.

YEAR	TEAM	G	REC	YDS	AVG	TD
			RECEIVING			
1993	Green Bay	14	2	13	6.5	0
1	YR TOTALS	14	2	13	6.5	0
1993	RANK NFL TE		61	63	60	46

Harry Galbreath   No. 76/G

Full name: Harry Curtis Galbreath
HT: 6-1   **WT:** 275
Born: 1-1-65, Clarksville, TN
High school: Clarksville (TN)
College: Tennessee
Galbreath gets out well on sweeps and screens.

YEAR	TEAM	G	ATT	YDS	AVG	RANK AV RUSH	PASS YDS	RANK PASS YDS	SACKS	YDS. LOST
			RUSHING			RANK	PASS	RANK		YDS.
1991	Miami	16	379	1352	3.6	21	4077	4	28	188
1992	Miami	16	407	1525	3.7	20	4148	2	28	173
1993	Green Bay	16	448	1619	3.6	19	3330	18	30	199
6	YR TOTALS	94								

John Jurkovic No. 64/NT

Full name: Ivan John Jurkovic
HT: 6-2 **WT:** 285
Born: 8-18-67, Friedrischafen, Germany
High school: Thornton Fractional N. (Calumet City, IL)
College: Eastern Illinois

Jurkovic started after injuries to Bill Maas.

YEAR	TEAM	G	INT	YDS	AVG	TD	SACKS	FUM REC	TD
1991	Green Bay	5	---	---	---	---	---	---	---
1992	Green Bay	16	---	---	---	---	2.0	---	---
1993	Green Bay	16	---	---	---	---	5.5	---	---
	3 YR TOTALS	37	0	0	NA	0	7.5	0	0
1993	RANK NFL DL		16	NA	NA	NA	43	71	NA
1994	PROJECTIONS	16	0	0	0	0	9	0	0

Wayne Simmons No. 59/LB

Full name: Wayne General Simmons
HT: 6-3 **WT:** 240
Born: 12-15-69, Beauford, SC
High school: Hilton Head (SC)
College: Clemson

Simmons was a first-round draft choice in '93.

YEAR	TEAM	G	INT	YDS	AVG	TD	SACKS	FUM REC	TD
1993	Green Bay	14	2	21	10.5	0	1.0	---	---
	1 YR TOTALS	14	2	21	10.5	0	1.0	0	0
1993	RANK NFL LB		4	14	17	5	62	81	NA

George Koonce No. 53/LB

Full name: George Earl Koonce Jr.
HT: 6-1 **WT:** 238
Born: 10-15-68, New Bern, NC
High school: West Craven (Vanceboro, NC)
College: East Carolina

Koonce's 108 tackles ranked second on the team.

YEAR	TEAM	G	INT	YDS	AVG	TD	SACKS	FUM REC	TD
1992	Green Bay	16	---	---	---	---	1.5	1	0
1993	Green Bay	15	---	---	---	---	3.0	1	0
	2 YR TOTALS	31	0	0	NA	0	4.5	2	0
1993	RANK NFL LB		47	NA	NA	NA	30	24	8
1994	PROJECTIONS	14	0	0	0	0	4	1	0

Roland Mitchell   No. 47/CB

Full name: Roland Earl Mitchell
HT: 5-11   **WT:** 195
Born: 3-15-64, Columbus, TX
High school: Bay City (TX)
College: Texas Tech
Mitchell started all 16 games at RCB.

YEAR	TEAM	G	INT	YDS	AVG	TD	SACKS	FUM REC	TD
1991	Green Bay	16	---	---	---	---	1.0	2	0
1992	Green Bay	15	2	40	20.0	0	---	1	0
1993	Green Bay	16	1	0	0.0	0	---	---	---
	7 YR TOTALS	88	6	56	9.3	0	1.0	3	0
1993	RANK NFL DB		95	124	122	27	49	94	NA
1994	PROJECTIONS	16	1	0	0.0	0	0	0	0

Terrell Buckley   No. 27/CB

Full name: Douglas Terrell Buckley
HT: 5-9   **WT:** 174
Born: 6-7-71, Pascagoula, MS
High school: Pascagoula (MS)
College: Florida State
Buckley started all 16 games for the Pack at LCB.

YEAR	TEAM	G	INT	YDS	AVG	TD	SACKS	FUM REC	TD
1992	Green Bay	14	3	33	11.0	1	—	1	0
1993	Green Bay	16	2	31	15.5	0	—	—	—
	2 YR TOTALS	30	5	64	12.8	1	0.0	1	0
1993	RANK NFL DB		54	60	48	27	49	94	NA
1994	PROJECTIONS	16	1	24	24.0	0	0	0	0

Bryan Wagner   No. 9/P

Full name: Bryan Jeffrey Wagner
HT: 6-2   **WT:** 200
Born: 3-28-62, Escondido, CA
High school: Hilltop (Chula Vista, CA)
College: Cal State-Northridge
1993 may have been this veteran's best season.

YEAR	TEAM	G	NO	YARDS	LONG	AVG	BLK	IN20
1990	Cleveland	16	74	2879	NA	38.9	4	NA
1991	New England	3	14	548	54	39.1	0	0
1992	Green Bay	7	30	1222	52	40.7	0	10
1993	Green Bay	16	74	3174	60	42.9	0	19
	7 YR TOTALS	84	404	16383	60	40.6	5	29
1993	RANK NFL Ps		14	15	17	13		15
1994	PROJECTIONS	16	77	3427	0	44.5	0	22

Los Angeles
RAMS

1994 Scouting Report

Offense

Although the Rams only gained 4,804 total yards in 1993 (eighteenth in the NFL), they had the league's fifth-best ground attack (2,014 rushing yards), thanks to rookie RB Jerome Bettis. Bettis will be the center of the offense in '94. After collecting only 2,790 passing yards in '93 (twenty-third in the NFL), and trading Jim Everett, the Rams surprised many by not drafting a QB. But it appears that the job is ex-Falcon Chris Miller's to lose. Veteran WR Henry Ellard left for the Redskins, but WR Willie "Flipper" Anderson returns, and will be joined by former Patriot Greg McMurtry. TE Troy Drayton could see more passes in his sophomore year. The Rams will miss T Irv Eatman, a salary cap casualty during the off-season.

Defense

The Rams allowed 5,411 total yards (twenty-fourth in the league)—1,851 yards rushing (eighteenth in the NFL) and 3,560 passing yards (twenty-second in the NFL). They have good personnel, but got hit hard by injuries. Pass-rushing DE Robert Young, CB Todd Lyght and LB Shane Conlan collectively missed 22 games last year. Young, DT Sean Gilbert, and DE Fred Stokes give the Rams a good pass rush, when they're all healthy. Free agent DT Jimmie Jones should improve the defensive line, as should top draft pick DT Wayne Gandy. Conlan and Roman Phifer are quality NFL LBs, but the secondary is still one of the league's weakest.

Special Teams

Tony Zendejas is a steady veteran kicker with a strong leg, and the Ram punting game should benefit from a full year from mid-season pickup Sean Landeta. Punt returner Todd Kinchen must rebound from a knee injury.

1994 Prospects

The Rams show signs of improving in '94. Jerome Bettis is a terrific RB, Miller has to be better than Everett was last year, and there are quality players on the defense, when everyone's healthy. Depth, the secondary, and lack of a standout receiver are the team's biggest problems. They're not a playoff team yet, but the Rams could get near .500, and should certainly top '93's 5-11 mark.

Team Directory

Owner/President: Georgia Frontiere
VP/Head coach: Chuck Knox
Director of player personnel: John Becker
VP of media and community relations: Marshall Klein

1993 Review

Sep. 5	at Green Bay	L	36-6
Sep. 12	PITTSBURGH	W	27-0
Sep. 19	at N.Y. Giants	L	20-10
Sep. 26	at Houston	W	28-13
Oct. 3	NEW ORLEANS	L	37-6
Oct. 10	OPEN DATE		
Oct. 14	at Atlanta	L	30-24
Oct. 24	DETROIT	L	16-13
Oct. 31	at San Francisco	L	40-17
Nov. 7	OPEN DATE		
Nov. 14	ATLANTA	L	13-0
Nov. 21	WASHINGTON	W	10-6
Nov. 28	SAN FRANCISCO	L	35-10
Dec. 5	at Phoenix	L	38-10
Dec. 12	at New Orleans	W	23-20
Dec. 19	at Cincinnati	L	15-3
Dec. 26	CLEVELAND	L	42-14
Jan. 2	CHICAGO	W	20-6

1994 Schedule

Sep. 4	ARIZONA	4:00
Sep. 11	at Atlanta	1:00
Sep. 18	SAN FRANCISCO	4:00
Sep. 25	at Kansas City	1:00
Oct. 2	ATLANTA	4:00
Oct. 9	at Green Bay	1:00
Oct. 16	N.Y. GIANTS	4:00
Oct. 23	at New Orleans	1:00
Oct. 30	OPEN DATE	
Nov. 6	DENVER	4:00
Nov. 13	L.A. RAIDERS	4:00
Nov. 20	at San Francisco	8:00
Nov. 27	at San Diego	4:00
Dec. 4	NEW ORLEANS	4:00
Dec. 11	at Tampa Bay	1:00
Dec. 18	at Chicago	1:00
Dec. 24	WASHINGTON	4:00

1993 finish: 5-11 (3-5 home, 2-6 away), fourth in NFC West

Team Leaders

PASSING	ATT	COM	COM%	YDS	YPA	TD	TD%	INT	INT%	RTG
Everett	274	135	49.3	1652	6.03	8	2.9	12	4.4	59.7
Rubley	189	108	57.1	1338	7.08	8	4.2	6	3.2	80.1
Pagel	9	3	33.3	23	2.56	0	0.0	1	11.1	2.8
TEAM	473	247	52.2	3021	6.39	16	3.4	19	4.0	66.8
OPPONENTS	488	299	61.3	3763	7.71	17	3.5	11	2.3	87.5

RECEIVING	REC	YDS	AVG	TD	RUSHING	ATT	YDS	AVG	TD
Ellard	61	945	15.5	2	Bettis	294	1429	4.9	7
Anderson	37	552	14.9	4	Gary	79	293	3.7	1
Gary	36	289	8.0	1	Rubley	29	102	3.5	0
Drayton	27	319	11.8	4	Lester	11	74	6.7	0
Bettis	26	244	9.4	0	Everett	19	38	2.0	0
TEAM	247	3021	12.2	16	TEAM	449	2014	4.5	8
OPPONENTS	299	3763	12.6	17	OPPONENTS	480	1851	3.9	18

INTERCEPTIONS	INT	YDS	AVG	LG	TD	SACKS	NO
Bailey	2	41	20.5	41	0	Gilbert	10.5
Rolling	2	21	10.5	12	0	Stokes	9.5
Terrell	2	1	0.5	1	0	Young	7.0
TEAM	11	127	11.5	41	0	TEAM	35.0
OPPONENTS	19	347	18.3	54	2	OPPONENTS	31.0

KICK RETURNS	NO	YDS	AV	LG	TD	PUNT RETURNS	NO	FC	YDS	AV	LG	TD
Boykin	13	216	16.6	29	0	Buchanan	8	1	41	5.1	12	0
Griffith	8	169	21.1	29	0	Kinchen	7	4	32	4.6	8	0
Price	8	144	18.0	23	0	Ellard	2	8	18	9.0	13	0
TEAM	49	824	16.8	35	0	TEAM	19	15	102	5.4	13	0
OPPONENTS	47	984	20.9	45	0	OPPONENTS	43	16	533	12.4	74t	2

KICKING	XPM	XPA	FGM	FGA	LG	PTS
Zendejas	23	25	16	23	54	71
TEAM	23	25	16	23	54	71
OPPONENTS	38	40	29	37	53	125

PUNTING	NO	YDS	LG	AVG	TB	BLK	RET	RYD	IN20	NAV
Bracken	17	651	51	38.3	0	0	8	86	3	33.2
Landeta	42	1825	66	43.5	7	0	25	304	7	32.9
McJulien	21	795	56	37.9	3	0	10	143	5	28.2
TEAM	80	3271	66	40.9	10	0	43	533	15	31.7
OPPONENTS	58	2451	68	42.3	9	0	19	102	18	37.4

FUMBLES	FUM	OFF.FUM.REC.	REC	TD	DEF.FUM.REC.	REC	TD
Everett	7	Rubley	2	0	Phifer	2	0
Bettis	4				Stokes	2	0
Rubley	4						
TEAM	20	TEAM	8	0	TEAM	9	1
OPPONENTS	26	OPPONENTS	17	0	OPPONENTS	11	1

1994 Draft Choices

ROUND	NAME	POS	SCHOOL	OVERALL SELECTION
1	Wayne Gandy	T	Auburn	15
2	Isaac Bruce	WR	Memphis State	33
2	Toby Wright	S	Nebraska	49
2	Brad Ottis	DT	Wayne State (NE)	56
3	Keith Lyle	S	Virginia	71
3	James Bostic	RB	Auburn	83
3	Ernest Jones	LB	Oregon	100
4	Chris Brantley	WR	Rutgers	108
6	Rickey Brady	TE	Oklahoma	167
6	Ronald Edwards	T	North Carolina A&T	189

HISTORY

TITLES

1945	NFL Championship	1974	NFC West Championship
1949	NFL West Championship	1975	NFC West Championship
1950	NFL West Championship	1976	NFC West Championship
1951	NFL Championship	1977	NFC West Championship
1955	NFL West Championship	1978	NFC West Championship
1967	NFL Coastal Div. Champ.	1979	NFC Championship
1969	NFL Coastal Div. Champ.	1985	NFC West Championship
1973	NFC West Championship		

ALL-TIME TEAM RECORDS

Rushing

Most yards, game:	248	Eric Dickerson	1/4/86
Most yards, season:	2,105	Eric Dickerson	1984
Most yards, career:	7,245	Eric Dickerson	1983-1987

Passing

Most yards, game:	554	Norm Van Brocklin	9/28/51
Most yards, season:	4,310	Jim Everett	1989
Most yards, career:	23,758	Jim Everett	1986-1993

Receiving

Most catches, game:	18	Tom Fears	12/3/50
Most catches, season:	86	Henry Ellard	1988
Most catches, career:	593	Henry Ellard	1983-1993

Scoring

Most points, game:	24	Bob Shaw	12/11/49
		Elroy Hirsch	9/28/57
		Harold Jackson	10/14/83
Most points, season:	130	David Ray	1973
Most points, career:	789	Mike Lansford	1982-1990

COACHES

Hugo Bezdek	1-13-0	1937-38	Sid Gillman	28-32-1	1955-59
Art Lewis	4-4-0	1938	Bob Waterfield	9-23-1	1960-62
Dutch Clark	16-26-2	1939-42	Harland Svare	14-32-3	1962-65
Buff Donelli	4-6-0	1944	George Allen	49-19-4	1966-70
Adam Walsh	16-5-1	1845-46	Tommy Prothro	14-12-2	1971-72
Bob Snyder	6-6-0	1947	Chuck Knox	68-41-1	1973-77,
C. Shaugnessy	14-8-3	1948-49			1992-93
Joe Stydahar	19-9-0	1950-52	Ray Malavasi	43-36-0	1978-82
Hamp Pool	23-11-2	1952-54	John Robinson	79-74-0	1983-91

LOS ANGELES RAMS
1994 TRAINING CAMP ROSTER

No.	Quarterbacks		Ht.	Wt.	Born	NFL Exp.	College	How acq.	93 GP/GS
17	Chandler, Chris	QB	6-4	225	10-17-65	7	Washington	FA '94	4/2
13	Miller, Chris	QB	6-2	212	8-9-65	8	Oregon	FA '94	3/2
12	Rubley, T.J.	QB	6-3	205	11-29-68	3	Tulsa	D9 '92	9/7
	Running backs								
36	Bettis, Jerome	RB	5-11	243	2-16-72	2	Notre Dame	D1 '93	16/12
33	Bostic, James	RB	5-11	230	N/A	R	Auburn	D3b '94	
43	Gary, Cleveland	RB	6-0	226	5-4-66	6	Miami (FL)	D1 '89	15/4
34	Lester, Tim	RB	5-9	215	6-15-68	3	East. Kentucky	D10 '92	16/15
44	White, Russell	RB	5-11	216	12-15-70	2	California	D3 '93	5/0
	Wide receivers								
83	Anderson, Willie	WR	6-0	175	3-7-65	7	UCLA	D2b '88	15/15
2	Brantley, Chris	WR	5-10	180	N/A	R	Rutgers	D4 '94	
80	Bruce, Isaac	WR	6-0	178	N/A	R	Memphis State	D2a '94	
	Hester, Jessie	WR	5-11	175	1-21-63	9	Florida State	FA '94	16/16
81	Kinchen, Todd	WR	6-0	187	1-7-69	3	Louisiana State	D3 '92	5/1
88	LaChapelle, Sean	WR	6-3	205	7-29-70	2	UCLA	D5 '93	10/0
87	Lewis, Nate	WR	5-11	198	10-19-66	5	Oregon Tech	T-SD '94	15/9
	McMurtry, Greg	WR	6-2	207	10-15-67	5	Michigan	FA '94	14/8
	Tight ends								
48	Brady, Rickey	TE	6-4	246	N/A	R	Oklahoma	D6a '94	
84	Drayton, Troy	TE	6-3	255	6-29-70	2	Penn State	D2 '93	16/2
**	McNeal, Travis	TE	6-3	244	1-10-67	6	Tenn.-Chattanooga	FA '92	16/6
	Offensive linemen								
77	Ashmore, Darryl	T	6-7	300	11-1-69	3	Northwestern	D7 '92	9/7
71	Belin, Chuck	G	6-2	312	10-27-70	1	Wisconsin	D5 '93	0/0
61	Brostek, Bern	C	6-3	300	9-11-66	5	Washington	D1 '90	16/16
67	Edwards, Ronald	T	6-5	311	N/A	R	North Carolina A&T	D6b '94	
70	Gandy, Wayne	T	6-4	289	N/A	R	Auburn	D1 '94	
79	Goeas, Leo	G-T	6-4	292	8-15-66	5	Hawaii	T-SD '93	16/16
	Jones, Clarence	T	6-6	280	5-6-68	4	Maryland	FA '94	4/0
66	Newberry, Tom	G	6-2	285	12-20-62	9	Wisc.-LaCrosse	D2 '86	9/9
69	Pahukoa, Jeff	G-T	6-2	298	2-2-69	4	Washington	D12 '91	16/3
78	Slater, Jackie	T	6-4	287	5-27-54	19	Jackson St.	D3 '76	8/8
	Defensive linemen								
96	Boutte, Marc	DT	6-4	298	7-26-69	3	Louisiana State	D3a '92	16/16
90	Gilbert, Sean	DT	6-4	315	4-10-70	3	Pittsburgh	D1 '92	16/16
98	Jones, Jimmie	DT	6-4	276	1-9-66	5	Miami (FL)	FA '94	15/2
95	Ottis, Brad	DT	6-4	271	N/A	R	Wayne State (NE)	D2c '94	
97	Robinson, Gerald	DE	6-3	262	5-4-63	7	Auburn	Plan B '91	16/3
92	Rocker, David	DT	6-4	267	3-12-69	4	Auburn	FA '91	14/0
60	Stokes, Fred	DE	6-3	274	3-14-64	8	Georgia Southern	FA '93	15/15
99	Tanuvasa, Maa	DT	6-2	277	11-6-70	1	Hawaii	D8 '93	0/0
76	Young, Robert	DE	6-6	273	1-29-69	4	Mississippi St.	D5 '91	6/6
	Linebackers								
56	Conlan, Shane	LB	6-3	235	3-4-64	8	Penn State	FA '93	12/11
57	Homco, Thomas	LB	6-0	245	1-8-70	2	Northwestern	FA '92	16/3
50	Jones, Ernest	LB	6-2	239	N/A	R	Oregon	D3c '94	
	Kelly, Joe	LB	6-2	235	12-11-64	9	Washington	FA '94	N/A
53	Martin, Chris	LB	6-2	241	12-19-60	12	Auburn	T-KC '93	16/4
58	Phifer, Roman	LB	6-2	230	3-5-68	4	UCLA	D2 '91	16/16
59	Rolling, Henry	LB	6-2	225	9-8-65	8	Nevada-Reno	FA '93	12/8
	Defensive backs								
28	Bailey, Robert	CB	5-9	176	9-3-68	4	Miami (FL)	D4 '91	9/3
21	Boykin, Deral	S	5-11	196	9-2-70	2	Louisville	D6 '93	16/0
29	Davis, Dexter	CB	5-10	185	3-20-70	4	Clemson	FA '93	6/3
**	Henderson, Wymon	CB	5-10	188	12-15-61	9	Nevada-Las Vegas	FA '93	9/4
23	Hicks, Clifford	S	5-10	187	8-18-64	8	Oregon	FA '94	11/0
31	Israel, Steve	CB	5-10	186	3-16-69	3	Pittsburgh	D2 '92	16/11
41	Lyght, Todd	CB	6-0	186	2-9-69	4	Notre Dame	D1 '91	9/9
35	Lyle, Keith	S	6-2	204	N/A	R	Virginia	D3a '94	
26	Newman, Anthony	S	6-0	199	11-25-65	7	Oregon	D2 '88	16/16
22	Pope, Marquez	S-CB	5-10	193	10-29-70	3	Fresno State	T-SD '94	16/1
	Taylor, Terry	CB	5-10	185	7-18-61	10	Southern Illinois	FA '94	10/7
32	Wright, Toby	S	5-11	203	N/A	R	Nebraska	D2b '94	
	Specialists								
5	Landeta, Sean	P	6-0	210	1-10-62	10	Towson State	FA '93	13/0
10	Zendejas, Tony	K	5-8	165	5-15-60	10	Nevada-Reno	Plan B '91	16/0

Chris Miller   No. 13/QB

Full name: Christopher James Miller
HT: 6-2   **WT:** 212
Born: 8-9-65, Pomona, CA
High school: Sheldon (Eugene, OR)
College: Oregon
Formerly the starting QB in Atlanta, Miller was on IR for Atlanta's last 11 games. He's been in just 11 games over the last 2 years.

YEAR	TEAM	G	PASSING ATT	CPL	CPL%	YDS	AVG	TDS	TD%	INT	INT%	RTG	RUSHING ATT	YDS	AVG
1987	Atlanta	3	92	39	42.4	552	6.0	1	1.1	9	9.8	28.4	4	21	5.3
1988	Atlanta	13	351	184	52.4	2133	6.1	11	3.1	12	3.4	67.3	31	138	4.5
1989	Atlanta	15	526	280	53.2	3459	6.6	16	3.0	10	1.9	76.1	10	20	2.0
1990	Atlanta	12	388	222	57.2	2735	7.0	17	4.4	14	3.6	78.7	26	99	3.8
1991	Atlanta	15	413	220	53.3	3103	7.5	26	6.3	18	4.4	80.6	32	229	7.2
1992	Atlanta	8	253	152	60.1	1739	6.9	15	5.9	6	2.4	90.7	23	89	3.9
1993	Atlanta	3	66	32	48.5	345	5.2	1	1.5	3	4.5	50.4	2	11	5.5
	7 YR TOTALS	69	2089	1129	54.0	14066	6.7	87	4.2	72	3.4		128	607	4.7
1993	RANK NFL QB		49	51	65	53	56	54	55	43	17	64	54	40	6
1994	PROJECTIONS	6	195	123	62.9	1325	6.8	13	6.4	3	1.8		20	68	3.4

Tim Lester   No. 34/RB

Full name: Tim Lee Lester
HT: 5-9   **WT:** 215
Born: 6-15-68, Miami, FL
High school: Miami Southridge (FL)
College: Eastern Kentucky
Lester is a key blocker for Jerome Bettis. He gained only 74 yards in '93, but could see more action in '94.

YEAR	TEAM	G	RUSHING ATT	YDS	AVG	TD	RECEIVING REC	YDS	AVG	TD	KICK RETURNS RET	YDS	AVG	TD
1992	LA Rams	11	---	---	---	---	---	---	---	---	---	---	---	---
1993	LA Rams	16	11	74	6.7	0	18	154	8.6	0	---	---	---	---
	2 YR TOTALS	27	11	74	6.7	0	18	154	8.6	0	0	0	NA	0
1993	RANK NFL RB		105	99	7	89	51	50	38	40	65	65	65	
1994	PROJECTIONS	16	22	148	6.7	0	36	308	8.6	0	0	0	NA	0

Jerome Bettis   No. 36/RB

Full name: Jerome Abram Bettis
HT: 5-11 **WT:** 243
Born: 2-16-72, Detroit, MI
High school: McKenzie (Detroit)
College: Notre Dame
Second in the NFL with 1,429 yards rushing, Bettis was named AP Rookie of the Year, AP All-Pro first team, and went to the Pro Bowl.

YEAR	TEAM	G	RUSHING ATT	YDS	AVG	TD	RECEIVING REC	YDS	AVG	TD	KICK RETURNS RET	YDS	AVG	TD
1993	LA Rams	16	294	1429	4.9	7	26	244	9.4	0	---	---	---	---
1 YR TOTALS		16	294	1429	4.9	7	26	244	9.4	0	0	0	NA	0
1993 RANK NFL RB			3	2	19	9	36	30	29	40	65	65	65	

Willie Anderson   No. 83/WR

Full name: Willie Lee Anderson Jr.
HT: 6-0 **WT:** 175
Born: 3-7-65, Paulsboro, NJ
High school: Paulsboro (NJ)
College: UCLA
With Henry Ellard gone, Anderson is the team's primary wideout. He's eighth on the all-time Rams reception list with 213.

YEAR	TEAM	G	RECEIVING REC	YDS	AVG	TD	RUSHING ATT	YDS	AVG	TD	PUNT RETURN RET	YDS	AVG	TD
1988	LA Rams	16	11	319	29.0	0	---	---	---	---	---	---	---	---
1989	LA Rams	16	44	1146	26.0	5	1	-1	-1.0	0	---	---	---	---
1990	LA Rams	16	51	1097	21.5	4	1	13	13.0	0	---	---	---	---
1991	LA Rams	12	32	530	16.6	1	---	---	---	---	---	---	---	---
1992	LA Rams	15	38	657	17.3	7	---	---	---	---	---	---	---	---
1993	LA Rams	15	37	552	14.9	4	---	---	---	---	---	---	---	---
6 YR TOTALS		90	213	4301	20.2	21	2	0.1	12.0	0	0	0	NA	0
1993 RANK NFL WR			53	48	45	28	42	42	42	4	28	27	23	
1994 PROJECTIONS		16	38	469	12.3	4	0	0	NA	0	0	0	NA	0

Greg McMurtry   WR

Full name: Greg Wendell McMurtry
HT: 6-2   **WT:** 207
Born: 10-15-67, Brockton, MA
High school: Brockton (MA)
College: Michigan
Ex-Patriot McMurtry (22 catches in 1993) should complement Willie Anderson.

YEAR	TEAM	G	RECEIVING				RUSHING				PUNT RETURN		
			REC	YDS	AVG	TD	ATT	YDS	AVG	TD	RET	YDS	AVG
1990	New England	13	22	240	10.9	0	---	---	---	---	---	---	---
1991	New England	15	41	614	15.0	2	---	---	---	---	---	---	---
1992	New England	16	35	424	12.1	1	---	---	---	---	---	---	---
1993	New England	14	22	241	11.0	1	---	---	---	---	---	---	---
	4 YR TOTALS	58	120	1519	12.7	4	0	0	NA	0	0	0	NA
1993	RANK NFL WR		76	80	119	72	42	42	42		30	30	29
1994	PROJECTIONS	15	17	150	8.8	1	0	0	NA	0	0	0	NA

Troy Drayton   No. 84/TE

Full name: Troy Anthony Drayton
HT: 6-3   **WT:** 255
Born: 6-29-70, Harrisburg, PA
High school: Steelton (PA)
College: Penn State
A rookie in '93, Drayton led Ram TEs in receiving with 27 catches for 319 yards and 4 TDs.

YEAR	TEAM	G	RECEIVING			
			REC	YDS	AVG	TD
1993	LA Rams	16	27	319	11.8	4
	1 YR TOTALS	16	27	319	11.8	4
1993	RANK NFL TE		17	18	22	8

Cleveland Gary No. 43/RB

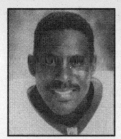

Full name: Cleveland Everette Gary
HT: 6-0   **WT:** 226
Born: 5-4-66, Stuart, FL
High school: South Fork (Indiantown, FL)
College: Miami (FL)

Gary rushed for 1,125 yards in '92, but lost his starting slot to rookie sensation Jerome Bettis in '93. He did have 36 catches.

		RUSHING				RECEIVING				KICK RETURNS			
YEAR	TEAM	G	ATT	YDS	AVG	TD	REC	YDS	AVG	TD	RET	YDS	AVG	TD
1989 LA Rams	10	37	163	4.4	1	2	13	6.5	0	1	4	4.0	0
1990 LA Rams	15	204	808	4.0	14	30	150	5.0	1	---	---	---	---
1991 LA Rams	10	68	245	3.6	1	13	110	8.5	0	---	---	---	---
1992 LA Rams	16	279	1125	4.0	7	52	293	5.6	3	---	---	---	---
1993 LA Rams	15	79	293	3.7	1	36	289	8.0	1	---	---	---	---
5 YR TOTALS	66	667	2634	3.9	24	133	855	6.4	5	1	4	4.0	0
1993 RANK NFL RB		49	51	70	58	23	26	53	13	65	65	65	
1994 PROJECTIONS	16	23	57	2.5	0	40	359	9.0	1	0	0	NA	0

Jimmie Jones   No. 98/DT

Full name: Jimmie Sims Jones
HT: 6-4   **WT:** 276
Born: 1-9-66, Lakeland, FL
High school: Okeechobee (FL)
College: Miami (FL)

A free-agent acquisition, Jones shared duty at DT with Tony Casillas in Dallas, where he recorded 24 tackles and 5.5 sacks.

YEAR	TEAM	G	INT	YDS	AVG	TD	SACKS	FUM REC	TD
1990 Dallas	16	---	---	---	---	7.5			
1991 Dallas	16	---	---	---	---	2.0	2	0	
1992 Dallas	16	---	---	---	---	4.0	---	---	
1993 Dallas	15	---	---	---	---	5.5	---	---	
4 YR TOTALS	63	0	0	NA	0	19.0	2	0	
1993 RANK NFL DL		16	NA	NA	NA	43	71	NA	
1994 PROJECTIONS	16	0	0	0	0	7	0	0	

Sean Gilbert   No. 90/DT

HT: 6-4   **WT:** 315
Born: 4-10-70, Aliquippa, PA
High school: Aliquippa (PA)
College: Pittsburgh
Pro Bowl starter Gilbert had 81 tackles (second on the team), and led Los Angeles with 10.5 sacks.

YEAR	TEAM	G	INT	YDS	AVG	TD	SACKS	FUM REC	TD
1992	LA Rams	16	---	---	---	---	5.0	1	---
1993	LA Rams	16	---	---	---	---	10.5	---	---
	2 YR TOTALS	32	0	0	NA	0	15.5	1	0
1993	RANK NFL DL		16	NA	NA	NA	14	71	NA
1994	PROJECTIONS	16	0	0	0	0	16	0	0

Roman Phifer   No. 58/LB

Full name: Roman Zubinski Phifer
HT: 6-2   **WT:** 230
Born: 3-5-68, Plattsburgh, NY
High school: S. Mecklenburg (Pineville, NC)
College: UCLA
Phifer was the Rams' leading tackler with 117, the highest total by a Ram since 1985. He's started 26 consecutive games.

YEAR	TEAM	G	INT	YDS	AVG	TD	SACKS	FUM REC	TD
1991	LA Rams	12	---	---	---	---	2.0	---	---
1992	LA Rams	16	1	3	3.0	0	---	2	---
1993	LA Rams	16	---	---	---	---	---	2	0
	3 YR TOTALS	44	1	3	3.0	0	2.0	4	0
1993	RANK NFL LB		47	NA	NA	NA	91	9	8
1994	PROJECTIONS	16	0	0	0	0	0	3	0

Tony Zendejas   No. 10/K

Full name: Anthony Guerrero Zendejas
HT: 5-8 **WT:** 165
Born. 5 15 66, Ourlmeu, Mexico
High school: Chino (CA)
College: Nevada-Reno
He's best all-time in the NFL from outside
the 50, converting 17 of 23 attempts (73.9%).
In '93, he made 6-of-8 FGs of over 50 yards.

YEAR	TEAM	G	XP	XPA	XP Pct.	FG	FGA	FG Pct.	PTS
1985	Houston	14	29	31	93.5	21	27	77.8	92
1986	Houston	15	28	29	96.6	22	27	81.5	94
1987	Houston	13	32	33	97.0	20	26	76.9	92
1988	Houston	16	48	50	96.0	22	34	64.7	114
1989	Houston	16	40	40	100.0	25	37	67.6	115
1990	Houston	7	20	21	95.2	7	12	58.3	41
1991	LA Rams	16	25	26	96.2	17	17	100.0	76
1992	LA Rams	16	38	38	100.0	15	20	75.0	83
1993	LA Rams	16	23	25	92.0	16	23	69.6	71
9 YR TOTALS		129	283	293	96.6	165	223	74.0	778
1993 RANK NFL			24	24	27	22	25	25	26

Chuck Knox   Head Coach

Full name: Charles Robert Knox Sr.
Born: 4-27-32, Sewickley, PA
High school: Sewickley (PA)
College: Juniata College (PA)
Knox is the only coach to twice inherit a los-
ing team and take it to the playoffs in their
first season (Rams in '73 and Seahawks in
'83).

		REGULAR SEASON				POSTSEASON		
YEAR	TEAM	W	L	T	PCT	FINISH	W	L	FINISH
1980	Buffalo	11	5	0	.688	1st/AFC East	0	1	lost 1st Rnd. game to San Diego, 20-14
1981	Buffalo	10	6	0	.625	3rd/AFC East	1	1	lost 2nd Rnd. game to Cinn., 28-21
1982	Buffalo	4	5	0	.444	T8th/AFC			
1983	Seattle	9	7	0	.563	2nd/AFC West	2	1	lost AFC Title game to LA Raiders, 30-14
1984	Seattle	12	4	0	.750	2nd/AFC West	1	1	lost 1st Rnd. game to Miami, 31-10
1985	Seattle	8	8	0	.500	T3rd/AFC West			
1986	Seattle	10	6	0	.625	T2nd/AFC West			
1987	Seattle	9	6	0	.600	2nd/AFC West	0	1	lost wild-card game to Houston, 23-20 (OT)
1988	Seattle	9	7	0	.563	1st/AFC West	0	1	lost 1st Rnd. game to Cinn., 21-13
1989	Seattle	7	9	0	.438	4th/AFC West			
1990	Seattle	9	7	0	.563	3rd/AFC West			
1991	Seattle	7	9	0	.438	4th/AFC West			
1992	LA Rams	6	10	0	.375	4th/NFC West			
1993	LA Rams	5	11	0	.313	4th/NFC West			
21 YR TOTALS		182	135	1	.574		7	11	

T.J. Rubley No. 12/QB

Full name: Theron Joseph Rubley
HT: 6-3 **WT:** 205
Born: 11-29-68, Davenport, IA
High school: Davenport West (IA)
College: Tulsa
Miller's backup, Rubley started 7 games in '93.

		PASSING										RUSHING		
YEAR	TEAM	G	ATT	CPL	CPL%	YDS	AVG	TDS	TD%	INT	INT%	RTG	ATT	YDS	AVG
1993	LA Rams	9	189	108	57.1	1338	7.1	8	4.2	6	3.2	80.1	29	102	3.5
	1 YR TOTALS	9	189	108	57.1	1338	7.1	8	4.2	6	3.2		29	102	3.5
1993	RANK NFL QB		31	32	35	32	24	24	20	31	37	26	15	14	23

Todd Kinchen No. 81/WR

Full name: Todd Whittington Kinchen
HT: 6-0 **WT:** 187
Born: 1-7-69, Baton Rouge, LA
High school: Trafton Academy (Baton Rouge)
College: Louisiana State
A knee injury hampered Kinchen in '93.

		RECEIVING				RUSHING				PUNT RETURN		
YEAR	TEAM	G	REC	YDS	AVG	TD	ATT	YDS	AVG	TD	RET	YDS	AVG
1992	LA Rams	14	---	---	---	---	---	---	---	---	4	103	25.8
1993	LA Rams	5	8	137	17.1	1	---	---	---	---	7	32	4.6
	2 YR TOTALS	19	8	137	17.1	1	0	0	NA	0	11	135	12.3
1993	RANK NFL WR		103	98	19	72	42	42	42		17	20	25
1994	PROJECTIONS	-4	0	0	NA	0	0	0	NA	0	0	0	NA

Bern Brostek No. 61/C

HT: 6-3 **WT:** 300
Born: 9-11-66, Honolulu, HI
High school: Iolani (Honolulu)
College: Washington
Brostek has only missed 3 plays in the last 32 games.

		RUSHING			RANK	PASS	RANK		YDS.
YEAR	TEAM	G	ATT	YDS	AVG	AV RUSH	YDS	PASS YDS	SACKS	LOST
1991	LA Rams	14	388	1285	3.3	26	3610	8	30	200
1992	LA Rams	16	393	1659	4.2	10	3422	10	26	204
1993	LA Rams	16	449	2014	4.5	2	3021	23	31	231
	4 YR TOTALS	62								

Fred Stokes

No. 60/DE

Full name: Louis Fred Stokes
HT: 6-3 **WT:** 274
Born: 2-14-64, Vidalia, GA
High school: Vidalia (GA)
College: Georgia Southern
Stokes had 9.5 sacks (second on the team).

YEAR	TEAM	G	INT	YDS	AVG	TD	SACKS	FUM REC	TD
1991	Washington	16	1	0	0.0	0	7.0	2	0
1992	Washington	16	---	---	---	---	3.5	1	---
1993	LA Rams	15	---	---	---	---	9.5	2	0
	7 YR TOTALS	92	1	0	0.0	0	32.0	13	0
1993	RANK NFL DL		16	NA	NA	NA	18	8	5
1994	PROJECTIONS	15	0	0	0	0	12	2	0

Robert Young

No. 76/DE

Full name: Robert E. Young
HT: 6-6 **WT:** 273
Born: 1-29-69, Jackson, MS
High school: Carthage (Jackson, MS)
College: Mississippi State
Young recorded 7 sacks in just 5 games.

YEAR	TEAM	G	INT	YDS	AVG	TD	SACKS	FUM REC	TD
1991	LA Rams	16	---	---	---	---	1.0	---	---
1992	LA Rams	11	---	---	---	---	2.0	---	---
1993	LA Rams	5	---	---	---	---	7.0	---	---
	3 YR TOTALS	32	0	0	NA	0	10.0	0	0
1993	RANK NFL DL		16	NA	NA	NA	29	71	NA
1994	PROJECTIONS	3	0	0	0	0	7	0	0

Shane Conlan

No. 56/LB

Full name: Shane Patrick Conlan
HT: 6-3 **WT:** 235
Born: 3-4-64, Frewsburg, NY
High school: Central (Frewsburg, NY)
College: Penn State
He recorded 75 tackles, third best on the team.

YEAR	TEAM	G	INT	YDS	AVG	TD	SACKS	FUM REC	TD
1991	Buffalo	16	---	---	---	---	---	2	0
1992	Buffalo	13	1	7	7.0	0	2.0	---	---
1993	LA Rams	12	1	28	28.0	0	---	---	---
	7 YR TOTALS	92	4	35	8.8	0	6.0	3	0
1993	RANK NFL LB		17	8	3	5	91	81	NA
1994	PROJECTIONS	15	2	57	28.5	0	0	0	0

Anthony Newman　No. 26/S

Full name: Anthony Q. Newman
HT: 6-0　　**WT:** 199
Born: 11-25-65, Bellingham, WA
High school: Beaverton (WA)
College: Oregon
FS Newman has started 32 consecutive games.

YEAR	TEAM	G	INT	YDS	AVG	TD	SACKS	FUM REC	TD
1988	LA Rams	16	2	27	13.5	0	---	1	0
1989	LA Rams	15	---	---	---	---	---	---	---
1990	LA Rams	16	2	0	0.0	0	---	1	0
1991	LA Rams	16	1	58	58.0	0	1.0	1	1
1992	LA Rams	16	4	33	8.3	0	---	3	0
	5 YR TOTALS	79	9	118	13.1	0	1.0	6	1
1994	PROJECTIONS	16	1	90	90.0	0	2	1	2

Todd Lyght　No. 41/CB

Full name: Todd William Lyght
HT: 6-0　　**WT:** 186
Born: 2-9-69, Kwajalein, Marshall Islands
High school: Luke M. Powers (Flint, MI)
College: Notre Dame
Starting CB Lyght had 44 tackles in 9 games.

YEAR	TEAM	G	INT	YDS	AVG	TD	SACKS	FUM REC	TD
1991	LA Rams	12	1	0	0.0	0	---	1	0
1992	LA Rams	12	3	80	26.7	0	---	---	---
1993	LA Rams	9	2	0	0.0	0	---	1	0
	3 YR TOTALS	33	6	80	13.3	0	0.0	2	0
1993	RANK NFL DB		54	124	122	27	49	37	14
1994	PROJECTIONS	10	2	0	0.0	0	0	2	0

Sean Landeta　No. 5/P

Full name: Sean Edward Landeta
HT: 6-0　　**WT:** 210
Born: 1-6-62, Baltimore, MD
High school: Loch Raven (Baltimore, MD)
College: Towson State
Landeta's 43.4 yard average is ninth all-time.

YEAR	TEAM	G	NO	YARDS	LONG	AVG	BLK	IN20
1991	NY Giants	15	64	2768	61	43.3	0	16
1992	NY Giants	11	53	2317	71	43.7	2	13
1993	NY Giants	8	33	1390	57	42.1	1	11
1993	LA Rams	8	42	1825	66	43.5	0	7
	9 YR TOTALS	119	568	24631	71	43.4	4	47
1993	RANK NFL		28	27	7	15	26	29
1994	PROJECTIONS	8	46	2032	75	44.2	0	5

Minnesota
VIKINGS

1994 Scouting Report

Offense

New faces Warren Moon, TE Adrian Cooper, and RT Chris Hinton will improve the Vikes' air attack from '93's 3,199 yards (fourteenth in the NFL). Moon should have a stellar season throwing to WRs Cris Carter and rookie David Palmer behind protection from Hinton, first-round pick T Todd Steussie, and Pro Bowl G Randall McDaniel. In '93, Minnesota gained just 1,623 rushing yards, placing them twenty-first in the league. There still isn't much of a running game, but young RB Scottie Graham showed promise by season's end.

Defense

Statistically, Minnesota had the NFL's stingiest defense in 1993, giving up 1,534 rushing yards (sixth in the NFL) and 2,870 passing yards (sixth in the NFL), for a total of 4,404 total yards allowed. The defense is led by Pro Bowler John Randle (12.5 sacks) at DE, NT Henry Thomas (9.0 sacks), DT Roy Barker, LBs Jack Del Rio (169 tackles) and Carlos Jenkins, CB Audray McMillian, and S Vencie Glenn (5 INTs). The Vikings will have to make up for the loss of DE Chris Doleman (12.5 sacks in '93), but they remain very strong on the defensive side of the ball.

Special Teams

The reliable Fuad Reveiz handles kicking duties for Minnesota and Qadry Ismail, the Vikings' primary kick returner, is always a threat to break one for a TD. Ex-Chief Bryan Barker takes over the punting duties.

1994 Prospects

The defense will miss Doleman's sacks, but it remains one of the league's best units, and should win a couple of games for the Vikes. The offense should be much steadier under Moon than it was under Jim McMahon and Sean Salisbury, and he's got a corps of speedy young receivers to work with. Minnesota will make the playoffs again, and should challenge Green Bay for first in the tough NFC Central. But Dennis Green's team lacks the proven running game needed to be considered a serious Super Bowl contender.

Team Directory

President/CEO: Roger L. Headrick

VP, administration and team operations: Jeff Diamond

Assistant GM for player personnel: Jerry Reichow

Director of public relations: David Pelletier

1993 Review			1994 Schedule		
Sep. 5	at L.A. Raiders	L 24-7	Sep. 4	at Green Bay	1:00
Sep. 12	CHICAGO	W 10-7	Sep. 11	DETROIT	1:00
Sep. 19	OPEN DATE		Sep. 18	at Chicago	1:00
Sep. 26	GREEN BAY	W 15-13	Sep. 25	MIAMI	1:00
Oct. 3	at San Francisco	L 38-19	Oct. 2	at Arizona	4:00
Oct. 10	TAMPA BAY	W 15-0	Oct. 10	at N.Y. Giants (Mon.)	9:00
Oct. 17	OPEN DATE		Oct. 16	OPEN DATE	
Oct. 25	at Chicago	W 19-12	Oct. 20	GREEN BAY (Thurs.)	8:00
Oct. 31	DETROIT	L 30-27	Oct. 30	at Tampa Bay	4:00
Nov. 7	SAN DIEGO	L 30-17	Nov. 6	NEW ORLEANS	1:00
Nov. 14	at Denver	W 26-23	Nov. 13	at New England	1:00
Nov. 21	at Tampa Bay	L 23-10	Nov. 20	N.Y. JETS	4:00
Nov. 28	NEW ORLEANS	L 17-14	Nov. 27	TAMPA BAY	1:00
Dec. 5	at Detroit	W 13-0	Dec. 1	CHICAGO (Thurs.)	8:00
Dec. 12	DALLAS	L 37-20	Dec. 11	at Buffalo	1:00
Dec. 19	vs. Green Bay (Mil.)	W 21-17	Dec. 17	at Detroit (Sat.)	12:30
Dec. 26	KANSAS CITY	W 30-10	Dec. 26	SAN FRANCISCO (Mon.)	9:00
Dec. 31	at Washington	W 14-9			

1993 finish: 9-7 (4-4 home, 5-3 away), second in NFC Central

Team Leaders

PASSING	ATT	COM	COM%	YDS	YPA	TD	TD%	INT	INT%	RTG
McMahon	331	200	60.4	1968	5.95	9	2.7	8	2.4	76.2
Salisbury	195	115	59.0	1413	7.25	9	4.6	6	3.1	84.0
TEAM	526	315	59.9	3381	6.43	18	3.4	14	2.7	79.1
OPPONENTS	478	310	64.9	3146	6.58	11	2.3	24	5.0	70.3

RECEIVING	REC	YDS	AVG	TD	RUSHING	ATT	YDS	AVG	TD
Carter, C.	86	1071	12.5	9	Graham	118	488	4.1	3
Carter, A.	60	775	12.9	5	Word	142	458	3.2	2
Jordan	56	542	9.7	1	Smith	82	399	4.9	2
Smith	24	111	4.6	0	Craig	38	119	3.1	1
Ismail	19	212	11.2	1	McMahon	33	96	2.9	0
TEAM	315	3381	10.7	18	TEAM	447	1624	3.6	8
OPPONENTS	310	3146	10.1	11	OPPONENTS	415	1536	3.7	14

INTERCEPTIONS	INT	YDS	AVG	LG	TD	SACKS	NO
Glenn	5	49	9.8	23	0	Doleman	12.5
McMillian	4	45	11.3	22t	1	Randle	12.5
Del Rio	4	3	0.8	3	0	Thomas	9.0
TEAM	24	211	8.8	63t	2	TEAM	45.0
OPPONENTS	14	166	11.9	41t	3	OPPONENTS	35.0

KICK RETURNS	NO	YDS	AV	LG	TD	PUNT RETURNS	NO	FC	YDS	AV	LG	TD
Ismail	42	902	21.5	47	0	Guliford	29	15	212	7.3	50	0
Guliford	5	101	20.2	29	0	Parker	9	6	64	7.1	20	0
Smith	3	41	13.7	16	0	Smith	1	2	4	4.0	4	0
TEAM	55	1086	19.7	47	0	TEAM	39	23	280	7.2	50	0
OPPONENTS	58	1420	24.5	99t	1	OPPONENTS	46	22	560	12.2	72t	1

KICKING	XPM	XPA	FGM	FGA	LG	PTS
Reveiz	27	28	26	35	51	105
TEAM	27	28	26	35	51	105
OPPONENTS	29	31	25	33	55	104

PUNTING	NO	YDS	LG	AVG	TB	BLK	RET	RYD	IN20	NAV
Newsome	90	3862	64	42.9	6	0	46	560	25	35.4
TEAM	90	3862	64	42.9	6	0	46	560	25	35.4
OPPONENTS	78	3307	59	42.4	4	0	39	280	23	37.8

FUMBLES	FUM	OFF.FUM.REC.	REC	TD	DEF.FUM.REC.	REC	TD
McMahon	4	Carter, C.	1	0	Strickland	4	0
Salisbury	3	Irwin	1	0			
Word	3	McMahon	1	0			
		Salisbury	1	0			
TEAM	15	TEAM	4	0	TEAM	10	0
OPPONENTS	24	OPPONENTS	13	0	OPPONENTS	10	1

1994 Draft Choices

ROUND	NAME	POS	SCHOOL	OVERALL SELECTION
1	DeWayne Washington	DB	North Carolina State	18
1	Todd Steussie	T	California	19
2	David Palmer	WR	Alabama	40
2	Fernando Smith	DE	Jackson State	55
4	Mike Wells	DT	Iowa	125
5	Shelly Hammonds	DB	Penn State	134
6	Andrew Jordan	TE	Western Carolina	179
7	Pete Bercich	LB	Notre Dame	211

HISTORY

TITLES

1968	NFL Central Championship	1976	NFC Championship
1969	NFC Championship	1977	NFC Central Championship
1970	NFC Central Championship	1978	NFC Central Championship
1971	NFC Central Championship	1980	NFC Central Championship
1973	NFC Championship	1989	NFC Central Championship
1974	NFC Championship	1992	NFC Central Championship
1975	NFC Central Championship		

ALL-TIME TEAM RECORDS

Rushing

Most yards, game:	200	Chuck Foreman	10/24/76
Most yards, season:	1,201	Terry Allen	1992
Most yards, career:	5,879	Chuck Foreman	1973-1979

Passing

Most yards, game:	490	Tommy Kramer	11/2/86
Most yards, season:	3,981	Tommy Kramer	1981
Most yards, career:	33,098	Fran Tarkenton	1961-1966 1972-1978

Receiving

Most catches, game:	15	Rickey Young	12/16/79
Most catches, season:	88	Rickey Young	1978
Most catches, career:	495	Steve Jordan	1982-1993

Scoring

Most points, game:	24	Chuck Foreman	12/20/75
		Ahmad Rashad	9/2/79
Most points, season:	132	Chuck Foreman	1975
Most points, career:	1,365	Fred Cox	1963-1977

COACHES

NAME	RECORD	YEARS
Norm Van Brocklin	29-51-4	1961-66
Bud Grant	168-108-5	1967-83, 1985
Les Steckel	3-13-0	1984
Jerry Burns	55-46-0	1986-91
Dennis Green	20-13-0	1992-93

MINNESOTA VIKINGS
1994 TRAINING CAMP ROSTER

No.	Quarterbacks		Ht.	Wt.	Born	NFL Exp.	College	How acq.	93 GP/GS
14	Johnson, Brad	QB	6-5	221	9-13-68	3	Florida State	D9 '92	0/0
1	Moon, Warren	QB	6-3	212	11-18-56	11	Washington	T-HOU '94	15/14
13	Torretta, Gino	QB	6-2	215	8-10-70	2	Miami (FL)	D7 '93	1/0
11	Ware, Andre	QB	6-2	205	7-31-68	5	Houston	D1 '90	5/2

Running backs

No.	Name	Pos.	Ht.	Wt.	Born	Exp.	College	How Acq.	G/S
21	Allen, Terry	RB	5-10	197	2-21-68	5	Clemson	D9 '90	0/0
**	Craig, Roger	RB	6-0	219	7-10-60	12	Nebraska	Plan B '92	14/2
29	Evans, Charles	RB	6-1	226	4-16-67	2	Clark	FA '93	3/0
31	Graham, Scottie	RB	5-9	215	3-28-69	2	Ohio State	FA '93	7/4
26	Smith, Robert	RB	6-0	195	3-4-72	2	Ohio State	D1 '93	10/2
**	Word, Barry	RB	6-2	245	1-17-63	6	Virginia	T-KC '93	13/8

Wide receivers

No.	Name	Pos.	Ht.	Wt.	Born	Exp.	College	How Acq.	G/S
80	Carter, Cris	WR	6-3	198	11-25-65	8	Ohio State	W-PHI '90	16/16
84	Guliford, Eric	WR	5-8	165	10-25-69	2	Arizona State	FA '93	10/0
82	Ismail, Qadry	WR	6-0	192	11-8-70	2	Syracuse	D2 '93	15/0
22	Palmer, David	WR	5-8	167	11-19-72	R	Alabama	D2a '94	
86	Reed, Jake	WR	6-3	212	9-28-67	4	Grambling	D3a '91	10/1
89	Truitt, Olanda	WR	6-0	186	1-4-71	2	Mississippi St.	W-RAI '93	8/0

Tight ends

No.	Name	Pos.	Ht.	Wt.	Born	Exp.	College	How Acq.	G/S
87	Cooper, Adrian	TE	6-5	263	4-27-68	4	Oklahoma	T-PIT '94	14/3
48	Harrison, Todd	TE	6-4	260	3-20-69	1	North Carolina St.	FA '93	0/0
43	Jordan, Andrew	TE	6-4	268	6-21-72	R	Western Carolina	D6 '94	14/12
**	Jordan, Steve	TE	6-3	240	1-10-61	13	Brown	D7 '82	14/12
**	Novoselsky, Brent	TE	6-2	237	1-8-66	7	Pennsylvania	FA '89	16/0
46	Tennell, Derek	TE	6-2	251	2-12-64	7	UCLA	FA '93	16/6
**	Tice, Mike	TE	6-7	253	2-2-59	14	Maryland	Plan B '92	15/12

Offensive linemen

No.	Name	Pos.	Ht.	Wt.	Born	Exp.	College	How Acq.	G/S
72	Adams, Scott	OL	6-5	293	9-28-66	3	Georgia	FA '91	15/9
62	Christy, Jeff	C	6-3	277	2-2-69	2	Pittsburgh	FA '93	8/0
75	Dafney, Bernard	T	6-5	331	11-1-69	3	Tennessee	FA '92	16/4
66	Gerak, John	G	6-3	285	1-6-70	2	Penn State	D3 '93	4/0
78	Hinton, Chris	T	6-4	305	7-31-61	12	Northwestern	FA '94	16/16
61	Lindsay, Everett	G	6-4	290	9-18-70	2	Mississippi	D5 '93	12/12
64	McDaniel, Randall	G	6-3	275	12-19-64	7	Arizona State	D1 '88	16/16
68	Morris, Mike	C	6-5	284	2-22-61	8	NE Missouri St.	FA '91	16/0
60	Schreiber, Adam	C	6-4	288	2-20-62	11	Texas	Plan B '90	16/16
73	Steussie, Todd	T	6-5	298	12-1-70	R	California	D1b '94	

Defensive linemen

No.	Name	Pos.	Ht.	Wt.	Born	Exp.	College	How Acq.	G/S
92	Barker, Roy	DT	6-4	280	2-14-69	3	North Carolina	D4 '92	16/16
77	Culpepper, Brad	DT	6-1	260	5-8-68	3	Florida	D10 '92	15/0
99	Harris, James	DE	6-4	270	5-13-68	2	Temple	FA '93	6/0
90	Harris, Robert	DE	6-4	270	6-13-69	3	Southern	D2 '92	16/0
93	Randle, John	DT	6-1	275	12-12-67	5	Texas A&I	FA '90	16/16
95	Smith, Fernando	DE	6-6	270	8-2-71	R	Jackson State	D2b '94	10/2
97	Thomas, Henry	DT	6-2	277	1-12-65	8	Louisiana State	D3 '87	13/13
98	Tuaolo, Esera	DT	6-2	274	7-11-68	4	Oregon State	FA '92	10/3
65	Wells, Mike	DT	6-3	287	1-6-71	R	Iowa	D4 '94	

Linebackers

No.	Name	Pos.	Ht.	Wt.	Born	Exp.	College	How Acq.	G/S
50	Abrams, Bobby	LB	6-3	230	7-1-67	5	Michigan	FA '93	4/0
56	Bercich, Pete	LB	6-1	248	12-23-71	R	Notre Dame	D7 '94	
55	Del Rio, Jack	LB	6-4	243	4-4-63	10	Southern California	Plan B '92	16/16
54	Garnett, Dave	LB	6-2	219	12-6-70	2	Stanford	FA '93	16/0
51	Jenkins, Carlos	LB	6-3	217	7-12-68	4	Michigan State	D3 '91	16/16
91	Manusky, Greg	LB	6-1	237	8-12-66	7	Colgate	Plan B '91	16/0
58	McDaniel, Ed	LB	5-11	230	2-23-69	3	Clemson	D5 '92	7/1
59	Sheppard, Ashley	LB	6-3	243	1-21-69	2	Clemson	D4 '93	10/0

Defensive backs

No.	Name	Pos.	Ht.	Wt.	Born	Exp.	College	How Acq.	G/S
25	Glenn, Vencie	S	6-0	201	10-26-64	9	Indiana State	Plan B '92	16/16
23	Hammonds, Shelly	CB	5-10	187	2-13-71	R	Penn State	D5 '94	
32	Jones, Shawn	S	6-1	203	6-16-70	2	Georgia Tech	FA '93	1/0
39	Lee, Carl	CB	5-11	182	4-6-61	12	Marshall	D7 '83	16/16
37	McGriggs, Lamar	S	6-3	210	5-9-68	4	Western Illinois	FA '93	9/4
26	McMillian, Audray	CB	6-0	190	8-13-62	9	Houston	Plan B '89	16/16
27	Parker, Anthony	CB	5-10	179	2-11-66	5	Arizona State	Plan B '92	14/0
28	Pool, David	CB	5-9	182	11-3-67	5	Carson-Newman	FA '94	0/0
38	Scott, Todd	S	5-10	207	1-23-68	4	SW Louisiana	D6 '91	13/12
20	Washington, DeWayne	DB	5-11	192	12-17-72	R	North Carolina State	D1a '94	

Specialists

No.	Name	Pos.	Ht.	Wt.	Born	Exp.	College	How Acq.	G/S
4	Barker, Bryan	P	6-1	187	6-28-64	5	Santa Clara	FA '94	16/0
19	Jones, Richard	P	6-3	198	3-25-65	1	Arizona State	FA '94	0/0
7	Reveiz, Fuad	K	5-11	223	2-24-63	10	Tennessee	FA '90	16/0

Warren Moon No. 1/QB

Full name: Harold Warren Moon
HT: 6-3 **WT:** 212
Born: 11-18-56, Los Angeles, CA
High school: Hamilton (Los Angeles)
College: Washington
After a slow start, Moon led the Oilers to 11 straight wins en route to his sixth straight Pro Bowl berth.

			PASSING											RUSHING		
YEAR	TEAM	G	ATT	CPL	CPL%	YDS	AVG	TDS	TD%	INT	INT%	RTG	ATT	YDS	AVG
1986	Houston	15	488	256	52.5	3489	7.1	13	2.7	26	5.3	62.3	42	157	3.7
1987	Houston	12	368	184	50.0	2806	7.6	21	5.7	18	4.9	74.2	34	112	3.3
1988	Houston	11	294	160	54.4	2327	7.9	17	5.8	8	2.7	88.4	33	88	2.7
1989	Houston	16	464	280	60.3	3631	7.8	23	5.0	14	3.0	88.9	70	268	3.8
1990	Houston	15	584	362	62.0	4689	8.0	33	5.7	13	2.2	96.8	55	215	3.9
1991	Houston	16	655	404	61.7	4690	7.2	23	3.5	21	3.2	81.7	33	68	2.1
1992	Houston	11	346	224	64.7	2521	7.3	18	5.2	12	3.5	89.3	27	147	5.4
1993	Houston	15	520	303	58.3	3485	6.7	21	4.0	21	4.0	75.2	48	145	3.0
	10 YR TOTALS	141	4546	2632	57.9	33685	7.4	196	4.3	166	3.7		439	1541	3.5
1993	RANK NFL QB		3	4	32	1	3	29	4	21	2	25	34	5	9	26
1994	PROJECTIONS	16	555	310	55.9	3507	6.3	20	3.6	25	4.5		55	137	2.5

Scottie Graham No. 31/RB

Full name: James Otis Graham
HT: 5-9 **WT:** 215
Born: 3-28-69, Long Beach, NY
High school: Long Beach (NY)
College: Ohio State
Graham spent the season's first 6 weeks on the practice squad, but still led Minnesota in rushing.

			RECEIVING				RUSHING				PUNT RETURN			
YEAR	TEAM	G	REC	YDS	AVG	TD	ATT	YDS	AVG	TD	RET	YDS	AVG	TD
1991	Pittsburgh	13	2	21	10.5	0	---	---	---	---	8	46	5.8	0
1992	Pittsburgh	14	49	711	14.5	1	---	---	---	---	---	---	---	---
1993	Pittsburgh	15	38	579	15.2	0	---	---	---	---	---	---	---	---
	3 YR TOTALS	42	89	1311	14.7	1	0	0.0	0.0	0	8	46	5.8	0
1993	RANK NFL WR		51	46	37	95	42	42	42		30	30	29	
1994	PROJECTIONS	16	42	668	15.9	0	0	0	NA	0	0	0	NA	0

Robert Smith   No. 20/RB

HT: 6-0 **WT:** 195
Born: 3-4-72, Euclid, OH
High school: Euclid (OH)
College: Ohio State
Smith averaged 4.9 yards per carry, which led the team, and caught 24 passes, tops among Viking RBs.

		RUSHING				RECEIVING				KICK RETURNS			
YEAR	TEAM	G	ATT	YDS	AVG	TD	REC	YDS	AVG	TD	RET	YDS	AVG	TD
1993	Minnesota	10	82	399	4.9	2	24	111	4.6	0	3	41	13.7	0
1 YR TOTALS		10	82	399	4.9	2	24	111	4.6	0	3	41	13.7	0
1993 RANK NFL RB			47	43	18	46	40	59	104	40	36	42	48	

Cris Carter   No. 80/WR

HT: 6-3 **WT:** 198
Born: 11-25-65, Middletown, OH
High school: Middletown (OH)
College: Ohio State
Carter set a team record for receptions by a wide receiver with 86, and became only the third Viking ever to have 70+ catches twice in his career (1991, 1993).

		RECEIVING				RUSHING				PUNT RETURN		
YEAR	TEAM	G	REC	YDS	AVG	TD	ATT	YDS	AVG	TD	RET	YDS	AVG
1987	Philadelphia	9	5	84	16.8	2	---	---	---	---	---	---	---
1988	Philadelphia	16	39	761	19.5	6	1	1	1.0	0	---	---	---
1989	Philadelphia	16	45	605	13.4	11	2	16	8.0	0	---	---	---
1990	Minnesota	16	27	413	15.3	3	2	6	3.0	0	---	---	---
1991	Minnesota	16	72	962	13.4	5	---	---	---	---	---	---	---
1992	Minnesota	12	53	681	12.8	6	5	15	3.0	0	---	---	---
1993	Minnesota	16	86	1071	12.5	9	---	---	---	---	---	---	---
7 YR TOTALS		101	327	4577	14.0	42	10	38	3.8	0	0	0	NA
1993 RANK NFL WR			4	7	92	5	42	42	42		30	30	29
1994 PROJECTIONS		16	99	1209	12.2	10	0	0	NA	0	0	0	NA

Qadry Ismail   No. 82/WR

Full name: Qadry Rahmadan Ismail
HT: 6-0   **WT:** 192
Born: 11-8-70, Newark, NJ
High school: E.L. Myers (Wilkes Barre, PA)
College: Syracuse
Ismail's 47 yard kickoff return December 12 vs. Dallas was the longest by a Viking in '93. Overall, he averaged 21.5 yards per return.

YEAR	TEAM	G	RECEIVING REC	YDS	AVG	TD	RUSHING ATT	YDS	AVG	TD	PUNT RETURN RET	YDS	AVG
1993	Minnesota	15	19	212	11.2	1	3	14	4.7	0	---	---	---
1 YR TOTALS		15	19	212	11.2	1	3	14	4.7	0	0	0	NA
1993 RANK NFL WR			80	84	113	72	12	19	20		30	30	29

Adrian Cooper   No. 87/TE

HT: 6-4   **WT:** 260
Born: 3-20-69, Denver, CO
High school: South (Denver)
College: North Carolina State
Cooper backed up star TE Eric Green in Pittsburgh, but should start in Minnesota, and will be a valuable blocker.

YEAR	TEAM	G	RUSHING ATT	AVG	AVG	RANK AV RUSH	PASS YDS	RANK PASS YDS	SACKS	YDS. LOST
1991	New Orleans	15	483	1709	3.5	22	3419	12	19	160
1992	New Orleans	16	454	1628	3.6	24	3297	16	15	119
1993	New Orleans	16	414	1766	4.3	6	3183	21	40	242
4 YR TOTALS		49								

Randall McDaniel   No. 64/G

Full name: Randall Cornell McDaniel
HT: 6-3   **WT:** 275
Born: 12-19-64, Phoenix, AZ
High school: Agua Fria Union (Avondale, AZ)
College: Arizona State
One of the NFL's top guards, McDaniel made the Pro Bowl for the fifth time in 6 seasons and was named AP first-team All-Pro.

YEAR	TEAM	G	RUSHING ATT	YDS	AVG	RANK AV RUSH	PASS YDS	RANK PASS YDS	SACKS	YDS. LOST
1991	Minnesota	16	464	2201	4.7	2	3016	24	28	133
1992	Minnesota	16	497	2030	4.1	14	3162	17	40	293
1993	Minnesota	16	447	1624	3.6	17	3381	17	35	181
	6 YR TOTALS	94								

Henry Thomas   No. 97/NT

Full name: Henry Lee Thomas Jr.
HT: 6-2   **WT:** 271
Born: 1-12-65, Houston, TX
High school: Eisenhower (Houston)
College: Louisiana State
Thomas' 12 solo tackles vs. San Diego November 7 tied for the team high in '93. He's started 101 of his 102 NFL games.

YEAR	TEAM	G	INT	YDS	AVG	TD	SACKS	FUM REC	TD
1987	Minnesota	12	1	0	0.0	0	2.5	1	0
1988	Minnesota	15	1	7	7.0	0	6.0	1	1
1989	Minnesota	14	---	---	---	---	9.0	3	1
1990	Minnesota	16	---	---	---	---	8.5	1	0
1991	Minnesota	16	---	---	---	---	8.0	1	0
1992	Minnesota	16	---	---	---	---	6.0	---	---
1993	Minnesota	13	---	---	---	---	9.0	---	---
	8 YR TOTALS	102	2	7	3.5	0	49.0	7	2
1993	RANK NFL DL		16	NA	NA	NA	19	71	NA
1994	PROJECTIONS	12	0	0	0	0	10	0	0

Carlos Jenkins   No. 51/LB

Full name: Carlos Edward Jenkins
HT: 6-3   **WT:** 217
Born: 7-12-68, Palm Beach, FL
High school: Santaluces CC (Lantana, FL)
College: Michigan State
Jenkins was third on the Vikings with 88 tackles. He gives the Vikings much-needed speed at OLB.

YEAR	TEAM	G	INT	YDS	AVG	TD	SACKS	FUM REC	TD
1991	Minnesota	3	—	—	—	—	—	—	—
1992	Minnesota	16	1	19	19.0	1	4.0	1	0
1993	Minnesota	16	2	7	3.5	0	2.5	1	0
	3 YR TOTALS	35	3	26	8.7	1	6.5	2	0
1993	RANK NFL LB		4	27	33	5	34	24	8
1994	PROJECTIONS	16	3	3	1.0	0	2	1	0

Vencie Glenn   No. 25/S

Full name: Vencie Leonard Glenn
HT: 6-0   **WT:** 201
Born: 10-26-64, Grambling, LA
High school: Kennedy (Silver Spring, MD)
College: Indiana State
Glenn notched a team-high 5 INTs. His father was an assistant under Grambling legend Eddie Robinson.

YEAR	TEAM	G	INT	YDS	AVG	TD	SACKS	FUM REC	TD
1986	New England	4	---	---	---	---	---	---	---
1986	San Diego	12	2	31	15.5	0	---	2	0
1987	San Diego	12	4	166	41.5	1	0.5	1	0
1988	San Diego	16	1	0	0.0	0	1.0	2	0
1989	San Diego	16	4	52	13.0	0	1.0	1	1
1990	San Diego	14	1	0	0.0	0	---	---	---
1991	New Orleans	16	4	35	8.8	0	---	1	0
1992	Minnesota	16	5	65	13.0	0	---	---	---
1993	Minnesota	16	5	49	9.8	0	---	---	---
	8 YR TOTALS	122	26	398	15.3	1	2.5	7	1
1993	RANK NFL DB		14	42	80	27	49	94	NA
1994	PROJECTIONS	16	6	51	8.5	0	0	0	0

Fuad Reveiz   No. 7/K

HT: 5-11 **WT:** 223
Born: 2-24-63, Bogota, Colombia
High school: Sunset (Miami, FL)
College: Tennessee
Reveiz has become one of the top 3 scorers among Viking kickers. He's done the color for 4 Super Bowl telecasts on Univision, the Colombian Spanish-language network.

YEAR	TEAM	G	XP	XPA	XP Pct.	FG	FGA	FG Pct.	PTS
1985	Miami	16	50	52	96.2	22	27	81.5	116
1986	Miami	16	52	55	94.5	14	22	63.6	94
1987	Miami	11	28	30	93.3	9	11	81.8	55
1988	Miami	11	31	32	96.9	8	12	66.7	55
1990	Miami	13	26	27	96.3	13	19	68.4	65
1991	SD (4)-Minn (9)	16	34	35	97.1	17	24	70.8	85
1992	Minnesota	16	45	45	100.0	19	25	76.0	102
1993	Minnesota	16	27	28	96.4	26	35	74.3	105
	8 YR.TOTALS	115	293	304	96.4	128	175	73.1	677
1993	RANK NFL		20	20	21	10	6	19	14

Dennis Green   Head Coach

Born: 2-17-49, Harrisburg, PA
High school: John Harris (Harrisburg, PA)
College: Iowa
Green has a 13–3 record against rivals in the NFC Central. He was named NFL Coach of the Year by UPI after the '92 season. He was also Big Ten coach of the year in '82 at Northwestern.

		REGULAR SEASON					POSTSEASON		
YEAR	TEAM	W	L	T	PCT	FINISH	W	L	FINISH
1992	Minnesota	11	5	0	.688	1st/NFC Central	0	1	lost 1st Rnd to Wash., 24-7
1993	Minnesota	9	7	0	.663	T2nd/NFC Central	0	1	lost wild card game to NY Giants 17-10
	2 YR TOTALS	20	12	0	.625		0	2	

Gino Torretta   No. 13/QB

HT: 6-2   **WT:** 215
Born: 8-10-70,
High school: Pinole Valley (CA)
College: Miami (FL)
Torretta, a former Heisman Trophy winner, will battle Andre Ware to back up Warren Moon in '94.

YEAR	TEAM	G	ATT	CPL	CPL%	YDS	AVG	TDS	TD%	INT	INT%	RTG	ATT	YDS	AVG
					PASSING									RUSHING	
1993	Minnesota	0	---	---	---	---	---	---	---	---	---	---	---	---	---
	1 YR TOTALS	0	0	0	NA	0	NA	0	NA	0	NA		0	0	NA

Jake Reed   No. 86/WR

HT: 6-3   **WT:** 212
Born: 9-28-67, Covington, GA
High school: Newton County (Covington, GA)
College: Grambling
Reed should see more passes with the departure of Anthony Carter.

YEAR	TEAM	G	REC	YDS	AVG	TD	ATT	YDS	AVG	TD	RET	YDS	AVG
			RECEIVING				RUSHING				PUNT RETURN		
1991	Minnesota	1	---	---	---	---	---	---	---	---	---	---	---
1992	Minnesota	16	6	142	23.7	0	---	---	---	---	---	---	---
1993	Minnesota	10	5	65	13.0	0	---	---	---	---	---	---	---
	3 YR TOTALS	27	11	207	18.8	0	0	0	NA	0	0	0	NA
1993	RANK NFL WR		116	114	82	95	42	42	42		30	30	29
1994	PROJECTIONS	10	7	69	9.9	0	0	0	NA	0	0	0	NA

Derek Tennell   No. 46/TE

Full name: Derek Wayne Tennell
HT: 6-2   **WT:** 251
Born: 2-12-64, Los Angeles, CA
High school: West Covina (CA)
College: UCLA
Tennell got a Super Bowl ring with Dallas in '92.

YEAR	TEAM	G	REC	YDS	AVG	TD
			RECEIVING			
1991	Detroit	15	4	43	10.8	0
1992	Minnesota	3	2	12	6.0	0
1993	Minnesota	16	15	122	8.1	0
	6 YR TOTALS	75	40	371	9.3	5
1993	RANK NFL TE		34	37	50	46
1994	PROJECTIONS	16	19	158	8.3	0

Chris Hinton   No. 78/T

Full name: Christopher Jerrod Hinton
HT: 6-4 **WT:** 300
Born: 7-01-01, Chicago, IL
High school: Wendell Phillips (Chicago)
College: Northwestern
Hinton started every game for the Falcons in '93.

YEAR	TEAM	G	RUSHING ATT	YDS	AVG	RANK AV RUSH	PASS YDS	RANK PASS YDS	SACKS	YDS. LOST
1991	Atlanta	16	410	1664	4.1	11	3634	7	31	185
1992	Atlanta	16	322	1270	3.9	16	3894	4	40	259
1993	Atlanta	16	395	1590	4.0	10	3787	6	40	267
11 YR TOTALS		157								

Roy Barker   No. 92/DT

HT: 6-4 **WT:** 280
Born: 2-14-69, New York, NY
High school: Central Islip (NY)
College: North Carolina
Starting every game for Minnesota, Barker had 47 tackles and 6 sacks, fourth highest on the team.

YEAR	TEAM	G	NO	YARDS	LONG	AVG	BLK	IN20
1990	Kansas City	13	64	2479	56	38.7	0	16
1991	Kansas City	16	57	2303	57	40.4	0	11
1992	Kansas City	15	75	3245	65	43.3	1	16
1993	Kansas City	16	76	3240	59	42.6	1	19
4 YR TOTALS		60	272	11267	65	41.4	2	62
1993 RANK NFL Ps			12	11	22	17		15
1994 PROJECTIONS	16		79	3364	54	42.6	1	22

John Randle   No. 93/DE

HT: 6-1 **WT:** 275
Born: 12-12-67, Hearne, TX
High school: Hearne (TX)
College: Trinity Valley CC (TX) and Texas A&I
Randle made the NFC Pro Bowl team for the first time and was also named AP first-team All-Pro.

YEAR	TEAM	G	INT	YDS	AVG	TD	SACKS	FUM REC	TD
1990	Minnesota	16	---	---	---	---	1.0	---	---
1991	Minnesota	16	---	---	---	---	9.5	---	---
1992	Minnesota	16	---	---	---	---	11.5	1	---
1993	Minnesota	16	---	---	---	---	12.5	---	---
4 YR TOTALS		64	0	0	NA	0	34.5	1	0
1993 RANK NFL DL			16	NA	NA	NA	5	71	NA
1994 PROJECTIONS	16	0	0	0	0	15	0	0

Jack Del Rio   No. 55/LB

Full name: Jack Del Rio Jr.
HT: 6-4   **WT:** 243
Born: 4-4-63, Castro Valley, CA
High school: Hayward (CA)
College: Southern California
Del Rio led the Vikings with 169 tackles in '93.

YEAR	TEAM	G	INT	YDS	AVG	TD	SACKS	FUM REC	TD
1991	Dallas	16	---	---	---	---	---	1	0
1992	Minnesota	16	2	92	46.0	1	2.0	2	0
1993	Minnesota	16	---	---	---	---	---	---	---
9 YR TOTALS		135	5	105	21.0	1	7.5	11	2
1993 RANK NFL LB			47	NA	NA	NA	91	81	NA
1994 PROJECTIONS		16	0	0	0	0	0	0	0

Audray McMillian   No. 26/CB

Full name: Audray Glenn McMillian
HT: 6-0   **WT:** 190
Born: 8-13-62, Carthage, TX
High school: Carthage (TX)
College: Houston
McMillian tied for the NFL lead with 8 INTs in '92.

YEAR	TEAM	G	INT	YDS	AVG	TD	SACKS	FUM REC	TD
1990	Minnesota	15	3	20	6.7	---	---	---	---
1991	Minnesota	16	4	5	1.3	0	---	1	0
1992	Minnesota	16	8	157	19.6	2	---	---	---
1993	Minnesota	16	4	45	11.3	1	---	1	0
8 YR TOTALS		123	19	227	11.9	3	0.0	4	0
1993 RANK NFL DB			21	44	71	2	49	37	14
1994 PROJECTIONS		16	3	17	5.7	1	0	1	0

Bryan Barker   No. 4/P

Full name: Bryan Christopher Barker
HT: 6-1   **WT:** 187
Born: 6-28-64, Jacksonville Beach, FL
High school: Miramonte (Orinda, CA)
College: Santa Clara
Barker replaces Harry Newsome, who was waived.

YEAR	TEAM	G	NO	YARDS	LONG	AVG	BLK	IN20
1990	Kansas City	13	64	2479	56	38.7	0	16
1991	Kansas City	16	57	2303	57	40.4	0	11
1992	Kansas City	15	75	3245	65	43.3	1	16
1993	Kansas City	16	76	3240	59	42.6	1	19
4 YR TOTALS		60	272	11267	65	41.4	2	62
1993 RANK NFL Ps			12	11	22	17		15
1994 PROJECTIONS		16	79	3364	54	42.6	1	22

New Orleans
SAINTS

1994 Scouting Report

Offense

Long plagued with problems passing the ball, New Orleans saw more of the same in 1993. The Saints' 2,941 yards in the air ranked twenty-first in the NFL. The Saints are counting on ex-Ram QB Jim Everett to thrive in new surroundings. Everett had his worst season by far in '93, but so did the man he replaces, Wade Wilson. Everett will throw to quality WRs Eric Martin, All-Pro Michael Haynes, who played for Atlanta in '93, and Quinn Early. The Saints hope Irv Smith will emerge as a premier TE in his second season. The running game is uneven—RB Derek Brown had a strong rookie year, but FB Brad Muster is coming off his worst season since 1988. T Willie Roaf had an impressive rookie campaign.

Defense

Once one of the NFL's best defenses, New Orleans now has trouble stopping the run. The defense allowed only 4,696 total yards in 1993 (seventh in the NFL) but gave up 2,090 rushing yards, twenty-fifth in the NFL. The Saints did have the league's top-rated pass defense, giving up only 2,606 yards through the air. The defense is led by CB Vince Buck, and LBs Vaughan Johnson and James Williams. The Saints will need another strong year from LB Renaldo Turnbull (13 sacks), and must hope DE Wayne Martin rebounds from an off-year in '93. New Orleans also bolstered its run defense in the draft, picking DE Joe Johnson and LB Winfred Tubbs.

Special Teams

Morten Anderson is a consistent, accurate kicker with one of the strongest legs in football, and Tommy Barnhardt ranked fourth in the NFC in punting. Fred McAfee was among the NFC leaders in kickoff returns.

1994 Prospects

A team that counts on Jim Everett to turn its offense around doesn't have a promising outlook. New Orleans does have great wideouts, but who's going to get the ball to them? The running game is mediocre at best, and opponents figure to run the ball at will. They could get off to a fast start, with 5 of their first 7 games at home, but, unless some surprising help arrives from unexpected places, look for the Saints to continue the decline they began in '93.

Team Directory

Owner: Tom Benson

Director of player personnel: Bill Kuharich

Director of media relations: Rusty Kasmiersky

1993 Review

Sep. 5	HOUSTON	W	33-21
Sep. 12	at Atlanta	W	34-31
Sep. 19	DETROIT	W	14-3
Sep. 26	SAN FRANCISCO	W	16-13
Oct. 3	at L.A. Rams	W	37-6
Oct. 10	OPEN DATE		
Oct. 17	at Pittsburgh	L	37-14
Oct. 24	ATLANTA	L	26-15
Oct. 31	at Phoenix	W	20-17
Nov. 7	OPEN DATE		
Nov. 14	GREEN BAY	L	19-17
Nov. 22	at San Francisco	L	42-7
Nov. 28	at Minnesota	W	17-14
Dec. 5	at Cleveland	L	17-13
Dec. 12	L.A. RAMS	L	23-20
Dec. 20	N.Y. GIANTS	L	24-14
Dec. 26	at Philadelphia	L	37-26
Jan. 2	CINCINNATI	W	20-13

1994 Schedule

Sep. 4	KANSAS CITY	1:00
Sep. 11	WASHINGTON	4:00
Sep. 18	at Tampa Bay	1:00
Sep. 25	at San Francisco	4:00
Sep. 2	N.Y. GIANTS	4:00
Oct. 9	at Chicago	1:00
Oct. 16	SAN DIEGO	4:00
Oct. 23	L.A. RAMS	1:00
Oct. 30	OPEN DATE	
Nov. 6	at Minnesota	1:00
Nov. 13	ATLANTA	1:00
Nov. 20	at L.A. Raiders	4:00
Nov. 28	SAN FRANCISCO (Mon.)	9:00
Dec. 4	at L.A. Rams	4:00
Dec. 11	at Atlanta	8:00
Dec. 19	DALLAS (Mon.)	9:00
Dec. 24	at Denver	4:00

1993 finish: 8-8 (4-4 home, 4-4 away), second in NFC West

Team Leaders

PASSING	ATT	COM	COM%	YDS	YPA	TD	TD%	INT	INT%	RTG
Wilson	388	221	57.0	2457	6.33	12	3.1	15	3.9	70.1
Buck	54	32	59.3	448	8.30	4	7.4	3	5.6	87.6
Walsh	38	20	52.6	271	7.13	2	5.3	3	7.9	60.3
TEAM	481	274	57.0	3183	6.62	18	3.7	21	4.4	71.4
OPPONENTS	444	259	58.3	2924	6.59	22	5.0	10	2.3	85.3

RECEIVING	REC	YDS	AVG	TD	RUSHING	ATT	YDS	AVG	TD
Martin	66	950	14.4	3	Brown	180	705	3.9	2
Early	45	670	14.9	6	Wilson	31	230	7.4	0
Hilliard	40	296	7.4	1	Muster	64	214	3.3	3
Muster	23	195	8.5	0	Neal	21	175	8.3	1
Brown	21	170	8.1	1	Hilliard	50	165	3.3	2
TEAM	274	3183	11.6	18	TEAM	414	1766	4.3	10
OPPONENTS	259	2924	11.3	22	OPPONENTS	513	2090	4.1	7

INTERCEPTIONS	INT	YDS	AVG	LG	TD	SACKS	NO
Atkins	3	59	19.7	37	0	Turnbull	13.0
Taylor	2	32	16.0	30	0	Jackson, R.	11.5
Buck	2	28	14.0	28	0	Johnson, V.	5.0
TEAM	10	133	13.3	37	0	TEAM	51.0
OPPONENTS	21	444	21.1	67t	6	OPPONENTS	40.0

KICK RETURNS	NO	YDS	AV	LG	TD	PUNT RETURNS	NO	FC	YDS	AV	LG	TD
Hughes	30	753	25.1	99t	1	Hughes	37	21	503	13.6	83t	2
McAfee	28	580	20.7	55	0	Newman	1	0	14	14.0	14	0
Brown	3	58	19.3	23	0							
TEAM	62	1460	23.5	99t	1	TEAM	38	21	517	13.6	83t	2
OPPONENTS	40	788	19.7	47	0	OPPONENTS	36	18	348	9.7	75t	1

KICKING	XPM	XPA	FGM	FGA	LG	PTS
Andersen	33	33	28	35	56	117
TEAM	33	33	28	35	56	117
OPPONENTS	35	39	24	30	53	107

PUNTING	NO	YDS	LG	AVG	TB	BLK	RET	RYD	IN20	NAV
Barnhardt	77	3356	58	43.6	6	0	36	348	26	37.5
TEAM	77	3356	58	43.6	6	0	36	348	26	37.5
OPPONENTS	80	3384	60	42.3	4	0	38	517	20	34.8

FUMBLES	FUM	OFF.FUM.REC.	REC	TD	DEF.FUM.REC.	REC	TD
Wilson	9	Wilson	4	0	Cook	3	0
McAfee	3	Hilliard	3	0	Jackson	3	0
Buck	2				Spencer	3	0
Hilliard	2						
TEAM	24	TEAM	11	0	TEAM	20	2
OPPONENTS	30	OPPONENTS	9	0	OPPONENTS	13	3

1994 Draft Choices

ROUND	NAME	POS	SCHOOL	OVERALL SELECTION
1	Joe Johnson	DE	Louisville	13
2	Mario Bates	RB	Arizona State	44
3	Winfred Tubbs	LB	Texas	79
4	Doug Nussmeier	QB	Idaho	116
5	Herman Carroll	DE	Mississippi State	142
5	Craig Novitsky	G	UCLA	143
6	Derrell Mitchell	WR	Texas Tech	176
7	Lance Lundberg	T	Nebraska	213

HISTORY

TITLES

1991   NFC West Championship

ALL-TIME TEAM RECORDS

Rushing

Most yards, game:	206	George Rogers	9/4/83
Most yards, season:	1,674	George Rogers	1981
Most yards, career:	4,267	George Rogers	1981-1984

Passing

Most yards, game:	377	Archie Manning	9/4/83
Most yards, season:	3,716	Archie Manning	1980
Most yards, career:	21,734	Archie Manning	1971-1982

Receiving

Most catches, game:	14	Tony Galbreath	9/10/78
Most catches, season:	85	Eric Martin	1988
Most catches, career:	532	Eric Martin	1985-1993

Scoring

Most points, game:	18	Many Times	
		Rueben Mayes	9/23/90
Most points, season:	121	Morten Andersen	1987
Most points, career:	1,202	Morten Andersen	1982-1993

COACHES

NAME	RECORD	YEARS
Tom Fears	13-34-2	1967-70
J.D. Roberts	7-25-3	1970-72
John North	11-23-0	1973-75
Ernie Hefferle	1-7-0	1975
Hank Stram	7-21-0	1976-77
Dick Nolan	15-29-0	1978-80
Dick Stanfel	1-3-0	1980
Bum Phillips	27-42-0	1981-85
Wade Phillips	1-3-0	1985
Jim Mora	77-54-0	1986-93

NEW ORLEANS SAINTS
1994 TRAINING CAMP ROSTER

No.	Quarterbacks		Ht.	Wt.	Born	NFL Exp.	College	How acq.	93 GP/GS
17	Everett, Jim	QB	6-5	212	1-3-63	9	Purdue	T-RAM '94	10/0
13	Nussmeier, Doug	QB	6-3	211	12-11-70	R	Idaho	D4 '94	
18	Wilson, Wade	QB	6-3	206	2-1-59	14	East Texas St.	FA '93	14/14
	Running backs								
28	Bates, Mario	RB	6-1	217	1-16-73	R	Arizona State	D2 '94	
24	Brown, Derek	RB	5-9	186	4-15-71	2	Nebraska	D4a '93	13/12
32	Dunbar, Vaughn	RB	5-10	204	9-4-68	3	Indiana	D1 '92	0/0
**	Hilliard, Dalton	RB	5-8	204	1-21-64	9	Louisiana State	D2 '86	16/0
25	McAfee, Fred	RB	5-10	195	6-20-68	4	Mississippi Coll.	D6 '91	15/4
22	Muster, Brad	FB	6-4	235	4-11-65	7	Stanford	FA '93	13/12
34	Ned, Derrick	FB	6-1	220	1-5-69	2	Grambling State	FA '92	14/3
23	Neal, Lorenzo	FB	5-11	240	12-27-70	2	Fresno State	D4 '93	2/2
	Wide receivers								
80	Dowdell, Marcus	WR	5-10	179	5-22-70	2	Tennessee St.	D10 '92	9/1
89	Early, Quinn	WR	6-0	190	4-13-65	7	Iowa	Plan B '91	16/15
81	Haynes, Michael	WR	6-0	184	12-24-65	7	Northern Arizona	FA '94	16/16
84	Martin, Eric	WR	6-1	207	11-8-61	10	Louisiana State	D7 '85	16/13
11	Mitchell, Derrell	WR	5-9	190	9-16-71	R	Texas Tech	D6 '94	
83	Small, Torrance	WR	6-3	201	9-6-70	3	Alcorn State	D5 '92	11/0
	Tight ends								
82	Smith, Irv	TE	6-3	246	10-13-71	2	Notre Dame	D1a '93	16/8
87	Wainright, Frank	TE	6-3	245	10-10-67	4	Northern Colorado	D8 '91	16/2
85	Walls, Wesley	TE	6-5	250	2-26-66	6	Mississippi	FA '94	16/0
	Offensive linemen								
71	Cooper, Richard	T	6-5	290	11-1-64	5	Tennessee	FA '89	16/16
72	Dombrowski, Jim	G-T	6-5	300	10-19-63	9	Virginia	D1 '86	16/2
**	Hilgenberg, Joel	C-G	6-2	252	7-10-62	11	Iowa	D4 '84	9/9
67	Lundberg, Lance	T	6-4	308	8-15-70	R	Nebraska	D7 '94	
79	Nelson, Royce	G	6-4	315	8-9-70	2	Nicholls State	FA '93	0/0
60	Novitsky, Craig	C-G	6-5	295	5-12-71	R	UCLA	D5b '94	
70	Port, Chris	G	6-5	295	11-2-67	4	Duke	D12 '90	15/15
64	Ricketts, Tom	G-T	6-5	305	11-21-65	5	Pittsburgh	FA '94	5/0
77	Roaf, William	T	6-5	299	4-18-70	2	Louisiana Tech	D1 '93	16/16
62	Uhlenhake, Jeff	C	6-3	284	1-28-66	6	Ohio State	FA '94	5/5
	Defensive linemen								
74	Carroll, Herman	DE	6-4	265	6-20-71	R	Mississippi State	D5a '94	
95	Dixon, Ronnie	NT	6-2	292	5-10-71	2	Cincinnati	D6 '93	2/0
63	Dunbar, Karl	DE	6-4	275	5-18-67	3	Louisiana State	FA '93	13/1
91	Goff, Robert	NT-DE	6-3	270	10-2-65	7	Auburn	T-TB '90	16/9
94	Johnson, Joe	DE	6-4	285	7-11-72	R	Louisville	D1 '94	
93	Martin, Wayne	DE	6-5	275	10-26-65	6	Arkansas	D1 '89	16/16
69	Miller, Les	DE-NT	6-7	285	3-1-65	8	Fort Hays State	FA '89	13/11
73	Warren, Frank	DE	6-4	290	9-14-59	13	Auburn	D3 '81	8/7
	Linebackers								
55	Freeman, Reggie	LB	6-1	233	5-8-70	2	Florida State	D2 '93	10/0
**	Jackson, Rickey	LB	6-2	243	3-20-58	14	Pittsburgh	D2 '81	16/16
53	Johnson, Vaughan	LB	6-3	240	3-24-62	9	North Carolina St.	D1 Sup '84	15/13
**	Mills, Sam	LB	5-9	225	6-3-59	9	Montclair State	FA '86	9/7
99	Smeenge, Joel	LB	6-5	250	4-1-68	5	Western Michigan	D3 '90	16/2
54	Tubbs, Winfred	LB	6-4	250	9-24-70	R	Texas	D3 '94	
97	Turnbull, Renaldo	LB	6-4	255	1-5-66	5	West Virginia	D1 '90	15/14
90	Williams, James	LB	6-0	230	10-10-68	5	Mississippi St.	D6a '90	16/9
**	Winston, DeMond	LB	6-2	239	9-14-68	5	Vanderbilt	D4 '90	16/0
	Defensive backs								
26	Buck, Vince	CB	6-0	198	1-12-68	5	Central State (OH)	D6 '91	16/16
40	Coghill, George	S	6-2	196	3-30-70	2	Wake Forest	FA '93	0/0
**	Cook, Toi	CB	5-11	188	12-3-64	8	Stanford	D8 '87	16/16
20	Henderson, Othello	S	6-0	192	8-23-72	2	UCLA	D7 '93	5/1
33	Hughes, Tyrone	CB	5-9	175	1-14-70	2	Nebraska	D5 '93	16/0
27	Jones, Reginald	CB	6-1	202	1-11-69	4	Memphis State	D5 '91	13/3
43	Legette, Tyrone	CB	5-9	177	2-15-70	3	Nebraska	D3 '92	14/1
46	Lumpkin, Sean	S	6-0	206	1-4-70	3	Minnesota	D4a '92	12/0
**	Maxie, Brett	S	6-2	194	1-13-62	10	Texas Southern	FA '85	1/1
37	Spencer, Jimmy	CB	5-9	180	3-29-69	3	Florida	FA '92	16/3
	Specialists								
7	Andersen, Morten	K	6-2	221	8-19-60	13	Michigan State	D4 '82	16/0
6	Barnhardt, Tommy	P	6-2	207	6-11-63	8	North Carolina	FA '89	16/0

Jim Everett   No. 17/QB

Full name: James Samuel Everett III
HT: 6-5 **WT:** 212
Born: 1-3-63, Emporia, KS
High school: Eldorado (Albuquerque, NM)
College: Purdue

Everett posted a career-worst 59.7 QB rating with just 8 TD passes for the Rams in 1993.

YEAR	TEAM	G	ATT	CPL	CPL%	YDS	AVG	TDS	TD%	INT	INT%	RTG	ATT	YDS	AVG	HO
				PASSING									RUSHING			SACKS
1986	LA Rams	6	147	73	49.7	1018	6.9	8	5.4	8	5.4	67.8	16	46	2.9	N/A
1987	LA Rams	11	302	162	53.6	2064	6.8	10	3.3	13	4.3	68.4	18	83	4.6	N/A
1988	LA Rams	16	517	308	59.6	3964	7.7	31	6.0	18	3.5	89.2	34	104	3.1	N/A
1989	LA Rams	16	518	304	58.7	4310	8.3	29	5.6	17	3.3	90.6	25	31	1.2	N/A
1990	LA Rams	16	554	307	55.4	3989	7.2	23	4.2	17	3.1	79.3	20	31	1.6	N/A
1991	LA Rams	16	490	277	56.5	3438	7.0	11	2.2	20	4.1	68.9	27	44	1.6	30
1992	LA Rams	16	475	281	59.2	3323	7.0	22	4.6	18	3.8	80.2	32	133	4.2	26
1993	LA Rams	10	274	135	49.3	1652	6.0	8	2.9	12	4.4	59.7	19	38	2.0	18
	8 YR TOTALS	107	3277	1847	56.4	23758	7.2	142	4.3	123	3.8		191	510	2.7	74
1993	RANK NFL QB		25	26	63	27	44	24	40	12	21		26	31	37	23
1994	PROJECTIONS	8	204	90	43.9	1079	5.3	4	2.2	10	4.8		16	25	1.6	17

Wade Wilson   No. 18/QB

Full name: Charles Wade Wilson
HT: 6-3 **WT:** 206
Born: 2-1-59, Greenville, TX
High school: Commerce (TX)
College: East Texas State

In 14 starts in '93, Wilson gave up 15 INTs, the most of his career.

YEAR	TEAM	G	ATT	CPL	CPL%	YDS	AVG	TDS	TD%	INT	INT%	RTG	ATT	YDS	AVG
				PASSING									RUSHING		
1986	Minnesota	9	143	80	55.9	1165	8.1	7	4.9	5	3.5	84.4	13	9	0.7
1987	Minnesota	12	264	140	53.0	2106	8.0	14	5.3	13	4.9	76.7	41	263	6.4
1988	Minnesota	14	332	204	61.4	2746	8.3	15	4.5	9	2.7	91.5	36	136	3.8
1989	Minnesota	14	362	194	53.6	2543	7.0	9	2.5	12	3.3	70.5	32	132	4.1
1990	Minnesota	6	146	82	56.2	1155	7.9	9	6.2	8	5.5	79.8	12	79	6.6
1991	Minnesota	5	122	72	59.0	825	6.8	3	2.5	10	8.2	53.5	13	33	2.5
1992	Atlanta	9	163	111	68.1	1368	8.4	13	8.0	4	2.5	110.2	15	62	4.1
1993	New Orleans	14	388	221	57.0	2457	6.3	12	3.1	15	3.9	70.1	31	230	7.4
	12 YR TOTALS	99	2216	1261	56.9	15980	7.2	91	4.1	94	4.2		205	971	4.7
1993	RANK NFL QB		17	18	38	17	36	18	39	9	28		41	14	4	1
1994	PROJECTIONS	16	495	274	55.4	2894	5.8	11	2.2	18	3.6		37	332	9.0

Brad Muster   No. 22/RB

Full name: Brad William Muster
HT: 6-4   **WT:** 235
Born: 4-11-65, Novato, CA
High school: San Marin (CA)
College: Stanford
Hobbled by injuries, Muster had just 214 rushing yards, his worst total since 1988.

YEAR	TEAM	G	RUSHING ATT	YDS	AVG	TD	RECEIVING REC	YDS	AVG	TD	KICK RETURNS RET	YDS	AVG	TD
1988	Chicago	16	44	197	4.5	0	21	236	11.2	1	---	---	---	---
1989	Chicago	16	82	327	4.0	5	32	259	8.1	3	---	---	---	---
1990	Chicago	16	141	664	4.7	6	47	452	9.6	0	---	---	---	---
1991	Chicago	11	90	412	4.6	6	35	287	8.2	1	---	---	---	---
1992	Chicago	16	98	414	4.2	3	34	389	11.4	2	---	---	---	---
1993	New Orleans	13	64	214	3.3	3	23	195	8.5	0	---	---	---	---
	6 YR TOTALS	88	519	2228	4.3	23	192	1818	9.5	7	0	0	NA	0
1993	RANK NFL RB		60	68	94	21	41	38	41	40	65	65	65	
1994	PROJECTIONS	13	50	119	2.4	2	18	131	7.3	0	0	0	NA	0

Derek Brown   No. 24/RB

HT: 5-9   **WT:** 186
Born: 4-15-71, Banning, CA
High school: Anaheim Servite (CA)
College: Nebraska
Rookie Brown's 705 yards rushing led the team and ranked tenth in the NFC.

YEAR	TEAM	G	RUSHING ATT	YDS	AVG	TD	RECEIVING REC	YDS	AVG	TD	KICK RETURNS RET	YDS	AVG	TD
1993	New Orleans	13	180	705	3.9	2	21	170	8.1	1	3	58	19.3	0
	1 YR TOTALS	13	180	705	3.9	2	21	170	8.1	1	3	58	19.3	0
1993	RANK NFL RB		22	21	57	46	43	44	48	13	36	34	19	

Eric Martin   No. 84/WR

HT: 6-1   **WT:** 207
Born: 11-8-61, Van Vleck, TX
High school: Van Vleck (TX)
College: Louisiana State
New Orleans' top all-time receiver, Martin led the Saints with 950 receiving yards, sixth-best in the NFC.

| YEAR | TEAM | G | RECEIVING | | | | RUSHING | | | | PUNT RETURN | | |
			REC	YDS	AVG	TD	ATT	YDS	AVG	TD	RET	YDS	AVG
1986	New Orleans	16	37	675	18.2	5	---	---	---	---	24	227	9.5
1987	New Orleans	15	44	778	17.7	7	---	---	---	---	14	88	6.3
1988	New Orleans	16	85	1083	12.7	7	2	12	6.0	0	---	---	---
1989	New Orleans	16	68	1090	16.0	8	---	---	---	---	---	---	---
1990	New Orleans	16	63	912	14.5	5	---	---	---	---	---	---	---
1991	New Orleans	16	66	803	12.2	4	---	---	---	---	---	---	---
1992	New Orleans	16	68	1041	15.3	5	---	---	---	---	---	---	---
1993	New Orleans	16	66	950	14.4	3	---	---	---	---	---	---	---
	9 YR TOTALS	143	532	7854	14.8	48	4	11	2.8	0	46	368	8.0
1993	RANK NFL WR		14	10	54	41	42	42	42		30	30	29
1994	PROJECTIONS	16	66	940	14.2	2	0	0	NA	0	0	0	NA

Michael Haynes No. 81/WR

Full name: Michael David Haynes
HT: 6-0   **WT:** 184
Born: 11-24-65, New Orleans, LA
High school: Joseph S. Clark (New Orleans)
College: E Arizona (JC) and Northern Arizona
All-Pro Haynes comes from Atlanta, where he posted a career-high 72 catches in 1993.

| YEAR | TEAM | G | RECEIVING | | | | RUSHING | | | | PUNT RETURN | | |
			REC	YDS	AVG	TD	ATT	YDS	AVG	TD	RET	YDS	AVG
1988	Atlanta	15	13	232	17.8	4	---	---	---	---	---	---	---
1989	Atlanta	13	40	681	17.0	4	4	35	8.8	0	---	---	---
1990	Atlanta	13	31	445	14.4	0	---	---	---	---	---	---	---
1991	Atlanta	16	50	1122	22.4	11	---	---	---	---	---	---	---
1992	Atlanta	14	48	808	16.8	10	---	---	---	---	---	---	---
1993	Atlanta	16	72	778	10.8	4	---	---	---	---	---	---	---
	6 YR TOTALS	87	254	4066	16.0	33	4	35	8.8	0	0	0	NA
1993	RANK NFL WR		12	25	120	28	42	42	42		30	30	29
1994	PROJECTIONS	16	83	714	8.6	2	0	0	NA	0	0	0	NA

Irv Smith   No. 82/TE

HT: 6-3   **WT:** 246
Born: 10-13-71, Trenton, NJ
High school: Pemberton Township (NJ)
College: Notre Dame
Smith started 8 games as a rookie, and should see more action in 1994.

| | | | RECEIVING | | | |
YEAR	TEAM	G	REC	YDS	AVG	TD
1993	New Orleans	16	16	180	11.3	2
1 YR TOTALS		16	16	180	11.3	2
1993 RANK NFL TE			31	28	26	15

Wayne Martin   No. 93/DE

Full name: Gerald Wayne Martin
HT: 6-5   **WT:** 275
Born: 10-26-65, Forrest City, AR
High school: Cross Cty. (Cherry Valley, AR)
College: Arkansas
Martin picked up just 5 sacks in 1993, after posting a whopping 15.5 in 1992.

YEAR	TEAM	G	INT	YDS	AVG	TD	SACKS	FUM REC	TD
1989	New Orleans	16	---	---	---	---	2.5	2	0
1990	New Orleans	11	---	---	---	---	4.0	---	---
1991	New Orleans	16	---	---	---	---	3.5	1	0
1992	New Orleans	16	---	---	---	---	15.5	2	0
1993	New Orleans	16	---	---	---	---	5.0	2	0
5 YR TOTALS		75	0	0	NA	0	30.5	7	0
1993 RANK NFL DL			16	NA	NA	NA	51.0	8	5
1994 PROJECTIONS		16	0	0	NA	0	3.0	2	0

Renaldo Turnbull   No. 97/LB

Full name: Renaldo Antonio Turnbull
HT: 6-4   **WT:** 255
Born: 1-5-66, St. Thomas, VI
High school: Charlotte Amalie (VI)
College: West Virginia
After averaging 3 sacks/year for his career, Turnbull exploded for a team-high 13 in 1993.

YEAR	TEAM	G	INT	YDS	AVG	TD	SACKS	FUM REC	TD
1990	New Orleans	16	---	---	---	---	9.0	1	0
1991	New Orleans	16	---	---	---	---	1.0	1	0
1992	New Orleans	14	---	---	---	---	1.5	---	---
1993	New Orleans	15	1	2	2.0	0	13.0	2	0
	4 YR TOTALS	61	1	2	2.0	0	24.5	4	0
1993	RANK NFL LB		17	37	36	5	2	9	8
1994	PROJECTIONS	16	2	3	1.5	0	21	3	0

Vince Buck   No. 26/CB

Full name: Vincent Lamont Buck
HT: 6-0   **WT:** 198
Born: 1-12-68, Owensboro, KY
High school: Owensboro (KY)
College: Central State (OH)
Buck led the Saints with 15 passes defensed and had 61 solo tackles.

YEAR	TEAM	G	INT	YDS	AVG	TD	SACKS	FUM REC	TD
1990	New Orleans	16	2	51	25.5	1	0.0	2	0
1991	New Orleans	13	5	12	2.4	0	---	3	0
1992	New Orleans	10	2	51	25.5	1	0.5	---	---
1993	New Orleans	16	2	28	14.0	0	3.0	2	0
	4 YR TOTALS	55	11	142	12.9	2	3.5	7	0
1993	RANK NFL DB		54	67	53	27	2	10	14
1994	PROJECTIONS	16	1	10	10.0	0	5	2	0

Morten Andersen   No. 7/K

HT: 6-2 **WT:** 221
Born: 8-19-60, Struer, Denmark
High school: Ben Davis (Indianapolis)
College: Michigan State
Andersen had 4 game-winning FGs and has scored 90+ points in each of the last 11 years.

YEAR	TEAM	G	XP	XPA	XP Pct	FG	FGA	FG Pct	PTS
1985	New Orleans	16	27	29	93.1	31	35	88.6	120
1986	New Orleans	16	30	30	100.0	26	30	86.7	108
1987	New Orleans	12	37	37	100.0	28	36	77.8	121
1988	New Orleans	16	23	33	69.7	26	36	72.2	101
1989	New Orleans	16	32	33	97.0	26	36	72.2	110
1990	New Orleans	16	29	29	100.0	21	27	77.8	92
1991	New Orleans	16	38	38	100.0	25	32	78.1	113
1992	New Orleans	16	33	34	97.1	29	34	85.3	120
1993	New Orleans	16	33	33	100.0	28	35	80.0	117
	12 YR TOTALS	140	282	296	96.0	240	301	78.4	1002
1993	RANK NFL		12	12	1	6	6	9	8
1994	PROJECTIONS	16	33	32	100.0	29	36	80.6	120

Jim Mora   Head Coach

Full name: James Ernest Mora
Born: 5-24-35, Los Angeles, CA
High school: University (Los Angeles)
College: Occidental and Southern California
Already the winningest coach in Saints history, Mora should surpass the wins of all other Saints coaches combined (83) in '94.

		REGULAR SEASON					POSTSEASON		
YEAR	TEAM	W	L	T	PCT	FINISH	W	L	FINISH
1986	New Orleans	7	9	0	.438	4th/NFC West			
1987	New Orleans	12	3	0	.800	2nd/NFC West	0	1	lost wild card game to Minn., 44-10
1988	New Orleans	10	6	0	.625	T1st/NFC West			
1989	New Orleans	9	7	0	.563	3rd/NFC West			
1990	New Orleans	8	8	0	.500	2nd/NFC West	0	1	lost 1st Rnd. game to Chicago, 16-6
1991	New Orleans	11	5	0	.688	1st/NFC West	0	1	lost 1st Rnd. game to Atlanta, 27-20
1992	New Orleans	12	4	0	.750	2nd/NFC West	0	1	lost 1st Rnd. game to Phila., 36-20
1993	New Orleans	8	8	0	.500	2nd/NFC West			
	8 YR TOTALS	77	50	0	.606		0	4	

Lorenzo Neal   No. 23/FB

HT: 5-11 **WT:** 240
Born: 12-27-70, Hanford, CA
High school: Lemoore (CA)
College: Fresno State
Rookie Neal started 2 games, then fractured his ankle and was out for the year.

YEAR	TEAM	G	RUSHING ATT	YDS	AVG	TD	RECEIVING REC	YDS	AVG	TD	KICK RETURNS RET	YDS	AVG	TD
1993	New Orleans	2	21	175	8.3	1	---	---	---	---	---	---	---	---
1 YR TOTALS		2	21	175	8.3	1	0	0	NA	0	0	0	NA	0
1993 RANK NFL RB			98	75	3	58	123	122	122	40	65	65	65	

Fred McAfee   No. 25/RB

Full name: Fred Lee McAfee
HT: 5-10 **WT:** 195
Born: 6-20-68, Meridian, MS
High school: Philadelphia (MS)
College: Mississippi College
McAfee ranked ninth in the NFC in kickoff returns.

YEAR	TEAM	G	RUSHING ATT	YDS	AVG	TD	RECEIVING REC	YDS	AVG	TD	KICK RETURNS RET	YDS	AVG	TD
1991	New Orleans	9	109	494	4.5	2	1	8	8.0	0	1	14	14.0	0
1992	New Orleans	14	39	114	2.9	1	1	16	16.0	0	19	393	20.7	0
1993	New Orleans	15	51	160	3.1	1	1	3	3.0	0	28	580	20.7	0
3 YR TOTALS		38	199	768	3.9	4	3	27	9.0	0	48	987	20.6	0
1993 RANK NFL RB			69	78	109	58	111	118	115	40	4	4	13	
1994 PROJECTIONS		16	24	14	0.6	0	1	0	0.0	0	41	852	20.8	0

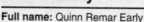

Quinn Early   No. 89/WR

Full name: Quinn Remar Early
HT: 6-0 **WT:** 190
Born: 4-13-65, West Hempstead, NY
High school: Great Neck South (NY)
College: Iowa
Early set personal bests in catches (45) and yards (670).

YEAR	TEAM	G	RECEIVING REC	YDS	AVG	TD	RUSHING ATT	YDS	AVG	TD	PUNT RETURN RET	YDS	AVG
1991	New Orleans	15	32	541	16.9	2	3	13	4.3	0	---	---	---
1992	New Orleans	16	30	566	18.9	5	3	-1	-0.3	0	---	---	---
1993	New Orleans	16	45	670	14.9	6	2	32	16.0	0	---	---	---
6 YR TOTALS		83	162	2516	15.5	18	16	126	7.9	0	0	0	NA
1993 RANK NFL WR			36	39	46	13	22	9	2		30	30	29
1994 PROJECTIONS		16	53	762	14.4	8	2	44	22.0	0	0	0	NA

William Roaf No. 77/T

HT: 6-4 **WT:** 299
Born: 4-18-70, Pine Bluff, AR
High school: Pine Bluff (AR)
College: Louisiana Tech
Rookie Roaf had an effective first campaign, starting all 16 games.

YEAR	TEAM	G	RUSHING ATT	YDS	AVG	RANK AV RUSH	PASS YDS	RANK PASS YDS	SACKS	YDS. LOST
1993	New Orleans	16	414	1766	4.3	6	3183	21	40	242
	1 YR TOTALS	16								

Les Miller No. 69/DE-NT

Full name: Leslie Paul Miller
HT: 6-7 **WT:** 285
Born: 3-1-65, Arkansas City, KS
High school: Arkansas City (KS)
College: Kansas State and Fort Hays State (KS)
Miller's 2.5 sacks were his best since 1987.

YEAR	TEAM	G	INT	YDS	AVG	TD	SACKS	FUM REC	TD
1991	New Orleans	16	—	—	—	—	1.0	—	—
1992	New Orleans	16	—	—	—	—	1.0	1	0
1993	New Orleans	13	—	—	—	—	2.5	—	—
	7 YR TOTALS	95	0	0	NA	0	11.0	6	3
1993	RANK NFL DL		16	NA	NA	NA	94	71	NA
1994	PROJECTIONS	15	0	0	0	0	4	0	0

Vaughan Johnson No. 53/LB

Full name: Vaughan Monroe Johnson
HT: 6-3 **WT:** 235
Born: 3-24-62, Morehead City, NC
High school: West Carteret (Morehead City, NC)
College: North Carolina St.
Johnson led the Saints with 111 tackles.

YEAR	TEAM	G	INT	YDS	AVG	TD	SACKS	FUM REC	TD
1991	New Orleans	13	1	19	19.0	0	---	1	0
1992	New Orleans	16	---	---	---	---	1.0	---	---
1993	New Orleans	15	---	---	---	---	5.0	---	---
	8 YR TOTALS	120	4	68	17.0	0	14.0	5	0
1993	RANK NFL LB		47	NA	NA	NA	22	81	NA
1994	PROJECTIONS	15	0	0	0	0	7	0	0

James Williams   No. 90/LB

Full name: James Edward Williams
HT: 6-0   **WT:** 230
Born: 10-10-68, Natchez, MS
High school: North Natchez (MS)
College: Mississippi State
Williams' 95 tackles were second on the team.

YEAR	TEAM	G	INT	YDS	AVG	TD	SACKS	FUM REC	TD
1991	New Orleans	16	---	---	---	---	1.0	1	0
1992	New Orleans	16	---	---	---	---	---	---	---
1993	New Orleans	16	---	---	---	---	2.0	---	---
	4 YR TOTALS	62	0	0.0	NA	0	3.0	1	0
1993	RANK NFL LB		47	NA	NA	NA	37	81	NA
1994	PROJECTIONS	16	0	0	0	0	3	0	0

Toi Cook   No. 41/CB

Full name: Toi Fitzgerald Cook
HT: 5-11   **WT:** 188
Born: 12-3-64, Chicago, IL
High school: Montclair (CA)
College: Stanford
His 9 passes defensed were second on the team.

YEAR	TEAM	G	INT	YDS	AVG	TD	SACKS	FUM REC	TD
1991	New Orleans	14	3	54.0	18.0	0	---	---	
1992	New Orleans	16	6	90.0	15.0	1	1 0	---	
1993	New Orleans	16	1	0.0	0.0	0	1.0	3	0
	7H TOTALS	101	16	280.0	17.5	1	4.0	3	0
1993	RANK NFL DB		95	124	122	27	13	1	-
1994	PROJECTIONS	16	0	0	0	0	1	5	0

Tommy Barnhardt   No. 6/P

Full name: Tommy Ray Barnhardt
HT: 6-2   **WT:** 207
Born: 6-11-63, Salisbury, NC
High school: South Rowan (China Grove, NC)
College: North Carolina
His 43.6 yards/punt ranked fourth in the NFC.

YEAR	TEAM	G	NO	YARDS	LONG	AVG	BLK	IN20
1990	New Orleans	16	70	2990	NA	42.7	1	NA
1991	New Orleans	16	86	3743	61	43.5	1	20
1992	New Orleans	16	67	2947	62	44.0	0	19
1993	New Orleans	16	77	3356	58	43.6	0	26
	7 YR TOTALS	84	387	16562	62	42.8	2	65
1993	RANK NFL Ps		11	9	25	9		4
1994	PROJECTIONS	16	80	3464	55	43.3	0	31

New York
GIANTS

1994 Scouting Report

Offense

New York had the league's best rushing offense last season, gaining 2,210 yards. Rodney Hampton is one of the best big RBs in football, gaining 1,000+ yards for the third straight year, and David Meggett remains one of the league's premier all-purpose backs. TE Howard Cross is a good blocker, and the Giants have a massive offensive line, led by Ts Doug Riesenberg and Jumbo Elliott and free-agent signee G Lance Smith. The passing game is suspect; with Phil Simms released during the off-season, little-used Kent Graham and Dave Brown will compete for the starting role. The WR corps is thin; often-injured WR Mike Sherrard is coming off of a hip injury, and Coach Dan Reeves is looking to rookie WR Thomas Lewis to replace the departed Mark Jackson.

Defense

The Giants still have one of the best defenses in football. In '93, the team allowed 4,663 total yards, fifth in the NFL—1,547 yards on the ground (fifth in the NFL) and 3,116 yards in the air (tenth in the NFL). Of course, the Giants have lost LB Lawrence Taylor to retirement, but due to age and injury, he had become just an average OLB. The Giants remain strong at LB with veterans Michael Brooks and Carlton Bailey. Keith Hamilton became a strong pass rusher at LDE. The defensive backfield is the team's weak point, and will miss the departed Mark Collins and Myron Guyton.

Special Teams

Brad Daluiso's strong leg usually prevents opponents from returning kickoffs; in 1994, he'll take over all of the kicking duties. P Mike Horan consistently puts punts inside the 20. Meggett is one of the most exciting return men in the league.

1994 Prospects

No matter how you look at it, the loss of Simms will seriously hurt the Giants. Still, they'll win games on defense and ball control, and, with Rodney Hampton and two easy games against both the Eagles and Washington, they should still have the talent to beat out Chicago and Detroit for the NFC's final wild card spot.

Team Directory

President/Co-CEO: Wellington Mara

Chairman/Co-CEO: Preston Robert Tisch

General manager: George Young

Director of player personnel: Tom Boisture

Director of public relations: Pat Hanlon

1993 Review		
Sep. 5	at Chicago	W 26-20
Sep. 12	TAMPA BAY	W 23-7
Sep. 19	L.A. RAMS	W 20-10
Sep. 26	OPEN DATE	
Oct. 3	at Buffalo	L 17-14
Oct. 10	at Washington	W 41-7
Oct. 17	PHILADELPHIA	W 21-10
Oct. 24	OPEN DATE	
Oct. 31	N.Y. JETS	L 10-6
Nov. 7	at Dallas	L 31-9
Nov. 14	WASHINGTON	W 20-6
Nov. 21	at Philadelphia	W 7-3
Nov. 28	PHOENIX	W 19-17
Dec. 5	at Miami	W 19-14
Dec. 12	INDIANAPOLIS	W 20-6
Dec. 20	at New Orleans	W 24-14
Dec. 26	at Phoenix	L 17-6
Jan. 2	DALLAS	L 16-13 (OT)

1994 Schedule		
Sep. 4	PHILADELPHIA	1:00
Sep. 11	at Arizona	8:00
Sep. 18	WASHINGTON	4:00
Sep. 25	OPEN DATE	
Oct. 2	at New Orleans	4:00
Oct. 10	MINNESOTA (Mon.)	9:00
Oct. 16	at L.A. Rams	4:00
Oct. 23	PITTSBURGH	1:00
Oct. 30	DETROIT	1:00
Nov. 7	at Dallas (Mon.)	9:00
Nov. 13	ARIZONA	1:00
Nov. 21	at Houston (Mon.)	9:00
Nov. 27	at Washington	4:00
Dec. 4	at Cleveland	4:00
Dec. 11	CINCINNATI	1:00
Dec. 18	at Philadelphia	4:00
Dec. 24	DALLAS	1:00

1993 finish: 11-5 (6-2 home, 5-3 away), second in NFC East

Team Leaders

PASSING	ATT	COM	COM%	YDS	YPA	TD	TD%	INT	INT%	RTG
Simms	400	247	61.8	3038	7.60	15	3.8	9	2.3	88.3
Graham	22	8	36.4	79	3.59	0	0.0	0	0.0	47.3
Meggett	2	2	100.0	63	31.50	2	100.0	0	0.0	158.3
TEAM	424	257	60.6	3180	7.50	17	4.0	9	2.1	88.4
OPPONENTS	514	298	58.0	3354	6.53	13	2.5	18	3.5	71.4

RECEIVING	REC	YDS	AVG	TD	RUSHING	ATT	YDS	AVG	TD
Jackson, M.	58	708	12.2	4	Hampton	292	1077	3.7	5
Meggett	38	319	8.4	0	Tillman	121	585	4.8	3
Calloway	35	513	14.7	3	Meggett	69	329	4.8	0
McCaffrey	27	335	12.4	2	Bunch	33	128	3.9	2
Sherrard	24	433	18.0	2	Rasheed	9	42	4.7	1
TEAM	257	3180	12.4	17	TEAM	560	2210	3.9	11
OPPONENTS	298	3354	11.3	13	OPPONENTS	395	1547	3.9	7

INTERCEPTIONS	INT	YDS	AVG	LG	TD
Collins	4	77	19.3	50t	1
Jackson, G.	4	32	8.0	29	0
Guyton	2	34	17.0	19	0
TEAM	18	184	10.2	50t	1
OPPONENTS	9	175	19.4	85t	1

SACKS	NO
Hamilton	11.5
Miller	6.5
Taylor	6.0
TEAM	41.0
OPPONENTS	40.0

KICK RETURNS	NO	YDS	AV	LG	TD
Meggett	24	403	16.8	35	0
Calloway	6	89	14.8	21	0
Cross	2	15	7.5	13	0
TEAM	32	507	15.8	35	0
OPPONENTS	29	646	22.3	68	0

PUNT RETURNS	NO	FC	YDS	AV	LG	TD
Meggett	32	20	331	10.3	75t	1
TEAM	32	20	331	10.3	75t	1
OPPONENTS	44	10	247	5.6	28	0

KICKING	XPM	XPA	FGM	FGA	LG	PTS
Treadwell	28	29	25	31	46	103
Daluiso	0	0	1	3	54	3
TEAM	28	30	26	34	54	106
OPPONENTS	22	22	17	23	52	73

PUNTING	NO	YDS	LG	AVG	TB	BLK	RET	RYD	IN20	NAV
Horan	44	1882	60	42.8	1	0	25	107	13	39.9
Landeta	33	1390	57	42.1	3	1	19	140	11	35.0
TEAM	78	3272	60	41.9	4	1	44	247	24	37.8
OPPONENTS	80	3224	54	40.3	6	0	32	331	23	34.7

FUMBLES	FUM
Simms	7
Bunch	2
Hampton	2
Pierce	2
TEAM	19
OPPONENTS	27

OFF.FUM.REC.	REC	TD
Simms	3	0
TEAM	10	0
OPPONENTS	13	0

DEF.FUM.REC.	REC	TD
Jackson, G.	2	0
Miller	2	0
TEAM	10	0
OPPONENTS	8	0

1994 Draft Choices

ROUND	NAME	POS	SCHOOL	OVERALL SELECTION
1	Thomas Lewis	WR	Indiana	24
2	Thomas Randolph	DB	Kansas State	47
2	Jason Sehorn	DB	Southern California	59
3	Gary Downs	RB	North Carolina State	95
4	Chris Maumalanga	DT	Kansas	128
5	Chad Bratzke	DE	Eastern Kentucky	155
6	Jason Winrow	G	Ohio State	186

HISTORY

TITLES

1927	NFL Championship	1956	NFL Championship
1933	NFL Championship	1958	NFL East Championship
1934	NFL Championship	1959	NFL East Championship
1935	NFL East Championship	1961	NFL East Championship
1938	NFL Championship	1962	NFL East Championship
1939	NFL East Championship	1963	NFL East Championship
1941	NFL East Championship	1986	Super Bowl Winner
1944	NFL East Championship	1989	NFC East Championship
1946	NFL East Championship	1990	Super Bowl Winner

ALL-TIME TEAM RECORDS

Rushing

Most yards, game:	218	Gene Roberts	11/12/50
Most yards, season:	1,516	Joe Morris	1986
Most yards, career:	5,296	Joe Morris	1982-1988

Passing

Most yards, game:	513	Phil Simms	10/13/85
Most yards, season:	4,044	Phil Simms	1984
Most yards, career:	33,462	Phil Simms	1979-1993

Receiving

Most catches, game:	12	Mark Bavaro	10/13/85
Most catches, season:	78	Earnest Gray	1983
Most catches, career:	395	Joe Morrison	1959-1972

Scoring

Most points, game:	24	Ron Johnson	10/2/72
		Earnest Gray	9/7/80
Most points, season:	127	Ali Haji-Sheikh	1983
Most points, career:	646	Pete Gogolak	1966-1974

COACHES

NAME	RECORD	YEARS	NAME	RECORD	YEARS
Bob Folwell	8-4-0	1925	Allie Sherman	57-54-4	1961-68
Joe Alexander	8-4-1	1926	Alex Webster	29-40-1	1969-73
Earl Potteiger	15-8-3	1927-28	Bill Arnsparger	7-28-0	1974-76
LeRoy Andrews	24-5-1	1929-30	John McVay	14-23-0	1976-78
Benny Freidman-Steve Owen	2-0-0	1930	Ray Perkins	24-35-0	1979-82
			Bill Parcells	85-82-1	1983-90
Steve Owen	153-108-17	1931-53	Ray Handley	14-18-0	1991-92
Jim Lee Howell	54-29-4	1954-60	Dan Reeves	11-5-0	1993

NEW YORK GIANTS
1994 TRAINING CAMP ROSTER

No.	Quarterbacks		Ht.	Wt.	Born	NFL Exp.	College	How acq.	93 GP/GS
17	Brown, Dave	QB	6-5	215	2-25-70	3	Duke	D1 Sup '92	1/0
10	Graham, Kent	QB	6-6	220	11-1-68	3	Ohio State	D8 '92	9/9
	Running backs								
33	Bunch, Jarrod	FB	6-2	248	8-9-68	4	Michigan	D1 '91	13/8
24	Downs, Gary	RB	6-0	212		R	North Carolina State	D3 '94	
27	Hampton, Rodney	RB	5-11	215	4-3-69	5	Georgia	D1 '90	12/10
30	Meggett, David	RB	5-7	180	4-30-66	6	Towson State	D5 '89	16/1
44	Rasheed, Kenyon	RB	5-10	245	8-23-70	2	Oklahoma	FA '93	5/3
	Wide receivers								
**	Calloway, Chris	WR	5-10	185	3-29-68	5	Michigan	FA '92	16/9
85	Crawford, Keith	WR	6-2	180	11-21-70	2	Howard Payne	FA '93	7/0
18	Lewis, Thomas	WR	6-1	185		R	Indiana	D1 '94	
19	Marshall, Arthur	WR	5-11	174	4-29-69	3	Georgia	T-DEN '94	16/9
81	McCaffrey, Ed	WR	6-5	215	8-17-68	4	Stanford	D3 '91	16/1
88	Sherrard, Mike	WR	6-2	187	6-21-63	9	UCLA	FA '93	6/6
82	Weir, Eric	WR	6-2	175	7-15-70	1	Vanderbilt	FA '93	0/0
	Tight ends								
86	Brown, Derek	TE	6-6	252	3-31-70	3	Notre Dame	D1 '92	16/0
87	Cross, Howard	TE	6-5	245	8-8-67	6	Alabama	D6 '89	16/16
84	Pierce, Aaron	TE	6-5	246	9-6-69	3	Washington	D3 '92	13/6
	Offensive linemen								
78	Bishop, Greg	T	6-5	298	5-2-71	2	Pacific	D4 '93	8/0
62	Davis, Scott	G	6-3	289	1-29-70	2	Iowa	D6 '93	4/0
76	Elliott, John	T	6-7	305	4-1-65	7	Michigan	D2 '88	11/11
69	Johnson, Chuck	G	6-3	305	5-22-69	3	Texas	FA '94	
**	Oates, Bart	C	6-3	265	12-16-58	10	Brigham Young	FA '85	16/15
72	Riesenberg, Doug	T	6-5	275	7-22-65	8	California	D6a '87	16/16
**	Roberts, William	T	6-5	280	8-5-62	10	Ohio State	D1a '84	16/16
61	Smith, Lance	G	6-3	285	11-1-63	10	Louisiana State	FA '94	16/16
59	Williams, Brian	C	6-5	300	6-8-66	6	Minnesota	D1 '89	16/1
60	Winrow, Jason	G	6-4	321		R	Ohio State	D6 '94	
	Defensive linemen								
77	Bratzke, Chad	DE	6-4	262		R	Eastern Kentucky	D5 '94	
71	Dillard, Stacey	DT	6-5	288	9-17-68	3	Oklahoma	D6 '92	16/16
95	Flythe, Mark	DE	6-7	290	5-16-68	2	Penn State	FA '93	2/0
93	Fox, Mike	DE	6-6	275	8-5-67	5	West Virginia	D2 '90	16/16
75	Hamilton, Keith	DE	6-6	280	5-5-71	3	Pittsburgh	D4 '92	16/16
74	Howard, Erik	NT	6-4	268	11-12-64	9	Washington St.	D2a '86	16/0
79	Maumalanga, Chris	DT	6-2	288		R	Kansas	D4 '94	
92	Strahan, Mike	DE	6-4	275	11-21-71	2	Texas Southern	D2 '93	9/0
	Linebackers								
98	Armstead, Jessie	LB	6-1	238	10-26-70	2	Miami (FL)	D8 '93	16/0
54	Bailey, Carlton	LB	6-3	235	12-15-64	7	North Carolina	FA '93	16/16
94	Brooks, Michael	LB	6-1	235	3-2-64	8	Louisiana State	FA '93	13/13
55	Buckley, Marcus	LB	6-3	235	2-3-71	2	Texas A&M	D3 '93	16/2
**	Dent, Burnell	LB	6-2	235	3-16-63	9	Tulane	FA '93	0/0
57	Miller, Corey	LB	6-2	255	10-25-68	4	South Carolina	D6 '91	16/14
51	Powell, Andre	LB	6-1	226	6-5-69	2	Penn State	FA '93	15/1
97	Thigpen, Tommy	LB	6-2	242	3-17-71	2	North Carolina	D5 '93	0/0
90	Widmer, Corey	LB	6-3	276	12-25-68	3	Montana State	D7 '92	11/0
	Defensive backs								
21	Beamon, Willie	S	5-11	170	6-14-70	2	Northern Iowa	FA '93	13/0
37	Campbell, Jesse	S	6-1	215	4-11-69	4	North Carolina St.	FA '92	16/0
**	Jackson, Greg	S	6-1	200	8-20-66	6	Louisiana State	D3a '89	16/16
**	Jenkins, Izel	CB	5-10	190	5-27-64	7	North Carolina St.	FA '93	5/0
23	Randolph, Thomas	CB	5-9	176		R	Kansas State	D2a '94	
39	Raymond, Corey	CB	5-11	180	7-28-69	3	Louisiana State	FA '92	16/8
31	Sehorn, Jason	S	6-2	212		R	Southern California	D2b '94	
22	Sparks, Phillippi	CB	5-11	186	4-15-69	3	Arizona State	D2 '92	5/3
**	Tate, David	S	6-1	200	11-22-64	7	Colorado	FA '93	14/1
	Specialists								
3	Daluiso, Brad	K	6-2	207	12-31-67	4	UCLA	FA '93	15/0
**	Horan, Mike	P	5-11	190	2-1-59	11	Long Beach State	FA '93	8/0

Kent Graham   No. 10/QB

Full name: Kent Douglas Graham
HT: 6-5   **WT:** 220
Born: 11-1-68, Winfield, IL
High school: Wheaton North (IL)
College: Ohio State

Kent Graham was No. 2 on the Giants' depth chart behind Phil Simms in '93. Now he's the front runner for the No. 1 job.

YEAR	TEAM		G	ATT	CPL	CPL%	YDS	AVG	TDS	TD%	INT	INT%	RTG	ATT	YDS	AVG
		PASSING													**RUSHING**	
1992	NY Giants		6	97	42	43.3	470	4.8	1	1.0	4	4.1	44.6	6	36	6.0
1993	NY Giants		9	22	8	36.4	79	3.6	0	0.0	0	0.0	47.3	2	-3	-1.5
	2 YR TOTALS		15	119	50	42.0	549	4.6	1	0.8	4	3.4		8	33	4.1
1993 RANK NFL QB				60	61	70	60	69	59	59	61	61	67	54	59	65
1994 PROJECTIONS			12	0	0	NA	0	NA	0	NA	0	NA		0	0	NA

Rodney Hampton No. 27/RB

HT: 5-11 **WT:** 215
Born: 4-3-69, Houston, TX
High school: Kashmere Senior (Houston)
College: Georgia

In '93 Hampton passed Frank Gifford to move into fourth place on the Giants' all-time rushing list. He also became the first Giant to gain 1,000+ yards in 3 consecutive years.

YEAR	TEAM	G	ATT	YDS	AVG	TD	REC	YDS	AVG	TD	RET	YDS	AVG	TD
				RUSHING				**RECEIVING**				**KICK RETURNS**		
1990	NY Giants	15	109	455	4.2	2	32	274	8.6	2	20	340	17.0	0
1991	NY Giants	14	256	1059	4.1	10	43	283	6.6	0	10	204	20.4	0
1992	NY Giants	16	257	1141	4.4	14	28	215	7.7	0	---	---	---	
1993	NY Giants	12	292	1077	3.7	5	18	210	11.7	0	---	---	---	
	4 YR TOTALS	57	914	3732	4.1	31	121	982	8.1	2	30	544	18.1	0
1993 RANK NFL RB			4	7	73	17	51	36	8	40	65	65	65	
1994 PROJECTIONS		12	360	1258	3.5	3	13	220	16.9	0	0	0	NA	0

David Meggett   No. 30/RB

Full name: David Lee Meggett
HT: 5-7   **WT:** 180
Born: 4-30-66, Charleston, SC
High school: Bonds-Wilson (N. Charleston, SC)
College: Towson State
Meggett is blessed with tremendous upper body strength, one reason why he hasn't missed a game in his five-year career.

YEAR	TEAM	G	RUSHING					RECEIVING					KICK RETURNS			
			ATT	YDS	AVG	TD	REC	YDS	AVG	TD	RET	YDS	AVG	TD
1989	NY Giants	16	28	117	4.2	0	34	531	15.6	4	27	577	21.4	0
1990	NY Giants	16	22	164	7.5	0	39	410	10.5	1	21	492	23.4	0
1991	NY Giants	16	29	153	5.3	1	50	412	8.2	3	25	514	20.6	0
1992	NY Giants	16	32	167	5.2	0	38	229	6.0	2	20	455	22.8	1
1993	NY Giants	16	69	329	4.8	0	38	319	8.4	0	24	403	16.8	0
	5 YR TOTALS	80	180	930	5.2	1	199	1901	9.6	10	117	2441	20.9	1
1993	RANK NFL RB		55	49	23	89	19	21	43	40	6	8	32	
1994	PROJECTIONS	16	90	419	4.7	0	37	309	8.4	0	25	358	14.3	0

Mike Sherrard   No. 88/WR

Full name: Michael Watson Sherrard
HT: 6-2   **WT:** 187
Born: 6-21-63, Oakland, CA
High school: Chino (CA)
College: UCLA
Cursed with injuries throughout his career, Sherrard's '93 campaign was cut short by a dislocated hip in October vs. Philadelphia.

YEAR	TEAM	G	RECEIVING					RUSHING					PUNT RETURN		
			REC	YDS	AVG	TD	ATT	YDS	AVG	TD	RET	YDS	AVG
1986	Dallas	16	41	744	18.1	5	2	11	5.5	0	---	---	---
1990	San Francisco	7	17	264	15.5	2	---	---	---	---	---	---	---
1991	San Francisco	16	24	296	12.3	2	---	---	---	---	---	---	---
1992	San Francisco	16	38	607	16.0	0	---	---	---	---	---	---	---
1993	NY Giants	6	24	433	18.0	2	---	---	---	---	---	---	---
	5 YR TOTALS	61	144	2344	16.3	11	2	11	5.5	0	0	0	NA
1993	RANK NFL WR		73	62	14	55	42	42	42		30	30	29
1994	PROJECTIONS	3	15	276	18.4	1	0	0	NA	0	0	0	NA

Ed McCaffrey   No. 81/WR

HT: 6-5   **WT:** 215
Born: 8-17-68, Allentown
High school: Allentown Central Catholic (PA)
College: Stanford

In '93, McCaffrey had just 1 start (against the Jets after Mike Sherrard's injury), but he should battle rookie Thomas Lewis for the second starting WR slot.

YEAR	TEAM	G	RECEIVING				RUSHING				PUNT RETURN		
			REC	YDS	AVG	TD	ATT	YDS	AVG	TD	RET	YDS	AVG
1991	NY Giants	16	16	146	9.1	0	---	---	---	---	---	---	---
1992	NY Giants	16	49	610	12.4	5	---	---	---	---	---	---	---
1993	NY Giants	16	27	335	12.4	2	---	---	---	---	---	---	---
	3 YR TOTALS	48	92	1091	11.9	7	0	0	NA	0	0	0	NA
1993	RANK NFL WR		68	74	94	55	42	42	42		30	30	-29
1994	PROJECTIONS	16	19	245	12.9	1	0	0	NA	0	0	0	NA

Howard Cross   No. 87/TE

HT: 6-5   **WT:** 245
Born: 8-8-67, Huntsville, AL
High school: New Hope (AL)
College: Alabama

An outstanding blocker, Cross started every Giants' game in '93 at TE, and he hasn't missed a game in 5 NFL seasons.

YEAR	TEAM	G	RECEIVING			
			REC	YDS	AVG	TD
1989	NY Giants	16	6	107	17.8	1
1990	NY Giants	16	8	106	13.3	0
1991	NY Giants	16	20	283	14.2	2
1992	NY Giants	16	27	357	13.2	2
1993	NY Giants	16	21	272	13.0	5
	5 YR TOTALS	80	82	1125	13.7	10
1993	RANK NFL TE		27	19	12	6
1994	PROJECTIONS	16	22	274	12.5	7

Doug Riesenberg No. 72/T

HT: 6-5 **WT:** 275
Born: 7-22-65, Moscow, ID
High school: Moscow (ID)
College: California
Riesenberg has missed just 1 start in the last
5 seasons, and the Giants paid big bucks to
keep him in New York.

YEAR	TEAM	G	RUSHING ATT	YDS	AVG	RANK AV RUSH	PASS YDS	RANK PASS YDS	SACKS	YDS. LOST
1991	NY Giants	15	487	2064	4.2	6	3025	23	36	181
1992	NY Giants	16	458	2077	4.5	4	2628	25	45	283
1993	NY Giants	16	560	2210	3.9	14	3180	22	40	245
	7 YR TOTALS	103								

Keith Hamilton No. 75/DE

Full name: Keith Lamarr Hamilton
HT: 6-6 **WT:** 280
Born: 5-5-71, Paterson, NJ
High school: Heritage (Lynchburg, VA)
College: Pittsburgh
Hamilton took over as a starting DE in '94
and had 2 sacks in a game 3 times last sea-
son.

YEAR	TEAM	G	INT	YDS	AVG	TD	SACKS	FUM REC	TD
1992	NY Giants	16	---	---	---	---	3.5	1	---
1993	NY Giants	16	---	---	---	---	11.5	1	0
	2 YR TOTALS	32	0	0	NA	0	15.0	2	0
1993	RANK NFL DL		16	NA	NA	NA	10	25	5
1994	PROJECTIONS	16	0	0	0	0	20	1	0

Michael Brooks No. 94/LB

HT: 6-1   **WT:** 235
Born: 3-2-64, Ruston, LA
High school: Ruston (LA)
College: Louisiana State
Another of the ex-Broncos brought to New York by Dan Reeves, Brooks led Denver in tackles every year between 1990 and 1992.

YEAR	TEAM	G	INT	YDS	AVG	TD	SACKS	FUM REC	TD
1987	Denver	12	---	---	---	---	1.0	1	0
1988	Denver	16	---	---	---	---	---	---	---
1989	Denver	16	---	---	---	---	1.0	2	0
1990	Denver	16	---	---	---	---	2.0	---	---
1991	Denver	14	2	7	3.5	0	---	---	---
1992	Denver	15	1	17	17.0	0	---	2	1
1993	NY Giants	13	---	---	---	---	1.0	1	0
	7 YR TOTALS	102	3	24	8.0	0	5.0	6	1
1993	RANK NFL LB		47	NA	NA	NA	62	24	8
1994	PROJECTIONS	13	0	9	0	0	1	1	0

Greg Jackson   No. 47/S

Full name: Greg Allen Jackson
HT: 6-1   **WT:** 200
Born: 8-20-66, Hialeah, FL
High school: American (Miami)
College: Louisiana State
Jackson tied for the team lead in INTs with 4, and was second with 9 passes defensed.

YEAR	TEAM	G	INT	YDS	AVG	TD	SACKS	FUM REC	TD
1989	NY Giants	16	---	---	---	---	---	1	0
1990	NY Giants	14	5	8	1.6	0	4.0	---	---
1991	NY Giants	13	1	3	3.0	0	---	---	---
1992	NY Giants	16	4	71	17.8	0	---	1	0
1993	NY Giants	16	4	32	8.0	0	---	2	0
	5 YR TOTALS	75	14	114	8.1	0	4.0	4	0
1993	RANK NFL DB		21	57	90	27	49	10	14
1994	PROJECTIONS	16	4	30	7.5	0	0	3	0

Brad Daluiso   No. 3/K

Full name: Bradley William Daluiso
HT: 6-2   **WT:** 207
Born: 12-31-67, San Diego, CA
High school: Valhalla (El Cajon, CA)
College: UCLA
Daluiso is known for his booming kickoffs; 79 of his 143 career kickoffs have gone for touchbacks.

YEAR	TEAM	G	XP	XPA	XP Pct.	FG	FGA	FG Pct.	PTS
1991	Atl (2)-Buf (14)	16	2	2	100.0	2	3	66.7	8
1992	Denver	16	0	0	—	0	1	0.0	0
1993	NY Giants	15	0	0	—	1	3	33.3	3
	3 YR TOTALS	47	2	2	100.0	3	7	42.9	11
1993	RANK NFL		31	31	31	31	31	31	31
1994	PROJECTIONS	16	0	0	NA	1	4	25.0	3

Dan Reeves   Head Coach

Full name: Daniel Edward Reeves
Born: 1-19-44, Rome, GA
High school: Americus (GA)
College: South Carolina
Reeves now has 121 regular season wins, third among active NFL coaches. He was never Coach of the Year while at Denver.

		REGULAR SEASON					POSTSEASON		
YEAR	TEAM	W	L	T	PCT	FINISH	W	L	FINISH
1981	Denver	10	6	0	.625	T1st/AFC West			
1982	Denver	2	7	0	.222	12th/AFC			
1983	Denver	9	7	0	.563	T2nd/AFC West	0	1	lost wild card game to Seattle, 31-7
1984	Denver	13	3	0	.813	1st/AFC West	0	1	lost 1st Rnd. game to Pitt., 24-17
1985	Denver	11	5	0	.688	2nd/AFC West			
1986	Denver	11	5	0	.688	1st/AFC West	2	1	lost Super Bowl XXI to NY Giants, 39-20
1987	Denver	10	4	1	.700	1st/AFC West	2	1	lost Super Bowl XXII to Wash., 42-10
1988	Denver	8	8	0	.500	2nd/AFC West			
1989	Denver	11	5	0	.688	1st/AFC West	2	1	lost Super Bowl XXIV to SF, 55-10
1990	Denver	5	11	0	.313	5th/AFC West			
1991	Denver	12	4	0	.750	1st/AFC West	1	1	lost AFC Title game to Buffalo, 10-7
1992	Denver	8	8	0	.500	3rd/AFC West			
1993	NY Giants	11	5	0	.688	2nd/NFC East	1	1	lost 2nd Rnd. game to SF, 44-3
	13 YR TOTALS	121	78	1	.608		8	7	

Dave Brown   No. 17/QB

Full name: David Michael Brown
HT: 6-5   **WT:** 215
Born: 2-25-70, Summit, NJ
High school: Westfield (NJ)
College: Duke
Brown was a first-round pick in the '92 supplemental draft.

YEAR	TEAM	G	PASSING ATT	CPL	CPL%	YDS	AVG	TDS	TD%	INT	INT%	RTG	RUSHING ATT	YDS	AVG
1992	NY Giants	2	7	4	57.1	21	3.0	0	0.0	0	0.0	62.2	2	-1	-0.5
1993	NY Giants	1	---	---	---	---	---	---	---	---	---	---	3	-4	-1.3
	2 YR TOTALS	3	7	4	57.1	21	3.0	0	0.0	0	0.0		5	-5	NA
1993	RANK NFL QB		NA	NA	NA	0	NA	0	NA	0	NA	NA	52	60	64
1994	PROJECTIONS	0	0	0	NA	0	NA	0	NA	0	NA		0	0	NA

Jarrod Bunch   No. 3/FB

HT: 6-2   **WT:** 248
Born: 8-9-68, Ashtabula, OH
High school: Ashtabula (OH)
College: Michigan
Bunch slumped from 501 rushing yards in '92 to 128 in '93, but could bounce back in '94.

YEAR	TEAM	G	RUSHING ATT	YDS	AVG	TD	RECEIVING REC	YDS	AVG	TD	KICK RETURNS RET	YDS	AVG	TD
1991	NY Giants	16	1	0	0.0	0	2	8	4.0	0	---	---	---	---
1992	NY Giants	16	104	501	4.8	3	11	50	4.5	1	2	27	13.5	0
1993	NY Giants	13	33	128	3.9	2	13	98	7.5	1	---	---	---	---
	3 YR TOTALS	45	138	629	4.6	5	26	156	6.0	2	2	27	13.5	0
1993	RANK NFL RB		89	89	62	46	63	64	63	13	65	65	65	
1994	PROJECTIONS	15	18	24	1.3	3	21	173	8.2	2	0	0	NA	0

Arthur Marshall   No. 19/WR

Full name: Arthur James Marshall Jr.
HT: 5-11   **WT:** 174
Born: 4-29-69, Ft. Gordon, GA
High school: Hephzibah (GA)
College: Georgia
Marshall could see action as the third wideout.

YEAR	TEAM	G	RECEIVING REC	YDS	AVG	TD	RUSHING ATT	YDS	AVG	TD	PUNT RETURN RET	YDS	AVG
1992	Denver	16	26	493	19.0	1	11	56	5.1	0	33	349	10.6
1993	Denver	16	28	360	12.9	2	---	---	---	---	---	---	---
	2 YR TOTALS	32	54	853	15.8	3	11	56	5.1	0	33	349	10.6
1993	RANK NFL WR		66	69	86	55	42	42	42		30	30	29
1994	PROJECTIONS	16	30	227	7.6	3	0	0	NA	0	0	0	NA

Aaron Pierce   No. 84/TE

HT: 6-5   **WT:** 246
Born: 9-6-69, Seattle, WA
High school: Franklin (Seattle)
College: Washington
Primarily a blocker, Pierce had 12 catches in his first full NFL season.

		RECEIVING			
YEAR	TEAM	G	REC	YDS	AVG	TD
1992 NY Giants	1		---	---	---
1993 NY Giants	13	12	212	17.7	0
2 YR TOTALS	14	12	212	17.7	0
1993 RANK NFL TE		39	26	1	46
1994 PROJECTIONS	16	30	522	17.4	0

John Elliott   No. 76/T

HT: 6-7   **WT:** 305
Born: 4-1-65, Lake Ronkonkoma, NY
High school: Sachem (Lake Ronkonkoma, NY)
College: Michigan
Elliott's string of 45 straight starts ended against Philadelphia November 21 due to back spasms.

		RUSHING			**RANK**	**PASS**	**RANK**		**YDS.**
YEAR TEAM	G	ATT	AVG	AVG AV RUSH	YDS	PASS YDS	SACKS	LOST
1991 NY Giants	16	487	2064	4.2	6	3025	23	36	181
1992 NY Giants	16	458	2077	4.5	4	2628	25	45	283
1993 NY Giants	11	560	2077	3.9	14	3180	22	40	245
6 YR TOTALS	80								

Carlton Bailey   No. 54/LB

Full name: Carlton Wilson Bailey
HT: 6-3   **WT:** 235
Born: 12-15-64, Baltimore, MD
High school: Woodlawn (Baltimore)
College: North Carolina
Bailey started all 16 games for the Giants in '93.

YEAR	TEAM	G	INT	YDS	AVG	TD	SACKS	FUM REC	TD
1991 Buffalo	16	---	---	---	---		1	0
1992 Buffalo	16	---	---	---	---	1.0	---	---
1993 NY Giants	16	---	---	---	---	1.5	---	---
6 YR TOTALS	86	1	16	16.0	0	4.5	2	0
1993 RANK NFL LB		47	NA	NA	NA	56	81	NA
1994 PROJECTIONS	16	0	0	NA	0	2	0	0

Corey Miller — No. 57/LB

HT: 6-2   **WT:** 255
Born: 10-25-68, Pageland, SC
High school: Central (Pageland, SC)
College: South Carolina
Miller had 6.5 sacks and 61 tackles in '93.

YEAR	TEAM	G	INT	YDS	AVG	TD	SACKS	FUM REC	TD
1991	NY Giants	16	---	---	---	---	2.5	---	---
1992	NY Giants	16	2	10	5.0	0	2.0	---	---
1993	NY Giants	16	2	18	9.0	0	6.5	2	0
	3 YR TOTALS	48	4	28	7.0	0	11.0	2	0
1993	RANK NFL LB		4	18	20	5	11	9	8
1994	PROJECTIONS	16	3	27	9.0	0	10	4	0

Corey Raymond — No. 39/S

HT: 5-11   **WT:** 180
Born: 7-28-69, New Iberia, LA
High school: New Iberia (LA)
College: Louisiana State
Raymond made the team in '92 as a special teams player but finished 1993 as the starting RCB.

YEAR	TEAM	G	INT	YDS	AVG	TD	SACKS	FUM REC	TD
1992	NY Giants	16	---	---	---	---	1.0	---	---
1993	NY Giants	16	2	11	5.5	0	---	---	---
	2 YR TOTALS	32	2	11	5.5	0	1.0	0	0
1993	RANK NFL DB		54	101	101	27	49	94	NA
1994	PROJECTIONS	16	4	22	5.5	0	0	0	0

Mike Horan — No. 2/P

Full name: Michael William Horan
HT: 5-11   **WT:** 190
Born: 2-1-59, Orange, CA
High school: Sunny Hills (Fullerton, CA)
College: Long Beach State
Horan has placed 149 of 557 punts inside the 20.

YEAR	TEAM	G	NO	YARDS	LONG	AVG	BLK	IN20
1990	Denver	15	58	2575	NA	44.4	1	NA
1991	Denver	16	72	3012	71	41.8	1	24
1992	Denver	7	37	1681	62	45.4	1	7
1993	NY Giants	8	44	1882	60	42.8	0	13
	10 YR TOTALS	46	211	9150	71	43.4	3	44
1993	RANK NFL		26	26	20	31	25	25
1994	PROJECTIONS	7	41	1734	60	42.3	0	14

Philadelphia
EAGLES

1994 Scouting Report

Offense
Philadelphia (4,922 total yards and 1,761 rushing yards, both fifteenth in the league) has had trouble running the ball since Wilbert Montgomery retired. Herschel Walker gave the team a boost in his first season as an Eagle, but he slumped last year (746 yards). Randall Cunningham has been seriously injured in 2 of Coach Rich Kotite's 3 seasons at the helm. With Bubby Brister at the helm through most of '93, the Eagles passed for 3,161 yards (sixteenth in the NFL). Philadelphia is not deep at WR. Fred Barnett, the team's leading deep threat, is coming off of an injury, and Calvin Williams is basically a possession receiver.

Defense
Once virtually impossible to run on, the Eagles allowed 2,080 rushing yards last year, twenty-fourth in the NFL. And with the departure of DT Clyde Simmons and LB Seth Joyner, the defensive talent is thin. Adding DE William Fuller and LB Mike Romanowski will help patch up the depleted defense, something oft-injured Keith Millard failed to do. The Eagles play the pass pretty well, ranking eighth in the NFL in '93 with 2,939 yards allowed. CB Eric Allen is a four-time Pro Bowler.

Special Teams
Free-agent K Eddie Murray will replace weak-legged Roger Ruzek. The Eagles will also have to replace P Jeff Feagles, who rejoined Buddy Ryan in Arizona, and main returner Vai Sikahema, who retired. Rookie Mitch Berger will get a shot at punter.

1994 Prospects
The Eagles are very similar to baseball's San Diego Padres. Both teams had a nucleus of star players, and were considered one or two players away from a title. But instead, ownership closed the checkbook and let their stars get away, receiving little or nothing in return. Now the Padres are one of their league's worst teams, and sadly, the same must be said of the Eagles. With an improving Arizona team, and a two-time Super Bowl champ in Dallas, it could be well into the next decade before Philadelphia is a serious contender once again.

Team Directory

Owner: Jeffrey Lurie
Director of player personnel: Joe Woolley
Director of public relations: Ron Howard

1993 Review				1994 Schedule		
Sep. 5	PHOENIX	W 23-17		Sep. 4	at N.Y. Giants	1:00
Sep. 12	at Green Bay	W 20-17		Sep. 12	CHICAGO (Mon.)	9:00
Sep. 19	WASHINGTON	W 34-31		Sep. 18	GREEN BAY	1:00
Sep. 26	OPEN DATE			Sep. 25	OPEN DATE	
Oct. 3	at N.Y. Jets	W 35-30		Oct. 2	at San Francisco	4:00
Oct. 10	CHICAGO	L 17-6		Oct. 9	WASHINGTON	8:00
Oct. 17	at N.Y. Giants	L 21-10		Oct. 16	at Dallas	4:00
Oct. 24	OPEN DATE			Oct. 24	HOUSTON (Mon.)	9:00
Oct. 31	DALLAS	L 23-10		Oct. 30	at Washington	1:00
Nov. 7	at Phoenix	L 16-3		Nov. 6	ARIZONA	4:00
Nov. 14	MIAMI	L 19-14		Nov. 13	CLEVELAND	1:00
Nov. 21	N.Y. GIANTS	L 7-3		Nov. 20	at Arizona	4:00
Nov. 28	at Washington	W 17-14		Nov. 27	at Atlanta	1:00
Dec. 6	at Dallas	L 23-17		Dec. 4	DALLAS	1:00
Dec. 12	BUFFALO	L 10-7		Dec. 11	at Pittsburgh	1:00
Dec. 19	at Indianapolis	W 20-10		Dec. 18	N.Y. GIANTS	4:00
Dec. 26	NEW ORLEANS	W 37-26		Dec. 24	at Cincinnati	4:00
Jan. 3	at San Francisco	W 37-34 OT				

1993 finish: 8-8 (3-5 home, 5-3 away), third in NFC East

Team Leaders

PASSING	ATT	COM	COM%	YDS	YPA	TD	TD%	INT	INT%	RTG
Brister	309	181	58.6	1905	6.17	14	4.5	5	1.6	84.9
O'Brien	137	71	51.8	708	5.17	4	2.9	3	2.2	67.4
Cunningham	110	76	69.1	850	7.73	5	4.5	5	4.5	88.1
TEAM	556	328	59.0	3463	6.23	23	4.1	13	2.3	81.2
OPPONENTS	463	251	54.2	3153	6.81	22	4.8	20	4.3	73.5

RECEIVING	REC	YDS	AVG	TD	RUSHING	ATT	YDS	AVG	TD
Walker	75	610	8.1	3	Walker	174	746	4.3	1
Williams	60	725	12.1	10	Sherman	115	406	3.5	2
Bavaro	43	481	11.2	6	Hebron	84	297	3.5	3
Bailey	41	545	13.3	1	Joseph	39	140	3.6	0
Joseph	29	291	10.0	1	Cunningham	18	110	6.1	1
TEAM	328	3463	10.6	23	TEAM	456	1761	3.9	7
OPPONENTS	251	3153	12.6	22	OPPONENTS	467	2080	4.5	11

INTERCEPTIONS	INT	YDS	AVG	LG	TD	SACKS	NO
Allen	6	201	33.5	94t	4	Harmon	11.5
Miano	4	26	6.5	16	0	Thomas	6.5
Thomas	2	39	19.5	21	0	Simmons	5.0
TEAM	20	324	16.2	94t	4	TEAM	36.0
OPPONENTS	13	107	8.2	41	0	OPPONENTS	42.0

KICK RETURNS	NO	YDS	AV	LG	TD	PUNT RETURNS	NO	FC	YDS	AV	LG	TD
Sikahema	30	579	19.3	35	0	Sikahema	33	20	275	8.3	25	0
Walker	11	184	16.7	30	0	Smith, O.	0	0	9	—	9	0
Sydner	9	158	17.6	36	0							
TEAM	54	987	18.3	36	0	TEAM	33	20	284	8.6	25	0
OPPONENTS	53	1133	21.4	60	0	OPPONENTS	35	19	311	8.9	83t	1

KICKING	XPM	XPA	FGM	FGA	LG	PTS
Ruzek	13	16	8	10	46	37
TEAM	31	35	16	23	48	79
OPPONENTS	34	35	23	34	56	103

PUNTING	NO	YDS	LG	AVG	TB	BLK	RET	RYD	IN20	NAV
Feagles	83	3323	60	40.0	4	0	35	311	31	35.3
TEAM	83	3323	60	40.0	4	0	35	311	31	35.3
OPPONENTS	75	3137	59	41.8	7	0	33	284	28	36.2

FUMBLES	FUM	OFF.FUM.REC.	REC	TD	DEF.FUM.REC.	REC	TD
Hebron	5	Walker	2	0	Evans	3	1
O'Brien	4				Thomas	3	0
Sikahema	4						
TEAM	32	TEAM	10	0	TEAM	15	1
OPPONENTS	33	OPPONENTS	18	0	OPPONENTS	21	1

1994 Draft Choices

ROUND	NAME	POS	SCHOOL	OVERALL SELECTION
1	Bernard Williams	T	Georgia	14
2	Bruce Walker	DT	UCLA	37
2	Charlie Garner	RB	Tennessee	42
3	Joe Panos	G	Wisconsin	77
3	Eric Zomalt	DB	California	103
5	Marvin Goodwin	S	UCLA	144
6	Ryan McCoy	LB	Houston	174
6	Mitch Berger	P	Colorado	193
7	Mark Montgomery	RB	Wisconsin	206

HISTORY

TITLES

1947	NFL East Championship
1948	NFL Championship
1949	NFL Championship
1960	NFL Championship
1980	NFC Championship
1988	NFC East Championship

ALL-TIME TEAM RECORDS

Rushing

Most yards, game:	205	Steve Van Buren	11/27/49
Most yards, season:	1,512	Wilbert Montgomery	1979
Most yards, career:	6,538	Wilbert Montgomery	1977-1984

Passing

Most yards, game:	437	Bobby Thomason	11/18/53
Most yards, season:	3,808	Randall Cunningham	1988
Most yards, career:	26,963	Ron Jaworski	1977-1986

Receiving

Most catches, game:	14	Dan Looney	12/1/40
Most catches, season:	81	Keith Jackson	1988
		Keith Byars	1990
Most catches, career:	589	Harold Carmichael	1971-1983

Scoring

Most points, game:	25	Bobby Walston	10/17/54
Most points, season:	116	Paul McFadden	1984
Most points, career:	881	Bobby Walston	1951-1962

COACHES

NAME	RECORD	YEARS	NAME	RECORD	YEARS
Lud Wray	9-21-1	1933-35	Jim Kuharich	28-41-1	1964-68
Bert Bell	10-44-2	1936-40	Jerry Williams	7-22-2	1969-71
Earle Neale	66-44-5	1941-50	Ed Khayat	8-15-2	1971-72
Bo McMillin	2-0-0	1951	Mike McCormack	16-25-1	1973-75
Wayne Millner	2-8-0	1951	Dick Vermeil	57-51-0	1976-82
Jim Trimble	25-20-3	1952-55	Marion Campbell	17-29-1	1983-85
Hugh Devore	7-16-1	1956-57	Ted Bruney	1-0-0	1985
Laurence Shaw	20-16-1	1958-60	Buddy Ryan	43-28-1	1986-90
Nick Skorich	15-24-3	1961-63	Rich Kotite	30-20-0	1991-93

PHILADELPHIA EAGLES
1994 TRAINING CAMP ROSTER

No.	Quarterbacks		Ht.	Wt.	Born	NFL Exp.	College	How acq.	93 GP/GS
6	Brister, Bubby	QB	6-3	207	8-15-62	9	NE Louisiana	FA '93	10/8
12	Cunningham, Randall	QB	6-4	205	3-27-63	10	Nevada-Las Vegas	D2 '85	4/4
8	Jones, Preston	QB	6-3	223	7-3-70	1	Georgia	FA '93	0/0
	Running backs								
36	Garner, Charlie	RB	5-9	187		R	Tennessee	D2b '94	
45	Hebron, Vaughn	RB	5-8	196	10-7-70	2	Virginia Tech	FA '93	16/4
32	Joseph, James	RB	6-2	222	10-28-67	4	Auburn	D7 '91	16/5
25	Montgomery, Mark	FB	5-11	220		R	Wisconsin	D7 '94	
23	Sherman, Heath	RB	6-0	205	3-27-67	6	Texas A&I	D6 '89	15/7
34	Walker, Herschel	RB	6-1	225	3-3-62	9	Georgia	FA '92	16/16
	Wide receivers								
82	Bailey, Victor	WR	6-2	196	7-30-70	2	Missouri	D2 '93	16/10
86	Barnett, Fred	WR	6-0	199	6-17-66	5	Arkansas State	D3 '90	4/4
85	Sydner, Jeff	WR	5-6	170	11-11-69	3	Hawaii	D6 '92	4/0
89	Williams, Calvin	WR	5-11	190	3-3-67	5	Purdue	D5 '90	16/14
**	Young, Michael	WR	6-1	183	2-21-62	9	UCLA	FA '93	10/0
	Tight ends								
84	Bavaro, Mark	TE	6-4	245	4-28-63	9	Notre Dame	FA '93	16/16
87	Johnson, Maurice	TE	6-2	243	1-9-67	4	Temple	FA '91	16/2
	Offensive linemen								
72	Alexander, David	C	6-3	275	7-28-64	8	Tulsa	D5 '87	16/16
78	Davis, Antone	T	6-4	325	2-28-67	4	Tennessee	D1 '91	16/16
**	Floyd, Eric	G	6-5	310	10-28-65	5	Auburn	Plan B '92	3/3
73	Holmes, Lester	G	6-3	301	9-27-69	2	Jackson St.	D1 '93	12/6
66	Hudson, John	G-C	6-2	275	1-29-68	5	Auburn	D11 '90	16/0
**	McHale, Tom	G	6-4	290	4-13-63	8	Cornell	FA '93	8/4
63	Panos, Joe	G	6-2	296		R	Wisconsin	D3a '94	
75	Selby, Rob	G-T	6-3	286	10-11-67	4	Auburn	D3 '91	2/0
76	Thompson, Broderick	T	6-5	295	8-14-60	9	Kansas	T-SD '93	10/10
74	Williams, Bernard	T	6-8	317		R	Georgia	D1 '94	
	Defensive linemen								
71	Chalenski, Mike	DL	6-5	258	1-28-70	2	UCLA	FA '93	15/0
95	Flores, Mike	DE	6-3	256	12-1-66	4	Louisville	D11 '91	16/11
93	Fuller, William	DE	6-3	274	3-6-62	9	North Carolina	FA '94	16/16
69	Grossman, Burt	DE	6-4	275	4-10-67	6	Pittsburgh	T-SD '93	10/10
91	Harmon, Andy	DE	6-4	265	4-6-69	4	Kent State	D6 '91	16/15
97	Harris, Tim	DE	6-6	258	9-10-64	9	Memphis State	FA '93	4/3
98	Jeter, Tommy	DT	6-5	282	9-20-69	3	Texas	D3 '92	6/0
90	Perry, William	DT	6-2	335	12-16-62	10	Clemson	W-CHI '93	8/8
94	Renfro, Leonard	DT	6-2	291	6-29-70	2	Colorado	D1a '93	14/2
92	Walker, Bruce	DT	6-4	326		R	UCLA	D2a '94	
	Linebackers								
**	Cooper, Louis	LB	6-1	245	8-5-63	9	Western Carolina	FA '93	11/0
56	Evans, Byron	LB	6-2	235	2-23-64	8	Arizona	D4 '87	11/10
54	Hager, Britt	LB	6-1	225	2-20-66	6	Texas	D3b '89	16/7
	Jones, Jock	LB	6-2	227	3-13-68	5	Virginia Tech	FA '94	7/0
52	McCoy, Ryan	LB	6-2	237		R	Houston	D6a '94	
58	Oden, Derrick	LB	5-11	230	9-29-70	2	Alabama	D6 '93	12/0
53	Romanowski, Bill	LB	6-4	231	4-2-66	7	Boston College	T-SF '94	16/16
55	Rose, Ken	LB	6-1	215	6-9-62	8	Nevada-Las Vegas	FA '90	5/0
51	Thomas, William	LB	6-2	218	8-13-68	4	Texas A&M	D4 '91	16/16
	Defensive backs								
21	Allen, Eric	CB	5-10	180	11-22-65	7	Arizona State	D2 '88	16/16
24	Booker, Corey	CB	5-9	182	11-1-70	2	Auburn	D5 '91	10/0
37	Frazier, Derrick	CB	5-10	178	4-29-70	1	Texas A&M	D3 '93	0/0
**	Frizzell, William	S	6-3	205	9-8-62	11	N. Carolina Cent.	FA '92	16/2
22	Goodwin, Marvin	FS	6-0	199		R	UCLA	D5 '94	
**	Hopkins, Wes	FS	6-1	215	9-26-61	12	Southern Methodist	D2a '83	15/8
29	McMillian, Mark	CB	5-7	162	4-29-70	3	Alabama	D10 '92	16/12
**	Miano, Rich	S	6-1	200	9-3-62	10	Hawaii	FA '91	16/14
42	Reid, Mike	S	6-1	218	11-24-70	2	North Carolina St.	D3a '94	9/0
30	Smith, Otis	CB	5-11	184	10-22-65	5	Missouri	FA '90	15/0
27	Zomalt, Eric	DB	5-11	197		R	California	D3b '94	
	Specialists								
17	Berger, Mitch	P	6-2	231		R	Colorado	D6b '94	
3	Murray, Eddie	K	5-11	195	8-29-56	16	Tulane	FA '94	14/0

Bubby Brister   No. 6/QB

Full name: Walter Andrew Brister III
HT: 6-3   **WT:** 207
Born: 8-15-62, Alexandria, LA
High school: Neville (Monroe, LA)
College: Northeast Louisiana

Brister finished the year as the fourth highest rated passer in the NFC. Philadelphia was 4-4 in his 8 starts.

YEAR	TEAM	G	ATT	CPL	CPL%	YDS	AVG	TDS	TD%	INT	INT%	RTG	ATT	YDS	AVG
			PASSING										RUSHING		
1986	Pittsburgh	2	60	21	35.0	291	13.9	0	0.0	2	9.5	37.6	6	10	1.7
1987	Pittsburgh	2	12	4	33.3	20	5.0	0	0.0	3	^^^^^	2.8	---	---	N/A
1988	Pittsburgh	13	370	175	47.3	2634	15.1	11	6.3	14	8.0	65.3	45	209	4.6
1989	Pittsburgh	14	342	187	54.7	2365	12.6	9	4.8	10	5.3	73.1	27	25	0.9
1990	Pittsburgh	16	387	223	57.6	2725	12.2	20	9.0	14	6.3	81.6	25	64	2.6
1991	Pittsburgh	8	190	103	54.2	1350	13.1	9	8.7	9	8.7	72.9	11	17	1.5
1992	Pittsburgh	6	116	63	54.3	719	11.4	2	3.2	5	7.9	61.0	10	16	1.6
1993	Philadelphia	10	309	181	58.6	1905	10.5	14	7.7	5	2.8	84.9	20	39	2.0
	8 YR TOTALS	71	1786	957	53.6	12009	6.7	65	3.6	62	3.5		144	380	2.6
1993	RANK NFL QB		23	21	31	23	39	13	17	35	55	17	25	29	39
1994	PROJECTIONS	11	392	234	59.7	2353	6.0	19	4.9	3	0.8		24	50	2.1

Randall Cunningham   QB

HT: 6-4   **WT:** 205
Born: 3-27-63, Santa Barbara, CA
High school: Santa Barbara (CA)
College: Nevada-Las Vegas

Cunningham again must return from a serious injury. When he was last hurt, in 1991, he went from 30 TD passes in 1990 (before hurting his knee) to just 19 in 1992.

YEAR	TEAM	G	ATT	CPL	CPL%	YDS	AVG	TDS	TD%	INT	INT%	RTG	ATT	YDS	AVG
			PASSING										RUSHING		
1986	Philadelphia	15	209	111	53.1	1391	6.7	8	3.8	7	3.3	72.9	66	540	8.2
1987	Philadelphia	12	406	223	54.9	2786	6.9	23	5.7	12	3.0	83.0	76	505	6.6
1988	Philadelphia	16	560	301	53.8	3808	6.8	24	4.3	16	2.9	77.6	93	624	6.7
1989	Philadelphia	16	532	290	54.5	3400	6.4	21	3.9	15	2.8	75.5	104	621	6.0
1990	Philadelphia	16	465	271	58.3	3466	7.5	30	6.5	13	2.8	91.6	118	942	8.0
1991	Philadelphia	1	4	1	25.0	19	4.8	0	0.0	0	0.0	46.9	---	---	N/A
1992	Philadelphia	15	384	233	60.7	2775	7.2	19	4.9	11	2.9	87.3	87	549	6.3
1993	Philadelphia	4	110	76	69.1	850	7.7	5	4.5	5	4.5	88.1	2	-2	-1.0
	9 YR TOTALS	97	2641	1464	55.4	18193	6.9	126	4.8	82	3.1		573	3986	7.0
1993	RANK NFL QB		42	39	4	38	12	35	15	35	17	13	54	56	58
1994	PROJECTIONS	16	469	297	63.3	3471	7.4	24	5.1	14	3.0		112	682	6.1

Heath Sherman No. 23/RB

HT: 6-0 **WT:** 205
Born: 3-27-67, Wharton, TX
High school: El Campo (TX)
College: Texas A&I

Sherman was second on the Eagles in rushing attempts (115) and yards (406). He started 7 games, all before November 14.

| YEAR | TEAM | G | RUSHING | | | | RECEIVING | | | | KICK RETURNS | | | |
			ATT	YDS	AVG	TD	REC	YDS	AVG	TD	RET	YDS	AVG	TD
1989	Philadelphia	15	40	177	4.4	2	8	85	10.6	0	13	222	17.1	0
1990	Philadelphia	14	164	685	4.2	1	23	167	7.3	3	---	---	---	---
1991	Philadelphia	16	106	279	2.6	0	14	59	4.2	0	4	61	15.3	0
1992	Philadelphia	16	112	583	5.2	5	18	219	12.2	1	---	---	---	---
1993	Philadelphia	15	115	406	3.5	2	12	78	6.5	0	---	---	---	---
	5 YR TOTALS	76	537	2130	4.0	10	75	608	8.1	4	17	283	16.6	0
1993	RANK NFL RB		41	41	84	46	66	73	86	40	65	65	65	
1994	PROJECTIONS	16	127	401	3.2	2	10	43	4.3	0	0	0	NA	0

Herschel Walker   No. 34/RB

HT: 6-1 **WT:** 225
Born: 3-3-62, Wrightsville, GA
High school: Johnson Cty. (Wrightville, GA)
College: Georgia

Walker's 1,356 total yards from scrimmage ranked fifth in the NFC and seventh in the NFL. His 4.3 yards per carry average was his best since 1987.

| YEAR | TEAM | G | RUSHING | | | | RECEIVING | | | | KICK RETURNS | | | |
			ATT	YDS	AVG	TD	REC	YDS	AVG	TD	RET	YDS	AVG	TD
1986	Dallas	16	151	737	4.9	12	76	837	11.0	2	---	---	---	---
1987	Dallas	12	209	891	4.3	7	60	715	11.9	1	---	---	---	---
1988	Dallas	16	361	1514	4.2	5	53	505	9.5	2	---	---	---	---
1989	Dal (5)-Minn (11)	16	250	915	3.7	7	40	423	10.6	2	13	374	28.8	1
1990	Minnesota	16	184	770	4.2	5	35	315	9.0	4	44	966	22.0	0
1991	Minnesota	15	198	825	4.2	10	33	204	6.2	0	5	83	16.6	0
1992	Philadelphia	16	267	1070	4.0	8	38	278	7.3	2	3	69	23.0	0
1993	Philadelphia	16	174	746	4.3	1	75	610	8.1	3	11	184	16.7	0
	8 YR TOTALS	139	2044	8383	4.1	62	450	4310	9.6	18	76	1676	22.1	1
1993	RANK NFL RB		25	17	37	58	1	4	47	2	15	15	33	
1994	PROJECTIONS	16	141	636	4.5	0	0	0	NA	4	11	148	13.5	0

Calvin Williams No. 89/WR

Full name: Calvin John Williams Jr.
HT: 5-11 **WT:** 190
Born: 3-3-67, Baltimore, MD
High school: Dunbar (Baltimore)
College: Purdue

Williams became the primary WR target after Fred Barnett went down with an injury. Williams was fourth in the NFL in TD catches.

YEAR	TEAM	G	RECEIVING				RUSHING				PUNT RETURN		
			REC	YDS	AVG	TD	ATT	YDS	AVG	TD	RET	YDS	AVG
1990	Philadelphia	16	37	602	16.3	9	2	20	10.0	0	2	-1	-0.5
1991	Philadelphia	12	33	326	9.9	3	---	---	---	---	---	---	---
1992	Philadelphia	16	42	598	14.2	7	---	---	---	---	---	---	---
1993	Philadelphia	16	60	725	12.1	10	---	---	---	---	---	---	---
	4 YR TOTALS	60	172	2251	13.1	29	2	20	10.0	0	2	-1	-0.5
1993	RANK NFL WR		24	33	102	4	42	42	42		30	30	29
1994	PROJECTIONS	16	71	829	11.7	12	0	0	NA	0	0	0	NA

Fred Barnett   No. 86/WR

Full name: Fred Lee Barnett Jr.
HT: 6-0 **WT:** 199
Born: 6-17-66, Shelby, MS
High school: Rosedale (MS)
College: Arkansas State

Barnett is returning from a torn ligament in his right knee. He has been the Eagles' best WR, with 182 catches in 4 seasons.

YEAR	TEAM	G	RECEIVING				RUSHING				PUNT RETURN		
			REC	YDS	AVG	TD	ATT	YDS	AVG	TD	RET	YDS	AVG
1990	Philadelphia	16	36	721	20.0	8	2	13	6.5	0	---	---	---
1991	Philadelphia	15	62	948	15.3	4	1	0	0.0	0	---	---	---
1992	Philadelphia	16	67	1083	16.2	6	1	-15	-15.0	0	---	---	---
1993	Philadelphia	4	17	170	10.0	0	---	---	---	---	---	---	---
	4 YR TOTALS	51	182	2922	16.1	18	4	-2	-0.5	0	0	0	NA
1993	RANK NFL WR		83	92	127	95	42	42	42		30	30	29
1994	PROJECTIONS	16	75	1209	16.1	6	1	0	0.0	0	0	0	NA

Mark Bavaro No. 84/TE

HT: 6-4 **WT:** 245
Born: 4-28-63, Winthrop, MA
High school: Danvers (MA)
College: Notre Dame

Bavaro's 6 TD catches ranked second on the team, and first among NFC TEs. He caught more passes and gained more yards in '93 than in any year since 1988.

YEAR	TEAM	G	RECEIVING REC	YDS	AVG	TD
1985	NY Giants	16	37	511	13.8	4
1986	NY Giants	16	66	1001	15.2	4
1987	NY Giants	12	55	867	15.8	8
1988	NY Giants	16	53	672	12.7	4
1989	NY Giants	7	22	278	12.6	3
1990	NY Giants	15	33	393	11.9	5
1992	Cleveland	16	25	315	12.6	2
1993	Philadelphia	16	43	481	11.2	6
	8 YR TOTALS	114	334	4518	13.5	36
1993	RANK NFL TE		10	12	27	3
1994	PROJECTIONS	16	47	505	10.7	7

William Fuller No. 93/DE

Full name: William Henry Fuller Jr.
HT: 6-3 **WT:** 274
Born: 3-6-62, Norfolk, VA
High school: Indian River (Chesapeake, VA)
College: North Carolina

Fuller is a top-notch pass rusher who started all 16 games for Houston in '93.

YEAR	TEAM	G	INT	YDS	AVG	TD	SACKS	FUM REC	TD
1986	Houston	13	---	---	---	---	1.0	---	---
1987	Houston	12	---	---	---	---	2.0	1	0
1988	Houston	16	1	9	9.0	0	8.5	---	---
1989	Houston	15	---	---	---	---	6.5	---	---
1990	Houston	16	---	---	---	---	8.0	1	0
1991	Houston	16	---	---	---	---	15.0	2	0
1992	Houston	15	---	---	---	---	8.5	1	1
1993	Houston	16	---	---	---	---	10.0	---	---
	8 YR TOTALS	119	1	9	9.0	0	59.5	5	1
1993	RANK NFL DL		16	NA	NA	NA	17	71	NA

Bill Romanowski No. 53/LB

Full name: William Thomas Romanowski
HT: 6-4 **WT:** 231
Born: 4-2-66, Vernon, CT
High school: Rockville (Vernon, CT)
College: Boston College
Obtained from San Francisco on Draft Day '94, Romanowski consistently ranked among his team's leaders.

YEAR	TEAM	G	INT	YDS	AVG	TD	SACKS	FUM REC	TD
1988	San Francisco	16	---	---	---	---	---	1	0
1989	San Francisco	16	1	13	13.0	0	1.0	2	0
1990	San Francisco	16	---	---	---	---	1.0	---	---
1991	San Francisco	16	1	7	7.0	0	1.0	2	0
1992	San Francisco	16	---	---	---	---	1.0	1	0
1993	San Francisco	16	---	---	---	---	3.0	1	0
	6 YR TOTALS	96	2	20	10.0	0	7.0	7	0
1993	RANK NFL LB		47	NA	NA	NA	30	24	8
1994	PROJECTIONS	16	0	0	0	0	4	1	0

Eric Allen No. 21/CB

Full name: Eric Andre Allen
HT: 5-10 **WT:** 180
Born: 11-22-65, San Diego, CA
High school: Point Loma (San Diego)
College: Arizona State
Allen made his fourth Pro Bowl in 6 seasons. His 31 career INTs are second among active NFC players (behind Darrell Green's 34).

YEAR	TEAM	G	INT	YDS	AVG	TD	SACKS	FUM REC	TD
1988	Philadelphia	10	5	76	15.2	0	---	---	---
1989	Philadelphia	15	8	38	4.8	0	---	---	---
1990	Philadelphia	16	3	37	12.3	1	---	1	0
1991	Philadelphia	16	5	20	4.0	0	---	1	0
1992	Philadelphia	16	4	49	12.3	0	---	2	---
1993	Philadelphia	16	6	201	33.5	4	2.0	---	---
	6 YR TOTALS	95	31	421	13.6	5	2.0	4	0
1993	RANK NFL DB		7	1	16	1	4	94	NA
1994	PROJECTIONS	16	7	285	40.7	6	3	0	0

Eddie Murray   No. 3/K

Full name: Edward Peter Murray
HT: 5-11 **WT:** 195
Born: 8-29-56, Halifax, NS
High school: Spectrum (Victoria, BC)
College: Tulane
Murray, a free agent pickup from Dallas, is a former Pro Bowl MVP (1980). He's tenth on the all-time NFL scoring list.

YEAR	TEAM	G	XP	XPA	XP Pct.	FG	FGA	FG Pct.	PTS
1985	Detroit	16	31	33	93.9	26	31	83.9	109
1986	Detroit	16	31	32	96.9	18	25	72.0	85
1987	Detroit	12	21	21	100.0	20	32	62.5	81
1988	Detroit	16	22	23	95.7	20	21	95.2	82
1989	Detroit	16	36	36	100.0	20	21	95.2	96
1990	Detroit	11	34	34	100.0	13	19	68.4	73
1991	Detroit	16	40	40	100.0	19	.28	67.9	97
1992	KC (1)-TB (7)	8	13	13	100.0	5	9	55.6	28
1993	Dallas	14	38	38	100.0	28	33	84.8	122
	14 YR TOTALS	196	432	437	98.9	277	367	75.5	1263
1993	RANK NFL		4	4	1	6	10	4	6
1994	PROJECTIONS	15	45	45	100.0	38	43	88.4	159

Rich Kotite   Head Coach

Full name: Richard Edward Kotite
Born: 10-13-42, Brooklyn, NY
High school: Poly Prep Country (Brooklyn, NY)
College: Wagner (NY)
Kotite has more wins (29) than any other Eagle coach in his first three seasons. But his '93 Eagles lost 8 of their last 12 games.

YEAR	TEAM	REGULAR SEASON					POSTSEASON		
		W	L	T	PCT	FINISH	W	L	FINISH
1991	Philadelphia	10	6	0	.625	3rd/NFC East			
1992	Philadelphia	11	5	0	.688	2nd/NFC East	1	1	lost 2nd Rnd. game to Dallas, 34-10
1993	Philadelphia	8	8	0	.500	3rd/NFC East			
	3 YR TOTALS	29	19	0	.604		1	1	

Vaughn Hebron   No. 45/RB

HT: 5-8   **WT:** 196
Born: 10-7-70, Baltimore, MD
College: Virginia Tech
Rookie free agent Hebron played in all 16 games
for the Eagles, with 4 starts.

| YEAR TEAM | G | RUSHING | | | | RECEIVING | | | | KICK RETURNS | | | |
		ATT	YDS	AVG	TD	REC	YDS	AVG	TD	RET	YDS	AVG	TD
1993 Philadelphia	16	84	297	3.5	3	11	82	7.5	0	3	35	11.7	0
1 YR TOTALS	16	84	297	3.5	3	11	82	7.5	0	3	35	11.7	0
1993 RANK NFL RB		46	50	83	21	67	71	66	40	36	45	56	

James Joseph   No. 32/RB

HT: 6-2   **WT:** 222
Born: 10-28-67, Phenix City, AL
High school: Central (Phenix City, AL)
College: Auburn
Joseph started 5 games for the '93 Eagles, and
led the team with 20 special teams tackles.

| YEAR TEAM | G | RUSHING | | | | RECEIVING | | | | KICK RETURNS | | | |
		ATT	YDS	AVG	TD	REC	YDS	AVG	TD	RET	YDS	AVG	TD
1991 Philadelphia	16	135	440	3.3	3	10	64	6.4	0	---	---	---	---
1992 Philadelphia	16	---	---	---	---	---	---	---	---	---	---	---	---
1993 Philadelphia	16	39	140	3.6	0	29	291	10.0	1	---	---	---	---
3 YR TOTALS	48	174	580	3.3	3	39	355	9.1	1	0	0	NA	0
1993 RANK NFL RB		81	86	78	89	33	25	18	13	65	65	65	
1994 PROJECTIONS	16	35	135	3.9	0	48	493	10.3	2	0	0	NA	0

Victor Bailey   No. 82/WR

HT: 6-2   **WT:** 196
Born: 7-30-70, Fort Worth, TX
High school: Fort Worth (TX)
College: Missouri
Bailey became a starter after Fred Barnett was
hurt. He was second in catches among rookies.

| YEAR TEAM | G | RECEIVING | | | | RUSHING | | | | PUNT RETURN | | | |
		REC	YDS	AVG	TD	ATT	YDS	AVG	TD	RET	YDS	AVG	TD
1993 Philadelphia	16	41	545	13.3	1	---	---	---	---	---	---	---	---
1 YR TOTALS	16	41	545	13.3	1	0	0.0	NA	0	0	0	NA	0
1993 RANK NFL WR		44	50	74	72	42	42	42		30	30	29	

David Alexander   No. 72/C

HT: 6-3   **WT:** 275
Born: 7-28-64, Silver Spring, MD
High school: Broken Arrow (OK)
College: Tulsa
Alexander has now started 92 consecutive games, Philadelphia's longest current streak.

YEAR	TEAM	G	RUSHING ATT	YDS	AVG	RANK AV RUSH	PASS YDS	RANK PASS YDS	SACKS	YDS. LOST
1991	Philadelphia	16	446	1396	3.1	28	3169	20	45	263
1992	Philadelphia	16	516	2388	4.6	2	3054	21	64	462
1993	Philadelphia	16	456	1761	3.9	15	3463	13	42	302
	7 YR TOTALS	108								

Andy Harmon   No. 91/DE

Full name: Andrew Phillip Harmon
HT: 6-4   **WT:** 265
Born: 4-6-69, Centerville, OH
High school: Centerville (OH)
College: Kent
Harmon posted a team-high 11.5 sacks.

YEAR	TEAM	G	INT	YDS	AVG	TD	SACKS	FUM REC	TD
1991	Philadelphia	16	---	---	---	---			---
1992	Philadelphia	16	---	---	---	---	7.0	1	---
1993	Philadelphia	16	---	---	---	---	11.5	2	0
	3 YR TOTALS	48	0	0	NA	0	18.5	3	0
1993	RANK NFL DL		16	NA	NA	NA	10	8	5
1994	PROJECTIONS	16	0	0	0	0	17	3	0

Burt Grossman   No. 69/DE

Full name: Burton Grossman
HT: 6-4   **WT:** 275
Born: 4-10-67, Philadelphia, PA
High school: Archbishop Carroll (Bala Cynwyd, PA)
College: Pittsburgh
Grossman started 10 games for San Diego in '93.

YEAR	TEAM	G	INT	YDS	AVG	TD	SACKS	FUM REC	TD
1989	San Diego	16	---	---	---	---	10.0	---	---
1990	San Diego	15	---	---	---	---	10.0	---	---
1991	San Diego	16	---	---	---	---	5.5	2	0
1992	San Diego	15	---	---	---	---	8.0	---	---
1993	San Diego	10	---	---	---	---	4.5	1	0
	6 YR TOTALS	72	0	0	NA	0	38.0	3	0
1993	RANK NFL DL		16	NA	NA	NA	57	25	5

William Thomas   No. 51/LB

Full name: William Harrison Thomas Jr.
HT: 6-2   **WT:** 218
Born: 8-13-68, Amarillo, TX
High school: Palo Duro (Amarillo, TX)
College: Texas A&M
He set career highs in nearly every category.

YEAR	TEAM	G	INT	YDS	AVG	TD	SACKS	FUM REC	TD
1991	Philadelphia	16	---	---	---	---	2.0	---	---
1992	Philadelphia	16	2	4	2.0	0	1.5	2	0
1993	Philadelphia	16	2	39	19.5	0	6.5	3	0
3 YR TOTALS		48	4	43	10.8	0	10.0	5	0
1993 RANK NFL LB			4	6	12	5	11	4	8
1994 PROJECTIONS		16	3	66	22.0	0	10	4	0

Byron Evans   No. 56/LB

Full name: Byron Nelson Evans
HT: 6-2   **WT:** 235
Born: 2-23-64, Phoenix, AZ
High school: South Mountain (Phoenix)
College: Arizona
Evans was second on the club with 109 tackles.

YEAR	TEAM	G	INT	YDS	AVG	TD	SACKS	FUM REC	TD
1990	Philadelphia	16	1	43	43.0	0	---	---	---
1991	Philadelphia	16	2	46	23.0	0	---	2	0
1992	Philadelphia	16	4	76	19.0	0	---	---	---
1993	Philadelphia	11	1	8	8.0	0	---	3	1
7 YR TOTALS		103	12	208	17.3	0	2.0	11	1
1993 RANK NFL LB			17	24	22	5	91	4	1
1994 PROJECTIONS		9	0	0	3	0	0	3	1

Mark McMillian   No. 29/CB

HT: 5-7   **WT:** 162
Born: 4-29-70, Los Angeles
High school: J. F. Kennedy (Granada Hills, CA)
College: Glendale (CA) and Alabama
McMillian started 12 games at LCB. Teams often go his way to avoid Pro Bowler Eric Allen.

YEAR	TEAM	G	INT	YDS	AVG	TD	SACKS	FUM REC	TD
1992	Philadelphia	16	1	0	0.0	0	---	---	---
1993	Philadelphia	16	2	25	12.5	0	---	1	0
2 YR TOTALS		32	3	25	8.3	0	0.0	1	0
1993 RANK NFL DB			54	73	61	27	49	37	14
1994 PROJECTIONS		16	3	50	16.7	0	0	2	0

San Francisco
49ERS

1994 Scouting Report

Offense

The Niners had the league's best offense last season (6,435 total yards gained, including 2,133 rushing yards, third in the NFL, and 4,302 passing yards, second in the NFL), and figure to do it again this year. San Francisco features one of the league's top QBs, Steve Young, passing to two of the best WRs in Jerry Rice and John Taylor. Young can also throw to Pro Bowl TE Brent Jones when Taylor and Rice are covered. Ricky Watters emerged in '93 as a genuine threat at RB. San Francisco has penciled in draft pick William Floyd to replace Tom Rathman as the blocking back. T Harris Barton and C Jesse Sapolu, both Pro Bowlers, anchor one of the best offensive lines in football.

Defense

The defense fell off in '93, ranking just fifteenth overall with 4,997 total yards, allowing 1,800 rushing yards (sixteenth in the NFL) and 3,197 passing yards (sixteenth in the league). Difficulty stopping the run prompted the 49ers to trade up to draft DT Bryant Young, and free to sign agents Richard Dent, Ken Norton, and Gary Plummer. Dana Stubblefield and Dennis Brown provide serious pressure on opposing QBs, and the defensive backfield features Pro Bowl S Tim McDonald, CB Eric Davis, and CB Merton Hanks. Look for the Niner defense to bounce back in '94, even without departed MLB Bill Romanowski.

Special Teams

Draft pick Doug Brien will be given a chance to win the kicking job in training camp, especially if free agent Mike Cofer (who always had problems from outside 40 yards) isn't resigned. P Klaus Wilmsmeyer is entering his third season. Dexter Carter is a terrific punt returner—his 12.1 yard average was second in the NFC last season.

1994 Prospects

The 49ers should have little difficulty taking the weak NFC West, and they've made smart moves to shore up their defense. San Francisco has lost two straight NFC title games to Dallas; the question is, have the Cowboys slipped enough to let the 49ers catch up with them? Not quite, this year.

Team Directory
Owner: Edward J. DeBartolo, Jr.   President: Carmen Policy

VP of football admin.: John G. McVay   Operations and personnel: Dwight Clark

Director of public relations: Rodney Knox

<table>
<tr><td colspan="3">### 1993 Review</td><td colspan="3">### 1994 Schedule</td></tr>
<tr><td>Sep. 5</td><td>at Pittsburgh</td><td>W 24-13</td><td>Sep. 5</td><td>L.A. RAIDERS (Mon.)</td><td>9:00</td></tr>
<tr><td>Sep. 13</td><td>at Cleveland</td><td>L 23-13</td><td>Sep. 11</td><td>at Kansas City</td><td>1:00</td></tr>
<tr><td>Sep. 19</td><td>ATLANTA</td><td>W 37-30</td><td>Sep. 18</td><td>at L.A. Rams</td><td>4:00</td></tr>
<tr><td>Sep. 26</td><td>at New Orleans</td><td>L 16-13</td><td>Sep. 25</td><td>NEW ORLEANS</td><td>4:00</td></tr>
<tr><td>Oct. 3</td><td>MINNESOTA</td><td>W 38-19</td><td>Oct. 2</td><td>PHILADELPHIA</td><td>4:00</td></tr>
<tr><td>Oct. 10</td><td>OPEN DATE</td><td></td><td>Oct. 9</td><td>at Detroit</td><td>1:00</td></tr>
<tr><td>Oct. 17</td><td>at Dallas</td><td>L 26-17</td><td>Oct. 16</td><td>at Atlanta</td><td>1:00</td></tr>
<tr><td>Oct. 24</td><td>PHOENIX</td><td>W 28-14</td><td>Oct. 23</td><td>TAMPA BAY</td><td>4:00</td></tr>
<tr><td>Oct. 31</td><td>L.A. RAMS</td><td>W 40-17</td><td>Oct. 30</td><td>OPEN DATE</td><td></td></tr>
<tr><td>Nov. 7</td><td>OPEN DATE</td><td></td><td>Nov. 6</td><td>at Washington</td><td>1:00</td></tr>
<tr><td>Nov. 14</td><td>at Tampa Bay</td><td>W 45-21</td><td>Nov. 13</td><td>DALLAS</td><td>4:00</td></tr>
<tr><td>Nov. 22</td><td>NEW ORLEANS</td><td>W 42-7</td><td>Nov. 20</td><td>L.A. RAMS</td><td>8:00</td></tr>
<tr><td>Nov. 28</td><td>at L.A. Rams</td><td>W 35-10</td><td>Nov. 28</td><td>at New Orleans (Mon.)</td><td>9:00</td></tr>
<tr><td>Dec. 5</td><td>CINCINNATI</td><td>W 21-8</td><td>Dec. 4</td><td>ATLANTA</td><td>4:00</td></tr>
<tr><td>Dec. 11</td><td>at Atlanta</td><td>L 27-24</td><td>Dec. 11</td><td>at San Diego</td><td>4:00</td></tr>
<tr><td>Dec. 19</td><td>at Detroit</td><td>W 55-17</td><td>Dec. 17</td><td>DENVER (Sat.)</td><td>4:00</td></tr>
<tr><td>Dec. 25</td><td>HOUSTON</td><td>L 10-7</td><td>Dec. 26</td><td>at Minnesota (Mon.)</td><td>9:00</td></tr>
<tr><td>Jan. 3</td><td>PHILADELPHIA</td><td>L 37-34 OT</td><td></td><td></td><td></td></tr>
</table>

1993 finish: 10-6 (6-2 home, 4-4 away), first in NFC West

Team Leaders

PASSING	ATT	COM	COM%	YDS	YPA	TD	TD%	INT	INT%	RTG
Young	462	314	68.0	4023	8.71	29	6.3	16	3.5	101.5
Bono	61	39	63.9	416	6.82	0	0.0	1	1.6	76.9
Taylor	1	1	100.0	41	41.00	0	0.0	0	0.0	118.8
TEAM	524	.354	67.6	4480	8.55	29	5.5	17	3.2	98.9
OPPONENTS	564	314	55.7	3513	6.23	23	4.1	19	3.4	74.0

RECEIVING	REC	YDS	AVG	TD	RUSHING	ATT	YDS	AVG	TD
Rice	98	1503	15.3	15	Watters	208	950	4.6	10
Jones	68	735	10.8	3	Young	69	407	5.9	2
Taylor	56	940	16.8	5	Logan	58	280	4.8	7
Logan	37	348	9.4	0	Lee	72	230	3.2	1
Watters	31	326	10.5	1	Rathman	19	80	4.2	3
TEAM	354	4480	12.7	29	TEAM	463	2133	4.6	26
OPPONENTS	314	3513	11.2	23	OPPONENTS	404	1800	4.5	6

INTERCEPTIONS	INT	YDS	AVG	LG	TD	SACKS	NO
McGruder	5	89	17.8	37	1	Stubblefield	10.5
Davis	4	45	11.3	41t	1	Harrison	6.0
Hanks	3	104	34.7	67t	1	Brown	5.5
TEAM	19	267	14.1	67t	3	TEAM	44.0
OPPONENTS	17	157	9.2	30	0	OPPONENTS	35.0

KICK RETURNS	NO	YDS	AV	LG	TD	PUNT RETURNS	NO	FC	YDS	AV	LG	TD
Carter	25	494	19.8	60	0	Carter	34	20	411	12.1	72t	1
Lee	10	160	16.0	28	0	Kelm	1	0	0	0.0	0	0
Walker	3	51	17.0	30	0							
TEAM	40	715	17.9	60	0	TEAM	35	20	411	11.7	72t	1
OPPONENTS	61	1196	19.6	50	0	OPPONENTS	15	8	171	11.4	50	0

KICKING	XPM	XPA	FGM	FGA	LG	PTS
Cofer	59	61	16	26	46	107
TEAM	59	61	16	26	46	107
OPPONENTS	30	30	27	30	51	111

PUNTING	NO	YDS	LG	AVG	TB	BLK	RET	RYD	IN20	NAV
Wilmsmeyer	42	1718	61	40.9	5	0	15	171	11	34.5
TEAM	42	1718	61	40.9	5	0	15	171	11	34.5
OPPONENTS	68	2985	57	43.9	5	0	35	411	12	36.4

FUMBLES	FUM	OFF.FUM.REC.	REC	TD	DEF.FUM.REC.	REC	TD
Young	8	Jones	2	0	Eleven Tied With	1	0
Carter	5	McIntyre	2	0			
Watters	5	Young	2	0			
TEAM	32	TEAM	16	1	TEAM	11	1
OPPONENTS	20	OPPONENTS	8	0	OPPONENTS	13	1

1994 Draft Choices

ROUND	NAME	POS	SCHOOL	OVERALL SELECTION
1	Bryant Young	DE	Notre Dame	7
1	William Floyd	RB	Florida State	28
2	Kevin Mitchell	LB	Syracuse	53
2	Tyronne Drakeford	CB	Virginia Tech	62
3	Doug Brien	K	California	85
3	Cory Fleming	WR	Tennessee	87
5	Anthony Peterson	LB	Notre Dame	153
6	Lee Woodall	LB	Westchester (PA)	182

HISTORY

TITLES

1970	NFC West Championship	1987	NFC West Championship
1971	NFC West Championship	1988	Super Bowl Winner
1972	NFC West Championship	1989	Super Bowl Winner
1981	Super Bowl Winner	1990	NFC West Championship
1983	NFC West Championship	1992	NFC West Championship
1984	Super Bowl Winner	1993	NFC West Championship
1986	NFC West Championship		

ALL-TIME TEAM RECORDS

Rushing

Most yards, game:	194	Delvin Williams	10/31/76
Most yards, season:	1,502	Roger Craig	1988
Most yards, career:	7,344	Joe Perry	1950-1960, 1963

Passing

Most yards, game:	476	Joe Montana	10/14/90
Most yards, season:	4,023	Steve Young	1993
Most yards, career:	35,124	Joe Montana	1979-1992

Receiving

Most catches, game:	13	Jerry Rice	10/14/90
Most catches, season:	100	Jerry Rice	1990
Most catches, career:	708	Jerry Rice	1985-1993

Scoring

Most points, game:	30	Jerry Rice	10/14/90
Most points, season:	138	Jerry Rice	1987
Most points, career:	979	Ray Wersching	1977-1987

COACHES

NAME	RECORD	YEARS
Buck Shaw	33-25-2	1950-54
Red Strader	4-8-0	1955
Frankie Albert	19-17-1	1956-58
Red Hickey	27-27-1	1959-63
Jack Christiansen	26-38-3	1963-67
Dick Nolan	56-56-5	1968-75
Monte Clark	8-6-0	1976
Ken Meyer	5-9-0	1977
Pete McCulley	1-8-0	1978
Fred O'Connor	1-6-0	1978
Bill Walsh	102-63-1	1979-88
George Seifert	68-21-0	1989-93

SAN FRANCISCO 49ERS
1994 TRAINING CAMP ROSTER

No.	Quarterbacks		Ht.	Wt.	Born	NFL Exp.	College	How acq.	GP/GS
18	Grbac, Elvis	QB	6-5	232	8-13-70	1	Michigan	D8 '93	0/0
14	Musgrave, Bill	QB	6-2	205	11-11-67	4	Oregon	FA '91	1/0
8	Young, Steve	QB	6-2	205	10-11-61	10	Brigham Young	T-TB '87	16/16
	Running backs								
35	Carter, Dexter	RB	5-9	174	9-15-67	5	Florida State	D1 '90	16/0
40	Floyd, William	FB	6-1	242		R	Florida State	D1b '94	
	Gainer, Derrick	RB	5-11	240	8-15-66	4	Florida A&M	T-DAL '94	11/0
43	Logan, Marc	FB	6-0	212	5-9-65	7	Kentucky	Plan B '92	14/11
**	Rathman, Tom	FB	6-1	232	10-7-62	9	Nebraska	D3 '86	8/4
32	Watters, Ricky	RB	6-1	212	4-7-69	3	Notre Dame	D2 '91	13/13
	Wide receivers								
83	Beach, Sanjay	WR	6-1	194	2-21-66	4	Colorado State	FA '94	9/0
89	Fleming, Cory	WR	6-1	207		R	Tennessee	D3b '94	
80	Rice, Jerry	WR	6-2	200	10-13-62	10	Miss. Valley St.	D1 '85	16/16
88	Singleton, Nate	WR	5-11	190	7-5-68	2	Grambling	FA '93	16/0
82	Taylor, John	WR	6-1	185	3-31-62	9	Delaware State	D3 '86	16/16
	Tight ends								
**	Brandes, John	TE	6-2	249	4-2-64	8	Cameron	FA '93	9/0
84	Jones, Brent	TE	6-4	230	2-12-63	8	Santa Clara	FA '87	16/16
	Offensive linemen								
79	Barton, Harris	T	6-4	286	4-19-64	8	North Carolina	D1a '87	15/15
65	Boatswain, Harry	T	6-4	295	6-26-69	4	New Haven	D5 '91	16/2
71	Bollinger, Brian	G	6-5	285	11-21-68	3	North Carolina	D3 '92	16/0
50	Dalman, Chris	C	6-3	285	3-15-70	2	Stanford	D6 '93	15/0
63	Deese, Derrick	G	6-3	270	5-17-70	3	Southern California	FA '92	0/0
**	Foster, Roy	G	6-4	290	5-24-60	13	Southern California	Plan B '91	0/0
**	McIntyre, Guy	G	6-3	265	2-17-61	11	Georgia	D3 '84	16/16
66	Millen, Alec	T	6-7	285	9-25-70	1	Georgia	FA '93	0/0
61	Sapolu, Jesse	C	6-4	278	3-10-61	12	Hawaii	D11 '83	16/16
64	Tamm, Ralph	G	6-4	280	3-11-66	7	West Chester	FA '92	16/16
74	Wallace, Steve	T	6-5	280	12-27-64	9	Auburn	D4 '86	15/15
	Defensive linemen								
96	Brown, Dennis	DE	6-4	290	11-6-67	5	Washington	D2 '90	16/16
91	Dent, Richard	DE	6-5	265	12-13-60	12	Tennessee	FA '94	16/16
**	Fagan, Kevin	DE	6-3	260	4-25-63	8	Miami (FL)	D4 '86	7/7
58	Kelly, Todd	DE	6-2	259	11-27-70	2	Tennessee	D1b '93	14/5
68	Roberts, Larry	DE	6-3	275	6-2-63	9	Alabama	D2 '86	6/0
95	Smith, Artie	DE	6-4	303	5-15-70	2	Louisiana Tech	D5 '93	16/5
94	Stubblefield, Dana	DE	6-2	302	11-14-70	2	Kansas	D1a '93	16/15
72	Thomas, Mark	DE	6-5	273	5-6-69	3	North Carolina St.	D4a '92	11/1
77	Wilson, Karl	DE	6-5	277	9-10-64	7	Louisiana State	FA '93	5/2
92	Wilson, Troy	DE	6-4	235	11-22-70	2	Pittsburg St. (KS)	D7 '93	10/0
97	Young, Bryant	DE	6-3	276		R	Notre Dame	D1a '94	
	Linebackers								
55	Johnson, John	LB	6-3	230	5-8-68	4	Clemson	D2 '91	15/12
**	Jordan, Darin	LB	6-2	245	12-4-64	5	Northeastern	Plan B '91	14/0
**	Kelm, Larry	LB	6-4	240	11-29-64	8	Texas A&M	FA '93	10/1
54	Mitchell, Kevin	LB	6-1	260		R	Syracuse	D2a '94	
51	Norton, Ken	LB	6-2	241	9-29-66	7	UCLA	FA '94	16/16
53	Peterson, Anthony	LB	6-0	223		R	Notre Dame	D5 '94	
50	Plummer, Gary	LB	6-2	247	1-26-60	9	California	FA '94	16/15
**	Walter, Mike	LB	6-3	238	11-30-60	12	Oregon	FA '84	15/8
	Defensive backs								
25	Davis, Eric	CB	5-11	178	1-26-68	5	Jacksonville St.	D2 '90	16/16
24	Drakeford, Tyronne	CB	5-9	185		R	Virginia Tech	D2b '94	
**	Gash, Thane	S	5-11	198	9-1-65	7	E. Tennessee St.	Plan B '92	0/0
28	Hall, Dana	S	6-2	206	7-8-69	3	Washington	D1 '92	13/7
36	Hanks, Merton	CB	6-2	185	3-12-68	4	Iowa	D5 '91	16/14
45	Hardy, Adrian	CB	5-11	194	8-16-70	2	Northwestern St.	D2 '93	10/0
46	McDonald, Tim	S	6-2	215	1-26-65	8	Southern California	FA '93	16/16
38	Russell, Damien	S	6-1	204	8-20-70	3	Virginia Tech	D6 '92	16/0
41	Woodall, Lee	S	6-0	220		R	Westchester (PA)	D6 '94	
	Specialists								
4	Brien, Doug	K	5-11	177		R	California	D3a '94	
10	Wilmsmeyer, Klaus	P	6-1	210	12-4-67	3	Louisville	FA '92	15/0

Steve Young　　No. 8/QB

Full name: Jon Steven Young
HT: 6-2　**WT:** 205
Born: 10-11-61, Salt Lake City, UT
High school: Greenwich (CT)
College: Brigham Young

With a 101.5 QB rating, Young became the first player ever to win 3 straight passing titles.

| YEAR | TEAM | G | PASSING | | | | | | | | | | RUSHING | | |
			ATT	CPL	CPL%	YDS	AVG	TDS	TD%	INT	INT%	RTG	ATT	YDS	AVG
1985	Tampa Bay	14	363	195	53.7	2282	6.3	8	2.2	13	3.6	65.5	74	425	5.7
1987	San Francisco	8	69	37	53.6	570	8.3	10	14.5	0	0.0	120.8	26	190	7.3
1988	San Francisco	11	101	54	53.5	680	6.7	3	3.0	3	3.0	72.2	27	184	6.8
1989	San Francisco	10	92	64	69.6	1001	10.9	8	8.7	3	3.3	120.8	38	126	3.3
1990	San Francisco	6	62	38	61.3	427	6.9	2	3.2	0	0.0	92.6	15	159	
1991	San Francisco	11	279	180	64.5	2517	9.0	17	6.1	8	2.9	101.8	66	415	6.3
1992	San Francisco	16	402	268	66.7	3465	8.6	25	6.2	7	1.7	107.0	76	537	7.1
1993	San Francisco	16	462	314	68.0	4023	8.7	29	6.3	16	3.5	101.5	69	407	5.9
	9 YR TOTALS	97	1968	1222	62.1	15900	8.1	105	5.3	58	2.9		431	2676	6.2
1993	RANK NFL QB		8	3		5	2	1		5	8	33	5	1	1	5
1994	PROJECTIONS	16	528	363	68.8	4599	8.7	34	6.4	21	4.0		67	361	5.4

Ricky Watters　　No. 32/RB

Full name: Richard James Watters
HT: 6-1　**WT:** 212
Born: 4-7-69, Harrisburg, PA
High school: Bishop McDevitt (Harrisburg)
College: Notre Dame

Watters led the team in rushing, and had a record 5 TDs against New York in the play-offs.

| YEAR | TEAM | G | RUSHING | | | | RECEIVING | | | | KICK RETURNS | | | |
			ATT	YDS	AVG	TD	REC	YDS	AVG	TD	RET	YDS	AVG	TD
1992	San Francisco	14	206	1013	4.9	9	43	405	9.4	2	---	---	---	---
1993	San Francisco	13	208	950	4.6	10	31	326	10.5	1	---	---	---	---
	2 YR TOTALS	27	414	1963	4.7	19	74	731	9.9	3	0	0	NA	0
1993	RANK NFL RB		14	12	33	2	31	19	14	13	65	65	65	
1994	PROJECTIONS	12	207	886	4.3	11	20	255	12.8	0	0	0	NA	0

Marc Logan   No. 43/RB

Full name: Marc Anthony Logan
HT: 6-0 **WT:** 212
Born: 5-9-65, Lexington, KY
High school: Bryan Station (Lexington, KY)
College: Kentucky
With a career-best 7 TDs, replacement starter Logan ranked third on the squad.

YEAR	TEAM	G	RUSHING ATT	YDS	AVG	TD	RECEIVING REC	YDS	AVG	TD	KICK RETURNS RET	YDS	AVG	TD
1987	Miami	3	37	203	5.5	0	3	14	4.7	0	3	31	10.3	0
1988	Miami	9	2	10	5.0	0	2	20	10.0	0	4	80	20.0	0
1989	Miami	10	57	201	3.5	0	5	34	6.8	0	24	613	25.5	1
1990	Miami	16	79	317	4.0	2	7	54	7.7	0	20	367	18.4	0
1991	Miami	16	4	5	1.3	0	---	---	---	---	12	191	15.9	0
1992	San Francisco	16	8	44	5.5	1	2	17	8.5	0	22	478	21.7	0
1993	San Francisco	14	58	280	4.8	7	37	348	9.4	0	---	---	---	---
	7 YR TOTALS	84	245	1060	4.3	11	56	487	8.7	0	85	1760	20.7	1
1993	RANK NFL RB		65	54	22	9	22	17	28	40	65	65	65	
1994	PROJECTIONS	14	75	375	5.0	10	55	519	9.4	0	0	0	NA	0

Jerry Rice   No. 80/WR

Full name: Jerry Lee Rice
HT: 6-2 **WT:** 200
Born: 10-13-62, Starkville, MS
High school: Moor (Crawford, MS)
College: Miss. Valley St.
Rice had his usual Pro Bowl year (1,503 yards), tying an NFL mark with his eighth 1,000+ yard season.

YEAR	TEAM	G	RECEIVING REC	YDS	AVG	TD	RUSHING ATT	YDS	AVG	TD	PUNT RETURN RET	YDS	AVG
1986	San Francisco	16	86	1570	18.3	15	10	72	7.2	1	---	---	---
1987	San Francisco	12	65	1078	16.6	22	8	51	6.4	1	---	---	---
1988	San Francisco	16	64	1306	20.4	9	13	107	8.2	1	---	---	---
1989	San Francisco	16	82	1483	18.1	17	5	33	6.6	0	---	---	---
1990	San Francisco	16	100	1502	15.0	13	2	0	0.0	0	---	---	---
1991	San Francisco	16	80	1206	15.1	14	1	2	2.0	0	---	---	---
1992	San Francisco	16	84	1201	14.3	10	9	58	6.4	1	---	---	---
1993	San Francisco	16	98	1503	15.3	15	3	69	23.0	1	---	---	---
	9 YR TOTALS	140	708	11776	16.6	118	57	418	7.3	6	0	0	NA
1993	RANK NFL WR		2	1	35	1	12	2	1		30	30	29
1994	PROJECTIONS	16	105	1617	15.4	16	2	88	44.0	1	0	0	NA

John Taylor　　No. 82/WR

Full name: John Gregory Taylor
HT: 6-1　**WT:** 185
Born: 3-31-62, Pennsauken, NJ
High school: Pennsauken (NJ)
College: Delaware State

Taylor had 5 TDs and 940 yards. His average (16.8 yards/catch) was better than Jerry Rice's (15.3).

YEAR	TEAM	G	RECEIVING REC	YDS	AVG	TD	RUSHING ATT	YDS	AVG	TD	PUNT RETURN RET	YDS	AVG
1987	San Francisco	12	9	151	16.8	0	---	---	---	---	---	---	---
1988	San Francisco	12	14	325	23.2	2	---	---	---	---	1	9	9.0
1989	San Francisco	15	60	1077	18.0	10	1	6	6.0	0	44	556	12.6
1990	San Francisco	14	49	748	15.3	7	---	---	---	---	36	417	11.6
1991	San Francisco	16	64	1011	15.8	9	---	---	---	---	31	267	8.6
1992	San Francisco	9	25	428	17.1	3	---	---	---	---	---	---	---
1993	San Francisco	16	56	940	16.8	5	2	17	8.5	0	---	---	---
	7 YR TOTALS	94	277	4680	16.9	36	3	23	7.7	0	112	1249	11.2
1993	RANK NFL WR		30	13	22	19	22	16	10		30	30	29
1994	PROJECTIONS	16	57	970	17.0	4	3	25	8.3	0	0	0	NA

Brent Jones　　No. 84/TE

Full name: Brent Michael Jones
HT: 6-4　**WT:** 230
Born: 2-12-63, San Jose, CA
High school: Leland (San Jose, CA)
College: Santa Clara

Another Pro Bowler, Jones led NFC TEs in catches (68) and yards (735).

YEAR	TEAM	G	RECEIVING REC	YDS	AVG	TD
1987	San Francisco	4	2	35	17.5	0
1988	San Francisco	11	8	57	7.1	2
1989	San Francisco	16	40	500	12.5	4
1990	San Francisco	16	56	747	13.3	5
1991	San Francisco	10	27	417	15.4	0
1992	San Francisco	15	45	628	14.0	4
1993	San Francisco	16	68	735	10.8	3
	7 YR TOTALS	88	246	3119	12.7	18
1993	RANK NFL TE		2	3	30	12
1994	PROJECTIONS	16	79	773	9.8	3

Dana Stubblefield No. 94/DE

Full name: Dana William Stubblefield
HT: 6-2 **WT:** 302
Born: 11-14-70, Cleves, OH
High school: Taylor (Cincinnati)
College: Kansas

Stubblefield led the squad with 10.5 sacks and was named Defensive Rookie of the Year by the AP.

YEAR	TEAM	G	INT	YDS	AVG	TD	SACKS	FUM REC	TD
1993	San Francisco	16	---	---	---	---	10.5	---	---
1 YR TOTALS		16	0	0	NA	0	10.5	0	0
1993 RANK NFL DL			16	NA	NA	NA	14	71	NA

Ken Norton No. 51/LB

Full name: Kenneth Howard Norton Jr.
HT: 6-2 **WT:** 241
Born: 9-29-66, Jacksonville, IL
High school: Westchester (Los Angeles)
College: UCLA

Free-agent signee Norton was a Pro Bowler for Dallas. His 159 tackles was the fourth-highest total in club history.

YEAR	TEAM	G	INT	YDS	AVG	TD	SACKS	FUM REC	TD
1988	Dallas	3	---	---	---	---	---	1	0
1989	Dallas	13	---	---	---	---	2.5	---	---
1990	Dallas	15	---	---	---	---	2.5	2	0
1991	Dallas	16	---	---	---	---	---	---	---
1992	Dallas	16	---	---	---	---	---	2	0
1993	Dallas	16	1	25	25.0	0	2.0	1	0
6 YR TOTALS		79	1	25	25.0	0	7.0	6	0
1993 RANK NFL LB			17	11	5	5	37	24	8
1994 PROJECTIONS		16	2	38	19.0	0	3	1	0

Tim McDonald No. 46/S

HT: 6-2 **WT:** 215
Born: 1-26-65, Fresno, CA
High school: Edison (CA)
College: Southern California
Yet another Pro Bowler, McDonald had 91 tackles (second on the team) and 3 INTs.

YEAR	TEAM	G	INT	YDS	AVG	TD	SACKS	FUM REC	TD
1987	St. Louis	3	---	---	---	---	---	---	---
1988	Phoenix	16	2	11	5.5	0	2.0	1	0
1989	Phoenix	16	7	140	20.0	1	---	1	0
1990	Phoenix	16	4	63	15.8	0	---	1	0
1991	Phoenix	13	5	36	7.2	0	---	1	0
1992	Phoenix	16	2	35	17.5	0	0.5	3	---
1993	San Francisco	16	3	23	7.7	0	---	1	0
	7 YR TOTALS	96	23	308	13.4	1	2.5	8	0
1993	RANK NFL DB		33	79	92	27	49	37	14
1994	PROJECTIONS	16	3	7	2.3	0	0	0	0

Harris Barton No. 79/T

Full name: Harris Scott Barton
HT: 6-4 **WT:** 286
Born: 4-19-64, Atlanta, GA
High school: Dunwoody (GA)
College: North Carolina
Barton started 15 games and was one of 3 Niner offensive linemen selected for the Pro Bowl.

YEAR	TEAM	G	RUSHING			RANK	PASS	RANK		YDS.
			ATT	YDS	AVG	AV RUSH	YDS	PASS YDS	SACKS	LOST
1991	San Francisco	16	440	1861	4.2	7	4167	2	24	170
1992	San Francisco	13	482	2315	4.8	1	4054	3	32	174
1993	San Francisco	15	463	2133	4.6	1	4480	2	35	178
	7 YR TOTALS	104								

Gary Plummer   No. 50/LB

Full name: Gary Lee Plummer
HT: 6-2   **WT:** 247
Born: 1-26-60, Fremont, CA
High school: Mission San Jose (Fremont)
College: California

Ex-Charger Plummer joins Ken Norton in a revamped LB corps. He had 93 tackles, 12 of them for a loss, in '93.

YEAR	TEAM	G	INT	YDS	AVG	TD	SACKS	FUM REC	TD
1986	San Diego	15	---	---	---	---	2.5	---	---
1987	San Diego	8	1	2	2.0	---	---	---	---
1988	San Diego	16	---	---	---	---	---	---	---
1989	San Diego	16	---	---	---	---	---	1	0
1990	San Diego	16	---	---	---	---	---	---	---
1991	San Diego	16	---	---	---	---	1.0	1	0
1992	San Diego	16	2	40	20.0	0	---	1	0
1993	San Diego	16	2	7	3.5	0	---	---	---
	8 YR TOTALS	119	5	49	9.8	0	3.5	3	0
1993	RANK NFL LB		4	27	33	5	91	81	NA
1994	PROJECTIONS	16	3	1	0.3	0	0	0	0

George Seifert Head Coach

Full name: George Gerald Seifert
Born: 12-22-40, San Francisco, CA
High school: Polytechnic (San Francisco)
College: Utah

Seifert has the best winning percentage of any active NFL coach: .775. No other active coach has a winning percentage over .700. Yet he was only 3–15 in 2 years at Cornell.

		REGULAR SEASON					POSTSEASON		
YEAR	TEAM	W	L	T	PCT	FINISH	W	L	FINISH
1989	San Francisco	14	2	0	.875	1st/NFC West	3	0	won Super Bowl XXIV over Denver, 55-10
1990	San Francisco	14	2	0	.875	1st/NFC West	1	1	lost NFC Title game to NY Giants, 15-13
1991	San Francisco	10	6	0	.625	2nd/NFC West			
1992	San Francisco	14	2	0	.875	1st/NFC West	1	1	lost NFC Title game to Dallas, 30-20
1993	San Francisco	10	6	0	.625	1st/NFC West	1	1	lost NFC Title game to Dallas, 38-21
	5 YR TOTALS	62	18	0	.775		6	3	

Elvis Grbac — No. 18/QB

HT: 6-5   **WT:** 232
Born: 8-13-70, Cleveland, OH
High school: St. Joseph's (OH)
College: Michigan
Ex-Wolverine Grbac has yet to see NFL action, but he'll take over Steve Bono's back-up role.

YEAR	TEAM	G	ATT	CPL	CPL%	YDS	AVG	TDS	TD%	INT	INT%	RTG	ATT	YDS	AVG
1993	San Francisco	---	---	---	---	---	---	---	---	---	---	---	---	---	---
	1 YR TOTALS	0	0	0	NA	0	NA	0	NA	0	NA		0	0	NA
	1993 RANK NFL QB														

Dexter Carter — No. 35/RB

Full name: Dexter Anthony Carter
HT: 5-9   **WT:** 174
Born: 9-15-67, Baxley, GA
High school: Appling County (Baxley, GA)
College: Florida State
His punt return average was second in the NFC.

			RUSHING				RECEIVING				KICK RETURNS			
YEAR	TEAM	G	ATT	YDS	AVG	TD	REC	YDS	AVG	TD	RET	YDS	AVG	TD
1990	San Francisco	16	114	460	4.0	1	25	217	8.7	0	41	783	19.1	0
1991	San Francisco	16	85	379	4.5	2	23	253	11.0	1	37	839	22.7	1
1992	San Francisco	3	4	9	2.3	0	1	43	43.0	1	2	55	27.5	0
1993	San Francisco	16	10	72	7.2	1	3	40	13.3	0	25	494	19.8	0
	4 YR TOTALS	51	213	920	4.3	4	52	553	10.6	2	105	2171	20.7	1
	1993 RANK NFL RB	108	101	5	58	105	91	5	40	5	6	18		
	1994 PROJECTIONS	16	0	0	NA	1	0	0	NA	0	26	471	18.1	0

Jesse Sapolu — No. 61/C

Full name: Manase Jesse Sapolu
HT: 6-4   **WT:** 278
Born: 3-10-61, Apla, Western Samoa
High school: Farrington (Honolulu, HI)
College: Hawaii
Center Sapolu started every game in 1993.

			RUSHING			RANK	PASS	RANK		YDS.
YEAR	TEAM	G	ATT	YDS	AVG	AV RUSH	YDS	PASS YDS	SACKS	LOST
1991	San Francisco	16	440	1861	4.2	7	4167	2	24	170
1992	San Francisco	16	482	2315	4.8	1	4054	3	32	174
1993	San Francisco	16	463	2133	4.6	1	4480	2	35	178
	9 YR TOTALS	125								

Dennis Brown　　　No. 96/DE

Full name: Dennis Trammel Brown
HT: 6-4　**WT:** 290
Born: 11-6-67, Los Angeles, CA
High school: Jordan (Long Beach, CA)
College: Washington
He had 5.5 sacks and a personal best 58 tackles.

YEAR	TEAM	G	INT	YDS	AVG	TD	SACKS	FUM REC	TD
1990	San Francisco	15	---	---	---	---	6.0	---	---
1991	San Francisco	16	---	---	---	---	3.0	---	---
1992	San Francisco	16	1	0	0.0	0	3.5	---	---
1993	San Francisco	16	---	---	---	---	5.5	---	---
4 YR TOTALS		63	1	0	0.0	0	18.0	0	0
1993 RANK NFL DL			16	NA	NA	NA	43	71	NA
1994 PROJECTIONS		16	0	0	0	0	6	0	0

Troy Wilson　　　No. 92/DE

HT: 6-4　**WT:** 235
Born: 11-22-70, Topeka, KS
High school: Shawnee Heights (KS)
College: Pittsburg State (KS)
Wilson missed 6 games but his 5.5 sacks tied for second on the team.

YEAR	TEAM	G	INT	YDS	AVG	TD	SACKS	FUM REC	TD
1993	San Francisco	10	---	---	---	---	5.5	---	---
1 YR TOTALS		10	0	0	NA	0	5.5	0	0
1993 RANK NFL DL			16	NA	NA	NA	43	71	NA

Artie Smith　　　No. 95/DE

Full name: Artie Enlow Smith
HT: 6-4　**WT:** 303
Born: 5-15-70, Stillwater, OK
High school: Stillwater (OK)
College: Louisiana Tech
He'll take over for Ted Washington on the DL.

YEAR	TEAM	G	INT	YDS	AVG	TD	SACKS	FUM REC	TD
1993	San Francisco	16	---	---	---	---	1.5	---	---
1 YR TOTALS		16	0	0	NA	0	1.5	0	0
1993 RANK NFL DL			16	NA	NA	NA	113	71	NA

Eric Davis   No. 25/CB

Full name: Eric Wayne Davis
HT: 5-11   **WT:** 178
Born: 1-26-68, Anniston. AL
High school: Anniston (AL)
College: Jacksonville State
Davis led the team with 21 passes defensed.

YEAR	TEAM	G	INT	YDS	AVG	TD	SACKS	FUM REC	TD
1990	San Francisco	16	1	13	13.0	---	---	1	0
1991	San Francisco	2	---	---	---	---	---	---	---
1992	San Francisco	16	3	52	17.3	0	---	2	---
1993	San Francisco	16	4	45	11.3	1	---	1	1
	4 YR TOTALS	50	8	110	13.8	1	0.0	4	1
1993	RANK NFL DB		21	44	71	2	49	37	2
1994	PROJECTIONS	16	5	54	10.8	2	0	1	2

Merton Hanks   No. 36/CB

Full name: Merton E. Hanks
HT: 6-2   **WT:** 185
Born: 3-12-68, Dallas, TX
High school: Lake Highlands (Dallas)
College: Iowa
Hanks finished third on the team in tackles (71).

YEAR	TEAM	G	INT	YDS	AVG	TD	SACKS	FUM REC	TD
1991	San Francisco	13	---	---	---	---	---	2	0
1992	San Francisco	16	2	5	2.5	0	---	---	---
1993	San Francisco	16	3	104	34.7	1	---	---	---
	3 YR TOTALS	45	5	109	21.8	1	0.0	2	0
1993	RANK NFL DB		33	9	15	2	49	94	NA
1994	PROJECTIONS	16	4	180	45.0	2	0	0	0

Klaus Wilmsmeyer   No. 10/P

Full name: Klaus Wilmsmeyer Jr.
HT: 6-1   **WT:** 210
Born: 12-4-67, Mississauga, Ontario
High school: Lorne Park (Mississauga)
College: Louisville
He's never had a punt blocked as a Niner.

YEAR	TEAM	G	NO	YARDS	LONG	AVG	BLK	IN20
1992	San Francisco	15	49	1918	58	39.1	0	19
1993	San Fran.	15	42	1718	61	40.9	0	11
	2 YR TOTALS	30	91	3636	61	40.0	0	30
1993	RANK NFL		27	27	13	19	29	27
1994	PROJECTIONS	15	35	1518	64	43.4	0	3

Tampa Bay
BUCCANEERS

1994 Scouting Report

Offense

Tampa Bay had difficulty moving the ball in 1993. They gained 4,311 total yards, twenty-fifth in the NFL—1,290 rushing yards (next to last in the NFL) and 3,021 passing yards (twentieth in the league). In '94, the Bucs should move the ball through the air, since QB Craig Erickson has a year of starting experience under his belt. His favorite targets will be WRs Courtney Hawkins and Horace Copeland, plus Vince Workman out of the backfield. But Tampa Bay could have even more trouble on the ground, with the loss of leading rusher Reggie Cobb to free agency. They'll be looking to Mazio Royster and rookie Errict Rhett to fill the void. Tampa Bay signed Minnesota free agent T Tim Irwin to strengthen the offensive line beside T Paul Gruber. Rookie QB Trent Dilfer is waiting in the wings.

Defense

Tampa Bay had one of the league's worst defenses, allowing 5,246 total yards, twenty-second in the NFL. The Bucs allowed 1,994 rushing yards (twenty-third in the league) and 3,252 passing yards (eighteenth in the NFL). Depth is the major problem—the Bucs have some talented defensive starters, including Pro Bowl LB Hardy Nickerson (214 tackles), DE Eric Curry and LB Broderick Thomas—but little else. Tampa Bay signed free agents LB Lonnie Marts and CB Tony Stargell and traded for FS Thomas Everett. They'll miss departed DE Ray Seals and his 8.5 sacks.

Special Teams

Special teams are a bright spot for Tampa. In his first year, K Michael Husted showed a strong leg; he hit 3 50+ yard FGs, and his 25% touchback percentage was among the league leaders. P Dan Stryzinski set a team record with 24 punts inside the 20 yard line. Courtney Hawkins, the team's punt returner, set a team record with his 11.1 yard average in '93.

1994 Prospects

The Bucs figure to be better in '94. The defense should improve, and they should move the ball through the air well enough to surprise some teams. But they're in a tough division, and they won't be in the playoff hunt, since the lack of a running game will force Craig Erickson to play catch up too much.

Team Directory

Owner: Hugh Culverhouse
VP, football operations: Richard McKay
Director of player personnel: Jerry Angelo
Director of public relations: Rick Odioso

1993 Review				1994 Schedule		
Sep. 5	KANSAS CITY	L 27-3		Sep. 4	at Chicago	1:00
Sep. 12	at N.Y. Giants	L 23-7		Sep. 11	INDIANAPOLIS	1:00
Sep. 19	OPEN DATE			Sep. 18	NEW ORLEANS	1:00
Sep. 26	at Chicago	L 47-17		Sep. 25	at Green Bay	1:00
Oct. 3	DETROIT	W 27-10		Oct. 2	DETROIT	1:00
Oct. 10	at Minnesota	L 15-0		Oct. 9	at Atlanta	1:00
Oct. 17	OPEN DATE			Oct. 16	OPEN DATE	
Oct. 24	GREEN BAY	L 37-14		Oct. 23	at San Francisco	4:00
Oct. 31	at Atlanta	W 31-24		Oct. 30	MINNESOTA	4:00
Nov. 7	at Detroit	L 23-0		Nov. 6	CHICAGO	1:00
Nov. 14	SAN FRANCISCO	L 45-21		Nov. 13	at Detroit	8:00
Nov. 21	MINNESOTA	W 23-10		Nov. 20	at Seattle	4:00
Nov. 28	at Green Bay	L 13-10		Nov. 27	at Minnesota	1:00
Dec. 5	WASHINGTON	L 23-17		Dec. 4	WASHINGTON	1:00
Dec. 12	CHICAGO	W 13-10		Dec. 11	L.A. RAMS	1:00
Dec. 19	at L.A. Raiders	L 27-20		Dec. 18	at Washington	1:00
Dec. 26	at Denver	W 17-10		Dec. 24	GREEN BAY	1:00
Jan. 2	SAN DIEGO	L 32-17				

1993 finish: 5-11 (3-5 home, 2-6 away), fifth in NFC Central

Team Leaders

PASSING	ATT	COM	COM%	YDS	YPA	TD	TD%	INT	INT%	RTG
Erickson	457	233	51.0	3054	6.68	18	3.9	21	4.6	66.4
DeBerg	39	23	59.0	186	4.77	1	2.6	3	7.7	47.6
Weldon	11	6	54.5	55	5.00	0	0.0	1	9.1	30.5
TEAM	508	262	51.6	3295	6.49	19	3.7	25	4.9	64.1
OPPONENTS	503	300	59.6	3384	6.73	22	4.4	9	1.8	86.9

RECEIVING	REC	YDS	AVG	TD	RUSHING	ATT	YDS	AVG	TD
Hawkins	62	933	15.0	5	Cobb	221	658	3.0	3
Workman	54	411	7.6	2	Workman	78	284	3.6	2
Copeland	30	633	21.1	4	Royster	33	115	3.5	1
Hall	23	268	11.7	1	Erickson	26	96	3.7	0
Wilson	15	225	15.0	0	Anderson	28	56	2.0	0
TEAM	262	3295	12.6	19	TEAM	402	1290	3.2	6
OPPONENTS	300	3384	11.3	22	OPPONENTS	479	1994	4.2	15

INTERCEPTIONS	INT	YDS	AVG	LG	TD	SACKS	NO
King	3	29	9.7	28	0	Seals	8.5
Mack	1	27	27.0	27t	1	Curry	5.0
Anderson	1	6	6.0	6	0	Dotson	5.0
TEAM	6	71	7.0	28	2	TEAM	39.0
OPPONENTS	25	280	11.2	59t	1	OPPONENTS	39.0

KICK RETURNS	NO	YDS	AV	LG	TD	PUNT RETURNS	NO	FC	YDS	AV	LG	TD
Wilson	23	454	19.7	42	0	Anderson	17	1	113	6.6	15	0
Anderson	12	181	15.1	24	0	Hawkins	15	8	166	11.1	35	0
Royster	8	102	12.8	26	0	Claiborne	6	6	32	5.3	13	0
TEAM	58	922	15.9	42	0	TEAM	38	15	311	8.2	35	0
OPPONENTS	28	499	17.8	46	0	OPPONENTS	53	23	394	7.4	54	0

KICKING	XPM	XPA	FGM	FGA	LG	PTS
Husted	27	27	16	22	57	75
TEAM	27	27	16	22	57	75
OPPONENTS	38	40	32	35	55	134

PUNTING	NO	YDS	LG	AVG	TB	BLK	RET	RYD	IN20	NAV
Stryzinski	93	3772	57	40.6	3	1	53	394	24	35.3
TEAM	94	3772	57	40.1	3	1	53	394	24	35.3
OPPONENTS	76	3290	64	43.3	11	0	38	311	20	36.3

FUMBLES	FUM	OFF.FUM.REC.	REC	TD	DEF.FUM.REC.	REC	TD
Erickson	9	Erickson	6	0	Carter	2	0
Cobb	5	Wilson	2	0	Jones	2	0
Anderson	3				King	2	0
TEAM	28	TEAM	16	0	TEAM	13	0
OPPONENTS	27	OPPONENTS	10	1	OPPONENTS	11	1

1994 Draft Choices

ROUND	NAME	POS	SCHOOL	OVERALL SELECTION
1	Trent Dilfer	QB	Fresno State	6
2	Errict Rhett	RB	Florida	34
3	Harold Bishop	TE	Louisiana State	69
5	Pete Pierson	T	Washington	136
6	Bernard Carter	LB	East Carolina	165
7	Jim Payne	C	Virginia Tech	200

HISTORY

TITLES

1979   NFC Central Championship
1981   NFC Central Championship

ALL-TIME TEAM RECORDS

Rushing

Most yards, game:	219	James Wilder	11/6/83
Most yards, season:	1,544	James Wilder	1984
Most yards, career:	5,957	James Wilder	1981-1989

Passing

Most yards, game:	486	Doug Williams	11/16/80
Most yards, season:	3,563	Doug Williams	1981
Most yards, career:	14,820	Vinny Testaverde	1987-1992

Receiving

Most catches, game:	13	James Wilder	9/15/85
Most catches, season:	85	James Wilder	1984
Most catches, career:	432	James Wilder	1981-1989

Scoring

Most points, game:	24	Jimmie Giles	10/20/85
Most points, season:	99	Donald Igwebuike	1989
Most points, career:	416	Donald Igwebuike	1985-1989

COACHES

NAME	RECORD	YEARS
John McKay	45-91-1	1976-84
Leeman Bennett	4-28-0	1985-86
Ray Perkins	19-41-0	1987-90
Richard Williamson	4-15-0	1990-91
Sam Wyche	10-22-0	1992-93

TAMPA BAY BUCCANEERS
1994 TRAINING CAMP ROSTER

No.	Quarterbacks		Ht.	Wt.	Born	NFL Exp.	College	How acq.	93 GP/GS
12	Dilfer, Trent	QB	6-4	230	3-13-72	R	Fresno State	D1 '94	
7	Erickson, Craig	QB	6-2	205	5-17-69	3	Miami (FL)	D4 '92	16/15
13	Vlasic, Mark	QB	6-3	205	10-25-63	6	Iowa	FA '93	0/0
11	Weldon, Casey	QB	6-1	200	2-3-69	3	Florida State	FA '93	4/0
	Running backs								
43	Harris, Rudy	FB	6-1	255	9-18-71	2	Clemson	D4 '93	10/2
33	McDowell, Anthony	FB	5-11	235	11-12-68	3	Texas Tech	D8 '92	4/3
32	Rhett, Errict	RB	5-11	210	12-11-70	R	Florida	D2 '94	
31	Royster, Mazio	RB	6-1	200	8-3-70	3	Southern California	D11 '92	14/0
46	Workman, Vince	RB	5-10	205	5-9-68	6	Ohio State	FA '93	16/10

Wide receivers

89	Collins, Shawn	WR	6-2	205	2-20-67	6	Northern Arizona	FA '93	0/0
88	Copeland, Horace	WR	6-2	195	1-1-71	2	Miami (FL)	D4a '93	14/8
80	Dawsey, Lawrence	WR	6-0	195	11-16-67	4	Florida State	D3 '91	4/4
85	Hawkins, Courtney	WR	5-9	180	12-12-69	3	Michigan State	D3a '92	16/12
87	Thomas, Lamar	WR	6-1	170	2-12-70	2	Miami (FL)	D3 '93	14/2
30	Turner, Vernon	WR-KR	5-8	185	1-6-67	5	Carson-Newman	FA '93	1/0
84	Wilson, Charles	WR	5-10	185	7-1-68	4	Memphis State	FA '92	15/1

Tight ends

86	Armstrong, Tyji	TE	6-4	250	10-3-70	3	Mississippi	D3a '92	12/7
82	Bishop, Harold	TE	6-4	250	4-8-70	R	Louisiana State	D3 '94	
83	Moore, Dave	TE	6-2	245	11-11-69	2	Pittsburgh	FA '92	15/1

Offensive linemen

73	Adams, Theo	OL	6-4	300	4-24-66	3	Hawaii	FA '93	7/0
62	Beckles, Ian	G	6-1	295	7-20-67	5	Indiana	D5 '90	14/14
76	Dill, Scott	OL	6-5	290	4-5-66	7	Memphis State	FA '90	16/16
75	Gruber, Paul	T	6-5	290	2-24-65	7	Wisconsin	D1 '88	10/10
78	Irwin, Tim	T	6-7	297	12-13-58	14	Tennessee	FA '94	16/16
79	Love, Sean	G	6-3	290	9-6-68	2	Penn State	FA '93	2/0
61	Mayberry, Tony	C	6-4	285	12-8-67	5	Wake Forest	D4 '91	16/16
70	McRae, Charles	T	6-7	300	9-16-68	4	Tennessee	D1 '90	13/4
**	Munoz, Anthony	T	6-6	285	8-19-58	15	Southern California	FA '93	0/0
69	Pierson, Pete	T	6-5	286	2-4-71	R	Washington	D5 '94	
65	Pyne, Jim	C	6-2	277	11-23-71	R	Virginia Tech	D7 '94	
66	Reimers, Bruce	G	6-7	300	9-28-60	11	Iowa State	Plan B '92	11/10
64	Ryan, Tim	G	6-2	280	9-2-68	4	Notre Dame	D5a '91	6/0
67	Sullivan, Mike	G	6-3	290	12-22-67	3	Miami (FL)	FA '92	11/3
94	Trumbull, Rick	OL	6-6	300	12-4-67	2	Missouri	T-CLE '93	0/0

Defensive linemen

72	Ahanotu, Chidi	DL	6-2	280	10-11-70	2	California	D6 '93	16/10
75	Curry, Eric	DE	6-5	270	2-3-70	2	Alabama	D1 '93	10/10
71	Dotson, Santana	DL	6-5	270	12-19-69	3	Baylor	D5a '92	16/13
97	Hunter, Jeff	DE	6-4	290	4-12-66	5	Albany State	FA '94	5/1
92	Price, Shawn	DL	6-5	260	3-28-70	2	Pacific	FA '93	9/6
77	Wheeler, Mark	DL	6-2	280	4-1-70	3	Texas A&M	D3 '92	10/10
99	Winter, Blaise	DL	6-4	295	1-31-62	10	Syracuse	T-SD '94	16/16
96	Wilson, Bernard	DL	6-2	295	8-17-70	2	Tennessee St.	FA '93	13/2

Linebackers

53	Brady, Ed	LB	6-2	235	6-17-62	11	Illinois	Plan B '92	16/0
95	Brady, Jeff	LB	6-1	235	11-9-68	4	Kentucky	FA '94	9/0
59	Carter, Bernard	LB	6-3	245	8-22-71	R	East Carolina	D6 '94	
93	DuBose, Demetrius	LB	6-1	240	3-23-71	2	Notre Dame	D2 '93	15/4
51	Marts, Lonnie	LB	6-1	230	11-10-68	5	Tulane	FA '94	16/15
56	Nickerson, Hardy	LB	6-2	230	9-1-65	8	California	FA '93	16/16
57	Thomas, Broderick	LB	6-4	250	2-20-67	6	Nebraska	D1 '89	16/8
**	Williams, Jimmy	LB	6-3	230	11-15-60	13	Nebraska	T-MIN '92	11/7

Defensive backs

44	Anderson, Darren	CB	5-10	180	1-11-69	2	Toledo	FA '92	14/1
28	Buckley, Curtis	DB	6-0	185	9-25-70	2	East Texas St.	FA '93	10/2
27	Bussey, Barney	S	6-0	210	5-20-62	9	S. Carolina St.	FA '94	16/7
23	Carter, Marty	S	6-1	200	12-17-69	4	Middle Tenn. St.	D8 '91	16/14
25	Covington, Tony	S	5-11	195	12-26-67	4	Virginia	D4 '91	0/0
	Dimry, Charles	CB	6-0	175	1-31-66	8	Nevada-Las Vegas	FA '94	12/11
22	Everett, Thomas	S	5-9	183	11-21-64	8	Baylor	T-DAL '94	16/16
**	Gray, Jerry	S	6-0	185	12-16-62	10	Texas	FA '93	14/5
26	Green, Rogerick	CB	6-0	180	12-15-69	3	Kansas State	D5 '92	0/0
24	Jones, Roger	CB	5-9	175	4-22-69	4	Tennessee St.	FA '92	16/5
41	King, Joe	S	6-2	195	5-7-68	4	Oklahoma St.	FA '92	15/10
21	Lynch, John	S	6-2	220	9-25-71	2	Stanford	D3a '93	15/4
21	Mack, Milton	CB	5-11	195	9-20-63	8	Alcorn State	FA '92	12/3
35	Mayhew, Martin	CB	5-8	175	10-8-65	7	Florida State	FA '93	14/14
	McGruder, Michael	CB	5-10	190	5-6-64	5	Kent	FA '94	16/5
36	Paul, Markus	S	6-2	200	4-1-66	6	Syracuse	FA '93	1/0
45	Stargell, Tony	DB	5-11	190	8-7-66	5	Tennessee St.	FA '94	16/1

Specialists

5	Husted, Michael	K	6-0	190	6-16-70	2	Virginia	FA '93	16/0
4	Stryzinksi, Dan	P	6-1	195	5-15-65	5	Indiana	FA '92	14/0

Craig Erickson   No. 7/QB

Full name: Craig Neil Erickson
HT: 6-2 **WT:** 205
Born: 5-17-69, Boynton Beach, FL
High school: Cardinal Newman (W. Palm Beach)
College: Miami (FL)

Erickson's 18 TD passes ranked fifth in the NFL. His 3,054 yards passing are the first 3,000 yards by a Tampa Bay QB since 1989.

YEAR	TEAM	G	PASSING ATT	CPL	CPL%	YDS	AVG	TDS	TD%	INT	INT%	RTG	RUSHING ATT	YDS	AVG
1992	Tampa Bay	6	26	15	57.7	121	4.7	0	0.0	0	0.0	69.6	1	-1	-1.0
1993	Tampa Bay	16	457	233	51.0	3054	6.7	18	3.9	21	4.6	66.4	26	96	3.7
2 YR TOTALS		22	483	248	51.3	3175	6.6	18	3.7	21	4.3		27	95	3.5
1993	RANK NFL QB		9	15	58	11	30	6	24	2	16	46	17	16	19
1994	PROJECTIONS	16	845	426	50.4	5785	6.8	36	4.3	42	5.0		49	195	4.0

Mazio Royster   No. 33/RB

Full name: Mazio Denmar Vesey Royster
HT: 6-1   **WT:** 200
Born: 8-3-70, Berkeley, CA
High school: Bishop Amat (La Puente, CA)
College: Southern California

Royster will be counted on to replace Reggie Cobb in the Tampa Bay backfield. He starred at USC, with 1,168 yards and 8 TDs in 1990.

YEAR	TEAM	G	RUSHING ATT	YDS	AVG	TD	RECEIVING REC	YDS	AVG	TD	KICK RETURNS RET	YDS	AVG	TD
1992	Tampa Bay	5	---	---	---	---	1	8	8.0	0	---	---	---	---
1993	Tampa Bay	14	33	115	3.5	1	5	18	3.6	0	8	102	12.8	0
2 YR TOTALS		19	33	115	3.5	1	6	26	4.3	0	8	102	12.8	0
1993	RANK NFL RB		89	91	86	58	92	104	112	40	20	24	50	
1994	PROJECTIONS	16	75	263	3.5	2	8	16	2.0	0	18	233	12.9	0

Vince Workman No. 46/RB

Full name: Vincent Innocent Workman Jr.
HT: 5-10 **WT:** 205
Born: 5-9-68, Buffalo, NY
High school: Dublin (OH)
College: Ohio State

Capable of playing FB or HB, Workman's 54 catches were the best by a Buc RB since James Wilder's 85 in 1984.

YEAR	TEAM	RUSHING					RECEIVING				KICK RETURNS			
		G	ATT	YDS	AVG	TD	REC	YDS	AVG	TD	RET	YDS	AVG	TD
1989	Green Bay	15	4	8	2.0	1	---	---	---	---	33	547	16.6	0
1990	Green Bay	15	8	51	6.4	0	4	30	7.5	1	14	210	15.0	0
1991	Green Bay	16	71	237	3.3	7	46	371	8.1	4	8	139	17.4	0
1992	Green Bay	10	159	631	4.0	2	47	290	6.2	0	1	17	17.0	0
1993	Tampa Bay	16	78	284	3.6	2	54	411	7.6	2	5	67	13.4	0
5 YR TOTALS		72	320	1211	3.8	12	151	1102	7.3	7	61	980	16.1	0
1993 RANK NFL RB			50	53	75	46	11	12	61	7	26	31	49	
1994 PROJECTIONS		16	45	145	3.2	1	57	460	8.1	2	3	23	7.7	0

Courtney Hawkins No. 85/WR

Full name: Courtney Tyrone Hawkins Jr.
HT: 5-9 **WT:** 180
Born: 12-12-69, Flint, MI
High school: Beacher (Flint, MI)
College: Michigan State

Hawkins had 565 yards in his last 6 games, a total exceeded only by Pro Bowlers Jerry Rice and Tim Brown.

YEAR	TEAM	RECEIVING					RUSHING				PUNT RETURN		
		G	REC	YDS	AVG	TD	ATT	YDS	AVG	TD	RET	YDS	AVG
1992	Tampa Bay	16	20	336	16.8	2	---	---	---	---	13	53	4.1
1993	Tampa Bay	16	62	933	15.0	5	---	---	---	---	15	166	11.1
2 YR TOTALS		32	82	1269	15.5	7	0	0	NA	0	28	219	7.8
1993 RANK NFL WR			21	15	40	19	42	42	42		15	13	6
1994 PROJECTIONS		16	104	1530	14.7	8	0	0	NA	0	17	279	16.4

Horace Copeland No. 88/WR

Full name: Horace Nathaniel Copeland
HT: 6-2　**WT:** 195
Born: 1-1-71, Orlando, FL
High school: Evans (Orlando)
College: Miami (FL)

Copeland had the Bucs' longest rush of 1993, 22 yards on a reverse. He's Tampa Bay's fastest player, with a 4.4 40-yard-dash time.

			RECEIVING				ROSHING				PUNT RETURN		
YEAR	TEAM	G	REC	YDS	AVG	TD	ATT	YDS	AVG	TD	RET	YDS	AVG
1993	Tampa Bay	13	30	633	21.1	4	3	34	11.3	0	---	---	---
1	YR TOTALS	13	30	633	21.1	4	3	34	11.3	0	0	0	NA
1993	RANK NFL WR		63	43	9	28	12	7	3		30	30	29

Tyji Armstrong　No. 86/TE

Full name: Tyji Donrapheal Armstrong
HT: 6-4　**WT:** 250
Born: 10-3-70, Inkster, MI
High school: Robichaud (Inkster, MI)
College: Mississippi State

Sam Wyche called blocking TE Armstrong the team's most improved player. He will replace the departed Ron Hall.

			RECEIVING			
YEAR	TEAM	G	REC	YDS	AVG	TD
1992	Tampa Bay	15	7	138	19.7	1
1993	Tampa Bay	12	9	86	9.6	1
2	YR TOTALS	27	16	224	14.0	2
1993	RANK NFL TE		44	45	42	22
1994	PROJECTIONS	9	9	46	5.1	1

Paul Gruber   No. 74/T

Full name: Paul Blake Gruber
HT: 6-5 **WT:** 290
Born: 2-24-65, Madison, WI
High school: Sauk Prairie (Prairie du Sac, WI)
College: Wisconsin

Designated as a franchise player in '93, Gruber once went 35 games—2,155 plays—without drawing a penalty.

YEAR	TEAM	G	RUSHING			RANK	PASS	RANK		YDS.
			ATT	YDS	AVG	AV RUSH	YDS	PASS YDS	SACKS	LOST
1991	Tampa Bay	16	371	1429	3.9	16	2955	28	56	383
1992	Tampa Bay	16	438	1706	3.9	17	3399	11	45	334
1993	Tampa Bay	10	402	1290	3.2	28	3295	20	39	274
	6 YR TOTALS	90								

Eric Curry   No. 75/DE

Full name: Eric Felece Curry
HT: 6-5 **WT:** 270
Born: 2-3-70, Thomasville, GA
High school: Thomasville (GA)
College: Alabama

Curry tied for second on the team in sacks with 5.0. At Alabama, only Derrick Thomas had more career sacks.

YEAR	TEAM	G	INT	YDS	AVG	TD	SACKS	FUM REC	TD
1993	Tampa Bay	10	---	---	---	---	5.0	1	0
	1 YR TOTALS	10	0	0	NA	0	5.0	1	0
1993	RANK NFL DL		16	NA	NA	NA	51	25	5

Hardy Nickerson   No. 56/LB

Full name: Hardy Otto Nickerson
HT: 6-2   **WT:** 230
Born: 9-1-65, Los Angeles, CA
High school: Verbum Dei (Los Angeles)
College: California

Nickerson was the first Tampa Bay Pro Bowl starter since 1984. He was also a first-team AP All-Pro, the first Buc since 1979.

YEAR	TEAM	G	INT	YDS	AVG	TD	SACKS	FUM REC	TD
1987	Pittsburgh	12	—	—	—	—	—	1	0
1988	Pittsburgh	15	1	0	0.0	0	3.5	1	0
1989	Pittsburgh	10	—	—	—	—	1.0	—	—
1990	Pittsburgh	16	—	—	—	—	2.0	—	—
1991	Pittsburgh	16	—	—	—	—	1.0	—	—
1992	Pittsburgh	15	—	—	—	—	2.0	2	0
1993	Tampa Bay	16	1	6	6.0	0	1.0	1	0
	7 YR TOTALS	100	2	6	3.0	0	10.5	5	0
1993	RANK NFL LB		17	29	25	5	62	24	8
1994	PROJECTIONS	16	2	9	4.5	0	1	1	0

Marty Carter   No. 23/S

Full name: Marty LaVincent Carter
HT: 6-1   **WT:** 200
Born: 12-17-69, LaGrange, GA
High school: LaGrange (GA)
College: Middle Tennessee State

Carter finished second on Tampa Bay with 130 tackles, setting a new team record for tackles by a DB.

YEAR	TEAM	G	INT	YDS	AVG	TD	SACKS	FUM REC	TD
1991	Tampa Bay	14	1	5	5.0	0	---	---	---
1992	Tampa Bay	16	3	1	0.3	0	2.0	---	---
1993	Tampa Bay	16	1	0	0.0	0	---	2	0
	3 YR TOTALS	46	5	6	1.2	0	2.0	2	0
1993	RANK NFL DB		95	124	122	27	49	10	14
1994	PROJECTIONS	16	0	0	0	0	0	4	0

Michael Husted   No. 5/K

HT: 6-0 **WT:** 190
Born: 6-16-70, El Paso, TX
High school: Hampton (VA)
College: Virginia
Rookie Husted tied a Buc record with 3 50+ yard FGs in '93, including a 57 yarder (a new team record). 25% of his kickoffs were touchbacks.

YEAR	TEAM	G	XP	XPA	XP Pct.	FG	FGA	FG Pct.	PTS
1993	Tampa Bay	16	27	27	100.0	16	22	72.7	75
	1 YR TOTALS	16	27	27	100.0	16	22	72.7	75
1993	RANK NFL		20	22	1	22	26	21	24

Sam Wyche   Head Coach

Full name: Samuel David Wyche
Born: 1-5-45, Atlanta, GA
High school: North Fulton (Atlanta)
College: Furman
Wyche's '93 team won 5 games, three against playoff teams. He won NFL Coach of the Year honors in Cincinnati in 1988.

		REGULAR SEASON					POSTSEASON		
YEAR	TEAM	W	L	T	PCT	FINISH	W	L	FINISH
1984	Cincinnati	8	8	0	.500	2nd/AFC Central			
1985	Cincinnati	7	9	0	.438	2nd/AFC Central			
1986	Cincinnati	10	6	0	.625	T2nd/AFC Central			
1987	Cincinnati	4	11	0	.267	4th/AFC Central			
1988	Cincinnati	12	4	0	.750	1st/AFC Central	2	1	lost Super Bowl XXIII to SF, 20-16
1989	Cincinnati	8	8	0	.500	4th/AFC Central			
1990	Cincinnati	9	7	0	.563	T1st/AFC Central	1	1	lost 2nd Rnd. game to LA Raiders, 20-10
1991	Cincinnati	3	13	0	.188	4th/AFC Central			
1992	Tampa Bay	5	11	0	.313	T3rd/NFC Central			
1993	Tampa Bay	5	11	0	.313	5th/NFC Central			
	10 YR TOTALS	71	88	0	.447		3	2	

Mark Vlasic   No. 13/QB

Full name: Mark Richard Vlasic
HT: 6-3   **WT:** 205
Born: 10-25-63, Rochester, PA
High school: Center (Monaca, PA)
College: Iowa
Vlasic saw no action in '93, his first year as a Buc.

YEAR	TEAM	PASSING										RUSHING		
		G	ATT	CPL	CPL%	YDS	AVG	TDS	TD%	INT	INT%	RTG	ATT	YDS	AVG
1987	San Diego	1	8	3	50.0	8	2.7	0	0.0	1	^^^^^	18.7	---	---	N/A
1988	San Diego	2	52	25	48.1	270	10.8	1	4.0	2	8.0	54.2	2	0	0.0
1990	San Diego	6	40	19	47.5	168	8.8	1	5.3	2	^^^^^	48.7	---	---	N/A
1991	Kansas City	6	44	28	63.6	316	11.3	2	7.1	0	0.0	100.2	1	-1	-1.0
	4 YR TOTALS	15	142	75	52.8	762	5.4	4	2.8	5	3.5		3	-1	-0.3
1994	PROJECTIONS	7	32	28	88.1	365	11.4	3	8.7	0	0.0		1	0	0.0

Charles Wilson   No. 84/WR

Full name: Charles Joseph Wilson II
HT: 5-10   **WT:** 185
Born: 7-1-68, Tallahassee, FL
High school: Godby (Tallahassee, FL)
College: Memphis State
Wilson is the Bucs' most elusive kick returner.

YEAR	TEAM		RECEIVING				RUSHING					PUNT RETURN		
		G	REC	YDS	AVG	TD	ATT	YDS	AVG	TD	RET	YDS	AVG
1991	Green Bay	15	19	305	16.1	1	3	3	1.0	0	---	---	---
1992	Tampa Bay	2	---	---	---	---	---	---	---	---	---	---	---
1993	Tampa Bay	15	15	225	15.0	0	2	7	3.5	0	---	---	---
	4 YR TOTALS	47	41	614	15.0	1	5	10	2.0	0	0	0	NA
1993	RANK NFL WR		88	83	41	95	22	23	24		30	30	29
1994	PROJECTIONS	16	22	322	14.6	0	3	11	3.7	0	0	0	NA

Tim Irwin   No. 78/T

Full name: Timothy Edward Irwin
HT: 6-7   **WT:** 297
Born: 12-13-58, Knoxville, TN
High school: Central (Knoxville, TN)
College: Pittsburgh
Irwin's 181 starts is the longest streak in the NFL.

YEAR	TEAM		RUSHING			RANK	PASS	RANK		YDS.
		G	ATT	YDS	AVG	AV RUSH	YDS	PASS YDS	SACKS	LOST
1991	Minnesota	16	464	2201	4.7	2	3016	24	28	133
1992	Minnesota	16	497	2030	4.1	14	3162	17	40	293
1993	Minnesota	16	447	1624	3.6	17	3381	17	35	181
	13 YR TOTALS	188								

Santana Dotson   No. 71/DT

HT: 6-5   **WT:** 270
Born: 4-5-66, New Orleans, LA
High school: Jack Yates (Houston)
College: Baylor

Dotson led the Tampa Bay DL in tackles for the second straight year with 63.

YEAR	TEAM	G	INT	YDS	AVG	TD	SACKS	FUM REC	TD
1992	Tampa Bay	16	—	—	—	—	10.0	2	0
1993	Tampa Bay	16	—	—	—	—	5.0	—	—
	2 YR TOTALS	32	0	0	NA	0	15.0	2	0
1993	RANK NFL DL		16	NA	NA	NA	51	71	NA
1994	PROJECTIONS	16	0	0	0	0	0	0	0

Broderick Thomas No. 51/LB

HT: 6-4   **WT:** 250
Born: 2-20-67, Houston, TX
High school: Madison (Houston)
College: Nebraska

Thomas set a Buc LB sack record with 11 in 1991. His uncle is former Bear MLB Mike Singletary.

YEAR	TEAM	G	INT	YDS	AVG	TD	SACKS	FUM REC	TD
1991	Tampa Bay	16	—	—	—	—	11.0	2	0
1992	Tampa Bay	16	2	81	40.5	1	5.0	3	0
1993	Tampa Bay	16	—	—	—	—	1.0	1	0
	5 YR TOTALS	80	2	81	40.5	1	26.5	8	0
1993	RANK NFL LB		47	NA	NA	NA	62	24	8
1994	PROJECTIONS	16	0	0	0	0	0	0	0

Lonnie Marts   No. 95/LB

HT: 6-1   **WT:** 243
Born: 11-10-68, New Orleans, LA
High school: St. Augustine (New Orleans)
College: Tulane

Marts started 15 games for Kansas City at RLB in '93, posting 73 tackles and 3 forced fumbles.

YEAR	TEAM	G	INT	YDS	AVG	TD	SACKS	FUM REC	TD
1991	Kansas City	16	—	—	—	—	1.0	1	0
1992	Kansas City	15	1	36	36.0	1	—	1	0
1993	Kansas City	16	1	20	20.0	0	2.0	1	0
	3 YR TOTALS	47	2	56	28.0	1	3.0	3	0
1993	RANK NFL LB		17	16	11	5	37	24	8
1994	PROJECTIONS	16	1	16	16.0	0	3	1	0

Thomas Everett   No. 22/S

Full name: Thomas Gregory Everett
HT: 5-9   **WT:** 183
Born: 11-21-64, Daingerfield, TX
High school: Daingerfield (TX)
College: Baylor
Everett was selected to the NFC Pro Bowl team.

YEAR	TEAM	G	INT	YDS	AVG	TD	SACKS	FUM REC	TD
1991	Pittsburgh	16	4	53	13.3	0	---	2	0
1992	Dallas	11	2	28	14.0	0	---	2	0
1993	Dallas	16	2	25	12.5	0	---	---	---
7 YR TOTALS		100	20	229	11.5	0	0.0	9	0
1993 RANK NFL DB			54	73	61	27	49	94	NA
1994 PROJECTIONS		16	1	17	17.0	0	0	0	0

Joe King   No. 41/S

Full name: Joe D. King
HT: 6-2   **WT:** 195
Born: 5-7-68, Dallas, TX
High school: South Oak Cliff (Dallas)
College: Oklahoma State
King had a career high 46 tackles and 10 starts.

YEAR	TEAM	G	INT	YDS	AVG	TD	SACKS	FUM REC	TD
1991	Cincinnati	6	---	---	---	---	---	---	---
1991	Cleveland	7	---	---	---	---	---	---	---
1992	Tampa Bay	14	2	24	12.0	0	---	---	---
1993	Tampa Bay	15	3	29	9.7	0	---	2	0
3 YR TOTALS		42	5	53	10.6	0	0.0	2	0
1993 RANK NFL DB			33	65	81	27	49	10	14
1994 PROJECTIONS		16	4	40	10.0	0	0	4	0

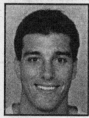

Dan Stryzinksi   No. 4/P

Full name: Daniel Thomas Stryzinksi
HT: 6-1   **WT:** 195
Born: 5-15-65, Indianapolis, IN
High school: Lincoln (Vincennes, IN)
College: Indiana
His 24 punts inside the 20 in '93 set a team record.

YEAR	TEAM	G	NO	YARDS	LONG	AVG	BLK	IN20
1990	Pittsburgh	16	65	2454	51	37.8	1	18
1991	Pittsburgh	16	74	2996	63	40.5	1	10
1992	Tampa Bay	16	74	3015	57	40.7	0	15
1993	Tampa Bay	14	93	3772	57	40.6	1	24
4 YR TOTALS		62	306	12237	63	40.0	3	67
1993 RANK NFL			1	5	27	25	1	8
1994 PROJECTIONS		15	119	4845	65	40.7	1	33

Washington
REDSKINS

1994 Scouting Report

Offense

QB Mark Rypien and WR Art Monk are both gone, so the 'Skins have to cast about for replacements. Washington's handed the starting QB job to first-round pick Heath Shuler. Unfortunately, his protection will be suspect. The Hogs–once the best offensive line in the league–are no more. Age and injury caught up with them. Second-round pick T Tre Johnson is expected to make a major contribution as a rookie, and Reggie Brooks was a pleasant surprise at RB. Although the team was plagued with injuries in '93, without a solid line or established QB, Washington will have trouble moving the ball in '94.

Defense

Last year, due to injuries, only three Redskin defenders started all 16 games–Darrell Green, Brad Edwards, and Kurt Gouveia. But some of those injuries were suffered by aging players–so many of last year's replacements will be this year's starters. Defensive backfield is the Redskins' only defensive strength: Darrell Green is an All-Pro caliber cornerback, but he's 34 this season. Tom Carter was a big plus at the other corner; his six interceptions ranked second in the conference. The 'Skins will miss retired S Danny Copeland, but they're hoping free agent signee S Keith Taylor will help.

Special Teams

Special teams are still a strength. Reggie Roby is one of the best punters in the league. Chip Lohmiller has a strong leg, although his 57% field goal percentage in 1993 was a career low.

1994 Prospects

Rebuilding is the name of the game here. Washington has holes to fill on the defensive line and at linebacker, and they're opening the season with a rookie QB and a spotty offensive line. Even so, the Redskins should certainly benefit from the fifth-place schedule and could slip past Philadelphia for fourth place. But the only thing this team has in common with the Super Bowl teams is the uniform. Norv Turner has a rebuilding job every bit as big as the one Jimmy Johnson faced in 1989—when the Cowboys were 1–15.

Team Directory

Chairman: Jack Kent Cooke
General mgr.: Charley Casserley
VP, Communications: Charlie Drayton

Exec. VP: John Kent Cooke
Dir. of player pers.: Kirk Mee
Director of media rel.: Mike McCall

1993 Review			1994 Schedule		
Sept. 6	DALLAS	W 35-16	Sep. 4	SEATTLE	1:00
Sept. 12	PHOENIX	L 17-10	Sep. 11	at New Orleans	4:00
Sept. 19	at Philadelphia	L 34-31	Sep. 18	at N.Y. Giants	4:00
Sept. 26	OPEN DATE		Sep. 25	ATLANTA	1:00
Oct. 4	MIAMI	L 17-10	Oct. 2	DALLAS	1:00
Oct. 10	N.Y. GIANTS	L 41-7	Oct. 9	at Philadelphia	8:00
Oct. 17	at Phoenix	L 36-6	Oct. 16	ARIZONA	1:00
Oct. 24	OPEN DATE		Oct. 23	at Indianapolis	1:00
Nov. 1	at Buffalo	L 24-10	Oct. 30	PHILADELPHIA	1:00
Nov. 7	INDIANAPOLIS	W 30-24	Nov. 6	SAN FRANCISCO	1:00
Nov. 14	at N.Y. Giants	L 20-6	Nov. 13	OPEN DATE	
Nov. 21	at L.A. Rams	L 10-6	Nov. 20	at Dallas	1:00
Nov. 28	PHILADELPHIA	L 17-14	Nov. 27	N.Y. GIANTS	4:00
Dec. 5	at Tampa Bay	W 23-17	Dec. 4	at Tampa Bay	1:00
Dec. 11	N.Y. Jets	L 3-0	Dec. 11	at Arizona	4:00
Dec. 19	ATLANTA	W 30-17	Dec. 18	TAMPA BAY	1:00
Dec. 26	at Dallas	L 38-3	Dec. 24	at L.A. Rams	4:00
Dec. 31	MINNESOTA	L 14-9			

1993 finish: 4-12 (3-5 home, 1-7 away), fifth in NFC East

Team Leaders

PASSING	ATT	COM	COM%	YDS	YPA	TD	TD%	INT	INT%	RTG
Rypien	319	166	52.0	1514	4.75	4	1.3	10	3.1	56.3
Gannon	125	74	59.2	704	5.63	3	2.4	7	5.6	59.6
Conklin	87	46	52.9	496	5.70	4	4.6	3	3.4	70.9
TEAM	533	287	53.8	2764	5.19	11	2.1	21	3.9	59.0
OPPONENTS	483	291	60.2	3584	7.42	24	5.0	17	3.5	85.1

RECEIVING	REC	YDS	AVG	TD	RUSHING	ATT	YDS	AVG	TD
Sanders	58	638	11.0	4	Brooks	223	1063	4.8	3
Monk	41	398	9.7	2	Mitchell	63	246	3.9	3
McGee	39	500	12.8	3	Ervins	50	201	4.0	0
Byner	27	194	7.2	0	Byner	23	105	4.6	1
Middleton	24	154	6.4	2	Gannon	21	88	4.2	1
TEAM	287	2764	9.6	11	TEAM	396	1728	4.4	11
OPPONENTS	291	3584	12.3	24	OPPONENTS	513	2112	4.1	14

INTERCEPTIONS	INT	YDS	AVG	LG	TD	SACKS	NO
Carter	6	54	9.0	29	0	Coleman	6.0
Green	4	10	2.5	6	0	Collins	6.0
Coleman	2	27	13.5	14	0	Palmer	4.5
TEAM	17	241	14.2	69t	2	TEAM	31.0
OPPONENTS	21	209	10.0	30	2	OPPONENTS	40.0

KICK RETURNS	NO	YDS	AV	LG	TD	PUNT RETURNS	NO	FC	YDS	AV	LG	TD
Mitchell	33	678	20.5	68	0	Mitchell	29	7	193	6.7	48	0
Howard	21	405	19.3	33	0	Howard	4	0	25	6.3	13	0
Ervins	2	29	14.5	18	0	Green	1	1	27	27.0	24	0
TEAM	59	1166	19.8	68	0	TEAM	35	8	245	7.0	48	0
OPPONENTS	36	722	20.1	43	0	OPPONENTS	34	23	343	10.1	62t	2

KICKING	XPM	XPA	FGM	FGA	LG	PTS
Lohmiller	24	26	16	28	51	72
TEAM	24	26	16	28	51	72
OPPONENTS	40	42	17	22	53	91

PUNTING	NO	YDS	LG	AVG	TB	BLK	RET	RYD	IN20	NAV
Roby	78	3447	60	44.2	10	0	31	343	25	37.2
TEAM	83	3644	60	43.9	10	0	34	343	28	37.4
OPPONENTS	73	2995	65	41.0	4	0	35	245	20	36.6

FUMBLES	FUM	OFF.FUM.REC.	REC	TD	DEF.FUM.REC.	REC	TD
Rypien	7	Elewonibi	2	0	Eilers	3	0
Brooks	4				Coleman	2	1
Gannon	3				Green	2	1
Mitchell	3						
TEAM	24	TEAM	14	0	TEAM	14	2
OPPONENTS	25	OPPONENTS	10	0	OPPONENTS	10	0

1994 Draft Choices

ROUND	NAME	POS	SCHOOL	OVERALL SELECTION
1	Heath Shuler	QB	Tennessee	3
2	Tre Johnson	T	Temple	31
3	Tydus Winans	WR	Fresno State	68
3	Joe Patton	G	Alabama A&M	97
4	Kurt Haws	TE	Utah	105
6	Dexter Nottage	DE	Florida A&M	163
7	Gus Frerotte	QB	Tulsa	197

HISTORY

TITLES

1936 NFL East Championship	1972 NFC Championshipship
1937 NFL Championship	1982 Super Bowl Winner
1940 NFL East Championship	1983 NFC Championship
1942 NFL Championship	1984 NFC East Championship
1943 NFL East Championship	1987 Super Bowl Winner
1945 NFL East Championship	1991 Super Bowl Winner

ALL-TIME TEAM RECORDS

Rushing

Most yards, game:	221	Gerald Riggs	9/17/89
Most yards, season:	1,347	John Riggins	1983
Most yards, career:	7,472	John Riggins	1976-1985

Passing

Most yards, game:	446	Sammy Baugh	10/31/48
Most yards, season:	4,109	Jay Schroeder	1986
Most yards, career:	25,206	Joe Theismann	1974-1985

Receiving

Most catches, game:	13	Art Monk	11/4/90
	13	Art Monk	12/15/85
	13	Kelvin Bryant	12/7/86
Most catches, season:	106	Art Monk	1984
Most catches, career:	801	Art Monk	1980-1993

Scoring

Most points, game:	24	Dick James	12/17/61
	24	Larry Brown	12/16/73
Most points, season:	161	Mark Moseley	1983
Most points, career:	1,207	Mark Moseley	1974-1986

COACHES

COACH	RECORD	YEARS	COACH	RECORD	YEARS
Lud Wray	4-4-2	1932	Joe Kuharich	26-32-2	1954-58
Lone Star Dietz	11-11-2	1933-34	Mike Dixon	4-18-2	1959-60
Eddie Casey	2-8-1	1935	Bill McPeak	21-46-3	1961-65
Ray Flaherty	56-23-3	1936-42	Otto Graham	17-22-3	1966-68
Dutch Bergman	7-4-1	1943	Vince Lombardi	7-5-2	1969
Dudley DeGroot	14-6-1	1944-45	Bill Austin	6-8-0	1970
Turk Edwards	16-81-1	1946-48	George Allen	69-35-1	1971-77
John Whelchel	3-3-1	1949	Jack Pardee	24-24-0	1978-80
Herman Ball	4-16-0	1949-51	Joe Gibbs	140-65-0	1981-92
Dick Todd	5-4-0	1951	Richie Petitbon	4-12	1993
Curly Lambeau	10-13-1	1952-53			

WASHINGTON REDSKINS
1994 TRAINING CAMP ROSTER

No.	Quarterbacks		Ht.	Wt.	Born	NFL Exp.	College	How acq.	93 GP/GS
14	Frerotte, Gus	QB	6-3	231	7-31-71	R	Tulsa	D7 '94	
19	Friesz, John	QB	6-4	210	5-17-67	1	Idaho	FA '94	17/6
5	Shuler, Heath	QB	6-2	221	12-31-71	R	Tennessee	D1 '94	
	Running backs								
40	Brooks, Reggie	RB	5-8	202	1-19-71	2	Notre Dame	D2 '93	16/11
32	Ervins, Ricky	RB	5-7	200	12-7-68	4	Southern California	D3 '91	15/1
30	Mitchell, Brian	RB	5-10	209	8-18-68	5	SW Louisiana	D5 '90	16/4
22	Wycheck, Frank	FB	6-3	235	10-14-71	2	Maryland	D6 '93	9/7
	Tight ends								
48	Haws, Kurt	TE	6-5	248	9-25-69	R	Utah	D4 '94	
89	Horton, Ethan	TE	6-4	240	12-19-62	8	North Carolina	FA '94	
87	Middleton, Ron	TE	6-2	270	7-17-65	9	Auburn	Plan B '89	16/16
88	Jenkins, James	TE	6-2	234	8-17-67	4	Rutgers	FA '91	15/5
	Wide receivers								
85	Ellard, Henry	WR	5-11	182	7-21-61	12	Fresno State	FA '94	16/16
80	Howard, Desmond	WR	5-9	183	5-15-70	3	Michigan	D1 '92	16/5
83	Sanders, Ricky	WR	5-11	180	8-30-62	9	Southwest Texas St.	T-NE/86	16/11
83	Winans, Tydus	WR	5-11	180	7-26-72	R	Fresno State	D3a '94	
	Offensive linemen								
57	Bingham, Guy	C	6-3	260	2-25-58	15	Montana	FA '92	14/0
67	Brown, Ray	T	6-5	310	12-12-62	9	Arkansas State	Plan B '89	16/14
64	Elewonibi, Moe	T	6-4	285	12-16-65	3	Brigham Young	D3 '90	15/15
75	Gesek, John	G	6-5	279	2-18-63	8	Sacramento State	FA '94	16/10
60	Huntington, Greg	C	6-3	278	9-22-70	2	Penn State	D5 '93	9/0
66	Jacoby, Joe	G-T	6-6	314	7-6-59	14	Louisville	FA '91	5/1
77	Johnson, Tre	T	6-3	315	8-30-71	R	Temple	D2 '94	
59	Matich, Trevor	C	6-4	297	10-9-61	10	Brigham Young	FA '94	16/4
63	McKenzie, Raleigh	C-G	6-2	279	2-8-63	10	Tennessee	D11 '85	16/16
62	Moore, Darryl	G	6-2	292	1-27-69	3	Texas-El Paso	D8 '92	12/0
68	Patton, Joe	G	6-5	288	1-5-72	R	Alabama A&M	D3b '94	
69	Schlereth, Mark	G	6-3	283	1-25-66	6	Idaho	D10 '89	9/8
76	Simmons, Ed	T	6-5	300	12-31-63	8	East. Washington	D6 '87	13/13
61	Smith, Vernice	G	6-3	298	10-24-65	6	Florida A&M	FA '93	8/3
	Defensive linemen								
**	Buck, Jason	DE	6-4	265	7-27-63	8	Brigham Young	FA '91	13/3
91	Collins, Shane	DE	6-3	267	4-11-69	3	Arizona State	D2 '92	7/5
93	Faulkner, Jeff	DE	6-4	300	4-4-64	4	Southern	FA '93	5/3
78	Johnson, Tim	DT	6-3	275	1-29-65	8	Penn State	T-PIT '90	15/15
72	Noga, Al	DE	6-1	269	9-16-65	7	Hawaii	FA '93	16/4
92	Nottage, Dexter	DE	6-4	273	11-14-70	R	Florida A&M	D6 '94	
97	Palmer, Sterling	DE	6-5	256	2-4-71	2	Florida State	D4 '93	14/10
75	Williams, Eric	DT	6-4	290	2-24-62	11	Washington St.	T-DET/90	4/4
94	Wilson, Bobby	DT	6-2	283	3-4-68	4	Michigan State	D1 '91	12/9
91	Woods, Tony	DE	6-4	269	9-11-65	8	Pittsburgh	FA '94	14/8
	Linebackers								
**	Coleman, Monte	LB	6-2	245	11-4-57	16	Central Arkansas	D11 '79	14/4
55	Collins, Andre	LB	6-1	233	5-4-68	5	Penn State	D2 '90	13/13
54	Gouveia, Kurt	LB	6-1	228	9-14-64	8	Brigham Young	D8 '86	16/16
56	Hamilton, Rick	LB	6-2	238	4-19-70	2	Central Florida	D3 '93	16/0
57	Harvey, Ken	OLB	6-3	230	5-6-65	7	California	FA '94	16/6
96	Hollinquest, Lamont	LB	6-3	225	10-24-70	2	Southern California	D8 '93	16/0
	Stowe, Tyronne	LB	6-2	250	5-31-65	8	Rutgers	T-AZ '94	15/15
	Defensive backs								
22	Bowles, Todd	DB	6-2	205	11-18-63	9	Temple	FA '92	10/2
25	Carter, Tom	CB	5-11	181	9-5-72	2	Notre Dame	D1 '93	14/11
27	Edwards, Brad	FS	6-2	207	3-22-66	7	South Carolina	Plan B '90	16/16
24	Eilers, Pat	FS	5-11	197	9-3-66	4	Notre Dame	FA '93	11/0
28	Green, Darrell	CB	5-8	170	2-15-60	12	Texas A&I	D1 '83	16/16
47	Johnson, A.J.	CB	5-8	170	6-22-67	6	SW Texas State	D6 '89	13/3
20	Mays, Alvoid	CB	5-9	180	7-10-66	5	West Virginia	FA '90	15/2
37	Morrison, Darryl	CB	5-11	189	5-19-71	2	Arizona	D6 '93	4/0
29	Taylor, Keith	S	5-11	206	12-21-64	6	Illinois	FA '94	16/14
	Specialists								
8	Lohmiller, Chip	K	6-3	210	7-16-66	7	Minnesota	D2 '88	16/0
1	Roby, Reggie	P	6-2	258	7-30-61	12	Iowa	FA '93	15/0

Heath Shuler   No. 5/QB

HT: 6-2   **WT:** 221
Born: 12-31-71
College: Tennessee
This rookie QB was Washington's top draft choice. He'll be the Redskins' starter come opening day.

		PASSING										RUSHING		
YEAR	TEAM	G	ATT	CPL	CPL%	YDS	AVG	TDS	TD%	INT	INT%	RTG	ATT	YDS	AVG
1993	Tennessee	11	285	184	64.6	2353	8.3	25	8.8	8	2.8		46	73	1.6
1994	first year in NFL														

Reggie Brooks   No. 40/RB

HT: 5-8   **WT:** 202
Born: 1-19-71, Tulsa, OK
High school: Tulsa (OK)
College: Notre Dame
Brooks led the Redskins in rushing in 1993. His 85-yard run against the Eagles was the longest in the NFL last season.

		RUSHING				RECEIVING				KICK RETURNS				
YEAR	TEAM	G	ATT	YDS	AVG	TD	REC	YDS	AVG	TD	RET	YDS	AVG	TD
1993	Washington	16	223	1063	4.8	3	21	186	8.9	0	1	12	12.0	0
	1 YR TOTALS	16	223	1063	4.8	3	21	186	8.9	0	1	12	12.0	0
1993 RANK NFL RB			10	9	24	21	43	43	36	40	51	57	53	

Ricky Ervins   No. 32/RB

HT: 5-7 **WT:** 200
Born: 12-7-68, Ft. Wayne, IN
High school: John Muir (Pasadena, CA)
College: Southern California
His first career start occurred vs. Atlanta in the Redskins' 14th game last season, yet Ervins was third on the team in rushing.

| | | RUSHING | | | | RECEIVING | | | | KICK RETURNS | | | |
YEAR	TEAM	G	ATT	YDS	AVG	TD	REC	YDS	AVG	TD	RET	YDS	AVG	TD
1991	Washington	15	145	680	4.7	3	16	181	11.3	1	11	232	21.1	0
1992	Washington	16	151	495	3.3	2	32	252	7.9	0	---	---	---	---
1993	Washington	15	50	201	4.0	0	16	123	7.7	0	2	29	14.5	0
	3 YR TOTALS	46	346	1376	4.0	5	64	556	8.7	1	13	261	20.1	0
1993	RANK NFL RB		72	72	49	89	55	55	60	40	44	47	44	
1994	PROJECTIONS	16	0	0	NA	0	10	55	5.5	0	1	0	0.0	0

Desmond Howard No. 80/WR

Full name: Desmond Kevin Howard
HT: 5-9 **WT:** 183
Born: 5-15-70, Cleveland, OH
High school: St. Joseph (Cleveland, OH)
College: Michigan
Howard saw duty as a receiver and kick returner. He should compete for more playing time on the 'Skins' young wideout corps.

| | | RECEIVING | | | | RUSHING | | | | PUNT RETURN | | |
YEAR	TEAM	G	REC	YDS	AVG	TD	ATT	YDS	AVG	TD	RET	YDS	AVG
1992	Washington	16	3	20	6.7	0	3	14	4.7	0	6	84	14.0
1993	Washington	16	23	286	12.4	0	2	17	8.5	0	4	25	6.3
	2 YR TOTALS	32	26	306	11.8	0	5	31	6.2	0	10	109	10.9
1993	RANK NFL WR		75	78	93	95	22	16	10		21	22	21
1994	PROJECTIONS	16	43	552	12.8	0	1	20	20.0	0	2	0	0.0

Henry Ellard   No. 85/WR

HT: 5-11 **WT:** 182
Born: 7-21-61, Fresno, CA
High school: Hoover (Fresno, CA)
College: Fresno State
Long-time Ram Ellard steps into the 'Skins'
top wideout slot. He'll be a popular target
for rookie QB Heath Shuler.

YEAR	TEAM	G	RECEIVING				RUSHING				PUNT RETURN		
			REC	YDS	AVG	TD	ATT	YDS	AVG	TD	RET	YDS	AVG
1986	LA Rams	9	34	447	13.1	4	1	-15	-15.0	0	14	127	9.1
1987	LA Rams	12	51	799	15.7	3	1	4	4.0	0	15	107	7.1
1988	LA Rams	16	86	1414	16.4	10	1	7	7.0	0	17	119	7.0
1989	LA Rams	14	70	1382	19.7	8	2	10	5.0	0	2	20	10.0
1990	LA Rams	15	76	1294	17.0	4	2	21	10.5	0	2	15	7.5
1991	LA Rams	16	64	1052	16.4	3	---	---	---	---	---	---	---
1992	LA Rams	16	47	727	15.5	3	---	---	---	---	---	---	---
1993	LA Rams	16	61	945	15.5	2	---	---	---	---	2	18	9.0
11	YR TOTALS	158	593	9761	16.5	48	16	37	2.3	0	135	1527	11.3
1993	RANK NFL WR		22	11	34	55	42	42	42		25	23	8
1994	PROJECTIONS	16	61	910	14.9	1	0	0	NA	0	3	25	8.3

Ethan Horton   No. 89/TE

Full name: Ethan Shane Horton
HT: 6-4 **WT:** 240
Born: 12-19-62, Kannapolis, NC
High school: A.L. Brown (Kannapolis, NC)
College: North Carolina
Horton was acquired from the Raiders, where
he averaged over 40 catches per year since
1990.

YEAR	TEAM	G	RECEIVING			
			REC	YDS	AVG	TD
1985	Kansas City	16	28	185	6.6	1
1987	LA Raiders	4	3	44	14.7	1
1989	LA Raiders	16	4	44	11.0	1
1990	LA Raiders	16	33	404	12.2	3
1991	LA Raiders	16	53	650	12.3	5
1992	LA Raiders	16	33	409	12.4	2
1993	LA Raiders	16	43	467	10.9	1
7	YR TOTALS	100	197	2203	11.2	14
1993	RANK NFL TE		10	13	29	22
1994	PROJECTIONS	16	48	490	10.2	0

John Friesz   No. 19/QB

Full name: John Melvin Friesz
HT: 6-4   **WT:** 218
Born: 5-19-67, Missoula, MT
High school: Coeur D'Alene (ID)
College: Idaho

Friesz was a disappointment as the Chargers' starting QB. He's the only veteran QB on the Redskins' roster.

YEAR	TEAM	G	ATT	CPL	CPL%	YDS	AVG	TDS	TD%	INT	INT%	RTG	ATT	YDS	AVG
1990	San Diego	1	22	11	50.0	98	4.5	1	4.5	1	4.5	58.5	1	3	3.0
1991	San Diego	16	487	262	53.8	2896	5.9	12	2.5	15	3.1	67.1	10	18	1.8
1993	San Diego	12	238	128	53.8	1402	5.9	6	2.5	4	1.7	72.8	10	3	0.3
	3 YR TOTALS	29	747	401	53.7	4396	5.9	19	2.5	20	2.7		21	24	1.1
1993	RANK NFL QB		27	29	49	31	47	31	46	40	53	38	34	47	50
1994	PROJECTIONS	13	182	100	55.2	1163	6.4	3	1.8	0	0.0		12	0	0.0

Table columns: PASSING — G, ATT, CPL, CPL%, YDS, AVG, TDS, TD%, INT, INT%, RTG; RUSHING — ATT, YDS, AVG

Tim Johnson   No. 78/DT

HT: 6-3   **WT:** 283
Born: 1-29-65, Sarasota, FL
High school: Sarasota (FL)
College: Penn State

Johnson's 18 quarterback hurries led the team, and his 4 sacks tied for fourth. He had 103 tackles, sixth on the Redskins.

YEAR	TEAM	G	INT	YDS	AVG	TD	SACKS	FUM REC	TD
1987	Pittsburgh	12	---	---	---	---	---	---	---
1988	Pittsburgh	15	---	---	---	---	4.0	---	---
1989	Pittsburgh	14	---	---	---	---	4.5	---	---
1990	Washington	16	---	---	---	---	3.0	1	0
1991	Washington	16	1	14	14.0	0	5.0	---	---
1992	Washington	16	---	---	---	---	6.0	1	---
1993	Washington	15	---	---	---	---	4.0	1	0
	7 YR TOTALS	104	1	14	14.0	0	26.5	3	0
1993	RANK NFL DL		16	NA	NA	NA	60	25	5
1994	PROJECTIONS	15	0	0	NA	0	4	1	0

Ken Harvey No. 57/OLB

Full name: Kenneth Ray Harvey
HT: 6-3 **WT:** 230
Born: 5-6-65, Austin, TX
High school: Lanier (Austin, TX)
College: California
Harvey played for Phoenix in 1993. He should be needed help for the beleaguered Redskin defense.

YEAR	TEAM	G	INT	YDS	AVG	TD	SACKS	FUM REC	TD
1989	Phoenix	16	---	---	---	---	6.0	---	---
1990	Phoenix	16	---	---	---	---	7.0	1	0
1991	Phoenix	16	---	---	---	---	9.0	2	0
1992	Phoenix	16	---	---	---	---	6.0	2	---
1993	Phoenix	---	---	---	---	---	9.5	---	---
	5 YR TOTALS	64	0	0	NA	0	37.5	5	0
1993	RANK NFL LB		47	NA	NA	NA	6	81	NA
1994	PROJECTIONS	-7	ERR	ERR	ERR	ERR	ERR	ERR	ERR

Darrell Green No. 28/CB

HT: 5-8 **WT:** 170
Born: 2-15-60, Houston, TX
High school: Jesse Jones (Houston, TX)
College: Texas A&I
Known as the fastest man in the NFL, Green was one of only three Redskin defenders to start every game. He's second on the Redskin career interception list with 34.

YEAR	TEAM	G	INT	YDS	AVG	TD	SACKS	FUM REC	TD
1985	Washington	16	2	0	0.0	0	---	1	0
1986	Washington	16	5	9	1.8	0	---	1	0
1987	Washington	12	3	65	21.7	0	---	1	1
1988	Washington	15	1	12	12.0	0	1.0	1	0
1989	Washington	7	2	0	0.0	0	---	1	0
1990	Washington	16	4	20	5.0	1	---	---	---
1991	Washington	16	5	47	9.4	0	---	---	---
1992	Washington	8	1	15	15.0	0	---	---	---
1993	Washington	16	4	10	2.5	0	---	2	1
	11 YR TOTALS	154	34	276	8.1	2	1.0	8	2
1993	RANK NFL DB		21	105	112	27	49	10	2
1994	PROJECTIONS	16	4	0	0.0	0	0	3	2

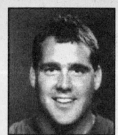

Chip Lohmiller No. 8/K

Full name: Chip Lohmiller
HT: 6-3 **WT:** 210
Born: 7-16-66, Woodbury, MN
High school: Woodbury (MN)
College: Minnesota

Lohmiller's streak of 213 consecutive extra points was broken against the Colts in game 8. He's made 8 game-winning kicks.

YEAR	TEAM	G	XP	XPA	XP Pct.	FG	FGA	FG Pct.	PTS
1988	Washington	16	40	41	97.6	19	26	73.1	97
1989	Washington	16	41	41	100.0	29	40	72.5	128
1990	Washington	16	41	41	100.0	30	40	75.0	131
1991	Washington	16	56	56	100.0	31	43	72.1	149
1992	Washington	16	30	30	100.0	30	40	75.0	120
1993	Washington	16	24	26	92.3	16	28	57.1	72
6	YR TOTALS	96	232	235	98.7	155	217	71.4	697
1993	RANK NFL		23	23	26	22	18	28	25
1994	PROJECTIONS	16	16	19	84.2	9	21	42.9	43

Norv Turner Head Coach

Full name: Norval Turner
Born: 5-17-52, LeJeune, NC
High school: Alhambra (CA)
College: Oregon

Turner, the most sought-after coaching recruit in 1994, was offensive coordinator for the Dallas Cowboys under Jimmy Johnson.

YEAR	TEAM	REGULAR SEASON					POSTSEASON			
		W	L	T	PCT	FINISH	W	L	FINISH
1994	Washington	first year in NFL							

Brian Mitchell   No. 30/RB

Full name: Brian Keith Mitchell
HT: 5-10 **WT:** 203
Born: 8-18-68, Fort Polk, LA
High school: Plaquemine (LA)
College: SW Louisiana
Mitchell tied for the team lead with 3 rushing TDs.

		RUSHING				RECEIVING				KICK RETURNS			
YEAR	TEAM	G	ATT	YDS	AVG	TD	REC	YDS	AVG	TD	RET	YDS	AVG	TD
1991 Washington	16	3	14	4.7	0	---	---	---		29	583	20.1	0
1992 Washington	16	6	70	11.7	0	3	30	10.0	0	23	492	21.4	0
1993 Washington	16	63	246	3.9	3	20	157	7.9	0	33	678	20.5	0
4 YR TOTALS	63	87	411	4.7	4	25	192	7.7	0	103	2118	20.6	0
1993 RANK NFL RB		62	61	59	21	47	49	57	40	2	3	14	
1994 PROJECTIONS	16	97	361	3.7	5	31	242	7.8	0	39	788	20.2	0

Stephen Hobbs   No. 86/WR

HT: 5-11 **WT:** 200
Born: 11-14-65, Mendenhall, MS
High school: Mendenhall (MS)
College: North Alabama
Hobbs was on the injured list throughout 1993.

		RECEIVING				RUSHING				PUNT RETURN		
YEAR	TEAM	G	REC	YDS	AVG	TD	ATT	YDS	AVG	TD	RET	YDS	AVG
1990 Washington	7	1	18	18.0	1	---	---	---		---	---	---
1991 Washington	16	3	24	8.0	0	---	---	---		1	10	10.0
1992 Washington	2	---	---	---	---		---	---	---		---	---	---
3 YR TOTALS	25	4	42	10.5	1	0	0	NA	0	1	10	10.0
1994 PROJECTIONS	16	4	7	1.8	0	0	0	NA	0	2	20	10.0

Ron Middleton   No. 87/TE

Full name: Ronald Allen Middleton
HT: 6-2 **WT:** 270
Born: 8–18–68, Atmore, AL
High school: Escambia County (Atmore, AL)
College: Auburn
Middleton's 23 receptions were his career best.

		RECEIVING			
YEAR	TEAM	G	REC	YDS	AVG	TD
1991 Washington	12	3	25	8.3	0
1992 Washington	16	7	50	7.1	0
1993 Washington	16	24	154	6.4	2
8 YR TOTALS	99	42	266	6.3	3
1993 RANK NFL TE		20	32	62	15
1994 PROJECTIONS	16	38	236	6.2	4

John Gesek No. 75/G

Full name: John Christian Gesek, Jr.
HT: 6-5 **WT:** 282
Born: 2-18-63, San Francisco, CA
High school: Bellflower (CA)
College: Sacramento State
He'll help an OL that allowed 40 sacks in '93.

YEAR	TEAM	G	RUSHING ATT	YDS	AVG	RANK AV RUSH	PASS YDS	RANK PASS YDS	SACKS	YDS. LOST
1991	Dallas	16	433	1711	4.0	14	3663	6	38	273
1992	Dallas	16	500	2121	4.2	9	3597	7	23	112
1993	Dallas	14	490	2161	4.4	3	3617	9	29	163
7 YR TOTALS		92								

Sterling Palmer No. 97/DE

HT: 6-3 **WT:** 256
Born: 2-4-71, Ft. Lauderdale, FL
College: Florida State
A rookie in '93, Palmer tied for the team lead with 5 tackles for losses, and was third on the team with 4.5 sacks.

YEAR	TEAM	G	INT	YDS	AVG	TD	SACKS	FUM REC	TD
1993	Washington	14	---	---	---	---	4.5	---	---
1 YR TOTALS		14	0	0	NA	0	4.5	0	0
1993 RANK NFL DL			16	NA	NA	NA	57	71	NA

Andre Collins No. 55/LB

Full name: Andre Pierre Collins
HT: 6-1 **WT:** 233
Born: 5-4-68, Riverside, NJ
High school: Cinnaminson (NJ)
College: Penn State
Collins had 3 sacks in game 6 vs. Phoenix.

YEAR	TEAM	G	INT	YDS	AVG	TD	SACKS	FUM REC	TD
1990	Washington	16	---	---	---	---	6.0	---	---
1991	Washington	16	2	33	16.5	1	3.0	---	---
1992	Washington	14	1	59	59.0	0	1.0	1	---
1993	Washington	13	1	5	5.0	0	6.0	---	---
4 YR TOTALS		59	4	97	24.3	1	16.0	1	0
1993 RANK NFL LB		-	17	32	30	5	16	81	NA
1994 PROJECTIONS		14	1	0	0.0	0	9	0	0

Tom Carter
No. 25/CB

HT: 5-11 **WT:** 181
Born: 9-5-72, St. Petersburg, FL
College: Notre Dame

As a rookie in '93, Carter had 6 INTs, tying for second in the NFC. He had a 29 yard interception return against Phoenix in Week 2.

YEAR	TEAM	G	INT	YDS	AVG	TD	SACKS	FUM REC	TD
1993	Washington	14	6	54.0	9.0	0	---	---	---
	1 YR TOTALS	14	6	54.0	9.0	0	0.0	0	0
1993	RANK NFL DB		7	35	85	27	49	94	NA

Brad Edwards
No. 27/FS

Full name: Bradford Wayne Edwards
HT: 6-2 **WT:** 207
Born: 3-22-66, Lumberton, NC
High school: Douglas Byrd (Fayetteville, NC)
College: South Carolina

Edwards was 1 of 3 'Skins to start all 16 games.

YEAR	TEAM	G	INT	YDS	AVG	TD	SACKS	FUM REC	TD
1991	Washington	16	4	52	13.0	0	---	---	---
1992	Washington	16	6	157	26.2	1	---	---	---
1993	Washington	16	1	17	17.0	0	---	1	0
	6 YR TOTALS	89	16	324	20.3	2	0.0	1	0
1993	RANK NFL DB		95	89	39	27	49	37	14
1994	PROJECTIONS	16	0	0	NA	0	0	2	0

Reggie Roby
No. 1/P

Full name: Reginald Henry Roby
HT: 6-2 **WT:** 243
Born: 7-30-61, Waterloo, IA
High school: East (Waterloo, IA)
College: Iowa

Roby's 44.2 average was second in the NFC.

YEAR	TEAM	G	NO	YARDS	LONG	AVG	BLK	IN20
1989	Miami	16	58	2458	NA	42.4	1	NA
1990	Miami	16	72	3022	NA	42.0	0	NA
1991	Miami	16	54	2466	64	45.7	1	17
1992	Miami	9	35	1443	60	41.2	0	11
1993	Washington	15	78	3447	60	44.2	0	25
	11 YR TOTALS	72	297	12836	64	43.2	2	53
1993	RANK NFL		10	8	18	4	19	6

1993 Playoff Recap

WILD CARD GAMES

  Green Bay 28, Detroit 24
  Kansas City 27, Pittsburgh 24 (OT)
  New York 17, Minnesota 10
  Los Angeles 42, Denver 24

NFC WILD CARD GAME

  At Pontiac, MI, January 8, 1994

Green Bay	0	7	14	7—28
Detroit	3	7	7	7—24

Scoring

Detroit: FG Hanson 47, 15:00 1st
Green Bay: Sharpe 12 pass from Favre (Jacke kick), 7:04 2nd
Detroit: Perriman 1 pass from Kramer (Hanson kick), 12:56 2nd
Detroit: Jenkins 15 interception return (Hanson kick), 6:40 3rd
Green Bay: Sharpe 28 pass from Favre (Jacke kick), 10:25 3rd
Green Bay: Teague 101 interception return (Jacke kick), 13:20 3rd
Detroit: D. Moore 5 run (Hanson kick), 6:33 4th
Green Bay: Sharpe 40 pass from Favre (Jacke kick), 14:05 4th
Attendance: 68, 479

Team Statistics

	Green Bay	Detroit
Points	28	24
Rushing yards	89	175
Passing yards	204	235
Return yards	233	101
Sacked–yards lost	0–0	5–13
Punts–average	4–40	3–48
Third downs	4–10	6–11
Fourth downs	0–0	0–1
Time of possession	24:26	35:34

Individual Statistics

Rushing: Green Bay, Thompson 12–41, E. Bennett 9–30, Favre 4–18; Detroit, Sanders 27–169, D. Moore 1–5, Kramer 1–1
Passing: Green Bay, Favre 15–26–1–204; Detroit, Kramer 22–31–2–248
Receiving: Green Bay, Sharpe 5–101, West 3–40, Thompson 3–32, E. Bennett 2–21, Clayton 1–9, Brooks 1–1; Detroit, Perriman 10–150, D. Moore 4–14, Holman 3–31, Green 2–33, Sanders 2–0, H. Moore 1–20
Interceptions: Green Bay, Teague 1–101, Buckley 1–0; Detroit, Jenkins 1–15
Sacks: Green Bay, White 2, T. Bennett 1.5, Holland 1.5
Missed Field Goals: None

AFC WILD CARD GAME

At Kansas City, MO, January 8, 1994

Pittsburgh	7	10	0	7	0—24
Kansas City	7	0	3	14	3—27

Scoring

Pittsburgh: Cooper 10 pass from O'Donnell (Anderson kick), 6:15 1st
Kansas City: Birden 23 pass from Krieg (Lowery kick), 13:21 1st
Pittsburgh: FG Anderson 30, 5:26 2nd
Pittsburgh: Mills 26 pass from O'Donnell (Anderson kick), 14:42 2nd
Kansas City: FG Lowery 23, 13:51 3rd
Kansas City: Allen 2 run (Lowery kick), 6:02 4th
Pittsburgh: Green 22 pass from O'Donnell (Anderson kick), 10:49 4th
Kansas City: Barnett 7 pass from Montana (Lowery kick), 13:17 4th
Kansas City: FG Lowery 32, 11:03 OT
Attendance: 74,515

Team Statistics

	Pittsburgh	Kansas City
Points	24	27
Rushing yards	97	125
Passing yards	276	276
Return yards	115	163
Sacked–yards lost	3–10	4–23
Punts-average	7–38	6–45
Third downs	9–19	4–13
Fourth downs	1–2	1–2
Time of possession	34:58	36:05

Individual Statistics

Rushing: Pittsburgh, L. Thompson 25–60, Hoge 6–27, Stone 3–11, O'Donnell 1–minus 1; Kansas City, Allen 21–67, Anders 5–27, Montana 4–13, McNair 2–9, Jones 1–9

Passing: Pittsburgh, O'Donnell 23–42–0–286; Kansas City, Montana 28–43–0–276, Krieg 1–1–0–23

Receiving: Pittsburgh, Graham 7–96, Mills 4–60, Hoge 3–43, Stone 3–36, L. Thompson 3–4, E. Green 2–37, Cooper 1–10; Kansas City, Cash 7–56, Birden 6–72, Allen 4–29, Anders 3–30, Barnett 3–30, Davis 2–47, Hayes 2–11, Hughes 1–15, McNair 1–9

Interceptions: None

Sacks: Pittsburgh, G. Williams 3, Lloyd 1; Kansas City, Smith 2, Bayless 1

Missed Field Goals: Kansas City, Lowery 43

NFC WILD CARD GAME

At East Rutherford, NJ, January 9, 1994

Minnesota	0	10	0	0—10
N.Y. Giants	3	0	14	0—17

Scoring

New York: FG Treadwell 26, 6:25 1st
Minnesota: C. Carter 40 pass from McMahon (Reveiz kick), 13:07 2nd
Minnesota: FG Reveiz 52, 14:58 2nd
New York: Hampton 51 run (Treadwell kick), 2:54 3rd
New York: Hampton 2 run (Treadwell kick), 9:23, 3rd
Attendance: 75,089

Team Statistics

	Minnesota	New York
Points	10	17
Rushing yards	79	176
Passing yards	181	94
Return yards	69	17
Sacked–yards lost	3–11	0–0
Punts-average	8–38	7–32
Third downs	2–13	7–17
Fourth downs	0–2	1–1
Time of possession	24:37	35:23

Individual Statistics

Rushing: Minnesota, Graham 19–69, McMahon 1–5, A. Carter 1–4, Craig 1–1; New York, Hampton 33–161, Simms 4–14, Bunch 1–1, Jackson 1–1, Tillman 2–minus 1

Passing: Minnesota, McMahon 12–25–0–145, Salisbury 3–9–0–47; New York, Simms 17–26–0–94

Receiving: Minnesota, C. Carter 4–83, Jordan 4–31, A. Carter 2–37, Graham 2–19, Reed 2–16, Ismail 1–6; New York, Hampton 6–24, Meggett 4–12, Calloway 2–30, Cross 2–11, M. Jackson 2–9, Pierce 1–8

Interceptions: None

Sacks: New York, Hamilton 2, Fox 1

Missed Field Goals: New York, Treadwell 34

AFC WILD CARD GAME

At Los Angeles, CA, January 9, 1994

Denver	7	14	0	3—24
L.A. Raiders	14	7	14	7—42

Scoring

Los Angeles: Horton 9 pass from Hostetler (Jaeger kick), 5:34 1st
Denver: Sharpe 23 pass from Elway (Elam kick), 8:48 1st
Los Angeles: T. Brown 65 pass from Hostetler (Jaeger kick), 12:35 1st
Denver: R. Johnson 16 pass from Elway (Elam kick), 4:54 2nd
Los Angeles: Jett 54 pass from Hostetler (Jaeger kick), 7:32 2nd
Denver: Russell 6 pass from Elway (Elam kick), 14:28 2nd
Los Angeles: McCallum 26 run (Jaeger kick), 6:52 3rd
Los Angeles: McCallum 2 run (Jaeger kick), 10:33 3rd
Denver: FG Elam 33, 2:24 4th
Los Angeles: McCallum 1 run (Jaeger kick), 8:17 4th
Attendance: 65,314

Team Statistics

	Denver	Los Angeles
Points	24	42
Rushing yards	56	136
Passing yards	331	291
Return yards	123	56
Sacked–yards lost	1–5	2–3
Punts-average	4–34	4–43
Third downs	4–14	5–9
Fourth downs	2–4	0–0
Time of possession	31:09	28:51

Individual Statistics

Rushing: Denver, Delpino 9–32, Elway 5–23, Rivers 1–2, Maddox 1–1, Milburn 2–minus 2; Los Angeles, McCallum 13–81, Montgomery 15–50, Hostetler 4–5

Passing: Denver, Elway 29–47–1–302, Maddox 3–7–0–34; Los Angeles, Hostetler 13–19–0–294

Receiving: Denver, Sharpe 13–156, Marshall 5–69, Milburn 5–8, Russell 2–31, Tillman 2–25, R. Johnson 2–19, K. Taylor 1–13, Rivers 1–8, Evans 1–7; Los Angeles, Jett 3–111, Brown 3–86, Horton 3–45, Montgomery 3–29, Wright 1–23

Interceptions: Los Angeles, Dorn 1–1

Sacks: Denver, Fletcher 2; Los Angeles, A. Smith 1

Missed Field Goals: None

SECOND ROUND GAMES

San Francisco 44, New York 3
Buffalo 29, Los Angeles 23
Dallas 27, Green Bay 17
Kansas City 20, Houston 20

NFC SECOND ROUND GAME

At San Francisco, CA, January 15, 1994

N.Y. Giants	0	3	0	0—3
San Francisco	9	14	14	7—44

Scoring

San Francisco: Watters 1 run (kick failed), 4:27 1st
San Francisco: FG Cofer 29, 10:07 1st
San Francisco: Watters 1 run (Cofer kick), :02 2nd
San Francisco: Watters 2 run (Cofer kick), 10:57 2nd
New York: FG Treadwell 25, 15:00 2nd
San Francisco: Watters 6 run (Cofer kick), 7:22 3rd
San Francisco: Watters 2 run (Cofer kick), 13:51 3rd
San Francisco: Logan 2 run (Cofer kick), 2:34 4th
Attendance: 67,143

Team Statistics

	New York	San Francisco
Points	3	44
Rushing yards	41	178
Passing yards	153	235
Return yards	108	60
Sacked–yards lost	4–27	1–6
Punts–average	5–40	3–45
Third downs	2–12	5–11
Fourth downs	1–4	0–1
Time of possession	25:15	34:45

Individual Statistics

Rushing: New York, Hampton 7–12, Brown 1–8, Tillman 4–8, Bunch 2–5, Meggett 2–5, Simms 2–3, M. Jackson 1–0; San Francisco, Watters 24–118, Logan 9–40, Young 3–17, Rathman 2–7, Lee 1–5, Rice 1–minus 9
Passing: New York, Simms 12–25–2–124, Brown 6–10–1–56; San Francisco, Young 17–22–0–226, Bono 2–2–0–15
Receiving: New York, McCaffrey 5–59, Meggett 3–17, Cross 2–32, Calloway 2–24, M. Jackson 2–16, Hampton 2–11, Tillman 1–14, Pierce 1–7; San Francisco, Watters 5–46, Jones 4–39, Rice 3–43, Taylor 2–74, Rathman 2–16, Lee 2–15, Logan 1–8
Interceptions: San Francisco, Caldwell 1–13, Davis 1–4, McDonald 1–4
Sacks: New York, Hamilton .5, McGhee .5; San Francisco, Stubblefield 2, T. Wilson 1, Washington .5, Walter .5
Missed Field Goals: None

AFC SECOND ROUND GAME

At Orchard Park, NY, January 15, 1994

L.A. Raiders	0	17	6	0—23	
Buffalo	0	13	9	7—29	

Scoring

Los Angeles: FG Jaeger 30, 1:13 2nd
Buffalo: K. Davis 1 run (kick failed), 1:30 2nd
Los Angeles: McCallum 1 run (Jaeger kick), 6:50 2nd
Los Angeles: McCallum 1 run (Jaeger kick), 13:03 2nd
Buffalo: T. Thomas 8 run (Christie kick), 14:10 2nd
Buffalo: Brooks 25 pass from Kelly (kick failed), 11:37 3rd
Buffalo: FG Christie 29, 14:01 3rd
Los Angeles: T. Brown 86 pass from Hostetler (kick failed), 14:30 3rd
Buffalo: Brooks 22 pass from Kelly (Christie kick), 2:55 4th
Attendance: 61,923

Team Statistics

	Los Angeles	Buffalo
Points	23	29
Rushing yards	110	75
Passing yards	215	280
Return yards	90	118
Sacked–yards lost	2–15	3–7
Punts–average	6–37	3–36
Third downs	2–11	7–14
Fourth downs	1–1	0–1
Time of possession	32:57	27:03

Individual Statistics

Rushing: Los Angeles, McCallum 19–56, Hostetler 5–29, Montgomery 9–22, Bell 2–3; Buffalo, T. Thomas 14–44, K. Davis 11–36, Kelly 5–minus 5

Passing: Los Angeles, Hostetler 14–20–0–230; Buffalo, Kelly 27–37–0–287

Receiving: Los Angeles, T. Brown 5–127, Montgomery 3–26, Horton 2–42, McCallum 1–15, Bell 1–2, Duff 1–5, Jett 1–3; Buffalo, Brooks 6–96, T. Thomas 6–48, Metzelaars 5–43, Reed 4–53, McKeller 3–21, K. Davis 1–16, Beebe 1–9, Gardner 1–1

Interceptions: None

Sacks: Los Angeles, M. Jones 1, A. Smith 1, Long 1; Buffalo, B. Smith 2

Missed Field Goals: Los Angeles, Jaeger 47; Buffalo, Christie 43

NFC SECOND ROUND GAME

At Irving, TX, January 16, 1994

Green Bay	3	0	7	7—17
Dallas	0	17	7	3—27

Scoring

Green Bay: FG Jacke 30, 11:40 1st
Dallas: Harper 25 pass from Aikman (Murray kick), 5:53 2nd
Dallas: FG Murray 41, 14:37 2nd
Dallas: Novacek 6 pass from Aikman (Murray kick), 14:55 2nd
Dallas: Irvin 19 pass from Aikman (Murray kick), 9:05 3rd
Green Bay: Brooks 13 pass from Favre (Jacke kick), 13:28 3rd
Dallas: FG Murray 38, 7:22 4th
Green Bay: Sharpe 29 pass from Favre (Jacke kick), 14:38 4th
Attendance: 64,790

Team Statistics

	Green Bay	Dallas
Points	17	27
Rushing yards	31	97
Passing yards	327	284
Return yards	143	53
Sacked–yards lost	2–4	4–18
Punts–average	3–9	3–44
Third downs	6–14	6–13
Fourth downs	1–3	0–1
Time of possession	25:28	34:32

Individual Statistics

Rushing: Green Bay, Thompson 7–28, E. Bennett 6–3; Dallas, E. Smith 13–60, Coleman 5–19, Johnston 3–12, Lassic 2–6, Aikman 3–0, Bates 1–0
Passing: Green Bay, Favre 28–45–2–331; Dallas, Aikman 28–37–2–302
Receiving: Green Bay, E. Bennett 9–53, Sharpe 6–128, West 4–41, Thompson 3–54, Brooks 3–39, Ingram 2–9, Lewis 1–7; Dallas, Irvin 9–126, Novacek 6–59, Johnston 6–43, Harper 2–33, E. Smith 2–27, Coleman 2–6, Lassic 1–8
Interceptions: Green Bay, Butler 1–14, Buckley 1–0; Dallas, Woodson 1–5, Haley 1–0
Sacks: Green Bay, T. Bennett 1.5, Paup 1, Butler 1, Brock .5; Dallas, Tolbert 1, Jeffcoat 1
Missed Field Goals: Green Bay, Jacke 49

AFC SECOND ROUND GAME

At Houston,TX, January 16, 1994

Kansas City	0	0	7	21—28
Houston	10	0	0	10—20

Scoring

Houston: FG Del Greco 49, 3:50 1st
Houston: G. Brown 2 run (Del Greco kick), 13:01 1st
Kansas City: Cash 7 pass from Montana (Lowery kick), 4:41 3rd
Houston: FG Del Greco 43, 5:23 4th
Kansas City: Birden 11 pass from Montana (Lowery kick), 6:22 4th
Kansas City: Davis 18 pass from Montana (Lowery kick), 7:16 4th
Houston: Givins 7 pass from Moon (Del Greco kick), 11:15 4th
Kansas City: Allen 21 run (Lowery kick), 13:05 4th
Attendance: 64,011

Team Statistics

	Kansas City	Houston
Points	28	20
Rushing yards	71	39
Passing yards	283	238
Return yards	94	76
Sacked–yards lost	2–16	9–68
Punts–average	5–45	5–49
Third downs	6–12	7–15
Fourth downs	0–1	0–1
Time of possession	24:18	35:42

Individual Statistics

Rushing: Kansas City, Allen 14–74, Anders 1–0, Montana 1–minus 1, Krieg 2–minus 2; Houston, Moon 3–22, G. Brown 11–17

Passing: Kansas City, Montana 22–38–2–299, Krieg 0–0–0–0; Houston, Moon 32–43–1–306

Receiving: Kansas City, Birden 6–60, Davis 5–96, Cash 4–80, Barnett 2–24, McNair 2–9, Allen 1–12, Hayes 1–9, F. Jones 1–9; Houston, Jeffires 9–88, Givins 7–63, Wellman 6–80, Duncan 6–49, G. Brown 4–26

Interceptions: Kansas City, Mincy 1–12; Houston, Hoage 1–0, Jackson 1–14

Sacks: Kansas City, B. Thompson 2, Thomas 2, Phillips 2, A. Lewis 2, Smith 1; Houston, Lathon 1, Fuller 1

Missed Field Goals: None

CONFERENCE CHAMPIONSHIPS

> Dallas 38, San Francisco 21
> Buffalo 30, Kansas City 13

NFC CHAMPIONSHIP

At Irving, TX, January 23, 1994

San Francisco	0	7	7	7—21
Dallas	7	21	7	3—38

Scoring

Dallas: E. Smith 5 run (Murray kick), 6:19 1st
San Francisco: Rathman 7 pass from Young (Cofer kick), :05 2nd
Dallas: Johnston 4 run (Murray kick), 5:12 2nd
Dallas: E. Smith 11 pass from Aikman (Murray kick), 8:56 2nd
Dallas: Novacek 19 pass from Aikman (Murray kick), 14:02 2nd
San Francisco: Watters 4 run (Cofer kick), 9:13 3rd
Dallas: Harper 42 pass from Kosar (Murray kick), 12:36 3rd
Dallas: FG Murray 50, 5:08 4th
San Francisco: Young 1 run (Cofer kick), 10:54 4th
Attendance: 64,902

Team Statistics

	San Francisco	Dallas
Points	21	38
Rushing yards	84	124
Passing yards	275	253
Return yards	95	49
Sacked–yards lost	4–12	2–7
Punts–average	4–46	4–41
Third downs	5–15	8–13
Fourth downs	1–2	0–0
Time of possession	26:27	33:33

Individual Statistics

Rushing: San Francisco, Young 7–38, Watters 12–37, Rathman 2–9; Dallas, E. Smith 23–88, Aikman 3–25, Johnston 4–13, Lassic 1–1, Kosar 2–minus 3

Passing: San Francisco, Young 27–45–1–287; Dallas, Aikman 14–18–0–177, Kosar 5–9–0–83, Harper 0–1–0–0

Receiving: San Francisco, Watters 7–33, Rice 6–83, Taylor 3–61, J. Williams 3–44, B. Jones 3–26, Logan 3–21, Turner 1–12, Rathman 1–7; Dallas, E. Smith 7–85, Harper 4–78, Novacek 4–57, Irvin 2–23, Johnston 2–17

Interceptions: Dallas, Everett 1–14

Sacks: San Francisco, Griffin 1, Brown 1; Dallas, Haley 1, Jeffcoat 1, Tolbert 1, Maryland 1

Missed Field Goals: None

AFC CHAMPIONSHIP

At Orchard Park, NY, January 23, 1994

Kansas City	6	0	7	0—13
Buffalo	7	13	0	10—30

Scoring

Buffalo: T. Thomas 12 run (Christie kick), 8:11 1st
Kansas City: FG Lowery 31, 12:46 1st
Kansas City: FG Lowery 31, 14.21 1st
Buffalo: T. Thomas 3 run (Christie kick), 2:58 2nd
Buffalo: FG Christie 23, 7:56 2nd
Buffalo: FG Christie 25, 12:59 2nd
Kansas City: Allen 1 run (Lowery kick), 11:54 3rd
Buffalo: FG Christie 18, 3:05 4th
Buffalo: T. Thomas 3 run (Christie kick), 9:30 4th
Attendance: 76,642

Team Statistics

	Kansas City	Buffalo
Points	13	30
Rushing yards	52	229
Passing yards	286	160
Return yards	100	153
Sacked–yards lost	4–37	0–0
Punts–average	6–41	4–33
Third downs	7–17	5–12
Fourth downs	1–1	0–0
Time of possession	29:20	30:40

Individual Statistics

Rushing: Kansas City, Allen 18–50, Anders 2–1, Montana 1–1; Buffalo, T. Thomas 33–186, K. Davis 10–32, Reed 1–8, Kelly 2–3
Passing: Kansas City, Montana 9–23–1–125, Krieg 16–29–1–198; Buffalo, Kelly 17–27–0–160
Receiving: Kansas City, Cash 6–87, W. Davis 5–57, Birden 4–60, Allen 2–36, McNair 2–33, Hayes 2–14, E. Thompson 1–12, Hughes 1–11, Anders 1–7, Szott 1–6; Buffalo, Reed 4–49, Brooks 4–34, Metzelaars 4–29, Thomas 2–22, Beebe 2–19, McKeller 1–7
Interceptions: Buffalo, Jones 1–15, Williams 1–0
Sacks: Buffalo, Smith 1, Wright 1, Hansen 1, Talley 1
Missed Field Goals: None

1994 Super Bowl recap

At Atlanta, GA, January 30, 1994

Dallas	6	0	14	10—30
Buffalo	3	10	0	0—13

SCORING SUMMARY

1ST QTR: DAL—FG, EDDIE MURRAY 41 YD, 2:19. Drive: 5 plays, 24 yards in 2:19.
Key plays: K. Williams 50–yard kickoff return to Buffalo 48; Aikman 20–yard pass to Irvin to Buffalo 28.

BUF—FG, STEVE CHRISTIE 54 YD, 4:41. Drive: 8 plays, 43 yards in 2:12.
Key plays: Kelly 11–yard pass to Reed to Buffalo 23; Kelly 24–yard pass to Thomas to Dallas 39.

DAL—FG, EDDIE MURRAY 24 YD, 11:05. Drive: 7 plays, 43 yards in 4:02.
Key plays: Woodson recovery of Thomas fumble at midfield; Aikman 8–yard pass to E. Smith to Buffalo 39; Aikman 24–yard pass to Harper to Buffalo 15.

2ND QTR: BUF—TD, THURMAN THOMAS 4 YD RUN (CHRISTIE KICK), 2:34. Drive: 17 plays, 80 yards in 6:29. Key plays: D. Thomas running into the kicker penalty to Buffalo 46; K. Davis 2–yard run on 3rd–and–1 to Dallas 32; Kelly 6–yard pass to Beebe on 3rd–and–3 to Dallas 3.

BUF—FG, STEVE CHRISTIE 28 YD, 15:00. Drive: 7 plays, 38 yards in 1:03.
Key plays: Odomes 40–yard interception return to Dallas 48; Kelly 13–yard pass to T. Thomas to Dallas 35; Kelly 22–yard pass to Reed to Dallas 13.

3RD QTR: DAL—TD, JAMES WASHINGTON 46 YD FUMBLE RETURN (MURRAY KICK), 0:55

DAL—TD, EMMITT SMITH 16 YD RUN (MURRAY KICK), 6:18. Drive: 8 plays, 64 yards in 4:32. Key plays: E. Smith 7 carries for 62 yards.

4TH QTR: DAL—TD, EMMITT SMITH 1 YD RUN (MURRAY KICK), 5:10. Drive: 9 plays, 34 yards in 5:03. Key plays: Washington 12–yard interception return to Buffalo 34; Aikman 16–yard pass to Harper on 3rd–and–8 to Buffalo 6.

DAL—FG, EDDIE MURRAY 20 YD, 12:10. Drive: 10 plays, 49 yards in 4:10.
Key plays: Aikman 4–yard pass to Novacek on 3rd–and–2 to Buffalo 39; Aikman 35–yard pass to Harper on 3rd–and–8 to Buffalo 1.

TEAM STATISTICS

	Dallas	Buffalo
FIRST DOWNS	20	22
Rushing	6	6
Passing	14	15
Penalty	0	1
THIRD DOWNS	5–13	5–17
FOURTH DOWNS	1–1	2–3
TOTAL NET YARDS	341	314
Total plays	64	80
Average gain	5.3	3.9
NET YARDS RUSHING	137	87
Rushes	35	27
Average per rush	3.9	3.2
NET YARDS PASSING	204	227
Completed–attempted	19–27	31–50
Yards per pass	7.6	4.5
Sacked–yards lost	2–3	3–33
Had intercepted	1	1
PUNTs–aVERAGE	4–43.8	5–37.6
RETURN YARDAGE	89	190
Punts–returns	1–5	1–5
Kickoffs–returns	2–72	6–144
Interceptions–returns	1–12	1–41
PENALTIES–YARDS	6–50	1–10
FUMBLES–LOST	0–0	3–2
TIME OF POSSESSION	34:29	25:31

INDIVIDUAL LEADERS

Dallas rushing: Emmitt Smith 30–132, Kevin Williams 1–6, Troy Aikman 1–3, Daryl Johnston 1–0, Bernie Kosar 1–(minus 1), Lincoln Coleman 1–(minus 3).

Buffalo rushing: Kenneth Davis 9–38, Thurman Thomas 16–37, Jim Kelly 2–12

Dallas passing: Troy Aikman 19–27–1–207

Buffalo passing: Jim Kelly 31–50–1–260

Dallas receiving: Michael Irvin 5–66, Jay Novacek 5–26, Emmitt Smith 4–26, Alvin Harper 3–75, Daryl Johnston 2–14

Buffalo receiving: Bill Brooks 7–63, Thurman Thomas 7–52, Andre Reed 6–75, Don Beebe 6–60, Kenneth Davis 3–(–5), Pete Metzelaars 1–8, Keith McKeller 1–7

Interceptions: Dallas (James Washington 1 for 12 yards); Buffalo (Nate Odomes 1 for 41 yards)

Officials: Referee–Bob McElwee, Umpire–Art Demmas, Head linesman–Sid Semon, Line judge–Tom Barnes, Back judge–Al Jury, Side judge–NathanJones, Field judge–Don Orr

Missed field goals: None

Attendance: 72,817

Time: 3:16

1994 Pro Bowl Rosters

(x–voted to start; y–did not play due to injury)

NATIONAL FOOTBALL CONFERENCE

OFFENSE

Quarterbacks — x–Troy Aikman, Dallas; Steve Young, San Francisco; Phil Simms, New York Giants

Running backs — x–Emmitt Smith, Dallas; x–Barry Sanders, Detroit; Jerome Bettis, L.A. Rams; Daryl Johnston, Dallas

Wide receivers — x–Jerry Rice, San Francisco; x–Michael Irvin, Dallas; Sterling Sharpe, Green Bay; Andre Rison, Atlanta

Tight ends — x–Jay Novacek, Dallas; Brent Jones, San Francisco

Tackles — x–Harris Barton, San Francisco; x–Eric Williams, Dallas; y–Jumbo Elliott, New York Giants; Lomas Brown, Detroit

Guards — x–Nate Newton, Dallas; x–Randall McDaniel, Minnesota; Guy McIntyre, San Francisco

Centers — x–y–Mark Stepnoski, Dallas; x–Jesse Sapolu, San Francisco; Bart Oates, New York Giants

Kicker — Norm Johnson, Atlanta

DEFENSE

Ends — x–Richard Dent, Chicago; x–Reggie White, Green Bay; Chris Doleman, Minnesota

Interior linemen — x–Sean Gilbert, L.A. Rams; x–John Randle, Minnesota; Russell Maryland, Dallas

Outside linebackers — x–Rickey Jackson, New Orleans; x–Renaldo Turnbull, New Orleans; Pat Swilling, Detroit

Inside linebackers — x–Hardy Nickerson, Tampa Bay; Ken Norton, Dallas

Cornerbacks — x–Deion Sanders, Atlanta; x–Eric Allen, Philadelphia; Donnell Woolford, Chicago

Safeties — x–Mark Carrier, Chicago; x–Tim McDonald, San Francisco; Thomas Everett, Dallas

Punter — Rich Camarillo, Phoenix

Kick returner — Tyrone Hughes, New Orleans

Special teams — Elbert Shelley, Atlanta

AMERICAN FOOTBALL CONFERENCE

OFFENSE

Quarterbacks — x–John Elway, Denver; y–Joe Montana, Kansas City; Warren Moon, Houston; Boomer Esiason, New York Jets

Running backs — x–Marcus Allen, Kansas City; x–Thurman Thomas, Buffalo; y–Barry Foster, Pittsburgh; Keith Byars, Miami; Chris Warren, Seattle

Wide receivers — x–y–Webster Slaughter, Houston; x–Tim Brown, L.A. Raiders; x–Anthony Miller, San Diego; Irving Fryar, Miami; Andre Reed, Buffalo

Tight ends — x–Shannon Sharpe, Denver; y–Keith Jackson, Miami; Eric Green, Pittsburgh

Tackles — x–Richmond Webb, Miami; x–Howard Ballard, Buffalo; John Alt, Kansas City

Guards — x–Mike Munchak, Houston; x–Steve Wisniewski, L.A. Raiders; Keith Sims, Miami

Centers — x–Bruce Matthews, Houston; Dermontti Dawson, Pittsburgh

Kicker — Gary Anderson, Pittsburgh

DEFENSE

Ends — x–Bruce Smith, Buffalo; x–Neil Smith, Kansas City; Leslie O'Neal, San Diego

Interior linemen — x–Cortez Kennedy, Seattle; x–Ray Childress, Houston; Michael Dean Perry, Cleveland

Outside linebackers — x–Derrick Thomas, Kansas City; x–Greg Lloyd, Pittsburgh; Cornelius Bennett, Buffalo

Inside linebackers — x–Junior Seau, San Diego; Karl Mecklenburg, Denver

Cornerbacks — x–Ron Woodson, Pittsburgh; x–Nate Odomes, Buffalo; Terry McDaniel, L.A. Raiders

Safeties — x–Steve Atwater, Denver; x–Dennis Smith, Denver; Eugene Robinson, Seattle

Punter — Greg Montgomery, Houston

Kick returner — Eric Metcalf, Cleveland

Special teams — Steve Tasker, Buffalo

NFL PRO BOWL
At Honolulu, HI, February 6, 1994

NFC	3	0	7	7—17
AFC	0	3	0	0—3

Scoring
NFC: FG Johnson 35, 10:28 1st
AFC: FG Anderson 25, 13:51 2nd
NFC: Bettis 4 run (Johnson kick), 13:33 3rd
NFC: C. Carter 15 pass from Hebert (Johnson kick), 0:53 4th
Attendance: 50,026

Team Statistics

	NFC	AFC
Points	17	3
Rushing yards	110	81
Passing yards	240	190
Return yards	61	219
Sacked–yards lost	1–11	3–10
Punts–average	5–43	5–42
Third downs	6–17	2–13
Fourth downs	2–2	1–1
Time of possession	38:22	21:38

Individual Statistics
Rushing: NFC, Bettis 14–49, Watters 11–25, Rice 1–12, Hampton 5–11, Young 1–7, Johnston 3–5, Favre 1–2, Hebert 1–minus 1; AFC, Warren 4–64, Thomas 4–11, Byars 3–8, Moon 1–3, Esiason 1–2, Allen 1–minus 1
Passing: NFC, Young 4–14–0–48, Favre 14–24–0–135 (2 INT), Hebert 4–6–1–68; AFC, Elway 5–13–0–45 (2 INT), Moon 3–8–0–26, Esiason 13–22–0–129 (2 INT)
Receiving: NFC, Rison 6–86, C. Carter 3–52, Novacek 3–21, Rison 6–86, C. Carter 3–52, Novacek 3–21, Hampton 3–13, Rice 2–30, B. Jones 1–13, Irvin 1–12, Bettis 1–10, Watters 1–9, Johnston 1–5; AFC, Byars 6–53, Sh. Sharpe 3–28, Green 2–35, Fryar 2–20, Miller 2–19, Brown 2–19, Allen 2–14, Metcalf 1–9, Jeffires 1–3
Interceptions: NFC, E. Allen 1, Sanders 1, Woolford 1, R. Jackson 1; AFC, Robinson 1, McDaniel 1
Sacks: NFC, Doleman 1, Randle 2; AFC, D. Thomas 1
Missed Field Goals: NFC, Johnson 39, 24

1993 NFL Statistics

RUSHING

NFL LEADING RUSHERS

PLAYER/TEAM	ATT	YARDS	AVG	LONG	TD
Emmitt Smith, DAL	283	1486	5.3	62t	9
Jerome Bettis, Rams	294	1429	4.9	71t	7
Thurman Thomas, BUF	355	1315	3.7	27	6
Erric Pegram, ATL	292	1185	4.1	29	3
Barry Sanders, DET	243	1115	4.6	42	3
Leonard Russell, NE	300	1088	3.6	21	7
Rodney Hampton, NYG	292	1077	3.7	20	5
Chris Warren, SEA	273	1072	3.9	45t	7
Reggie Brooks, WAS	223	1063	4.8	85t	3
Ron Moore, PHO	263	1018	3.9	20	9
Gary Brown, HOU	195	1002	5.1	26	6
Ricky Watters, SF	208	950	4.6	39	10
Johnnie Johnson, NYJ	198	821	4.1	57t	3
Rod Bernstine, DEN	223	816	3.7	24	4
Marcus Allen, KC	206	764	3.7	39	12
Leroy Thompson, PIT	205	763	3.7	36	3
Herschel Walker, PHI	174	746	4.3	35	1
Marion Butts, SD	185	746	4.0	27	4
Barry Foster, PIT	177	711	4.0	38	8
Roosevelt Potts, IND	179	711	4.0	34	0

NFL LEADERS — TOTAL YARDS FROM SCRIMMAGE

PLAYER/TEAM	TOTAL	RUSH	REC
Emmitt Smith, DAL	1900	1486	414
Thurman Thomas, BUF	1702	1315	387
Jerome Bettis, Rams	1673	1429	244
Jerry Rice, SF	1572	69	1503
Erric Pegram, ATL	1487	1185	302
Johnnie Johnson, NYJ	1462	821	641
Herschel Walker, PHI	1356	746	610
Michael Irvin, DAL	1336	6	1330
Leonard Russell, NE	1333	1088	245
Barry Sanders, DET	1320	1115	205
Rodney Hampton, NYG	1287	1077	210
Sterling Sharpe, GB	1282	8	1274
Ricky Watters, SF	1276	950	326
Terry Kirby, MIA	1264	390	874
Reggie Brooks, WAS	1249	1063	186
Andre Rison, ATL	1242	0	1242
Gary Brown, HOU	1242	1002	240
Rod Bernstine, DEN	1188	816	372
Tim Brown, Raiders	1187	7	1180
Chris Warren, SEA	1171	1072	99

RUSHING-AFC

PLAYER/TEAM	ATT	YARDS	AVG	LONG	TD
Aguiar, L., NYJ	3	−27	−9.0	5	0
Allen, M., KC	206	764	3.7	39	12
Anders, K., KC	75	291	3.9	18	0
Baldwin, R., CLE	18	61	3.4	11	0
Ball, E., CIN	8	37	4.6	18	1
Barnett, T., KC	1	3	3.0	3	0
Bates, M., SEA	2	12	6.0	6	0
Baxter, B., NYJ	174	559	3.2	16	7

PLAYER/TEAM	ATT	YARDS	AVG	LONG	TD
Bell, N., Raiders	67	180	2.7	12	1
Benjamin, R., CIN	3	5	1.7	2	0
Bernstine, R., DEN	223	816	3.7	24	4
Bieniemy, E., SD	33	135	4.1	12	1
Bledsoe, D., SEA	6	62	10.4	26	0
Bledsoe, D., NE	32	82	2.6	15	0
Brooks, B., BUF	3	30	10.0	15	0
Brown, G., HOU	195	1002	5.1	26	6
Brown, Tim, Raiders	2	7	3.5	14	0
Butts, M., SD	185	746	4.0	27	4
Byars, K., MIA	64	269	4.2	77t	3
Carlson, C., HOU	14	41	2.9	10t	2
Carrier, M., CLE	4	26	6.5	15t	1
Carter, Dale, KC	1	2	2.0	2	0
Cash, Keith, KC	1	0	0.0	0	0
Chaffey, P., NYJ	5	17	3.4	7	0
Coleman, P., HOU	1	1	1.0	1	0
Crittenden, R., NE	1	−3	−3.0	−3	0
Croom, C., NE	60	198	3.3	22	1
Culver, R., IND	65	150	2.3	9	3
Cuthbert, R., PIT	1	7	7.0	7	0
Davis, K., BUF	109	391	3.6	19	6
DeBerg, S., MIA	4	−4	−1.0	−1	0
Delpino, R., DEN	131	445	3.4	18	8
Elway, J., DEN	44	153	3.5	18	0
Esiason, B., NYJ	45	118	2.6	17	1
Evans, V., Raiders	14	51	3.6	17	0
Fenner, D., CIN	121	482	4.0	26	1
Fina, J., BUF	1	−2	−2.0	−2	0
Foster, B., PIT	177	711	4.0	38	8
Friesz, J., SD	10	3	0.3	2	0
Fryar, I., MIA	3	−4	−1.3	2	0
Gardner, C., BUF	20	56	2.8	8	0
Gash, S., NE	48	149	3.1	14	1
Gelbaugh, S., SEA	1	−1	−1.0	−1	0
George, J., IND	13	39	3.0	14	0
Givins, E., HOU	6	19	3.2	16	0
Gossett, J., Raiders	1	−10	−10.0	−10	0
Green, H., CIN	215	589	2.7	25	0
Harmon, R., SD	46	216	4.7	19	0
Hendrickson, S., SD	1	0	0.0	0	0
Higgs, M., MIA	186	693	3.7	31	3
Hoard, L., CLE	56	227	4.1	30	0
Hoge, M., PIT	51	249	4.9	30	1
Hostetler, J., Raiders	55	202	3.7	19	5
Humphries, S., SD	8	37	4.6	27	0
Ismail, R., Raiders	4	−5	−1.3	10	0
Jackson, Mi., CLE	1	1	1.0	1	0
Jefferson, S., SD	5	53	10.6	33	0
Jett, Ja., Raiders	1	0	0.0	0	0
Johnson, A., IND	95	331	3.5	14	1
Johnson, J., NYJ	198	821	4.1	57t	3
Johnson, Tr., SEA	2	8	4.0	5	0
Jones, F., KC	5	34	6.8	13	0
Jones, James, CLE	2	2	1.0	1t	1
Jordan, R., Raiders	12	33	2.8	12	0

PLAYER/TEAM	ATT	YARDS	AVG	LONG	TD
Kelly, Ji., BUF	36	102	2.8	17	0
Kidd, J., SD	3	-13	-4.3	2t	1
Kirby, T., MIA	119	390	3.3	20	3
Klingler, D., CIN	41	282	6.9	29	0
Kosar, B., CLE	14	19	1.4	10	0
Krieg, D., KC	21	24	1.1	20	0
Lewis, N., SD	3	2	0.7	7	0
Mack, K., CLE	10	33	3.3	7	1
Maddox, T., DEN	2	-2	-1.0	-1	0
Majkowski, D., IND	2	4	2.0	4	0
Marino, D., MIA	9	-4	-0.4	4t	1
Martin, K., SEA	1	0	0.0	0	0
Martin, T., MIA	1	6	6.0	6	0
Maston, L., HOU	1	10	10.0	10	0
Mathis, T., NYJ	2	20	10.0	17t	1
Mayes, R., SEA	1	2	2.0	2	0
McCallum, N., Raiders	37	114	3.1	14	3
McDuffie, O.J., MIA	1	-4	-4.0	-4	0
McGwire, D., SEA	1	-1	-1.0	-1	0
McNair, T., KC	51	278	5.5	47	2
Means, N., SD	160	645	4.0	65t	8
Metcalf, E., CLE	129	611	4.7	55	1
Milburn, G., DEN	52	231	4.4	26	0
Miles, O., CIN	22	56	2.5	15	1
Miller, A., SD	1	0	0.0	0	0
Mills, E., PIT	3	12	4.0	19	0
Mirer, R., SEA	68	343	5.0	33	3
Mitchell, S., MIA	21	89	4.2	32	0
Montana, J., KC	25	64	2.6	17	0
Montgomery, T., Raiders	37	106	2.9	15	0
Moon, W., HOU	48	145	3.0	35	1
Moore, R., NYJ	1	-6	-6.0	-6	0
Murrell, A., NYJ	34	157	4.6	37t	1
Parmalee, B., MIA	4	16	4.0	12	0
Pederson, D., MIA	2	-1	-0.5	0	0
Philcox, T., CLE	2	3	1.5	3t	1
Potts, R., IND	179	711	4.0	34	0
Query, J., CIN	2	13	6.5	8	0
Reed, A., BUF	9	21	2.3	15	0
Reich, F., BUF	6	-6	-1.0	-1	0
Richardson, B., HOU	2	9	4.5	11	0
Rivers, R., DEN	15	50	3.3	14	1
Robinson, Gr., Raiders	156	591	3.8	16	1
Robinson, P., CIN	1	6	6.0	6	0
Rouen, T., DEN	1	0	0.0	0	0
Russell, L., NE	300	1088	3.6	21	7
Saxon, J., MIA	5	13	2.6	9	0
Saxon, M., NE	2	2	1.0	2	0
Schroeder, J., CIN	10	41	4.1	20	0
Secules, S., NE	8	33	4.1	13	0
Smith, St., Raiders	47	156	3.3	13	0
Stark, R., IND	1	11	11.0	11	0
Stephens, J., KC	6	18	3.0	7	0
Stone, D., PIT	12	121	10.1	38t	1
Testaverde, V., CLE	18	74	4.1	14	0
Thomas, B., NYJ	59	221	3.7	24	1

PLAYER/TEAM	ATT	YARDS	AVG	LONG	TD
Thomas, Do., SEA	1	4	4.0	4	0
Thomas, T., BUF	355	1315	3.7	27	6
Thompson, E., KC	11	28	2.5	14	0
Thompson, L., PIT	205	763	3.7	36	3
Tillman, O., HOU	0	01	10.1	01	0
Tomczak, M., PIT	5	−4	−0.8	2	0
Toner, E., IND	2	6	3.0	6	0
Trudeau, J., IND	5	3	0.6	2	0
Turner, K., NE	50	231	4.6	49	0
Turner, N., BUF	11	36	3.3	10	0
Vardell, T., CLE	171	644	3.8	54	3
Vaughn, J., SEA	36	153	4.3	37	0
Verdin, C., IND	3	33	11.0	29	0
Warren, C., SEA	273	1072	3.9	45t	7
Wellman, G., HOU	2	6	3.0	4	0
White, Lo., HOU	131	465	3.5	14	2
Williams, H., KC	42	149	3.5	19	0
Williams, J.L., SEA	82	371	4.5	38	3
Woodson, R., PIT	1	0	0.0	0	0
Worley, T., PIT	10	33	3.3	8	0
Zolak, S., NE	1	0	0.0	0	0

RUSHING-NFC

PLAYER/TEAM	ATT	YARDS	AVG	LONG	TD
Agee, T., DAL	6	13	2.2	6	0
Aikman, T., DAL	32	125	3.9	20	0
Alexander, H., ATL	2	−7	−3.5	0	0
Anderson, Ga., TB/DET	28	56	2.0	13	0
Anderson, N., CHI	202	646	3.2	45	4
Armstrong, Ty., TB	2	5	2.5	4	0
Bailey, J., PHO	49	253	5.2	31	1
Barnhardt, T., NO	1	18	18.0	18	0
Bennett, E., GB	159	550	3.5	19	9
Bettis, J., Rams	294	1429	4.9	71t	7
Beuerlein, S., PHO	22	45	2.0	20	0
Blount, E., PHO	5	28	5.6	7	1
Bono, S., SF	12	14	1.2	10	1
Brister, B., PHI	20	39	2.0	13	0
Brooks, Re., WAS	223	1063	4.8	85t	3
Brooks, Ro., GB	3	17	5.7	21	0
Broussard, S., ATL	39	206	5.3	26	1
Brown, Da., NYG	3	−4	−1.3	−1	0
Brown, Derek, NO	180	705	3.9	60	2
Buck, M., NO	1	0	0.0	0	0
Bunch, J., NYG	33	128	3.9	13	2
Byner, E., WAS	23	105	4.6	16	1
Camarillo, R., PHO	1	0	0.0	0	0
Carter, A., MIN	7	19	2.7	9	0
Carter, De., SF	10	72	7.2	50t	1
Centers, L., PHO	25	152	6.1	33	0
Chandler, C., PHO	3	2	0.7	1	0
Christian, B., CHI	8	19	2.4	12	0
Cobb, R., TB	221	658	3.0	16	3
Coleman, L., DAL	34	132	3.9	16	2
Conklin, C., WAS	2	−2	−1.0	−1	0
Conway, C., CHI	5	44	8.8	18	0

PLAYER/TEAM	ATT	YARDS	AVG	LONG	TD
Copeland, H., TB	3	34	11.3	22	0
Craig, R., MIN	38	119	3.1	11	1
Cunningham, R., PHI	18	110	6.1	26	1
Detmer, Ty, GB	1	−2	−2.0	−2	0
Dickerson, E., ATL	26	91	3.5	10	0
Drayton, T., Rams	1	7	7.0	7	0
Early, Q., NO	2	32	16.0	26	0
Ellard, H., Rams	2	18	9.0	15	0
Erickson, C., TB	26	96	3.7	15	0
Ervins, R., WAS	50	201	4.0	18	0
Evans, C., MIN	14	32	2.3	5	0
Everett, J., Rams	19	38	2.0	14	0
Favre, B., GB	58	216	3.7	27	1
Feagles, J., PHI	2	6	3.0	6	0
Gainer, D., DAL	9	29	3.2	8	0
Gannon, R., WAS	21	88	4.2	12	1
Garrett, J., DAL	8	−8	−1.0	0	0
Gary, C., Rams	79	293	3.7	15	1
Graham, K., NYG	2	−3	−1.5	−1	0
Graham, S., MIN	118	488	4.1	31	3
Green, Ro., CHI	15	29	1.9	10	0
Hampton, R., NYG	292	1077	3.7	20	5
Harbaugh, J., CHI	60	277	4.6	25	4
Harris, Ru., TB	7	29	4.1	12	0
Hearst, G., PHO	76	264	3.5	57	1
Hebert, B., ATL	24	49	2.0	14	0
Hebron, V., PHI	84	297	3.5	33	3
Heyward, C., CHI	68	206	3.0	11	0
Hilliard, D., NO	50	165	3.3	16	2
Howard, De., WAS	2	17	8.5	9	0
Irvin, M., DAL	2	6	3.0	9	0
Ismail, Q., MIN	3	14	4.7	6	0
Jackson, M., NYG	3	25	8.3	20	0
Johnston, D., DAL	24	74	3.1	11	3
Jones, Er., Rams	1	4	4.0	4	0
Joseph, J., PHI	39	140	3.6	12	0
Kinchen, T., Rams	2	10	5.0	8	0
Kosar, B., DAL	9	7	0.8	4	0
Kramer, E., DET	10	5	0.5	4	0
Lang, D., Rams	9	29	3.2	28	0
Lassic, D., DAL	75	269	3.6	15	3
Lee, A., SF	72	230	3.2	13	1
Lester, T., Rams	11	74	6.7	26	0
Lewis, D., CHI	7	13	1.9	3	0
Logan, M., SF	58	280	4.8	45	7
Lynch, E., DET	53	207	3.9	15	2
Matthews, A., DET	2	7	3.5	9	0
McAfee, F., NO	51	160	3.1	27	1
McDowell, A., TB	2	6	3.0	3	0
McMahon, J., MIN	33	96	2.9	16	0
Meggett, D., NYG	69	329	4.8	23	0
Miller, C., ATL	2	11	5.5	6	0
Mims, D., ATL	1	3	3.0	3	0
Mitchell, B., WAS	63	246	3.9	29t	3
Monk, A., WAS	1	−1	−1.0	−1	0
Moore, De., DET	88	405	4.6	48	3

PLAYER/TEAM	ATT	YARDS	AVG	LONG	TD
Moore, Ro., PHO	263	1018	3.9	20	9
Musgrave, B., SF	3	–3	–1.0	–1	0
Muster, B., NO	64	214	3.3	18	3
Neal, L., NO	21	175	8.3	74t	1
Ned, D., NO	9	71	7.9	35t	1
Novacek, J., DAL	1	2	2.0	2t	1
O'Brien, K., PHI	4	17	4.3	11	0
Peete, R., DET	45	165	3.7	28	1
Pegram, E., ATL	292	1185	4.1	29	3
Perriman, B., DET	4	16	4.0	16	0
Pritchard, M., ATL	2	4	2.0	4	0
Proehl, R., PHO	8	47	5.9	17	0
Rasheed, K., NYG	9	42	4.7	23t	1
Rathman, T., SF	19	80	4.2	19	3
Rice, J., SF	3	69	23.0	43t	1
Richards, C., DET	4	1	0.3	1	0
Roby, R., WAS	1	0	0.0	0	0
Royster, M., TB	33	115	3.5	19	1
Rubley, T., Rams	29	102	3.5	13	0
Rypien, M., WAS	9	4	0.4	5	3
Salisbury, S., MIN	10	–1	–0.1	6	0
Sanders, B., DET	243	1115	4.6	42	3
Sanders, R., WAS	1	7	7.0	7	0
Sharpe, S., GB	4	8	2.0	5	0
Sherman, H., PHI	115	406	3.5	19	2
Simms, P., NYG	28	31	1.1	9	0
Smith, E., DAL	283	1486	5.3	62t	9
Smith, Ro., MIN	82	399	4.9	26t	2
Stephens, J., GB	48	173	3.6	22	1
Taylor, J., SF	2	17	8.5	12	0
Thompson, Da., GB	169	654	3.9	60t	3
Tillman, Le., NYG	121	585	4.8	58	3
Tolliver, B., ATL	7	48	6.9	24	0
Walker, A., SF	5	17	3.4	11	0
Walker, H., PHI	174	746	4.3	35	1
Walsh, S., NO	4	–4	–1.0	–1	0
Ware, A., DET	7	23	3.3	8	0
Watters, R., SF	208	950	4.6	39	10
White, Ru., Rams	2	10	5.0	5	0
Williams, K., DAL	7	26	3.7	12	2
Willis, P., CHI	2	6	3.0	6	0
Wilmsmeyer, K., SF	2	0	0.0	0	0
Wilson, C., TB	2	7	3.5	4	0
Wilson, Marcus, GB	6	3	0.5	5	0
Wilson, W., NO	31	230	7.4	44	0
Word, B., MIN	142	458	3.2	14	2
Workman, V., TB	78	284	3.6	21	2
Worley, T., CHI	110	437	4.0	28	2
Young, S., SF	69	407	5.9	35	2

PASSING

NFL LEADING PASSERS

PLAYER/TEAM	ATT	CMP	PCT	YDG	AV YDS PASS	TD	PCT TD	INT	PCT INT	LNG	RTG PTS
Steve Young, SF	462	314	68.0	4023	8.71	29	6.3	16	3.5	80t	101.5
Troy Aikman, DAL	392	271	69.1	3100	7.91	15	3.8	6	1.5	80t	99.0
John Elway, DEN	551	348	63.2	4030	7.31	25	4.5	10	1.8	63	92.8
Phil Simms, NYG	400	247	61.8	3038	7.60	15	3.8	9	2.3	62	88.3
Joe Montana, KC	298	181	60.7	2144	7.19	13	4.4	7	2.3	50t	87.4
V. Testaverde, CLE	230	130	56.5	1797	7.81	14	6.1	9	3.9	62t	85.7
Bubby Brister, PHI	309	181	58.6	1905	6.17	14	4.5	5	1.6	58	84.9
Boomer Esiason, NYJ	473	288	60.9	3421	7.23	16	3.4	11	2.3	77	84.5
Scott Mitchell, MIA	233	133	57.1	1773	7.61	12	5.2	8	3.4	77t	84.2
Bobby Hebert, ATL	430	263	61.2	2978	6.93	24	5.6	17	4.0	98t	84.0
Jeff Hostetler, Raiders	419	236	56.3	3242	7.74	14	3.3	10	2.4	74t	82.5
Steve Beuerlein, PHO	418	258	61.7	3164	7.57	18	4.3	17	4.1	65t	82.5
Jim Kelly, BUF	470	288	61.3	3382	7.20	18	3.8	18	3.8	65t	79.9
Neil O'Donnell, PIT	486	270	55.6	3208	6.60	14	2.9	7	1.4	71t	79.5
Jeff George, IND	407	234	57.5	2526	6.21	8	2.0	6	1.5	72t	76.3
Jim McMahon, MIN	331	200	60.4	1967	5.94	9	2.7	8	2.4	58	76.2
S. DeBerg, TB–MIA	227	136	59.9	1707	7.52	7	3.1	10	4.4	47	75.3
Warren Moon, HOU	520	303	58.3	3485	6.70	21	4.0	21	4.0	80t	75.2
John Friesz, SD	238	128	53.8	1402	5.89	6	2.5	4	1.7	66t	72.8
Brett Favre, GB	522	318	60.9	3303	6.33	19	3.6	24	4.6	66t	72.2

PASSERS — AFC

PLAYER/TEAM	ATT	CMP	PCT	YDG	AV YDS PASS	TD	PCT TD	INT	PCT INT	LNG	RTG PTS
Aguiar, L., NYJ	2	0	0.0	0	0.00	0	0.0	1	50.0	0	0
Anders, K., KC	0	0	—	0	—	0	—	0	—	0	-1
Bledsoe, D., NE	429	214	49.9	2494	5.81	15	3.5	15	3.5	54t	65.0
Blundin, M., KC	3	1	33.3	2	0.67	0	0.0	0	0.0	2	42.4
Byars, K., MIA	2	1	50.0	11	5.50	1	50.0	0	0.0	11t	106.3
Carlson, C., HOU	90	51	56.7	605	6.72	2	2.2	4	4.4	47	66.2
DeBerg, S., MIA	188	113	60.1	1521	8.09	6	3.2	7	3.7	47	81.0
Elway, J., DEN	551	348	63.2	4030	7.31	25	4.5	10	1.8	63	92.8
Esiason, B., NYJ	473	288	60.9	3421	7.23	16	3.4	11	2.3	77	84.5
Evans, V., PIT	76	45	59.2	640	8.42	3	3.9	4	5.3	68t	77.7
Friesz, J., SD	238	128	53.8	1402	5.89	6	2.5	4	1.7	66t	72.8
Gelbaugh, S., SEA	5	3	60.0	39	7.80	0	0.0	1	20.0	22	45.0
George, J., IND	407	234	57.5	2526	6.21	8	2.0	6	1.5	72t	76.3
Hoard, J., CLE	1	0	0.0	0	0.00	0	0.0	0	0.0	0	39.6
Hostetler, J., PIT	419	236	56.3	3242	7.74	14	3.3	10	2.4	74t	82.5
Humphries, S., SD	324	173	53.4	1981	6.11	12	3.7	10	3.1	48t	71.5
Jackson, Mi., CLE	1	1	100.0	25	25.00	0	0.0	0	0.0	25	118.8
Johnson, A., IND	1	0	0.0	0	0.00	0	0.0	1	100.0	0	0
Johnson, L., CIN	1	0	0.0	0	0.00	0	0.0	0	0.0	0	39.6
Kelly, Ji., BUF	470	288	61.3	3382	7.20	18	3.8	18	3.8	65t	79.9
Klingler, D., CIN	343	190	55.4	1935	5.64	6	1.7	9	2.6	51	66.6
Kosar, B., CLE	138	79	57.2	807	5.85	5	3.6	3	2.2	38t	77.2
Krieg, D., KC	189	105	55.6	1238	6.55	7	3.7	3	1.6	66t	81.4
Maddox, T., DEN	1	1	100.0	1	1.00	1	100.0	0	0.0	1t	118.8
Majkowski, D., IND	24	13	54.2	105	4.38	0	0.0	1	4.2	17	48.1
Marino, D., MIA	150	91	60.7	1218	8.12	8	5.3	3	2.0	80t	95.9
Marshall, A., DEN	1	1	100.0	30	30.00	1	100.0	0	0.0	30t	158.3
McGwire, D., SEA	5	3	60.0	24	4.80	1	20.0	0	0.0	17t	111.7
Means, N., SD	1	0	0.0	0	0.00	0	0.0	0	0.0	0	39.6

PLAYER/TEAM	ATT	CMP	PCT	YDG	AV YDS PASS	TD	PCT TD	INT	PCT INT	LNG	RTG PTS
Mirer, R., SEA	486	274	56.4	2833	5.83	12	2.5	17	3.5	53t	67.0
Mitchell, S., MIA	233	133	57.1	1773	7.61	12	5.2	8	3.4	77t	84.2
Montana, J., KC	298	181	60.7	2144	7.19	13	4.4	7	2.3	50t	87.4
Moon, W., HOU	520	303	58.3	3485	6.70	21	4.0	21	4.0	80t	75.2
Nagle, B., NYJ	14	6	42.9	71	5.07	0	0.0	0	0.0	18	58.9
O'Donnell, N., PIT	486	270	55.6	3208	6.60	14	2.9	7	1.4	71t	79.5
Pederson, D., MIA	8	4	50.0	41	5.13	0	0.0	0	0.0	12	65.1
Philcox, T., CLE	108	52	48.1	699	6.47	4	3.7	7	6.5	56	54.5
Pickens, C., CIN	1	0	0.0	0	0.00	0	0.0	0	0.0	0	39.6
Reich, F., BUF	26	16	61.5	153	5.88	2	7.7	0	0.0	30t	103.5
Richardson, B., HOU	4	3	75.0	55	13.75	0	0.0	0	0.0	34	116.7
Schroeder, J., CIN	159	78	49.1	832	5.23	5	3.1	2	1.3	37	70.0
Secules, S., NE	134	75	56.0	918	6.85	2	1.5	9	6.7	82	54.3
Testaverde, V., CLE	230	130	56.5	1797	7.81	14	6.1	9	3.9	62t	85.7
Thomas, T., BUF	1	0	0.0	0	0.00	0	0.0	0	0.0	0	39.6
Tomczak, M., PIT	54	29	53.7	398	7.37	2	3.7	5	9.3	39t	51.3
Trudeau, J., IND	162	85	52.5	992	6.12	2	1.2	7	4.3	68	57.4
Turner, K., NE	1	0	0.0	0	0.00	0	0.0	0	0.0	0	39.6
Tuten, R., SEA	1	0	0.0	0	0.00	0	0.0	0	0.0	0	39.6
Wilhelm, E., CIN	6	4	66.7	63	10.50	0	0.0	0	0.0	27	101.4
Williams, J.L., SEA	1	0	0.0	0	0.00	0	0.0	0	0.0	0	39.6
Zolak, S., NE	2	0	0.0	0	0.00	0	0.0	0	0.0	0	39.6

PASSERS — NFC

PLAYER/TEAM	ATT	CMP	PCT	YDG	AV YDS PASS	TD	PCT TD	INT	PCT INT	LNG	RTG PTS
Aikman, T., DAL	392	271	69.1	3100	7.91	15	3.8	6	1.5	80t	99.0
Anderson, N., CHI	1	0	0.0	0	0.00	0	0.0	0	0.0	0	39.6
Barnhardt, T., NO	1	1	100.0	7	7.00	0	0.0	0	0.0	7	95.8
Beuerlein, S., PHO	418	258	61.7	3164	7.57	18	4.3	17	4.1	65t	82.5
Bono, S., SF	61	39	63.9	416	6.82	0	0.0	1	1.6	33	76.9
Brister, B., PHI	309	181	58.6	1905	6.17	14	4.5	5	1.6	58	84.9
Buck, M., NO	54	32	59.3	448	8.30	4	7.4	3	5.6	63t	87.6
Chandler, C., PHO	103	52	50.5	471	4.57	3	2.9	2	1.9	27t	64.8
Conklin, C., WAS	87	46	52.9	496	5.70	4	4.6	3	3.4	34t	70.9
Cunningham, R., PHI	110	76	69.1	850	7.73	5	4.5	5	4.5	80t	88.1
DeBerg, S., TB	39	23	59.0	186	4.77	1	2.6	3	7.7	24	47.6
Detmer, T., GB	5	3	60.0	26	5.20	0	0.0	0	0.0	25	73.8
Erickson, C., TB	457	233	51.0	3054	6.68	18	3.9	21	4.6	67t	66.4
Everett, J., Rams	274	135	49.3	1652	6.03	8	2.9	12	4.4	60t	59.7
Favre, B., GB	522	318	60.9	3303	6.33	19	3.6	24	4.6	66t	72.2
Gannon, R., WAS	125	74	59.2	704	5.63	3	2.4	7	5.6	54	59.6
Gardocki, C., CHI	2	0	0.0	0	0.00	0	0.0	0	0.0	0	39.6
Garrett, J., DAL	19	9	47.4	61	3.21	0	0.0	0	0.0	16	54.9
Gary, C., Rams	1	1	100.0	8	8.00	0	0.0	0	0.0	8	100
Graham, K., NYG	22	8	36.4	79	3.59	0	0.0	0	0.0	18	47.3
Harbaugh, J., CHI	325	200	61.5	2002	6.16	7	2.2	11	3.4	48	72.1
Harper, A., DAL	1	1	100.0	46	46.00	0	0.0	0	0.0	46	118.8
Hearst, G., PHO	1	0	0.0	0	0.00	0	0.0	1	100.0	0	0
Hebert, B., ATL	430	263	61.2	2978	6.93	24	5.6	17	4.0	98t	84.0
Kosar, B., DAL	63	36	57.1	410	6.51	3	4.8	0	0.0	86	92.7
Kramer, E., DET	138	87	63.0	1002	7.26	8	5.8	3	2.2	48	95.1
McMahon, J., MIN	331	200	60.4	1968	5.95	9	2.7	8	2.4	58	76.2
Meggett, D., NYG	2	2	100.0	63	31.50	2	100.0	0	0.0	42t	158.3
Miller, C., ATL	66	32	48.5	345	5.23	1	1.5	3	4.5	32t	50.4

PLAYER/TEAM	ATT	CMP	PCT	YDG	AV YDS PASS	TD	PCT TD	INT	PCT INT	LNG	RTG PTS
Mitchell, B., WAS	2	1	50.0	50	25.00	0	0.0	1	50.0	50	56.3
Moore, D., TB	1	0	0.0	0	0.00	0	0.0	0	0.0	0	39.6
O'Brien, K., PHI	137	71	51.8	708	5.17	4	2.9	3	2.2	41	67.4
Pagel, M., Rams	9	3	33.3	23	2.56	0	0.0	1	11.1	10	2.8
Peete, R., DET	252	157	62.3	1670	6.63	6	2.4	14	5.6	93t	66.4
Rubley, T., Rams	189	108	57.1	1338	7.08	8	4.2	6	3.2	54	80.1
Rypien, M., WAS	319	166	52.0	1514	4.75	4	1.3	10	3.1	43	56.3
Salisbury, S., MIN	195	115	59.0	1413	7.25	9	4.6	6	3.1	55	84
Sanders, D., ATL	1	0	0.0	0	0.00	0	0.0	0	0.0	0	39.6
Sharpe, S., GB	1	1	100.0	1	1.00	0	0.0	0	0.0	1	79.2
Simms, P., NYG	400	247	61.8	3038	7.60	15	3.8	9	2.3	62	88.3
Taylor, J., SF	1	1	100.0	41	41.00	0	0.0	0	0.0	41	118.8
Tolliver, B., ATL	76	39	51.3	464	6.11	3	3.9	5	6.6	42t	56
Walker, H., PHI	0	0	—	0	—	0	—	0	—	—	-1
Walsh, S., NO	38	20	52.6	271	7.13	2	5.3	3	7.9	54t	60.3
Ware, A., DET	45	20	44.4	271	6.02	1	2.2	2	4.4	47	53.1
Weldon, C., TB	11	6	54.5	55	5.00	0	0.0	1	9.1	20	30.5
Willis, P., CHI	60	30	50.0	268	4.47	0	0.0	5	8.3	29	27.6
Wilson, W., NO	388	221	57.0	2457	6.33	12	3.1	15	3.9	42t	70.1
Young, S., SF	462	314	68.0	4023	8.71	29	6.3	16	3.5	80t	101.5

RECEIVING

NFL LEADERS — RECEPTIONS

PLAYER/TEAM	NO	YDS	AVG	LONG	TD
Sterling Sharpe, GB	112	1274	11.4	54	11
Jerry Rice, SF	98	1503	15.3	80t	15
Michael Irvin, DAL	88	1330	15.1	61t	7
Andre Rison, ATL	86	1242	14.4	53t	15
Chris Carter, MIN	86	1071	12.5	58	9
Reggie Langhorne, IND	85	1038	12.2	72t	3
Anthony Miller, SD	84	1162	13.8	66t	7
Shannon Sharpe, DEN	81	995	12.3	63	9
Tim Brown, Raiders	80	1180	14.8	71t	7
Brian Blades, SEA	80	945	11.8	41	3
Webster Slaughter, HOU	77	904	11.7	41	5
Herschel Walker, PHI	75	610	8.1	55	3
Terry Kirby, MIA	75	874	11.7	47	3
Mike Pritchard, ATL	74	736	9.9	34	7
Ronnie Harmon, SD	73	671	9.2	37	2
Michael Haynes, ATL	72	778	10.8	98t	4
Pete Metzelaars, BUF	68	609	9.0	51	4
Brent Jones, SF	68	735	10.8	29	3
Ernest Givins, HOU	68	887	13.0	80t	4
Johnny Johnson, NYJ	67	641	9.6	48	1

NFL LEADERS — RECEIVING YARDS

PLAYER/TEAM	YARDS	NO	AVG	LONG	TD
Jerry Rice, SF	1503	98	15.3	80t	15
Michael Irvin, DAL	1330	88	15.1	61t	7
Sterling Sharpe, GB	1274	112	11.4	54	11
Andre Rison, ATL	1242	86	14.4	53t	15
Tim Brown, Raiders	1180	80	14.8	71t	7
Anthony Miller, SD	1162	84	13.8	66t	7
Chris Carter, MIN	1071	86	12.5	58	9
Reggie Langhorne, IND	1038	85	12.2	72t	3

PLAYER/TEAM	NO	YARDS	AVG	LONG	TD
Irving Fryar, MIA	1010	64	15.8	65t	5
Shannon Sharpe, DEN	995	81	12.3	63	9
Eric Martin, NO	950	66	14.4	54t	3
Henry Ellard, Rams	945	61	15.5	54	2
Brian Blades, SEA	945	80	11.8	41	3
Eric Green, PIT	942	63	15.0	71t	5
John Taylor, SF	940	56	16.8	76t	5
Herman Moore, DET	935	61	15.3	93t	6
Courtney Hawkins, TB	933	62	15.0	67	5
Willie Davis, KC	909	52	17.5	66t	7
Webster Slaughter, HOU	904	77	11.7	41	5
Ernest Givins, HOU	887	68	13.0	80t	4

RECEIVING — AFC

PLAYER/TEAM	NO	YARDS	AVG	LONG	TD
Allen, M., KC	34	238	7.0	18t	3
Anders, K., KC	40	326	8.2	27	1
Arbuckle, C., IND	15	90	6.0	23	0
Awalt, R., BUF	2	19	9.5	10	0
Baldwin, R., CLE	1	5	5.0	5t	1
Ball, E., CIN	4	39	9.8	24	0
Banks, F., MIA	1	26	26.0	26	0
Barnes, J., SD	10	137	13.7	21	0
Barnett, T., KC	17	182	10.7	25	1
Bates, M., SEA	1	6	6.0	6	0
Baty, G., MIA	5	78	15.6	32	1
Baxter, B., NYJ	20	158	7.9	24	0
Baxter, F., NYJ	3	48	16.0	25	1
Beebe, D., BUF	31	504	16.3	65t	3
Bell, N., Raiders	11	111	10.1	18	0
Benjamin, R., CIN	1	16	16.0	16	0
Bernstine, R., DEN	44	372	8.5	41	0
Bieniemy, E., SD	1	0	0.0	0	0
Birden, J.J., KC	51	721	14.1	50t	2
Blades, B., SEA	80	945	11.8	41	3
Brisby, V., NE	45	626	13.9	39	2
Brooks, B., BUF	60	714	11.9	32	5
Brown, G., HOU	21	240	11.4	38t	2
Brown, Re., HOU	2	30	15.0	26	0
Brown, Tim, Raiders	80	1180	14.8	71t	7
Brown, Tr., NE	2	22	11.0	14	0
Burkett, C., NYJ	40	531	13.3	77	4
Butts, M., SD	15	105	7.0	23	0
Byars, K., MIA	61	613	10.0	27	3
Carpenter, R., NYJ	6	83	13.8	18	0
Carrier, M., CLE	43	746	17.3	55	3
Carroll, W., CIN	6	81	13.5	28	0
Cash, Keith, KC	24	242	10.1	24	4
Cash, Kerry, IND	43	402	9.3	37	3
Chaffey, P., NYJ	4	55	13.8	20t	1
Coates, B., NE	53	659	12.4	54t	8
Coleman, P., HOU	9	129	14.3	25	0
Cook, M., NE	22	154	7.0	17	1
Cooper, A., PIT	9	112	12.4	38	0
Copeland, R., BUF	13	242	18.6	60	0
Cox, A., IND	4	59	14.8	24	0

PLAYER/TEAM	NO	YARDS	AVG	LONG	TD
Crittenden, R., NE	16	293	18.3	44	1
Croom, C., NE	8	92	11.5	21	0
Culver, R., IND	11	112	10.2	26	1
Cuthbert, R., PIT	1	3	3.0	3	0
Davenport, C., PIT	4	51	12.8	19	0
Davis, K., BUF	21	95	4.5	28	0
Davis, Wi., KC	52	909	17.5	66t	7
Dawkins, S., IND	26	430	16.5	68	1
Delpino, R., DEN	26	195	7.5	25	0
Drewrey, W., HOU	1	3	3.0	3	0
Duncan, C., HOU	41	456	11.1	47	3
Dyal, M., KC/SD	7	83	11.9	31	0
Edmunds, F., SEA	24	239	10.0	32	2
Esiason, B., NYJ	1	-8	-8.0	-8	0
Fenner, D., CIN	48	427	8.9	40	0
Foster, B., PIT	27	217	8.0	21	1
Frisch, D., CIN	6	43	7.2	12	0
Fryar, I., MIA	64	1010	15.8	65t	5
Gardner, C., BUF	4	50	12.5	22	1
Gash, S., NE	14	93	6.6	15	0
Gault, W., Raiders	8	64	8.0	12	0
Givins, E., HOU	68	887	13.0	80t	4
Glover, A., Raiders	4	55	13.8	26	1
Graham, Je., PIT	38	579	15.2	51	0
Green, E., PIT	63	942	15.0	71t	5
Green, H., CIN	22	115	5.2	16	0
Green, P., SEA	23	178	7.7	20	1
Harmon, R., SD	73	671	9.2	37	2
Harris, L., HOU	4	53	13.3	17t	1
Hastings, A., PIT	3	44	14.7	18	0
Hayes, J., KC	24	331	13.8	49	1
Hester, J., IND	64	835	13.0	58	1
Higgs, M., MIA	10	72	7.2	15	0
Hoard, L., CLE	35	351	10.0	41	0
Hoge, M., PIT	33	247	7.5	18	4
Horton, E., Raiders	43	467	10.9	32	1
Ingram, M., MIA	44	707	16.1	77t	6
Ismail, R., Raiders	26	353	13.6	43t	1
Jackson, K., MIA	39	613	15.7	57t	6
Jackson, Mi, CLE	41	756	18.4	62t	8
Jefferson, S., SD	30	391	13.0	39t	2
Jeffires, H., HOU	66	753	11.4	66t	6
Jett, Ja., Raiders	33	771	23.4	74t	3
Johnson, A., IND	55	443	8.1	36	0
Johnson, J., NYJ	67	641	9.6	48	1
Johnson, Re., DEN	20	243	12.2	38	1
Johnson, Tr., SEA	3	15	5.0	8	1
Johnson, Vance, DEN	36	517	14.4	56	5
Jones, F., KC	9	111	12.3	19	0
Jones, H., KC	7	91	13.0	22	0
Jordan, R., Raiders	4	42	10.5	33	0
Jorden, T., PIT	1	12	12.0	12	0
Kimbrough, T., DEN	8	79	9.9	16	0
Kinchen, B., CLE	29	347	12.0	40	2
Kirby, T., MIA	75	874	11.7	47	3
Langhorne, R., IND	85	1038	12.2	72t	3

PLAYER/TEAM	NO	YARDS	AVG	LONG	TD
Lewis, N., SD	38	463	12.2	47	4
Marshall, A., DEN	28	360	12.9	40	2
Martin, K., SEA	57	798	14.0	53t	5
Martin, T., MIA	20	347	17.4	80t	3
Maston, L., HOU	1	14	14.0	14	0
Mathis, T., NYJ	24	352	14.7	46	0
McCallum, N., Raiders	2	5	2.5	3	0
McCardell, K., CLE	13	234	18.0	43	4
McDuffie, O.J., MIA	19	197	10.4	18	0
McGee, To., CIN	44	525	11.9	37	0
McKeller, K., BUF	3	35	11.7	13t	1
McMurtry, G., NE	22	241	11.0	20	1
McNair, T., KC	10	74	7.4	24	0
Means, N., SD	10	59	5.9	11	0
Metcalf, E., CLE	63	539	8.6	49t	2
Metzelaars, P., BUF	68	609	9.0	51	4
Milburn, G., DEN	38	300	7.9	50	3
Miles, O., CIN	6	89	14.8	27	0
Miller, A., SD	84	1162	13.8	66t	7
Miller, S., MIA	2	15	7.5	8	0
Mills, E., PIT	29	386	13.3	30	1
Mitchell, J., NYJ	39	630	16.2	65t	6
Montgomery, T., Raiders	10	43	4.3	9	0
Moore, R., NYJ	64	843	13.2	51	1
Murrell, A., NYJ	5	12	2.4	8	0
Norgard, E., HOU	1	13	13.0	13	0
Parmalee, B., MIA	1	1	1.0	1	0
Pickens, C., CIN	43	565	13.1	36	6
Potts, R., IND	26	189	7.3	24	0
Pupunu, A., SD	13	142	10.9	28	0
Query, J., CIN	56	654	11.7	51	4
Reed, A., BUF	52	854	16.4	65t	6
Rembert, R., CIN	8	101	12.6	21	0
Rivers, R., DEN	6	59	9.8	17	1
Roberts, R., SEA	1	4	4.0	4	0
Robinson, Gr., Raiders	15	142	9.5	58	0
Robinson, P., CIN	8	72	9.0	14	0
Rowe, P., CLE	3	37	12.3	16	0
Russell, D., DEN	44	719	16.3	43	3
Russell, L., NE	26	245	9.4	69	0
Sadowski, T., NYJ	2	14	7.0	11	0
Sharpe, Sh., DEN	81	995	12.3	63	9
Slaughter, W., HOU	77	904	11.7	41	5
Smith, Ri., CLE	4	55	13.8	17	0
Smith, St., Raiders	18	187	10.4	22	0
Stegall, M., CIN	1	8	8.0	8	0
Stone, D., PIT	41	587	14.3	44	2
Tasker, S., BUF	2	26	13.0	22	0
Taylor, Ki., DEN	1	28	28.0	28	0
Thigpen, Y., PIT	9	154	17.1	39t	3
Thomas, B., NYJ	7	25	3.6	7	0
Thomas, Do., SEA	11	95	8.6	20	0
Thomas, Rob, SEA	7	67	9.6	16	0
Thomas, T., BUF	48	387	8.1	37	0
Thomason, J., CIN	2	8	4.0	5	0
Thompson, C., CIN	17	87	5.1	10	1

PLAYER/TEAM	NO	YARDS	AVG	LONG	TD
Thompson, E., KC	4	33	8.3	13	0
Thompson, L., PIT	38	259	6.8	28	0
Thornton, J., NYJ	12	108	9.0	22	2
Tillman, C., DEN	17	193	11.4	30	2
Tillman, La., CLE	5	68	13.6	18	1
Tillman, S., HOU	1	4	4.0	4t	1
Timpson, M., NE	42	654	15.6	48	2
Toner, E., IND	1	5	5.0	5	0
Turner, K., NE	39	333	8.5	26	2
Valerio, J., KC	1	1	1.0	1t	1
Vardell, T., CLE	19	151	7.9	28t	1
Verdin, C., IND	2	20	10.0	19	1
Walker, De., SD	21	212	10.1	25t	1
Warren, C., SEA	15	99	6.6	21	0
Wellman, G., HOU	31	430	13.9	44	1
White, Lo., HOU	34	229	6.7	20	0
Williams, Cl., CLE	1	14	14.0	14	0
Williams, H., KC	7	42	6.0	14	0
Williams, J.L., SEA	58	450	7.8	25	1
Williams, M., MIA	1	11	11.0	11	0
Wolfley, R., CLE	5	25	5.0	9	1
Worley, T., PIT	3	13	4.3	9	0
Wright, Al., Raiders	27	462	17.1	68t	4
Wyman, D., DEN	1	1	1.0	1t	1
Young, D., SD	6	41	6.8	12t	2

RECEIVING — NFC

PLAYER/TEAM	NO	YARDS	AVG	LONG	TD
Anderson, Ga., TB/DET	11	89	8.1	28	1
Anderson, N., CHI	31	160	5.2	35	0
Anderson, W., Rams	37	552	14.9	56t	4
Armstrong, Ty., TB	9	86	9.6	29	1
Bailey, J., PHO	32	243	7.6	30	0
Bailey, V., PHI	41	545	13.3	58	1
Banks, F., CHI	1	19	19.0	19	0
Barnett, F., PHI	17	170	10.0	21	0
Bavaro, M., PHI	43	481	11.2	27	6
Beach, S., SF	5	59	11.8	20t	1
Bennett, E., GB	59	457	7.7	39t	1
Bettis, J., Rams	26	244	9.4	28	0
Blount, E., PHO	5	36	7.2	9	0
Brenner, H., NO	11	171	15.5	27	1
Brooks, Re., WAS	21	186	8.9	43	0
Brooks, Ro., GB	20	100	9.0	25	0
Broussard, S., ATL	1	4	4.0	4	0
Brown, Derek, NYG	7	56	8.0	14	0
Brown, Derek, NO	21	170	8.1	19	1
Bunch, J., NYG	13	98	7.5	15	1
Byner, E., WAS	27	194	7.2	20	0
Calloway, C., NYG	35	513	14.7	47	3
Campbell, J., DET	7	55	7.9	12	0
Carter, A., MIN	60	775	12.9	39	5
Carter, C., MIN	86	1071	12.5	58	9
Carter, D., SF	3	40	13.3	14	0
Carter, P., Rams	14	166	11.9	38	1
Centers, L., PHO	66	603	9.1	29	3

PLAYER/TEAM	NO	YARDS	AVG	LONG	TD
Chmura, M., GB	2	13	6.5	7	0
Christian, B., CHI	16	160	10.0	36	0
Claiborne, R., TB	5	61	12.2	16	0
Clark, G., PHO	63	818	13.0	55	4
Clayton, M., GB	32	331	10.3	32	3
Clifton, G., WAS	2	15	7.5	10	0
Cobb, R., TB	9	61	6.8	19	1
Coleman, L., DAL	4	24	6.0	10	0
Conway, C., CHI	19	231	12.2	38t	2
Copeland, H., TB	30	633	21.1	67t	4
Craig, R., MIN	19	169	8.9	31	1
Crawford, K., NYG	1	6	6.0	6	0
Cross, H., NYG	21	272	13.0	32	5
Davis, W., CHI	12	132	11.0	17	0
Dawsey, L., TB	15	203	13.5	24	0
Dickerson, E., ATL	6	58	9.7	30	0
Dowdell, M., NO	6	46	7.7	11t	1
Drayton, T., Rams	27	319	11.8	27	4
Early, Q., NO	45	670	14.9	63t	6
Edwards, An., PHO	13	326	25.1	65t	1
Ellard, H., Rams	61	945	15.5	54	2
Ervins, R., WAS	16	123	7.7	20	0
Evans, C., MIN	4	39	9.8	21	0
Fralic, B., DET	1	−4	−4.0	−4	0
Gainer, D., DAL	6	37	6.2	8	0
Galbraith, S., DAL	1	1	1.0	1t	1
Gary, C., Rams	36	289	8.0	60t	1
Gedney, C., CHI	10	98	9.8	24	0
Graham, S., MIN	7	46	6.6	11	0
Green, Ro., CHI	13	63	4.8	9	0
Green, W., DET	28	462	16.5	47	2
Guliford, E., MIN	1	45	45.0	45	0
Hall, R., TB	23	268	11.7	37t	1
Hallock, T., DET	8	88	11.0	24	2
Hampton, R., NYG	18	210	11.7	62	0
Harbaugh, J., CHI	1	1	1.0	1	0
Harper, A., DAL	36	777	21.6	80t	5
Harris, C., GB	2	11	5.5	6	0
Harris, J., GB	42	604	14.4	66t	4
Harris, Ru., TB	4	48	12.0	25	0
Hawkins, C., TB	62	933	15.0	67	5
Haynes, M., ATL	72	778	10.8	98t	4
Hearst, G., PHO	6	18	3.0	9	0
Hebron, V., PHI	11	82	7.5	12	0
Heyward, C., CHI	16	132	8.3	20	0
Hill, D., ATL	34	384	11.3	30	0
Hill, R., PHO	35	519	14.8	58t	4
Hilliard, D., NO	40	296	7.4	34	1
Hinton, C., ATL	1	−8	−8.0	−8	0
Holman, R., DET	25	244	9.8	28t	2
Howard, De., WAS	23	286	12.4	27	0
Irvin, M., DAL	88	1330	15.1	61t	7
Ismail, Q., MIN	19	212	11.2	37	1
Jackson, M., NYG	58	708	12.2	40t	4
Jennings, K., CHI	14	150	10.7	29	0
Johnson, Ji., DET	2	18	9.0	9	0

PLAYER/TEAM	NO	YARDS	AVG	LONG	TD
Johnson, Ma., PHI	10	81	8.1	17	0
Johnston, D., DAL	50	372	7.4	20	1
Jones, B., SF	68	735	10.8	29	3
Jones, Er., Rams	5	56	11.2	21t	2
Jordan, S., MIN	56	542	9.7	53	1
Joseph, J., PHI	29	291	10.0	48	1
Kinchen, T., Rams	8	137	17.1	35t	1
LaChapelle, S., Rams	2	23	11.5	14	0
Lang, D., Rams	4	45	11.3	21	0
Lassic, D., DAL	9	37	4.1	9	0
Lawrence, R., PHI	1	5	5.0	5	0
Lee, A., SF	16	115	7.2	22	2
Lester, T., Rams	18	154	8.6	21	0
Lewis, D., CHI	4	26	6.5	18	0
Lewis, R., GB	2	21	10.5	17	0
Lofton, J., Rams/PH	14	183	13.1	32	0
Logan, M., SF	37	348	9.4	24	0
Lynch, E., DET	13	82	6.3	11	0
Lyons, M., ATL	8	63	7.9	14	0
Martin, E., NO	66	950	14.4	54t	3
Matthews, A., DET	11	171	15.5	40	0
McAfee, F., NO	1	3	3.0	3	0
McCaffrey, E., NYG	27	335	12.4	31	2
McDowell, A., TB	8	26	3.3	9	1
McGee, T., WAS	39	500	12.8	54	3
McNeal, T., Rams	8	75	9.4	22t	1
Meggett, D., NYG	38	319	8.4	50	0
Middleton, R., WAS	24	154	6.4	18	2
Mims, D., ATL	12	107	8.9	19	1
Mitchell, B., WAS	20	157	7.9	18	0
Monk, A., WAS	41	398	9.7	29	2
Moore, Da., TB	4	47	11.8	19t	1
Moore, De., DET	21	169	8.0	20	1
Moore, H., DET	61	935	15.3	93t	6
Moore, Ro., PHO	3	16	5.3	6	0
Morgan, A., GB	1	8	8.0	8	0
Muster, B., NO	23	195	8.5	31	0
Ned, D., NO	9	54	6.0	14	0
Newman, P., NO	8	121	15.1	32	1
Novacek, J., DAL	44	445	10.1	30	1
Obee, T., CHI	26	351	13.5	48	3
Pegram, E., ATL	33	302	9.2	30	0
Perriman, B., DET	49	496	10.1	34	2
Phillips, Ja., ATL	1	15	15.0	15	0
Pierce, A., NYG	12	212	17.7	54	0
Price, J., DAL	1	4	4.0	4	0
Pritchard, M., ATL	74	736	9.9	34	7
Proehl, R., PHO	65	877	13.5	51t	7
Rasheed, K., NYG	1	3	3.0	3	0
Rathman, T., SF	10	86	8.6	17	0
Reed, J., MIN	5	65	13.0	18	0
Reeves, W., PHO	9	67	7.4	18	1
Rice, J., SF	98	1503	15.3	80t	15
Rison, A., ATL	86	1242	14.4	53t	15
Rolle, R., PHO	10	67	6.7	22	1

PLAYER/TEAM	NO	YARDS	AVG	LONG	TD
Royster, M., TB	5	18	3.6	10	0
Sanders, B., DET	36	205	5.7	17	0
Sanders, D., ATL	6	106	17.7	70t	1
Sanders, R., WAS	58	638	11.0	50	4
Sharpe, S., GB	112	1274	11.4	54	11
Sherman, H., PHI	12	78	6.5	21	0
Sherrard, M., NYG	24	433	18.0	55t	2
Simms, P., NYG	1	–6	–6.0	–6	0
Singleton, N., SF	8	126	15.8	33	1
Small, T., NO	16	164	10.3	17	1
Smith, E., DAL	57	414	7.3	86	1
Smith, I., NO	16	180	11.3	23	2
Smith, Ro., MIN	24	111	4.6	12	0
Stephens, J., GB	5	31	6.2	10	0
Sydner, J., PHI	2	42	21.0	31	0
Taylor, J., SF	56	940	16.8	76t	5
Tennell, D., MIN	15	122	8.1	17	0
Thomas, L., TB	8	186	23.3	62t	2
Thompson, Da., GB	18	129	7.2	34	0
Thompson, M., DET	1	15	15.0	15	0
Tice, M., MIN	6	39	6.5	21	1
Tillman, Le., NYG	1	21	21.0	21	0
Truitt, O., MIN	4	40	10.0	13	0
Turner, F., NO	12	163	13.6	52	1
Turner, O., SF	3	64	21.3	32	0
Turner, V., DET/TB	1	7	7.0	7	0
Waddle, T., CHI	44	552	12.5	38	1
Walker, A., SF	1	4	4.0	4	0
Walker, H., PHI	75	610	8.1	55	3
Ware, D., PHO	3	45	15.0	27	0
Watters, R., SF	31	326	10.5	48t	1
West, E., GB	25	253	10.1	24	0
Wetnight, R., CHI	9	93	10.3	25t	1
Whitaker, D., CHI	6	53	8.8	18	0
Williams, C., PHI	60	725	12.1	80t	10
Williams, Ja., SF	16	132	8.3	15	1
Williams, K., DAL	20	151	7.6	33	2
Williams, T., DAL	1	25	25.0	25	0
Wilson, C., TB	15	225	15.0	24	0
Wilson, Marcus, GB	2	18	9.0	11	0
Word, B., MIN	9	105	11.7	27	0
Workman, V., TB	54	411	7.6	42t	2
Worley, T., CHI	8	49	6.1	15	0
Wycheck, F., WAS	16	113	7.1	20	0
Young, M., PHI	14	186	13.3	49t	2
Young, S., SF	2	2	1.0	6	0

INTERCEPTIONS

NFL INTERCEPTION LEADERS

PLAYER/TEAM	INT	YDS	LONG	TD
Eugene Robinson, SEA	9	80	28	0
Nate Odomes, BUF	9	65	25	0
Rod Woodson, PIT	8	138	63t	1
Deion Sanders, ATL	7	91	41	0
Marcus Robertson, HOU	7	137	69	0
Darren Carrington, SD	7	104	28	0

PLAYER/TEAM	INT	YDS	LONG	TD
Eric Allen, PHI	6	201	94t	4
LeRoy Butler, GB	6	131	39	0
Kevin Smith, DAL	6	56	32t	1
Tom Carter, WAS	6	54	29	0
Brian Washington, NYJ	6	128	62t	1
Cris Dishman, HOU	6	74	30	0
Albert Lewis, KC	6	61	24	0
Michael McGruder, SF	5	89	37	1
Vencie Glenn, MIN	5	49	23	0
Terry McDaniel, Raiders	5	87	36t	1
Steve Jackson, HOU	5	54	22t	1
Charles Mincy, KC	5	44	20	0
J.B. Brown, MIA	5	43	29	0
Eric Turner, CLE	5	25	19	0

INTERCEPTIONS — AFC

PLAYER/TEAM	NO	YARDS	AVG	LONG	TD
Anderson, E., Raiders	2	52	26.0	27	0
Atwater, S., DEN	2	81	40.5	68	0
Barnett, H., NE	1	40	40.0	40	0
Bates, P., Raiders	1	0	0.0	0	0
Bayless, M., KC	2	14	7.0	16	0
Baylor, J., IND	3	11	3.7	7	0
Belser, J., IND	1	14	14.0	11	0
Bennett, C., BUF	1	5	5.0	5	0
Bishop, B., HOU	1	1	1.0	1	0
Blackmon, R., SEA	2	0	0.0	0	0
Bradford, R., DEN	1	0	0.0	0	0
Braxton, T., DEN	3	37	12.3	25	0
Brim, M., CIN	3	74	24.7	30	1
Brown, J.B., MIA	5	43	8.6	29	0
Brown, V., NE	1	24	24.0	24	0
Buchanan, Ra., IND	4	45	11.3	28	0
Carrington, D., SD	7	104	14.9	28	0
Carter, Da., KC	1	0	0.0	0	0
Clifton, K., NYJ	1	3	3.0	3	0
Collins, T., NE	1	8	8.0	8	0
Cox, B., MIA	1	26	26.0	26	0
Croel, M., DEN	1	22	22.0	22t	1
Daniel, E., IND	1	17	17.0	17	0
Darby, M., BUF	2	32	16.0	32	0
Davidson, K., PIT	1	6	6.0	6	0
Davis, B., SD	1	0	0.0	0	0
Dimry, C., DEN	1	0	0.0	0	0
Dishman, C., HOU	6	74	12.3	30	0
Dronett, S., DEN	2	13	6.5	7	0
Figures, D., PIT	1	78	78.0	78	0
Francis, J., CIN	2	12	6.0	12	0
Frank, D., SD	3	119	39.7	102t	1
Gordon, D., SD	1	3	3.0	3	0
Grant, A., CIN	1	17	17.0	17	0
Gray, C., SEA	3	33	11.0	16	0
Green, C., MIA	2	0	0.0	0	0
Hall, Da., DEN	1	0	0.0	0	0
Harper, D., SEA	1	0	0.0	0	0
Hasty, J., NYJ	2	22	11.0	22	0

PLAYER/TEAM	NO	YARDS	AVG	LONG	TD
Hendrickson, S., SD	1	16	16.0	16	0
Henry, K., PIT	1	10	10.0	10	0
Herrod, J., IND	1	29	29.0	29	0
Hilliard, R., CLE	1	54	54.0	54	0
Hobley, L., MIA	1	17	17.0	17	0
Hoskins, D., Raiders	2	34	17.0	20	0
Houston, B., NYJ	1	0	0.0	0	0
Hunter, P., SEA	4	54	13.5	34	0
Hurst, M., NE	4	53	13.3	24	0
Jackson, S., HOU	5	54	10.8	22t	1
Jefferson, J., SEA	1	12	12.0	12	0
Johnson, D.J., PIT	3	51	17.0	26	0
Johnson, M., CLE	1	0	0.0	0	0
Jones, G., PIT	2	11	5.5	11	0
Jones, He., BUF	2	92	46.0	85t	1
Jones, Ro., CIN	1	0	0.0	0	0
Jones, Se., CLE	3	0	0.0	0	0
Lageman, J., NYJ	1	15	15.0	15	0
Lake, C., PIT	4	31	7.8	26	0
Lambert, D., NE	1	0	0.0	0	0
Lang, L., DEN	2	4	2.0	4	0
Lewis, A., KC	6	61	10.2	24	0
Lewis, Da., HOU	1	47	47.0	47t	1
Lewis, M., NYJ	2	4	2.0	3	0
Lott, R., NYJ	3	35	11.7	29	0
Marts, L., KC	1	20	20.0	20	0
Matthews, C., CLE	1	10	10.0	10	0
McDaniel, T., Raiders	5	87	17.4	36t	1
McDowell, B., HOU	3	31	10.3	13	0
McGlockton, C., Raiders	1	19	19.0	19	0
Mincy, C., KC	5	44	8.8	20	0
Mustafaa, N., CLE	1	97	97.0	97t	1
Nash, J., SEA	1	13	13.0	13t	1
Odomes, N., BUF	9	65	7.2	25	0
Oliver, L., MIA	2	60	30.0	56t	1
Orlando, B., HOU	3	68	22.7	38t	1
Patton, M., BUF	2	0	0.0	0	0
Perry, D., PIT	4	61	15.3	30	0
Plummer, G., SD	2	7	3.5	6	0
Pope, M., SD	2	14	7.0	12	0
Porter, R., SEA	1	4	4.0	4	0
Ray, T., NE	1	0	0.0	0	0
Richard, S., SD	1	−2	−2.0	−2	0
Robertson, M., HOU	7	137	19.6	69	0
Robinson, E., SEA	9	80	8.9	28	0
Robinson, F., DEN	1	13	13.0	13	0
Ross, K., KC	2	49	24.5	48	0
Saleaumua, D., KC	1	13	13.0	13	0
Seau, J., SD	2	58	29.0	42	0
Smith, B., BUF	1	0	0.0	0	0
Smith, De., DEN	3	57	19.0	36	0
Smith, N., KC	1	3	3.0	3	0
Speer, D., CLE	1	22	22.0	22	0
Talley, D., BUF	3	74	24.7	61t	1
Taylor, Ja., KC	1	0	0.0	0	0
Terry, D., KC	1	21	21.0	21	0

PLAYER/TEAM	NO	YARDS	AVG	LONG	TD
Thomas, E., NYJ	2	20	10.0	20	0
Thompson, R., NE	1	4	4.0	4	0
Tovar, S., CIN	1	0	0.0	0	0
Trapp, J., Raiders	1	7	7.0	7	0
Turner, E., CLE	5	25	5.0	19	0
Vanhorse, S., SD	2	0	0.0	0	0
Vincent, T., MIA	2	29	14.5	23	0
Washington, B., NYJ	6	128	21.3	62t	1
Washington, L., Raiders	2	0	0.0	0	0
Washington, Mi., BUF	1	27	27.0	27t	1
Wheeler, L., CIN	0	24	N/A	24	0
White, S., CIN	2	19	9.5	14	0
Williams, D., CIN	2	126	63.0	97t	1
Williams, James, BUF	2	11	5.5	6	0
Woodson, R., PIT	8	138	17.3	63t	1
Wren, D., NE	3	-7	-2.3	2	0
Wyman, D., DEN	1	9	9.0	9	0
Young, L., NYJ	1	6	6.0	6	0

INTERCEPTIONS — NFC

PLAYER/TEAM	INT	YDS	AVG	LG	TD
Allen, E., PHI	6	201	33.5	94t	4
Anderson, D., TB	1	6	6.0	6	0
Armstead, J., NYG	1	0	0.0	0	0
Atkins, G., NO	3	59	19.7	37	0
Bailey, R., Rams	2	41	20.5	41	0
Bates, B., DAL	2	25	12.5	22	0
Beamon, W., NYG	1	0	0.0	0	0
Blaylock, A., CHI	2	3	1.5	3	0
Booty, J., PHO	2	24	12.0	19	0
Brock, M., GB	1	0	0.0	0	0
Buck, V., NO	2	28	14.0	28	0
Buckley, T., GB	2	31	15.5	31	0
Butler, L., GB	6	131	21.8	39	0
Campbell, Je., NYG	1	0	0.0	0	0
Carrier, Ma., CHI	4	94	23.5	34t	1
Carter, Ma., TB	1	0	0.0	0	0
Carter, T., WAS	6	54	9.0	29	0
Case, S., ATL	0	3	N/A	3	0
Clark, V., ATL	2	59	29.5	38	0
Coleman, M., WAS	2	27	13.5	14	0
Collins, A., WAS	1	5	5.0	5	0
Collins, M., NYG	4	77	19.3	50t	1
Colon, H., DET	2	28	14.0	27	0
Conlan, S., Rams	1	28	28.0	28	0
Cook, T., NO	1	0	0.0	0	0
Copeland, D., WAS	1	0	0.0	0	0
Crockett, R., DET	2	31	15.5	31	0
Davis, E., SF	4	45	11.3	41t	1
Dent, R., CHI	1	24	24.0	24	0
Doleman, C., MIN	1	-3	-3.0	-3	0
Eaton, T., ATL	1	0	0.0	0	0
Edwards, B., WAS	1	17	17.0	17	0
Evans, B., PHI	1	8	8.0	7	0
Evans, Do., GB	1	0	0.0	0	0
Everett, T., DAL	2	25	12.5	17	0

PLAYER/TEAM	NO	YARDS	AVG	LONG	TD
Gant, K., DAL	1	0	0.0	0	0
Gibson, D., DET	1	0	0.0	0	0
Glenn, V., MIN	5	49	9.8	23	0
Gouveia, K., WAS	1	59	59.0	59t	1
Green, D., WAS	4	10	2.5	8	0
Griffin, D., SF	3	6	2.0	3	0
Guyton, M., NYG	2	34	17.0	19	0
Hager, B., PHI	1	19	19.0	19	0
Hanks, M., SF	3	104	34.7	67t	1
Holland, Jo., GB	2	41	20.5	30	0
Homco, T., Rams	1	6	6.0	6	0
Hopkins, W., PHI	1	0	0.0	0	0
Jackson, G., NYG	4	32	8.0	29	0
Jamison, G., DET	2	48	24.0	35t	1
Jenkins, C., MIN	2	7	3.5	4	0
Johnson, A.J., WAS	1	69	69.0	69t	1
Johnson, Jo., SF	1	0	0.0	0	0
Jones, Da., CHI	4	52	13.0	22	0
Jones, R., NO	1	12	12.0	12	0
Joyner, S., PHI	1	6	6.0	6	0
King, J., TB	3	29	9.7	28	0
Lee, C., MIN	3	20	6.7	19	0
Lincoln, J., CHI	3	109	36.3	80t	1
Lyght, T., Rams	2	0	0.0	0	0
Lynch, L., PHO	3	13	4.3	13	0
Mack, M., TB	1	27	27.0	27t	1
Mangum, J., CHI	1	0	0.0	0	0
Marion, B., DAL	1	2	2.0	2	0
McDonald, T., SF	3	23	7.7	21	0
McGriggs, L., MIN	1	63	63.0	63t	1
McGruder, M., SF	5	89	17.8	37	1
McKyer, T., DET	2	10	5.0	10	0
McMichael, S., CHI	1	0	0.0	0	0
McMillian, A., MIN	4	45	11.3	22t	1
McMillian, M., PHI	2	25	12.5	17	0
McNeil, R., DET	2	19	9.5	16	0
Miano, R., PHI	4	26	6.5	16	0
Miller, Co., NYG	2	18	9.0	11	0
Mitchell, R., GB	1	0	0.0	0	0
Nickerson, H., TB	1	6	6.0	6	0
Norton, K., DAL	1	25	25.0	25	0
Oldham, C., PHO	1	0	0.0	0	0
Owens, D., DET	1	1	1.0	1	0
Parker, A., MIN	1	1	1.0	1	0
Paup, B., GB	1	8	8.0	8	0
Pearson, Ja., MIN	1	0	0.0	0	0
Prior, M., GB	1	1	1.0	1	0
Raymond, C., NYG	2	11	5.5	11	0
Reynolds, R., TB	1	3	3.0	3	0
Rolling, B., Rams	2	21	10.5	12	0
Sanders, D., ATL	7	91	13.0	41	0
Scott, T., MIN	2	26	13.0	26	0
Scroggins, T., DET	1	0	0.0	0	0
Seals, R., TB	1	0	0.0	0t	1
Simmons, C., PHI	1	0	0.0	0	0
Simmons, W., GB	2	21	10.5	19	0

PLAYER/TEAM	NO	YARDS	AVG	LONG	TD
Smith, K., DAL	6	56	9.3	32t	0
Smith, O., PHI	1	0	0.0	0	0
Spielman, C., DET	2	-2	-1.0	0	0
Stewart, M., Rams	1	30	30.0	30	0
Swilling, P., DET	3	16	5.3	14	0
Tate, D., NYG	1	12	12.0	12	0
Taylor, K., NO	2	32	16.0	30	0
Teague, G., GB	1	22	22.0	22	0
Terrell, P., Rams	2	1	0.5	1	0
Thomas, Wi., PHI	2	39	19.5	21	0
Turnbull, R., NO	1	2	2.0	2	0
Walker, D., ATL	3	7	2.3	7	0
Washington, Ja., DAL	1	38	38.0	24	0
White, W., DET	1	5	5.0	5	0
Williams, A., PHO	2	87	43.5	46t	1
Woolford, D., CHI	2	18	9.0	18	0
Zordich, M., PHO	1	0	0.0	0	0

PUNT RETURNS

NFL PUNT RETURN LEADERS

PLAYER/TEAM	NO	YARDS	AVG	LONG	TD
Tyrone Hughes, NO	37	503	13.6	83t	2
Eric Metcalf, CLE	36	464	12.9	91t	2
Darrien Gordon, SD	31	395	12.7	54	0
Dexter Carter, SF	34	411	12.1	72t	1
Tim Brown, Raiders	40	465	11.6	74t	1
O.J. McDuffie, MIA	28	317	11.3	72t	2
Kevin Williams, DAL	36	381	10.6	64t	2
Glyn Milburn, DEN	40	425	10.6	54	0
David Meggett, NYG	32	331	10.3	75t	1
Dale Carter, KC	27	247	9.1	30	0
Troy Brown, NE	25	224	9.0	19	0
Russell Copeland, BUF	31	274	8.8	47t	1
Ron Harris, NE	23	201	8.7	21	0
Mel Gray, DET	23	197	8.6	35	0
Kelvin Martin, SEA	32	270	8.4	33	0
Vai Sikahema, PHI	33	275	8.3	25	0
Terry Obee, CHI	35	289	8.3	28	0
Johnny Bailey, PHO	35	282	8.1	58t	1
Tony Smith, ATL	32	255	8.0	51	0
Eric Guliford, MIN	29	212	7.3	50	0

PUNT RETURNS — AFC

PLAYER/TEAM	RET	FC	YDS	AVG	LG	TD
Birden, J.J., KC	5	3	43	8.6	12	0
Bradford, R., DEN	1	0	0	0.0	0	0
Brooks, B., BUF	1	0	3	3.0	3	0
Brown, Tim, Raiders	40	20	465	11.6	74t	1
Brown, Troy, NE	25	9	224	9.0	19	0
Carrier, Ma., CLE	6	1	92	15.3	56t	1
Carter, Da., KC	27	4	247	9.1	30	0
Copeland, R., BUF	31	7	274	8.8	47t	1
Crittenden, R., NE	2	1	37	18.5	30	0
Drewrey, W., HOU	41	19	275	6.7	18	0
Figures, D., PIT	5	2	15	3.0	6	0
Gordon, D., SD	31	15	395	12.7	54	0

PLAYER/TEAM	NO	YARDS	AVG	LONG	TD	
Harris, Ro., NE	23	4	201	8.7	21	0
Hicks, C., NYJ	17	4	157	9.2	20	0
Hughes, D., KC	3	0	49	16.3	29	0
Lewis, N., SD	3	2	17	5.7	7	0
Martin, K., SEA	32	15	270	8.4	33	0
Mathis, T., NYJ	14	8	99	7.1	16	0
McCloughan, D., SEA	1	0	10	10.0	10	0
McDuffie, O.J., MIA	28	22	317	11.3	72t	2
Metcalf, E., CLE	36	11	464	12.9	91t	2
Milburn, G., DEN	40	11	425	10.6	54	0
Mincy, C., KC	2	0	9	4.5	9	0
Pickens, C., CIN	4	2	16	4.0	9	0
Robinson, P., CIN	43	6	305	7.1	36	0
Simmons, M., CIN	1	0	0	0.0	0	0
Smith, R., NE	1	0	0	0.0	0	0
Tasker, S., BUF	1	0	0	0.0	0	0
Turner, E., CLE	0	0	7	N/A	7	0
Verdin, C., IND	30	17	173	5.8	24	0
Vincent, T., MIA	0	0	9	N/A	9	0
Woodson, R., PIT	42	10	338	8.0	39	0

PUNT RETURNS — NFC

PLAYER/TEAM	RET	FC	YDS	AVG	LG	TD
Anderson, Ga., TB/DET	17	1	113	6.6	15	0
Bailey, J., PHO	35	5	282	8.1	58t	1
Blount, E., PHO	9	3	90	10.0	25	0
Brooks, Ro., GB	16	4	135	8.4	35	0
Buchanan, R., Rams	8	1	41	5.1	12	0
Buckley, T., GB	11	5	76	6.9	39	0
Carter, D., SF	34	20	411	12.1	72t	1
Claiborne, R., TB	6	6	32	5.3	13	0
Clark, V., ATL	1	0	0	0.0	0	0
Edwards, An., PHO	3	3	12	4.0	11	0
Ellard, H., Rams	2	8	18	9.0	13	0
Gray, M., DET	23	14	197	8.6	35	0
Green, D., WAS	1	1	27	27.0	24	0
Guliford, E., MIN	29	15	212	7.3	50	0
Hawkins, C., TB	15	8	166	11.1	35	0
Henley, D., Rams	1	0	8	8.0	8	0
Howard, De., WAS	4	0	25	6.3	13	0
Hughes, T., NO	37	21	503	13.6	83t	2
Kelm, L., SF	1	0	0	0.0	0	0
Kinchen, T., Rams	7	4	32	4.6	8	0
Mays, A., WAS	1	0	0	0.0	0	0
Meggett, D., NYG	32	20	331	10.3	75t	1
Mitchell, B., WAS	29	7	193	6.7	48	0
Newman, P., NO	1	0	14	14.0	14	0
Obee, T., CHI	35	20	289	8.3	28	0
Parker, A., MIN	9	6	64	7.1	20	0
Price, M., Rams	1	2	3	3.0	3	0
Prior, M., GB	17	3	194	11.4	24	0
Sanders, D., ATL	2	1	21	10.5	16	0
Sikahema, V., PHI	33	20	275	8.3	25	0
Smith, O., PHI	0	0	9	N/A	9	0
Smith, Ro., MIN	1	2	4	4.0	4	0
Smith, T., ATL	22	17	255	8.0	51	0

Teague, G., GB------------------------1	0	-1	-1.0	-1	0
Turner, V., DET/TB------------------17	4	152	8.9	53	0
Washington, Ja., DAL-----------------1	0	0	0.0	0	0
Williams, K., DAL-----------------------36	14	381	10.6	64t	2

KICKOFF RETURNS

NFL KICKOFF RETURN LEADERS

PLAYER/TEAM	NO	YARDS	AVG	LONG	TD
Robert Brooks, GB---------------------23	611	26.6	95t	1
Tyrone Hughes, NO--------------------30	753	25.1	99t	1
Tony Smith, ATL-------------------------38	948	24.9	97t	1
Mel Gray, DET --------------------------28	688	24.6	95t	1
Raghib Ismail, Raiders ---------------25	605	24.2	66	0
O.J. McDuffie, MIA ---------------------32	755	23.6	48	0
Johnny Bailey, PHO ------------------31	699	22.5	48	0
Kevin Williams, DAL -------------------31	689	22.2	49	0
Eric Ball, CIN --------------------------23	501	21.8	45	0
Qadry Ismail, MIN ----------------------42	902	21.5	47	0
Curtis Conway, CHI---------------------21	450	21.4	55	0
Clarence Verdin, IND------------------50	1050	21.0	38	0
Ray Crittenden, NE --------------------23	478	20.8	44	0
Fred McAfee, NO-----------------------28	580	20.7	55	0
Nate Lewis, SD--------------------------33	684	20.7	60	0
Brian Mitchell, WAS--------------------33	678	20.5	68	0
Michael Bates, SEA--------------------30	603	20.1	46	0
Patrick Robinson, CIN----------------30	567	18.9	42	0
Randy Baldwin, CLE-------------------24	444	18.5	31	0
Russell Copeland, BUF---------------24	436	18.2	28	0

KICKOFF RETURNS — AFC

PLAYER/TEAM	RET	YDS	AVG	LG	TD
Anders, K., KC -----------------------1	47	47.0	47	0
Anderson, R., NYJ ---------------------4	66	16.5	22	0
Baldwin, R., CLE------------------------24	444	18.5	31	0
Ball, E., CIN----------------------------23	501	21.8	45	0
Bates, M., SEA-------------------------30	603	20.1	46	0
Baty, G., MIA --------------------------1	7	7.0	7	0
Beebe, D., BUF -----------------------10	160	16.0	22	0
Benjamin, R., CIN---------------------4	78	19.5	24	0
Bieniemy, E., SD ----------------------7	110	15.7	18	0
Birden, J.J., KC-----------------------0	0	N/A	—	0
Brown, G., HOU -----------------------2	29	14.5	16	0
Brown, Troy, NE ----------------------15	243	16.2	29	0
Butcher, P., IND-----------------------2	2	1.0	2	0
Cash, K., IND--------------------------1	11	11.0	11	0
Coates, B., NE-------------------------0	0	N/A	—	0
Coleman, P., HOU --------------------3	37	12.3	16	0
Cook, M., NE---------------------------1	8	8.0	8	0
Cooper, A., PIT------------------------1	2	2.0	2	0
Copeland, R., BUF--------------------24	436	18.2	28	0
Crittenden, R., NE--------------------23	478	20.8	44	0
Culver, R., IND-------------------------3	51	17.0	20	0
Davis, K., BUF8------------------------8	100	12.5	18	0
Delpino, R., DEN7 --------------------7	146	20.9	49	0
Dickerson, R., KC11------------------11	237	21.5	44	0
Drewrey, W., HOU15 ----------------15	293	19.5	34	0
Fryar, I., MIA---------------------------1	10	10.0	10	0

PLAYER/TEAM	NO	YARDS	AVG	LONG	TD
Gault, W., Raiders	7	187	26.7	60	0
Harmon, R., SD	1	18	18.0	18	0
Harris, Ro., NE	6	90	15.0	19	0
Hastings, A., PIT	12	177	14.8	22	0
Hendrickson, S., SD	2	25	12.5	19	0
Hoard, L., CLE	13	286	22.0	39	0
Hoge, M., PIT	3	33	11.0	15	0
Hughes, D., KC	14	266	19.0	30	0
Ismail, R., Raiders	25	605	24.2	66	0
Jones, F., KC	9	156	17.3	29	0
Kinchen, B., CLE	1	0	0.0	0	0
Kirby, T., MIA	4	85	21.3	26	0
Lamb, B., BUF	2	40	20.0	23	0
Lewis, N., SD	33	684	20.7	60	0
Martin, K., SEA	3	38	12.7	15	0
Marts, L., KC	1	0	0.0	0	0
Mathis, T., NYJ	7	102	14.6	28	0
McCallum, N., Raiders	1	12	12.0	12	0
McDuffie, O.J., MIA	32	755	23.6	48	0
McNair, T., KC	1	28	28.0	28	0
Means, N., SD	2	22	11.0	14	0
Meeks, B., DEN	1	9	9.0	9	0
Metcalf, E., CLE	15	318	21.2	47	0
Milburn, G., DEN	12	188	15.7	26	0
Miles, O., CIN	4	65	16.3	24	0
Miller, A., SD	2	42	21.0	29	0
Miller, S., MIA	2	22	11.0	16	0
Mills, Jo., HOU	11	230	20.9	37	0
Murrell, A., NYJ	23	342	14.9	23	0
Peat, T., Raiders	2	18	9.0	10	0
Prior, A., NYJ	9	126	14.0	27	0
Radecic, S., IND	1	10	10.0	10	0
Robinson, Gr., Raiders	4	57	14.3	33	0
Robinson, P., CIN	30	567	18.9	42	0
Russell, D., DEN	18	374	20.8	49	0
Sabb, D., NE	2	0	0.0	0	0
Sadowski, T., NYJ	1	0	0.0	0	0
Saxon, J., MIA	1	7	7.0	7	0
Sharpe, Sh., DEN	1	0	0.0	0	0
Shaw, E., CIN	0	0	N/A	—	0
Smith, Ke., Raiders	2	15	7.5	8	0
Smith, Ri., CLE	1	13	13.0	13	0
Stephens, J., KC	5	88	17.6	25	0
Stone, D., PIT	11	168	15.3	30	0
Thigpen, Y., PIT	1	23	23.0	23	0
Thomas, B., NYJ	2	39	19.5	28	0
Thompson, L., PIT	4	77	19.3	27	0
Tuatagaloa, N., SEA	1	10	10.0	10	0
Turk, D., Raiders	1	0	0.0	0	0
Turner, N., BUF	1	10	10.0	10	0
Vardell, T., CLE	4	58	14.5	16	0
Vaughn, J., SEA	16	280	17.5	31	0
Verdin, C., IND	50	1050	21.0	38	0
Vincent, T., MIA	0	2	N/A	2	0
Williams, H., KC	3	53	17.7	26	0
Williams, M., MIA	8	180	22.5	39	0

PLAYER/TEAM	RET	YDS	AVG	LG	TD
Williams, Wi., PIT	1	19	19.0	19	0
Woodson, R., PIT	15	294	19.6	44	0
Worley, T., PIT	4	85	21.3	26	0
Wright, Al., Raiders	10	167	16.7	28	0

KICKOFF RETURNS — NFC

PLAYER/TEAM	RET	YDS	AVG	LG	TD
Anderson, Ga., TB/DET	15	232	15.5	24	0
Bailey, J., PHO	31	699	22.5	48	0
Blount, E., PHO	8	163	20.4	27	0
Bowles, T., WAS	1	27	27.0	27	0
Boykin, D., Rams	13	216	16.6	29	0
Brandes, J., SF	1	10	10.0	10	0
Brooks, Re., WAS	1	12	12.0	12	0
Brooks, Ro., GB	23	611	26.6	95t	1
Brown, Derek, NO	3	58	19.3	23	0
Buck, J., WAS	1	15	15.0	15	0
Calloway, C., NYG	6	89	14.8	21	0
Carter, De., SF	25	494	19.8	60	0
Chmura, M., GB	1	0	0.0	0	0
Claiborne, R., TB	4	57	14.3	33	0
Clay, W., DET	2	34	17.0	20	0
Conway, C., CHI	21	450	21.4	55	0
Craig, R., MIN	1	11	11.0	11	0
Cross, H., NYG	2	15	7.5	13	0
Del Rio, J., MIN	1	4	4.0	4	0
Dowdell, M., NO	0	52	N/A	52	0
Drayton, T., Rams	1	−15	−15.0	−15	0
Edwards, An., PHO	3	51	17.0	20	0
Ervins, R., WAS	2	29	14.5	18	0
Evans, C., MIN	1	11	11.0	11	0
Fontenot, A., CHI	1	8	8.0	8	0
Gant, K., DAL	1	18	18.0	18	0
Graham, S., MIN	1	16	16.0	16	0
Gray, M., DET	28	688	24.6	95t	1
Green, Ro., CHI	9	141	15.7	30	0
Griffith, H., Rams	8	169	21.1	29	0
Guliford, E., MIN	5	101	20.2	29	0
Hallock, T., DET	1	11	11.0	11	0
Harris, C., GB	16	482	30.1	65	0
Hebron, V., PHI	3	35	11.7	18	0
Hennings, C., DAL	1	7	7.0	7	0
Heyward, C., CHI	1	12	12.0	12	0
Hilliard, D., NO	1	17	17.0	17	0
Howard, De., WAS	21	405	19.3	33	0
Hughes, T., NO	30	753	25.1	99t	1
Ismail, Q., MIN	42	902	21.5	47	0
Israel, S., Rams	5	92	18.4	23	0
Jamison, G., DET	1	0	0.0	0	0
Johnson, Ma., PHI	1	7	7.0	7	0
Jones, Robert, DAL	1	12	12.0	12	0
Jones, V., DET	0	0	N/A	—	0
Jurkovic, J., GB	2	22	11.0	13	0
Kelm, L., SF	1	0	0.0	0	0
Kinchen, T., Rams	6	96	16.0	22	0
Lee, A., SF	10	160	16.0	28	0

PLAYER/TEAM	NO	YARDS	AVG	LONG	TD
Lofton, S., PHO	1	18	18.0	18	0
Lynch, E., DET	1	22	22.0	22	0
Mangum, J., CHI	1	0	0.0	0	0
McAfee, F., NO	28	580	20.7	55	0
McMillian, A., MIN	1	0	0.0	0	0
Meggett, D., NYG	24	403	16.8	35	0
Mims, D., ATL	1	22	22.0	22	0
Mitchell, B., WAS	33	678	20.5	68	0
Montgomery, A., ATL	2	53	26.5	33	0
Moore, De., DET	1	68	68.0	68	0
Moore, Ro., PHO	1	9	9.0	9	0
Novacek, J., DAL	1	−1	−1.0	−1	0
Obee, T., CHI	9	159	17.7	34	0
Pegram, E., ATL	4	63	15.8	28	0
Phillips, Ja., ATL	2	38	19.0	29	0
Price, M., Rams	8	144	18.0	23	0
Royster, M., TB	8	102	12.8	26	0
Ruether, M., ATL	1	7	7.0	7	0
Ryan, T., CHI	1	5	5.0	5	0
Sanders, D., ATL	7	169	24.1	31	0
Sikahema, V., PHI	30	579	19.3	35	0
Smith, K., DAL	1	33	33.0	33	0
Smith, La., PHO	1	11	11.0	11	0
Smith, O., PHI	0	24	N/A	24	0
Smith, Ro., MIN	3	41	13.7	16	0
Smith, T., ATL	38	948	24.9	97t	1
Sydner, J., PHI	9	158	17.6	36	0
Thompson, Da., GB	9	171	19.0	42	0
Turner, V., DET/TB	21	391	18.6	46	0
Vanderbeek, M., DAL	0	0	N/A	—	0
Walker, A., SF	3	51	17.0	30	0
Walker, H., PHI	11	184	16.7	30	0
Walls, W., SF	0	0	N/A	—	0
White, Ru., Rams	8	122	15.3	35	0
Williams, Ja., SF	0	0	N/A	—	0
Williams, K., DAL	31	689	22.2	49	0
Wilson, C., TB	23	454	19.7	42	0
Wilson, Marcus, GB	9	197	21.9	37	0
Workman, V., TB	5	67	13.4	19	0
Worley, T., CHI	2	36	18.0	24	0

PUNTING

LEADING PUNTERS

	NO	YDS	LG	AVG	TB	BLK	RET	RET YDS	IN 20	NET AVG
Greg Montgomery, HOU	54	2462	77	45.6	5	0	28	249	13	39.1
Tom Rouen, DEN	67	3017	62	45.0	8	1	33	337	17	37.1
Jim Arnold, DET	72	3207	68	44.5	9	0	45	377	15	36.8
Rick Tuten, SEA	90	4007	64	44.5	7	1	47	475	21	37.3
Brian Hansen, CLE	82	3632	72	44.3	10	2	48	438	15	35.6
Reggie Roby, WAS	78	3447	60	44.2	10	0	31	343	25	37.2
Lee Johnson, CIN	90	3954	60	43.9	12	0	47	416	24	36.6
Rich Camarillo, PHO	73	3189	61	43.7	8	0	30	267	23	37.8
Tommy Barnhardt, NO	77	3356	58	43.6	6	0	36	348	26	37.5
Harold Alexander, ATL	72	3114	75	43.3	3	0	41	050	21	37.6

	NO	YDS	LG	AVG	TB	BLK	RET	RET YDS	IN 20	NET AVG
Rohn Stark, IND	83	3595	65	43.3	13	0	41	352	18	35.9
Harry Newsome, MIN	90	3864	64	42.9	6	0	46	560	25	35.4
Bryan Wagner, GB	74	3174	60	42.9	7	0	38	350	19	36.3
Sean Landeta, NYG/Rams	75	3215	66	42.9	10	1	44	444	18	33.8
Mike Horan, NYG	44	1882	60	42.8	1	0	25	107	13	39.9
John Kidd, SD	57	2431	67	42.0	7	0	28	243	16	35.9
Bryan Barker, KC	76	3240	59	42.6	8	1	43	352	19	35.4
Mark Royals, PIT	89	3781	61	42.5	3	0	50	678	28	34.2
Mike Saxon, NE	73	3096	59	42.4	7	3	34	313	25	34.8
John Jett, DAL	56	2342	59	41.8	3	0	32	169	22	37.7

PUNTERS — AFC

PLAYER/TEAM	NO	YDS	LG	AVG	TB	BLK	RET	RET YDS	IN 20	NET AVG
Aguiar, L., NYJ	73	2806	71	38.4	7	0	26	156	21	34.4
Barker, B., KC	76	3240	59	42.6	8	1	43	352	19	35.4
Carney, J., SD	4	155	46	38.8	0	0	2	16	1	34.8
Gossett, J., Raiders	71	2971	61	41.8	9	0	35	301	19	35.1
Hansen, B., CLE	82	3632	72	44.3	10	2	49	438	15	35.6
Hatcher, D., MIA	58	2304	56	39.7	4	0	32	359	13	32.2
Johnson, L., CIN	90	3954	60	43.9	12	0	47	416	24	36.6
Kidd, J., SD	57	2431	67	42.6	7	0	28	243	16	35.9
Mohr, C., BUF	74	2991	58	40.4	4	0	29	247	19	36.0
Montgomery, Gr., HOU	54	2462	77	45.6	5	0	28	249	13	39.1
Rouen, T., DEN	67	3017	62	45.0	8	1	33	337	17	37.1
Royals, M., PIT	89	3781	61	42.5	3	0	50	678	28	34.2
Saxon, M., NE	73	3096	59	42.4	7	3	34	313	25	34.8
Stark, R., IND	83	3595	65	43.3	13	0	41	352	18	35.9
Sullivan, K., SD/HOU	15	614	50	40.9	1	0	6	33	4	38.7
Tuten, R., SEA	90	4007	64	44.5	7	1	47	475	21	37.3

PUNTERS — NFC

PLAYER/TEAM	NO	YDS	LG	AVG	TB	BLK	RET	RET YDS	IN 20	NET AVG
Alexander, H., ATL	72	3114	75	43.3	3	0	41	350	21	37.6
Arnold, J., DET	72	3207	68	44.5	9	0	45	377	15	36.8
Barnhardt, T., NO	77	3356	58	43.6	6	0	36	348	26	37.5
Bracken, D., Rams	17	651	51	38.3	0	0	8	86	3	33.2
Camarillo, R., PHO	73	3189	61	43.7	8	0	30	267	23	37.8
Feagles, J., PHI	83	3323	60	40.0	4	0	35	311	31	35.3
Gardocki, C., CHI	80	3080	58	38.5	2	0	22	115	28	36.6
Goodburn, K., WAS	6	107	49	39.4	0	0	3	0	3	39.4
Horan, M., NYG	44	1882	60	42.8	1	0	25	107	13	39.9
Jett, J., DAL	56	2342	59	41.8	3	0	32	169	22	37.7
Landeta, S., NYG/Rams	75	3215	66	42.9	10	1	44	444	18	33.8
McJulien, P., Rams	21	795	56	37.9	3	0	10	143	5	28.2
Newsome, H., MIN	90	3862	64	42.9	6	0	46	560	25	35.4
Roby, R., WAS	78	3447	60	44.2	10	0	31	343	25	37.2
Stryzinski, D., TB	93	3772	57	40.6	3	1	53	394	24	35.3
Wagner, B., GB	74	3174	60	42.9	7	0	38	350	19	36.3
Wilmsmeyer, K., SF	42	1718	61	40.9	5	0	15	171	11	34.5

SCORING

KICKING LEADERS

PLAYER/TEAM	XPM	XPA	XP PCT.	FGM	FGA	FG PCT.	LNG	PTS
Jeff Jaeger, Raiders	27	29	93.1	35	44	79.5	53	132
Jason Hanson, DET	28	28	100.0	34	43	79.1	53	130
Chris Jacke, GB	35	35	100.0	31	37	83.8	54	128
Al Del Greco, HOU	39	40	97.5	29	34	85.3	52	126
John Carney, SD	31	33	93.9	31	40	77.5	51	124
Eddie Murray, DAL	38	38	100.0	28	33	84.8	52	122
Jason Elam, DEN	41	42	97.6	26	35	74.3	54	119
Morten Andersen, NO	33	33	100.0	28	35	80.0	56	117
Gary Anderson, PIT	32	32	100.0	28	30	93.3	46	116
Norm Johnson, ATL	34	34	100.0	26	27	96.3	54	112
Pete Stoyanovich, MIA	37	37	100.0	24	32	75.0	52	109
Mike Cofer, SF	59	61	96.7	16	26	61.5	46	107
Nick Lowery, KC	37	37	100.0	23	29	79.3	52	106
Fuad Reveiz, MIN	27	28	96.4	26	35	74.3	51	105
Steve Christie, BUF	36	37	97.3	23	32	71.9	59	105
David Treadwell, NYG	28	29	96.6	25	31	80.6	46	103
Kevin Butler, CHI	21	22	95.5	27	36	75.0	55	102
Greg Davis, PHO	37	37	100.0	21	28	75.0	55	100
John Kasay, SEA	29	29	100.0	23	28	82.1	55	98
Dean Biasucci, IND	15	16	93.8	26	31	83.9	53	93

KICKING — AFC

PLAYER/TEAM	XPM	XPA	XP PCT.	FGM	FGA	FG PCT.	LNG	PTS
Anderson, G., PIT	32	32	100.0	28	30	93.3	46	116
Bahr, M.,PHI/NE	28	29	96.6	13	18	72.2	48	67
Biasucci, D., IND	15	16	93.8	26	31	83.9	53	93
Blanchard, C., NYJ	31	31	100.0	17	26	65.4	45	82
Carney, J., SD	31	33	93.9	31	40	77.5	51	124
Christie, S., BUF	36	37	97.3	23	32	71.9	59	105
Del Greco, A., HOU	39	40	97.5	29	34	85.3	52	126
Elam, J., DEN	41	42	97.6	26	35	74.3	54	119
Jaeger, J., Raiders	27	29	93.1	35	44	79.5	53	132
Kasay, J., SEA	29	29	100.0	23	28	82.1	55	98
Lowery, N., KC	37	37	100.0	23	29	79.3	52	106
Pelfrey, T., CIN	13	16	81.3	24	31	77.4	53	85
Sisson, S., NE	15	15	100.0	14	26	53.8	40	57
Stover, M., CLE	36	36	100.0	16	22	72.7	53	84
Stoyanovich, P., MIA	37	37	100.0	24	32	75.0	52	109

KICKING — NFC

PLAYER/TEAM	XPM	XPA	XP PCT.	FGM	FGA	FG PCT.	LNG	PTS
Andersen, M., NO	33	33	100.0	28	35	80.0	56	117
Butler, K., CHI	21	22	95.5	27	36	75.0	55	102
Cofer, M., SF	59	61	96.7	16	26	61.5	46	107
Daluiso, B., NYG	0	0	NA	1	3	33.3	54	3
Davis, G., PHO	37	37	100.0	21	28	75.0	55	100
Elliott, L., ATL	2	3	66.7	2	4	50.0	43	8
Hanson, J., DET	28	28	100.0	34	43	79.1	53	130
Husted, M., TB	27	27	100.0	16	22	72.7	57	75
Jacke, C., GB	35	35	100.0	31	37	83.8	54	128
Johnson, N., ATL	34	34	100.0	26	27	96.3	54	112
Lohmiller, C., WAS	24	26	92.3	16	28	57.1	51	72

PLAYER/TEAM	XPM	XPA	XP PCT.	FGM	FGA	FG PCT.	LNG	PTS
Murray, E., DAL ------------	38	38	100.0	28	33	84.8	52	122
Reveiz, F., MIN -------------	27	28	96.4	26	35	74.3	51	105
Ruzek, R., PHI -------------	13	16	81.3	8	10	80.0	46	37
Treadwell, D., NYG --------	28	29	96.6	25	31	80.6	46	103
Zendejas, T., Rams--------	23	25	92.0	16	23	69.6	54	71

NFL LEADERS — TOUCHDOWNS

PLAYER/TEAM	TD	RUSH	REC	RET	PTS
Jerry Rice, SF ------------------------	16	1	15	0	96
Marcus Allen, KC ----------------------	15	12	3	0	90
Andre Rison, ATL----------------------	15	0	15	0	90
Sterling Sharpe, GB-------------------	11	0	11	0	66
Ricky Watters, SF -------------------	11	10	1	0	66
Edgar Bennett, GB --------------------	10	9	1	0	60
Emmitt Smith, DAL --------------------	10	9	1	0	60
Calvin Williams, PHI ------------------	10	0	10	0	60
Barry Foster, PIT --------------------	9	8	1	0	54
Cris Carter, MIN ----------------------	9	0	9	0	54
Ron Moore, PHO----------------------	9	9	0	0	54
Shannon Sharpe, DEN ----------------	9	0	9	0	54
Greg Brown, HOU--------------------	8	6	2	0	48
Tim Brown, Raiders---------------------	8	0	7	1	48
Ben Coates, NE ---------------------	8	0	8	0	48
Robert Delpino, DEN-------------------	8	0	8	0	48
Michael Jackson, CLE -----------------	8	0	8	0	48
Natrone Means, SD -------------------	8	8	0	0	48
Jerome Bettis, Rams ------------------	7	7	0	0	42
Michael Irvin, DAL---------------------	7	0	7	0	42

TOUCHDOWNS — AFC

PLAYER/TEAM	TOT	RUSH	REC	RET	PTS
Allen, M., KC---------------------------	15	12	3	0	90
Anders, K., KC ------------------------	1	0	1	0	6
Baldwin, R., CLE -----------------------	1	0	1	0	6
Ball, E., CIN---------------------------	1	1	0	0	6
Barnett, T., KC ------------------------	1	0	1	0	6
Baty, G., MIA --------------------------	1	0	1	0	6
Baxter, B., NYJ ------------------------	7	7	0	0	42
Baxter, F., NYJ-------------------------	1	0	1	0	6
Beebe, D., BUF-------------------------	3	0	3	0	18
Bell, N., Raiders -----------------------	1	1	0	0	6
Bernstine, R., DEN---------------------	4	4	0	0	24
Bieniemy, E., SD ------------------------	1	1	0	0	6
Birden, J.J., KC -----------------------	2	0	2	0	12
Blackmon, R., SEA ---------------------	1	0	0	1	6
Blades, B., SEA------------------------	3	0	3	0	18
Brim, M., CIN--------------------------	1	0	0	1	6
Brisby, V., NE -------------------------	2	0	2	0	12
Brooks, B., BUF -----------------------	5	0	5	0	30
Brown, G., HOU -----------------------	8	6	2	0	48
Brown, Tim, Raiders--------------------	8	0	7	1	48
Burkett, C., NYJ -----------------------	4	0	4	0	24
Butts, M., SD -------------------------	4	4	0	0	24
Byars, K., MIA-------------------------	6	3	3	0	36
Carlson, C., HOU-----------------------	2	2	0	0	12

TOUCHDOWNS — AFC

PLAYER/TEAM	TOT	RUSH	REC	RET	PTS
Carrier, M., CLE	5	1	3	1	30
Cash, Keith, KC	4	0	4	0	24
▮▮▮▮, ▮▮▮▮, IND	3	0	3	0	18
Chaffey, P., NYJ	1	0	1	0	0
Childress, R., HOU	1	0	0	1	6
Coates, B., NE	8	0	8	0	48
Cook, M., NE	1	0	1	0	6
Copeland, R., BUF	1	0	0	1	6
Crittenden, R., NE	1	0	1	0	6
Croel, M., DEN	1	0	0	1	6
Croom, C., NE	1	1	0	0	6
Culver, R., IND	5	3	1	1	30
Davidson, K., PIT	1	0	0	1	6
Davis, K., BUF	6	6	0	0	36
Davis, Wi., KC	7	0	7	0	42
Dawkins, S., IND	1	0	1	0	6
Delpino, R., DEN	8	8	0	0	48
Dishman, C., HOU	1	0	0	1	6
Duncan, C., HOU	3	0	3	0	18
Edmunds, F., SEA	2	0	2	0	12
Edwards, An., SEA	0	0	0	0	0
Esiason, B., NYJ	1	1	0	0	6
Fenner, D., CIN	1	1	0	0	6
Foster, B., PIT	9	8	1	0	54
Frank, D., SD	1	0	0	1	6
Fryar, I., MIA	5	0	5	0	30
Gardner, C., BUF	1	0	1	0	6
Gash, S., NE	1	1	0	0	6
Givins, E., HOU	4	0	4	0	24
Glover, A., Raiders	1	0	1	0	6
Green, E., PIT	5	0	5	0	30
Green, P., SEA	1	0	1	0	6
Harmon, R., SD	2	0	2	0	12
Harris, L., HOU	1	0	1	0	6
Hayes, J., KC	1	0	1	0	6
Herrod, J., IND	1	0	0	1	6
Hester, J., IND	1	0	1	0	6
Higgs, M., MIA	3	3	0	0	18
Hoge, M., PIT	5	1	4	0	30
Horton, E., Raiders	1	0	1	0	6
Hostetler, J., Raiders	5	5	0	0	30
Ingram, M., MIA	6	0	6	0	36
Ismail, R., Raiders	1	0	1	0	6
Jackson, K., MIA	6	0	6	0	36
Jackson, Mi., CLE	8	0	8	0	48
Jackson, S., HOU	1	0	0	1	6
Jefferson, S., SD	2	0	2	0	12
Jeffires, H., HOU	6	0	6	0	36
Jett, Ja., Raiders	3	0	3	0	18
Johnson, A., IND	1	1	0	0	6
Johnson, J., NYJ	4	3	1	0	24
Johnson, Re., DEN	1	0	1	0	6
Johnson, Tr., SEA	1	0	1	0	6
Johnson, Vance, DEN	5	0	5	0	30
Jones, He., BUF	1	0	0	1	6

TOUCHDOWNS — AFC

PLAYER/TEAM	TOT	RUSH	REC	RET	PTS
Jones, Ja., CLE	1	1	0	0	6
Kidd, J., SD	1	1	0	0	6
Kinchen, B., CLE	2	0	2	0	12
Kirby, T., MIA	6	3	3	0	36
Kirkland, L., PIT	1	0	0	1	6
Langhorne, R., IND	3	0	3	0	18
Lewis, A., KC	1	0	0	1	6
Lewis, Da., HOU	1	0	0	1	6
Lewis, N., SD	4	0	4	0	24
Mack, K., CLE	1	1	0	0	6
Marino, D., MIA	1	1	0	0	6
Marshall, A., DEN	2	0	2	0	12
Martin, K., SEA	5	0	5	0	30
Martin, T., MIA	3	0	3	0	18
Mathis, T., NYJ	1	1	0	0	6
McCallum, N., Raiders	3	3	0	0	18
McCardell, K., CLE	4	0	4	0	24
McDaniel, T., Raiders	1	0	0	1	6
McDuffie, O.J., MIA	2	0	0	2	12
McKeller, K., BUF	1	0	1	0	6
McMurtry, G., NE	1	0	1	0	6
McNair, T., KC	2	2	0	0	12
Means, N., SD	8	8	0	0	48
Metcalf, E., CLE	5	1	2	2	30
Metzelaars, P., BUF	4	0	4	0	24
Milburn, G., DEN	3	0	3	0	18
Miles, O., CIN	1	1	0	0	6
Miller, A., SD	7	0	7	0	42
Mills, E., PIT	1	0	1	0	6
Mirer, R., SEA	3	3	0	0	18
Mitchell, J., NYJ	6	0	6	0	36
Moon, W., HOU	1	1	0	0	6
Moore, R., NYJ	1	0	1	0	6
Moore, St., CLE	1	0	0	1	6
Murrell, A., NYJ	1	1	0	0	6
Mustafaa, N., CLE	1	0	0	1	6
Nash, J., SEA	1	0	0	1	6
Odomes, N., BUF	1	0	0	1	6
Oliver, L., MIA	1	0	0	1	6
Orlando, B., HOU	1	0	0	1	6
Philcox, T., CLE	1	1	0	0	6
Pickens, C., CIN	6	0	6	0	36
Pleasant, A., CLE	0	0	0	0	0
Query, J., CIN	4	0	4	0	24
Reed, A., BUF	6	0	6	0	36
Riddick, L., CLE	0	0	0	0	0
Rivers, R., DEN	2	1	1	0	12
Robertson, M., HOU	1	0	0	1	6
Robinson, Gr., Raiders	1	1	0	0	6
Russell, D., DEN	4	0	3	1	24
Russell, L., NE	7	7	0	0	42
Saleaumua, D., KC	1	0	0	1	6
Sharpe, Sh., DEN	9	0	9	0	54
Slaughter, W., HOU	5	0	5	0	30
Stephens, J., KC	1	1	0	0	6

TOUCHDOWNS — AFC

PLAYER/TEAM	TOT	RUSH	REC	RET	PTS
Stephens, R., SEA	1	0	0	1	6
Stone, D., PIT	3	1	2	0	18
Talley, D., BUF	1	0	0	1	6
Thigpen, Y., PIT	3	0	3	0	18
Thomas, B., NYJ	1	1	0	0	6
Thomas, D., KC	1	0	0	1	6
Thomas, T., BUF	6	6	0	0	36
Thompson, C., CIN	1	0	1	0	6
Thompson, L., PIT	3	3	0	0	18
Thornton, J., NYJ	2	0	2	0	12
Tillman, C., DEN	2	0	2	0	12
Tillman, L., CLE	1	0	1	0	6
Tillman, S., HOU	1	0	1	0	6
Timpson, M., NE	2	0	2	0	12
Turner, K., NE	2	0	2	0	12
Valerio, J., KC	1	0	1	0	6
Vardell, T., CLE	4	3	1	0	24
Verdin, C., IND	1	0	1	0	6
Walker, De., SD	1	0	1	0	6
Warren, C., SEA	7	7	0	0	42
Washington, B., NYJ	1	0	0	1	6
Washington, Mi., BUF	1	0	0	1	6
Wellman, G., HOU	1	0	1	0	6
White, Lo., HOU	2	2	0	0	12
Williams, Al., CIN	0	0	0	0	0
Williams, D., CIN	1	0	0	1	6
Williams, J.L., SEA	4	3	1	0	24
Wolfley, R., CLE	1	0	1	0	6
Woodson, R., PIT	1	0	0	1	6
Wright, Al., Raiders	4	0	4	0	24
Wyman, D., DEN	1	0	1	0	6
Young, D., SD	2	0	2	0	12

TOUCHDOWNS—NFC

PLAYER/TEAM	TOT	RUSH	REC	RET	PTS
Allen, E., PHI	4	0	0	4	24
Anderson, Ga., TB/DET	1	0	1	0	6
Anderson, N., CHI	4	4	0	0	24
Anderson, W., Rams	4	0	4	0	24
Armstrong, Ty., TB	1	0	1	0	6
Bailey, J., PHO	2	1	0	1	12
Bailey, V., PHI	1	0	1	0	6
Baker, Sh., CHI	2	0	0	2	12
Bavaro, M., PHI	6	0	6	0	36
Beach, S., SF	1	0	1	0	6
Bennett, E., GB	10	9	1	0	60
Bettis, J., Rams	7	7	0	0	42
Blount, E., PHO	1	1	0	0	6
Bono, S., SF	1	1	0	0	6
Boykin, D., Rams	1	0	0	1	6
Brenner, H., NO	1	0	1	0	6
Brooks, Re., WAS	3	3	0	0	18
Brooks, Ro., GB	1	0	0	1	6
Broussard, S., ATL	1	1	0	0	6
Brown, Derek, NO	3	2	1	0	18
Bunch, J., NYG	3	2	1	0	18

TOUCHDOWNS—NFC

PLAYER/TEAM	TOT	RUSH	REC	RET	PTS
Butler, L., GB	1	0	0	1	6
Byner, E., WAS	1	1	0	0	6
Calloway, C., NYG	3	0	3	0	18
Carrier, Ma., CHI	1	0	0	1	6
Carter, A., MIN	5	0	5	0	30
Carter, C., MIN	9	0	9	0	54
Carter, De., SF	2	1	0	1	12
Carter, P., Rams	1	0	1	0	6
Centers, L., PHO	3	0	3	0	18
Clark, G., PHO	4	0	4	0	24
Clark, V., ATL	1	0	0	1	6
Clay, W., DET	2	0	0	2	12
Clayton, M., GB	3	0	3	0	18
Cobb, R., TB	4	3	1	0	24
Coleman, L., DAL	2	2	0	0	12
Coleman, M., WAS	1	0	0	1	6
Collins, M., NYG	1	0	0	1	6
Conway, C., CHI	2	0	2	0	12
Copeland, H., TB	4	0	4	0	24
Craig, R., MIN	2	1	1	0	12
Cross, H., NYG	5	0	5	0	30
Cunningham, R., PHI	1	1	0	0	6
Davis, E., SF	2	0	0	2	12
Dowdell, M., NO	1	0	1	0	6
Drayton, T., Rams	4	0	4	0	24
Early, Q., NO	6	0	6	0	36
Edwards, An., PHO	1	0	1	0	6
Ellard, H., Rams	2	0	2	0	12
Evans, B., PHI	1	0	0	1	6
Favre, B., GB	1	1	0	0	6
Flores, M., PHI	0	0	0	0	0
Galbraith, S., DAL	1	0	1	0	6
Gannon, R., WAS	1	1	0	0	6
Gary, C., Rams	2	1	1	0	12
Gouveia, K., WAS	1	0	0	1	6
Graham, S., MIN	3	3	0	0	18
Gray, M., DET	1	0	0	1	6
Green, D., WAS	1	0	0	1	6
Green, W., DET	2	0	2	0	12
Hall, R., TB	1	0	1	0	6
Hallock, T., DET	2	0	2	0	12
Hamilton, K., NYG	0	0	0	0	0
Hampton, R., NYG	5	5	0	0	30
Hanks, M., SF	1	0	0	1	6
Harbaugh, J., CHI	4	4	0	0	24
Harper, A., DAL	5	0	5	0	30
Harris, J., GB	4	0	4	0	24
Hawkins, C., TB	5	0	5	0	30
Haynes, M., ATL	4	0	4	0	24
Hearst, G., PHO	1	1	0	0	6
Hebron, V., PHI	3	3	0	0	18
Hill, R., PHO	4	0	4	0	24
Hilliard, D., NO	3	2	1	0	18
Holman, R., DET	2	0	2	0	12
Hughes, T., NO	3	0	0	3	18

TOUCHDOWNS—NFC

PLAYER/TEAM	TOT	RUSH	REC	RET	PTS
Irvin, M., DAL	7	0	7	0	42
Ismail, Q., MIN	1	0	1	0	6
Jackson, M., NYG	4	0	4	0	24
Jamison, G., DET	1	0	0	1	6
Johnson, A.J., WAS	1	0	0	1	6
Johnston, D., DAL	4	3	1	0	24
Jones, B., SF	3	0	3	0	18
Jones, Da, CHI	1	0	0	1	6
Jones, Er., Rams	2	0	2	0	12
Jordan, S., MIN	1	0	1	0	6
Joseph, J., PHI	1	0	1	0	6
Kinchen, T., Rams	1	0	1	0	6
Lassic, D., DAL	3	3	0	0	18
Lee, A., SF	3	1	2	0	18
Lincoln, J., CHI	1	0	0	1	6
Logan, M., SF	7	7	0	0	42
Lynch, E., DET	2	2	0	0	12
Lynch, L., PHO	1	0	0	1	6
Mack, M., TB	1	0	0	1	6
Martin, E., NO	3	0	3	0	18
McAfee, F., NO	1	1	0	0	6
McCaffrey, E., NYG	2	0	2	0	12
McDowell, A., TB	1	0	1	0	6
McGee, Ti., WAS	3	0	3	0	18
McGriggs, L., MIN	1	0	0	1	6
McGruder, M., SF	1	0	0	1	6
McMillian, A., MIN	1	0	0	1	6
McNeal, T., Rams	1	0	1	0	6
Meggett, D., NYG	1	0	0	1	6
Middleton, R., WAS	2	0	2	0	12
Mills, S., NO	1	0	0	1	6
Mims, D., ATL	1	0	1	0	6
Mitchell, B., WAS	3	3	0	0	18
Monk, A., WAS	2	0	2	0	12
Moore, Da., TB	1	0	1	0	6
Moore, De., DET	4	3	1	0	24
Moore, H., DET	6	0	6	0	36
Moore, Ro., PHO	9	9	0	0	54
Muster, B., NO	3	3	0	0	18
Neal, L., NO	1	1	0	0	6
Ned, D., NO	1	1	0	0	6
Newman, P., NO	1	0	1	0	6
Novacek, J., DAL	2	1	1	0	12
Obee, T., CHI	3	0	3	0	18
Peete, R., DET	1	1	0	0	6
Pegram, E., ATL	3	3	0	0	18
Perriman, B., DET	2	0	2	0	12
Pritchard, M., ATL	7	0	7	0	42
Proehl, R., PHO	7	0	7	0	42
Rasheed, K., NYG	1	1	0	0	6
Rathman, T., SF	3	3	0	0	18
Reeves, W., PHO	1	0	1	0	6
Rice, J., SF	16	1	15	0	96
Rison, A., ATL	15	0	15	0	90
Rolle, B., PHO	1	0	1	0	6

TOUCHDOWNS—NFC

PLAYER/TEAM	TOT	RUSH	REC	RET	PTS
Royster, M., TB	1	1	0	0	6
Rypien, M., WAS	3	3	0	0	18
Sanders, B., DET	3	3	0	0	18
Sanders, D., ATL	1	0	1	0	6
Sanders, R., WAS	4	0	4	0	24
Seals, R., TB	1	0	0	1	6
Sharpe, S., GB	11	0	11	0	66
Sherman, H., PHI	2	2	0	0	12
Sherrard, M., NYG	2	0	2	0	12
Singleton, N., SF	1	0	1	0	6
Small, T., NO	1	0	1	0	6
Smith, E., DAL	10	9	1	0	60
Smith, I., NO	2	0	2	0	12
Smith, K., DAL	1	0	0	1	6
Smith, Ro., MIN	2	2	0	0	12
Smith, T., ATL	1	0	0	1	6
Tamm, R., SF	1	0	0	1	6
Taylor, J., SF	5	0	5	0	30
Thomas, L., TB	2	0	2	0	12
Thompson, Da, GB	3	3	0	0	18
Tice, M., MIN	1	0	1	0	6
Tillman, Le., NYG	3	3	0	0	18
Turner, F., NO	1	0	1	0	6
Waddle, T., CHI	1	0	1	0	6
Walker, H., PHI	4	1	3	0	24
Warren, F., NO	1	0	0	1	6
Watters, R., SF	11	10	1	0	66
Wetnight, R., CHI	1	0	1	0	6
Williams, A., PHO	2	0	0	2	12
Williams, C., PHI	10	0	10	0	60
Williams, Ja., SF	1	0	1	0	6
Williams, K., DAL	6	2	2	2	36
Word, B., MIN	2	2	0	0	12
Workman, V., TB	4	2	2	0	24
Worley, T., CHI	2	2	0	0	12
Young, M., PHI	2	0	2	0	12
Young, S., SF	2	2	0	0	12

SACKS

NFL LEADERS — SACKS

PLAYER/TEAM	NO.	PLAYER/TEAM	NO.
Neil Smith, KC	15.0	Anthony Smith, Raiders	12.5
Simon Fletcher, DEN	13.5	Leslie O'Neal, SD	12.0
Bruce Smith, BUF	13.5	Trace Armstrong, CHI	11.5
Renaldo Turnbull, NO	13.0	Keith Hamilton, NYG	11.5
Reggie White, GB	13.0	Andy Harmon, PHI	11.5
Sean Jones, HOU	13.0	Rickey Jackson, NO	11.5
Richard Dent, CHI	12.5	Bryce Paup, GB	11.0
Chris Doleman, MIN	12.5	Anthony Pleasant, CLE	11.0
John Randle, MIN	12.5	Jeff Cross, MIA	10.5
Kevin Greene, PIT	12.5	William Fuller, HOU	10.0

SACKS — AFC

PLAYER/TEAM	NO.	PLAYER/TEAM	NO.
Agnew, R., NE	1.5	Johnson, Bi., CLE	1.0
Alexander, B., MIA	1.0	Johnson, M., CLE	4.0
Anderson, E., Raiders	1.0	Johnson, P., CLE	1.0
Atwater, S., DEN	1.0	Jones, A., NE	3.5
Ball, J., CLE	3.0	Jones, Do., NYJ	1.0
Barnett, O., BUF	2.0	Jones, He., BUF	2.0
Barrow, M., HOU	1.0	Jones, James, CLE	5.5
Bayless, M., KC	1.0	Jones, S., HOU	13.0
Bennett, C., BUF	4.5	Kelly, Joe, Raiders	1.0
Bickett, D., IND	4.0	Kennedy, C., SEA	6.5
Bishop, B., HOU	1.0	Kirkland, L., PIT	1.0
Bowden, J., HOU	1.0	Klingbeil, C., MIA	1.5
Broughton, W., Raiders	1.0	Kragen, G., DEN	3.0
Brown, C., PIT	3.0	Krumrie, T., CIN	3.0
Brown, V., NE	1.0	Lageman, J., NYJ	8.5
Bruce, A., Raiders	2.0	Lake, C., PIT	5.0
Bryant, J., SEA	1.0	Lathon, L., HOU	2.0
Burnett, R., CLE	9.0	Lee, S., SD	3.0
Carrington, D., SD	1.0	Lewis, M., NYJ	4.0
Childress, R., HOU	9.0	Lloyd, G., PIT	6.0
Clancy, S., IND	1.0	Lodish, M., BUF	0.5
Clifton, K., NYJ	1.0	Long, H., Raiders	6.0
Coleman, Ma., MIA	5.5	Lott, R., NYJ	1.0
Collins, T., NE	1.0	Marshall, L., NYJ	2.0
Copeland, J., CIN	3.0	Marshall, W., HOU	2.0
Coryatt, Q., IND	1.0	Marts, L., KC	2.0
Cox, B., MIA	5.0	Matthews, C., CLE	5.5
Croel, M., DEN	5.0	McClendon, S., IND	1.5
Cross, J., MIA	10.5	McCrary, M., SEA	4.0
Davidson, K., PIT	2.5	McDonald, R., CIN	1.0
Dronett, S., DEN	7.0	McDowell, B., HOU	1.0
Edwards, An., SEA	3.0	McGlockton, C., Raiders	7.0
Emtman, S., IND	1.0	Mecklenburg, K., DEN	9.0
Evans, D., PIT	6.5	Mersereau, S., NYJ	1.0
Fletcher, S., DEN	13.5	Mickell, D., KC	1.0
Footman, D., CLE	1.0	Mims, C., SD	7.0
Francis, J., CIN	2.0	Montgomery, Gl., HOU	6.0
Frase, P., NYJ	1.0	Nash, J., SEA	0.5
Frier, M., CIN	1.0	Newton, T., KC	1.0
Fuller, W., HOU	10.0	O'Neal, L., SD	12.0
Goad, T., NE	0.5	Oshodin, W., DEN	1.0
Goganious, K., BUF	1.0	Parrella, J., BUF	1.0
Gray, C., SEA	1.0	Patton, M., BUF	1.0
Greene, K., PIT	12.5	Peguese, W., IND	2.0
Griggs, D., MIA	0.5	Perry, M., CLE	6.0
Grossman, B., SD	4.5	Phillips, J., KC	1.5
Hand, J., IND	5.0	Pitts, M., NE	3.0
Hansen, P., BUF	3.5	Pleasant, A., CLE	11.0
Harrison, N., Raiders	3.0	Pope, M., SD	0.5
Henry, K., PIT	1.0	Porter, R., SEA	1.0
Herrod, J., IND	2.0	Richard, S., SD	2.0
Hinkle, G., CIN	1.0	Robinson, Eu., SEA	2.0
Houston, B., NYJ	3.0	Robinson, Ed., HOU	1.0
Hunter, J., MIA	3.0	Robinson, J., DEN	3.5
Hurst, M., NE	1.0	Robinson, R., SEA	1.5

SACKS—AFC

PLAYER/TEAM	NO.
Rodgers, T., SEA	1.0
Ross, K., KC	0.5
Sabb, D., NE	2.0
Saleaumua, D., KC	3.5
Sims, T., IND	1.0
Sinclair, M., SEA	8.0
Siragusa, T., IND	1.5
Slade, C., NE	9.0
Smith, An., Raiders	12.5
Smith, B., BUF	13.5
Smith, N., KC	15.0
Stargell, T., IND	1.0
Steed, J., PIT	1.5
Stephens, R., SEA	2.5
Stubbs, D., CIN	5.0
Talley, D., BUF	2.0
Teeter, M., HOU	1.0
Terry, D., KC	1.0
Thomas, D., KC	8.0
Thompson, B., KC	0.5
Thompson, R., NE	1.0
Tippett, A., NE	8.5
Townsend, G., Raiders	7.5
Tuatagaloa, N., SEA	3.5
Turner, M., NYJ	1.0
Veasey, C., MIA	2.0
Wallace, A., Raiders	2.0
Walls, E., CLE	1.0
Washington, L., Raiders	1.0
Washington, Ma., NYJ	5.5
Washington, Mi., BUF	0.5
Williams, Al., CIN	4.0
Williams, B., NE	2.0
Williams, Dan, DEN	1.0
Williams, Darryl, CIN	2.0
Williams, G., PIT	1.0
Williams, L., HOU	3.0
Winter, B., SD	2.0
Wooden, T., SEA	2.5
Woodson, R., PIT	2.0
Wright, J., BUF	5.5
Wyman, D., DEN	2.0
Young, L., NYJ	1.0

SACKS — NFC

PLAYER/TEAM	NO.
Agee, M., ATL	2.5
Ahanotu, C., TB	1.5
Allen, E., PHI	2.0
Armstrong, T., CHI	11.5
Atkins, G., NO	1.0
Bailey, C., NYG	1.5
Banks, Ca., WAS	1.0
Bankston, M., PHO	3.0
Barker, R., MIN	6.0

PLAYER/TEAM	NO.
Bennett, T., GB	6.5
Booty, J., PHO	3.0
Boutte, M., Rams	1.0
Brock, M., GB	2.0
Brooks, M., NYG	1.0
Brown, Dennis, SF	5.5
Buck, V., NO	3.0
Butler, L., GB	1.0
Case, S., ATL	1.5
Casillas, T., DAL	2.0
Clay, W., DET	1.0
Coleman, M., WAS	6.0
Collins, A., WAS	6.0
Collins, M., NYG	1.0
Colon, H., DET	1.0
Conner, D., ATL	1.5
Cook, T., NO	1.0
Cox, Ro., CHI	2.0
Crockett, R., DET	1.0
Curry, E., TB	5.0
Davis, R., PHO	1.0
Del Rio, J., MIN	0.5
Dent, R., CHI	12.5
Dillard, S., NYG	3.0
Doleman, C., MIN	12.5
Dotson, S., TB	5.0
Edwards, D., DAL	1.5
Fagan, K., SF	1.0
Faulkner, J., WAS	1.0
Flores, M., PHI	3.0
Fontenot, A., CHI	1.0
Fox, M., NYG	4.5
Gann, M., ATL	1.0
Gardner, M., ATL	2.0
Gayle, S., CHI	1.0
Geathers, J., ATL	3.5
George, R., ATL	1.0
Gibson, D., DET	1.0
Gilbert, S., Rams	10.5
Goff, R., NO	2.0
Gouveia, K., WAS	1.5
Hager, B., PHI	1.0
Haley, C., DAL	4.0
Hamilton, K., NYG	11.5
Harmon, A., PHI	11.5
Harris, R., MIN	1.0
Harrison, M., SF	6.0
Harvey, K., PHO	9.5
Hayworth, T., DET	2.0
Henderson, W., Rams	1.0
Hill, E., PHO	1.0
Holland, Jo., GB	2.0
Holt, P., ATL	6.5
Howard, E., NYG	3.5
Jackson, R., NO	11.5

PLAYER/TEAM	NO.	PLAYER/TEAM	NO.
Jamison, G., DET	2.0	Rocker, D., Rams	1.0
Jeffcoat, J., DAL	6.0	Romanowski, B., SF	3.0
Jenkins, C., MIN	2.5	Roper, J., DAL	2.0
Johnson, Jo., SF	2.0	Scroggins, T., DET	8.0
Johnson, Ti., WAS	4.0	Seals, R., TB	8.5
Johnson, V., NO	5.0	Sheppard, A., MIN	1.0
Jones, Da, CHI	1.0	Simmons, C., PHI	5.0
Jones, Jim, DAL	5.5	Simmons, W., GB	1.0
Jones, Mike, PHO	3.0	Simpson, C., CHI	0.5
Jones, Re., NO	1.0	Smeenge, J., NO	1.0
Jones, Ro., TB	1.0	Smith, Ar., SF	1.5
Joyner, S., PHI	2.0	Smith, C., ATL	3.5
Jurkovic, J., GB	5.5	Smith, D., DAL	1.0
Kelly, T., SF	1.0	Spellman, A., CHI	2.5
Koonce, G., GB	3.0	Spielman, C., DET	0.5
Logan, E., ATL	1.0	Spindler, M., DET	2.0
London, A., DET	1.0	Stewart, M., Rams	1.0
Lynch, L., PHO	1.0	Stokes, F., Rams	9.5
Mann, C., WAS	1.0	Stowe, T., PHO	1.5
Martin, W., NO	5.0	Strahan, M., NYG	1.0
Maryland, R., DAL	2.5	Stubblefield, D., SF	10.5
McGhee, K., NYG	1.5	Swann, E., PHO	3.5
McMichael, S., CHI	6.0	Swilling, P., DET	6.5
Millard, K., PHI	4.0	Taylor, L., NYG	6.0
Miller, Co., NYG	6.5	Thomas, Br., TB	1.0
Miller, L., NO	2.5	Thomas, H., MIN	9.0
Mills, S., NO	2.0	Thomas, M., SF	0.5
Nickerson, H., TB	1.0	Thomas, Wi., PHI	6.5
Noga, A., WAS	4.0	Tolbert, T., DAL	7.5
Norton, K., DAL	2.0	Tuggle, J., ATL	2.0
Nunn, C., PHO	6.5	Turnbull, R., NO	13.0
Oldham, C., PHO	1.0	Warren, F., NO	1.0
Owens, D., DET	3.0	Washington, T., SF	3.0
Palmer, S., WAS	4.5	Wheeler, M., TB	2.0
Patterson, S., GB	1.0	White, R., GB	13.0
Paup, B., GB	11.0	White, W., DET	1.5
Perry, W., PHI	1.0	Williams, James, NO	2.0
Porcher, R., DET	8.5	Wilson, B., WAS	2.0
Price, S., TB	3.0	Wilson, K., SF	3.0
Pritchett, K., DET	4.0	Wilson, T., SF	5.5
Randle, J., MIN	12.5	Woods, T., Rams	1.0
Reynolds, R., TB	1.0	Young, R., Rams	7.0
Roberts, L., SF	1.5	Zorich, C., CHI	7.0
Robinson, G., Rams	3.0		

FUMBLES

FUMBLES -- AFC

PLAYER/TEAM	FUM	OFF.FUM.REC.		DEF.FUM.REC.	
		REC	TD	REC	TD
Aguiar, L., NYJ	2	1	0	0	0
Alexander, B., MIA	0	0	0	1	0
Allen, M., KC	4	1	0	0	0
Anders, K., KC	1	0	0	0	0
Anderson, E., Raiders	0	0	0	1	0
Anderson, R., NYJ	1	1	0	0	0
Arbuckle, C., IND	1	0	0	0	0
Armstrong, B., NE	0	1	0	0	0
Arthur, M., NE	0	1	0	0	0

PLAYER/TEAM	FUM	OFF.FUM.REC. REC	OFF.FUM.REC. TD	DEF.FUM.REC. REC	DEF.FUM.REC. TD
Baldwin, R., CLE	2	1	0	0	0
Bates, M., SEA	1	0	0	2	0
Bavaro, D., NE	0	1	0	1	0
Baxter, B., NYJ	3	2	0	0	0
Beebe, D., BUF	1	1	0	0	0
Bell, N., Raiders	2	0	0	0	0
Belser, J., IND	0	0	0	3	0
Bennett, C., BUF	1	1	0	1	0
Bernstine, R., DEN	3	1	0	0	0
Bickett, D., IND	0	0	0	1	0
Bieniemy, E., SD	1	0	0	0	0
Birden, J.J., KC	1	0	0	0	0
Bishop, B., HOU	1	0	0	1	0
Blackmon, R., SEA	0	0	0	1	1
Blades, B., SEA	1	0	0	0	0
Bledsoe, D., NE	8	5	0	0	0
Bowden, J., HOU	0	0	0	1	0
Bradford, R., DEN	1	0	0	0	0
Brady, J., SD	0	0	0	1	0
Braxton, T., DEN	0	0	0	2	0
Brim, M., CIN	0	1	0	1	0
Brisby, V., NE	1	1	0	0	0
Brown, Ch., NE	0	0	0	1	0
Brown, G., HOU	4	2	0	0	0
Brown, J.B., MIA	1	0	0	0	0
Brown, Tim, Raiders	1	0	0	0	0
Brown, Tr., NE	2	1	0	0	0
Bruce, A., Raiders	0	0	0	1	0
Burkett, C., NYJ	1	0	0	0	0
Burnett, R., CLE	0	0	0	2	0
Byars, K., MIA	3	0	0	0	0
Caldwell, M., CLE	0	0	0	1	0
Carlson, C., HOU	3	2	0	0	0
Carrington, D., SD	1	0	0	1	0
Carter, Da., KC	4	2	0	0	0
Cash, Keith, KC	1	1	0	0	0
Cash, Kerry, IND	2	1	0	0	0
Childress, R., HOU	0	0	0	3	1
Clancy, S., IND	0	0	0	1	0
Clifton, K., NYJ	0	0	0	2	0
Collins, T., NE	0	0	0	1	0
Cook, M., NE	1	0	0	0	0
Cooper, A., PIT	1	0	0	0	0
Copeland, R., BUF	1	0	0	0	0
Cox, B., MIA	0	0	0	4	0
Croel, M., DEN	0	0	0	2	0
Croom, C., NE	1	0	0	0	0
Cross, J., MIA	0	0	0	2	0
Culver, R., IND	3	1	0	1	1
Dahl, B., CLE	0	1	0	0	0
Darby, M., BUF	0	0	0	1	0
Davidson, K., PIT	0	0	0	1	1
Davis, K., BUF	3	1	0	0	0
Dawson, D., PIT	0	0	0	0	0
DeBerg, S., MIA	1	0	0	0	0
Dellenbach, J., MIA	1	0	0	1	0
Delpino, R., DEN	1	0	0	0	0
Dennis, M., MIA	0	1	0	0	0
Dishman, C., HOU	0	0	0	2	1

PLAYER/TEAM	FUM	OFF.FUM.REC. REC	TD	DEF.FUM.REC. REC	TD
Donaldson, R., SEA	1	0	0	0	0
Drewrey, W., HOU	2	1	0	0	0
Duffy, R., NYJ	0	1	0	0	0
Dyal, M., KC	1	0	0	0	0
Edmunds, F., SEA	1	0	0	0	0
Elway, J., DEN	8	5	0	0	0
Esiason, B., NYJ	13	5	0	0	0
Evans, V., Raiders	4	0	0	0	0
Everitt, S., CLE	0	2	0	0	0
Fenner, D., CIN	1	2	0	0	0
Figures, D., PIT	2	0	0	2	0
Fletcher, S., DEN	0	0	0	1	0
Foster, B., PIT	3	0	0	0	0
Francis, J., CIN	0	0	0	1	0
Frase, P., NYJ	0	0	0	2	0
Friesz, J., SD	2	1	0	0	0
Gardner, C., BUF	1	0	0	0	0
Gash, S., NE	1	0	0	0	0
Gelbaugh, S., SEA	1	0	0	0	0
George, J., IND	4	0	0	0	0
Givins, E., HOU	2	0	0	0	0
Goad, T., NE	0	0	0	1	0
Goganious, K., BUF	0	0	0	1	0
Gordon, D., SD	4	1	0	1	0
Gray, D., IND	0	0	0	1	0
Green, E., PIT	3	0	0	0	0
Green, H., CIN	3	0	0	0	0
Greene, K., PIT	0	0	0	3	0
Grossman, B., SD	0	0	0	1	0
Grunhard, T., KC	1	0	0	0	0
Gunn, L., CIN	0	0	0	1	0
Harper, D., SEA	0	0	0	1	0
Harris, Ro., NE	2	1	0	0	0
Harrison, N., Raiders	0	0	0	1	0
Hasty, J., NYJ	0	0	0	2	0
Hayes, J., KC	1	0	0	0	0
Heck, A., SEA	0	2	0	0	0
Heller, Ro., MIA	0	1	0	0	0
Henderson, J., BUF	0	0	0	1	0
Hendrickson, S., SD	0	0	0	1	0
Herrod, J., IND	0	0	0	1	1
Hester, J., IND	1	0	0	0	0
Hicks, C., NYJ	2	1	0	0	0
Higgs, M., MIA	1	0	0	0	0
Hoard, L., CLE	4	0	0	0	0
Hoge, M., PIT	0	1	0	0	0
Hollier, D., MIA	0	0	0	1	0
Hoover, H., CLE	0	1	0	0	0
Horton, E., Raiders	0	1	0	0	0
Hoskins, D., Raiders	0	0	0	1	0
Hostetler, J., Raiders	6	2	0	0	0
Houston, B., NYJ	0	0	0	1	0
Humphries, S., SD	2	1	0	0	0
Hunter, P., SEA	0	0	0	3	0
Ingram, M., MIA	3	1	0	0	0
Ismail, R., Raiders	0	1	0	0	0
Jackson, John, PIT	0	1	0	0	0
Jackson, K., MIA	2	0	0	0	0
Jackson, Mi., CLE	1	0	0	1	0

PLAYER/TEAM	FUM	OFF.FUM.REC.		DEF.FUM.REC.	
		REC	TD	REC	TD
Jeffires, H., HOU	5	0	0	0	0
Jett, Ja., Raiders	1	0	0	0	0
Johnson, A., IND	5	2	0	0	0
Johnson, J., NYJ	5	2	0	0	0
Johnson, Re., DEN	1	0	0	0	0
Jones, F., KC	1	0	0	0	0
Jones, G., PIT	0	1	0	0	0
Jones, He., BUF	0	0	0	1	0
Jones, Ma., NYJ	0	1	0	1	0
Jones, Ro., CIN	0	0	0	1	0
Jones, S., HOU	0	0	0	2	0
Jones, Se., CLE	0	0	0	1	0
Jordan, R., Raiders	2	0	0	0	0
Jorden, T., PIT	0	1	0	0	0
Junior, E.J., SEA	0	1	0	0	0
Kartz, K., DEN	2	0	0	0	0
Kasay, J., SEA	0	0	0	1	0
Kelly, Ji., BUF	7	3	0	0	0
Kelly, Joe, Raiders	0	0	0	1	0
Kelso, M., BUF	0	0	0	1	0
Kennedy, C., SEA	0	0	0	1	0
Kinchen, B., CLE	1	0	0	0	0
Kirby, T., MIA	5	4	0	0	0
Kirkland, L., PIT	0	0	0	2	1
Klingler, D., CIN	7	2	0	0	0
Kosar, B., CLE	4	3	0	0	0
Kozerski, B., CIN	3	1	0	0	0
Kragen, G., DEN	0	0	0	1	0
Krieg, D., KC	6	1	0	0	0
Lake, C., PIT	0	0	0	2	0
Langhorne, R., IND	4	1	0	1	0
Lathon, L., HOU	0	0	0	1	0
Lee, S., SD	0	0	0	1	0
Lewis, A., KC	0	0	0	2	0
Lewis, B., NE	2	0	0	0	0
Lewis, N., SD	2	2	0	0	0
Lloyd, G., PIT	0	0	0	1	0
Lodish, M., BUF	0	0	0	1	0
Lott, R., NYJ	0	0	0	2	0
Lowdermilk, K., IND	0	1	0	0	0
Maddox, M., BUF	0	0	0	2	0
Majkowski, D., IND	1	1	0	0	0
Malamala, S., NYJ	0	1	0	0	0
Marino, D., MIA	4	2	0	0	0
Marshall, I., NY.I	0	0	0	1	0
Marshall, W., HOU	0	0	0	1	0
Martin, K., SEA	1	1	0	0	0
Martin, T., MIA	1	0	0	0	0
Marts, L., KC	0	0	0	1	0
Maston, L., HOU	1	0	0	0	0
Mathis, T., NYJ	5	1	0	0	0
McCallum, N., Raiders	1	0	0	0	0
McClendon, S., IND	0	0	0	2	0
McDuffie, O.J., MIA	4	1	0	0	0
McGee, To., CIN	1	0	0	0	0
McGlockton, C., Raiders	0	0	0	1	0
McMurtry, G., NE	1	1	0	0	0
McNair, T., KC	2	0	0	0	0
Means, N., SD	1	1	0	0	0

PLAYER/TEAM	FUM	OFF.FUM.REC.		DEF.FUM.REC.	
		REC	TD	REC	TD
Mecklenburg, K., DEN	0	0	0	2	0
Metcalf, E., CLE	4	0	0	0	0
Metzelaars, P., BUF	1	0	0	0	0
Mickell, D., KC	0	0	0	1	0
Milburn, G., DEN	9	1	0	0	0
Mims, C., SD	0	0	0	2	0
Mincy, C., KC	0	0	0	2	0
Mirer, R., SEA	13	5	0	0	0
Mitchell, S., MIA	3	1	0	0	0
Mohr, C., BUF	1	1	0	0	0
Montana, J., KC	1	0	0	0	0
Montgomery, Gl., HOU	0	0	0	3	0
Montgomery, T., Raiders	2	1	0	0	0
Moon, W., HOU	13	5	0	0	0
Moore, R., NYJ	2	0	0	0	0
Moore, St., CLE	0	0	0	1	1
Murrell, A., NYJ	4	2	0	0	0
Muster, B., NO	0	0	0	1	0
Newton, T., KC	0	0	0	3	0
Norgard, E., HOU	0	1	0	0	0
Odomes, N., BUF	0	0	0	1	1
O'Donnell, N., PIT	5	0	0	0	0
Oliver, L., MIA	0	0	0	1	0
O'Neal, L., SD	0	0	0	1	0
Patton, M., BUF	0	0	0	3	0
Pederson, D., MIA	2	1	0	0	0
Perry, G., Raiders	0	1	0	0	0
Perry, M., CLE	0	0	0	2	0
Philcox, T., CLE	2	0	0	0	0
Pickel, B., NYJ	0	0	0	3	0
Pickens, C., CIN	1	0	0	0	0
Pool, D., BUF	0	0	0	1	0
Port, C., NO	0	1	0	0	0
Potts, R., IND	8	2	0	0	0
Prior, A., NYJ	0	1	0	0	0
Pupunu, A., SD	0	1	0	0	0
Query, J., CIN	1	0	0	0	0
Rayam, T., CIN	0	2	0	0	0
Reed, A., BUF	3	0	0	0	0
Richard, S., SD	0	0	0	1	0
Rivers, R., DEN	0	0	0	1	0
Robertson, M., HOU	0	0	0	3	1
Robinson, E., SEA	0	0	0	2	0
Robinson, Gr., Raiders	3	1	0	0	0
Robinson, J., DEN	1	0	0	1	0
Robinson, P., CIN	2	1	0	0	0
Robinson, R., SEA	0	0	0	1	0
Rogers, T., KC	0	0	0	1	0
Ross, K., KC	0	0	0	1	0
Rowe, P., CLE	1	0	0	0	0
Russell, D., DEN	1	1	1	0	0
Russell, L., NE	4	2	0	0	0
Saleaumua, D., KC	0	0	0	1	1
Saxon, M., NE	1	1	0	0	0
Schroeder, J., CIN	5	1	0	0	0
Scott, To., CIN	0	2	0	0	0
Searcy, L., PIT	0	1	0	0	0
Seau, J., SD	0	0	0	1	0
Secules, S., NE	4	2	0	0	0

PLAYER/TEAM	FUM	OFF.FUM.REC.		DEF.FUM.REC.	
		REC	TD	REC	TD
Sharpe, Sh., DEN	1	0	0	0	0
Shaw, E., CIN	0	0	0	1	0
Shields, W., KC	0	2	0	0	0
Sims, K., MIA	0	1	0	0	0
Slade, C., NE	0	0	0	1	0
Slaughter, W., HOU	4	0	0	0	0
Smith, B., BUF	0	0	0	1	0
Smith, N., KC	0	0	0	3	0
Smith, St., Raiders	1	3	0	0	0
Smith, Th., BUF	0	0	0	1	0
Speer, D., CLE	1	0	0	1	0
Steed, J., PIT	0	0	0	1	0
Stephens, J., KC	1	0	0	0	0
Stephens, R., SEA	0	0	0	1	1
Stone, D., PIT	2	1	0	0	0
Strzelczyk, J., PIT	0	0	0	1	0
Stubbs, D., CIN	0	0	0	1	0
Talley, D., BUF	0	0	0	2	0
Tasker, S., BUF	1	0	0	1	0
Testaverde, V., CLE	4	0	0	0	0
Thomas, B., NYJ	0	1	0	0	0
Thomas, D., KC	0	0	0	1	1
Thomas, E., NYJ	0	1	0	0	0
Thomas, T., BUF	6	1	0	0	0
Thompson, C., CIN	0	1	0	0	0
Thompson, L., PIT	7	1	0	0	0
Tillman, C., DEN	1	1	0	0	0
Timpson, M., NE	1	0	0	0	0
Tippett, A., NE	0	0	0	4	0
Tomczak, M., PIT	2	1	0	0	0
Tovar, S., CIN	0	0	0	1	0
Trudeau, J., IND	2	1	0	0	0
Tuatagaloa, N., SEA	0	0	0	1	0
Turk, D., Raiders	0	0	0	1	0
Turner, K., NE	1	2	0	0	0
Turner, M., NYJ	0	0	0	1	0
Vardell, T., CLE	3	0	0	0	0
Vaughn, J., SEA	1	0	0	0	0
Verdin, C., IND	3	1	0	0	0
Vincent, T., MIA	0	0	0	1	0
Vinson, F., CIN	0	0	0	3	0
Wallace, A., Raiders	0	0	0	2	0
Warren, C., SEA	3	0	0	0	0
Washington, B., NYJ	0	0	0	1	0
Washington, Mi., BUF	0	0	0	2	0
Webster, L., MIA	0	0	0	1	0
Weidner, B., MIA	0	1	0	0	0
Wellman, G., HOU	1	0	0	0	0
Wheeler, L., CIN	0	0	0	1	0
White, Lo., HOU	1	0	0	0	0
White, S., CIN	0	0	0	1	0
Wilkerson, B., Raiders	0	1	0	0	0
Williams, D., CIN	0	0	0	2	0
Williams, David, HOU	0	1	0	0	0
Williams, Dan, DEN	0	0	0	1	0
Williams, H., KC	3	0	0	0	0
Williams, Jarvis, MIA	0	0	0	2	0
Williams, James, BUF	0	0	0	2	0
Williams, J.L., SEA	2	1	0	0	0

PLAYER/TEAM	FUM	OFF.FUM.REC.		DEF.FUM.REC.	
		REC	TD	REC	TD
Williams, M., MIA	1	0	0	0	0
Williams, R., MIA	0	1	0	0	0
Wilson, K., NYJ	0	0	0	1	0
Winter, B., SD	0	0	0	1	0
Wooden, T., SEA	0	0	0	1	0
Woodson, R., PIT	2	1	0	0	0
Wright, J., BUF	0	0	0	1	0
Wyman, D., DEN	0	0	0	2	0
Young, L., NYJ	0	0	0	1	0
Zgonina, J., PIT	0	0	0	1	0
Zimmerman, G., DEN	0	1	0	0	0

FUMBLES-- NFC

PLAYER/TEAM	FUM	OFF.FUM.REC.		DEF.FUM.REC.	
		REC	TD	REC	TD
Aikman, T., DAL	7	3	0	0	0
Alexander, H., ATL	0	1	0	0	0
Anderson, Ga., TB/DET	4	0	0	0	0
Anderson, N., CHI	2	1	0	0	0
Anderson, W., Rams	0	1	0	0	0
Armstrong, T., CHI	0	0	0	3	0
Atkins, G., NO	0	0	0	2	0
Bailey, C., NYG	1	1	0	0	0
Bailey, J., PHO	4	0	0	0	0
Baker, Sh., CHI	0	0	0	2	1
Bankston, M., PHO	0	0	0	5	0
Barker, R., MIN	0	0	0	1	0
Barlow, C., PHI	0	1	0	0	0
Barnett, F., PHI	1	0	0	0	0
Bates, B., DAL	0	0	0	1	0
Beach, S., SF	0	0	0	1	0
Beckles, I., TB	0	1	0	0	0
Bennett, E., GB	0	1	0	0	0
Bettis, J., Rams	4	0	0	0	0
Beuerlein, S., PHO	8	2	0	0	0
Bingham, G., WAS	1	0	0	0	0
Bortz, M., CHI	0	1	0	0	0
Boutte, M., Rams	0	0	0	1	0
Bowles, T., WAS	0	0	0	1	0
Boykin, D., Rams	1	1	0	1	1
Brandes, J., SF	1	0	0	1	0
Brister, B., PHI	3	0	0	0	0
Brock, M., GB	0	0	0	1	0
Brooks, M., NYG	0	0	0	1	0
Brooks, Re., WAS	4	1	0	0	0
Brooks, Ro., GB	1	1	0	0	0
Brostek, B., Rams	1	0	0	0	0
Brown, Derek, NO	1	0	0	0	0
Buck, M., NO	2	0	0	0	0
Buck, V., NO	0	0	0	2	0
Buckley, M., NYG	0	0	0	1	0
Buckley, T., GB	1	0	0	0	0
Bunch, J., NYG	2	0	0	0	0
Bussey, B., TB	0	0	0	1	0
Butler, L., GB	0	0	0	1	1
Byner, E., WAS	0	1	0	0	0
Calloway, C., NYG	0	1	0	0	0
Camarillo, R., PHO	0	1	0	0	0
Campen, J., GB	0	1	0	0	0

PLAYER/TEAM	FUM	OFF.FUM.REC. REC	TD	DEF.FUM.REC. REC	TD
Carter, A., MIN	1	0	0	0	0
Carter, C., MIN	0	1	0	0	0
Carter, D., SF	5	1	0	0	0
Carter, Ma., TB	0	0	0	2	0
Casillas, T., DAL	0	0	0	1	0
Centers, L., PHO	1	2	0	0	0
Chandler, C., PHO	2	0	0	0	0
Chmura, M., GB	1	1	0	0	0
Claiborne, R., TB	2	0	0	0	0
Clark, G., PHO	1	0	0	0	0
Clark, V., ATL	1	0	0	1	1
Clay, W., DET	0	0	0	2	2
Cobb, R., TB	5	1	0	0	0
Coleman, K., GB	0	0	0	1	0
Coleman, L., DAL	1	0	0	0	0
Coleman, M., WAS	0	0	0	2	1
Collins, Sh., WAS	0	0	0	1	0
Conklin, C., WAS	1	0	0	0	0
Conway, C., CHI	1	0	0	0	0
Cook, T., NO	0	0	0	3	0
Cooper, R., NO	0	1	0	0	0
Cox, Ro., CHI	0	0	0	1	0
Craig, R., MIN	1	0	0	0	0
Crockett, R., DET	0	0	0	1	0
Cross, H., NYG	0	0	0	1	0
Cunningham, Ra., PHI	3	0	0	0	0
Cunningham, Ri., PHO	0	1	0	0	0
Curry, E., TB	0	0	0	1	0
Dalman, C., SF	0	1	0	0	0
Davis, E., SF	0	0	0	1	1
Davis, R., PHO	0	0	0	1	0
DeBerg, S., TB	1	0	0	0	0
DeLong, K., SF	0	0	0	1	0
Dickerson, E., ATL	0	1	0	0	0
Dill, S., TB	0	1	0	0	0
Doleman, C., MIN	0	0	0	1	0
Dowdell, M., NO	1	0	0	0	0
Drayton, T., Rams	1	0	0	0	0
Dukes, J., ATL	0	0	0	1	0
Early, Q., NO	1	0	0	0	0
Eatman, I., Rams	0	1	0	0	0
Edwards, B., WAS	0	0	0	1	0
Edwards, D., DAL	0	0	0	1	0
Eilers, P., WAS	0	0	0	3	0
Flewonihi, M., WAS	0	2	0	0	0
Erickson, C., TB	9	6	0	0	0
Ervins, R., WAS	2	0	0	0	0
Evans, B., PHI	0	0	0	3	1
Evans, Do., GB	0	0	0	2	0
Everett, J., Rams	7	1	0	0	0
Favre, B., GB	14	2	0	0	0
Feagles, J., PHI	0	1	0	0	0
Flores, M., PHI	0	0	0	1	0
Floyd, E., PHI	0	1	0	0	0
Fontenot, J., CHI	0	1	0	0	0
Fox, M., NYG	0	0	0	1	0
Gannon, R., WAS	3	1	0	0	0
Gardocki, C., CHI	1	1	0	0	0
Garrett, J., DAL	1	0	0	0	0

PLAYER/TEAM	FUM	OFF.FUM.REC. REC	TD	DEF.FUM.REC. REC	TD
Gary, C., Rams	1	0	0	0	0
Gedney, C., CHI	1	0	0	0	0
Gibson, D., DET	0	0	0	1	0
Gordon, Dw., ATL	1	0	0	0	0
Gray, J., TB	0	1	0	0	0
Gray, M., DET	3	0	0	0	0
Green, D., WAS	0	0	0	2	1
Guliford, E., MIN	1	0	0	0	0
Guyton, M., NYG	0	1	0	0	0
Haley, C., DAL	0	0	0	1	0
Hamilton, K., NYG	0	0	0	1	0
Hamilton, R., WAS	0	0	0	1	0
Hampton, R., NYG	2	1	0	0	0
Hanks, M., SF	0	1	0	0	0
Harbaugh, J., CHI	15	4	0	0	0
Harmon, A., PHI	0	0	0	2	0
Harper, A., DAL	1	0	0	0	0
Harper, R., ATL	1	0	0	1	0
Hauck, T., GB	0	0	0	1	0
Hawkins, C., TB	2	0	0	0	0
Haynes, M., ATL	1	0	0	0	0
Hearst, G., PHO	2	0	0	0	0
Hebert, B., ATL	11	3	0	0	0
Hebron, V., PHI	5	1	0	0	0
Henley, D., Rams	0	0	0	1	0
Heyward, C., CHI	1	0	0	0	0
Hilgenberg, Ja., NO	1	0	0	0	0
Hilgenberg, Jo., NO	1	0	0	0	0
Hill, E., PHO	0	0	0	1	0
Hilliard, D., NO	2	3	0	0	0
Holland, Jo., GB	2	0	0	2	0
Holman, R., DET	1	0	0	0	0
Holmes, L., PHI	0	1	0	0	0
Hopkins, W., PHI	0	0	0	2	0
Hudson, J., PHI	1	0	0	0	0
Irwin, T., MIN	0	1	0	0	0
Ismail, Q., MIN	1	0	0	0	0
Jackson, G., NYG	0	1	0	2	0
Jackson, M., NYG	1	0	0	0	0
Jackson, R., NO	0	0	0	3	0
Jeffries, G., DET	0	1	0	0	0
Jenkins, C., MIN	0	0	0	1	0
Jenkins, M., ATL	0	0	0	1	0
Jennings, K., CHI	1	1	0	0	0
Johnson, A.J., WAS	0	1	0	0	0
Johnson, Jo., SF	0	0	0	1	0
Johnson, Ma., PHI	1	1	0	0	0
Johnson, Ti., WAS	0	0	0	1	0
Johnston, D., DAL	1	1	0	0	0
Jones, B., SF	2	2	0	0	0
Jones, Da., CHI	1	1	0	2	1
Jones, Roger, TB	0	1	0	2	0
Kauahi, K., PHO	1	0	0	0	0
Kelm, L., SF	1	1	0	0	0
Kennedy, L., ATL	0	1	0	0	0
Kinchen, T., Rams	1	0	0	0	0
King, J., TB	0	0	0	2	0
Koonce, G., GB	0	0	0	1	0
Kubar, B., DAL	2	0	0	0	0

PLAYER/TEAM	FUM	OFF.FUM.REC.		DEF.FUM.REC.	
		REC	TD	REC	TD
Kramer, E., DET	1	0	0	0	0
Lassic, D., DAL	2	1	0	0	0
Le Bel, H., ATL	1	0	0	0	0
Lee, A., SF	1	0	0	0	0
Lee, C., MIN	0	0	0	1	0
Lett, L., DAL	1	0	0	0	0
Logan, M., SF	2	1	0	0	0
Lyght, T., Rams	0	0	0	1	0
Lynch, E., DET	1	0	0	0	0
Lynch, L., PHO	0	0	0	3	1
Marion, B., DAL	0	0	0	1	0
Martin, C., Rams	0	0	0	1	0
Martin, W., NO	0	0	0	2	0
Maryland, R., DAL	0	0	0	2	0
Massey, R., PHO	0	0	0	2	0
May, M., PHO	0	1	0	0	0
Mayberry, T., TB	1	1	0	0	0
Mays, A., WAS	1	0	0	0	0
McAfee, F., NO	3	0	0	0	0
McDonald, T., SF	0	0	0	1	0
McDowell, A., TB	2	1	0	0	0
McIntyre, G., SF	0	2	0	0	0
McKyer, T., DET	0	0	0	1	0
McMahon, J., MIN	4	1	0	0	0
McMichael, S., CHI	0	0	0	2	0
McMillian, A., MIN	0	0	0	1	0
McMillian, M., PHI	1	0	0	1	0
McNeal, T., Rams	0	1	0	0	0
Meggett, D., NYG	1	1	0	0	0
Miano, R., PHI	0	0	0	1	0
Middleton, R., WAS	0	1	0	0	0
Millard, K., PHI	0	0	0	1	0
Miller, Ch., ATL	2	0	0	0	0
Miller, Co, NYG	1	0	0	2	0
Mills, S., NO	0	0	0	1	1
Mitchell, B., WAS	3	1	0	0	0
Moore, Da., TB	0	0	0	1	0
Moore, De, DET	4	3	0	0	0
Moore, H., DET	2	0	0	0	0
Moore, Ro., PHO	3	1	0	0	0
Morrissey, J., GB	0	0	0	1	0
Neal, L., NO	1	0	0	0	0
Ned, D., NO	1	0	0	0	0
Newberry, T., Rams	0	1	0	0	0
Nickerson, H., TB	0	0	0	1	0
Noble, B., GB	0	0	0	1	0
Noga, A., WAS	0	0	0	1	0
Norton, K., DAL	0	0	0	1	0
Novacek, J., DAL	3	1	0	0	0
Nunn, C., PHO	0	0	0	1	0
Obee, T., CHI	1	1	0	0	0
O'Brien, K., PHI	4	0	0	0	0
Owens, D., DET	0	0	0	2	0
Peete, R., DET	11	4	0	0	0
Pegram, E., ATL	6	4	0	0	0
Perriman, B., DET	1	0	0	0	0
Pete, L., DET	0	0	0	2	0
Phifer, R., Rams	0	0	0	2	0
Pierce, A., NYG	2	0	0	0	0

PLAYER/TEAM	FUM	OFF.FUM.REC.		DEF.FUM.REC.	
		REC	TD	REC	TD
Prior, M., GB	3	2	0	0	0
Pritchard, M., ATL	1	0	0	0	0
Prophl, B., PHO	1	0	0	0	0
Reeves, W., PHO	0	1	0	0	0
Rice, J., SF	3	1	0	0	0
Richards, D., DET	0	1	0	0	0
Rison, A., ATL	2	0	0	0	0
Roberts, W., NYG	0	1	0	0	0
Roby, R., WAS	0	1	0	0	0
Romanowski, B., SF	0	0	0	1	0
Roper, J., PHI	0	0	0	1	0
Rose, K., PHI	0	1	0	0	0
Rubley, T., Rams	4	2	0	0	0
Rucker, K., PHO	0	0	0	1	0
Ruettgers, K., GB	0	2	0	0	0
Russell, Da., SF	0	0	0	1	0
Rypien, M., WAS	7	0	0	0	0
Salisbury, S., MIN	3	1	0	0	0
Sanders, B., DET	3	3	0	0	0
Sanders, R., WAS	1	1	0	0	0
Schad, M., PHI	0	1	0	0	0
Schlereth, M., WAS	0	1	0	0	0
Scott, K., DET	0	0	0	1	0
Scott, T., MIN	0	0	0	1	0
Scroggins, T., DET	0	0	0	1	0
Seals, R., TB	0	0	0	1	0
Sharpe, S., GB	1	0	0	0	0
Sherman, H., PHI	3	0	0	0	0
Sikahema, V., PHI	4	0	0	0	0
Simmons, E., WAS	0	1	0	0	0
Simmons, W., GB	0	1	0	0	0
Simms, P., NYG	7	3	0	0	0
Smith, C., ATL	0	0	0	2	0
Smith, D., DAL	0	0	0	1	0
Smith, E., DAL	4	3	0	0	0
Smith, I., NO	1	1	0	0	0
Smith, K., DAL	0	0	0	1	0
Smith, La., PHO	0	2	0	0	0
Smith, T., ATL	4	1	0	0	0
Solomon, J., ATL	0	0	0	1	0
Spencer, J., NO	0	0	0	3	0
Spielman, C., DET	0	0	0	2	0
Spindler, M., DET	0	0	0	2	0
Stephens, J., GB	0	1	0	0	0
Stepnoski, M., DAL	1	0	0	0	0
Stokes, F., Rams	0	0	0	2	0
Strickland, F., MIN	0	0	0	4	0
Swann, E., PHO	0	0	0	1	0
Swilling, P., DET	0	0	0	1	0
Sydner, J., PHI	3	0	0	0	0
Tamm, R., SF	0	1	1	0	0
Tate, D., NYG	1	0	0	0	0
Taylor, J., SF	1	0	0	0	0
Taylor, K., NO	0	1	0	0	0
Taylor, L., NYG	0	0	0	1	0
Teague, G., GB	0	0	0	2	0
Thomas, Br., TB	0	0	0	1	0
Thomas, I., WAS	0	1	0	1	0
Thomas, M., SF	0	0	0	1	0

Thomas, Wi., PHI	0	0	3	0
Thompson, Da., GB	2	1	0	0
Tice, M., MIN	1	0	0	0
Tillman, Le., NYG	1	0	0	0
Tippins, K., ATL	0	0	1	0
Tuggle, J., ATL	0	0	1	0
Tuinei, M., DAL	0	1	0	0
Turnbull, R., NO	0	0	2	0
Turner, O., SF	1	0	0	0
Turner, V., DET	1	0	0	0
Walker, H., PHI	3	2	0	0
Wallace, S., SF	0	0	1	0
Walls, W., SF	0	1	0	0
Warren, F., NO	0	0	1	1
Washington, C., ATL	0	0	2	0
Washington, Ja., DAL	1	0	1	0
Washington, T., SF	0	0	1	0
Watters, R., SF	5	1	0	0
White, R., GB	0	1	1	0
Whitfield, B., ATL	0	2	0	0
Williams, A., PHO	0	0	2	1
Williams, Ji., TB	0	0	1	0
Williams, K., DAL	8	4	0	0
Willis, J., GB	0	1	0	0
Willis, P., CHI	2	1	0	0
Wilmsmeyer, K., SF	2	1	0	0
Wilson, C., TB	1	2	0	0
Wilson, Marcus, GB	1	0	1	0
Wilson, W., NO	9	4	0	0
Wojciechowski, J., CHI	0	2	0	0
Woodson, D., DAL	0	0	3	0
Word, B., MIN	3	0	0	0
Workman, V., TB	2	1	0	0
Worley, T., CHI	3	0	0	0
Wycheck, F., WAS	1	1	0	0
Young, S., SF	8	2	0	0
Zorich, C., CHI	0	0	2	0

TEAM BY TEAM SUMMARY

American Football Conference Rankings

	Offense			Defense		
	Total	Rush	Pass	Total	Rush	Pass
Buffalo Bills	4	3	7	13	11	11
Cincinnati Bengals	14	11	14	8	13	*1
Cleveland Browns	11	8	12	5	7	5
Denver Broncos	3	9	3	10	4	13
Houston Oilers	2	6	2	7	*1	10
Indianapolis Colts	12	14	5	14	14	4
Kansas City Chiefs	10	10	10	4	6	6
L.A. Raiders	8	13	4	3	10	3
Miami Dolphins	*1	12	*1	11	9	9
New England Patriots	7	7	8	6	12	2
N.Y. Jets	6	4	6	2	5	8
Pittsburgh Steelers	5	2	9	*1	3	7
San Diego Chargers	9	5	11	9	2	14
Seattle Seahawks	13	*1	13	12	8	12

* conference leader

National Football Conference Rankings

	Offense			Defense		
	Total	Rush	Pass	Total	Rush	Pass
Atlanta Falcons	5	13	2	13	6	14
Chicago Bears	14	10	14	3	8	2
Dallas Cowboys	2	2	3	7	5	7T
Detroit Lions	11	5	12	5	4	6
Green Bay Packers	9	12	7	2	3	4
L.A. Rams	8	4	11	12	9	13
Minnesota Vikings	7	11	5	*1	*1	3
New Orleans Saints	10	7	9	6	13	*1
N.Y. Giants	4	*1	10	4	2	7T
Philadelphia Eagles	6	8	6	9	12	5
Phoenix Cardinals	3	6	4	10	10	11
San Francisco 49ers	*1	3	*1	8	7	9
Tampa Bay Buccaneers	12	14	8	11	11	10
Washington Redskins	13	9	13	14	14	12

*conference leader

National Football League Rankings

	Offense			Defense		
	Total	Rush	Pass	Total	Rush	Pass
Atlanta Falcons	11	23	6	25	15	25
Buffalo Bills	6	8	11	27	21	24
Chicago Bears	28	19	28	4	17	3
Cincinnati Bengals	27	24	27	16	27	2
Cleveland Browns	20	17	19	12	12	13
Dallas Cowboys	4	2	7	10	11	10T
Denver Broncos	5	18	4	19	4	27
Detroit Lions	24	7	24	6	10	9
Green Bay Packers	19	22	18	2	8	7
Houston Oilers	3	12	3	14	*1	23
Indianapolis Colts	22	28	8	28	28	12
Kansas City Chiefs	16	20	15	11	9	14
L.A. Raiders	13	26	5	9	20	5
L.A. Rams	18	5	23	24	18	22
Miami Dolphins	2	25	*1	20	14	21
Minnesota Vikings	17	21	14	*1	6	6
New England Patriots	12	13	12	13	22	4
New Orleans Saints	21	14	21	7	25	*1
N.Y. Giants	10	*1	22	5	7	10T
N.Y. Jets	9	9	10	8	5	17
Philadelphia Eagles	15	15	16	17	24	8
Phoenix Cardinals	8	11	9	21	19	19
Pittsburgh Steelers	7	6	13	3	3	15
San Diego Chargers	14	10	17	18	2	28
San Francisco 49ers	*1	3	2	15	16	16
Seattle Seahawks	23	4	25	23	13	26
Tampa Bay Buccaneers	25	27	20	22	23	18
Washington Redskins	26	16	26	26	26	20

* league leader

AMERICAN FOOTBALL CONFERENCE OFFENSE

	BUF	CIN	CLE	DEN	HOU	IND	KC
FIRST DOWNS	316	239	264	327	330	269	300
Rushing	117	89	91	105	101	71	94
Passing	176	133	152	187	208	180	180
Penalty	23	17	21	35	21	18	26
YDS GAINED (tot)	5260	4052	4740	5461	5658	4705	4835
Avg per Game	328.8	253.3	296.3	341.3	353.6	294.1	302.2
RUSHING (net)	1943	1511	1701	1693	1792	1288	1655
Avg per Game	121.4	94.4	106.3	105.8	112	80.5	103.4
Rushes	550	423	425	468	409	365	445
Yards per Rush	3.5	3.6	4.0	3.6	4.4	3.5	3.7
PASSING (net)	3317	2541	3039	3768	3866	3417	3180
Avg per Game	207.3	158.8	189.9	235.5	241.6	213.6	198.8
Passes Att.	497	510	478	553	614	594	490
Completed	304	272	262	350	357	332	287
Pct Completed	61.2	53.3	54.8	63.3	58.1	55.9	58.6
Yards Gained	3535	2830	3328	4061	4145	3623	3384
Sacked	31	53	45	39	43	29	35
Yards Lost	218	289	289	293	279	206	204
Had Intercepted	18	11	19	10	25	15	10
Yards Opp Ret	174	49	246	79	309	247	111
Opp TDs on INT	0	0	0	0	0	1	0
PUNTS	74	90	84	68	56	83	77
Avg Yards	40.4	43.9	43.2	44.4	45.3	43.3	42.1
PUNT RETURNS	33	48	42	41	41	30	37
Avg Return	8.4	6.7	13.4	10.4	6.7	5.8	9.4
Returned for TD	1	0	3	0	0	0	0
KICKOFF RETURNS	45	61	58	39	31	57	45
Avg Return	16.6	19.9	19.3	18.4	19	19.7	19.4
Returned for TD	0	0	0	0	0	0	0
PENALTIES	94	105	121	112	132	94	121
Yards Penalized	630	773	842	822	1005	685	969
FUMBLES BY	26	24	27	29	37	34	28
Fumbles Lost	17	9	17	18	20	20	18
Opp Fumbles	35	22	28	27	31	25	30
Opp Fumbles Lost	24	14	9	13	17	11	17
POSS. TIME (avg)	27:30	28:58	29:32	31:23	31:48	27:55	29:29
TOUCHDOWNS	37	16	36	42	40	16	37
Rushing	12	3	8	13	11	4	14
Passing	20	11	23	27	23	10	20
Returns	5	2	5	2	6	2	3
EXTRA POINTS	36	13	36	41	39	15	37
FIELD GOALS/FGA	23/32	24/31	16/22	26/35	29/34	26/31	23/29
POINTS SCORED	329	187	304	373	368	189	328
POINTS ALLOWED	242	319	307	284	238	378	291

Rdrs	MIA	NYJ	NE	PIT	SEA	SD	AFC/Avg	NFL/Avg
292	309	304	315	307	279	313	297.4	290.2
88	86	100	116	116	114	120	101.4	102.4
168	207	173	169	180	144	171	173.4	167.7
29	17	25	30	11	21	22	22.6	20.1
5014	5812	5212	5065	5235	4669	4967	5048.9	4970.2
313.4	363.3	325.8	316.6	327.2	291.8	310.4	315.6	310.6
1425	1459	1880	1780	2003	2015	1824	1712.1	1760.4
89.1	91.2	117.5	111.3	125.2	125.9	114	107	110
433	419	521	502	491	473	455	455.6	453
3.3	3.5	3.6	3.5	4.1	4.3	4.0	3.8	3.9
3589	4353	3332	3285	3232	2654	3143	3336.9	3209.8
224.3	272.1	208.3	205.3	202	165.9	196.4	208.6	200.6
495	581	489	566	540	498	563	533.4	514.8
281	342	294	289	299	280	301	303.6	298.3
56.8	58.9	60.1	51.1	55.4	56.2	53.5	56.9	57.9
3882	4564	3492	3412	3606	2896	3383	3581.5	3446
50	30	21	23	48	48	32	37.6	37.7
293	211	160	127	374	242	240	244.6	236.3
14	18	12	24	12	18	14	15.7	16.8
289	329	310	201	216	159	271	213.6	218.9
2	2	3	1	2	0	2	0.9	1.3
71	58	73	76	89	91	74	76	75.6
41.8	39.7	38.4	40.7	42.5	44.0	42.3	42.3	42.2
40	28	31	51	46	33	34	38.2	37.3
11.6	11.6	8.3	9.1	7.7	8.5	12.1	9.2	9.1
1	2	0	0	0	0	0	0.5	0.5
52	49	46	47	52	50	47	48.5	49.3
20.4	21.8	14.7	17.4	16.9	18.6	19.2	18.7	19.5
0	0	0	0	0	0	0	0	0.1
148	81	86	64	100	99	87	103.1	96.4
1181	663	555	468	861	745	699	778.4	736.9
23	32	38	30	27	25	13	28.1	27
11	16	16	10	15	13	5	14.6	13.7
23	30	30	20	37	23	19	27.1	27
9	14	18	9	14	15	12	14	13.7
30:33	28:59	32:16	29:43	32:15	29:02	29:52	29:57	30:00
29	40	31	26	32	29	33	31.7	32.4
10	10	14	9	13	13	14	10.6	10.9
17	27	16	17	16	13	18	18.4	18.5
2	3	1	0	3	3	1	2.7	3
27	37	31	25	32	29	31	30.6	31.3
35/44	24/32	19/31	17/26	28/30	23/28	31/40	25/32	24/31
306	349	270	238	308	280	322	296.5	299.2
326	351	247	286	281	314	290	296.7	299.2

AMERICAN FOOTBALL CONFERENCE DEFENSE

	BUF	CIN	CLE	DEN	HOU	IND	KC
OPP FIRST DOWNS	331	306	290	280	289	334	300
Rushing	114	134	94	86	73	151	103
Passing	199	159	170	181	184	166	161
Penalty	18	13	26	13	32	17	36
OPP YARDS GAINED	5554	5018	4778	5149	4874	5638	4771
Avg per Game	347.1	313.6	298.6	321.8	304.6	352.4	298.2
OPP RUSHING (net)	1921	2220	1654	1418	1273	2521	1620
Avg per Game	120.1	138.8	103.4	88.6	79.6	157.6	101.3
Rushes	500	521	451	397	369	575	453
Yards per Rush	3.8	4.3	3.7	3.6	3.4	4.4	3.6
OPP PASSING (net)	3633	2798	3124	3731	3601	3117	3151
Avg per Game	227.1	174.9	195.3	233.2	225.1	194.8	196.9
Passes Att.	582	457	541	562	582	454	525
Completed	323	251	306	314	302	270	312
Pct Completed	55.5	54.9	56.6	55.9	51.9	59.5	59.4
Sacked	37	22	48	46	52	21	35
Yards Lost	256	154	342	238	313	121	228
INTERCEPTED BY	23	12	13	18	26	10	21
Yards Returned	306	272	208	236	412	116	225
Returned for TD	3	2	1	1	3	0	0
OPP PUNT RETURNS	29	47	48	33	28	41	43
Avg Return	8.5	8.9	9.1	10.2	8.9	8.6	8.2
OPP KICKOFF RET	43	38	46	63	60	37	49
Avg Return	19.8	21.9	17.7	17.8	17.7	14.9	20.6
OPP TOUCHDOWNS	25	37	30	27	26	45	30
Rushing	7	15	9	6	9	20	11
Passing	18	20	19	21	16	22	18
Returns	0	2	2	0	1	3	1

NATIONAL FOOTBALL CONFERENCE OFFENSE

	ATL	CHI	DAL	DET	GB	Rams	MIN
FIRST DOWNS	292	226	322	248	282	279	283
Rushing	91	98	120	101	98	117	85
Passing	185	113	172	139	166	147	182
Penalty	16	15	30	8	18	15	16
YDS GAINED (tot)	5110	3717	5615	4658	4750	4804	4822
Avg per Game	319.4	232.3	350.9	291.1	296.9	300.3	301.4
RUSHING (net)	1590	1677	2161	1944	1619	2014	1623
Avg per Game	99.4	104.8	135.1	121.5	101.2	125.9	101.4
Rushes	395	477	490	456	448	449	447
Yards per Rush	4.0	3.5	4.4	4.3	3.6	4.5	3.6
PASSING (net)	3520	2040	3454	2714	3131	2790	3199
Avg per Game	220	127.5	215.9	169.6	195.7	174.4	199.9
Passes Att.	573	388	475	435	528	473	526
Completed	334	230	317	264	322	247	315
Pct Completed	58.3	59.3	66.7	60.7	61.0	52.2	59.9
Yards Gained	3787	2270	3617	2943	3330	3021	3380
Sacked	40	48	29	46	30	31	35
Yards Lost	267	230	163	229	199	231	181
Had Intercepted	25	16	6	19	24	19	14
Yards Opp Ret	345	105	47	177	437	347	166
Opp TDs on INT	2	1	0	1	3	2	3
PUNTS	72	80	56	72	74	80	90
Avg Yards	43.3	38.5	41.8	44.5	42.9	40.9	42.9

Rdrs	MIA	NYJ	NE	PIT	SEA	SD	AFC/Avg	NFL/Avg
302	332	266	269	267	322	299	299.1	290.2
111	103	93	97	74	106	86	101.8	102.4
151	005	161	161	163	193	192	174.9	167.7
37	24	12	11	30	23	21	22.4	20.1
4723	5150	4712	4796	4531	5313	5066	5005.2	4970.2
295.2	321.9	294.5	299.8	283.2	332.1	316.6	312.8	310.6
1865	1665	1473	1951	1368	1660	1314	1708.8	1760.4
116.6	104.1	92.1	121.9	85.5	103.8	82.1	106.8	110.0
494	460	420	505	399	452	414	457.9	453
3.8	3.6	3.5	3.9	3.4	3.7	3.2	3.7	3.9
2858	3485	3239	2845	3163	3653	3752	3296.4	3209.8
178.6	217.8	202.4	177.8	197.7	228.3	234.5	206.0	200.6
457	572	497	474	521	595	556	526.8	514.8
258	350	296	280	277	333	329	300.1	298.3
56.5	61.2	59.6	59.1	53.2	56.0	59.2	57.0	57.9
45	29	32	34	42	38	32	36.6	37.7
283	197	195	242	277	244	206	235.4	236.3
14	13	19	13	24	22	22	17.9	16.8
199	175	233	122	386	196	319	243.2	218.9
1	1	1	0	1	1	1	1.1	1.3
35	32	26	34	50	47	36	37.8	37.3
8.6	11.2	6.0	9.2	13.6	10.1	8.1	9.4	9.1
45	62	47	44	54	52	64	50.3	49.3
17.4	20.0	19.4	20.9	21.6	18.6	16.6	18.9	19.5
37	43	26	32	30	32	30	32.1	32.4
17	12	8	9	6	12	10	10.8	10.9
17	26	15	20	16	16	17	18.6	18.5
3	5	3	3	8	4	3	2.7	3

NYG	NO	PHI	PHO	SF	TB	WAS	NFC/Avg	NFL/Avg
300	264	303	295	372	241	255	283	290.2
127	94	104	107	134	80	92	103.4	102.4
153	158	184	173	212	141	143	162	167.7
20	12	15	15	26	20	20	17.6	20.1
5145	4707	4922	5213	6435	4311	4271	4891.4	4970.2
321.6	294.2	307.6	325.8	402.2	269.4	266.9	305.7	310.6
2210	1766	1761	1809	2133	1290	1726	1808.8	1760.4
138.1	110.4	110.1	113.1	133.3	80.6	107.9	113	110
560	414	456	452	463	402	396	450.4	453
3.9	4.3	3.9	4.0	4.6	3.2	4.4	4.0	3.9
2935	2941	3161	3404	4302	3021	2545	3082.6	3209.8
183.4	183.8	197.6	212.8	268.9	188.8	159.1	192.7	200.6
424	481	556	522	524	508	533	496.1	514.8
257	274	328	310	354	262	287	292.9	298.3
60.6	57.0	59.0	59.4	67.6	51.6	53.8	59.0	57.9
3180	3183	3463	3635	4480	3295	2764	3310.6	3446
40	40	42	33	35	39	40	37.7	37.7
245	242	302	231	178	274	219	227.9	236.3
9	21	13	20	17	25	21	17.8	16.8
175	444	107	143	157	280	209	224.2	218.9
1	6	0	0	0	1	2	1.6	1.3
78	77	83	73	42	94	83	75.3	75.6
41.9	43.6	40.0	43.7	40.9	40.1	43.9	42.1	42.2

NATIONAL FOOTBALL CONFERENCE OFFENSE (cont.)

	ATL	CHI	DAL	DET	GB	Rams	MIN
PUNT RETURNS	35	35	37	40	45	19	39
Avg Return	7.9	8.3	10.3	8.7	9.0	5.4	7.2
Returned for TD	0	0	2	0	0	0	0
KICKOFF RETURNS	55	45	36	52	60	49	55
Avg Return	23.6	18	21.1	23.2	24.7	16.8	19.7
Returned for TD	1	0	0	1	1	0	0
PENALTIES	111	68	94	93	85	71	109
Yards Penalized	838	587	744	665	734	526	806
FUMBLES BY	31	29	33	29	26	20	15
Fumbles Lost	17	14	16	13	10	11	10
Opp Fumbles	25	24	22	34	33	26	24
Opp Fumbles Lost	11	12	14	16	15	9	10
POSS. TIME (avg)	31:23	28:36	30:56	29:27	30:53	28:18	30:27
TOUCHDOWNS	34	22	41	28	35	25	28
Rushing	4	10	20	9	14	8	8
Passing	28	7	18	15	19	16	18
Returns	2	5	3	4	2	1	2
EXTRA POINTS	34	21	40	28	35	23	27
FIELD GOALS/FGA	26/27	27/36	30/37	34/43	31/37	16/23	26/35
POINTS SCORED	316	234	376	298	340	221	277

NATIONAL FOOTBALL CONFERENCE DEFENSE

	ATL	CHI	DAL	DET	GB	Rams	MIN
POINTS ALLOWED	385	230	229	292	282	367	290
OPP FIRST DOWNS	278	290	297	279	261	304	259
Rushing	79	112	94	108	88	117	98
Passing	180	163	176	154	157	179	139
Penalty	19	15	27	17	16	8	22
OPP YARDS GAINED	5421	4653	4767	4669	4482	5411	4404
Avg per Game	338.8	290.8	297.9	291.8	280.1	338.2	275.3
OPP RUSHING (net)	1784	1835	1651	1649	1582	1851	1534
Avg per Game	111.5	114.7	103.2	103.1	98.9	115.7	95.9
Rushes	419	476	423	433	424	480	415
Yards per Rush	4.3	3.9	3.9	3.8	3.7	3.9	3.7
OPP PASSING (net)	3637	2818	3116	3020	2900	3560	2870
Avg per Game	227.3	176.1	194.8	188.8	181.3	222.5	179.4
Passes Att.	505	504	555	514	529	488	478
Completed	308	306	334	309	290	299	310
Pct Completed	61.0	60.7	60.2	60.1	54.8	61.3	64.9
Sacked	27	46	34	43	46	35	45
Yards Lost	149	287	231	253	301	203	276
INTERCEPTED BY	13	18	14	19	18	11	24
Yards Returned	160	300	171	156	255	127	211
Returned for TD	0	2	1	1	0	0	2
OPP PUNT RETURNS	41	22	32	45	38	43	46
Avg Return	8.5	5.2	5.3	8.4	9.2	12.4	12.2
OPP KICKOFF RET	55	53	66	30	70	47	58
Avg Return	19.3	17.3	18.6	20.3	20.1	20.9	24.5
OPP TOUCHDOWNS	46	22	23	32	27	40	31
Rushing	14	9	7	12	6	18	14
Passing	27	12	14	19	16	17	11
Returns	5	1	2	1	5	5	6

NYG	NO	PHI	PHO	SF	TB	WAS	NFC/Avg	NFL/Avg
32	38	33	47	35	38	35	36.3	37.3
10.3	13.6	8.6	8.2	11.7	8.2	7.0	9.0	9.1
1	2	0	1	1	0	0	0.5	0.5
0L	0L	04	43	40	36	39	30.1	48.3
15.8	23.5	18.3	21.1	17.9	15.9	19.8	20.2	19.5
0	1	0	0	0	0	0	0.3	0.1
90	81	101	77	95	89	90	89.6	96.4
596	663	770	644	800	765	596	695.3	736.9
19	24	32	23	31	28	24	26	27
8	13	21	11	13	11	10	12.7	13.7
27	30	33	27	20	27	25	26.9	27
10	20	15	17	11	13	14	13.4	13.7
32:18	28:31	31:00	31:54	30:24	28:38	27:58	30:03	30:00
30	33	35	37	61	27	26	33	32.4
11	10	7	12	26	6	11	11.1	10.9
17	18	23	21	29	19	11	18.5	18.5
2	5	5	4	6	2	4	3.4	3
28	33	31	37	59	27	24	31.9	31.3
26/34	28/35	16/23	21/28	16/26	16/22	16/28	24/31	24/31
288	317	293	326	473	237	230	301.9	299.2

NYG	NO	PHI	PHO	SF	TB	WAS	NFC/Avg	NFL/Avg
205	343	315	269	295	376	345	301.6	299.2
268	273	271	278	297	280	304	281.4	290.2
89	116	91	106	109	109	127	103.1	102.4
161	145	155	158	171	152	157	160.5	167.7
18	12	25	14	17	19	20	17.8	20.1
4663	4696	5019	5167	4997	5246	5497	4935.1	4970.2
291.4	293.5	313.7	322.9	312.3	327.9	343.6	308.4	310.6
1547	2090	2080	1861	1800	1994	2111	1812.1	1760.4
96.7	130.6	130	116.3	112.5	124.6	131.9	113.3	110
395	513	467	433	404	479	513	448.1	453
3.9	4.1	4.5	4.3	4.5	4.2	4.1	4.1	3.9
3116	2606	2939	3306	3197	3252	3386	3123.1	3209.8
194.8	162.9	183.7	206.6	199.8	203.3	211.6	195.2	200.6
514	444	463	495	564	503	483	502.8	514.8
298	259	251	281	314	300	291	296.4	298.3
58.0	58.3	54.2	56.8	55.7	59.6	60.2	59.0	57.9
41	51	36	34	44	29	31	38.7	37.7
238	318	214	205	316	132	197	237.1	236.3
18	10	20	9	19	9	17	15.6	16.8
184	133	324	124	267	71	241	194.6	218.9
1	0	4	1	3	2	2	1.4	1.3
44	36	35	30	15	53	34	36.7	37.3
5.6	9.7	8.9	8.9	11.4	7.4	10.1	8.8	9.1
29	40	53	51	61	28	36	48.4	49.3
22.3	19.7	21.4	19.5	19.6	17.8	20.1	20.1	19.5
22	39	35	27	30	40	42	32.6	32.4
7	7	11	13	6	15	14	10.9	10.9
13	22	22	14	23	22	24	18.3	18.5
2	10	2	0	1	3	4	3.4	3

1994 Draft

Player	Overall	Pos	College	Team	Rnd	No.
Abrams, Anthony	188	DT	Clark (GA)	BUF	6	27
Abrams, Brice	209	FB	Michigan State	PIT	7	15
Adams, Sam	8	DE	Texas A&M	SEA	1	8
Alberts, Trev	5	LB	Nebraska	IND (from Rams)	1	5
Aldridge, Allen	51	LB	Houston	DEN	2	22
Alexander, Derrick	29	WR	Michigan	CLE (from PHI)	1	29
Allen, Larry	46	G	Sonoma State	DAL (comp.)	2	17
Anderson, Jamal	201	RB	Utah	ATL	7	7
Bandison, Romeo	75	DT	Oregon	CLE	3	10
Banta, Bradford	106	TE	So. California	IND	4	3
Bates, Mario	44	RB	Arizona State	NO	2	15
Beavers, Aubrey	54	LB	Oklahoma	MIA	2	25
Beehn, Zane	207	DE	Kentucky	SD	7	13
Beer, Tom	215	LB	Wayne State (MI)	DET	7	21
Bell, Myron	140	DB	Michigan State	PIT (from CHI)	5	9
Benfatti, Lou	94	DT	Penn State	NYJ (from Raiders)	3	29
Bennett, Donnell	58	RB	Miami (FL)	KC	2	29
Bercich, Pete	211	LB	Notre Dame	MIN	7	17
Berger, Mitch	193	P	Colorado	PHI (comp.)	6	32
Bishop, Harold	69	TE	Louisiana State	TB	3	4
Bonham, Shane	93	DT	Tennessee	DET	3	28
Boot, Isaac	141	DB	California	CLE	5	10
Borgella, Jocelyn	183	DB	Cincinnati	DET	6	22
Bostic, James	83	RB	Auburn	Rams (from ATL thr. IND)(cmp.)	3	18
Bowens, Tim	20	DT	Mississippi	MIA (from GB)	1	20
Boyer, Brant	177	LB	Arizona	MIA	6	16
Brady, Rickey	167	TE	Oklahoma	Rams	6	6
Braham, Rich	76	G	West Virginia	AZ	3	11
Brantley, Chris	108	WR	Rutgers	Rams	4	5
Bratzke, Chad	155	DE	Eastern Kentucky	NYG	5	24
Brien, Doug	85	K	California	SF (comp.)	3	20
Brooks, Bucky	48	WR	North Carolina	BUF (comp.)	2	19
Brown, Gary	148	G	Georgia Tech	PIT	5	17
Bruce, Isaac	33	WR	Memphis State	Rams	2	4
Bryant, Vaughn	124	DB	Stanford	DET	4	21
Buckner, Brentson	50	DT	Clemson	PIT	2	21
Burch, Joe	90	C	Texas Southern	NE (from MIA)	3	25
Burke, John	121	TE	Virginia Tech	NE (from MIA thr. AZ)	4	18
Burns, Keith	210	LB	Oklahoma State	DEN	7	16
Burris, Jeff	27	DB	Notre Dame	BUF	1	27
Burton, James	151	DB	Fresno State	KC (from MIN)	5	20
By'not'e, Butler	212	RB	Ohio State	DEN (from GB)	7	18
Carroll, Herman	142	DE	Mississippi State	NO	5	11
Carter, Bernard	165	LB	East Carolina	TB	6	4
Carter, Perry	107	DB	So. Mississippi	AZ (from NE)	4	4
Carver, Shante	23	DE/LB	Arizona State	DAL (from SF)	1	23
Clark, Willie	82	DB	Notre Dame	SD (comp.)	3	17
Coleman, Andre	70	WR	Kansas State	SD (from NE)	3	5
Collier, Dennis	205	S	Colorado	CHI	7	11
Collier, Ervin	78	DT	Florida A&M	NE (from SD)	3	13
Cothran, Jeff	66	RB	Ohio State	CIN	3	1
Covington, John	133	DB	Notre Dame	IND	5	2
Crocker, Sean	130	DB	North Carolina	BUF	4	27
Crumpler, Carlester	202	TE	East Carolina	SEA	7	8

Player	Overall	Pos	College	Team	Rnd	No.
Daigle, Anthony	185	RB	Fresno State	KC	6	24
Davis, Isaac	43	G	Arkansas	SD	2	14
Davis, Michael	119	DB	Cincinnati	HOU (from MIN)	4	16
Davis, Mitch	118	LB	Georgia	ATL (from PHI)	4	15
Dawson, Lake	92	WR	Notre Dame	KC (from SF)	3	27
Dilfer, Trent	6	QB	Fresno State	TB	1	6
Dotson, Dewayne	131	LB	Mississippi	DAL	4	28
Downs, Gary	95	RB	North Carolina St.	NYG	3	30
Drakeford, Tyronne	62	DB	Virginia Tech	SF (from DAL)	2	33
Duckworth, Paul	190	LB	Connecticut	GB (from PHI thr. SF)(comp.)	6	29
Edwards, Ronald	189	T	N. Carolina A&T	Rams (from DAL)	6	28
Emanuel, Bert	45	WR	Rice	ATL (from MIN) (comp.)	2	16
England, Erik	89	DE	Texas A&M	AZ (from GB thr. MIA)	3	24
Faulk, Marshall	2	RB	San Diego State	IND	1	2
Faumoli, Taase	122	DE	Hawaii	PIT	4	19
Flanigan, Jim	74	DT	Notre Dame	CHI	3	9
Fleming, Cory	87	WR	Tennessee	SF (from DEN)	3	22
Floyd, William	28	RB	Florida State	SF (from DAL)	1	28
Foley, Glenn	208	QB	Boston College	NYJ	7	14
Folston, James	52	LB	NE Louisiana	Raiders (from MIN)	2	23
Ford, Henry	26	DE	Arkansas	HOU	1	26
Fredrickson, Rob	22	LB	Michigan State	Raiders	1	22
Frerotte, Gus	197	QB	Tulsa	WAS	7	3
Fuller, Randy	123	DE	Tennessee State	DEN	4	20
Gaines, William	147	DT	Florida	MIA	5	16
Gandy, Wayne	15	T	Auburn	Rams (from SD thr. SF)	1	15
Garner, Charlie	42	RB	Tennessee	PHI	2	13
Gildon, Jason	88	LB	Oklahoma State	PIT (from MIN)	3	23
Gissendaner, Lee	187	WR	Northwestern	HOU	6	26
Glenn, Aaron	12	DB	Texas A&M	NYJ (from NO)	1	12
Goodwin, Marvin	144	S	UCLA	PHI	5	13
Greene, Tracy	219	TE	Grambling	KC	7	25
Hall, Lemanski	220	LB	Alabama	HOU	7	26
Hamilton, Ruffin	175	LB	Tulane	GB (from SD thr. SF)	6	14
Hammonds, Shelly	134	DB	Penn State	MIN (from WAS)	5	3
Harris, Raymont	114	RB	Ohio State	CHI	4	11
Harrison, Rodney	145	DB	Western Illinois	SD	5	14
Harvey, Frank	204	FB	Georgia	AZ	7	10
Hawkins, Steve	166	DB	West. Michigan	NE	6	5
Haws, Kurt	105	TE	Utah	WAS	4	2
Hegamin, George	102	T	North Carolina St.	DAL (comp.)	3	37
Hewitt, Andre	203	OL	Clemson	CLE	7	9
Hill, Greg	25	RB	Texas A&M	KC	1	25
Hill, Lloyd	170	WR	Texas Tech	CHI	6	9
Hill, Sean	214	DB	Montana State	MIA	7	20
Holmberg, Rob	217	LB	Penn State	Raiders (from SF thr. DAL)	7	23
Houston, Harrison	138	WR	Florida	ATL	5	7
Irving, Terry	115	LB	McNeese State	AZ (from SD thr. MIA)	4	12
Jackson, Sean	129	RB	Florida State	HOU	4	26
Jackson, Willie	109	WR	Florida	DAL (from TB)	4	6
Johnson, Charles	17	WR	Colorado	PIT	1	17
Johnson, Filmel	221	DB	Illinois	BUF	7	27
Johnson, Joe	13	DE	Louisville	NO (from NYJ)	1	13
Johnson, LeShon	84	RB	Northern Illinois	GB (from SF) (comp.)	3	19
Johnson, Lonnie	61	TE	Florida State	BUF	2	32
Johnson, Tre	31	T	Temple	WAS	2	2

Player	Overall	Pos	College	Team	Rnd	No.
Jones, Calvin	80	RB	Nebraska	Raiders (from NYJ)	3	15
Jones, Ernest	100	LB	Oregon	Rams (from PHI thr. SF)(comp.)	3	35
Jordan, Andrew	179	TE	Western Carolina	MIN (from DEN)	6	18
Kalaniuvalu, Alai	99	G	Oregon State	ATL (from DAL thr. DEN&SF)	3	34
Kearney, Jay	169	WR	West Virginia	GB (from ATL thr. Raiders)	6	8
Klein, Perry	111	QB	C.W. Post	ATL	4	8
Knox, Kevin	192	WR	Florida State	BUF (comp.)	6	31
Krein, Darren	150	DE	Miami (FL)	SD (from SEA)	5	19
Laing, Aaron	137	TE	New Mexico St.	SD (from NE)	5	6
Lane, Max	168	T	Navy	NE (from SEA)	6	7
Langham, Antonio	9	DB	Alabama	CLE	1	9
Lee, Kevin	35	WR	Alabama	NE	2	6
Lester, Fred	173	RB	Alabama A&M	NYJ	6	12
Levens, Dorsey	149	RB	Georgia Tech	GB (from DEN thr. SF)	5	18
Levy, Chuck	38	RB	Arizona	AZ	2	9
Lewis, Roderick	157	TE	Arizona	HOU	5	26
Lewis, Thomas	24	WR	Indiana	NYG	1	24
Loucheiy, Corey	98	T	South Carolina	BUF	3	33
Lundberg, Lance	213	OL	Nebraska	NO	7	19
Lyle, Keith	71	DB	Virginia	Rams	3	6
Mahlum, Eric	32	C	California	IND	2	3
Malone, Van	57	DB	Texas	DET	2	28
Mathews, Jason	67	T	Texas A&M	IND	3	2
Matthews, Steve	199	QB	Memphis State	KC (from Rams)	7	5
Maumalanga, Chris	128	DT	Kansas	NYG	4	25
Mawae, Kevin	36	C	Louisiana State	SEA	2	7
McCoy, Ryan	174	LB	Houston	PHI	6	13
McGinest, Willie	4	LB	So. California	NE	1	4
McIntosh, Toddrick	216	DE	Florida State	DAL (from Raiders)	7	22
Mickens, Terry	146	WR	Florida A&M	GB	5	15
Miller, Jamir	10	LB	UCLA	AZ	1	10
Miller, Jim	178	QB	Michigan State	PIT	6	17
Mitchell, Derrell	176	WR	Texas Tech	NO	6	15
Mitchell, Kevin	53	DE	Syracuse	SF (from GB)	2	24
Montgomery, Mark	206	RB	Wisconsin	PHI	7	12
Moore, Marty	222	LB	Kentucky	NE (from DAL)	7	28
Morris, Byron "Bam"	91	RB	Texas Tech	PIT	3	26
Morris, Horace	152	LB	Tennessee	NYJ (from Raiders)	5	21
Morton, Johnnie	21	WR	So. California	DET	1	21
Nalen, Tom	218	C	Boston College	DEN (from NYG)	7	24
Nottage, Dexter	163	DE	Florida A&M	WAS	6	2
Novitsky, Craig	143	G	UCLA	NO (from NYJ)	5	12
Nunley, Jeremy	60	DE	Alabama	HOU	2	31
Nussmeier, Doug	116	QB	Idaho	NO	4	13
O'Neill, Pat	135	P	Syracuse	NE (from Rams thr. AZ)	5	4
Ofodile, A.J.	158	TE	Missouri	BUF	5	27
Ottis, Brad	56	DT	Wayne State (NE)	Rams (from SF)	2	27
Palmer, David	40	WR	Alabama	MIN (from CLE thr. PHI&ATL)	2	11
Panos, Joe	77	G	Wisconsin	PHI	3	12
Parker, Orlando	117	WR	Troy State	NYJ	4	14
Parker, Vaughn	63	G	UCLA	SD (comp.)	2	34
Patterson, Roosevelt	159	T	Alabama	Raiders (from DAL)	5	28
Patton, Joe	97	G	Alabama A&M	WAS (from HOU)	3	32
Penn, Chris	96	WR	Tulsa	KC	3	31
Perry, Marlo	81	LB	Jackson State	BUF (comp.)	3	16
Peterson, Tony	153	LB	Notre Dame	SF	5	22

Player	Overall	Pos	College	Team	Rnd	No.
Phillips, Anthony	72	DB	Tex. A&M–K'ville	ATL	3	7
Pierson, Pete	136	T	Washington	TB	5	5
Pollard, Trent	132	T	East. Washington	CIN	5	1
Pyne, Jim	200	C	Virginia Tech	TB	7	6
Randolph, Thomas	47	DB	Kansas State	NYG (comp.)	2	18
Ravotti, Eric	180	LB	Penn State	PIT (from MIN)	6	19
Redmon, Anthony	139	G	Auburn	AZ	5	8
Reece, John	113	DB	Nebraska	AZ	4	10
Reid, Jim	161	T	Virginia	HOU (comp.)	5	30
Reynolds, Jerry	184	T	UNLV	CIN (from Raiders)	6	23
Rhett, Errict	34	RB	Florida	TB	2	5
Robbins, Austin	120	DT	North Carolina	Raiders (from GB)	4	17
Rogers, Sam	64	LB	Colorado	BUF (comp.)	2	35
Ruddy, Tim	65	C	Notre Dame	MIA (from AZ) (comp.)	2	36
Samuels, Terry	172	TE	Kentucky	AZ	6	11
Sawyer, Corey	104	CB	Florida State	CIN	4	1
Schroeder, Bill	181	WR	Wisc.–LaCrosse	GB	6	20
Scott, Darnay	30	WR	San Diego State	CIN	2	1
Seabron, Malcolm	101	WR	Fresno State	HOU (comp.)	3	36
Sehorn, Jason	59	DB	So. California	NYG	2	30
Semple, Tony	154	T	Memphis State	DET	5	23
Shine, Steve	86	LB	Northwestern	CIN (comp.)	3	21
Shuler, Heath	3	QB	Tennessee	WAS	1	3
Smith, Fernando	55	DE	Jackson State	MIN (from Raiders)	2	26
Smith, Lamar	73	RB	Houston	SEA	3	8
Spears, Marcus	39	T	NW Louisiana	CHI	2	10
Stallings, Ramondo	195	DE	San Diego State	CIN	7	1
Steussie, Todd	19	T	California	MIN	1	19
Strait, Robert	171	RB	Baylor	CLE	6	10
Studstill, Darren	191	DB	West Virginia	DAL (from Rams) (comp.)	6	30
Taylor, Aaron	16	T	Notre Dame	GB (from MIA)	1	16
Teichelman, Lance	196	DT	Texas A&M	IND	7	2
Thierry, John	11	LB	Alcorn State	CHI	1	11
Tubbs, Winfred	79	LB	Texas	NO	3	14
Vinson, Tony	160	RB	Towson State	SD (comp.)	5	29
Von Oelhoffen, Kimo	162	DT	Boise State	CIN	6	1
Waldrop, Rob	156	DT	Arizona	KC	5	25
Walker, Bracey	127	DB	North Carolina	KC	4	24
Walker, Bruce	37	DT	UCLA	PHI (from ATL)	2	8
Walker, Jay	198	QB	Howard	NE	7	4
Warren, Lamont	164	RB	Colorado	IND	6	3
Washington, DeWayne	18	DB	North Carolina St.	MIN (from DEN)	1	18
Wells, Mike	125	DT	Iowa	MIN (from Raiders)	4	22
Whigham, Larry	110	DB	NE Louisiana	SEA	4	7
Wilkins, Dave	126	DE	Gardner–Webb	GB (from SF thr. Raiders)	4	23
Wilkinson, Dan	1	DT	Ohio State	CIN	1	1
Williams, Bernard	14	T	Georgia	PHI	1	14
Winans, Tydus	68	WR	Fresno State	WAS	3	3
Windrow, Jason	186	G	Ohio State	NYG	6	25
Woodall, Lee	182	LB	Westchester (PA)	SF	6	21
Woolfork, Ronnie	112	LB	Colorado	MIA (from CLE)	4	9
Wortham, Barron	194	LB	Texas–El Paso	HOU (comp.)	6	33
Wright, Toby	49	DB	Nebraska	Rams (comp.)	2	20
Yarborough, Ryan	41	WR	Wyoming	NYJ	2	12
Young, Bryant	7	DE	Notre Dame	SF (from ATL thr. IND&Rams)	1	7
Zomalt, Eric	103	DB	California	PHI (comp.)	3	38

NFL Standings 1921-1993

1921 NFL

	W	L	T	Pct.
Chicago Staleys	10	1	1	.909
Buffalo All–Americans	9	1	2	.900
Akron Pros	7	2	1	.778
Green Bay Packers	6	2	2	.750
Canton Bulldogs	4	3	3	.571
Dayton Triangles	4	3	1	.571
Rock Island Independents	5	4	1	.556
Chicago Cardinals	2	3	2	.400
Cleveland Indians	2	6	0	.250
Rochester Jeffersons	2	6	0	.250
Detroit Heralds	1	7	1	.125
Cincinnati Celts	0	8	0	.000
Columbus Panhandles	0	6	0	.000

1922 NFL

	W	L	T	Pct.
Canton Bulldogs	10	0	2	1.000
Chicago Bears	9	3	0	.750
Chicago Cardinals	8	3	0	.727
Toledo Maroons	5	2	2	.714
Rock Island Independents	4	2	1	.667
Dayton Triangles	4	3	1	.571
Green Bay Packers	4	3	3	.571
Racine Legion	5	4	1	.556
Akron Pros	3	4	2	.429
Buffalo All–Americans	3	4	1	.429
Milwaukee Badgers	2	4	3	.333
Marion Oorang Indians	2	6	0	.250
Minneapolis Marines	1	3	0	.250
Columbus Panhandles	0	7	0	.000
Evansville Crimson Giants	0	2	0	.000
Hammond Pros	0	4	1	.000
Louisville Brecks	0	3	0	.000
Rochester Jeffersons	0	3	1	.000

1923 NFL

	W	L	T	Pct.
Canton Bulldogs	11	0	1	1.000
Frankford Yellow Jackets	11	2	1	.846
Duluth Kelleys	5	1	0	.833
Chicago Bears	9	2	1	.818
Green Bay Packers	7	2	1	.778
Milwaukee Badgers	7	2	3	.778
Cleveland Indians	3	1	3	.750
Rock Island Independents	6	2	2	.750
Chicago Cardinals	8	4	0	.667
Buffalo Bisons	6	4	0	.600
Duluth Kelleys	4	3	0	.571
Racine Legion	4	3	3	.571
Buffalo All–Americans	5	4	3	.556
Columbus Tigers	5	4	1	.556
Hammond Pros	2	2	1	.500
Racine Legion	4	4	2	.500
Rock Island Independents	2	3	3	.400
Toledo Maroons	2	3	2	.400
Milwaukee Badgers	5	8	0	.385
Minneapolis Marines	2	5	2	.286
Dayton Triangles	2	7	0	.222
St. Louis All–Stars	1	4	2	.200
Hammond Pros	1	5	1	.167
Akron Indians	1	6	0	.143
Dayton Triangles	1	6	1	.143
Marion Oorang Indians	1	10	0	.091
Kansas City Cowboys	0	5	1	.000
Kenosha Maroons	0	5	1	.000
Louisville Brecks	0	3	0	.000
Minneapolis Marines	0	6	0	.000
Rochester Jeffersons	0	2	0	.000

1924 NFL

	W	L	T	Pct.
Cleveland Bulldogs	7	1	1	.875
Chicago Bears	6	1	4	.857
Frankford Yellow Jackets	11	2	1	.846
Duluth Kelleys	5	1	0	.833
Rock Island Independents	6	2	2	.750
Green Bay Packers	8	4	0	.667
Buffalo Bisons	6	4	0	.600
Racine Legion	4	3	3	.571
Chicago Cardinals	5	4	1	.556
Columbus Tigers	4	4	0	.500
Hammond Pros	2	2	1	.500
Milwaukee Badgers	5	8	0	.385
Dayton Triangles	2	7	0	.222
Kansas City Cowboys	2	7	0	.222
Akron Indians	1	6	0	.143
Kenosha Maroons	0	5	1	.000
Minneapolis Marines	0	6	0	.000
Rochester Jeffersons	0	7	0	.000

1925 NFL

	W	L	T	Pct.
Chicago Cardinals	11	2	1	.846
Pottsville Maroons	10	2	0	.833
Detroit Panthers	8	2	2	.800
Akron Indians	4	2	2	.667
N.Y. Giants	8	4	0	.667
Frankford Yellow Jackets	13	7	0	.650
Chicago Bears	9	5	3	.643
Rock Island Independents	5	3	3	.625
Green Bay Packers	8	5	0	.615
Providence Steamroller	6	5	1	.545
Canton Bulldogs	4	4	0	.500
Cleveland Bulldogs	5	8	1	.385
Kansas City Cowboys	2	5	1	.286
Hammond Pros	1	3	0	.250
Buffalo Bisons	1	6	2	.143
Columbus Tigers	0	9	0	.000
Dayton Triangles	0	7	1	.000
Duluth Kelleys	0	3	0	.000
Milwaukee Badgers	0	6	0	.000
Rochester Jeffersons	0	6	1	.000

1926 NFL

	W	L	T	Pct.
Frankford Yellow Jackets	14	1	1	.933
Chicago Bears	12	1	3	.923
Pottsville Maroons	10	2	1	.833
Kansas City Cowboys	8	3	1	.727
Green Bay Packers	7	3	3	.700
Los Angeles Buccaneers	6	3	1	.667
N.Y. Giants	8	4	1	.667
Duluth Eskimos	6	5	2	.545
Buffalo Rangers	4	4	2	.500
Chicago Cardinals	5	6	1	.455
Providence Steamroller	5	7	0	.417
Detroit Panthers	4	6	2	.400
Hartford Blues	3	7	0	.300
Brooklyn Lions	3	8	0	.273
Milwaukee Badgers	2	7	0	.222
Akron Indians	1	4	3	.200
Dayton Triangles	1	4	1	.200
Racine Legion	1	4	0	.200
Columbus Tigers	1	6	0	.143
Canton Bulldogs	1	9	3	.100
Hammond Pros	0	4	0	.000
Louisville Colonels	0	4	0	.000

1927 NFL

	W	L	T	Pct.
N.Y. Giants	11	1	1	.917
Green Bay Packers	7	2	1	.778
Chicago Bears	9	3	2	.750
Cleveland Bulldogs	8	4	1	.667
Providence Steamroller	8	5	1	.615
N.Y. Yankees	7	8	1	.467
Frankford Yellow Jackets	6	9	3	.400
Pottsville Maroons	5	8	0	.385
Chicago Cardinals	3	7	1	.300
Dayton Triangles	1	6	1	.143
Duluth Eskimos	1	8	0	.111
Buffalo Bisons	0	5	0	.000

1928 NFL

	W	L	T	Pct.
Providence Steamroller	8	1	2	.889
Frankford Yellow Jackets	11	3	2	.786
Detroit Wolverines	7	2	1	.778
Green Bay Packers	6	4	3	.600
Chicago Bears	7	5	1	.583
N.Y. Giants	4	7	2	.364
N.Y. Yankees	4	8	1	.333
Pottsville Maroons	2	8	0	.200
Chicago Cardinals	1	5	0	.167
Dayton Triangles	0	7	0	.000

1929 NFL

	W	L	T	Pct.
Green Bay Packers	12	0	1	1.000
N.Y. Giants	13	1	1	.929
Frankford Yellow Jackets	9	4	5	.692
Boston Bulldogs	4	4	0	.500
Chicago Cardinals	6	6	1	.500
Orange NJ Tornadoes	3	4	4	.429
Stapleton Stapes	3	4	3	.429
Providence Steamroller	4	6	2	.400
Chicago Bears	4	8	2	.333
Buffalo Bisons	1	7	1	.125
Minneapolis Red Jackets	1	9	0	.100
Dayton Triangles	0	6	0	.000

1930 NFL

	W	L	T	Pct.
Green Bay Packers	10	3	1	.769
N.Y. Giants	13	4	0	.765
Chicago Bears	9	4	1	.692
Brooklyn Dodgers	7	4	1	.636
Providence Steamroller	6	4	1	.000
Stapleton Stapes	5	5	2	.500
Chicago Cardinals	5	6	2	.455
Portsmouth Spartans	5	6	3	.455
Frankford Yellow Jackets	4	14	1	.222
Minneapolis Red Jackets	1	7	1	.125
Newark Tornadoes	1	10	1	.091

1931 NFL

	W	L	T	Pct.
Green Bay Packers	12	2	0	.857
Portsmouth Spartans	11	3	0	.786
Chicago Bears	8	4	0	.667
Chicago Cardinals	5	4	0	.556
N.Y. Giants	7	6	1	.538
Providence Steamroller	4	4	3	.500
Stapleton Stapes	4	6	1	.400
Cleveland Indians	2	8	0	.200
Brooklyn Dodgers	2	12	0	.143
Frankford Yellow Jackets	1	6	1	.143

1932 NFL

	W	L	T	Pct.
Chicago Bears	7	1	6	.875
Green Bay Packers	10	3	1	.769
Portsmouth Spartans	6	2	4	.750
Boston Braves	4	4	2	.500
N.Y. Giants	4	6	2	.400
Brooklyn Dodgers	3	9	0	.250
Chicago Cardinals	2	6	2	.250
Stapleton Stapes	2	7	3	.222

1933 NFL

EASTERN DIVISION

	W	L	T	PCT.	PF	PA
N.Y. Giants	11	3	0	.786	244	101
Brooklyn	5	4	1	.556	93	54
Boston	5	5	2	.500	103	97
Philadelphia	3	5	1	.375	77	158
Pittsburgh	3	6	2	.333	67	208

WESTERN DIVISION

	W	L	T	PCT.	PF	PA
Chicago Bears	10	2	1	.833	133	82
Portsmouth	6	5	0	.545	128	87
Green Bay	5	7	1	.417	170	107
Cincinnati	3	6	1	.333	38	110
Chicago Cardinals	1	9	1	.100	52	101

NFL Championship: Chicago Bears 23, N.Y. Giants 21

1934 NFL

EASTERN DIVISION

	W	L	T	PCT.	PF	PA
N.Y. Giants	8	5	0	.615	147	107
Boston	6	6	0	.500	107	94
Brooklyn	4	7	0	.364	61	153
Philadelphia	4	7	0	.364	127	85
Pittsburgh	2	10	0	.167	51	206

WESTERN DIVISION

	W	L	T	PCT.	PF	PA
Chicago Bears	13	0	0	1.000	286	86
Detroit	10	3	0	.769	238	59
Green Bay	7	6	0	.538	156	112
Chicago Cardinals	5	6	0	.455	80	84
St. Louis	1	2	0	.333	27	61
Cincinnati	0	8	0	.000	10	243

NFL Championship: N.Y. Giants 30, Chicago Bears 13

1935 NFL

EASTERN DIVISION	W	L	T	PCT.	PF	PA
N.Y. Giants	9	3	0	.750	180	96
Brooklyn	5	6	1	.455	90	141
Pittsburgh	4	8	0	.333	100	209
Boston	2	8	1	.200	65	123
Philadelphia	2	9	0	.182	60	179

WESTERN DIVISION	W	L	T	PCT.	PF	PA
Detroit	7	3	2	.700	191	11
Green Bay	8	4	0	.667	181	96
Chicago Bears	6	4	2	.600	192	106
Chicago Cardinals	6	4	2	.600	99	97

NFL Championship: Detroit 26, N.Y. Giants 7

1936 NFL

EASTERN DIVISION	W	L	T	PCT.	PF	PA
Boston	7	5	0	.583	149	110
Pittsburgh	6	6	0	.500	98	187
N.Y. Giants	5	6	1	.455	115	163
Brooklyn	3	8	1	.273	92	161
Philadelphia	1	11	0	.083	51	206

WESTERN DIVISION	W	L	T	PCT.	PF	PA
Green Bay	10	1	1	.909	248	118
Chicago Bears	9	3	0	.750	222	94
Detroit	8	4	0	.667	235	102
Chicago Cardinals	3	8	1	.273	74	143

NFL Championship: Green Bay 21, Boston 6

1937 NFL

EASTERN DIVISION	W	L	T	PCT.	PF	PA
Washington	8	3	0	.727	195	120
N.Y. Giants	6	3	2	.667	128	109
Pittsburgh	4	7	0	.364	122	145
Brooklyn	3	7	1	.300	82	174
Philadelphia	2	8	1	.200	86	177

WESTERN DIVISION	W	L	T	PCT.	PF	PA
Chicago Bears	9	1	1	.900	201	100
Detroit	7	4	0	.636	180	105
Green Bay	7	4	0	.636	220	122
Chicago Cardinals	5	5	1	.500	135	165
Cleveland Rams	1	10	0	.091	75	207

NFL Championship: Washington 28, Chicago Bears 7

1938 NFL

EASTERN DIVISION	W	L	T	PCT.	PF	PA
N.Y. Giants	8	2	1	.800	194	79
Washington	6	3	2	.667	148	154
Brooklyn	4	4	3	.500	131	161
Philadelphia	5	6	0	.455	154	164
Pittsburgh	2	9	0	.182	79	169

WESTERN DIVISION	W	L	T	PCT.	PF	PA
Green Bay	8	3	0	.727	220	122
Detroit	7	4	0	.636	119	108
Chicago Bears	6	5	0	.545	194	148
Cleveland	4	7	0	.364	131	215
Chicago Cardinals	2	9	0	.182	111	168

NFL Championship: N.Y. Giants 23, Green Bay 17

1939 NFL

EASTERN DIVISION	W	L	T	PCT.	PF	PA
N.Y. Giants	9	1	1	.900	168	85
Washington	8	2	1	.800	242	94
Brooklyn	4	6	1	.400	108	219
Philadelphia	1	9	1	.100	105	200
Pittsburgh	1	9	1	.100	114	216

WESTERN DIVISION	W	L	T	PCT.	PF	PA
Green Bay	9	2	0	.818	233	153
Chicago Bears	8	3	0	.727	298	157
Detroit	6	5	0	.545	145	150
Cleveland	5	5	1	.500	195	164
Chicago Cardinals	1	10	0	.091	84	254

NFL Championship: Green Bay 27, N.Y. Giants 0

1940 NFL

EASTERN DIVISION	W	L	T	PCT.	PF	PA
Washington	9	2	0	.818	245	142
Brooklyn	8	3	0	.727	186	120
N.Y. Giants	6	4	1	.600	131	133
Pittsburgh	2	7	2	.222	60	178
Philadelphia	1	10	0	.091	111	211

WESTERN DIVISION	W	L	T	PCT.	PF	PA
Chicago Bears	8	3	0	.727	238	152
Green Bay	6	4	1	.600	238	155
Detroit	5	5	1	.500	138	153
Cleveland	4	6	1	.400	171	191
Chicago Cardinals	2	7	2	.222	139	222

NFL Championship: Chicago Bears 73, Washington 0

1941 NFL

EASTERN DIVISION	W	L	T	PCT.	PF	PA	WESTERN DIVISION	W	L	T	PCT.	PF	PA
N.Y. Giants	8	3	0	.727	238	114	Chicago Bears	10	1	0	.909	396	147
Brooklyn	7	4	0	.636	158	127	Green Bay	10	1	0	.909	258	120
Washington	6	5	0	.545	176	174	Detroit	4	6	1	.400	121	195
Philadelphia	2	8	1	.200	119	218	Chicago Cardinals	3	7	1	.300	127	197
Pittsburgh	1	9	1	.100	103	276	Cleveland	2	9	0	.182	116	244

Western Division playoff: Chicago Bears 33, Green Bay 14
NFL Championship: Chicago Bears 37, N.Y. Giants 9

1942 NFL

EASTERN DIVISION	W	L	T	PCT.	PF	PA	WESTERN DIVISION	W	L	T	PCT.	PF	PA
Washington	10	1	0	.909	227	102	Chicago Bears	11	0	0	1.000	376	84
Pittsburgh	7	4	0	.636	167	119	Green Bay	8	2	1	.800	300	215
N.Y. Giants	5	5	1	.500	155	139	Cleveland	5	6	0	.455	150	207
Brooklyn	3	8	0	.273	100	168	Chicago Cardinals	3	8	0	.273	98	209
Philadelphia	2	9	0	.182	134	239	Detroit	0	11	0	.000	38	263

NFL Championship: Washington 14, Chicago Bears 6

1943 NFL

EASTERN DIVISION	W	L	T	PCT.	PF	PA	WESTERN DIVISION	W	L	T	PCT.	PF	PA
Washington	6	3	1	.667	229	137	Chicago Bears	8	1	1	.889	303	157
N.Y. Giants	6	3	1	.667	197	170	Green Bay	7	2	1	.778	264	172
Phil–Pitt	5	4	1	.556	225	230	Detroit	3	6	1	.333	178	218
Brooklyn	2	8	0	.200	65	234	Chicago Cardinals	0	10	0	.000	95	238

Eastern Division playoff: Washington 28, N.Y. Giants 0
NFL Championship: Chicago Bears 41, Washington 21

1944 NFL

EASTERN DIVISION	W	L	T	PCT.	PF	PA	WESTERN DIVISION	W	L	T	PCT.	PF	PA
N.Y. Giants	8	1	1	.889	206	75	Green Bay	8	2	0	.800	238	141
Philadelphia	7	1	2	.875	267	131	Chicago Bears	6	3	1	.667	258	172
Washington	6	3	1	.667	169	180	Detroit	6	3	1	.667	216	151
Boston	2	8	0	.200	82	233	Cleveland	4	6	0	.400	188	224
Brooklyn	0	10	0	.000	69	166	Card–Pitt	0	10	0	.000	108	328

NFL Championship: Green Bay 14, N.Y. Giants 7

1945 NFL

EASTERN DIVISION	W	L	T	PCT.	PF	PA	WESTERN DIVISION	W	L	T	PCT.	PF	PA
Washington	8	2	0	.800	209	121	Cleveland	9	1	0	.900	244	136
Philadelphia	7	3	0	.700	272	133	Detroit	7	3	0	.700	195	194
Boston	3	6	1	.333	123	211	Green Bay	6	4	0	.600	258	173
N.Y. Giants	3	6	1	.333	179	198	Chicago Bears	3	7	0	.300	192	235
Pittsburgh	2	8	0	.200	79	220	Chicago Cardinals	1	9	0	.100	98	228

NFL Championship: Cleveland 15, Washington 14

1946 NFL

EASTERN DIVISION	W	L	T	PCT.	PF	PA	WESTERN DIVISION	W	L	T	PCT.	PF	PA
N.Y. Giants	7	3	1	.700	236	162	Chicago Bears	8	2	1	.800	289	193
Philadelphia	6	5	0	.545	231	220	L.A. Rams	6	4	1	.600	277	257
Pittsburgh	5	5	1	.500	136	117	Chicago Cardinals	6	5	0	.545	260	198
Washington	5	5	1	.500	171	191	Green Bay	6	5	0	.545	148	158
Boston	2	8	1	.200	189	273	Detroit	1	10	0	.091	142	310

NFL Championship: Chicago Bears 24, N.Y. Giants 14

1947 NFL

EASTERN DIVISION	W	L	T	PCT.	PF	PA	WESTERN DIVISION	W	L	T	PCT.	PF	PA
Philadelphia	8	4	0	.667	308	242	Chicago Cardinals	9	3	0	.750	306	231
Pittsburgh	8	4	0	.667	240	259	Chicago Bears	8	4	0	.667	363	241
Boston	4	7	1	.364	168	256	Green Bay	6	5	1	.545	274	210
Washington	4	8	0	.333	295	367	L.A. Rams	6	6	0	.500	259	214
N.Y. Giants	2	8	2	.200	190	309	Detroit	3	9	0	.250	231	305

Eastern Division playoff: Philadelphia 21, Pittsburgh 0
NFL Championship: Chicago Cardinals 28, Philadelphia 21

1948 NFL

EASTERN DIVISION	W	L	T	PCT.	PF	PA	WESTERN DIVISION	W	L	T	PCT.	PF	PA
Philadelphia	9	2	1	.818	376	156	Chicago Cardinals	11	1	0	.917	395	226
Washington	7	5	0	.583	291	287	Chicago Bears	10	2	0	.833	375	151
N.Y. Giants	4	8	0	.333	297	388	L.A. Rams	6	5	1	.545	327	269
Pittsburgh	4	8	0	.333	200	243	Green Bay	3	9	0	.250	154	290
Boston	3	9	0	.250	174	372	Detroit	2	10	0	.167	200	407

NFL Championship: Philadelphia 7, Chicago Cardinals 0

1949 NFL

EASTERN DIVISION	W	L	T	PCT.	PF	PA	WESTERN DIVISION	W	L	T	PCT.	PF	PA
Philadelphia	11	1	0	.917	364	134	L.A. Rams	8	2	2	.800	360	239
Pittsburgh	6	5	1	.545	224	214	Chicago Bears	9	3	0	.750	332	218
N.Y. Giants	6	6	0	.500	287	298	Chicago Cardinals	6	5	1	.545	360	301
Washington	4	7	1	.364	268	339	Detroit	4	8	0	.333	237	259
N.Y. Bulldogs	1	10	1	.091	153	368	Green Bay	2	10	0	.167	114	329

NFL Championship: Philadelphia 14, L. A. Rams 0

1950 NFL

AMERICAN CONFERENCE	W	L	T	PCT.	PF	PA	NATIONAL CONFERENCE	W	L	T	PCT.	PF	PA
Cleveland	10	2	0	.833	310	144	L.A. Rams	9	3	0	.750	466	309
N.Y. Giants	10	2	0	.833	268	150	Chicago Bears	9	3	0	.750	279	207
Philadelphia	6	6	0	.500	254	141	N.Y. Yanks	7	5	0	.583	366	367
Pittsburgh	6	6	0	.500	180	195	Detroit	6	6	0	.500	321	285
Chicago Cardinals	5	7	0	.417	233	287	Green Bay	3	9	0	.250	244	406
Washington	3	9	0	.250	232	326	San Francisco	3	9	0	.250	213	300
							Baltimore	1	11	0	.083	213	462

American Conference playoff: Cleveland 8, N.Y. Giants 3
National Conference playoff: L. A. Rams 24, Chicago Bears 14
NFL Championship: Cleveland 30, L. A. Rams 28

1951 NFL

AMERICAN CONFERENCE	W	L	T	PCT.	PF	PA	NATIONAL CONFERENCE	W	L	T	PCT.	PF	PA
Cleveland	11	1	0	.917	331	152	L.A. Rams	8	4	0	.667	392	261
N.Y. Giants	9	2	1	.818	254	161	Detroit	7	4	1	.636	336	259
Washington	5	7	0	.417	183	296	San Francisco	7	4	1	.636	255	205
Pittsburgh	4	7	1	.364	183	235	Chicago Bears	7	5	0	.583	286	282
Philadelphia	4	8	0	.333	234	264	Green Bay	3	9	0	.250	254	375
Chicago Cardinals	3	9	0	.250	210	287	N.Y. Yanks	1	9	2	.100	241	382

NFL Championship: L. A. Rams 24, Cleveland 17

1952 NFL

AMERICAN CONFERENCE	W	L	T	PCT.	PF	PA
Cleveland	8	4	0	.667	310	213
N.Y. Giants	7	5	0	.583	234	231
Philadelphia	7	5	0	.583	252	271
Pittsburgh	5	7	0	.417	300	273
Chicago Cardinals	4	8	0	.333	172	221
Washington	4	8	0	.333	240	287

NATIONAL CONFERENCE	W	L	T	PCT.	PF	PA
Detroit	9	3	0	.750	344	192
L.A. Rams	9	3	0	.750	349	234
San Francisco	7	5	0	.583	285	221
Green Bay	6	6	0	.500	295	312
Chicago Bears	5	7	0	.417	245	326
Dallas	1	11	0	.083	182	427

National Conference playoff: Detroit 31, L. A. Rams 21
NFL Championship: Detroit 17, Cleveland 7

1953 NFL

AMERICAN CONFERENCE	W	L	T	PCT.	PF	PA
Cleveland	11	1	0	.917	348	162
Philadelphia	7	4	1	.636	352	215
Washington	6	5	1	.545	208	215
Pittsburgh	6	6	0	.500	211	263
N.Y. Giants	3	9	0	.250	179	277
Chicago Cardinals	1	10	1	.091	190	337

NATIONAL CONFERENCE	W	L	T	PCT.	PF	PA
Detroit	10	2	0	.833	271	205
San Francisco	9	3	0	.750	372	237
L.A. Rams	8	3	1	.727	366	236
Chicago Bears	3	8	1	.273	218	262
Baltimore	3	9	0	.250	182	350
Green Bay	2	9	1	.182	200	338

NFL Championship: Detroit 17, Cleveland 16

1954 NFL

EASTERN CONFERENCE	W	L	T	PCT.	PF	PA
Cleveland	9	3	0	.750	336	162
Philadelphia	7	4	1	.636	284	230
N.Y. Giants	7	5	0	.583	293	184
Pittsburgh	5	7	0	.417	219	263
Washington	3	9	0	.250	207	432
Chicago Cardinals	2	10	0	.167	183	347

WESTERN CONFERENCE	W	L	T	PCT.	PF	PA
Detroit	9	2	1	.818	337	189
Chicago Bears	8	4	0	.667	301	279
San Francisco	7	4	1	.636	313	251
L.A. Rams	6	5	1	.545	314	285
Green Bay	4	8	0	.333	234	251
Baltimore	3	9	0	.250	131	279

NFL Championship: Cleveland 56, Detroit 10

1955 NFL

EASTERN CONFERENCE	W	L	T	PCT.	PF	PA
Cleveland	9	2	1	.818	349	218
Washington	8	4	0	.667	246	222
N.Y. Giants	6	5	1	.545	267	223
Chicago Cardinals	4	7	1	.364	224	252
Philadelphia	4	7	1	.364	248	231
Pittsburgh	4	8	0	.333	195	285

WESTERN CONFERENCE	W	L	T	PCT.	PF	PA
L.A. Rams	8	3	1	.727	260	231
Chicago Bears	8	4	0	.667	294	251
Green Bay	6	6	0	.500	258	276
Baltimore	5	6	1	.455	214	239
San Francisco	4	8	0	.333	216	298
Detroit	3	9	0	.250	230	275

NFL Championship: Cleveland 38, L. A. Rams 14

1956 NFL

EASTERN CONFERENCE	W	L	T	PCT.	PF	PA
N.Y. Giants	8	3	1	.727	264	197
Chicago Cardinals	7	5	0	.583	240	182
Washington	6	6	0	.500	183	225
Cleveland	5	7	0	.417	167	177
Pittsburgh	5	7	0	.417	217	250
Philadelphia	3	8	1	.273	143	215

WESTERN CONFERENCE	W	L	T	PCT.	PF	PA
Chicago Bears	9	2	1	.818	363	246
Detroit	9	3	0	.750	300	188
San Francisco	5	6	1	.455	233	284
Baltimore	5	7	0	.417	270	322
Green Bay	4	8	0	.333	264	342
L.A. Rams	4	8	0	.333	291	307

NFL Championship: N.Y. Giants 47, Chicago Bears 7

1957 NFL

EASTERN CONFERENCE	W	L	T	PCT.	PF	PA
Cleveland	9	2	1	.818	269	172
N.Y. Giants	7	5	0	.583	254	211
Pittsburgh	6	6	0	.500	161	178
Washington	5	6	1	.455	251	230
Philadelphia	4	8	0	.333	173	230
Chicago Cardinals	3	9	0	.250	200	299

WESTERN CONFERENCE	W	L	T	PCT.	PF	PA
Detroit	8	4	0	.667	251	231
San Francisco	8	4	0	.667	260	264
Baltimore	7	5	0	.583	303	235
L.A. Rams	6	6	0	.500	307	278
Chicago Bears	5	7	0	.417	203	211
Green Bay	3	9	0	.250	218	311

Western Conference playoff: Detroit 31, San Francisco 27
NFL Championship: Detroit 59, Cleveland 14

1958 NFL

EASTERN CONFERENCE	W	L	T	PCT.	PF	PA
N.Y. Giants	9	3	0	.750	246	183
Cleveland	9	3	0	.750	302	217
Pittsburgh	7	4	1	.636	261	230
Washington	4	7	1	.364	214	268
Chicago Cardinals	2	9	1	.182	261	356
Philadelphia	2	9	1	.182	235	306

WESTERN CONFERENCE	W	L	T	PCT.	PF	PA
Baltimore	9	3	0	.750	381	203
Chicago Bears	8	4	0	.667	298	230
L.A. Rams	8	4	0	.667	344	278
San Francisco	6	6	0	.500	257	324
Detroit	4	7	1	.364	261	276
Green Bay	1	10	1	.091	193	382

Eastern Conference playoff: N.Y. Giants 10, Cleveland 0
NFL Championship: Baltimore 23, N.Y. Giants 17 (OT)

1959 NFL

EASTERN CONFERENCE	W	L	T	PCT.	PF	PA
N.Y. Giants	10	2	0	.833	284	170
Cleveland	7	5	0	.583	270	214
Philadelphia	7	5	0	.583	268	278
Pittsburgh	6	5	1	.545	257	216
Washington	3	9	0	.250	185	350
Chicago Cardinals	2	10	0	.167	234	324

WESTERN CONFERENCE	W	L	T	PCT.	PF	PA
Baltimore	9	3	0	.750	374	251
Chicago Bears	8	4	0	.667	252	196
Green Bay	7	5	0	.583	248	246
San Francisco	7	5	0	.583	255	237
Detroit	3	8	1	.273	203	275
L.A. Rams	2	10	0	.167	242	315

NFL Championship: Baltimore 31, N.Y. Giants 16

1960 AFL

EASTERN DIVISION	W	L	T	PCT.	PF	PA
Houston	10	4	0	.714	379	285
N.Y. Titans	7	7	0	.500	382	399
Buffalo	5	8	1	.385	296	303
Boston	5	9	0	.357	286	349

WESTERN DIVISION	W	L	T	PCT.	PF	PA
L.A. Chargers	10	4	0	.714	373	336
Dallas Texans	8	6	0	.571	362	253
Oakland	6	8	0	.429	319	399
Denver	4	9	1	.308	309	393

AFL Championship: Houston 24, L.A. Chargers 16

1960 NFL

EASTERN CONFERENCE	W	L	T	PCT.	PF	PA
Philadelphia	10	2	0	.833	321	246
Cleveland	8	3	1	.727	362	217
N.Y. Giants	6	4	2	.600	271	261
St. Louis	6	5	1	.545	288	230
Pittsburgh	5	6	1	.455	240	275
Washington	1	9	2	.100	178	309

WESTERN CONFERENCE	W	L	T	PCT.	PF	PA
Green Bay	8	4	0	.667	332	209
Detroit	7	5	0	.583	239	212
San Francisco	7	5	0	.583	208	205
Baltimore	6	6	0	.500	288	234
Chicago	5	6	1	.455	194	299
L.A. Rams	4	7	1	.364	265	297
Dallas	0	12	0	.000	177	369

NFL Championship: Philadelphia 17, Green Bay 13

1961 AFL

EASTERN DIVISION	W	L	T	PCT.	PF	PA
Houston	10	3	1	.769	513	242
Boston	9	4	1	.692	413	313
N.Y. Titans	7	7	0	.500	301	390
Buffalo	6	8	0	.429	294	342

WESTERN DIVISION	W	L	T	PCT.	PF	PA
San Diego	12	2	0	.857	396	219
Dallas Texans	6	8	0	.429	334	343
Denver	3	11	0	.214	251	432
Oakland	2	12	0	.143	237	458

AFL Championship: Houston 10, San Diego 3

1961 NFL

EASTERN CONFERENCE	W	L	T	PCT.	PF	PA	WESTERN CONFERENCE	W	L	T	PCT.	PF	PA
N.Y. Giants	10	3	1	.769	368	220	Green Bay	11	3	0	.786	391	223
Philadelphia	10	4	0	.714	361	297	Detroit	8	5	1	.615	270	258
Cleveland	8	5	1	.615	319	270	Baltimore	8	6	0	.571	302	307
St. Louis	7	7	0	.500	279	267	Chicago	8	6	0	.571	326	302
Pittsburgh	6	8	0	.429	295	287	San Francisco	7	6	1	.538	346	272
Dallas	4	9	1	.308	236	380	L.A. Rams	4	10	0	.286	263	333
Washington	1	12	1	.077	174	392	Minnesota	3	11	0	.214	285	407

NFL Championship: Green Bay 37, N.Y. Giants 0

1962 AFL

EASTERN DIVISION	W	L	T	PCT.	PF	PA	WESTERN DIVISION	W	L	T	PCT.	PF	PA
Houston	11	3	0	.786	387	270	Dallas Texans	11	3	0	.786	389	233
Boston	9	4	1	.692	346	295	Denver	7	7	0	.500	353	334
Buffalo	7	6	1	.538	309	272	San Diego	4	10	0	.286	314	392
N.Y. Titans	5	9	0	.357	278	423	Oakland	1	13	0	.071	213	370

AFL Championship: Dallas Texans 20, Houston 17 (OT)

1962 NFL

EASTERN CONFERENCE	W	L	T	PCT.	PF	PA	WESTERN CONFERENCE	W	L	T	PCT.	PF	PA
N.Y. Giants	12	2	0	.857	398	283	Green Bay	13	1	0	.929	415	148
Pittsburgh	9	5	0	.643	312	363	Detroit	11	3	0	.786	315	177
Cleveland	7	6	1	.538	291	257	Chicago	9	5	0	.643	321	287
Washington	5	7	2	.417	305	376	Baltimore	7	7	0	.500	293	288
Dallas	5	8	1	.385	398	402	San Francisco	6	8	0	.429	282	331
St. Louis	4	9	1	.308	287	361	Minnesota	2	11	1	.154	254	410
Philadelphia	3	10	1	.231	282	356	L.A. Rams	1	12	1	.077	220	334

NFL Championship: Green Bay 16, N.Y. Giants 7

1963 AFL

EASTERN DIVISION	W	L	T	PCT.	PF	PA	WESTERN DIVISION	W	L	T	PCT.	PF	PA
Boston	7	6	1	.538	327	257	San Diego	11	3	0	.786	399	256
Buffalo	7	6	1	.538	304	291	Oakland	10	4	0	.714	363	288
Houston	6	8	0	.429	302	372	Kansas City	5	7	2	.417	347	293
N.Y. Jets	5	8	1	.385	249	399	Denver	2	11	1	.154	301	473

Eastern Division playoff: Boston 26, Buffalo 7
AFL Championship: San Diego 51, Boston 10

1963 NFL

EASTERN CONFERENCE	W	L	T	PCT.	PF	PA	WESTERN CONFERENCE	W	L	T	PCT.	PF	PA
N.Y. Giants	11	3	0	.786	448	280	Chicago	11	1	2	.917	301	144
Cleveland	10	4	0	.714	343	262	Green Bay	11	2	1	.846	369	206
St. Louis	9	5	0	.643	341	283	Baltimore	8	6	0	.571	316	285
Pittsburgh	7	4	3	.636	321	295	Detroit	5	8	1	.385	326	265
Dallas	4	10	0	.286	305	378	Minnesota	5	8	1	.385	309	390
Washington	3	11	0	.214	279	398	L.A. Rams	5	9	0	.357	210	350
Philadelphia	2	10	2	.167	242	381	San Francisco	2	12	0	.143	198	391

NFL Championship: Chicago 14, N.Y. Giants 10

1964 AFL

EASTERN DIVISION	W	L	T	PCT.	PF	PA	WESTERN DIVISION	W	L	T	PCT.	PF	PA
Buffalo	12	2	0	.857	400	242	San Diego	8	5	1	.615	341	300
Boston	10	3	1	.769	365	297	Kansas City	7	7	0	.500	366	306
N.Y. Jets	5	8	1	.385	278	315	Oakland	5	7	2	.417	303	350
Houston	4	10	0	.286	310	355	Denver	2	11	1	.154	240	438

AFL Championship: Buffalo 20, San Diego 7

1964 NFL

EASTERN CONFERENCE	W	L	T	PCT.	PF	PA	WESTERN CONFERENCE	W	L	T	PCT.	PF	PA
Cleveland	10	3	1	.769	415	293	Baltimore	12	2	0	.857	428	225
St. Louis	9	3	2	.750	357	331	Green Bay	8	5	1	.615	342	245
Philadelphia	6	8	0	.429	312	313	Minnesota	8	5	1	.615	355	296
Washington	6	8	0	.429	307	305	Detroit	7	5	2	.583	280	260
Dallas	5	8	1	.385	250	289	L.A. Rams	5	7	2	.417	283	339
Pittsburgh	5	9	0	.357	253	315	Chicago	5	9	0	.357	260	379
N.Y. Giants	2	10	2	.167	241	399	San Francisco	4	10	0	.286	236	330

NFL Championship: Cleveland 27, Baltimore 0

1965 AFL

EASTERN DIVISION	W	L	T	PCT.	PF	PA	WESTERN DIVISION	W	L	T	PCT.	PF	PA
Buffalo	10	3	1	.769	313	226	San Diego	9	2	3	.818	340	227
N.Y. Jets	5	8	1	.385	285	303	Oakland	8	5	1	.615	298	239
Boston	4	8	2	.333	244	302	Kansas City	7	5	2	.583	322	285
Houston	4	10	0	.286	298	429	Denver	4	10	0	.286	303	392

AFL Championship: Buffalo 23, San Diego 0

1965 NFL

EASTERN CONFERENCE	W	L	T	PCT.	PF	PA	WESTERN CONFERENCE	W	L	T	PCT.	PF	PA
Cleveland	11	3	0	.786	363	325	Green Bay	10	3	1	.769	316	224
Dallas	7	7	0	.500	325	280	Baltimore	10	3	1	.769	389	284
N.Y. Giants	7	7	0	.500	270	338	Chicago	9	5	0	.643	409	275
Washington	6	8	0	.429	257	301	San Francisco	7	6	1	.538	421	402
Philadelphia	5	9	0	.357	363	359	Minnesota	7	7	0	.500	383	403
St. Louis	5	9	0	.357	296	309	Detroit	6	7	1	.462	257	295
Pittsburgh	2	12	0	.143	202	397	L.A. Rams	4	10	0	.286	269	328

Western Conference playoff: Green Bay 13, Baltimore 10 (OT)
NFL Championship: Green Bay 23, Cleveland 12

1966 AFL

EASTERN DIVISION	W	L	T	PCT.	PF	PA	WESTERN DIVISION	W	L	T	PCT.	PF	PA
Buffalo	9	4	1	.692	358	255	Kansas City	11	2	1	.846	448	276
Boston	8	4	2	.667	315	283	Oakland	8	5	1	.615	315	288
N.Y. Jets	6	6	2	.500	322	312	San Diego	7	6	1	.538	335	284
Houston	3	11	0	.214	335	396	Denver	4	10	0	.286	196	381
Miami	3	11	0	.214	213	362							

AFL Championship: Kansas City 31, Buffalo 7

1966 NFL

EASTERN CONFERENCE	W	L	T	PCT.	PF	PA	WESTERN CONFERENCE	W	L	T	PCT.	PF	PA
Dallas	10	3	1	.769	445	239	Green Bay	12	2	0	.857	335	163
Cleveland	9	5	0	.643	403	259	Baltimore	9	5	0	.643	314	226
Philadelphia	9	5	0	.643	326	340	L.A. Rams	8	6	0	.571	289	212
St. Louis	8	5	1	.615	264	265	San Francisco	6	6	2	.500	320	325
Washington	7	7	0	.500	351	355	Chicago	5	7	2	.417	234	272
Pittsburgh	5	8	1	.385	316	347	Detroit	4	9	1	.308	206	317
Atlanta	3	11	0	.214	204	437	Minnesota	4	9	1	.308	292	304
N.Y. Giants	1	12	1	.077	263	501							

NFL Championship: Green Bay 34, Dallas 27
Super Bowl I: Green Bay (NFL) 35, Kansas City (AFL) 10

1967 AFL

EASTERN DIVISION	W	L	T	PCT.	PF	PA
Houston	9	4	1	.692	258	199
N.Y. Jets	8	5	1	.615	371	329
Buffalo	4	10	0	.286	237	285
Miami	4	10	0	.286	219	407
Boston	3	10	1	.231	280	389

WESTERN DIVISION	W	L	T	PCT.	PF	PA
Oakland	13	1	0	.929	468	233
Kansas City	9	5	0	.643	408	254
San Diego	8	5	1	.615	360	352
Denver	3	11	0	.214	256	409

AFL Championship: Oakland 40, Houston 7

1967 NFL

EASTERN CONFERENCE

CAPITOL DIVISION	W	L	T	PCT.	PF	PA
Dallas	9	5	0	.643	342	268
Philadelphia	6	7	1	.462	351	409
Washington	5	6	3	.455	347	353
New Orleans	3	11	0	.214	233	379

CENTURY DIVISION	W	L	T	PCT.	PF	PA
Cleveland	9	5	0	.643	334	297
N.Y. Giants	7	7	0	.500	369	379
St. Louis	6	7	1	.462	333	356
Pittsburgh	4	9	1	.308	281	320

WESTERN CONFERENCE

CENTRAL DIVISION	W	L	T	PCT.	PF	PA
Green Bay	9	4	1	.692	332	209
Chicago	7	6	1	.538	239	218
Detroit	5	7	2	.417	260	259
Minnesota	3	8	3	.273	233	294

COASTAL DIVISION	W	L	T	PCT.	PF	PA
L.A. Rams	11	1	2	.917	398	196
Baltimore	11	1	2	.917	398	198
San Francisco	7	7	0	.500	273	337
Atlanta	1	12	1	.077	175	422

Conference Championships: Dallas 52, Cleveland 14; Green Bay 28, L.A. Rams 7.
NFL Championship: Green Bay 21, Dallas 17
Super Bowl II: Green Bay (NFL) 33, Oakland (AFL) 14

1968 AFL

EASTERN DIVISION	W	L	T	PCT.	PF	PA
N.Y. Jets	11	3	0	.786	419	280
Houston	7	7	0	.500	303	248
Miami	5	8	1	.385	276	355
Boston	4	10	0	.286	229	406
Buffalo	1	12	1	.077	199	367

WESTERN DIVISION	W	L	T	PCT.	PF	PA
Oakland	12	2	0	.857	453	233
Kansas City	12	2	0	.857	371	170
San Diego	9	5	0	.643	382	310
Denver	5	9	0	.357	255	404
Cincinnati	3	11	0	.214	215	329

Eastern Division playoff: Oakland 41, Kansas City 6
AFL Championship: N.Y. Jets 27, Oakland 23

1968 NFL

EASTERN CONFERENCE

CAPITOL DIVISION	W	L	T	PCT.	PF	PA
Dallas	12	2	0	.857	431	186
N.Y. Giants	7	7	0	.500	294	325
Washington	5	9	0	.357	249	358
Philadelphia	2	12	0	.143	202	351

CENTURY DIVISION	W	L	T	PCT.	PF	PA
Cleveland	10	4	0	.714	394	273
St. Louis	9	4	1	.692	325	289
New Orleans	4	9	1	.308	246	327
Pittsburgh	2	11	1	.154	244	397

WESTERN CONFERENCE

CENTRAL DIVISION	W	L	T	PCT.	PF	PA
Minnesota	8	6	0	.571	282	242
Chicago	7	7	0	.500	250	333
Green Bay	6	7	1	.462	281	227
Detroit	4	8	2	.333	207	241

COASTAL DIVISION	W	L	T	PCT.	PF	PA
Baltimore	13	1	0	.929	402	144
L.A. Rams	10	3	1	.769	312	200
San Francisco	7	6	1	.538	303	310
Atlanta	2	12	0	.143	170	389

Conference Championships: Cleveland 31, Dallas 20; Baltimore 24, Minnesota 14
NFL Championship: Baltimore 34, Cleveland 0
Super Bowl III: N.Y. Jets (AFL) 16, Baltimore (NFL) 7

1969 AFL

EASTERN DIVISION

	W	L	T	PCT.	PF	PA
N.Y. Jets	10	4	0	.714	353	269
Houston	6	6	2	.500	278	279
Boston	4	10	0	.286	266	316
Buffalo	4	10	0	.286	230	359
Miami	3	10	1	.250	233	332

WESTERN DIVISION

	W	L	T	PCT.	PF	PA
Oakland	12	1	1	.893	377	242
Kansas City	11	3	0	.786	359	177
San Diego	8	6	0	.571	288	276
Denver	5	8	1	.393	297	344
Cincinnati	4	9	1	.321	280	367

Divisional playoffs: Kansas City 13, N.Y. Jets 6; Oakland 56, Houston 7
AFL Championship: Kansas City 17, Oakland 7

1969 NFL

EASTERN CONFERENCE
CAPITOL DIVISION

	W	L	T	PCT.	PF	PA
Dallas	11	2	1	.821	369	223
Washington	7	5	2	.571	307	319
New Orleans	5	9	0	.357	311	393
Philadelphia	4	9	1	.321	279	377

CENTURY DIVISION

	W	L	T	PCT.	PF	PA
Cleveland	10	3	1	.750	351	300
N.Y. Giants	6	8	0	.429	264	298
St. Louis	4	9	1	.321	314	389
Pittsburgh	1	13	0	.071	218	404

WESTERN CONFERENCE
CENTRAL DIVISION

	W	L	T	PCT.	PF	PA
Minnesota	12	2	0	.857	379	133
Detroit	9	4	1	.679	259	188
Green Bay	8	6	0	.571	269	221
Chicago	1	13	0	.071	210	339

COASTAL DIVISION

	W	L	T	PCT.	PF	PA
L.A. Rams	11	3	0	.786	320	243
Baltimore	8	5	1	.607	279	268
Atlanta	6	8	0	.429	276	268
San Francisco	4	8	2	.357	277	319

Conference Championships: Cleveland 38, Dallas 14; Minnesota 23, Los Angeles 20
NFL Championship: Minnesota 27, Cleveland 7
Super Bowl IV: Kansas City (AFL) 23, Minnesota (NFL) 7

1970 NFL

AMERICAN CONFERENCE
EASTERN DIVISION

	W	L	T	PCT.	PF	PA
Baltimore	11	2	1	.821	321	234
Miami*	10	4	0	.714	297	228
N.Y. Jets	4	10	0	.286	255	286
Buffalo	3	10	1	.250	204	337
Boston	2	12	0	.143	149	361

NATIONAL CONFERENCE
EASTERN DIVISION

	W	L	T	PCT.	PF	PA
Dallas	10	4	0	.714	299	221
N.Y. Giants	9	5	0	.643	301	270
St. Louis	8	5	1	.607	325	228
Washington	6	8	0	.429	297	314
Philadelphia	3	10	1	.250	241	332

CENTRAL DIVISION

	W	L	T	PCT.	PF	PA
Cincinnati	8	6	0	.571	312	255
Cleveland	7	7	0	.500	286	265
Pittsburgh	5	9	0	.357	210	272
Houston	3	10	1	.250	217	352

CENTRAL DIVISION

	W	L	T	PCT.	PF	PA
Minnesota	12	2	0	.857	335	143
Detroit*	10	4	0	.714	347	202
Green Bay	6	8	0	.429	196	293
Chicago	6	8	0	.429	256	261

WESTERN DIVISION

	W	L	T	PCT.	PF	PA
Oakland	8	4	2	.643	300	293
Kansas City	7	5	2	.571	272	244
San Diego	5	6	3	.464	282	278
Denver	5	8	1	.393	253	264

WESTERN DIVISION

	W	L	T	PCT.	PF	PA
San Francisco	10	3	1	.750	352	267
L.A. Rams	9	4	1	.679	325	202
Atlanta	4	8	2	.357	206	261
New Orleans	2	11	1	.179	172	347

* Wild Card qualifier for playoffs
AFC Divisional playoffs: Baltimore 17, Cincinnati 0; Oakland 21, Miami 14
NFC Divisional playoffs: Dallas 5, Detroit 0; San Francisco 17, Minnesota 14
AFC Championship: Baltimore 27, Oakland 17
NFC Championship: Dallas 17, San Francisco 10
Super Bowl V: Baltimore 16, Dallas 13

1971 NFL

AMERICAN CONFERENCE
EASTERN DIVISION

	W	L	T	PCT.	PF	PA
Miami	10	3	1	.750	315	174
Baltimore	10	1	0	.711	919	140
N.Y. Jets	6	8	0	.429	212	299
New England	6	8	0	.429	238	325
Buffalo	1	13	0	.071	184	394

CENTRAL DIVISION

	W	L	T	PCT.	PF	PA
Cleveland	9	5	0	.643	285	273
Pittsburgh	6	8	0	.429	246	292
Houston	4	9	1	.321	251	330
Cincinnati	4	10	0	.286	284	265

WESTERN DIVISION

	W	L	T	PCT.	PF	PA
Kansas City	10	3	1	.750	302	208
Oakland	8	4	2	.643	344	278
San Diego	6	8	0	.429	311	341
Denver	4	9	1	.321	203	275

NATIONAL CONFERENCE
EASTERN DIVISION

	W	L	T	PCT.	PF	PA
Dallas	11	3	0	.786	406	222
Washington*	9	4	1	.679	276	190
Philadelphia	6	7	1	.464	221	302
St. Louis	4	9	1	.321	231	279
N.Y. Giants	4	10	0	.286	228	362

CENTRAL DIVISION

	W	L	T	PCT.	PF	PA
Minnesota	11	3	0	.786	245	139
Detroit	7	6	1	.536	341	286
Chicago	6	8	0	.429	185	276
Green Bay	4	8	2	.357	274	298

WESTERN DIVISION

	W	L	T	PCT.	PF	PA
San Francisco	9	5	0	.643	300	216
L.A. Rams	8	5	1	.607	313	260
Atlanta	7	6	1	.536	274	277
New Orleans	4	8	2	.357	266	347

* Wild Card qualifier for playoffs
AFC Divisional playoffs: Miami 27, Kansas City 24 (OT); Baltimore 20, Cleveland 3
NFC Divisional playoffs: Dallas 20, Minnesota 12; San Francisco 24, Washington 20
AFC Championship: Miami 21, Baltimore 0
NFC Championship: Dallas 14, San Francisco 3
Super Bowl VI: Dallas 24, Miami 3

1972 NFL

AMERICAN CONFERENCE
EASTERN DIVISION

	W	L	T	PCT.	PF	PA
Miami	14	0	0	1.000	385	171
N.Y. Jets	7	7	0	.500	367	324
Baltimore	5	9	0	.357	235	252
Buffalo	4	9	1	.321	257	377
New England	3	11	0	.214	192	446

CENTRAL DIVISION

	W	L	T	PCT.	PF	PA
Pittsburgh	11	3	0	.786	343	175
Cleveland*	10	4	0	.714	268	249
Cincinnati	8	6	0	.571	299	229
Houston	1	13	0	.071	164	380

WESTERN DIVISION

	W	L	T	PCT.	PF	PA
Oakland	10	3	1	.750	365	248
Kansas City	8	6	0	.571	287	254
Denver	5	9	0	.357	325	350
San Diego	4	9	1	.321	264	344

NATIONAL CONFERENCE
EASTERN DIVISION

	W	L	T	PCT.	PF	PA
Washington	11	3	0	.786	336	218
Dallas*	10	4	0	.714	319	240
N.Y. Giants	8	6	0	.571	331	247
St. Louis	4	9	1	.321	193	303
Philadelphia	2	11	1	.179	145	352

CENTRAL DIVISION

	W	L	T	PCT.	PF	PA
Green Bay	10	4	0	.714	304	226
Detroit	8	5	1	.607	339	290
Minnesota	7	7	0	.500	301	252
Chicago	4	9	1	.321	225	275

WESTERN DIVISION

	W	L	T	PCT.	PF	PA
San Francisco	8	5	1	.607	353	249
Atlanta	7	7	0	.500	269	274
L.A. Rams	6	7	1	.464	291	286
New Orleans	2	11	1	.179	215	361

* Wild Card qualifier for playoffs
AFC Divisional playoffs: Pittsburgh 13, Oakland 7; Miami 20, Cleveland 14
NFC Divisional playoffs: Dallas 30, San Francisco 28; Washington 16, Green Bay 3
AFC Championship: Miami 21, Pittsburgh 17
NFC Championship: Washington 26, Dallas 3
Super Bowl VII: Miami 14, Washington 7

1973 NFL

AMERICAN CONFERENCE
EASTERN DIVISION

	W	L	T	PCT.	PF	PA
Miami	12	2	0	.857	343	150
Buffalo	9	5	0	.643	259	230
New England	5	9	0	.357	258	300
Baltimore	4	10	0	.286	226	341
N.Y. Jets	4	10	0	.286	240	306

CENTRAL DIVISION

	W	L	T	PCT.	PF	PA
Cincinnati	10	4	0	.714	286	231
Pittsburgh*	10	4	0	.714	347	210
Cleveland	7	5	2	.571	234	255
Houston	1	13	0	.071	199	447

WESTERN DIVISION

	W	L	T	PCT.	PF	PA
Oakland	9	4	1	.679	292	175
Denver	7	5	2	.571	354	296
Kansas City	7	7	0	.500	231	192
San Diego	2	11	1	.179	188	386

NATIONAL CONFERENCE
EASTERN DIVISION

	W	L	T	PCT.	PF	PA
Dallas	10	4	0	.714	382	203
Washington*	10	4	0	.714	325	198
Philadelphia	5	8	1	.393	310	393
St. Louis	4	9	1	.321	286	365
N.Y. Giants	2	11	1	.179	226	362

CENTRAL DIVISION

	W	L	T	PCT.	PF	PA
Minnesota	12	2	0	.857	296	168
Detroit	6	7	1	.464	271	247
Green Bay	5	7	2	.429	202	259
Chicago	3	11	0	.214	195	334

WESTERN DIVISION

	W	L	T	PCT.	PF	PA
L.A. Rams	12	2	0	.857	388	178
Atlanta	9	5	0	.643	318	224
New Orleans	5	9	0	.357	163	312
San Francisco	5	9	0	.357	262	319

* Wild Card qualifier for playoffs
AFC Divisional playoffs: Oakland 33, Pittsburgh 14; Miami 34, Cincinnati 16
NFC Divisional playoffs: Minnesota 27, Washington 20; Dallas 27, L. A. Rams 16
AFC Championship: Miami 27, Oakland 10
NFC Championship: Minnesota 27, Dallas 10
Super Bowl VIII: Miami 24, Minnesota 7

1974 NFL

AMERICAN CONFERENCE
EASTERN DIVISION

	W	L	T	PCT.	PF	PA
Miami	11	3	0	.786	327	216
Buffalo*	9	5	0	.643	264	244
N.Y. Jets	7	7	0	.500	279	300
New England	7	7	0	.500	348	289
Baltimore	2	12	0	.143	190	321

CENTRAL DIVISION

	W	L	T	PCT.	PF	PA
Pittsburgh	10	3	1	.750	305	189
Houston	7	7	0	.500	236	282
Cincinnati	7	7	0	.500	283	259
Cleveland	4	10	0	.286	251	344

WESTERN DIVISION

	W	L	T	PCT.	PF	PA
Oakland	12	2	0	.857	355	228
Denver	7	6	1	.536	302	294
Kansas City	5	9	0	.357	233	293
San Diego	5	9	0	.357	212	285

NATIONAL CONFERENCE
EASTERN DIVISION

	W	L	T	PCT.	PF	PA
St. Louis	10	4	0	.714	285	218
Washington*	10	4	0	.714	320	196
Dallas	8	6	0	.571	297	235
Philadelphia	7	7	0	.500	242	217
N.Y. Giants	2	12	0	.143	195	299

CENTRAL DIVISION

	W	L	T	PCT.	PF	PA
Minnesota	10	4	0	.714	310	195
Detroit	7	7	0	.500	256	270
Green Bay	6	8	0	.429	210	206
Chicago	4	10	0	.286	152	279

WESTERN DIVISION

	W	L	T	PCT.	PF	PA
L.A. Rams	10	4	0	.714	263	181
San Francisco	6	8	0	.429	226	236
New Orleans	5	9	0	.357	166	263
Atlanta	3	11	0	.214	111	271

* Wild Card qualifier for playoffs
AFC Divisional playoffs: Oakland 28, Miami 26; Pittsburgh 32, Buffalo 14
NFC Divisional playoffs: Minnesota 30, St. Louis 14; L. A. Rams 19, Washington 10
AFC Championship: Pittsburgh 24, Oakland 13
NFC Championship: Minnesota 14, L. A. Rams 10
Super Bowl IX: Pittsburgh 16, Minnesota 6

1975 NFL

AMERICAN CONFERENCE

EASTERN DIVISION

	W	L	T	PCT.	PF	PA
Baltimore	10	4	0	.714	395	269
Miami	10	4	0	.714	357	222
Buffalo	8	6	0	.571	420	355
N.Y. Jets	3	11	0	.214	256	433
New England	3	11	0	.214	258	358

CENTRAL DIVISION

	W	L	T	PCT.	PF	PA
Pittsburgh	12	2	0	.857	373	162
Cincinnati*	11	3	0	.786	340	246
Houston	10	4	0	.714	293	226
Cleveland	3	11	0	.214	218	372

WESTERN DIVISION

	W	L	T	PCT.	PF	PA
Oakland	11	3	0	.786	375	255
Denver	6	8	0	.429	254	307
Kansas City	5	9	0	.357	282	341
San Diego	2	12	0	.143	189	345

NATIONAL CONFERENCE

EASTERN DIVISION

	W	L	T	PCT.	PF	PA
St. Louis	11	3	0	.786	356	276
Dallas*	10	4	0	.714	350	268
Washington	8	6	0	.571	325	276
N.Y. Giants	5	9	0	.357	216	306
Philadelphia	4	10	0	.286	225	302

CENTRAL DIVISION

	W	L	T	PCT.	PF	PA
Minnesota	12	2	0	.857	377	180
Detroit	7	7	0	.500	245	262
Green Bay	4	10	0	.286	226	285
Chicago	4	10	0	.286	191	379

WESTERN DIVISION

	W	L	T	PCT.	PF	PA
L.A. Rams	12	2	0	.857	312	135
San Francisco	5	9	0	.357	255	286
Atlanta	4	10	0	.286	240	289
New Orleans	2	12	0	.143	165	360

* Wild Card qualifier for playoffs

AFC Divisional playoffs: Pittsburgh 28, Baltimore 10; Oakland 31, Cincinnati 28
NFC Divisional playoffs: L. A. Rams 35, St. Louis 23; Dallas 17, Minnesota 14
AFC Championship: Pittsburgh 16, Oakland 10
NFC Championship: Dallas 37, L. A. Rams 7
Super Bowl X: Pittsburgh 21, Dallas 17

1976 NFL

AMERICAN CONFERENCE

EASTERN DIVISION

	W	L	T	PCT.	PF	PA
Baltimore	11	3	0	.786	417	246
New England*	11	3	0	.786	376	236
Miami	6	8	0	.429	263	264
N.Y. Jets	3	11	0	.214	169	383
Buffalo	2	12	0	.143	245	363

CENTRAL DIVISION

	W	L	T	PCT.	PF	PA
Pittsburgh	10	4	0	.714	342	138
Cincinnati	10	4	0	.714	335	210
Cleveland	9	5	0	.643	267	287
Houston	5	9	0	.357	222	273

WESTERN DIVISION

	W	L	T	PCT.	PF	PA
Oakland	13	1	0	.929	350	237
Denver	9	5	0	.643	315	206
San Diego	6	8	0	.429	248	285
Kansas City	5	9	0	.357	290	376
Tampa Bay	0	14	0	.000	125	412

NATIONAL CONFERENCE

EASTERN DIVISION

	W	L	T	PCT.	PF	PA
Dallas	11	3	0	.786	296	194
Washington*	10	4	0	.714	291	217
St. Louis	10	4	0	.714	309	267
Philadelphia	4	10	0	.286	165	286
N.Y. Giants	3	11	0	.214	170	250

CENTRAL DIVISION

	W	L	T	PCT.	PF	PA
Minnesota	11	2	1	.821	305	176
Chicago	7	7	0	.500	253	216
Detroit	6	8	0	.429	262	220
Green Bay	5	9	0	.357	218	299

WESTERN DIVISION

	W	L	T	PCT.	PF	PA
L.A. Rams	10	3	1	.75	351	190
San Francisco	8	6	0	.571	270	190
New Orleans	4	10	0	.286	253	346
Atlanta	4	10	0	.286	172	312
Seattle	2	12	0	.143	229	429

* Wild Card qualifier for playoffs

AFC Divisional playoffs: Oakland 24, New England 21; Pittsburgh 40, Baltimore 14
NFC Divisional playoffs: Minnesota 35, Washington 20; L. A. Rams 14, Dallas 12
AFC Championship: Oakland 24, Pittsburgh 7
NFC Championship: Minnesota 24, L. A. Rams 13
Super Bowl XI: Oakland 32, Minnesota 14

1977 NFL

AMERICAN CONFERENCE
EASTERN DIVISION

	W	L	T	PCT.	PF	PA
Baltimore	10	4	0	.714	295	221
Miami	10	4	0	.714	313	197
New England	9	5	0	.643	278	217
N.Y. Jets	3	11	0	.214	191	300
Buffalo	3	11	0	.214	160	313

CENTRAL DIVISION

	W	L	T	PCT.	PF	PA
Pittsburgh	9	5	0	.643	283	243
Houston	8	6	0	.571	299	230
Cincinnati	8	6	0	.571	238	235
Cleveland	6	8	0	.429	269	267

WESTERN DIVISION

	W	L	T	PCT.	PF	PA
Denver	12	2	0	.857	274	148
Oakland*	11	3	0	.786	351	230
San Diego	7	7	0	.500	222	205
Seattle	5	9	0	.357	282	373
Kansas City	2	12	0	.143	225	349

NATIONAL CONFERENCE
EASTERN DIVISION

	W	L	T	PCT.	PF	PA
Dallas	12	2	0	.857	345	212
Washington	9	5	0	.643	196	189
St. Louis	7	7	0	.500	272	287
N.Y. Giants	5	9	0	.357	181	265
Philadelphia	5	9	0	.357	220	207

CENTRAL DIVISION

	W	L	T	PCT.	PF	PA
Minnesota	9	5	0	.643	231	227
Chicago*	9	5	0	.643	255	253
Detroit	6	8	0	.429	183	252
Green Bay	4	10	0	.286	134	219
Tampa Bay	2	12	0	.143	103	223

WESTERN DIVISION

	W	L	T	PCT.	PF	PA
L.A. Rams	10	4	0	.714	302	146
Atlanta	7	7	0	.500	179	129
San Francisco	5	9	0	.357	220	260
New Orleans	3	11	0	.214	232	336

* Wild Card qualifier for playoffs
AFC Divisional playoffs: Denver 34, Pittsburgh 21; Oakland 37, Baltimore 31 (OT)
NFC Divisional playoffs: Dallas 37, Chicago 7; Minnesota 14, L. A. Rams 7
AFC Championship: Denver 20, Oakland 17; NFC Championship: Dallas 23, Minnesota 6
Super Bowl XII: Dallas 27, Denver 10

1978 NFL

AMERICAN CONFERENCE
EASTERN DIVISION

	W	L	T	PCT.	PF	PA
New England	11	5	0	.688	358	286
Miami*	11	5	0	.688	372	254
N.Y. Jets	8	8	0	.500	359	364
Baltimore	5	11	0	.313	239	421
Buffalo	5	11	0	.313	302	354

CENTRAL DIVISION

	W	L	T	PCT.	PF	PA
Pittsburgh	14	2	0	.875	356	195
Houston*	10	6	0	.625	283	298
Cleveland	8	8	0	.500	334	356
Cincinnati	4	12	0	.250	252	284

WESTERN DIVISION

	W	L	T	PCT.	PF	PA
Denver	10	6	0	.625	282	198
Seattle	9	7	0	.563	345	358
San Diego	9	7	0	.563	355	309
Oakland	9	7	0	.563	311	283
Kansas City	4	12	0	.250	243	327

NATIONAL CONFERENCE
EASTERN DIVISION

	W	L	T	PCT.	PF	PA
Dallas	12	4	0	.750	384	208
Philadelphia*	9	7	0	.563	270	250
Washington	8	8	0	.500	273	283
N.Y. Giants	6	10	0	.375	264	298
St. Louis	6	10	0	.375	248	296

CENTRAL DIVISION

	W	L	T	PCT.	PF	PA
Minnesota	8	7	1	.531	294	306
Green Bay	8	7	1	.531	249	269
Chicago	7	9	0	.438	253	274
Detroit	7	9	0	.438	290	300
Tampa Bay	5	11	0	.313	241	259

WESTERN DIVISION

	W	L	T	PCT.	PF	PA
L.A. Rams	12	4	0	.750	316	245
Atlanta*	9	7	0	.563	240	290
New Orleans	7	9	0	.438	281	298
San Francisco	2	14	0	.125	219	350

* Wild Card qualifier for playoffs
AFC Wild Card game: Houston 17, Miami 9
NFC Wild Card game: Atlanta 14, Philadelphia 13
AFC Divisional playoffs: Houston 31, New England 14; Pittsburgh 33, Denver 10
NFC Divisional playoffs: Dallas 27, Atlanta 20; L. A. Rams 34, Minnesota 10
AFC Championship: Pittsburgh 34, Houston 5; NFC Championship: Dallas 28, L. A. Rams 0
Super Bowl XIII: Pittsburgh 35, Dallas 31

1979 NFL

AMERICAN CONFERENCE
EASTERN DIVISION

	W	L	T	PCT.	PF	PA
Miami	10	6	0	.625	341	257
New England	9	7	0	.563	411	326
N.Y. Jets	8	8	0	.500	337	383
Buffalo	7	9	0	.438	268	279
Baltimore	5	11	0	.313	271	351

CENTRAL DIVISION

	W	L	T	PCT.	PF	PA
Pittsburgh	12	4	0	.750	416	262
Houston*	11	5	0	.688	362	331
Cleveland	9	7	0	.563	359	352
Cincinnati	4	12	0	.250	337	421

WESTERN DIVISION

	W	L	T	PCT.	PF	PA
San Diego	12	4	0	.750	411	246
Denver*	10	6	0	.625	289	262
Oakland	9	7	0	.563	365	337
Seattle	9	7	0	.563	378	372
Kansas City	7	9	0	.438	238	262

NATIONAL CONFERENCE
EASTERN DIVISION

	W	L	T	PCT.	PF	PA
Dallas	11	5	0	.688	371	313
Philadelphia	11	5	0	.688	339	282
Washington	10	6	0	.625	348	295
N.Y. Giants	6	10	0	.375	237	323
St. Louis	5	11	0	.313	307	358

CENTRAL DIVISION

	W	L	T	PCT.	PF	PA
Tampa Bay	10	6	0	.625	273	237
Chicago*	10	6	0	.625	306	249
Minnesota	7	9	0	.438	259	337
Green Bay	5	11	0	.313	246	316
Detroit	2	14	0	.125	219	365

WESTERN DIVISION

	W	L	T	PCT.	PF	PA
L.A. Rams	9	7	0	.563	323	309
New Orleans	8	8	0	.500	370	360
Atlanta	6	10	0	.375	300	388
San Francisco	2	14	0	.125	308	416

* Wild Card qualifier for playoffs
AFC Wild Card game: Houston 13, Denver 7
NFC Wild Card game: Philadelphia 27, Chicago 17
AFC Divisional playoffs: Houston 17, San Diego 14; Pittsburgh 34, Miami 14
NFC Divisional playoffs: Tampa Bay 24, Philadelphia 17; L. A. Rams 21, Dallas 19
AFC Championship: Pittsburgh 27, Houston 13; NFC Championship: L. A. Rams 9, Tampa Bay 0
Super Bowl XIV: Pittsburgh 31, L.A. Rams 19

1980 NFL

AMERICAN CONFERENCE
EASTERN DIVISION

	W	L	T	PCT.	PF	PA
Buffalo	11	5	0	.688	320	260
New England	10	6	0	.625	441	325
Miami	8	8	0	.500	266	305
Baltimore	7	9	0	.438	355	387
N.Y. Jets	4	12	0	.250	302	395

CENTRAL DIVISION

	W	L	T	PCT.	PF	PA
Cleveland	11	5	0	.688	357	310
Houston*	11	5	0	.688	295	251
Pittsburgh	9	7	0	.563	352	313
Cincinnati	6	10	0	.375	244	312

WESTERN DIVISION

	W	L	T	PCT.	PF	PA
San Diego	11	5	0	.688	418	327
Oakland*	11	5	0	.688	364	306
Denver	8	8	0	.500	310	323
Kansas City	8	8	0	.500	319	336
Seattle	4	12	0	.250	291	408

NATIONAL CONFERENCE
EASTERN DIVISION

	W	L	T	PCT.	PF	PA
Philadelphia	12	4	0	.750	384	222
Dallas*	12	4	0	.750	454	311
Washington	6	10	0	.375	261	293
St. Louis	5	11	0	.313	299	350
N.Y. Giants	4	12	0	.250	249	425

CENTRAL DIVISION

	W	L	T	PCT.	PF	PA
Minnesota	9	7	0	.563	317	308
Detroit	9	7	0	.563	334	272
Chicago	7	9	0	.438	304	264
Tampa Bay	5	10	1	.344	271	341
Green Bay	5	10	1	.344	231	371

WESTERN DIVISION

	W	L	T	PCT.	PF	PA
Atlanta	12	4	0	.750	405	272
L.A. Rams*	11	5	0	.688	424	289
San Francisco	6	10	0	.375	320	415
New Orleans	1	15	0	.063	291	487

* Wild Card qualifier for playoffs
AFC Wild Card game: Oakland 27, Houston 7
NFC Wild Card game: Dallas 34, L. A. Rams 13
AFC Divisional playoffs: San Diego 20, Buffalo 14; Oakland 14, Cleveland 12
NFC Divisional playoffs: Philadelphia 31, Minnesota 16; Dallas 30, Atlanta 27
AFC Championship: Oakland 34, San Diego 27; NFC Championship: Philadelphia 20, Dallas 7
Super Bowl XV: Oakland 27, Philadelphia 10

1981 NFL

AMERICAN CONFERENCE

EASTERN DIVISION

	W	L	T	PCT.	PF	PA
Miami	11	4	1	.719	345	275
N.Y. Jets*	10	5	1	.656	355	287
Buffalo*	10	6	0	.625	311	276
New England	2	14	0	.125	322	370
Baltimore	2	14	0	.125	259	533

CENTRAL DIVISION

	W	L	T	PCT.	PF	PA
Cincinnati	12	4	0	.750	421	304
Pittsburgh	8	8	0	.500	356	297
Houston	7	9	0	.438	281	355
Cleveland	5	11	0	.313	276	375

WESTERN DIVISION

	W	L	T	PCT.	PF	PA
San Diego	10	6	0	.625	478	390
Denver	10	6	0	.625	321	289
Kansas City	9	7	0	.563	343	290
Oakland	7	9	0	.438	273	343
Seattle	6	10	0	.375	322	388

NATIONAL CONFERENCE

EASTERN DIVISION

	W	L	T	PCT.	PF	PA
Dallas	12	4	0	.750	367	277
Philadelphia*	10	6	0	.625	368	221
N.Y. Giants*	9	7	0	.563	295	257
Washington	8	8	0	.500	347	349
St. Louis	7	9	0	.438	315	408

CENTRAL DIVISION

	W	L	T	PCT.	PF	PA
Tampa Bay	9	7	0	.563	315	268
Detroit	8	8	0	.500	397	322
Green Bay	8	8	0	.500	324	361
Minnesota	7	9	0	.438	325	369
Chicago	6	10	0	.375	253	324

WESTERN DIVISION

	W	L	T	PCT.	PF	PA
San Francisco	13	3	0	.813	357	250
Atlanta	7	9	0	.438	426	355
L.A. Rams	6	10	0	.375	303	351
New Orleans	4	12	0	.250	207	378

* Wild Card qualifier for playoffs

AFC Wild Card game: Buffalo 31, N.Y. Jets 27
NFC Wild Card game: N.Y. Giants 27, Philadelphia 21
AFC Divisional playoffs: San Diego 41, Miami 38 (OT); Cincinnati 28, Buffalo 21
NFC Divisional playoffs: Dallas 38, Tampa Bay 0; San Francisco 38, N.Y. Giants 24
AFC Championship: Cincinnati 27, San Diego 7
NFC Championship: San Francisco 28, Dallas 27
Super Bowl XVI: San Francisco 26, Cincinnati 21

1982 NFL*

AMERICAN CONFERENCE

	W	L	T	PCT.	PF	PA
L.A. Raiders	8	1	0	.889	260	200
Cincinnati	7	2	0	.778	232	177
Miami	7	2	0	.778	198	131
N.Y. Jets	6	3	0	.667	245	166
San Diego	6	3	0	.667	288	221
Pittsburgh	6	3	0	.667	204	146
New England	5	4	0	.556	143	157
Cleveland	4	5	0	.444	140	182
Buffalo	4	5	0	.444	150	154
Seattle	4	5	0	.444	127	147
Kansas City	3	6	0	.333	176	184
Denver	2	7	0	.222	148	226
Houston	1	8	0	.111	136	245
Baltimore	0	8	1	.056	113	236

NATIONAL CONFERENCE

	W	L	T	PCT.	PF	PA
Washington	8	1	0	.889	190	128
Dallas	6	3	0	.667	226	145
Green Bay	5	3	1	.611	226	169
Tampa Bay	5	4	0	.556	158	178
Minnesota	5	4	0	.556	187	198
St. Louis	5	4	0	.556	135	170
Atlanta	5	4	0	.556	183	199
Detroit	4	5	0	.444	181	176
N.Y. Giants	4	5	0	.444	164	160
New Orleans	4	5	0	.444	129	160
San Francisco	3	6	0	.333	209	206
Chicago	3	6	0	.333	141	174
Philadelphia	3	6	0	.333	191	195
L.A. Rams	2	7	0	.222	200	250

*Players' Strike—top eight teams in each conference qualified for playoffs due to shortened season

AFC First–round playoffs: Miami 28, New England 13; L.A. Raiders 27, Cleveland 10; N.Y. Jets 44, Cincinnati 17; San Diego 31, Pittsburgh 28
NFC First–round playoffs: Green Bay 41, St. Louis 16; Washington 31, Detroit 7; Minnesota 30, Atlanta 24; Dallas 30, Tampa Bay 17
AFC Second–round playoffs: N.Y. Jets 17, L.A. Raiders 14; Miami 34, San Diego 13
NFC Second–round playoffs: Washington 21, Minnesota 7; Dallas 37, Green Bay 26
AFC Championship: Miami 14, N.Y. Jets 0
NFC Championship: Washington 31, Dallas 17
Super Bowl XVII: Washington 27, Miami 17

1983 NFL

AMERICAN CONFERENCE
EASTERN DIVISION

	W	L	T	PCT.	PF	PA
Miami	12	4	0	.750	389	250
Buffalo	8	8	0	.500	283	351
New England	8	8	0	.500	274	289
N.Y. Jets	7	9	0	.438	313	331
Baltimore	7	9	0	.438	264	354

CENTRAL DIVISION

	W	L	T	PCT.	PF	PA
Pittsburgh	10	6	0	.625	355	303
Cleveland	9	7	0	.563	356	342
Cincinnati	7	9	0	.438	346	302
Houston	2	14	0	.125	288	460

WESTERN DIVISION

	W	L	T	PCT.	PF	PA
L.A. Raiders	12	4	0	.750	442	338
Seattle*	9	7	0	.563	403	397
Denver*	9	7	0	.563	302	327
San Diego	6	10	0	.375	358	462
Kansas City	6	10	0	.375	386	367

NATIONAL CONFERENCE
EASTERN DIVISION

	W	L	T	PCT.	PF	PA
Washington	14	2	0	.875	541	332
Dallas	12	4	0	.750	479	360
St. Louis	8	7	1	.531	374	428
Philadelphia	5	11	0	.313	233	322
N.Y. Giants	3	12	1	.219	267	347

CENTRAL DIVISION

	W	L	T	PCT.	PF	PA
Detroit	9	7	0	.563	347	286
Green Bay	8	8	0	.500	429	439
Minnesota	8	8	0	.500	316	348
Chicago	8	8	0	.500	311	301
Tampa Bay	2	14	0	.125	241	380

WESTERN DIVISION

	W	L	T	PCT.	PF	PA
San Francisco	10	6	0	.625	432	293
L.A. Rams*	9	7	0	.563	361	344
New Orleans	8	8	0	.500	319	337
Atlanta	7	9	0	.438	370	389

* Wild Card qualifier for playoffs
AFC Wild Card game: Seattle 31, Denver 7
NFC Wild Card game: L.A. Rams 24, Dallas 17
AFC Divisional playoffs: Seattle 27, Miami 20; L.A. Raiders 38, Pittsburgh 10
NFC Divisional playoffs: San Francisco 24, Detroit 23; Washington 51, L.A. Rams 7
AFC Championship: L.A. Raiders 30, Seattle 14; NFC Championship: Washington 24, San Francisco 21
Super Bowl XVIII: L.A. Raiders 38, Washington 9

1984 NFL

AMERICAN CONFERENCE
EASTERN DIVISION

	W	L	T	PCT.	PF	PA
Miami	14	2	0	.875	513	298
New England	9	7	0	.563	362	352
N.Y. Jets	7	9	0	.438	332	364
Indianapolis	4	12	0	.250	239	414
Buffalo	2	14	0	.125	250	454

CENTRAL DIVISION

	W	L	T	PCT.	PF	PA
Pittsburgh	9	7	0	.563	387	310
Cincinnati	8	8	0	.500	339	339
Cleveland	5	11	0	.313	250	297
Houston	3	13	0	.188	240	437

WESTERN DIVISION

	W	L	T	PCT.	PF	PA
Denver	13	3	0	.813	353	241
Seattle*	12	4	0	.750	418	282
L.A. Raiders*	11	5	0	.688	368	278
Kansas City	8	8	0	.500	314	324
San Diego	7	9	0	.438	394	413

NATIONAL CONFERENCE
EASTERN DIVISION

	W	L	T	PCT.	PF	PA
Washington	11	5	0	.688	426	310
N.Y. Giants*	9	7	0	.563	299	301
Dallas	9	7	0	.563	308	308
St. Louis	9	7	0	.563	423	345
Philadelphia	6	9	1	.406	278	320

CENTRAL DIVISION

	W	L	T	PCT.	PF	PA
Chicago	10	6	0	.625	325	248
Green Bay	8	8	0	.500	390	309
Tampa Bay	6	10	0	.375	335	380
Detroit	4	11	1	.281	283	408
Minnesota	3	13	0	.188	276	484

WESTERN DIVISION

	W	L	T	PCT.	PF	PA
San Francisco	15	1	0	.938	475	227
L.A. Rams*	10	6	0	.625	346	316
New Orleans	7	9	0	.438	298	361
Atlanta	4	12	0	.250	281	382

* Wild Card qualifier for playoffs
AFC Wild Card game: Seattle 13, L.A. Raiders 7
NFC Wild Card game: N.Y. Giants 16, L.A. Rams 13
AFC Divisional playoffs: Miami 31, Seattle 10; Pittsburgh 24, Denver 17
NFC Divisional playoffs: San Francisco 21, N.Y. Giants 10; Chicago 23, Washington 19
AFC Championship: Miami 45, Pittsburgh 28; NFC Championship: San Francisco 23, Chicago 0
Super Bowl XVIII: San Francisco 38, Miami 16

1985 NFL

AMERICAN CONFERENCE
EASTERN DIVISION

	W	L	T	PCT.	PF	PA
Miami	12	4	0	.750	428	320
N.Y. Jets*	11	5	0	.688	393	264
New England*	11	5	0	.688	362	290
Indianapolis	5	11	0	.313	320	386
Buffalo	2	14	0	.125	200	381

CENTRAL DIVISION

	W	L	T	PCT.	PF	PA
Cleveland	8	8	0	.500	287	294
Cincinnati	7	9	0	.438	441	437
Pittsburgh	7	9	0	.438	379	355
Houston	5	11	0	.313	284	412

WESTERN DIVISION

	W	L	T	PCT.	PF	PA
L.A. Raiders	12	4	0	.750	354	308
Denver	11	5	0	.688	380	329
San Diego	8	8	0	.500	467	435
Seattle	8	8	0	.500	349	313
Kansas City	6	10	0	.375	317	360

NATIONAL CONFERENCE
EASTERN DIVISION

	W	L	T	PCT.	PF	PA
Dallas	10	6	0	.625	357	333
N.Y. Giants*	10	6	0	.625	399	283
Washington	10	6	0	.625	297	312
Philadelphia	7	9	0	.438	286	310
St. Louis	5	11	0	.313	278	414

CENTRAL DIVISION

	W	L	T	PCT.	PF	PA
Chicago	15	1	0	.938	456	198
Green Bay	8	8	0	.500	337	355
Detroit	7	9	0	.438	307	366
Minnesota	7	9	0	.438	346	359
Tampa Bay	2	14	0	.125	294	448

WESTERN DIVISION

	W	L	T	PCT.	PF	PA
L.A. Rams	11	5	0	.688	340	277
San Francisco*	10	6	0	.625	411	263
New Orleans	5	11	0	.313	294	401
Atlanta	4	12	0	.250	282	452

* Wild Card qualifier for playoffs

AFC Wild Card game: New England 26, N.Y. Jets 14
NFC Wild Card game: N.Y. Giants 17, San Francisco 3
AFC Divisional playoffs: Miami 24, Cleveland 21; New England 27, L.A. Raiders 20
NFC Divisional playoffs: L.A. Rams 20, Dallas 0; Chicago 21, N.Y. Giants 0
AFC Championship: New England 31, Miami 14; NFC Championship: Chicago 24, L.A. Rams 0
Super Bowl XX: Chicago 46, New England 10

1986 NFL

AMERICAN CONFERENCE
EASTERN DIVISION

	W	L	T	PCT.	PF	PA
New England	11	5	0	.688	412	307
N.Y. Jets*	10	6	0	.625	364	386
Miami	8	8	0	.500	430	405
Buffalo	4	12	0	.250	287	348
Indianapolis	3	13	0	.188	229	400

CENTRAL DIVISION

	W	L	T	PCT.	PF	PA
Cleveland	12	4	0	.750	391	310
Cincinnati	10	6	0	.625	409	394
Pittsburgh	6	10	0	.375	307	336
Houston	5	11	0	.313	274	329

WESTERN DIVISION

	W	L	T	PCT.	PF	PA
Denver	11	5	0	.688	378	327
Kansas City*	10	6	0	.625	358	326
Seattle	10	6	0	.625	366	293
L.A. Raiders	8	8	0	.500	323	346
San Diego	4	12	0	.250	335	396

NATIONAL CONFERENCE
EASTERN DIVISION

	W	L	T	PCT.	PF	PA
N.Y. Giants	14	2	0	.875	371	236
Washington*	12	4	0	.750	368	296
Dallas	7	9	0	.438	346	337
Philadelphia	5	10	1	.344	256	312
St. Louis	4	11	1	.281	218	351

CENTRAL DIVISION

	W	L	T	PCT.	PF	PA
Chicago	14	2	0	.875	352	187
Minnesota	9	7	0	.563	398	273
Detroit	5	11	0	.313	277	326
Green Bay	4	12	0	.250	254	418
Tampa Bay	2	14	0	.125	239	473

WESTERN DIVISION

	W	L	T	PCT.	PF	PA
San Francisco	10	6	0	.625	374	247
L.A. Rams*	10	6	0	.625	309	267
Atlanta	7	8	1	.469	280	280
New Orleans	7	9	0	.438	288	287

* Wild Card qualifier for playoffs

AFC Wild Card game: N.Y. Jets 35, Kansas City 15
NFC Wild Card game: Washington 19, L.A. Rams 7
AFC Divisional playoffs: Cleveland 23, N.Y. Jets 20 (2 OT); Denver 22, New England 17
NFC Divisional playoffs: Washington 27, Chicago 13; N.Y. Giants 49, San Francisco 3
AFC Championship: Denver 23, Cleveland 20; NFC Championship: N.Y. Giants 17, Washington 0
Super Bowl XXI: N.Y. Giants 39, Denver 20

1987 NFL*

AMERICAN CONFERENCE

EASTERN DIVISION

	W	L	T	PCT.	PF	PA
Indianapolis	9	6	0	.600	300	238
Miami	8	7	0	.533	362	335
New England	8	7	0	.533	320	293
Buffalo	7	8	0	.467	270	305
N.Y. Jets	6	9	0	.400	334	360

CENTRAL DIVISION

	W	L	T	PCT.	PF	PA
Cleveland	10	5	0	.667	390	239
Houston**	9	6	0	.600	345	349
Pittsburgh	8	7	0	.533	285	299
Cincinnati	4	11	0	.267	285	370

WESTERN DIVISION

	W	L	T	PCT.	PF	PA
Denver	10	4	1	.700	379	288
Seattle**	9	6	0	.600	371	314
San Diego	8	7	0	.533	253	317
L.A. Raiders	5	10	0	.333	301	289
Kansas City	4	11	0	.267	273	388

NATIONAL CONFERENCE

EASTERN DIVISION

	W	L	T	PCT.	PF	PA
Washington	11	4	0	.733	379	285
Dallas	7	8	0	.467	340	348
St. Louis	7	8	0	.467	362	368
Philadelphia	7	8	0	.467	337	380
N.Y. Giants	6	9	0	.400	280	312

CENTRAL DIVISION

	W	L	T	PCT.	PF	PA
Chicago	11	4	0	.733	356	282
Minnesota**	8	7	0	.533	336	335
Green Bay	5	9	1	.367	255	300
Tampa Bay	4	11	0	.267	286	360
Detroit	4	11	0	.267	269	384

WESTERN DIVISION

	W	L	T	PCT.	PF	PA
San Francisco	13	2	0	.867	459	253
New Orleans**	12	3	0	.800	422	283
L.A. Rams	6	9	0	.400	317	361
Atlanta	3	12	0	.200	205	436

*Players' Strike—one game cancelled due to strike
** Wild Card qualifier for playoffs
AFC Wild Card game: Houston 23, Seattle 20 (OT); NFC Wild Card game: Minn. 44, New Orleans 10
AFC Divisional playoffs: Cleveland 38, Indianapolis 21; Denver 34, Houston 10
NFC Divisional playoffs: Minnesota 36, San Francisco 24; Washington 21, Chicago 17
AFC Championship: Denver 38, Cleveland 33; NFC Championship: Washington 17, Minnesota 10
Super Bowl XXII: Washington 42, Denver 10

1988 NFL

AMERICAN CONFERENCE

EASTERN DIVISION

	W	L	T	PCT.	PF	PA
Buffalo	12	4	0	.750	329	237
New England	9	7	0	.563	250	284
Indianapolis	9	7	0	.563	354	315
N.Y. Jets	8	7	1	.531	372	354
Miami	6	10	0	.375	319	380

CENTRAL DIVISION

	W	L	T	PCT.	PF	PA
Cincinnati	12	4	0	.750	448	329
Cleveland*	10	6	0	.625	304	288
Houston*	10	6	0	.625	424	365
Pittsburgh	5	11	0	.313	336	421

WESTERN DIVISION

	W	L	T	PCT.	PF	PA
Seattle	9	7	0	.563	339	329
Denver	8	8	0	.500	327	352
L.A. Raiders	7	9	0	.438	325	369
San Diego	6	10	0	.375	231	332
Kansas City	4	11	1	.281	254	320

NATIONAL CONFERENCE

EASTERN DIVISION

	W	L	T	PCT.	PF	PA
Philadelphia	10	6	0	.625	379	319
N.Y. Giants	10	6	0	.625	359	304
Phoenix	7	9	0	.438	344	398
Washington	7	9	0	.438	345	387
Dallas	3	13	0	.188	265	381

CENTRAL DIVISION

	W	L	T	PCT.	PF	PA
Chicago	12	4	0	.750	312	215
Minnesota*	11	5	0	.688	406	233
Tampa Bay	5	11	0	.313	261	350
Detroit	4	12	0	.250	220	313
Green Bay	4	12	0	.250	240	315

WESTERN DIVISION

	W	L	T	PCT.	PF	PA
San Francisco	10	6	0	.625	369	294
L.A. Rams*	10	6	0	.625	407	293
New Orleans	10	6	0	.625	312	283
Atlanta	5	11	0	.313	244	315

* Wild Card qualifier for playoffs
AFC Wild Card game: Houston 24, Cleve. 23; NFC Wild Card game: Minn. 28, L.A. Rams 17
AFC Divisional playoffs: Cincinnati 21, Seattle 13; Buffalo 17, Houston 10
NFC Divisional playoffs: Chicago 20, Philadelphia 12; San Francisco 34, Minnesota 9
AFC Championship: Cincinnati 21, Buffalo 10; NFC Championship: San Francisco 28, Chicago 3
Super Bowl XXIII: San Francisco 20, Cincinnati 16

1989 NFL

AMERICAN CONFERENCE

EASTERN DIVISION

	W	L	T	PCT.	PF	PA
Buffalo	9	7	0	.563	409	317
Miami	8	8	0	.500	331	379
Indianapolis	8	8	0	.500	298	301
New England	5	11	0	.313	297	391
N.Y. Jets	4	12	0	.250	253	411

CENTRAL DIVISION

	W	L	T	PCT.	PF	PA
Cleveland	9	6	1	.594	334	254
Houston*	9	7	0	.563	365	412
Pittsburgh*	9	7	0	.563	265	326
Cincinnati	8	8	0	.500	404	285

WESTERN DIVISION

	W	L	T	PCT.	PF	PA
Denver	11	5	0	.688	362	226
Kansas City	8	7	1	.531	318	286
L.A. Raiders	8	8	0	.500	315	297
Seattle	7	9	0	.438	241	327
San Diego	6	10	0	.375	266	290

NATIONAL CONFERENCE

EASTERN DIVISION

	W	L	T	PCT.	PF	PA
N.Y. Giants	12	4	0	.750	348	252
Philadelphia*	11	5	0	.688	342	274
Washington	10	6	0	.625	386	308
Phoenix	5	11	0	.313	258	377
Dallas	1	15	0	.063	204	393

CENTRAL DIVISION

	W	L	T	PCT.	PF	PA
Minnesota	10	6	0	.625	351	275
Green Bay	10	6	0	.625	362	356
Detroit	7	9	0	.438	312	364
Chicago	6	10	0	.375	358	377
Tampa Bay	5	11	0	.313	320	419

WESTERN DIVISION

	W	L	T	PCT.	PF	PA
San Francisco	14	2	0	.875	442	253
L.A. Rams*	11	5	0	.688	426	344
New Orleans	9	7	0	.563	386	301
Atlanta	3	13	0	.188	279	437

* Wild Card qualifier for playoffs

AFC Wild Card game: Pittsburgh 26, Houston 23; NFC Wild Card game: L.A. Rams 21, Phila. 7
AFC Divisional playoffs: Cleveland 34, Buffalo 30; Denver 24, Pittsburgh 23
NFC Divisional playoffs: L.A. Rams 19, N.Y. Giants 13 (OT); San Francisco 41, Minnesota 13
AFC Championship: Denver 37, Cleveland 21
NFC Championship: San Francisco 30, L.A. Rams 3
Super Bowl XXIV: San Francisco 55, Denver 10

1990 NFL

AMERICAN CONFERENCE

EASTERN DIVISION

	W	L	T	PCT.	PF	PA
Buffalo	13	3	0	.813	428	263
Miami*	12	4	0	.750	336	242
Indianapolis	7	9	0	.438	281	353
N.Y. Jets	6	10	0	.375	295	345
New England	1	15	0	.063	181	446

CENTRAL DIVISION

	W	L	T	PCT.	PF	PA
Houston	9	7	0	.563	405	307
Cincinnati*	9	7	0	.563	360	352
Pittsburgh	9	7	0	.563	292	240
Cleveland	3	13	0	.188	228	462

WESTERN DIVISION

	W	L	T	PCT.	PF	PA
L.A. Raiders	12	4	0	.750	337	268
Kansas City*	11	5	0	.688	369	257
Seattle	9	7	0	.563	306	286
San Diego	6	10	0	.375	315	281
Denver	5	11	0	.313	331	374

NATIONAL CONFERENCE

EASTERN DIVISION

	W	L	T	PCT.	PF	PA
N.Y. Giants	13	3	0	.813	335	211
Philadelphia*	10	6	0	.625	396	299
Washington*	10	6	0	.625	381	301
Dallas	7	9	0	.438	244	308
Phoenix	5	11	0	.313	268	396

CENTRAL DIVISION

	W	L	T	PCT.	PF	PA
Chicago	11	5	0	.688	348	280
Minnesota	6	10	0	.375	351	326
Green Bay	6	10	0	.375	271	347
Tampa Bay	6	10	0	.375	264	367
Detroit	6	10	0	.375	373	413

WESTERN DIVISION

	W	L	T	PCT.	PF	PA
San Francisco	14	2	0	.875	353	239
New Orleans*	8	8	0	.500	274	275
Atlanta	5	11	0	.313	348	365
L.A. Rams	5	11	0	.313	345	412

* Wild Card qualifier for playoffs

AFC First Round playoffs: Miami 17, Kansas City 16; Cincinnati 41, Houston 14
NFC First Round playoffs: Washington 20, Philadelphia 6; Chicago 16, New Orleans 6
AFC Divisional playoffs: Buffalo 44, Miami 34; L.A. Raiders 20, Cincinnati 10
NFC Divisional playoffs: San Francisco 28, Washington 10; N.Y. Giants 31, Chicago 3
AFC Championship: Buffalo 51, L.A. Raiders 3; NFC Championship: N.Y. Giants 15, San Fran. 13
Super Bowl XXV: N.Y. Giants 20, Buffalo 19

1991 NFL

AMERICAN CONFERENCE

EASTERN DIVISION

	W	L	T	PCT.	PF	PA
Buffalo	13	3	0	.813	458	318
N.Y. Jets*	8	8	0	.500	314	293
Miami	8	8	0	.500	343	349
New England	6	10	0	.375	211	305
Indianapolis	1	15	0	.063	143	381

CENTRAL DIVISION

	W	L	T	PCT.	PF	PA
Houston	11	5	0	.688	386	251
Pittsburgh	7	9	0	.438	292	344
Cleveland	6	10	0	.375	293	298
Cincinnati	3	13	0	.188	263	435

WESTERN DIVISION

	W	L	T	PCT.	PF	PA
Denver	12	4	0	.750	304	235
Kansas City*	10	6	0	.625	322	252
L.A. Raiders*	9	7	0	.563	298	297
Seattle	7	9	0	.438	276	261
San Diego	4	12	0	.250	274	342

NATIONAL CONFERENCE

EASTERN DIVISION

	W	L	T	PCT.	PF	PA
Washington	14	2	0	.875	485	224
Dallas*	11	5	0	.688	342	310
Philadelphia	10	6	0	.625	285	244
N.Y. Giants	8	8	0	.500	281	297
Phoenix	4	12	0	.250	196	344

CENTRAL DIVISION

	W	L	T	PCT.	PF	PA
Detroit	12	4	0	.750	339	295
Chicago*	11	5	0	.688	299	269
Minnesota	8	8	0	.500	301	306
Green Bay	4	12	0	.250	273	313
Tampa Bay	3	13	0	.188	199	365

WESTERN DIVISION

	W	L	T	PCT.	PF	PA
New Orleans	11	5	0	.688	341	211
Atlanta*	10	6	0	.625	361	338
San Francisco	10	6	0	.625	393	239
L.A. Rams	3	13	0	.188	234	390

* Wild Card qualifier for playoffs

AFC First Round playoffs: Kansas City 10, L.A. Raiders 6; Houston 17, N.Y. Jets 10
NFC First Round playoffs: Atlanta 27, New Orleans 20; Dallas 17, Chicago 13
AFC Divisional playoffs: Buffalo 37, Kansas City 14; Denver 26, Houston 24
NFC Divisional playoffs: Washington 24, Atlanta 7; Detroit 38, Dallas 6
AFC Championship: Buffalo 10, Denver 7; NFC Championship: Washington 41, Detroit 10
Super Bowl XXVI: Washington 37, Buffalo 24

1992 NFL

AMERICAN CONFERENCE

EASTERN DIVISION

	W	L	T	PCT.	PF	PA
Miami	11	5	0	.688	340	281
Buffalo*	11	5	0	.688	381	283
Indianapolis	9	7	0	.563	216	302
N.Y. Jets	4	12	0	.250	220	315
New England	2	14	0	.125	205	363

CENTRAL DIVISION

	W	L	T	PCT.	PF	PA
Pittsburgh	11	5	0	.688	299	225
Houston*	10	6	0	.625	352	258
Cleveland	7	9	0	.438	272	275
Cincinnati	5	11	0	.313	274	364

WESTERN DIVISION

	W	L	T	PCT.	PF	PA
San Diego	11	5	0	.688	335	241
Kansas City*	10	6	0	.625	348	282
Denver	8	8	0	.500	262	329
L.A. Raiders	7	9	0	.438	249	281
Seattle	2	14	0	.125	140	312

NATIONAL CONFERENCE

EASTERN DIVISION

	W	L	T	PCT.	PF	PA
Dallas	13	3	0	.813	409	243
Philadelphia*	11	5	0	.688	354	245
Washington*	9	7	0	.563	300	255
N.Y. Giants	6	10	0	.375	306	367
Phoenix	4	12	0	.250	243	332

CENTRAL DIVISION

	W	L	T	PCT.	PF	PA
Minnesota	11	5	0	.688	374	249
Green Bay	9	7	0	.563	276	296
Tampa Bay	5	11	0	.313	267	365
Chicago	5	11	0	.313	295	361
Detroit	5	11	0	.313	273	332

WESTERN DIVISION

	W	L	T	PCT.	PF	PA
San Francisco	14	2	0	.875	431	236
New Orleans*	12	4	0	.750	330	202
L.A. Rams	6	10	0	.375	313	383
Atlanta	6	10	0	.375	327	414

* Wild Card qualifier for playoffs

AFC First Round playoffs: San Diego 17, Kansas City 0; Buffalo 41, Houston 38
NFC First Round playoffs: Washington 24, Minnesota 7; Philadelphia 36, New Orleans 20
AFC Divisional playoffs: Buffalo 24, Pittsburgh 3; Miami 31, San Diego 0
NFC Divisional playoffs: San Francisco 20, Washington 13; Dallas 34, Philadelphia 10
AFC Championship: Buffalo 29, Miami 10; NFC Championship: Dallas 30, San Francisco 20
Super Bowl XXVII: Dallas 52, Buffalo 17

Pro Football Hall of Fame

1963, Johnny Blood (McNally), Halfback; Sammy Baugh, Quarterback/Coach; Bert Bell, Commissioner; Joe Carr, President; Earl "Dutch" Clark, Quarterback; Red Grange, Halfback; George Halas, Player/Coach/Founder; Mel Hein, Center; Wilbur "Pete" Henry, Tackle; Cal Hubbard, Tackle/End; Don Hutson, End; Earl "Curly" Lambeau, Founder/Player/Coach; Tim Mara, Founder; George Preston Marshall, Founder; Bronko Nagurski, Fullback; Ernie Nevers, Fullback; Jim Thorpe, Halfback

1964, Jimmy Conzelman, Halfback/Coach/Executive; Ed Healey, Tackle; Clark Hinkle, Fullback; Roy "Link" Lyman, Tackle; Mike Michalske, Halfback; Art Rooney, Founder; George Trafton, Center

1965, Guy Chamberlain, Player/Coach; Paddy Driscoll, Player/Coach; Dan Fortmann, Guard; Otto Graham, Quarterback/Coach; Sid Luckman, Quarterback; Steve Van Buren, Halfback; Bob Waterfield, Quarterback/Coach

1966, Bill Dudley, Halfback; Joe Guyon, Halfback; Arnie Herber, Halfback; Walt Kiesling, Player/Coach; George McAfee, Halfback; Steve Owen, Player/Coach; Hugh "Shorty" Ray, Official; Clyde "Bulldog" Turner, Center/Linebacker

1967, Chuck Bednarik, Center/Linebacker; Charlie Bidwill, Owner; Paul Brown, Coach; Bobby Layne, Quarterback; Dan Reeves, Founder; Ken Strong, Halfback/Placekicker; Joe Stydahar, Tackle; Em Tunnell, Defensive Back

1968, Cliff Battles, Halfback/Quarterback, Coach; Art Donovan, Defensive Tackle; Elroy "Crazy Legs" Hirsch, End/Halfback; Wayne Millner, End; Marion Motley, Fullback/Linebacker; Charlie Trippi, Halfback; Alex Wojciechowicz, Center/Linebacker

1969, Glen "Turk" Edwards, Tackle; Earle "Greasy" Neale, Coach; Leo Nomellini, Defensive Tackle; Joe Perry, Fullback; Ernie Stautner, Defensive Tackle

1970, Jack Christiansen, Defensive Back/Coach; Tom Fears, End/Coach; Hugh McElhenny, End; Pete Pihos, End

1971, Jim Brown, Fullback; Bill Hewitt, Fullback; Frank "Bruiser" Kinard, Tackle; Vince Lombardi, Coach; Andy Robustelli, Defensive End; Y. A. Tittle, Quarterback; Norm Van Brocklin, Quarterback/Coach

1972, Lamar Hunt, Founder; Gino Marchetti, Defensive End; Ollie Matson, Halfback; Clarence "Ace" Parker, Halfback

1973, Raymond Berry, End/Coach; Jim Parker, Guard; Joe Schmidt, Linebacker

1974, Tony Canadeo, Halfback; Bill George, Linebacker; Lou Groza, Tackle/Placekicker; Dick "Night Train" Lane, Defensive Back

1975, Roosevelt Brown, Tackle; George Connor, Tackle/Linebacker; Dante Lavelli, End; Lenny Moore, Halfback

1976, Ray Flaherty, Player/Coach; Len Ford, End; Jim Taylor, Fullback

1977, Frank Gifford, Halfback/End; Forrest Gregg, Tackle/Coach; Gale Sayers, Running Back; Bart Starr, Quarterback; Bill Willis, Guard

1978, Lance Alworth, Wide Receiver; Weeb Ewbank, Coach; Alphonse "Tuffy" Leemans, Fullback; Ray Nitschke, Linebacker; Larry Wilson, Defensive Back

1979, Dick Butkus, Linebacker; Yale Lary, Defensive Back; Ron Mix, Offensive Tackle; Johnny Unitas, Quarterback

1980, Herb Adderley, Cornerback; Deacon Jones, Defensive End; Bob Lilly, Defensive Tackle; Jim Otto, Center

1981, Morris "Red" Badgro, End; George Blanda, Quarterback/Placekicker; Willie Davis, Defensive End; Jim Ringo, Center

1982, Doug Atkins, Defensive End; Sam Huff, Linebacker; George Musso, Guard/Defensive Tackle; Merlin Olsen, Defensive Tackle

1983, Bobby Bell, Linebacker; Sid Gillman, End/Coach; Sonny Jurgensen, Quarterback; Bobby Mitchell, Running Back/Wide Receiver; Paul Warfield, Wide Receiver

1984, Willie Brown, Defensive Back; Mike McCormack, Tackle; Charley Taylor, Wide Receiver; Arnie Weinmeister, Tackle

1985, Frank Gatski, Center; Joe Namath, Quarterback; Pete Rozelle, Commissioner; O. J. Simpson, Running Back; Roger Staubach, Quarterback

1986, Paul Hornung, Running Back; Ken Houston, Defensive Back; Willie Lanier, Linebacker; Fran Tarkenton, Quarterback; Doak Walker, Running Back

1987, Larry Csonka, Running Back; Len Dawson, Quarterback; Joe Greene, Defensive Tackle; John Henry Johnson, Fullback; Jim Langer, Center; Don Maynard, Wide Receiver; Gene Upshaw, Guard

1988, Fred Biletnikoff, Wide Receiver; Mike Ditka, Tight End/Coach; Jack Ham, Linebacker; Alan Page, Defensive Tackle

1989, Mel Blount, Cornerback; Terry Bradshaw, Quarterback; Art Shell, Tackle; Willie Wood, Safety

1990, Junious "Buck" Buchanan, Defensive Tackle; Bob Griese, Quarterback; Franco Harris, Running Back; Ted Hendricks, Linebacker; Jack Lambert, Linebacker; Tom Landry, Coach; Bob St. Clair, Tackle

1991, Earl Campbell, Running Back; John Hannah, Guard; Stan Jones, Guard/Defensive Tackle; Tex Schramm, President/General Manager; Jan Stenerud, Placekicker

1992, Lem Barney, Cornerback; Al Davis, Coach/General Manager/President; John Mackey, Tight End; John Riggins, Fullback

1993, Dan Fouts, Quarterback; Larry Little, Guard; Chuck Noll, Coach; Walter Payton, Running Back; Bill Walsh, Coach

1994, Tony Dorsett, Running Back; Bud Grant, Wide Receiver/Coach; Jimmy Johnson, Defensive Back; Leroy Kelly, Running Back; Jackie Smith, Tight End; Randy White, Defensive Tackle

America's most respected pro football magazine's 32nd year!

Street & Smith's
Pro Football

JERRY RICE ON
RECORD
PACE

80

**On Sale
June 28**